The Photographic History
of The Civil War

TWO VOLUMES IN ONE.
The Armies and Leaders

ACKNOWLEDGMENT

The publishers desire to express in this final volume a particular obligation to members of the special editorial force which has carried the Photographic History to completion. It was impossible for the staff of the Review of Reviews, at the beginning of the undertaking, to estimate its extent. To construct ten large volumes, to avoid controversy throughout, yet to obtain an unique comprehensiveness by a concentration of interest on the particular war-time activity treated in each volume separately—this involved a new departure in editorial effort. Even with the cordial cooperation of many distinguished contributors, the task—as a result of the novelty of the plan—far exceeded expectations, and called for a high degree of discrimination, application, and resource. These calls have been met most faithfully. Special mention is due George L. Kilmer, late U. S. V., Military Editor, whose lifelong devotion to the literature and records of the Civil War has endowed him with a sympathy, and an exact knowledge of events, that have rendered of utmost value his critical reading of both text and captions. From Mr. George H. Casamajor, Historical Editor, the text has received a minute scrutiny in manuscript and proof, coupled with painstaking historical research and investigation, imparting in no small degree its accuracy of statement and harmony of narrative. Mr. Herbert T. Wade, as Literary Editor, has developed and organized the text, from the initial extensive correspondence and negotiations in the obtaining of adequate contributions, to seeing the pages through the press. One and all have cooperated unsparingly, with many personal sacrifices. No small stimulus has come from the actuality of the photographic collection which the text seeks to complement. And all have felt the inspiration of this opportunity—to present the immense facts of Civil War bravery and tragedy in a form that is sympathetic and universal.

Thanks are due to many friends who have supplied rare and valuable photographs since the acknowledgments in Volume I went to press: Gen. G. W. C. Lee, C. S. A.; Col. E. F. Austin; R. B. Breen; Berry Benson, C. S. A.; Miss Sarah A. Smyth; W. H. Chamberlain, U. S. V.; Lieut-Col. Andrew Cowan U. S. V.; John Daniel, Jr., Late 7th Infantry, N. G. N. Y.; E. Drigg; Loyall Farragut; Miss A. L. Gill; Gen. Theodore S. Peck, U. S. V.; Col. C. F. Horner; James Howe; Mrs. T. M. Steger; C. D. MacDougall; Miss Cordelia Jackson; Mrs. John M. Keii· Gen. W. E. LeDuc, U. S. V.; A. W. Lanneau, C. S. A.; J. T. Lockwood, U. S. V.; Chas. L. McClung, U. S. N.; E. E. Patton; Walter A. Clark; A. K. Clark, C. S. A.; F. T. Peet; Miss Vera Pettit; Capt. Geo. J. Schmutz; A. Smith; Thomas W. Smith; Hon. H. L. Wait; D. H. Kerner; Rev. Thos. C. Walker; Jas. H. Ware; Mrs. Thos. S. Williams; Dr. D. H. Lamb; Capt. Robert L. Morris, C. S. A.; Ambrose Lee.

COPYRIGHT, 1911, REVIEW OF REVIEWS CO.

"SOLDIERS AND CITIZENS"

ROBERT E. LEE WITH FORMER UNION AND CONFEDERATE LEADERS
AFTER THE ARMIES' WORK WAS DONE

By great good fortune this unique photograph, taken at White Sulphur Springs, Virginia, in August, 1869, was preserved more than forty years by a Confederate veteran of Richmond, Mr. James Blair, through whose courtesy it appears here—to sound the key-note of this volume as no preface could. Such a fraternal gathering could have been paralleled after no other great war in history. For in this neighborly group, side by side, are bitter foemen of not five years past. Near the unmistakable figure of Lee stands Lew Wallace, the commander who in 1864 had opposed Lee's lieutenant—Early—at the Monocacy; the division leader who at Shiloh, first grand battle of the war, had fired on the lines in gray commanded by the dashing Confederate general who now touches him on the right—Beauregard. To the left stand Connor and Geary, formerly generals of opposing forces in the Carolinas. There is the tall "Prince John" Magruder, the venerable Henry A. Wise, and other one-time leaders of the Gray. And for a further touch of good citizenship, there is added the distinguished presence of George Peabody of Massachusetts, and W. W. Corcoran of Washington— philanthropists of the noblest type, but not alone in this group "as having helped their fellow men."

The Photographic History of The Civil War

Complete and Unabridged

TWO VOLUMES IN ONE.

Volume 5
*The Armies and Leaders
Poetry and Eloquence

Contributors

ROBERT S. LANIER
Managing Editor

WILLIAM CONANT CHURCH
Brevet Lieutenant-Colonel, U. S. V.; Editor of "The Army and Navy Journal"; Author of "Life of Ulysses S. Grant," "Life of John Ericsson," etc.

WILLIAM PETERFIELD TRENT, LL.D.
Professor of English Literature in Columbia University; Author of "Robert E. Lee," "Southern Statesmen of the Old Regime," etc.

WALTER LYNWOOD FLEMING, PH.D.
Professor of History, Louisiana State University; Author of "Secession and Reconstruction of Alabama," etc.

JOHN E. GILMAN
Commander-in-Chief, Grand Army of the Republic, 1910–1911

ALLEN C. REDWOOD
Artist and Author; Late Army of Northern Virginia; Author of "Johnny Reb Papers," etc.

HILARY A. HERBERT
Late Colonel, Eighth Alabama Infantry; Late Secretary of Navy of the United States

MARCUS J. WRIGHT
Late Brigadier-General, Confederate States Army; Agent for the Collection of War Records, United States War Department

SAMUEL A. CUNNINGHAM
Late Sergeant-Major, Confederate States Army; Founder and Editor of "The Confederate Veteran"

THE BLUE & GREY PRESS

PHOTOGRAPHIC HISTORY OF THE CIVIL WAR

Vol. 5
The Armies and Leaders
Poetry and Eloquence

Two Volumes in One.

Copyright © 1987 by The Blue & Grey Press,
a division of Book Sales, Inc.
110 Enterprise Avenue
Secaucus, NJ 07094

Printed in the United States of America.

ISBN: 1-55521-202-6

CONTENTS

PHOTOGRAPHIC DESCRIPTIONS THROUGHOUT THE VOLUME
  Roy Mason
  George L. Kilmer, Late U. S. V.

INTRODUCTION

SOLDIERS
AND
CITIZENS

VETERANS AFTER ONE YEAR

SELF-RELIANCE, COURAGE AND DIGNITY ARE IMPRINTED ON THE FACES OF THESE "VETERANS"—MEN OF MCCLERNAND'S CORPS IN THEIR QUARTERS AT MEMPHIS, TENNESSEE, AFTER THE COSTLY ATTEMPT ON VICKSBURG BY WAY OF CHICKASAW BLUFFS. YET THEY HAVE BEEN SOLDIERS HARDLY A YEAR—THE BOY ON THE RIGHT, SO SLIGHT AND YOUNG, MIGHT ALMOST BE MASQUERADING IN AN OFFICER'S UNIFORM. OF SUCH WERE THE SOLDIERS WHO EARLY IN THE WAR FOUGHT THE SOUTH IN THE FLUSH OF HER STRENGTH AND ENTHUSIASM

EDWIN M. STANTON
Secretary of War.

MONTGOMERY BLAIR
Postmaster-General.

GIDEON WELLES
Secretary of the Navy.

SALMON P. CHASE
Secretary of the Treasury.

HANNIBAL HAMLIN
Vice-President.

WILLIAM H. SEWARD
Secretary of State.

CALEB B. SMITH
Secretary of the Interior.

MEMBERS OF PRESIDENT LINCOLN'S OFFICIAL FAMILY

Other members were: War, Simon Cameron (1861); Treasury, W. P. Fessenden, July 1, 1864, and Hugh McCulloch, March 4, 1865; Interior, John P. Usher, January 8, 1863; Attorney-General, James Speed, December 2, 1864; Postmaster-General, William Dennison, September 24, 1864.

EDWARD BATES
Attorney-General.

JAMES A. SEDDON
Secretary of War.

CHRISTOPHER G. MEMMINGER
Secretary of the Treasury.

STEPHEN R. MALLORY
Secretary of the Navy.

JOHN H. REAGAN
Postmaster-General.

ALEXANDER H. STEPHENS
Vice-President.

JUDAH P. BENJAMIN
Secretary of State.

MEN WHO HELPED PRESIDENT DAVIS GUIDE THE SHIP OF STATE

The members of the Cabinet were chosen not from intimate friends of the President, but from the men preferred by the States they represented. There was no Secretary of the Interior in the Confederate Cabinet.

GEORGE DAVIS
Attorney-General.

VICE-PRESIDENT STEPHENS AND MEMBERS OF THE CONFEDERATE CABINET

Judah P. Benjamin, Secretary of State, has been called the brain of the Confederacy. President Davis wished to appoint the Honorable Robert Barnwell, Secretary of State, but Mr. Barnwell declined the honor.

AFTER THE GREAT MASS MEETING IN UNION SQUARE, NEW YORK, APRIL 20, 1861

Knots of citizens still linger around the stands where Anderson, who had abandoned Sumter only six days before, had just roused the multitude to wild enthusiasm. Of this gathering in support of the Government the *New York Herald* said at the time: "Such a mighty uprising of the people has never before been witnessed in New York, nor throughout the whole length and breadth of the Union. Five stands were erected, from which some of the most able speakers of the city and state addressed the multitude on the necessity of rallying around the flag of the Republic in this hour of its danger. A series of resolutions was proposed and unanimously adopted, pledging the meeting to use every means to preserve the Union intact and inviolate. Great unanimity prevailed throughout the whole proceedings; party politics were ignored, and the entire meeting—speakers and listeners—were a unit in maintaining the national honor unsullied. Major Anderson, the hero of Fort Sumter, was present, and showed himself at the various stands, at each of which he was most enthusiastically received. An impressive feature of the occasion was the flag of Sumter, hoisted on the stump of the staff that had been shot away, placed in the hand of the equestrian statue of Washington."

[14]

RECRUITING ON BROADWAY, 1861

Looking north on Broadway from "The Park" (later City Hall Park) in war time, one sees the Stars and Stripes waving above the recruiting station, p a s t which the soldiers stroll. There is a convenient booth with liquid refreshments. To the right of the picture the rear end of a street car is visible, but passenger travel on Broadway itself is by stage. On the left is the Astor House, then one of the foremost hostelries of the city. In the lower photograph the view is from the

balcony of the Metropolitan looking north on Broadway. The twin towers on the left are those of St. Thomas's Church. The lumbering stages, with the deafening noise of their rattling windows as they drive over the cobblestones, are here in force. More hoop-skirts are retreating in the distance, and a gentleman in the tall hat of the period is on his way down town. Few of the buildings seen here remained half a century later. The time is summer, as the awnings attest.

THE WAR'S GREAT "CITIZEN" AT HIS MOMENT OF TRIUMPH

Just behind the round table to the right, rising head and shoulders above the distinguished bystanders, grasping his manuscript in both hands, stands Abraham Lincoln. Of all the occasions on which he talked to his countrymen, this was most significant. The time and place marked the final and lasting approval of his political and military policies. Despite the bitter opposition of a majority of the Northern political and social leaders, the people of the Northern States had renominated Lincoln in June, 1864. In November, encouraged by the victories of Farragut at Mobile, Sherman in Georgia, and Sheridan in the Shenandoah Valley, they had reëlected him President of the United States by an electoral vote of 212 to 21. Since the election, continued Northern victories had made certain the

LINCOLN READING HIS SECOND INAUGURAL ADDRESS ON MARCH 4, 1865

speedy termination of the war. Not long since, his opponents had been so numerous and so powerful that they fully expected to prevent his renomination. Lincoln himself, shortly after his renomination, had come to believe that reelection was improbable, and had expressed himself as ready "to cooperate with the President-elect to save the Union." Yet neither in Lincoln's demeanor nor in his inaugural address is there the slighest note of personal exultation. For political and military enemies alike he has " malice toward none; charity for all." Indeed the dominant feeling in his speech is one of sorrow and sympathy for the cruel sufferings of both North and South. Not only in the United States, but throughout the civilized world, the address made a profound and immediate impression.

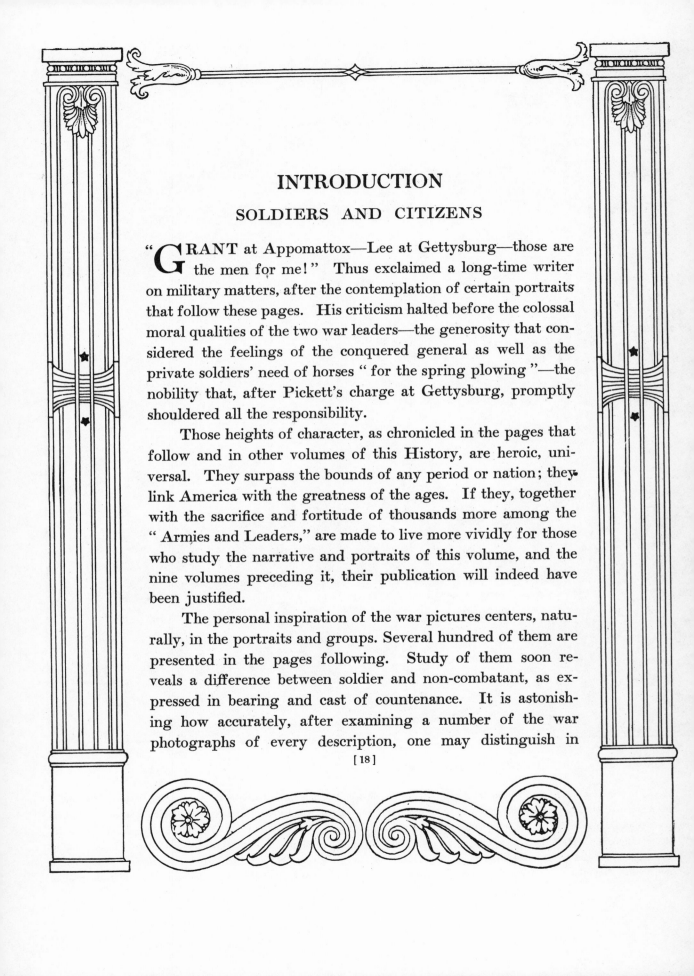

INTRODUCTION

SOLDIERS AND CITIZENS

"GRANT at Appomattox—Lee at Gettysburg—those are the men for me!" Thus exclaimed a long-time writer on military matters, after the contemplation of certain portraits that follow these pages. His criticism halted before the colossal moral qualities of the two war leaders—the generosity that considered the feelings of the conquered general as well as the private soldiers' need of horses "for the spring plowing"—the nobility that, after Pickett's charge at Gettysburg, promptly shouldered all the responsibility.

Those heights of character, as chronicled in the pages that follow and in other volumes of this History, are heroic, universal. They surpass the bounds of any period or nation; they link America with the greatness of the ages. If they, together with the sacrifice and fortitude of thousands more among the "Armies and Leaders," are made to live more vividly for those who study the narrative and portraits of this volume, and the nine volumes preceding it, their publication will indeed have been justified.

The personal inspiration of the war pictures centers, naturally, in the portraits and groups. Several hundred of them are presented in the pages following. Study of them soon reveals a difference between soldier and non-combatant, as expressed in bearing and cast of countenance. It is astonishing how accurately, after examining a number of the war photographs of every description, one may distinguish in

**FROM
THE ARMY
TO THE
WHITE HOUSE**

War-time portraits of
six soldiers whose
military records
assisted them
to the Pres-
idential
Chair.

Garfield in '63—(left to right) Thomas, Wiles, Tyler, Simmons, Drillard, Ducat, Barnett, Goddard,
Rosecrans, Garfield, Porter, Bond, Thompson, Sheridan.

Brig.-Gen. Andrew Johnson
President, 1865–69.

General Ulysses S. Grant
President, 1869–77.

Bvt. Maj.-Gen. Rutherford B. Hayes
President, 1877–81.

Maj.-Gen. James A. Garfield
President, March to September, 1881.

Bvt. Brig.-Gen. Benjamin Harrison
President, 1889–93.

Brevet Major William McKinley
President, 1897–1901.

many cases between fighters and non-combatants. This is true, even when the latter are represented in full army over-coats, with swords and the like, as was customary to some extent with postmasters, quartermasters, commissariat and hospital attendants.

The features are distinctive of the men who have stood up under fire, and undergone the even severer ordeal of submission to a will working for the common good, involving the sacrifice of personal independence. Their dignity and quiet self-confidence are obscured neither by the extreme growth of facial hair fashionable in the sixties, nor by the stains of marching and camping. Where the photograph "caught" the real soldiers under any circumstances of dress or undress, health or disease, camp-ease, or wounds that had laid the subjects low, the stamp of discipline stands revealed.

The young officers' portraits afford particularly interesting study. The habit of quick decision, the weighing of responsibilities involving thousands of human lives which has become a daily matter, like the morning and evening train-catching of the modern business commuter—these swift and tremendous affairs are borne with surprising calmness upon the young shoulders.

To represent in some coherent form the men of Civil War time, this volume has been set aside. It becomes highly desirable to the fundamental plan of this history.

The first three volumes, devoted to narrative in the largest sense, and to scenes, could present portraits only of officers and men connected with particular operations. Each of the next six volumes, occupied as it is with a special phase of war-time activity—cavalry, artillery, prisons and hospitals, or the like

Brevet Major George Haven Putnam, 176th New York, Prisoner at Libby and Danville in the Winter cf 1864-65.

Brevet Lieut.-Colonel Harrison Gray Otis: Twice Wounded; Brig.-Gen. in Spanish War, Maj.-Gen. in Philippines.

Chief of Scouts Henry Watterson, C. S. A., Aide-de-Camp to General Forrest, Chief of Scouts under General Jcs. E. Johnston.

REPRESENTATIVE CIVIL WAR OFFICERS—SUCCESSFUL ALSO IN LATER LIFE

Andrew Carnegie Superintended Military Railways and Government Telegraph Lines in 1861.

George Haven Putnam, publisher and author, led in the move for international copyright. Harrison Gray Otis served as an editor in California more than 30 years, and fought again in the Spanish War. Henry Watterson, as editor of the Louisville *Courier-Journal*, did much to reconcile North and South. Andrew Carnegie's millions, made from iron and steel, went largely to philanthropy and the advancement of peace. Nathan B. Forrest, the daring Confederate cavalryman, later developed two vast plantations. Thomas T. Eckert became President of the Western Union Telegraph Company. Grenville M. Dodge, Chief Engineer of the Union Pacific, built thousands of miles of railroads, opening up the Western empire.

Lieut.-General Nathan B. Forrest, C. S. A., Entered as Private; Lieut.-Col., 1861, Maj.-Gen., 1864.

Brevet Brig.-General Thomas T. Eckert, Superintendent of Military Telegraph; Asst. Sec. of War, 1864–66.

Maj.-General Grenville M. Dodge, Wounded Before Atlanta; Succeeded Rosecrans in the Department of Missouri.

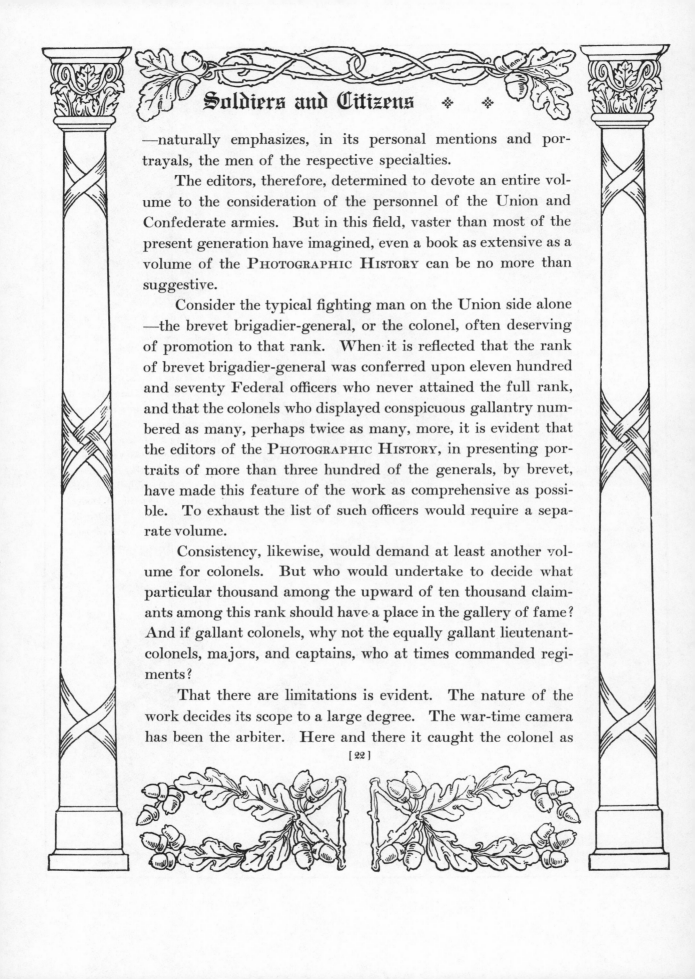

—naturally emphasizes, in its personal mentions and portrayals, the men of the respective specialties.

The editors, therefore, determined to devote an entire volume to the consideration of the personnel of the Union and Confederate armies. But in this field, vaster than most of the present generation have imagined, even a book as extensive as a volume of the PHOTOGRAPHIC HISTORY can be no more than suggestive.

Consider the typical fighting man on the Union side alone —the brevet brigadier-general, or the colonel, often deserving of promotion to that rank. When it is reflected that the rank of brevet brigadier-general was conferred upon eleven hundred and seventy Federal officers who never attained the full rank, and that the colonels who displayed conspicuous gallantry numbered as many, perhaps twice as many, more, it is evident that the editors of the PHOTOGRAPHIC HISTORY, in presenting portraits of more than three hundred of the generals, by brevet, have made this feature of the work as comprehensive as possible. To exhaust the list of such officers would require a separate volume.

Consistency, likewise, would demand at least another volume for colonels. But who would undertake to decide what particular thousand among the upward of ten thousand claimants among this rank should have a place in the gallery of fame? And if gallant colonels, why not the equally gallant lieutenant-colonels, majors, and captains, who at times commanded regiments?

That there are limitations is evident. The nature of the work decides its scope to a large degree. The war-time camera has been the arbiter. Here and there it caught the colonel as

Brevet Brigadier-General Stewart L. Woodford, Lieut.-Gov. of New York, 1866–68; President Electoral College, 1872; M. C., 1873–75; U. S. Dist. Atty., 1877–83; U. S. Minister to Spain, 1879–98.

Brevet Brigadier-General James Grant Wilson, Author of Addresses on Lincoln, Grant, Hull, Farragut, etc.; President New York Gen. and Biog. Soc. and of Am. Ethnological Society.

Brevet Major-General William B. Hazen, Chief Signal Officer, Raised 41st Ohio Volunteers; Marched with Sherman to the Sea; Commanded 15th Army Corps; U. S Military Attaché to France.

WAR–TIME PORTRAITS OF TYPICAL SOLDIERS WHO TURNED TO PUBLIC LIFE AND EDUCATION

Notable as lawyers, writers and statesmen are General Carl Schurz (on the left), who became Minister to Spain, Secretary of the Interior, and editor of the New York *Evening Post;* and General Lewis Wallace (to the right), Governor of New Mexico, Minister to Turkey, and author of "Ben Hur" and other historical novels.

Major-General Carl Schurz.

Major-General Lewis Wallace.

Colonel George E. Waring, Jr., Led a Brigade of Cavalry; Reorganized Street Cleaning System of New York City; Died in Havana, Cuba, Fighting Yellow Fever.

Brevet Brigadier-General Francis W. Palfrey, Register in Bankruptcy in 1872; Author of "Antietam and Fredericksburg" in 1882; Author of Many Scholarly and Important Papers.

Lieutenant E. Benjamin Andrews: Wounded at Petersburg, 1864; Professor of History and Political Economy, Brown University, 1882–88; President thereof, 1889–98.

Brevet Brigadier-General Francis A. Walker, Superintendent Ninth and Tenth Censuses; Commissioner of Indian Affairs in 1872; President Mass. Inst. of Technology, 1881.

well as the general, the captain as well as the colonel, and the private as well as the captain. On the whole, its work was well balanced, marvelously so, and the results are before the readers of the PHOTOGRAPHIC HISTORY.

If so slight a proportion can be shown of the men distinguished for their fighting, it obviously becomes impossible, even should the ten volumes consist of portraits alone, to represent adequately the soldiers whose fame has come since 1865.

Merely to suggest the function of the Civil War as a school of citizenship, portraits are presented with this introduction of six soldiers who became President; of a group like Grenville M. Dodge, Harrison Gray Otis, and Thomas T. Eckert, who helped to develop American material resources; together with several, such as Henry Watterson, Carl Schurz, George E. Waring, Jr., and Francis A. Walker, whose influence has put much of our journalism and public life on a higher plane.

As these lines are penned, no less than four Civil War soldiers—two Union, two Confederate—are serving as members of the highest American tribunal—the Supreme Court:—Chief Justice White and Justice Lurton (Confederate); Justices Harlan and Holmes (Union). Ex-Confederates again have been found in the cabinets of both Republican and Democratic Presidents, as well as in the National Congress.

But immense indeed would be the literary enterprise undertaking to cover all the results in American civic life of Civil War training. There have been State governors by the hundreds who could look back upon service with the armies. There have been members of legislatures by the tens of thou-

WAR–TIME POR-
TRAITS OF FEDERAL
SOLDIERS WHO CON-
TRIBUTED TO THE
PHOTOGRAPHIC
HISTORY HALF A
CENTURY LATER

Captain A. W. Greely, 1863; Later Maj.-
Gen., U. S. A.; Chief Signal Service
("Signals"; "Telegraph").

Private Geo. L. Kilmer in '64, Wearing
the "Veteran Stripe" at 18
(Military Editor).

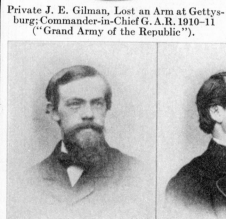

Private J. E. Gilman, Lost an Arm at Gettysburg; Commander-in-Chief G. A.R. 1910–11
("Grand Army of the Republic").

Bvt. Brig.-Gen. T. F. Roden-
bough, U. S. A., in 1865;
Wounded at Trevilian and
Winchester; Later Sec-
retary U. S. Military
Service Institution
("Cavalry" Editor).

Capt. F. Y. Hedley in '64, Age 20; Later Editor
and Author of "Marching Through Georgia"
("School of the Soldier," "Marching
and Foraging").

Col. W. C. Church; Later Edi-
tor of the *Army and Navy
Journal* and Author of Life of
Ulysses S. Grant ("Grant").

T. S. C. Lowe, Military Bal-
loonist in the Peninsula Campaign, 1862—the First War
Aeronaut ("Balloons").

Capt. T.S. Peck; Medal of Hon-
or in 1864; Later Adj.-Gen.
of Vermont (Contributor of
many rare photographs).

Col. L. R. Stegman, Wounded
at Cedar Creek, Gettysburg,
Ringgold and Pine Moun-
tain (Consulting Editor).

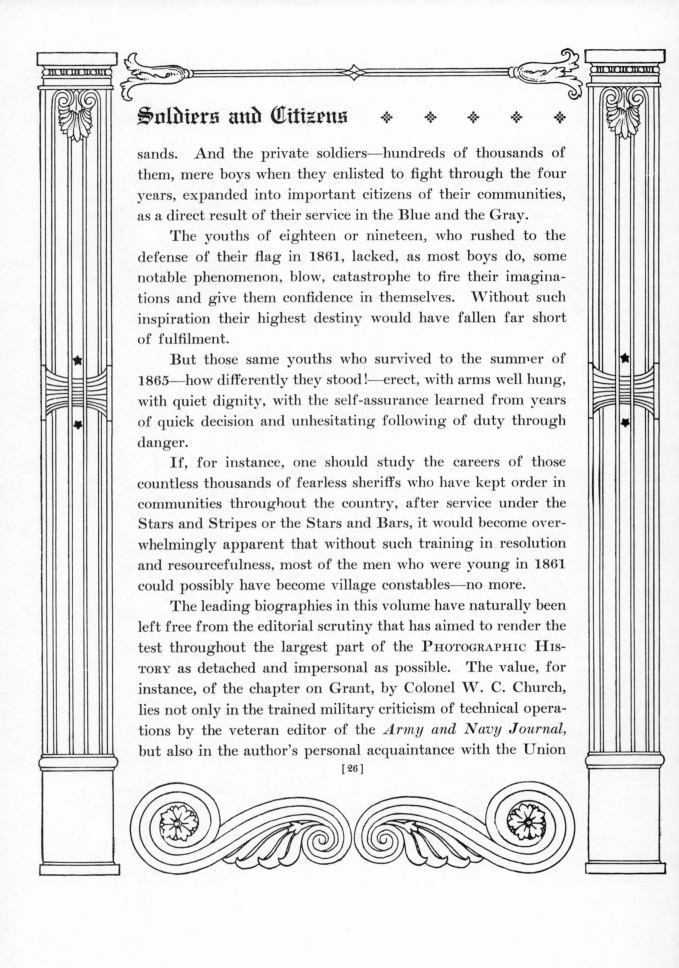

Soldiers and Citizens ✦ ✦ ✦ ✦ ✦

sands. And the private soldiers—hundreds of thousands of them, mere boys when they enlisted to fight through the four years, expanded into important citizens of their communities, as a direct result of their service in the Blue and the Gray.

The youths of eighteen or nineteen, who rushed to the defense of their flag in 1861, lacked, as most boys do, some notable phenomenon, blow, catastrophe to fire their imaginations and give them confidence in themselves. Without such inspiration their highest destiny would have fallen far short of fulfilment.

But those same youths who survived to the summer of 1865—how differently they stood!—erect, with arms well hung, with quiet dignity, with the self-assurance learned from years of quick decision and unhesitating following of duty through danger.

If, for instance, one should study the careers of those countless thousands of fearless sheriffs who have kept order in communities throughout the country, after service under the Stars and Stripes or the Stars and Bars, it would become overwhelmingly apparent that without such training in resolution and resourcefulness, most of the men who were young in 1861 could possibly have become village constables—no more.

The leading biographies in this volume have naturally been left free from the editorial scrutiny that has aimed to render the test throughout the largest part of the PHOTOGRAPHIC HISTORY as detached and impersonal as possible. The value, for instance, of the chapter on Grant, by Colonel W. C. Church, lies not only in the trained military criticism of technical operations by the veteran editor of the *Army and Navy Journal*, but also in the author's personal acquaintance with the Union

WAR–TIME
PHOTOGRAPHS OF
CONFEDERATE SOLDIERS

CONTRIBUTORS TO THE
PHOTOGRAPHIC
HISTORY

Col. Hilary A. Herbert; Later Member of Congress and Secretary of the Navy ("The Meaning of Losses in Battle").

Lieut.-Col. J. W. Mallet; Later Professor of Chemistry, University of Virginia ("Confederate Ordnance").

Private John A. Wyeth in '61, at 16; Later Organizer of the New York "Polyclinic" ("Confederate Raids").

Lieut. R. H. McKim in '62; Later Rector Church of the Epiphany, Washington, and Military and Religious Writer ("The Confederate Army").

Captain F. M. Colston, Artillery Officer with Alexander ("Memoirs of Gettysburg" and Many Rare Photographs).

Allen C. Redwood, of the 55th Virginia, with "Stonewall" Jackson; Later Artist and Author (Confederate Reminiscences; "Jackson").

Brig.-Gen. M. J. Wright; Later U. S. War Dept. Agent ("Records of the War" and Statistics).

Col. D. G. McIntosh; Later Attorney-at-Law ("Artillery of the Confederacy").

Col. T. M. R. Talcott; Later Civil Engineer ("Reminiscences of the Confederate Engineers").

S. A. Cunningham; Later Editor Confederate Veteran ("United Confederate Veterans").

Deering J. Roberts, Surgeon; Later Editor Southern Practitioner ("Confederate Medical Service").

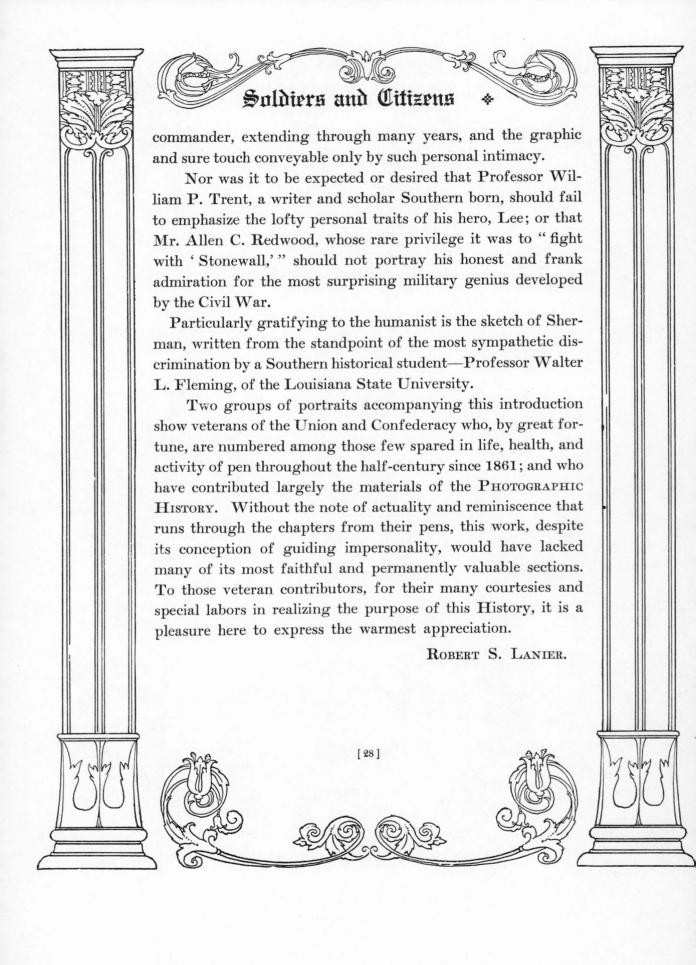

commander, extending through many years, and the graphic and sure touch conveyable only by such personal intimacy.

Nor was it to be expected or desired that Professor William P. Trent, a writer and scholar Southern born, should fail to emphasize the lofty personal traits of his hero, Lee; or that Mr. Allen C. Redwood, whose rare privilege it was to "fight with 'Stonewall,'" should not portray his honest and frank admiration for the most surprising military genius developed by the Civil War.

Particularly gratifying to the humanist is the sketch of Sherman, written from the standpoint of the most sympathetic discrimination by a Southern historical student—Professor Walter L. Fleming, of the Louisiana State University.

Two groups of portraits accompanying this introduction show veterans of the Union and Confederacy who, by great fortune, are numbered among those few spared in life, health, and activity of pen throughout the half-century since 1861; and who have contributed largely the materials of the PHOTOGRAPHIC HISTORY. Without the note of actuality and reminiscence that runs through the chapters from their pens, this work, despite its conception of guiding impersonality, would have lacked many of its most faithful and permanently valuable sections. To those veteran contributors, for their many courtesies and special labors in realizing the purpose of this History, it is a pleasure here to express the warmest appreciation.

ROBERT S. LANIER.

I

GRANT

DURING THE WILDERNESS CAMPAIGN, 1864

WHEN GRANT LOST AN ARMY BUT SAVED A NATION

GRANT ON LOOKOUT MOUNTAIN—1863

Wearing epaulets and a sword—quite unusual for him—but calm and imperturbable as of old, with his crumpled army hat, plain blouse, his trousers tucked into his boot-tops, and the inevitable cigar, Ulysses S. Grant stands at a historic spot. Less than a week before, when the Union soldiers under Thomas, still smarting from their experience at Chickamauga, stood gazing at the Confederate works behind which rose the crest of Missionary Ridge, the Stars and Stripes were thrown to the breeze on the crest of Lookout Mountain. Eager hands pointed, and a great cheer went up from the Army of the Cumberland. They knew that the Union troops with Hooker had carried the day in their "battle above the clouds." That was the 25th of November, 1863; and that same afternoon the soldiers

AT THE SPOT WHERE HOOKER SIGNALED VICTORY THE WEEK BEFORE

of Thomas swarmed over the crest of Missionary Ridge while Grant himself looked on and wondered. When a few days later Grant visited the spot whence the flag was waved, an enterprising photographer, already on the spot, preserved the striking scene. Seated with his back against a tree, General J. A. Rawlins gazes at his leader. Behind him stands General Webster, and leaning against the tree in Colonel Clark B. Lagow. The figure in the right foreground is Colonel William S. Hillyer. Seated by the path is an orderly. They have evidently come to survey the site of Hooker's battle from above. Colonel Lagow is carrying a pair of field glasses. Less than four months later Grant was commissioned lieutenant-general and placed in general command of the Union armies.

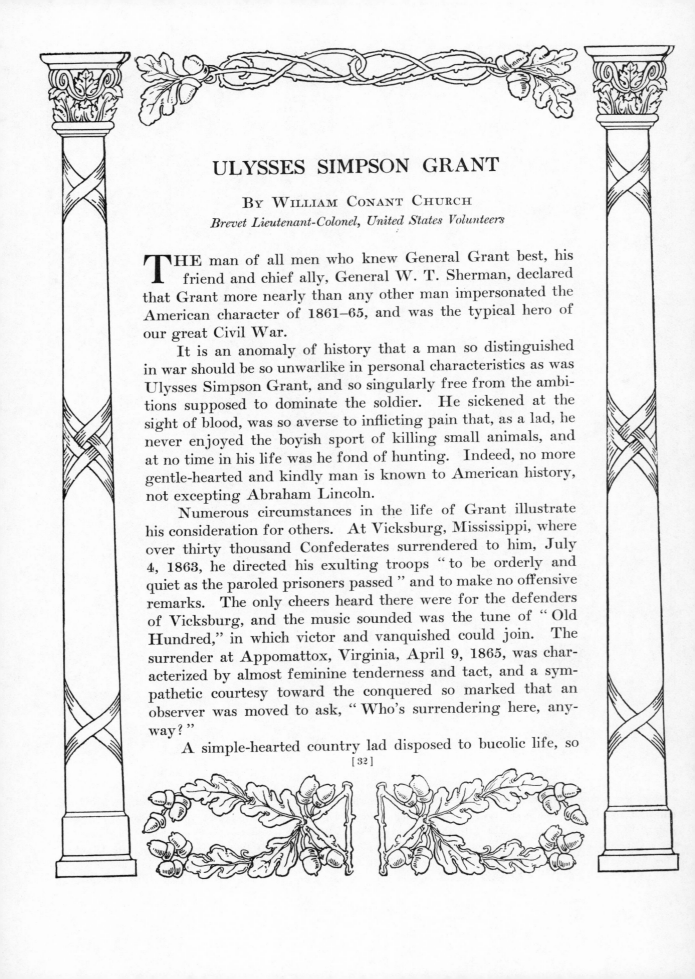

ULYSSES SIMPSON GRANT

BY WILLIAM CONANT CHURCH
Brevet Lieutenant-Colonel, United States Volunteers

THE man of all men who knew General Grant best, his friend and chief ally, General W. T. Sherman, declared that Grant more nearly than any other man impersonated the American character of 1861–65, and was the typical hero of our great Civil War.

It is an anomaly of history that a man so distinguished in war should be so unwarlike in personal characteristics as was Ulysses Simpson Grant, and so singularly free from the ambitions supposed to dominate the soldier. He sickened at the sight of blood, was so averse to inflicting pain that, as a lad, he never enjoyed the boyish sport of killing small animals, and at no time in his life was he fond of hunting. Indeed, no more gentle-hearted and kindly man is known to American history, not excepting Abraham Lincoln.

Numerous circumstances in the life of Grant illustrate his consideration for others. At Vicksburg, Mississippi, where over thirty thousand Confederates surrendered to him, July 4, 1863, he directed his exulting troops "to be orderly and quiet as the paroled prisoners passed" and to make no offensive remarks. The only cheers heard there were for the defenders of Vicksburg, and the music sounded was the tune of "Old Hundred," in which victor and vanquished could join. The surrender at Appomattox, Virginia, April 9, 1865, was characterized by almost feminine tenderness and tact, and a sympathetic courtesy toward the conquered so marked that an observer was moved to ask, "Who's surrendering here, anyway?"

A simple-hearted country lad disposed to bucolic life, so

[32]

GRANT IN 1863—BEFORE THE FIRST OF HIS GREAT VICTORIES

Grant was described in 1861 as a man "who knows how to do things." In February, 1862, he captured Forts Henry and Donelson, thus opening the way for a Federal advance up the Tennessee River, and was promptly commissioned major-general. His experience at Shiloh in April, coupled with failures in official routine during the Donelson campaign which were not approved by his superiors, left him under a cloud which was not removed until the capture of Vicksburg, July 4, 1863, revealed capacity of a high order. The government's plan of conducting the war was then entrusted to him to work out with practically unlimited power.

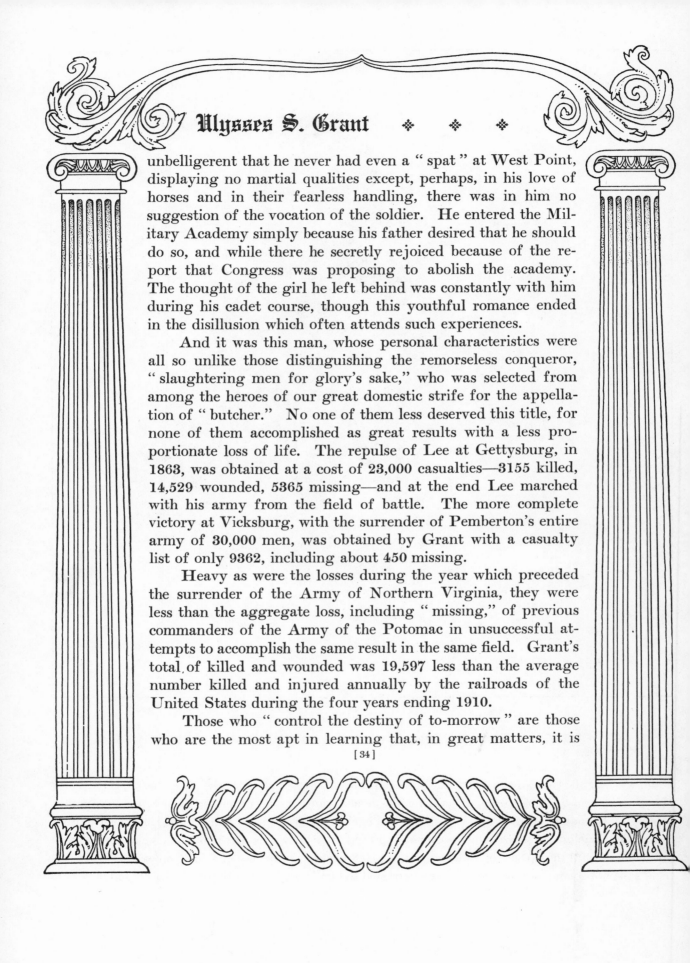

unbelligerent that he never had even a " spat " at West Point, displaying no martial qualities except, perhaps, in his love of horses and in their fearless handling, there was in him no suggestion of the vocation of the soldier. He entered the Military Academy simply because his father desired that he should do so, and while there he secretly rejoiced because of the report that Congress was proposing to abolish the academy. The thought of the girl he left behind was constantly with him during his cadet course, though this youthful romance ended in the disillusion which often attends such experiences.

And it was this man, whose personal characteristics were all so unlike those distinguishing the remorseless conqueror, " slaughtering men for glory's sake," who was selected from among the heroes of our great domestic strife for the appellation of " butcher." No one of them less deserved this title, for none of them accomplished as great results with a less proportionate loss of life. The repulse of Lee at Gettysburg, in 1863, was obtained at a cost of 23,000 casualties—3155 killed, 14,529 wounded, 5365 missing—and at the end Lee marched with his army from the field of battle. The more complete victory at Vicksburg, with the surrender of Pemberton's entire army of 30,000 men, was obtained by Grant with a casualty list of only 9362, including about 450 missing.

Heavy as were the losses during the year which preceded the surrender of the Army of Northern Virginia, they were less than the aggregate loss, including " missing," of previous commanders of the Army of the Potomac in unsuccessful attempts to accomplish the same result in the same field. Grant's total of killed and wounded was 19,597 less than the average number killed and injured annually by the railroads of the United States during the four years ending 1910.

Those who " control the destiny of to-morrow " are those who are the most apt in learning that, in great matters, it is

BEFORE VICKSBURG

AFTER VICKSBURG

The close-set mouth, squared shoulders and lowering brow in this photograph of Grant, taken in December, 1862, tell the story of the intensity of his purpose while he was advancing upon Vicksburg—only to be foiled by Van Dorn's raid on his line of communications at Holly Springs. His grim expression and determined jaw betokened no respite for the Confederates, however. Six months later he marched into the coveted stronghold. This photograph was taken by James Mullen at Oxford, Mississippi, in December, 1862, just before Van Dorn's raid balked the general's plans.

This photograph was taken in the fall of 1863, after the capture of the Confederacy's Gibraltar had raised Grant to secure and everlasting fame. His attitude is relaxed and his eyebrows no longer mark a straight line across the grim visage. The right brow is slightly arched with an almost jovial expression. But the jaw is no less vigorous and determined, and the steadfast eyes seem to be peering into that future which holds more victories. He still has Chattanooga and his great campaigns in the East to fight and the final magnificent struggle in the trenches at Petersburg.

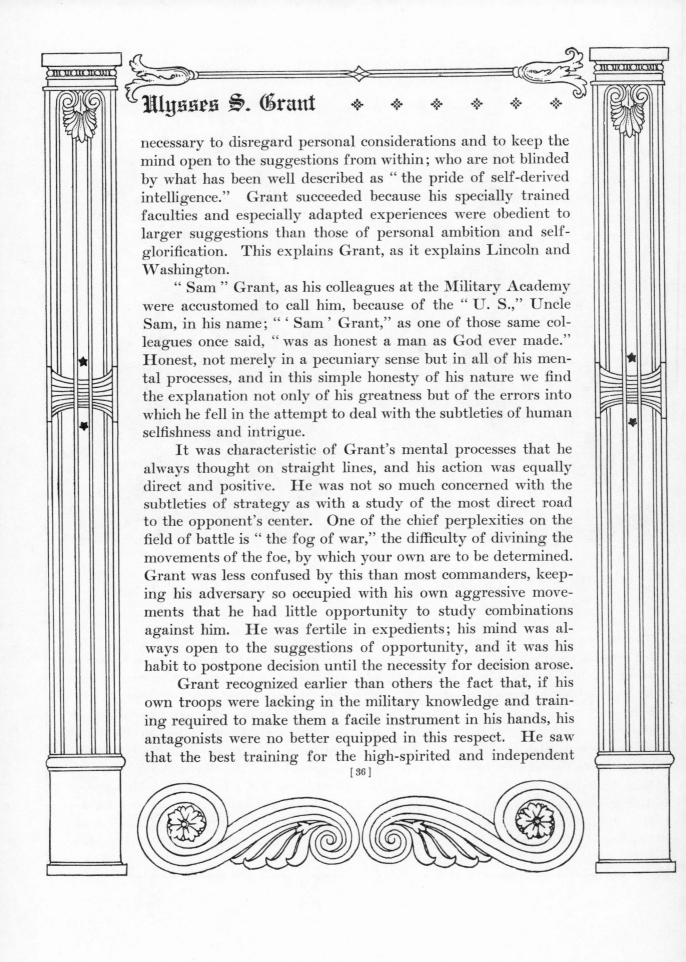

necessary to disregard personal considerations and to keep the mind open to the suggestions from within; who are not blinded by what has been well described as " the pride of self-derived intelligence." Grant succeeded because his specially trained faculties and especially adapted experiences were obedient to larger suggestions than those of personal ambition and self-glorification. This explains Grant, as it explains Lincoln and Washington.

" Sam " Grant, as his colleagues at the Military Academy were accustomed to call him, because of the " U. S.," Uncle Sam, in his name; " ' Sam ' Grant," as one of those same colleagues once said, " was as honest a man as God ever made." Honest, not merely in a pecuniary sense but in all of his mental processes, and in this simple honesty of his nature we find the explanation not only of his greatness but of the errors into which he fell in the attempt to deal with the subtleties of human selfishness and intrigue.

It was characteristic of Grant's mental processes that he always thought on straight lines, and his action was equally direct and positive. He was not so much concerned with the subtleties of strategy as with a study of the most direct road to the opponent's center. One of the chief perplexities on the field of battle is " the fog of war," the difficulty of divining the movements of the foe, by which your own are to be determined. Grant was less confused by this than most commanders, keeping his adversary so occupied with his own aggressive movements that he had little opportunity to study combinations against him. He was fertile in expedients; his mind was always open to the suggestions of opportunity, and it was his habit to postpone decision until the necessity for decision arose.

Grant recognized earlier than others the fact that, if his own troops were lacking in the military knowledge and training required to make them a facile instrument in his hands, his antagonists were no better equipped in this respect. He saw that the best training for the high-spirited and independent

On this page are three photographs of General Grant, taken in the most critical year of his career, the year when he took Vicksburg in July, then in November gazed in wonder at his own soldiers as they swarmed up the heights of Missionary Ridge. The following March he was made general-in-chief of the armies of the United States. Congress passed a vote of thanks to General Grant and his army, and ordered a gold medal to be struck in his honor. But as we see him here, none of these honors had come to him; and the deeds themselves were only in process of accomplishment. Even Sherman, the staunch friend and supporter of Grant, had doubts which were only dispelled by the master stroke at Vicksburg, as to the outcome of Grant's extraordinary methods and plans. He was himself conscious of the heavy responsibility resting upon him and of the fact that he stood on trial before the country. Other faithful generals had been condemned at the bar of public opinion before their projects matured. The eyes in these portraits are stern, and the expressions intense.

GRANT IN 1863

PORTRAITS OF 1863—SHOWING GRANT IN REPOSE

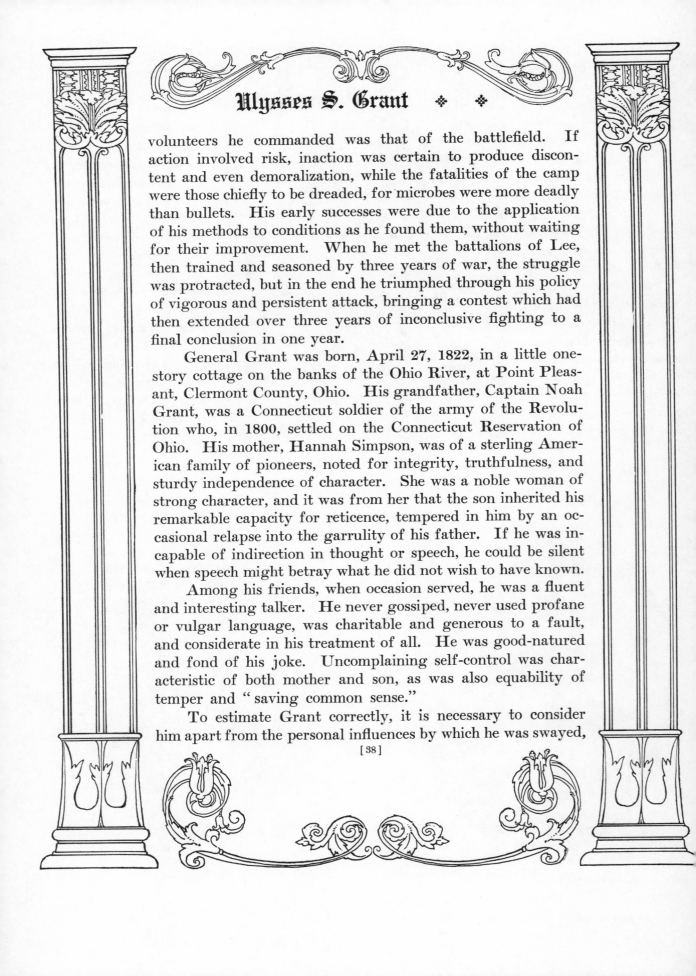

volunteers he commanded was that of the battlefield. If action involved risk, inaction was certain to produce discontent and even demoralization, while the fatalities of the camp were those chiefly to be dreaded, for microbes were more deadly than bullets. His early successes were due to the application of his methods to conditions as he found them, without waiting for their improvement. When he met the battalions of Lee, then trained and seasoned by three years of war, the struggle was protracted, but in the end he triumphed through his policy of vigorous and persistent attack, bringing a contest which had then extended over three years of inconclusive fighting to a final conclusion in one year.

General Grant was born, April 27, 1822, in a little one-story cottage on the banks of the Ohio River, at Point Pleasant, Clermont County, Ohio. His grandfather, Captain Noah Grant, was a Connecticut soldier of the army of the Revolution who, in 1800, settled on the Connecticut Reservation of Ohio. His mother, Hannah Simpson, was of a sterling American family of pioneers, noted for integrity, truthfulness, and sturdy independence of character. She was a noble woman of strong character, and it was from her that the son inherited his remarkable capacity for reticence, tempered in him by an occasional relapse into the garrulity of his father. If he was incapable of indirection in thought or speech, he could be silent when speech might betray what he did not wish to have known.

Among his friends, when occasion served, he was a fluent and interesting talker. He never gossiped, never used profane or vulgar language, was charitable and generous to a fault, and considerate in his treatment of all. He was good-natured and fond of his joke. Uncomplaining self-control was characteristic of both mother and son, as was also equability of temper and " saving common sense."

To estimate Grant correctly, it is necessary to consider him apart from the personal influences by which he was swayed,

IN THE AUTUMN OF 1863—GRANT'S CHANGING EXPRESSIONS

Although secure in his fame as the conqueror of Vicksburg, Grant still has the greater part of his destiny to fulfil as he faces the camera. Before him lie the Wilderness, Spotsylvania, Cold Harbor, and the slow investment of Petersburg. This series forms a particularly interesting study in expression. At the left hand, the face looks almost amused. In the next the expression is graver, the mouth close set. The third picture looks plainly obstinate, and in the last the stern fighter might have been declaring, as in the following spring: "I propose to fight it out on this line if it takes all summer." The eyes, first unveiled fully in this fourth view, are the unmistakable index to Grant's stern inflexibility, once his decision was made.

IN THE AUTUMN OF 1864—AFTER THE STRAIN OF THE WILDERNESS CAMPAIGN

Here is a furrowed brow above eyes worn by pain. In the pictures of the previous year the forehead is more smooth, the expression grave yet confident. Here the expression is that of a man who has won, but won at a bitter cost. It is the memory of the 50,000 men whom he left in the Wilderness campaign and at Cold Harbor that has lined this brow, and closed still tighter this inflexible mouth. Again, as in the series above, the eyes are not revealed until the last picture. Then again flashes the determination of a hero. The great general's biographers say that Grant was a man of sympathy and infinite pity. It was the more difficult for him, spurred on to the duty by grim necessity, to order forward the lines in blue that withered, again and again, before the Confederate fire, but each time weakened the attenuated line which confronted them.

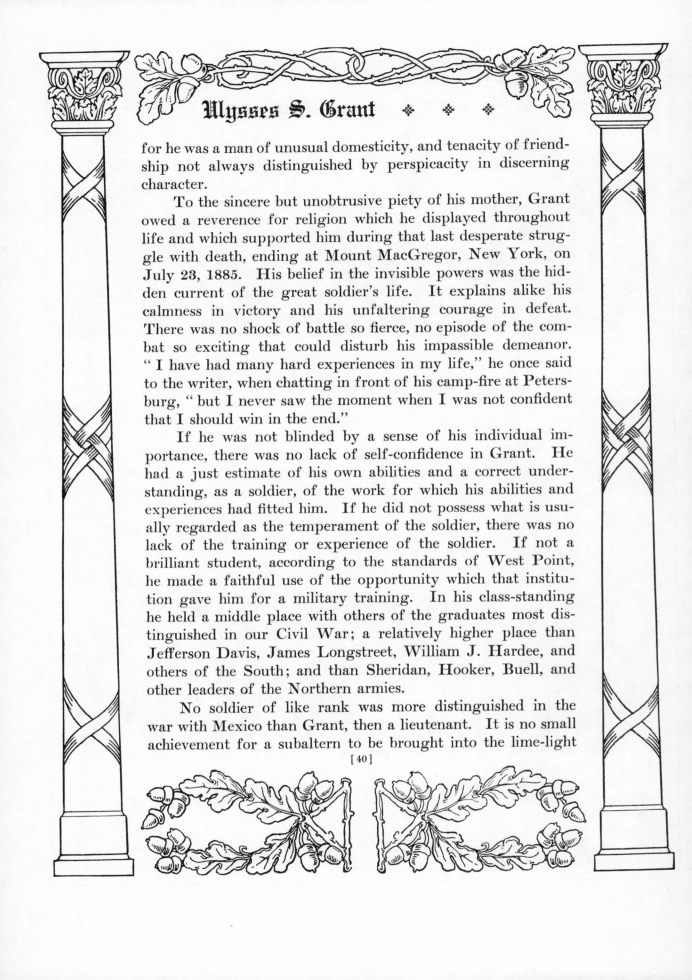

for he was a man of unusual domesticity, and tenacity of friendship not always distinguished by perspicacity in discerning character.

To the sincere but unobtrusive piety of his mother, Grant owed a reverence for religion which he displayed throughout life and which supported him during that last desperate struggle with death, ending at Mount MacGregor, New York, on July 23, 1885. His belief in the invisible powers was the hidden current of the great soldier's life. It explains alike his calmness in victory and his unfaltering courage in defeat. There was no shock of battle so fierce, no episode of the combat so exciting that could disturb his impassible demeanor. " I have had many hard experiences in my life," he once said to the writer, when chatting in front of his camp-fire at Petersburg, " but I never saw the moment when I was not confident that I should win in the end."

If he was not blinded by a sense of his individual importance, there was no lack of self-confidence in Grant. He had a just estimate of his own abilities and a correct understanding, as a soldier, of the work for which his abilities and experiences had fitted him. If he did not possess what is usually regarded as the temperament of the soldier, there was no lack of the training or experience of the soldier. If not a brilliant student, according to the standards of West Point, he made a faithful use of the opportunity which that institution gave him for a military training. In his class-standing he held a middle place with others of the graduates most distinguished in our Civil War; a relatively higher place than Jefferson Davis, James Longstreet, William J. Hardee, and others of the South; and than Sheridan, Hooker, Buell, and other leaders of the Northern armies.

No soldier of like rank was more distinguished in the war with Mexico than Grant, then a lieutenant. It is no small achievement for a subaltern to be brought into the lime-light

GRANT

IN JUNE, 1864—

A SUMMER DAY AT CITY POINT

Third from the left sits General Grant at his headquarters at City Point, on a high bluff at the junction of the James and the Appomattox rivers. At this moment his reputation hangs in the balance. In the three successive battles of the Wilderness, Spotsylvania, and Cold Harbor, he has lost 49,000 men, but the still-trusting North hurries fresh men and vast supplies to the front. Always unassuming in appearance, General Grant had changed in this photograph to his summer garb. The general's blouse, like the others, was of plain material, single-breasted, and had four regulation brass buttons in front. It was substantially the coat of a private soldier, with nothing to indicate the rank of an officer except the three gold stars of a lieutenant-general on the shoulder-straps. Judging from the experience of the past few weeks, the outlook for the future was far from bright. Yet here Grant sits serene, undaunted, confident that no army with ever lessening resources can stand the weight of metal and men which he has been hurling for many weeks against Lee.

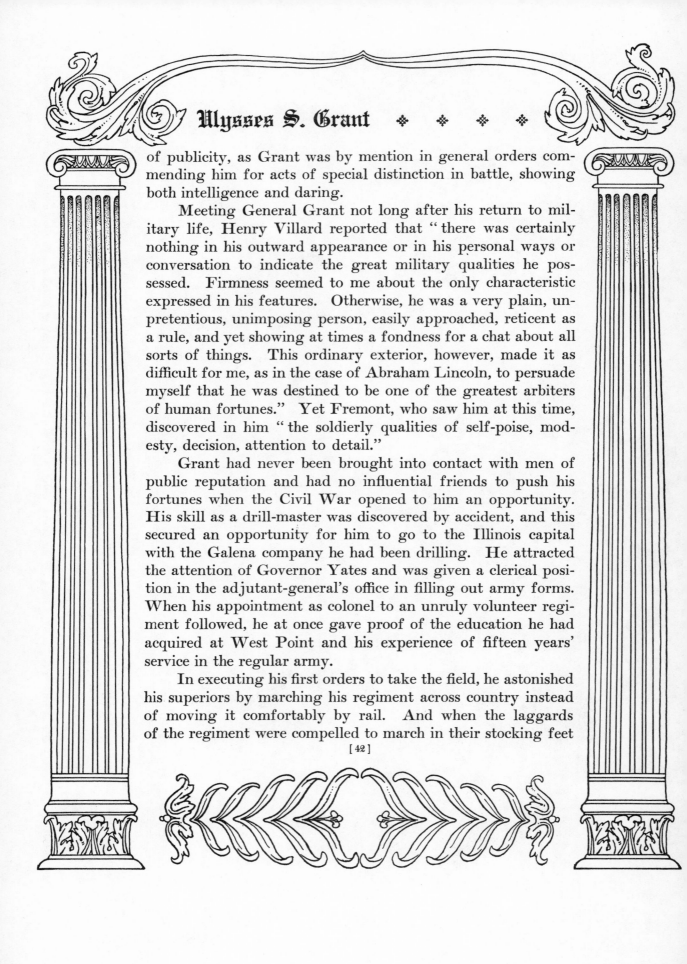

of publicity, as Grant was by mention in general orders commending him for acts of special distinction in battle, showing both intelligence and daring.

Meeting General Grant not long after his return to military life, Henry Villard reported that "there was certainly nothing in his outward appearance or in his personal ways or conversation to indicate the great military qualities he possessed. Firmness seemed to me about the only characteristic expressed in his features. Otherwise, he was a very plain, unpretentious, unimposing person, easily approached, reticent as a rule, and yet showing at times a fondness for a chat about all sorts of things. This ordinary exterior, however, made it as difficult for me, as in the case of Abraham Lincoln, to persuade myself that he was destined to be one of the greatest arbiters of human fortunes." Yet Fremont, who saw him at this time, discovered in him "the soldierly qualities of self-poise, modesty, decision, attention to detail."

Grant had never been brought into contact with men of public reputation and had no influential friends to push his fortunes when the Civil War opened to him an opportunity. His skill as a drill-master was discovered by accident, and this secured an opportunity for him to go to the Illinois capital with the Galena company he had been drilling. He attracted the attention of Governor Yates and was given a clerical position in the adjutant-general's office in filling out army forms. When his appointment as colonel to an unruly volunteer regiment followed, he at once gave proof of the education he had acquired at West Point and his experience of fifteen years' service in the regular army.

In executing his first orders to take the field, he astonished his superiors by marching his regiment across country instead of moving it comfortably by rail. And when the laggards of the regiment were compelled to march in their stocking feet

GRANT—ON HIS FIRST TRIP NORTH

The war is over. Grant has received in a magnanimous spirit, rarely paralleled in history, the surrender of Lee. Here he appears in Philadelphia on his first trip North after the war. His bearing is that of a man relieved of a vast responsibility, but with the marks of it still upon him. He is thinner than the full-chested soldier in the photograph taken in 1863, after the fall of Vicksburg. His dress is careless, as always, but shows more attention than when he was in the field. He looks out of the picture with the unflinching eyes that had been able to penetrate the future and see the wisdom of the plan that proved the final undoing of the Confederacy.

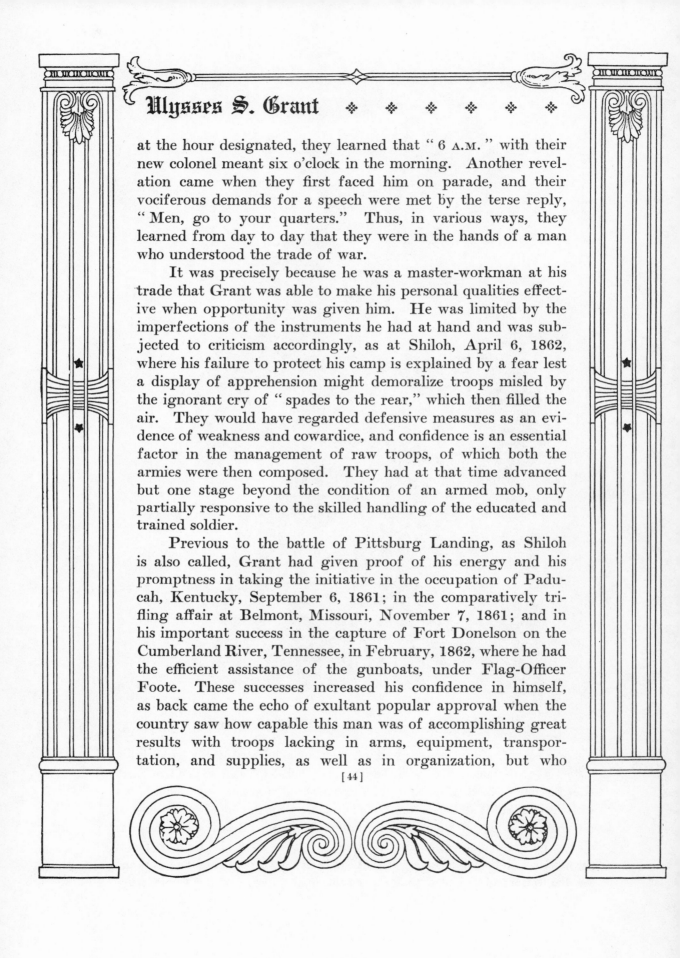

at the hour designated, they learned that " 6 A.M. " with their new colonel meant six o'clock in the morning. Another revelation came when they first faced him on parade, and their vociferous demands for a speech were met by the terse reply, " Men, go to your quarters." Thus, in various ways, they learned from day to day that they were in the hands of a man who understood the trade of war.

It was precisely because he was a master-workman at his trade that Grant was able to make his personal qualities effective when opportunity was given him. He was limited by the imperfections of the instruments he had at hand and was subjected to criticism accordingly, as at Shiloh, April 6, 1862, where his failure to protect his camp is explained by a fear lest a display of apprehension might demoralize troops misled by the ignorant cry of " spades to the rear," which then filled the air. They would have regarded defensive measures as an evidence of weakness and cowardice, and confidence is an essential factor in the management of raw troops, of which both the armies were then composed. They had at that time advanced but one stage beyond the condition of an armed mob, only partially responsive to the skilled handling of the educated and trained soldier.

Previous to the battle of Pittsburg Landing, as Shiloh is also called, Grant had given proof of his energy and his promptness in taking the initiative in the occupation of Paducah, Kentucky, September 6, 1861; in the comparatively trifling affair at Belmont, Missouri, November 7, 1861; and in his important success in the capture of Fort Donelson on the Cumberland River, Tennessee, in February, 1862, where he had the efficient assistance of the gunboats, under Flag-Officer Foote. These successes increased his confidence in himself, as back came the echo of exultant popular approval when the country saw how capable this man was of accomplishing great results with troops lacking in arms, equipment, transportation, and supplies, as well as in organization, but who

GRANT IN 1865—THE ZENITH OF HIS CAREER

Behind Grant in 1865 lay all his victories on the field of battle; before him the highest gift within the power of the American people—the presidency.   He says in his memoirs that after Vicksburg he had a presentment that he was to bring the war to a successful end and become the head of the nation.   Grant's sturdy, persistent Scottish ancestry stood him in good stead.   He was a descendant of Matthew Grant, one of the settlers of Windsor, Connecticut, in 1635, and a man of much importance in the infant colony.   His American ancestors were fighting stock.   His great-grandfather, Noah Grant, held a military commission in the French and Indian War, and his grandfather, also named Noah, fought in the Revolution.   Henry Ward Beecher summed up the causes of Grant's meteoric rise from store clerk in 1861, to president in 1869, as follows: "Grant was available and lucky."   His dominant trait was determination.

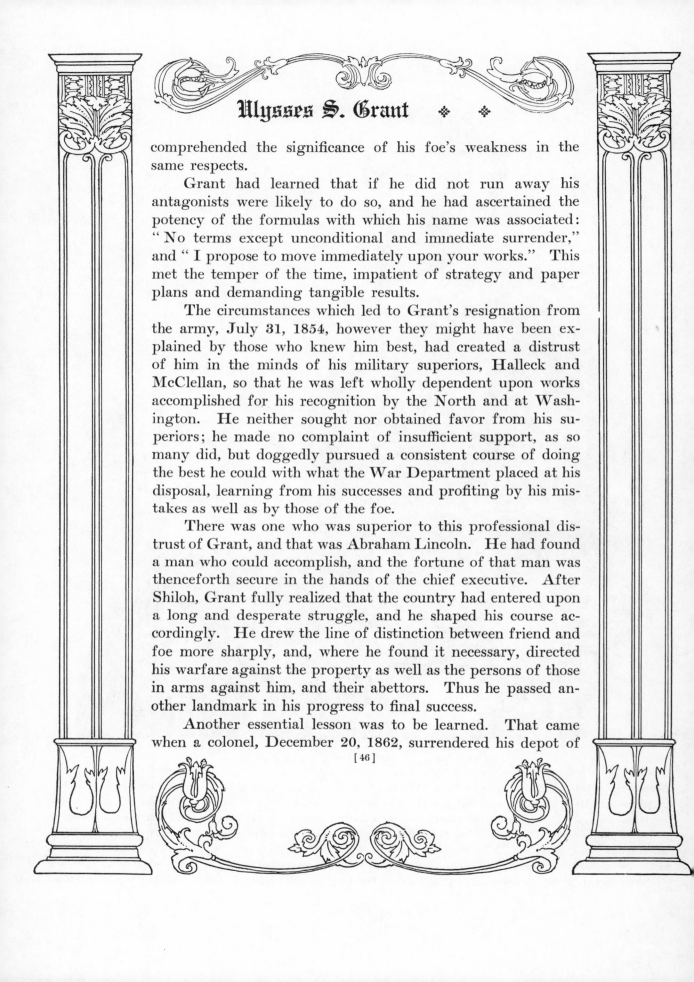

comprehended the significance of his foe's weakness in the same respects.

Grant had learned that if he did not run away his antagonists were likely to do so, and he had ascertained the potency of the formulas with which his name was associated: "No terms except unconditional and immediate surrender," and "I propose to move immediately upon your works." This met the temper of the time, impatient of strategy and paper plans and demanding tangible results.

The circumstances which led to Grant's resignation from the army, July 31, 1854, however they might have been explained by those who knew him best, had created a distrust of him in the minds of his military superiors, Halleck and McClellan, so that he was left wholly dependent upon works accomplished for his recognition by the North and at Washington. He neither sought nor obtained favor from his superiors; he made no complaint of insufficient support, as so many did, but doggedly pursued a consistent course of doing the best he could with what the War Department placed at his disposal, learning from his successes and profiting by his mistakes as well as by those of the foe.

There was one who was superior to this professional distrust of Grant, and that was Abraham Lincoln. He had found a man who could accomplish, and the fortune of that man was thenceforth secure in the hands of the chief executive. After Shiloh, Grant fully realized that the country had entered upon a long and desperate struggle, and he shaped his course accordingly. He drew the line of distinction between friend and foe more sharply, and, where he found it necessary, directed his warfare against the property as well as the persons of those in arms against him, and their abettors. Thus he passed another landmark in his progress to final success.

Another essential lesson was to be learned. That came when a colonel, December 20, 1862, surrendered his depot of

GRANT IN CHARACTERISTIC POSE, WITH HIS STAFF IN 1864

The indifferent attitude of the general-in-chief is most characteristic.   Grant had begun the investment of Petersburg when this photograph was taken.   Around him are the men who had followed him faithfully through the faith-shaking campaigns of the Wilderness.   He never made known his plans for an advance to anyone, but his calm confidence communicated itself to all who listened to him.   In the most critical moments he manifested no perceptible anxiety, but gave his orders with coolness and deliberation.   At the left of the photograph sits General John A. Rawlins, who has foresworn his customary mustache and beard which the next picture shows him as wearing.   He was first aide-de-camp to Grant, then assistant adjutant-general and chief of staff.   Behind Grant, who stands in the center with one hand thrust carelessly into his pocket, sits Lieutenant Frederick Grant, later major-general in the United States Army.   In front of Grant stands Colonel M. B. Ryan, and on the extreme right sits Colonel Ely S. Parker, military secretary, who was a full-blooded Indian, a grandnephew of the famous Red Jacket, and chief of the tribes known as the Six Nations.

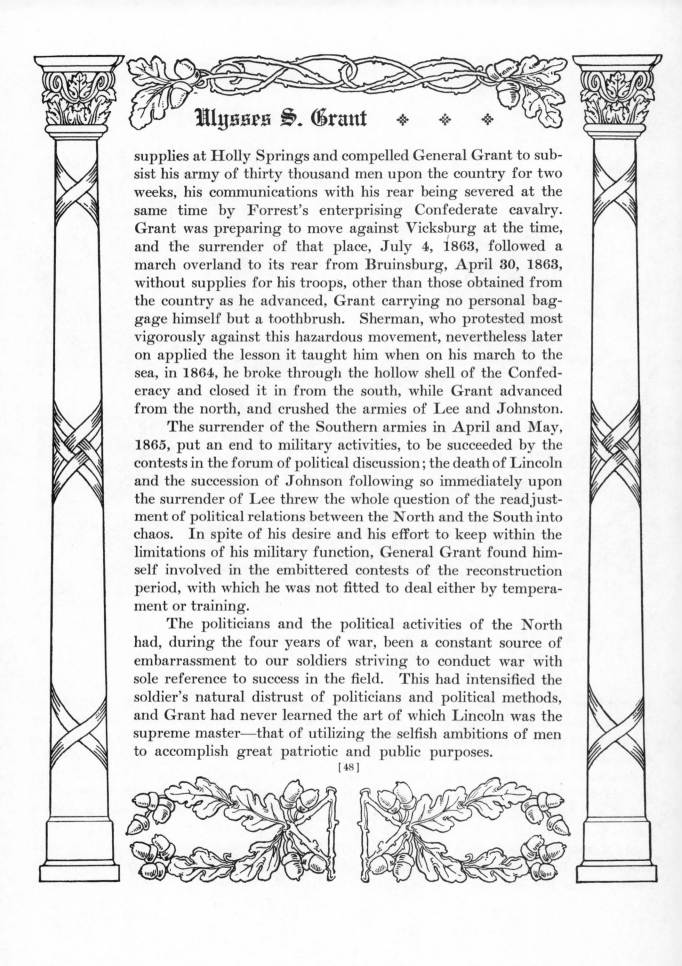

Ulysses S. Grant ✦ ✦ ✦

supplies at Holly Springs and compelled General Grant to subsist his army of thirty thousand men upon the country for two weeks, his communications with his rear being severed at the same time by Forrest's enterprising Confederate cavalry. Grant was preparing to move against Vicksburg at the time, and the surrender of that place, July 4, 1863, followed a march overland to its rear from Bruinsburg, April 30, 1863, without supplies for his troops, other than those obtained from the country as he advanced, Grant carrying no personal baggage himself but a toothbrush. Sherman, who protested most vigorously against this hazardous movement, nevertheless later on applied the lesson it taught him when on his march to the sea, in 1864, he broke through the hollow shell of the Confederacy and closed it in from the south, while Grant advanced from the north, and crushed the armies of Lee and Johnston.

The surrender of the Southern armies in April and May, 1865, put an end to military activities, to be succeeded by the contests in the forum of political discussion; the death of Lincoln and the succession of Johnson following so immediately upon the surrender of Lee threw the whole question of the readjustment of political relations between the North and the South into chaos. In spite of his desire and his effort to keep within the limitations of his military function, General Grant found himself involved in the embittered contests of the reconstruction period, with which he was not fitted to deal either by temperament or training.

The politicians and the political activities of the North had, during the four years of war, been a constant source of embarrassment to our soldiers striving to conduct war with sole reference to success in the field. This had intensified the soldier's natural distrust of politicians and political methods, and Grant had never learned the art of which Lincoln was the supreme master—that of utilizing the selfish ambitions of men to accomplish great patriotic and public purposes.

1. COLONEL
HORACE
PORTER

3. COLONEL
T. S.
BOWERS

5. GENERAL
JOHN G.
BARNARD

7. GENERAL
U. S.
GRANT

9. GENERAL
SETH
WILLIAMS

11. COLONEL
ADAM
BADEAU

2. COLONEL
WILLIAM
DUFF

4. COLONEL
J. D.
WEBSTER

6. GENERAL
JOHN A.
RAWLINS

8. GENERAL
M. R.
PATRICK

10. GENERAL
RUFUS
INGALLS

12. COLONEL
E. S.
PARKER

MEN ABOUT TO WITNESS APPOMATTOX

No photographer was present at Appomattox, that supreme moment in our national history, when Americans met for the last time as foes on the field. Nothing but fanciful sketches exist of the scene inside the McLean home. But here is a photograph that shows most of the Union officers present at the conference. Nine of the twelve men standing above stood also at the signing of Lee's surrender, a few days later. The scene is City Point, in March, 1865. Grant is surrounded by a group of the officers who had served him so faithfully. At the surrender, it was Colonel T. S. Bowers (third from left) upon whom Grant called to make a copy of the terms of surrender in ink. Colonel E. S. Parker, the full-blooded Indian on Grant's staff, an excellent penman, wrote

GRANT BETWEEN RAWLINS AND BOWERS

out the final copy. Nineteen years later, General Horace Porter recorded with pride that he loaned General Lee a pencil to make a correction in the terms. Colonels William Duff and J. D. Webster, and General M. R. Patrick, are the three men who were not present at the interview. All of the remaining officers were formally presented to Lee. General Seth Williams had been Lee's adjutant when the latter was superintendent at West Point some years before the war. In the lower photograph General Grant stands between General Rawlins and Colonel Bowers. The veins standing out on the back of his hand are plainly visible. No one but he could have told how calmly the blood coursed through them during the four tremendous years.

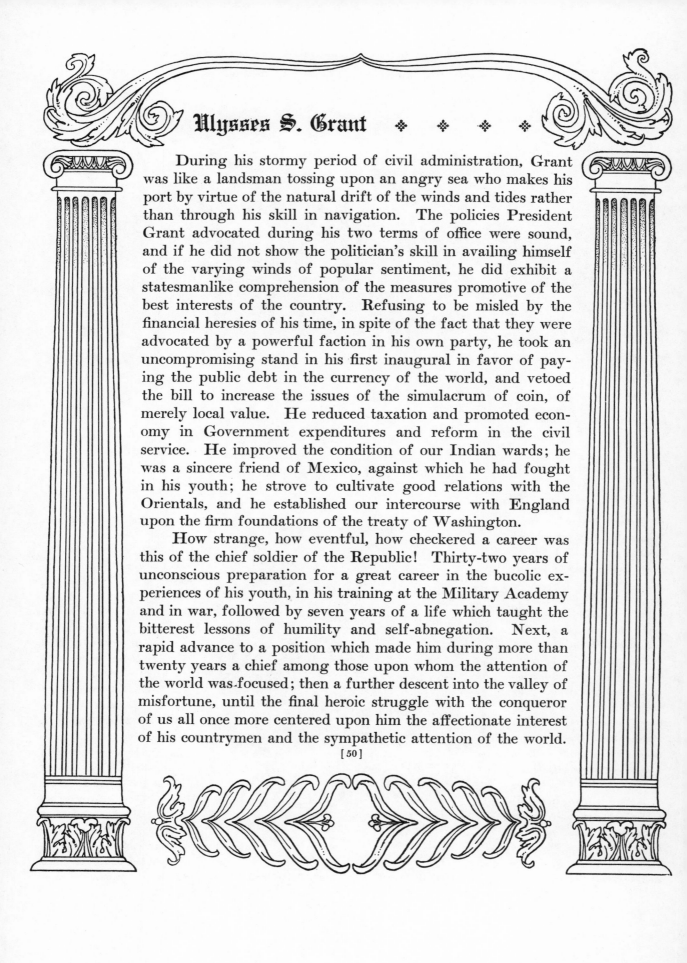

Ulysses S. Grant ✦ ✦ ✦ ✦

During his stormy period of civil administration, Grant was like a landsman tossing upon an angry sea who makes his port by virtue of the natural drift of the winds and tides rather than through his skill in navigation. The policies President Grant advocated during his two terms of office were sound, and if he did not show the politician's skill in availing himself of the varying winds of popular sentiment, he did exhibit a statesmanlike comprehension of the measures promotive of the best interests of the country. Refusing to be misled by the financial heresies of his time, in spite of the fact that they were advocated by a powerful faction in his own party, he took an uncompromising stand in his first inaugural in favor of paying the public debt in the currency of the world, and vetoed the bill to increase the issues of the simulacrum of coin, of merely local value. He reduced taxation and promoted economy in Government expenditures and reform in the civil service. He improved the condition of our Indian wards; he was a sincere friend of Mexico, against which he had fought in his youth; he strove to cultivate good relations with the Orientals, and he established our intercourse with England upon the firm foundations of the treaty of Washington.

How strange, how eventful, how checkered a career was this of the chief soldier of the Republic! Thirty-two years of unconscious preparation for a great career in the bucolic experiences of his youth, in his training at the Military Academy and in war, followed by seven years of a life which taught the bitterest lessons of humility and self-abnegation. Next, a rapid advance to a position which made him during more than twenty years a chief among those upon whom the attention of the world was focused; then a further descent into the valley of misfortune, until the final heroic struggle with the conqueror of us all once more centered upon him the affectionate interest of his countrymen and the sympathetic attention of the world.

II

LEE

RESIDENCE OF ROBERT E. LEE, ON FRANKLIN STREET,
RICHMOND, OCCUPIED BY HIS FAMILY DURING THE WAR—
THREE OF THE PORTRAITS OF GENERAL LEE THAT FOLLOW
WERE TAKEN IN THE BASEMENT OF THIS HOUSE—IT LATER
BECAME THE HOME OF THE VIRGINIA HISTORICAL SOCIETY

ROBERT E. LEE

BY WILLIAM P. TRENT

Professor of English Literature in Columbia University

"GENERAL LEE has been the only great man with whom I have been thrown who has not dwindled upon a near approach." This is the significant remark of one of his personal friends, Major A. R. H. Ranson of the Confederate artillery. The present writer, who never had the privilege of seeing General Lee, finds himself, in a sense, completely in accord with the veteran staff-officer, since he, too, can say that of all the great figures in history and literature whom he has had occasion to study through books, no one has stood out freer from human imperfections, of whatever sort, than the man and soldier upon whom were centered the affections, the admiration, and the hopes of the Southern people during the great crisis of their history. General Lee is the hero of his surviving veterans, of his fellow Virginians and Southerners, of many of those Americans of the North and West against whom he fought, and of his biographers. He is the Hector of a still-unwritten Iliad—a fact which the sketch that follows cannot prove, any more than it can set forth his claims to military fame in an adequately expert fashion, but to the truth of which it may perhaps bring a small bit of not valueless testimony—the testimony of personal conviction.*

Robert Edward Lee, the third son of the cavalry leader "Light Horse Harry" Lee by his second wife, Anne Hill Carter, was born at the family mansion, "Stratford," in Westmoreland County, Virginia, on January 19, 1807. On

*For a fuller, though necessarily limited treatment of Lee's character and career reference may be made to the writer's volume in the "Beacon Biographies," which has guided him in the present sketch.

COPYRIGHT, 1911, REVIEW OF REVIEWS CO.

"LEE WAS ESSENTIALLY A VIRGINIAN"

Old Christ Church at Alexandria, Virginia. The church attended by both Washington and Lee calls up associations that explain the reference of General Adams. In 1811, at the age of four, Robert E. Lee removed from Westmoreland County to Alexandria, which remained his home until he entered West Point, in 1825. During these years he was gaining his education from private tutors and devoting himself to the care of his invalid mother. Many a Sunday he passed through the trees around this church, of which Washington had been one of the first vestrymen, to occupy the pew that is still pointed out to visitors. The town serves to intensify love of Virginia; here Braddock made his headquarters before marching against the French, in 1755, with young George Washington as an aide on his staff; and here on April 13th of that year the Governors of New York, Massachusetts, Pennsylvania, Maryland, and Virginia had met, in order to determine upon plans for the expedition. In the vicinity were Mount Vernon, the estate of Washington, and Arlington, which remained in the family of Washington's wife. The whole region was therefore full of inspiration for the youthful Lee.

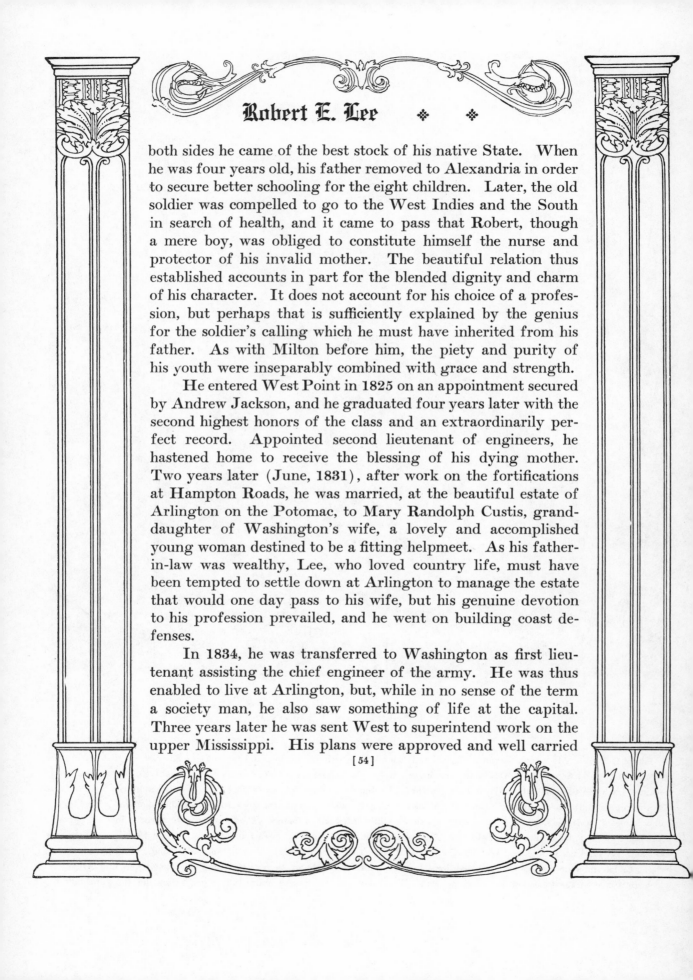

Robert E. Lee ❖ ❖

both sides he came of the best stock of his native State. When he was four years old, his father removed to Alexandria in order to secure better schooling for the eight children. Later, the old soldier was compelled to go to the West Indies and the South in search of health, and it came to pass that Robert, though a mere boy, was obliged to constitute himself the nurse and protector of his invalid mother. The beautiful relation thus established accounts in part for the blended dignity and charm of his character. It does not account for his choice of a profession, but perhaps that is sufficiently explained by the genius for the soldier's calling which he must have inherited from his father. As with Milton before him, the piety and purity of his youth were inseparably combined with grace and strength.

He entered West Point in 1825 on an appointment secured by Andrew Jackson, and he graduated four years later with the second highest honors of the class and an extraordinarily perfect record. Appointed second lieutenant of engineers, he hastened home to receive the blessing of his dying mother. Two years later (June, 1831), after work on the fortifications at Hampton Roads, he was married, at the beautiful estate of Arlington on the Potomac, to Mary Randolph Custis, granddaughter of Washington's wife, a lovely and accomplished young woman destined to be a fitting helpmeet. As his father-in-law was wealthy, Lee, who loved country life, must have been tempted to settle down at Arlington to manage the estate that would one day pass to his wife, but his genuine devotion to his profession prevailed, and he went on building coast defenses.

In 1834, he was transferred to Washington as first lieutenant assisting the chief engineer of the army. He was thus enabled to live at Arlington, but, while in no sense of the term a society man, he also saw something of life at the capital. Three years later he was sent West to superintend work on the upper Mississippi. His plans were approved and well carried

LEE IN 1850

FROM THE ORIGINAL DAGUERREOTYPE—WITHOUT THE UNIFORM
PAINTED ON LATER

Through the courtesy of General G. W. C. Lee—who furnished information of much value concerning several portraits in this chapter—there is reproduced above the actual appearance of his distinguished father in 1850. This portrait was copied, embellished with a uniform painted on by hand, and widely circulated. To study the unretouched original is particularly interesting. Lee at this period was in Baltimore, in charge of defenses then being constructed. Three years before, in the Mexican War, he had posted batteries before Vera Cruz so that the town was reduced in a week. After each of the battles of Cerro Gordo, Churubusco, and Chapultepec, he received promotion, and for his services in the last he was breveted colonel. A born soldier, the son of a soldier, this handsome young man is not as handsome by far as the superb general who later lent grace and dignity to the Confederate gray. He little realized the startling future when this photograph was taken.

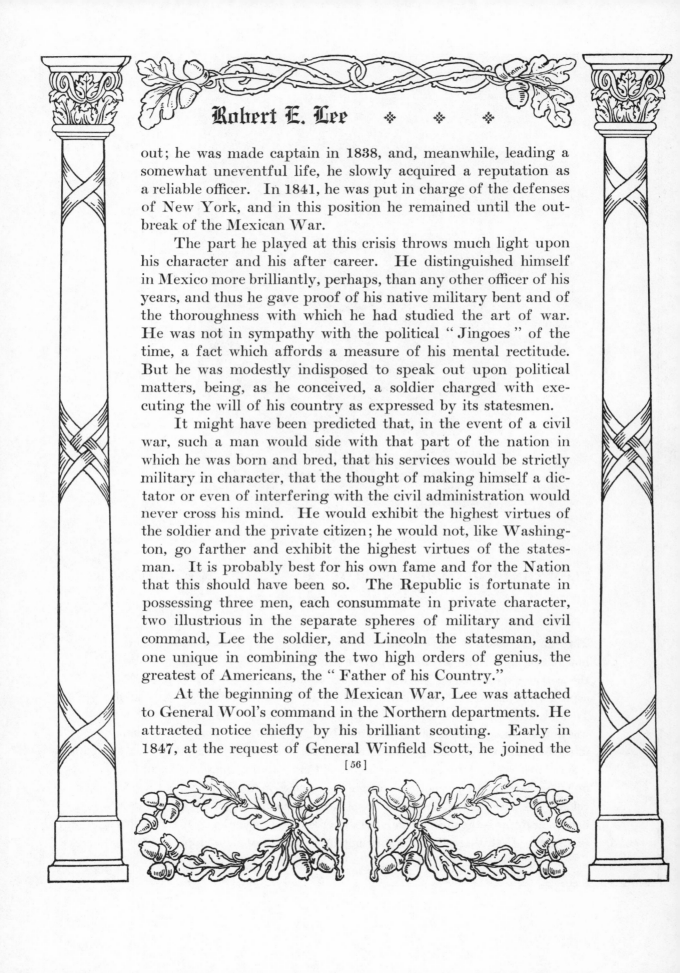

out; he was made captain in 1838, and, meanwhile, leading a
somewhat uneventful life, he slowly acquired a reputation as
a reliable officer. In 1841, he was put in charge of the defenses
of New York, and in this position he remained until the outbreak of the Mexican War.

The part he played at this crisis throws much light upon
his character and his after career. He distinguished himself
in Mexico more brilliantly, perhaps, than any other officer of his
years, and thus he gave proof of his native military bent and of
the thoroughness with which he had studied the art of war.
He was not in sympathy with the political "Jingoes" of the
time, a fact which affords a measure of his mental rectitude.
But he was modestly indisposed to speak out upon political
matters, being, as he conceived, a soldier charged with executing the will of his country as expressed by its statesmen.

It might have been predicted that, in the event of a civil
war, such a man would side with that part of the nation in
which he was born and bred, that his services would be strictly
military in character, that the thought of making himself a dic-
tator or even of interfering with the civil administration would
never cross his mind. He would exhibit the highest virtues of
the soldier and the private citizen; he would not, like Washington, go farther and exhibit the highest virtues of the statesman. It is probably best for his own fame and for the Nation
that this should have been so. The Republic is fortunate in
possessing three men, each consummate in private character,
two illustrious in the separate spheres of military and civil
command, Lee the soldier, and Lincoln the statesman, and
one unique in combining the two high orders of genius, the
greatest of Americans, the "Father of his Country."

At the beginning of the Mexican War, Lee was attached
to General Wool's command in the Northern departments. He
attracted notice chiefly by his brilliant scouting. Early in
1847, at the request of General Winfield Scott, he joined the

ARLINGTON, THE HOME OF LEE, FROM THE GREAT OAK

The beautiful estate by the Potomac came to General Lee from the family of George Washington. While Lee, as a boy and youth, lived in Alexandria he was a frequent caller at the Arlington estate, where Mary Lee Custis, the only daughter of George Washington Parke Custis, was his companion and playfellow. Before he had completed his course at West Point the friendship had ripened into love and the two became engaged. Her father is said to have considered her entitled to a more wealthy match than young Lee, who looked forward to a career in the army. But in 1831, two years after his graduation, the ceremony was performed and on the death of Custis in 1857, the estate passed into the possession of Robert E. Lee as trustee for his children. The management had already been in his hands for many years, and though constantly absent on duty, he had ordered it so skilfully that its value steadily increased. On the outbreak of the Civil War and his decision to cast in his lot with Virginia, he was obliged to leave the mansion that overlooked the national capital. It at once fell into the hands of Federal troops. Nevermore was he to dwell in the majestic home that had sheltered his family for thirty years. When the war was over, he gave the Pamunkey estate to his son Robert and himself retired to the quiet, simple life of Lexington, Virginia, as president of the institution that is now known, in his honor, as Washington and Lee University.

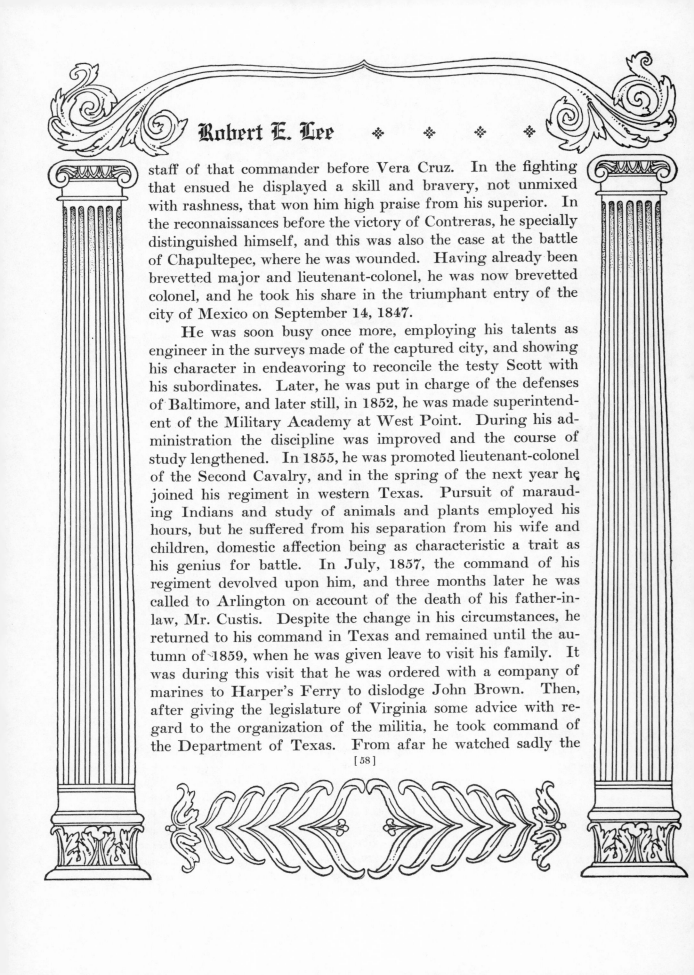

staff of that commander before Vera Cruz. In the fighting that ensued he displayed a skill and bravery, not unmixed with rashness, that won him high praise from his superior. In the reconnaissances before the victory of Contreras, he specially distinguished himself, and this was also the case at the battle of Chapultepec, where he was wounded. Having already been brevetted major and lieutenant-colonel, he was now brevetted colonel, and he took his share in the triumphant entry of the city of Mexico on September 14, 1847.

He was soon busy once more, employing his talents as engineer in the surveys made of the captured city, and showing his character in endeavoring to reconcile the testy Scott with his subordinates. Later, he was put in charge of the defenses of Baltimore, and later still, in 1852, he was made superintendent of the Military Academy at West Point. During his administration the discipline was improved and the course of study lengthened. In 1855, he was promoted lieutenant-colonel of the Second Cavalry, and in the spring of the next year he joined his regiment in western Texas. Pursuit of marauding Indians and study of animals and plants employed his hours, but he suffered from his separation from his wife and children, domestic affection being as characteristic a trait as his genius for battle. In July, 1857, the command of his regiment devolved upon him, and three months later he was called to Arlington on account of the death of his father-in-law, Mr. Custis. Despite the change in his circumstances, he returned to his command in Texas and remained until the autumn of 1859, when he was given leave to visit his family. It was during this visit that he was ordered with a company of marines to Harper's Ferry to dislodge John Brown. Then, after giving the legislature of Virginia some advice with regard to the organization of the militia, he took command of the Department of Texas. From afar he watched sadly the

LEE'S BOYHOOD PLAYGROUND

When Robert E. Lee came over from Alexandria as a boy, to play soldier in the gardens and grounds around this beautiful mansion overlooking the Potomac, he could hardly have thought of its occupation during his life-time by a hostile force determined to bend his native State to its will. When he was graduated from West Point in 1829 and proudly donned the army blue, he little imagined that thirty-two years later, after he had paced his room all night in terrible perplexity, he would doff the blue for another color sworn to oppose it. The estate about Arlington house was a fair and spacious domain. Every part of it had rung in his early youth and young manhood with the voice of her who later became his wife. He had whispered his love in its shaded alleys, and here his children had come into the world. Yet here stand men with swords and muskets ready to take his life if they should meet him on the field of battle. Arlington, once famous for its hospitality, has since extended a silent welcome to 20,000 dead. Lee's body is not here, but reposes in a splendid marble tomb at Washington and Lee University, where he ruled with simple dignity after the finish of the war.

drift of the two sections toward war, and in February, 1861, upon the secession of Texas, he was recalled to Washington.

It is needless to discuss exhaustively Lee's attitude on the questions that were dividing the country. He did not believe in slavery or secession, but, on the other hand, he did not admit that the general Government had the right to invade and coerce sovereign States, and he shared the conviction of his fellow Southerners that their section had been aggrieved and was threatened with grave losses. He sided with those whom he regarded as his " people," and they have continued to honor his decision,·which, as we have seen, was inevitable, given his training and character.

It was equally inevitable, in view of the oaths he had taken, and of the existence of theories of government to which he did not subscribe, that his entering the service of the Confederacy should seem to many Americans a wilful act of treason. His conduct will probably continue to furnish occasion for censure to those who judge actions in the light of rigid political, social, and ecclesiastical theories instead of in the light of circumstances and of the phases of character. To his admirers, on the other hand, who will increase rather than diminish, Lee will remain a hero without fear and without reproach.

Lee spent the weeks immediately following the inauguration of Lincoln in a state of great nervous tension. There seems to be little reason to doubt that, had he listened to the overtures made him, he could have had charge of the Union forces to be put in the field. On April 20, 1861, he resigned the colonelcy of the First Cavalry, and on the 23d he accepted the command of the military forces of Virginia in a brief speech worthy of the career upon which he was entering. A little less than a month later he became a brigadier of the Confederacy, that being then the highest grade in the Southern service.

For some time he chafed at not being allowed to take the field, but he could not be spared as an organizer of troops and

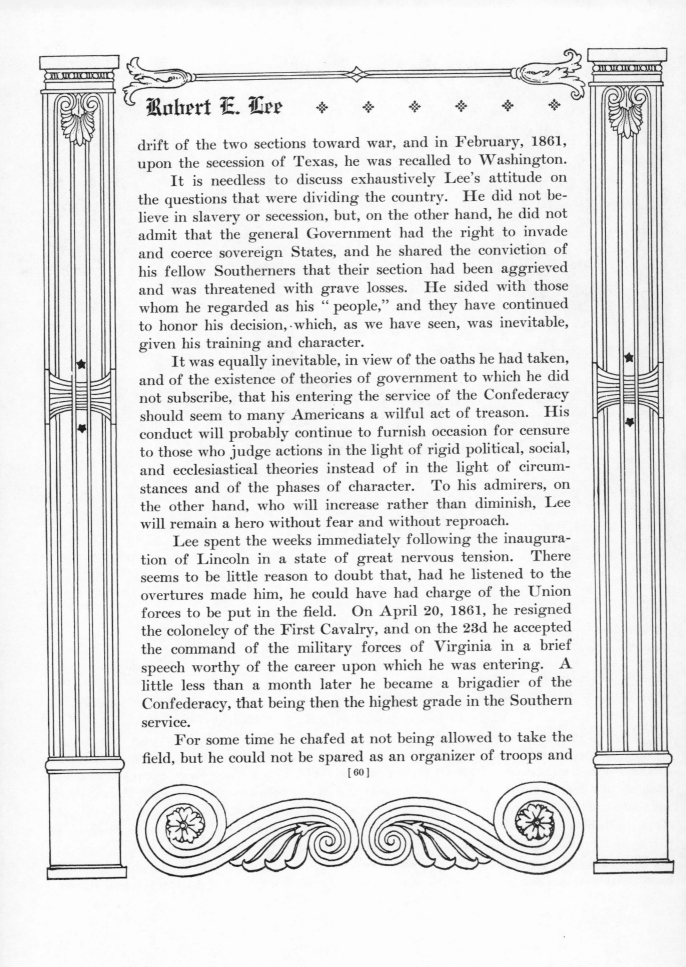

WHERE LEE STOOD SUPREME—THE WILDERNESS IN 1864

From the point of view of the military student Lee's consummate feats of generalship were performed in the gloom of the Wilderness. On this ground he presented an always unbroken front against which Grant dashed his battalions in vain. Never were Lee's lines here broken; the assailants must always shift their ground to seek a fresh opportunity for assault. At this spot on the battlefield of the Wilderness the opposing forces lay within twenty-four feet of each other all night. The soldiers, too, had learned by this 1864 campaign to carry out orders with judgment of their own. The rank and file grew to be excellent connoisseurs of the merits of a position. "If they only save a finger it will do some good," was General Longstreet's reply, when his engineer officers complained that their work on Marye's Hill was being spoiled by being built higher by the gunners of the Washington artillery—who had to fight behind them. For this reason the significance of the lines as shown in many war maps is often very puzzling to the students of to-day, who have never seen the actual field of operations and have no other guide. Much of the ground disputed by the contending forces in our Civil War was quite unlike the popular conception of a battlefield, derived from descriptions of European campaigns, or from portrayals of the same, usually fanciful. For at this variety of warfare, Lee was a master, as well as on the rolling open plains of the Virginia farm. The portrait of Lee opposite was taken during the campaign preceding this test of the Wilderness. The reproduction here is directly from the photograph—taken at Lee's first sitting in war-time, and his only one "in the field." Reproductions of this picture painted, engraved, and lithographed were widely circulated after the war. The likeness was much impaired.

LEE IN THE FIELD
THE BEST KNOWN PORTRAIT

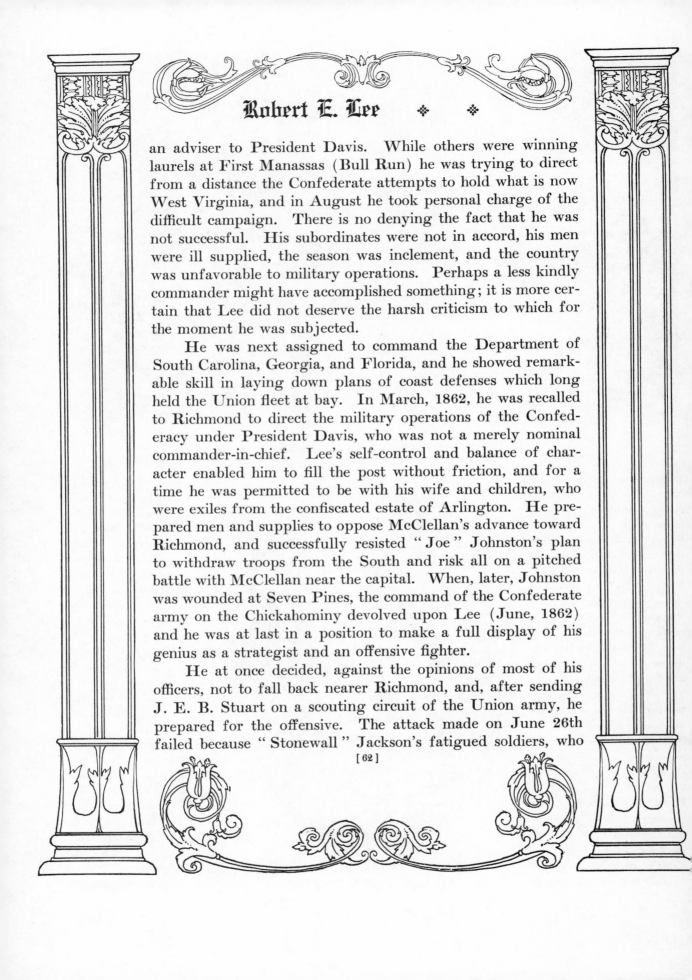

an adviser to President Davis. While others were winning laurels at First Manassas (Bull Run) he was trying to direct from a distance the Confederate attempts to hold what is now West Virginia, and in August he took personal charge of the difficult campaign. There is no denying the fact that he was not successful. His subordinates were not in accord, his men were ill supplied, the season was inclement, and the country was unfavorable to military operations. Perhaps a less kindly commander might have accomplished something; it is more certain that Lee did not deserve the harsh criticism to which for the moment he was subjected.

He was next assigned to command the Department of South Carolina, Georgia, and Florida, and he showed remarkable skill in laying down plans of coast defenses which long held the Union fleet at bay. In March, 1862, he was recalled to Richmond to direct the military operations of the Confederacy under President Davis, who was not a merely nominal commander-in-chief. Lee's self-control and balance of character enabled him to fill the post without friction, and for a time he was permitted to be with his wife and children, who were exiles from the confiscated estate of Arlington. He prepared men and supplies to oppose McClellan's advance toward Richmond, and successfully resisted "Joe" Johnston's plan to withdraw troops from the South and risk all on a pitched battle with McClellan near the capital. When, later, Johnston was wounded at Seven Pines, the command of the Confederate army on the Chickahominy devolved upon Lee (June, 1862) and he was at last in a position to make a full display of his genius as a strategist and an offensive fighter.

He at once decided, against the opinions of most of his officers, not to fall back nearer Richmond, and, after sending J. E. B. Stuart on a scouting circuit of the Union army, he prepared for the offensive. The attack made on June 26th failed because "Stonewall" Jackson's fatigued soldiers, who

ALL

THE ORIGINAL

WAR–TIME PHOTOGRAPHS

OF

ROBERT E. LEE

AS

PRESENTED

IN THIS CHAPTER

AND IN

OTHER VOLUMES

LEE
AT THE HEIGHT OF
HIS FAME
1863

"I believe there were none of the little things of life so irksome to him as having his picture taken in any way," writes Captain Robert E. Lee of his illustrious father. Lee was photographed in war-time on three occasions only: one was in the field, about '62–'63; the second in Richmond in 1863; and the third immediately after the surrender, at his Richmond home. Several of the portraits resulting have appeared in other volumes of this history; all the rest are presented with this chapter. Lee's first sitting produced the full-length on page 235, Volume II, and the full-face on the page preceding this—the popular portrait, much lithographed and engraved, but rarely shown, as here, from an original photograph, with the expression not distorted into a false amiability, but calm and dignified as in nature. Lee's second sitting was before Vannerson's camera in Richmond, 1863. Richmond ladies had made for their hero a set of shirts, and had begged him to sit for a portrait. Lee, yielding, courteously wore one of the gifts. The amateur shirtmaking is revealed in the set of the collar, very high in the neck, as seen in the photographs on this page. Another negative of this second oc-

casion, a full-length, is reproduced in Volume IX, page 123. The third photographing of Lee was done by Brady. It was the first opportunity of the camera wizard since the war began to preserve for posterity the fine features of the Southern hero. The position selected by Brady was under the back porch of Lee's home in Richmond, near the basement door, on account of the better light. The results were excellent. Three appear with this chapter: a magnificent three-quarter view, enlarged on page 63; a full-length, on page 69; and a group with Custis Lee and Colonel Taylor, on page 67. Another view of this group will be found on page 83 of Volume I; and the fifth of these Brady pictures, a seated profile of Lee alone, on page 23 of Volume III. An early daguerreotypist had portrayed Lee in 1850 as a young engineer-colonel —see page 55. The general's later life is covered by his celebrated photograph on "Traveler" in September, 1866, on page 121 of Volume IX; by the two portraits of '67 and '69 on page 73; by the photograph with Johnston, taken in 1869, on page 341 of Volume I, and by the striking group photograph that forms the frontispiece to this volume.

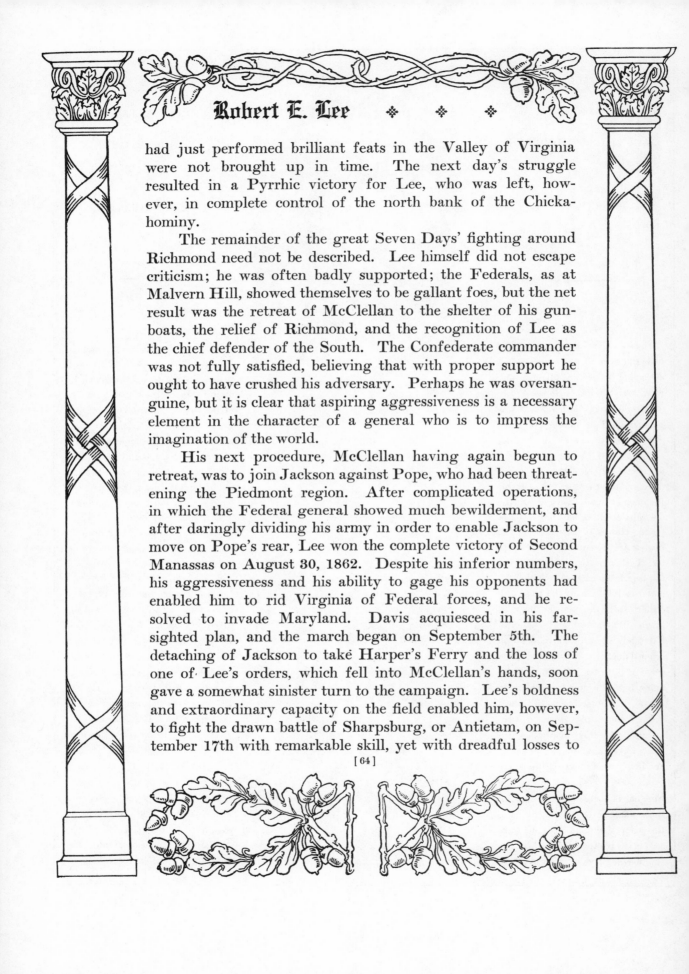

had just performed brilliant feats in the Valley of Virginia were not brought up in time. The next day's struggle resulted in a Pyrrhic victory for Lee, who was left, however, in complete control of the north bank of the Chickahominy.

The remainder of the great Seven Days' fighting around Richmond need not be described. Lee himself did not escape criticism; he was often badly supported; the Federals, as at Malvern Hill, showed themselves to be gallant foes, but the net result was the retreat of McClellan to the shelter of his gunboats, the relief of Richmond, and the recognition of Lee as the chief defender of the South. The Confederate commander was not fully satisfied, believing that with proper support he ought to have crushed his adversary. Perhaps he was oversanguine, but it is clear that aspiring aggressiveness is a necessary element in the character of a general who is to impress the imagination of the world.

His next procedure, McClellan having again begun to retreat, was to join Jackson against Pope, who had been threatening the Piedmont region. After complicated operations, in which the Federal general showed much bewilderment, and after daringly dividing his army in order to enable Jackson to move on Pope's rear, Lee won the complete victory of Second Manassas on August 30, 1862. Despite his inferior numbers, his aggressiveness and his ability to gage his opponents had enabled him to rid Virginia of Federal forces, and he resolved to invade Maryland. Davis acquiesced in his farsighted plan, and the march began on September 5th. The detaching of Jackson to take Harper's Ferry and the loss of one of Lee's orders, which fell into McClellan's hands, soon gave a somewhat sinister turn to the campaign. Lee's boldness and extraordinary capacity on the field enabled him, however, to fight the drawn battle of Sharpsburg, or Antietam, on September 17th with remarkable skill, yet with dreadful losses to

LEE—THE GENERAL WHO SHOULDERED "ALL THE RESPONSIBILITY"

The nobility revealed by the steadfast lips, the flashing eyes in this magnificent portrait is reflected by a happening a few days before its taking. It was 1865. The forlorn hope of the Confederacy had failed. Gordon and Fitzhugh Lee had attacked the Federal lines on April 9th, but found them impregnable. Lee heard the news, and said: "Then there is nothing left me but to go and see General Grant."—"Oh, General, what will history say to the surrender of the army in the field?"—Lee's reply is among the finest of his utterances: "Yes, I know they will say hard things of us; they will not understand how we were overwhelmed by numbers; but that is not the question, Colonel; the question is, is it right to surrender this army? If it is right, then I will take all the responsibility."

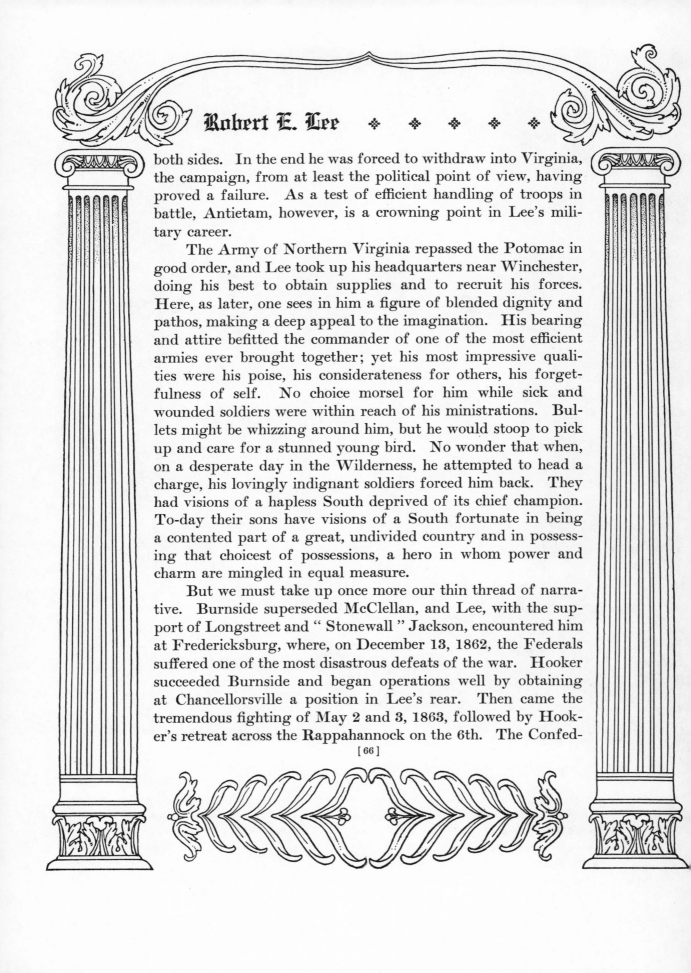

both sides. In the end he was forced to withdraw into Virginia, the campaign, from at least the political point of view, having proved a failure. As a test of efficient handling of troops in battle, Antietam, however, is a crowning point in Lee's military career.

The Army of Northern Virginia repassed the Potomac in good order, and Lee took up his headquarters near Winchester, doing his best to obtain supplies and to recruit his forces. Here, as later, one sees in him a figure of blended dignity and pathos, making a deep appeal to the imagination. His bearing and attire befitted the commander of one of the most efficient armies ever brought together; yet his most impressive qualities were his poise, his considerateness for others, his forgetfulness of self. No choice morsel for him while sick and wounded soldiers were within reach of his ministrations. Bullets might be whizzing around him, but he would stoop to pick up and care for a stunned young bird. No wonder that when, on a desperate day in the Wilderness, he attempted to head a charge, his lovingly indignant soldiers forced him back. They had visions of a hapless South deprived of its chief champion. To-day their sons have visions of a South fortunate in being a contented part of a great, undivided country and in possessing that choicest of possessions, a hero in whom power and charm are mingled in equal measure.

But we must take up once more our thin thread of narrative. Burnside superseded McClellan, and Lee, with the support of Longstreet and " Stonewall " Jackson, encountered him at Fredericksburg, where, on December 13, 1862, the Federals suffered one of the most disastrous defeats of the war. Hooker succeeded Burnside and began operations well by obtaining at Chancellorsville a position in Lee's rear. Then came the tremendous fighting of May 2 and 3, 1863, followed by Hooker's retreat across the Rappahannock on the 6th. The Confed-

LEE IN RICHMOND AFTER THE WAR

The quiet distinction and dignity of the Confederate leader appears particularly in this group portrait—always a trying ordeal for the central figure.   Superbly calm he sits, the general who laid down arms totally unembittered, and set a magnificent example to his followers in peace as he had in war.   Lee strove after the fall of the Confederacy, with all his far-reaching influence, to allay the feeling aroused by four years of the fiercest fighting in history.   This photograph was taken by Brady in 1865, in the basement below the back porch of Lee's Franklin Street house in Richmond.   On his right stands General G. W. C. Lee, on his left, Colonel Walter Taylor.   This is one of five photographs taken by Brady at this time.   A second and third are shown on pages 65 and 69, a fourth on page 83 of Volume I, and a fifth on page 23 of Volume III.

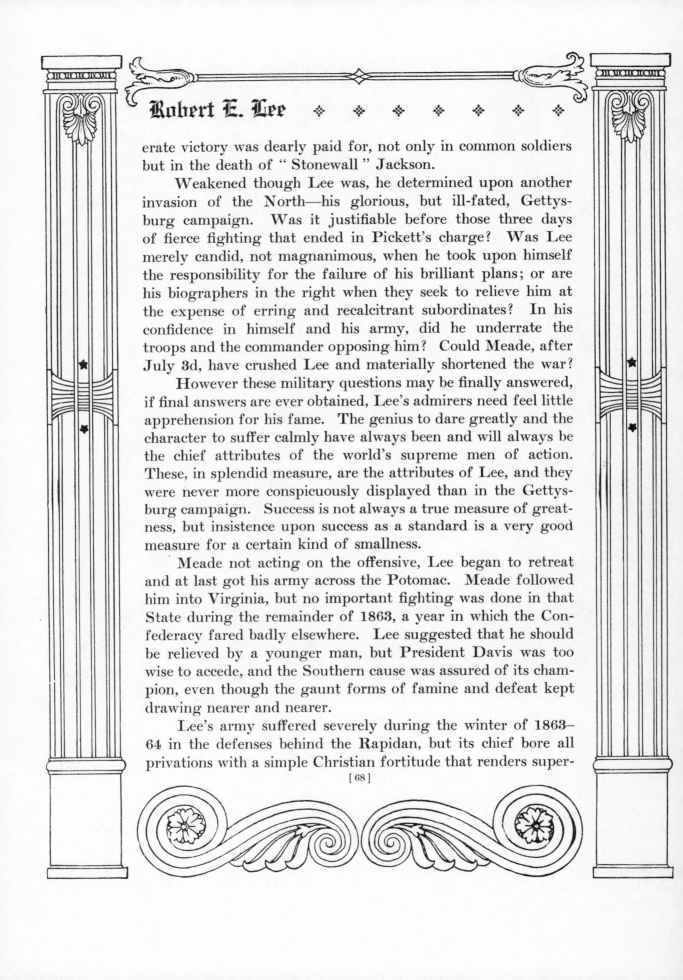

erate victory was dearly paid for, not only in common soldiers but in the death of "Stonewall" Jackson.

Weakened though Lee was, he determined upon another invasion of the North—his glorious, but ill-fated, Gettysburg campaign. Was it justifiable before those three days of fierce fighting that ended in Pickett's charge? Was Lee merely candid, not magnanimous, when he took upon himself the responsibility for the failure of his brilliant plans; or are his biographers in the right when they seek to relieve him at the expense of erring and recalcitrant subordinates? In his confidence in himself and his army, did he underrate the troops and the commander opposing him? Could Meade, after July 3d, have crushed Lee and materially shortened the war?

However these military questions may be finally answered, if final answers are ever obtained, Lee's admirers need feel little apprehension for his fame. The genius to dare greatly and the character to suffer calmly have always been and will always be the chief attributes of the world's supreme men of action. These, in splendid measure, are the attributes of Lee, and they were never more conspicuously displayed than in the Gettysburg campaign. Success is not always a true measure of greatness, but insistence upon success as a standard is a very good measure for a certain kind of smallness.

Meade not acting on the offensive, Lee began to retreat and at last got his army across the Potomac. Meade followed him into Virginia, but no important fighting was done in that State during the remainder of 1863, a year in which the Confederacy fared badly elsewhere. Lee suggested that he should be relieved by a younger man, but President Davis was too wise to accede, and the Southern cause was assured of its champion, even though the gaunt forms of famine and defeat kept drawing nearer and nearer.

Lee's army suffered severely during the winter of 1863–64 in the defenses behind the Rapidan, but its chief bore all privations with a simple Christian fortitude that renders super-

LEE IN 1865

The gray-haired man who wears his uniform with such high distinction is the general who had shown every kind of bravery known to the soldier, including the supreme courage to surrender his army in the field when he saw that further fighting would be a useless sacrifice of lives. This was a photograph taken by Brady, shortly before Lee left his home to become president of Washington University.

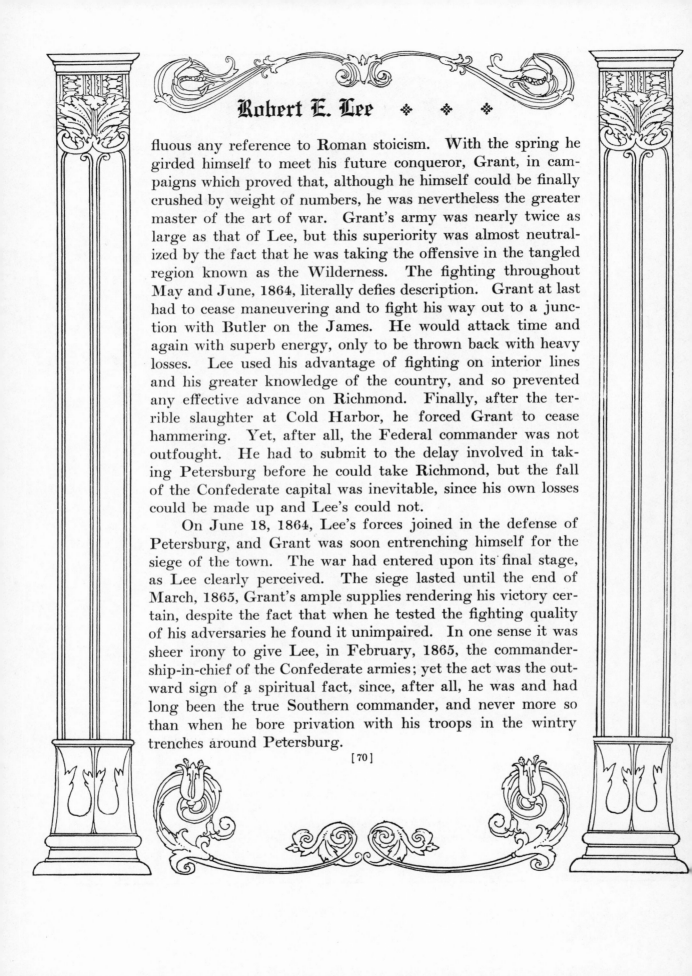

fluous any reference to Roman stoicism. With the spring he girded himself to meet his future conqueror, Grant, in campaigns which proved that, although he himself could be finally crushed by weight of numbers, he was nevertheless the greater master of the art of war. Grant's army was nearly twice as large as that of Lee, but this superiority was almost neutralized by the fact that he was taking the offensive in the tangled region known as the Wilderness. The fighting throughout May and June, 1864, literally defies description. Grant at last had to cease maneuvering and to fight his way out to a junction with Butler on the James. He would attack time and again with superb energy, only to be thrown back with heavy losses. Lee used his advantage of fighting on interior lines and his greater knowledge of the country, and so prevented any effective advance on Richmond. Finally, after the terrible slaughter at Cold Harbor, he forced Grant to cease hammering. Yet, after all, the Federal commander was not outfought. He had to submit to the delay involved in taking Petersburg before he could take Richmond, but the fall of the Confederate capital was inevitable, since his own losses could be made up and Lee's could not.

On June 18, 1864, Lee's forces joined in the defense of Petersburg, and Grant was soon entrenching himself for the siege of the town. The war had entered upon its final stage, as Lee clearly perceived. The siege lasted until the end of March, 1865, Grant's ample supplies rendering his victory certain, despite the fact that when he tested the fighting quality of his adversaries he found it unimpaired. In one sense it was sheer irony to give Lee, in February, 1865, the commander-ship-in-chief of the Confederate armies; yet the act was the outward sign of a spiritual fact, since, after all, he was and had long been the true Southern commander, and never more so than when he bore privation with his troops in the wintry trenches around Petersburg.

LEE

AND HIS STAFF

AS THE WAR ENDED

MEN

WHO STAYED

THROUGH APPOMATTOX

These twelve members of General Robert E. Lee's staff surrendered with him at Appomattox Court House, and with him signed a parole drawn up by Grant, to the effect that they would not take up arms against the United States until or unless they were exchanged. This military medallion was devised by the photographer Rockwell during General Lee's stay in Richmond in April, 1865. These facts are furnished by Major Giles B. Cooke (No. 12, above), who had verified them by writing General Lee himself after the surrender.

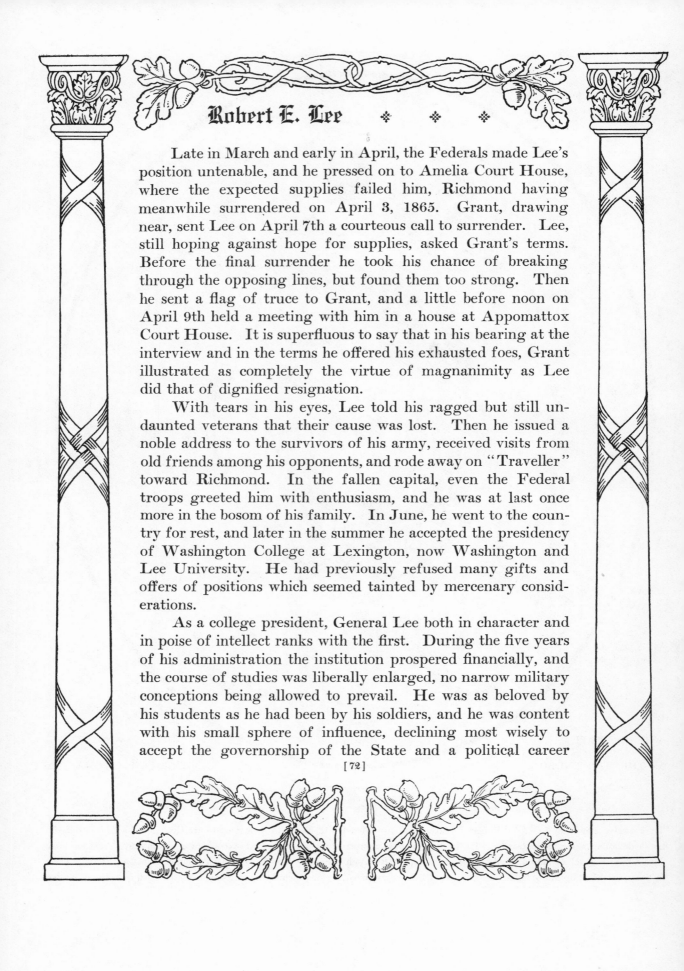

Robert E. Lee ❖ ❖ ❖

Late in March and early in April, the Federals made Lee's position untenable, and he pressed on to Amelia Court House, where the expected supplies failed him, Richmond having meanwhile surrendered on April 3, 1865. Grant, drawing near, sent Lee on April 7th a courteous call to surrender. Lee, still hoping against hope for supplies, asked Grant's terms. Before the final surrender he took his chance of breaking through the opposing lines, but found them too strong. Then he sent a flag of truce to Grant, and a little before noon on April 9th held a meeting with him in a house at Appomattox Court House. It is superfluous to say that in his bearing at the interview and in the terms he offered his exhausted foes, Grant illustrated as completely the virtue of magnanimity as Lee did that of dignified resignation.

With tears in his eyes, Lee told his ragged but still undaunted veterans that their cause was lost. Then he issued a noble address to the survivors of his army, received visits from old friends among his opponents, and rode away on "Traveller" toward Richmond. In the fallen capital, even the Federal troops greeted him with enthusiasm, and he was at last once more in the bosom of his family. In June, he went to the country for rest, and later in the summer he accepted the presidency of Washington College at Lexington, now Washington and Lee University. He had previously refused many gifts and offers of positions which seemed tainted by mercenary considerations.

As a college president, General Lee both in character and in poise of intellect ranks with the first. During the five years of his administration the institution prospered financially, and the course of studies was liberally enlarged, no narrow military conceptions being allowed to prevail. He was as beloved by his students as he had been by his soldiers, and he was content with his small sphere of influence, declining most wisely to accept the governorship of the State and a political career

LEE IN 1867

PRESIDENT OF WASHINGTON COLLEGE, LATER
WASHINGTON AND LEE UNIVERSITY

LEE IN 1869

THE YEAR BEFORE HIS DEATH AT THE AGE
OF SIXTY-THREE

THE DECLINING YEARS

In these portraits the bright eyes of the daring leader have lost none of their fire; the handsome head still remains erect.   In October, 1865, Lee had been installed as president of Washington College at Lexington, Virginia, later named in his honor Washington and Lee University.   Under his management new chairs were founded, the scheme of study enlarged, and from the moral side it would have been impossible to secure finer results.   Lee's greatness of soul was shown in the way in which he urged the Southern people loyally to accept the result of the war.   On the morning of October 12, 1870, at the age of sixty-three, he died—mourned throughout the Union which he had helped to reunite, and throughout the civilized world, which had watched with admiration his gallant fight and nobility of soul.   "To those who saw his composure under the greater and lesser trials of life," wrote Colonel William Preston Johnson, his intimate friend, "and his justice and forbearance with the most unjust and uncharitable, it seemed scarcely credible that his serene soul was shaken by the evil that raged around him."   On his dying bed he fought over the great battles of the war.   How strongly he felt his responsibility is shown by nearly his last words: "Tell Hill he must come up."

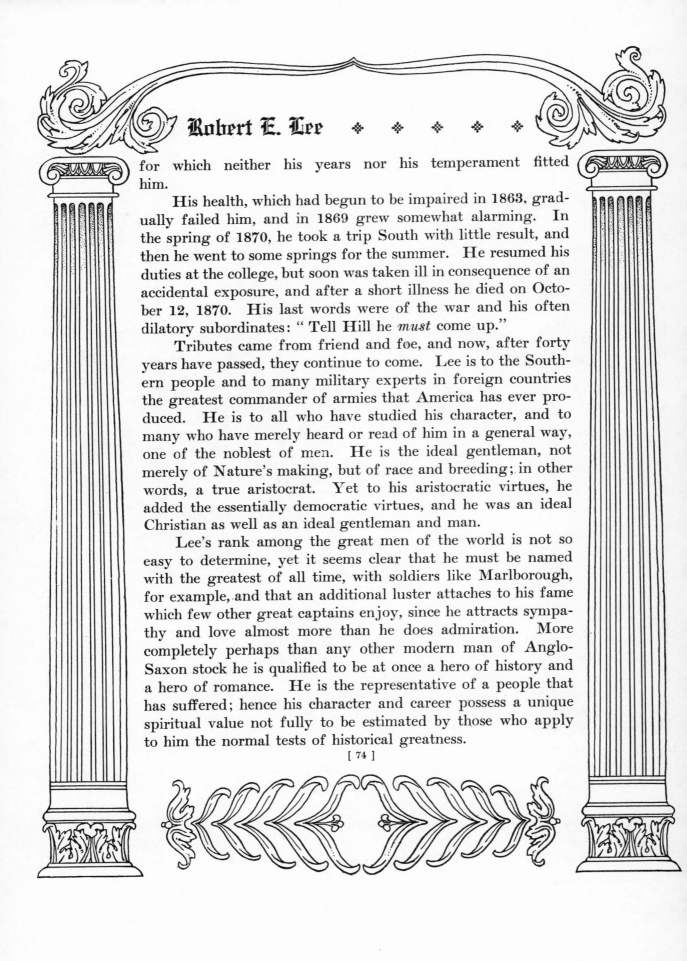

for which neither his years nor his temperament fitted him.

His health, which had begun to be impaired in 1863, gradually failed him, and in 1869 grew somewhat alarming. In the spring of 1870, he took a trip South with little result, and then he went to some springs for the summer. He resumed his duties at the college, but soon was taken ill in consequence of an accidental exposure, and after a short illness he died on October 12, 1870. His last words were of the war and his often dilatory subordinates: "Tell Hill he *must* come up."

Tributes came from friend and foe, and now, after forty years have passed, they continue to come. Lee is to the Southern people and to many military experts in foreign countries the greatest commander of armies that America has ever produced. He is to all who have studied his character, and to many who have merely heard or read of him in a general way, one of the noblest of men. He is the ideal gentleman, not merely of Nature's making, but of race and breeding; in other words, a true aristocrat. Yet to his aristocratic virtues, he added the essentially democratic virtues, and he was an ideal Christian as well as an ideal gentleman and man.

Lee's rank among the great men of the world is not so easy to determine, yet it seems clear that he must be named with the greatest of all time, with soldiers like Marlborough, for example, and that an additional luster attaches to his fame which few other great captains enjoy, since he attracts sympathy and love almost more than he does admiration. More completely perhaps than any other modern man of Anglo-Saxon stock he is qualified to be at once a hero of history and a hero of romance. He is the representative of a people that has suffered; hence his character and career possess a unique spiritual value not fully to be estimated by those who apply to him the normal tests of historical greatness.

III

SHERMAN

A LEADER WHO FOUGHT, BUT WHO WON MORE
BY MARCHES THAN OTHERS WON BY FIGHTING

MAJOR–GENERAL
WILLIAM T. SHERMAN
AND HIS GENERALS

This photograph shows Sherman with seven major-generals who "went through" with him —fighting their way to Atlanta, and marching on the famous expedition from Atlanta to the sea and north through the Carolinas to the battle of Bentonville and Johnston's surrender.

From left to right they are:

MAJOR–GENERAL
O. O. HOWARD
Commanding the Army of the
Tennessee

MAJOR–GENERAL
J. A. LOGAN
Formerly Commanding the
Army of the Tennessee

MAJOR–GENERAL
W. B. HAZEN
Commanding a Division in the
Fifteenth Army Corps

MAJOR–GENERAL
W. T. SHERMAN
Commanding the Military Division of the Mississippi

MAJOR–GENERAL
JEFF C. DAVIS
Commanding the Fourteenth
Army Corps

MAJOR–GENERAL
H. W. SLOCUM
Commanding the Army of
Georgia

MAJOR–GENERAL
J. A. MOWER
Commanding the Twentieth
Army Corps

WILLIAM TECUMSEH SHERMAN

By WALTER L. FLEMING, PH.D.
Professor of History, Louisiana State University

THE armies of the United States were led in 1864–65 by two generals, to whom, more than to any other military leaders, was due the final victory of the Northern forces. Both Grant and Sherman were Western men; both were somewhat unsuccessful in the early years of the war and attained success rather late; to both of them the great opportunity finally came, in 1863, in the successful movement which opened the Mississippi, and their rewards were the two highest commands in the Federal army and the personal direction of the two great masses of men which were to crush the life out of the weakening Confederacy. Grant was the chief and Sherman his lieutenant, but some military critics hold that the latter did more than his chief to bring the war to an end. They were friends and were closely associated in military matters after 1862; in temperament and in military methods each supplemented the other, and each enabled the other to push his plans to success.

William Tecumseh Sherman was born in Lancaster, Ohio, February 8, 1820. The family was of New England origin, and had come to America from England in the seventeenth century. About two hundred years later, Sherman's father and mother migrated to what was then the unsettled West and made their home in Ohio. His father, a lawyer and in his later years a justice of the Ohio Supreme Court, died in 1829, leaving a large family of children without adequate support. The subject of this sketch was adopted into the family of Thomas Ewing, who was later United States senator, and Secretary of the Interior in the cabinets of Harrison and Tyler. The boy

BEFORE THE MARCH TO THE SEA

These two photographs of General Sherman were taken in 1864—the year that made him an international figure, before his march to the sea which electrified the civilized world, and exposed once for all the crippled condition of the Confederacy. After that autumn expedition, the problem of the Union generals was merely to contend with detached armies, no longer with the combined States of the Confederacy. The latter had no means of extending further support to the dwindling troops in the field. Sherman was the chief Union exponent of the tactical gift that makes marches count as much as fighting. In the early part of 1864 he made his famous raid across Mississippi from Jackson to Meridian and back again, destroying the railroads, Confederate stores, and other property, and desolating the country along the line of march. In May he set out from Chattanooga for the invasion of Georgia. For his success in this campaign he was appointed, on August 12th, a major-general in the regular army. On November 12th, he started with the pick of his men on his march to the sea. After the capture of Savannah, December 21st, Sherman's fame was secure; yet he was one of the most heartily execrated leaders of the war. There is a hint of a smile in the right-hand picture. The left-hand portrait reveals all the sternness and determination of a leader surrounded by dangers, about to penetrate an enemy's country against the advice of accepted military authorities.

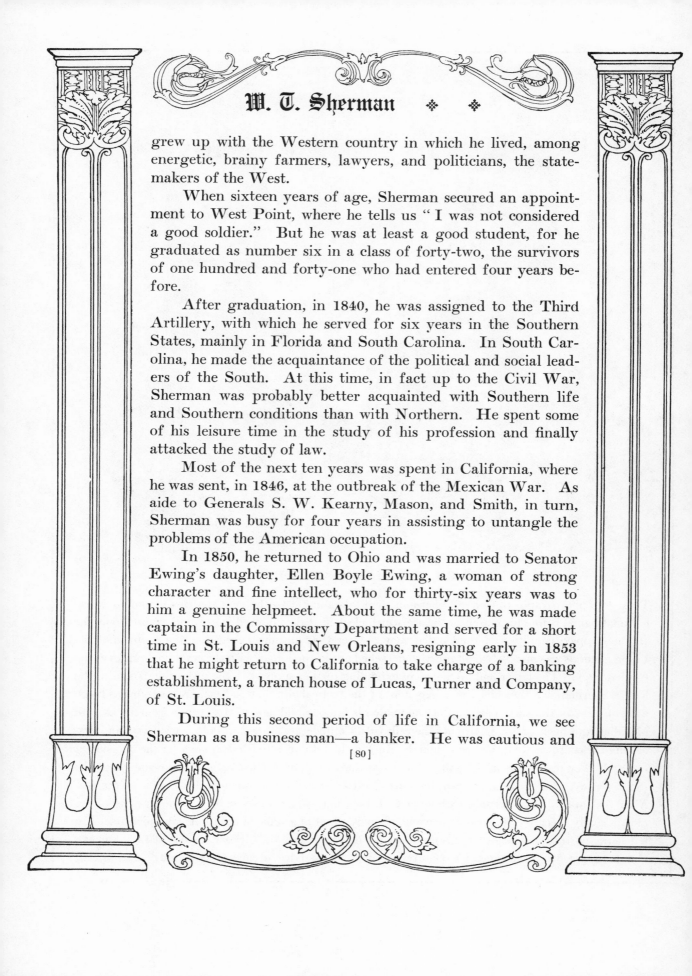

grew up with the Western country in which he lived, among energetic, brainy farmers, lawyers, and politicians, the state-makers of the West.

When sixteen years of age, Sherman secured an appointment to West Point, where he tells us " I was not considered a good soldier." But he was at least a good student, for he graduated as number six in a class of forty-two, the survivors of one hundred and forty-one who had entered four years before.

After graduation, in 1840, he was assigned to the Third Artillery, with which he served for six years in the Southern States, mainly in Florida and South Carolina. In South Carolina, he made the acquaintance of the political and social leaders of the South. At this time, in fact up to the Civil War, Sherman was probably better acquainted with Southern life and Southern conditions than with Northern. He spent some of his leisure time in the study of his profession and finally attacked the study of law.

Most of the next ten years was spent in California, where he was sent, in 1846, at the outbreak of the Mexican War. As aide to Generals S. W. Kearny, Mason, and Smith, in turn, Sherman was busy for four years in assisting to untangle the problems of the American occupation.

In 1850, he returned to Ohio and was married to Senator Ewing's daughter, Ellen Boyle Ewing, a woman of strong character and fine intellect, who for thirty-six years was to him a genuine helpmeet. About the same time, he was made captain in the Commissary Department and served for a short time in St. Louis and New Orleans, resigning early in 1853 that he might return to California to take charge of a banking establishment, a branch house of Lucas, Turner and Company, of St. Louis.

During this second period of life in California, we see Sherman as a business man—a banker. He was cautious and

SHERMAN IN 1865

If Sherman was deemed merciless in war, he was superbly generous when the fighting was over.   To Joseph E. Johnston he offered most liberal terms of surrender for the Southern armies.   Their acceptance would have gone far to prevent the worst of the reconstruction enormities.   Unfortunately his first convention with Johnston was disapproved.   The death of Lincoln had removed the guiding hand that would have meant so much to the nation. To those who have read his published correspondence and his memoirs Sherman appears in a very human light.   He was fluent and frequently reckless in speech and writing, but his kindly humanity is seen in both.

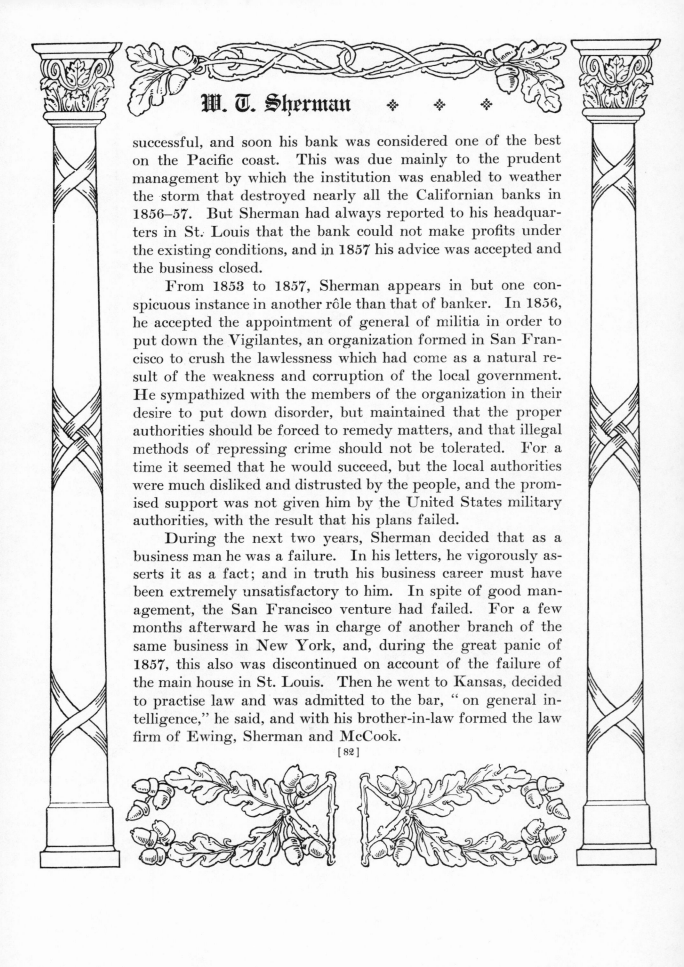

successful, and soon his bank was considered one of the best on the Pacific coast. This was due mainly to the prudent management by which the institution was enabled to weather the storm that destroyed nearly all the Californian banks in 1856–57. But Sherman had always reported to his headquarters in St. Louis that the bank could not make profits under the existing conditions, and in 1857 his advice was accepted and the business closed.

From 1853 to 1857, Sherman appears in but one conspicuous instance in another rôle than that of banker. In 1856, he accepted the appointment of general of militia in order to put down the Vigilantes, an organization formed in San Francisco to crush the lawlessness which had come as a natural result of the weakness and corruption of the local government. He sympathized with the members of the organization in their desire to put down disorder, but maintained that the proper authorities should be forced to remedy matters, and that illegal methods of repressing crime should not be tolerated. For a time it seemed that he would succeed, but the local authorities were much disliked and distrusted by the people, and the promised support was not given him by the United States military authorities, with the result that his plans failed.

During the next two years, Sherman decided that as a business man he was a failure. In his letters, he vigorously asserts it as a fact; and in truth his business career must have been extremely unsatisfactory to him. In spite of good management, the San Francisco venture had failed. For a few months afterward he was in charge of another branch of the same business in New York, and, during the great panic of 1857, this also was discontinued on account of the failure of the main house in St. Louis. Then he went to Kansas, decided to practise law and was admitted to the bar, "on general intelligence," he said, and with his brother-in-law formed the law firm of Ewing, Sherman and McCook.

SHERMAN IN 1876

A SOLDIER TO THE END

The tall figure of "Old Tecumseh" in 1876, though crowned with gray, still stood erect and commanding. Upon the appointment of Grant as full general, in July, 1866, Sherman had been promoted to the lieutenant-generalship. When Grant became President of the United States, March 4, 1869, Sherman succeeded him as general. An attempt was made to run him against Grant in 1872, but he emphatically refused to allow his name to be used. He retired from the army on full pay in February, 1884. Although he was practically assured of the Republican nomination for President that year, he telegraphed that he would not accept the nomination if given, and would not serve if elected. He spent his later years among his old army associates, attending reunions, making speeches at soldiers' celebrations, and putting his papers in order for future historians. He resolutely refused all inducements to enter the political arena, and to the end he remained a soldier.

[D—6]

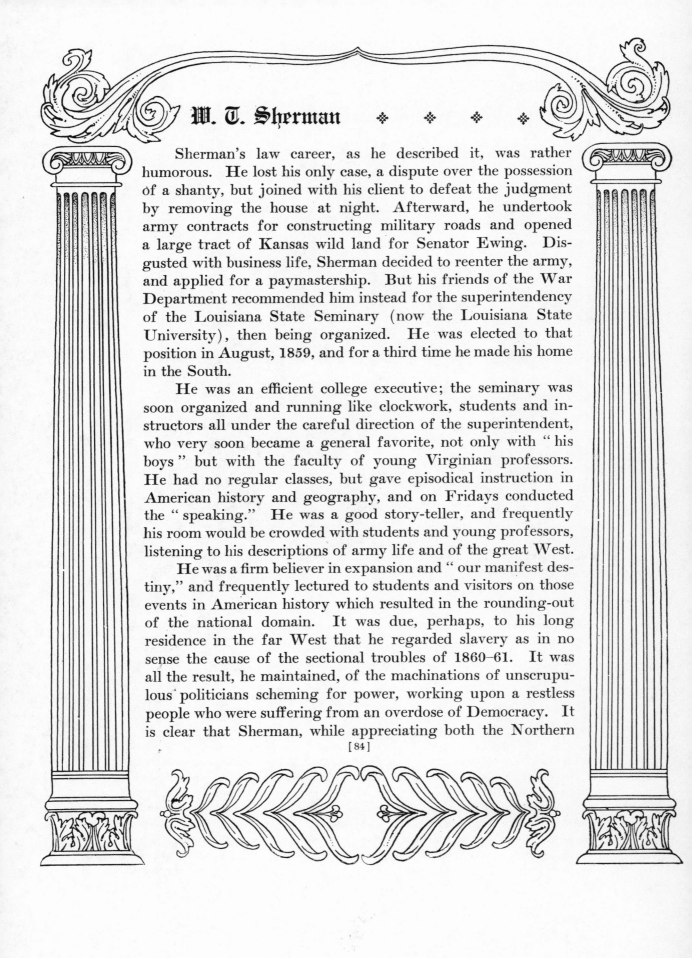

W. T. Sherman ❖ ❖ ❖ ❖

Sherman's law career, as he described it, was rather humorous. He lost his only case, a dispute over the possession of a shanty, but joined with his client to defeat the judgment by removing the house at night. Afterward, he undertook army contracts for constructing military roads and opened a large tract of Kansas wild land for Senator Ewing. Disgusted with business life, Sherman decided to reenter the army, and applied for a paymastership. But his friends of the War Department recommended him instead for the superintendency of the Louisiana State Seminary (now the Louisiana State University), then being organized. He was elected to that position in August, 1859, and for a third time he made his home in the South.

He was an efficient college executive; the seminary was soon organized and running like clockwork, students and instructors all under the careful direction of the superintendent, who very soon became a general favorite, not only with " his boys " but with the faculty of young Virginian professors. He had no regular classes, but gave episodical instruction in American history and geography, and on Fridays conducted the " speaking." He was a good story-teller, and frequently his room would be crowded with students and young professors, listening to his descriptions of army life and of the great West.

He was a firm believer in expansion and " our manifest destiny," and frequently lectured to students and visitors on those events in American history which resulted in the rounding-out of the national domain. It was due, perhaps, to his long residence in the far West that he regarded slavery as in no sense the cause of the sectional troubles of 1860–61. It was all the result, he maintained, of the machinations of unscrupulous politicians scheming for power, working upon a restless people who were suffering from an overdose of Democracy. It is clear that Sherman, while appreciating both the Northern

SHERMAN'S LEADERS IN THE ATLANTA CAMPAIGN

THE FIRST · OF FIVE GROUPS OF LEADERS WHO MADE POSSIBLE SHERMAN'S LACONIC MESSAGE
OF SEPTEMBER, 1864: "ATLANTA IS OURS AND FAIRLY WON"

James D. Morgan, Leader of a Division
in Palmer's Corps.

R. M. Johnson, Leader of a Division
in the Fourteenth Corps.

John Newton Led the Second Division
of the Fourth Corps.

Alpheus S. Williams, Leader of a Division
under General Joseph Hooker.

Edward M. McCook, Dashing Leader of a
Cavalry Division in Front of Atlanta.

Wager Swayne, Originally Colonel of the
43d Ohio, Brevetted Major-General.

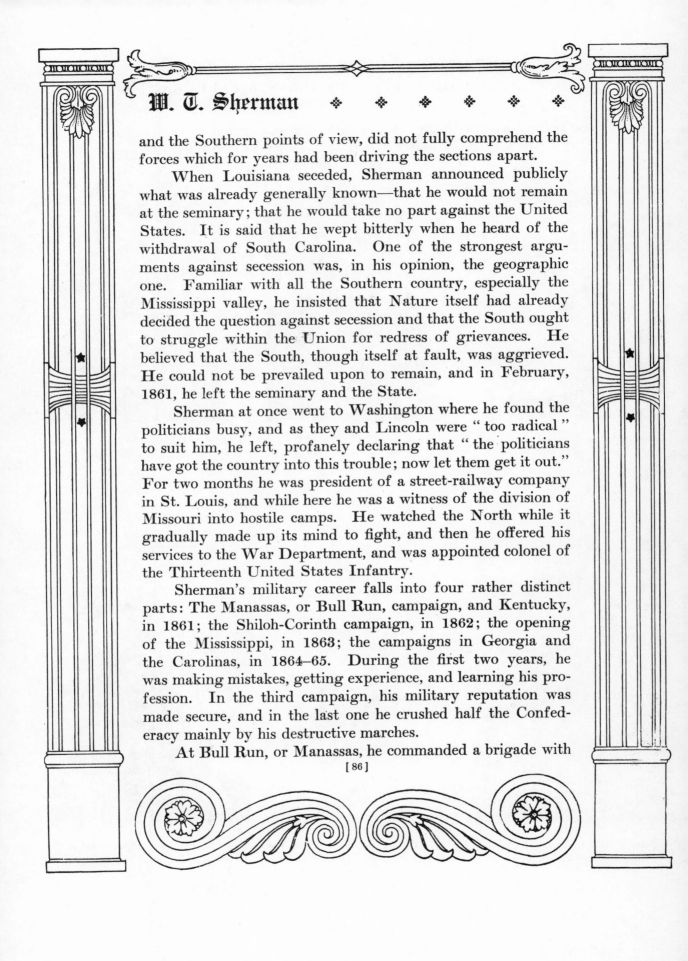

and the Southern points of view, did not fully comprehend the forces which for years had been driving the sections apart.

When Louisiana seceded, Sherman announced publicly what was already generally known—that he would not remain at the seminary; that he would take no part against the United States. It is said that he wept bitterly when he heard of the withdrawal of South Carolina. One of the strongest arguments against secession was, in his opinion, the geographic one. Familiar with all the Southern country, especially the Mississippi valley, he insisted that Nature itself had already decided the question against secession and that the South ought to struggle within the Union for redress of grievances. He believed that the South, though itself at fault, was aggrieved. He could not be prevailed upon to remain, and in February, 1861, he left the seminary and the State.

Sherman at once went to Washington where he found the politicians busy, and as they and Lincoln were " too radical " to suit him, he left, profanely declaring that " the politicians have got the country into this trouble; now let them get it out." For two months he was president of a street-railway company in St. Louis, and while here he was a witness of the division of Missouri into hostile camps. He watched the North while it gradually made up its mind to fight, and then he offered his services to the War Department, and was appointed colonel of the Thirteenth United States Infantry.

Sherman's military career falls into four rather distinct parts: The Manassas, or Bull Run, campaign, and Kentucky, in 1861; the Shiloh-Corinth campaign, in 1862; the opening of the Mississippi, in 1863; the campaigns in Georgia and the Carolinas, in 1864–65. During the first two years, he was making mistakes, getting experience, and learning his profession. In the third campaign, his military reputation was made secure, and in the last one he crushed half the Confederacy mainly by his destructive marches.

At Bull Run, or Manassas, he commanded a brigade with

Thos. H. Ruger Commanded a Brigade
under General Hooker.

J. C. Veatch, Division Leader in the
Sixteenth Army Corps.

Morgan L. Smith, Leader of the
Second Division, Fourteenth Corps.

LEADERS IN THE
ATLANTA CAMPAIGN—
GROUP No. 2

COMMANDERS OF BRIGADES
AND DIVISIONS WHICH FOUGHT
UNDER McPHERSON, THOMAS
AND HOOKER IN THE CAMPAIGN
FOR ATLANTA, SUMMER OF '64

J. D. Cox Commanded a Division
under General Schofield.

M. D. Manson, Brigade Leader in the
Twenty-third Corps.

Charles Cruft Commanded a Brigade
under General Stanley.

J. A. J. Lightburn Led a Division in
the Army of the Tennessee.

W. L. Elliott, Chief of Cavalry under
General Thomas

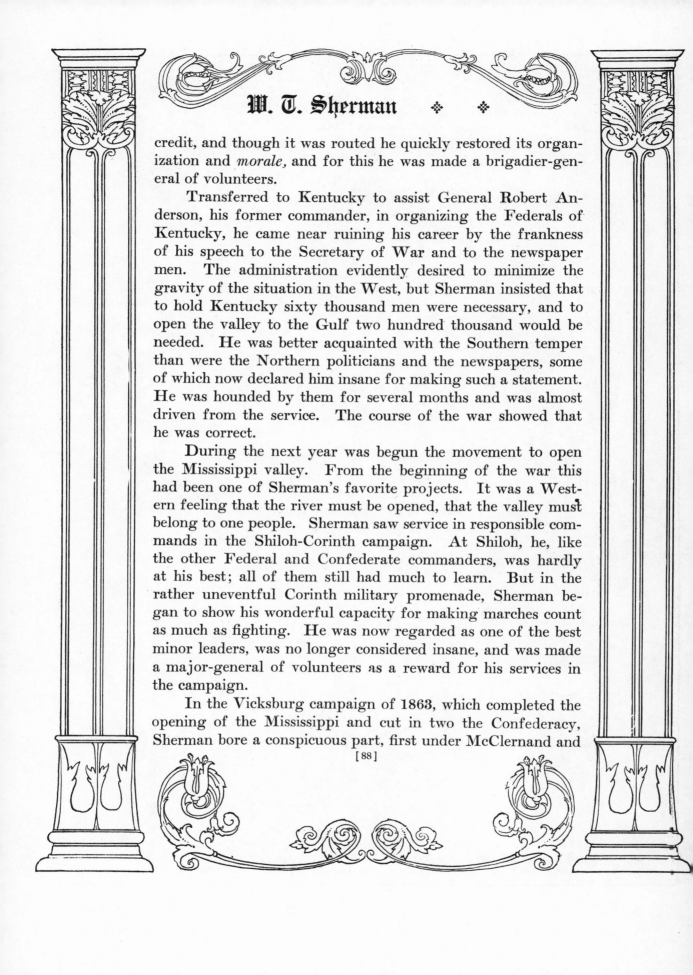

credit, and though it was routed he quickly restored its organization and *morale,* and for this he was made a brigadier-general of volunteers.

Transferred to Kentucky to assist General Robert Anderson, his former commander, in organizing the Federals of Kentucky, he came near ruining his career by the frankness of his speech to the Secretary of War and to the newspaper men. The administration evidently desired to minimize the gravity of the situation in the West, but Sherman insisted that to hold Kentucky sixty thousand men were necessary, and to open the valley to the Gulf two hundred thousand would be needed. He was better acquainted with the Southern temper than were the Northern politicians and the newspapers, some of which now declared him insane for making such a statement. He was hounded by them for several months and was almost driven from the service. The course of the war showed that he was correct.

During the next year was begun the movement to open the Mississippi valley. From the beginning of the war this had been one of Sherman's favorite projects. It was a Western feeling that the river must be opened, that the valley must belong to one people. Sherman saw service in responsible commands in the Shiloh-Corinth campaign. At Shiloh, he, like the other Federal and Confederate commanders, was hardly at his best; all of them still had much to learn. But in the rather uneventful Corinth military promenade, Sherman began to show his wonderful capacity for making marches count as much as fighting. He was now regarded as one of the best minor leaders, was no longer considered insane, and was made a major-general of volunteers as a reward for his services in the campaign.

In the Vicksburg campaign of 1863, which completed the opening of the Mississippi and cut in two the Confederacy, Sherman bore a conspicuous part, first under McClernand and

Nathan Kimball Led a Division in the Fourth Corps.

Samuel Beatty, Leader of a Brigade in the Fourth Corps.

William B. Hazen Commanded a Division under McPherson.

J. M. Corse "Held the Fort" at Alatoona Pass.

Joseph F. Knipe, Leader of a Brigade in the Twentieth Corps.

LEADERS IN THE ATLANTA
CAMPAIGN
GROUP No. 3

GENERAL OFFICERS WHO LED BRIGADES OR DIVISIONS IN THE HUNDRED DAYS' MARCHING AND FIGHTING FROM RESACA TO ATLANTA

Charles Candy Led a Brigade in Geary's Division of the Twentieth Corps.

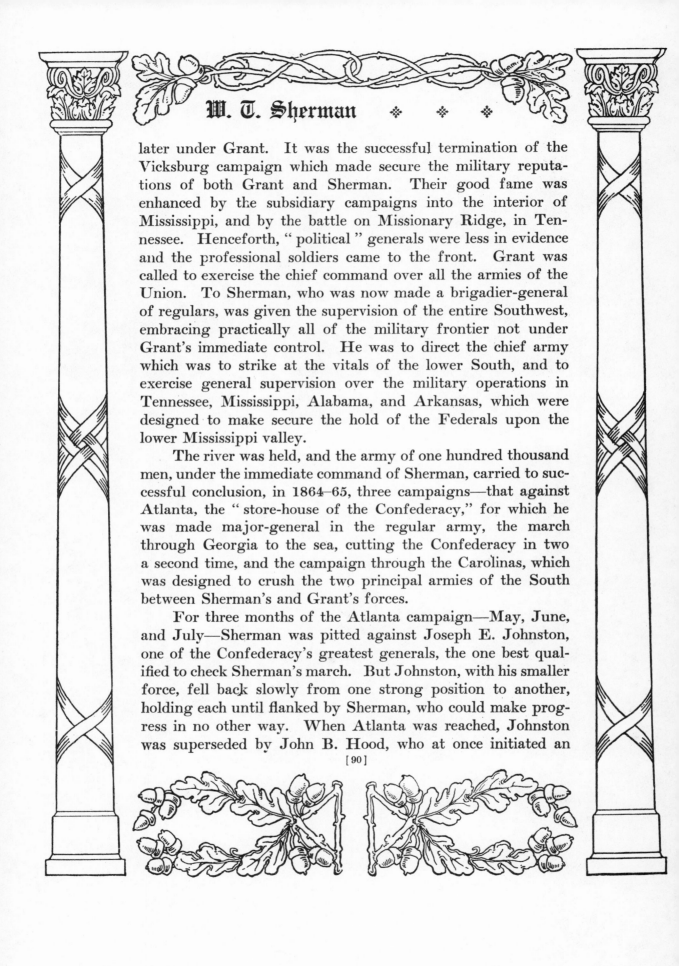

later under Grant. It was the successful termination of the Vicksburg campaign which made secure the military reputations of both Grant and Sherman. Their good fame was enhanced by the subsidiary campaigns into the interior of Mississippi, and by the battle on Missionary Ridge, in Tennessee. Henceforth, " political " generals were less in evidence and the professional soldiers came to the front. Grant was called to exercise the chief command over all the armies of the Union. To Sherman, who was now made a brigadier-general of regulars, was given the supervision of the entire Southwest, embracing practically all of the military frontier not under Grant's immediate control. He was to direct the chief army which was to strike at the vitals of the lower South, and to exercise general supervision over the military operations in Tennessee, Mississippi, Alabama, and Arkansas, which were designed to make secure the hold of the Federals upon the lower Mississippi valley.

The river was held, and the army of one hundred thousand men, under the immediate command of Sherman, carried to successful conclusion, in 1864–65, three campaigns—that against Atlanta, the " store-house of the Confederacy," for which he was made major-general in the regular army, the march through Georgia to the sea, cutting the Confederacy in two a second time, and the campaign through the Carolinas, which was designed to crush the two principal armies of the South between Sherman's and Grant's forces.

For three months of the Atlanta campaign—May, June, and July—Sherman was pitted against Joseph E. Johnston, one of the Confederacy's greatest generals, the one best qualified to check Sherman's march. But Johnston, with his smaller force, fell back slowly from one strong position to another, holding each until flanked by Sherman, who could make progress in no other way. When Atlanta was reached, Johnston was superseded by John B. Hood, who at once initiated an

M. D. Leggett, Division Leader in Blair's Corps.

William Harrow Commanded Division in Logan's Corps.

John W. Fuller, Leader of a Division in Dodge's Corps.

Thomas W. Sweeny Led a Division in Dodge's Corps.

LEADERS IN THE ATLANTA CAMPAIGN—No. 4

PROMINENT LEADERS IN THE ARMY OF THE CUMBERLAND AND THE TENNESSEE IN SHERMAN'S MASTERLY MOVEMENT TO THE HEART OF GEORGIA

George D. Wagner Commanded a Division under Howard.

William F. Barry, Chief of Artillery on Sherman's Staff.

W. W. Belknap, Promoted in Front of Atlanta.

John B. Turchin, Leader in the Fourteenth Corps.

William T. Ward Led a Division under Hooker.

John W. Sprague, Leader in the Sixteenth Corps.

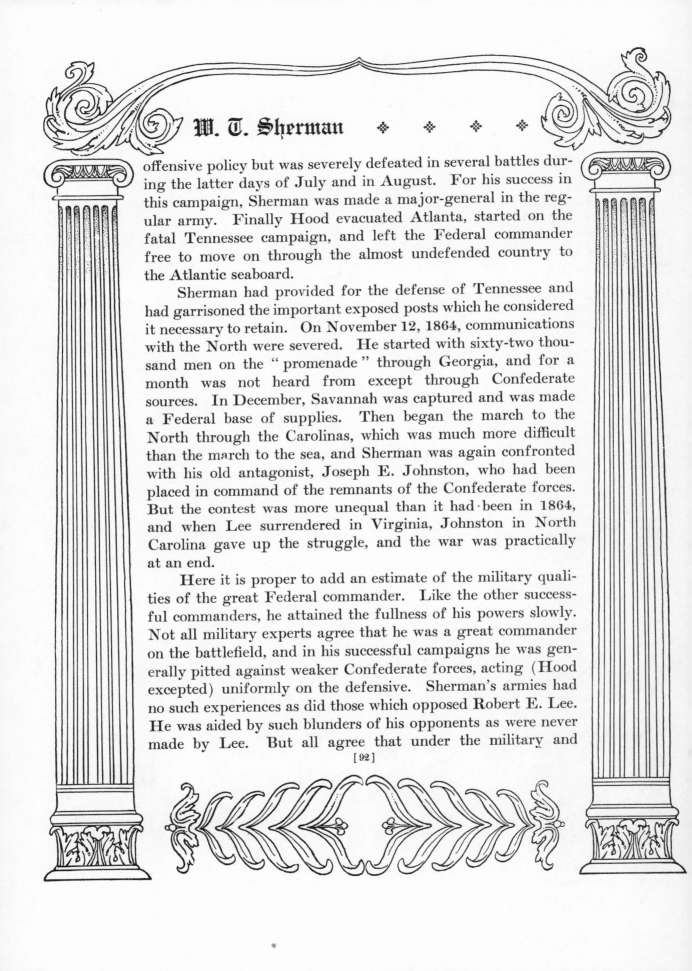

offensive policy but was severely defeated in several battles during the latter days of July and in August. For his success in this campaign, Sherman was made a major-general in the regular army. Finally Hood evacuated Atlanta, started on the fatal Tennessee campaign, and left the Federal commander free to move on through the almost undefended country to the Atlantic seaboard.

Sherman had provided for the defense of Tennessee and had garrisoned the important exposed posts which he considered it necessary to retain. On November 12, 1864, communications with the North were severed. He started with sixty-two thousand men on the "promenade" through Georgia, and for a month was not heard from except through Confederate sources. In December, Savannah was captured and was made a Federal base of supplies. Then began the march to the North through the Carolinas, which was much more difficult than the march to the sea, and Sherman was again confronted with his old antagonist, Joseph E. Johnston, who had been placed in command of the remnants of the Confederate forces. But the contest was more unequal than it had been in 1864, and when Lee surrendered in Virginia, Johnston in North Carolina gave up the struggle, and the war was practically at an end.

Here it is proper to add an estimate of the military qualities of the great Federal commander. Like the other successful commanders, he attained the fullness of his powers slowly. Not all military experts agree that he was a great commander on the battlefield, and in his successful campaigns he was generally pitted against weaker Confederate forces, acting (Hood excepted) uniformly on the defensive. Sherman's armies had no such experiences as did those which opposed Robert E. Lee. He was aided by such blunders of his opponents as were never made by Lee. But all agree that under the military and

Jos. A. Cooper Commanded a Brigade in the Twenty-third Corps.

M. F. Force Commanded a Brigade under Blair.

John H. King Commanded a Division in the Fourteenth Corps.

LEADERS IN THE

ATLANTA AND

NASHVILLE CAMPAIGNS

Milo S. Hascall, Leader of a Division in the Twenty-third Corps.

GENERAL OFFICERS

CONSPICUOUS IN SHERMAN'S

ADVANCE AND SOME

WHO PROTECTED THE FLANK

AND REAR OF HIS ARMY

David S. Stanley, Leader of the Fourth Corps; an All-around Soldier.

H. M. Judah Commanded a Division of the Twenty-third Corps.

Charles C. Walcutt, Leader of a Brigade in the Fifteenth Corps.

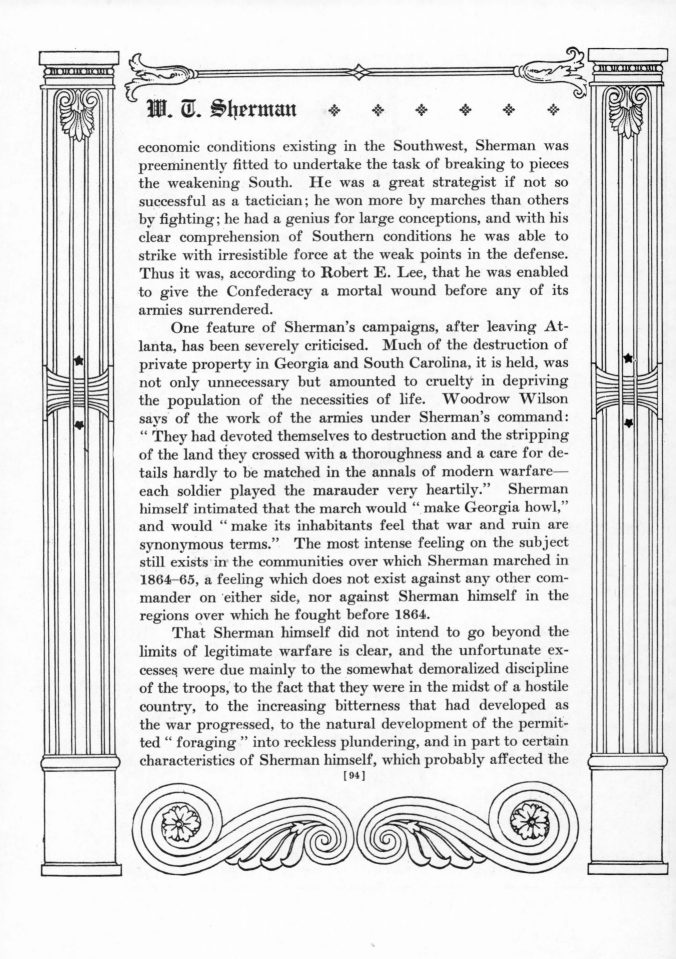

economic conditions existing in the Southwest, Sherman was preeminently fitted to undertake the task of breaking to pieces the weakening South. He was a great strategist if not so successful as a tactician; he won more by marches than others by fighting; he had a genius for large conceptions, and with his clear comprehension of Southern conditions he was able to strike with irresistible force at the weak points in the defense. Thus it was, according to Robert E. Lee, that he was enabled to give the Confederacy a mortal wound before any of its armies surrendered.

One feature of Sherman's campaigns, after leaving Atlanta, has been severely criticised. Much of the destruction of private property in Georgia and South Carolina, it is held, was not only unnecessary but amounted to cruelty in depriving the population of the necessities of life. Woodrow Wilson says of the work of the armies under Sherman's command: "They had devoted themselves to destruction and the stripping of the land they crossed with a thoroughness and a care for details hardly to be matched in the annals of modern warfare— each soldier played the marauder very heartily." Sherman himself intimated that the march would "make Georgia howl," and would "make its inhabitants feel that war and ruin are synonymous terms." The most intense feeling on the subject still exists in the communities over which Sherman marched in 1864–65, a feeling which does not exist against any other commander on either side, nor against Sherman himself in the regions over which he fought before 1864.

That Sherman himself did not intend to go beyond the limits of legitimate warfare is clear, and the unfortunate excesses were due mainly to the somewhat demoralized discipline of the troops, to the fact that they were in the midst of a hostile country, to the increasing bitterness that had developed as the war progressed, to the natural development of the permitted "foraging" into reckless plundering, and in part to certain characteristics of Sherman himself, which probably affected the

ARMY AND CORPS LEADERS WHO ENDED THE WAR IN THE NORTHWEST AND SOUTHWEST

As Sherman cut the southeastern Confederacy in two by his march to the sea, so Sheridan (center of group above) and Canby (shown below) wiped off the map the theaters of war in the northwest and southwest respectively. With Merritt and Torbert, and the dashing Custer, Sheridan swept the Shenandoah Valley. Canby, as commander of the military division of West Mississippi, directed the Mobile campaign of March-April, 1865, which resulted in the occupation by the Federals of Mobile and Montgomery. A raid by James H. Wilson (second from right) had prepared the way for this result. In May, 1865, Canby received the surrender of the Confederate forces under Generals R. Taylor and E. Kirby Smith, the largest Confederate forces which sur-

GENERAL EDWARD R. S. CANBY

rendered at the end of the war. The cavalry leaders in the upper picture are, from left to right: Generals Wesley Merritt, David McM. Gregg, Philip Henry Sheridan, Henry E. Davies, James Harrison Wilson, and Alfred T. A. Torbert. Wilson was given the cavalry corps of the military district of the Mississippi in 1865, and Torbert commanded the cavalry corps of the Army of the Shenandoah under Sheridan. These six great leaders are among the men who handled the Federal cavalry in its last days, welding it into the splendid, efficient, aggressive, fighting force that finally overwhelmed the depleted ranks of their Confederate opponents, Forrest and Wheeler in the West and Rosser, Lomax, Stuart, the two Lees and Hampton in the East.

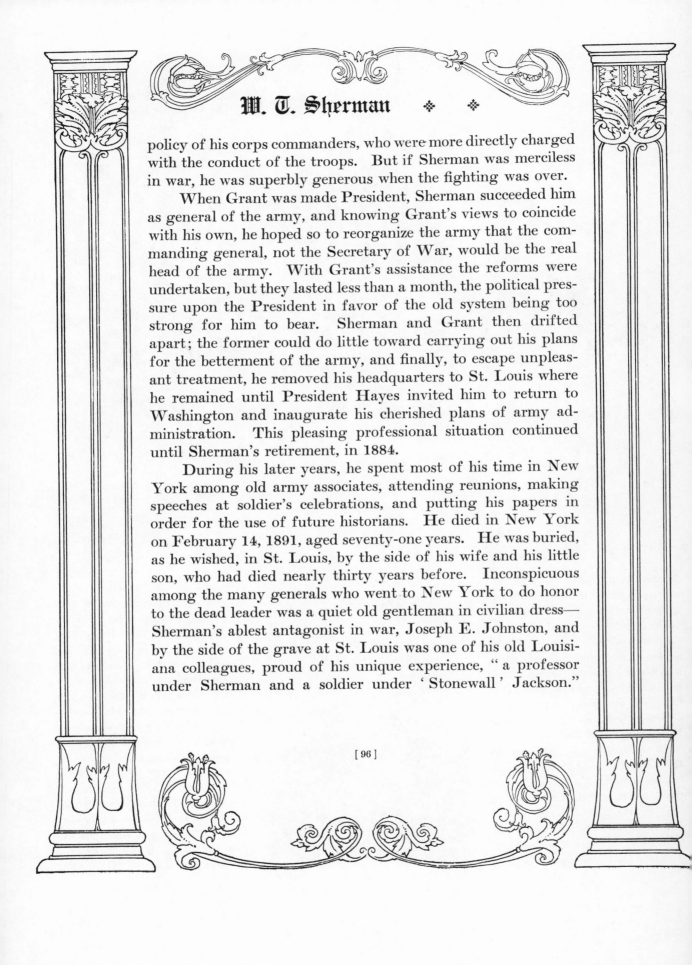

policy of his corps commanders, who were more directly charged with the conduct of the troops. But if Sherman was merciless in war, he was superbly generous when the fighting was over.

When Grant was made President, Sherman succeeded him as general of the army, and knowing Grant's views to coincide with his own, he hoped so to reorganize the army that the commanding general, not the Secretary of War, would be the real head of the army. With Grant's assistance the reforms were undertaken, but they lasted less than a month, the political pressure upon the President in favor of the old system being too strong for him to bear. Sherman and Grant then drifted apart; the former could do little toward carrying out his plans for the betterment of the army, and finally, to escape unpleasant treatment, he removed his headquarters to St. Louis where he remained until President Hayes invited him to return to Washington and inaugurate his cherished plans of army administration. This pleasing professional situation continued until Sherman's retirement, in 1884.

During his later years, he spent most of his time in New York among old army associates, attending reunions, making speeches at soldier's celebrations, and putting his papers in order for the use of future historians. He died in New York on February 14, 1891, aged seventy-one years. He was buried, as he wished, in St. Louis, by the side of his wife and his little son, who had died nearly thirty years before. Inconspicuous among the many generals who went to New York to do honor to the dead leader was a quiet old gentleman in civilian dress— Sherman's ablest antagonist in war, Joseph E. Johnston, and by the side of the grave at St. Louis was one of his old Louisiana colleagues, proud of his unique experience, " a professor under Sherman and a soldier under ' Stonewall ' Jackson."

IV

JACKSON

THOMAS J. JACKSON IN THE FORTIES

A PORTRAIT TAKEN DURING THE MEXICAN WAR,
WHERE JACKSON SERVED AS A SECOND
LIEUTENANT, THE YEAR AFTER HIS
GRADUATION FROM WEST POINT

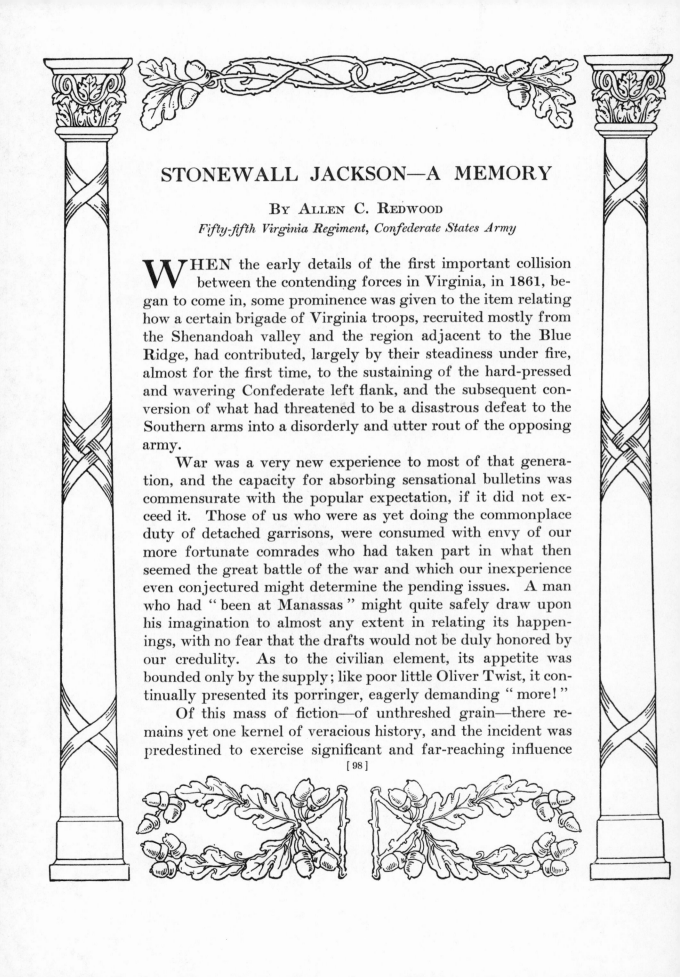

STONEWALL JACKSON—A MEMORY

By Allen C. Redwood
Fifty-fifth Virginia Regiment, Confederate States Army

WHEN the early details of the first important collision between the contending forces in Virginia, in 1861, began to come in, some prominence was given to the item relating how a certain brigade of Virginia troops, recruited mostly from the Shenandoah valley and the region adjacent to the Blue Ridge, had contributed, largely by their steadiness under fire, almost for the first time, to the sustaining of the hard-pressed and wavering Confederate left flank, and the subsequent conversion of what had threatened to be a disastrous defeat to the Southern arms into a disorderly and utter rout of the opposing army.

War was a very new experience to most of that generation, and the capacity for absorbing sensational bulletins was commensurate with the popular expectation, if it did not exceed it. Those of us who were as yet doing the commonplace duty of detached garrisons, were consumed with envy of our more fortunate comrades who had taken part in what then seemed the great battle of the war and which our inexperience even conjectured might determine the pending issues. A man who had "been at Manassas" might quite safely draw upon his imagination to almost any extent in relating its happenings, with no fear that the drafts would not be duly honored by our credulity. As to the civilian element, its appetite was bounded only by the supply; like poor little Oliver Twist, it continually presented its porringer, eagerly demanding "more!"

Of this mass of fiction—of unthreshed grain—there remains yet one kernel of veracious history, and the incident was predestined to exercise significant and far-reaching influence

[98]

THOMAS JONATHAN JACKSON

AS FIRST LIEUTENANT, U. S. A.

Jackson's very soul impressed itself on the glass of this early negative through his striking features—more clearly read than later, when a heavy beard had covered the resolute lips, and the habit of command had veiled the deep-seeing, somber eyes. When the quiet Virginia boy with the strong religious bent graduated eighteenth in his class of seventy from West Point in 1846, his comrades little thought that he was destined to become the most suddenly famous of American generals. The year after his graduation he attracted attention by his performances as lieutenant of artillery under General Scott in Mexico, and was brevetted captain and major for bravery at Contreras, Churubusco, and Chapultepec. Fourteen years later he earned his sobriquet of "Stonewall" in the first great battle of the Civil War. Within two years more he had risen to international fame—and received his mortal wound on the field of battle. He was reserved, almost somber with his men, yet he earned the love and enthusiastic devotion of the soldiers who came to be known as "Jackson's foot cavalry," so unparalleled were the marches they made under his leadership. They came to trust his judgment as infallible, and in spite of overwhelming odds they followed no matter where he led.

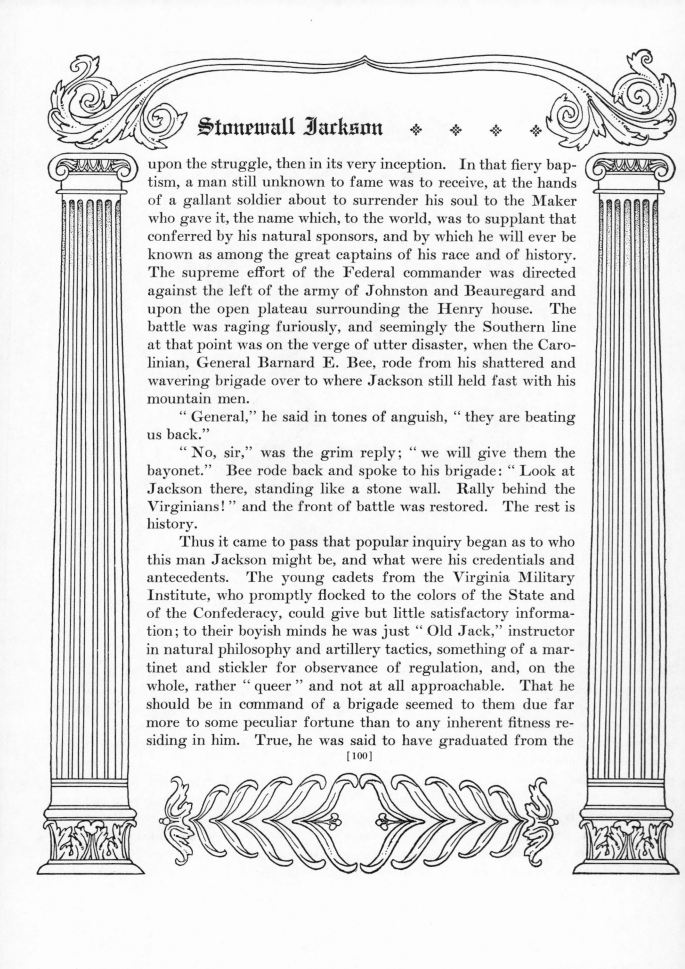

upon the struggle, then in its very inception. In that fiery baptism, a man still unknown to fame was to receive, at the hands of a gallant soldier about to surrender his soul to the Maker who gave it, the name which, to the world, was to supplant that conferred by his natural sponsors, and by which he will ever be known as among the great captains of his race and of history. The supreme effort of the Federal commander was directed against the left of the army of Johnston and Beauregard and upon the open plateau surrounding the Henry house. The battle was raging furiously, and seemingly the Southern line at that point was on the verge of utter disaster, when the Carolinian, General Barnard E. Bee, rode from his shattered and wavering brigade over to where Jackson still held fast with his mountain men.

"General," he said in tones of anguish, "they are beating us back."

"No, sir," was the grim reply; "we will give them the bayonet." Bee rode back and spoke to his brigade: "Look at Jackson there, standing like a stone wall. Rally behind the Virginians!" and the front of battle was restored. The rest is history.

Thus it came to pass that popular inquiry began as to who this man Jackson might be, and what were his credentials and antecedents. The young cadets from the Virginia Military Institute, who promptly flocked to the colors of the State and of the Confederacy, could give but little satisfactory information; to their boyish minds he was just "Old Jack," instructor in natural philosophy and artillery tactics, something of a martinet and stickler for observance of regulation, and, on the whole, rather "queer" and not at all approachable. That he should be in command of a brigade seemed to them due far more to some peculiar fortune than to any inherent fitness residing in him. True, he was said to have graduated from the

[100]

JACKSON—HIS MOST REVEALING PHOTOGRAPH

A PICTURE SECURED ONLY BY THE URGING
OF GENERAL BRADLEY T. JOHNSON

Jackson, a modest hero, nearly always shrank from being photographed. At the height of his fame he answered a publisher's letter with a refusal to write the desired magazine article or to send any picture of himself, though the offer was a very flattering one. The photograph above was made in Winchester, in February, 1862, at the Rontzohn gallery, where Jackson had been persuaded to spend a few minutes by the earnest entreaties of General Bradley T. Johnson. Some five months later Jackson was to send Banks whirling down the Shenandoah Valley, to the friendly shelter of the Potomac and Harper's Ferry, keep three armies busy in pursuit of him, and finally turn upon them and defeat two of them. This, with the profile portrait taken near Fredericksburg, shown on page 115 of Volume II, represents the only two sittings of Jackson during the war. Captain Frank P. Clark, who served three years in close association with the general, considered this the best likeness.

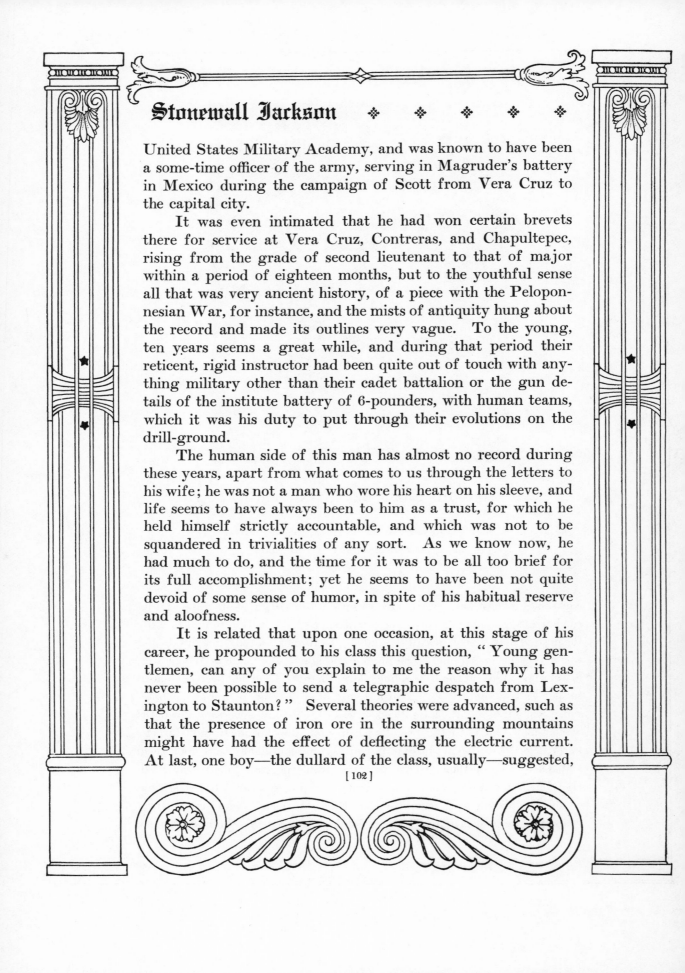

United States Military Academy, and was known to have been a some-time officer of the army, serving in Magruder's battery in Mexico during the campaign of Scott from Vera Cruz to the capital city.

It was even intimated that he had won certain brevets there for service at Vera Cruz, Contreras, and Chapultepec, rising from the grade of second lieutenant to that of major within a period of eighteen months, but to the youthful sense all that was very ancient history, of a piece with the Peloponnesian War, for instance, and the mists of antiquity hung about the record and made its outlines very vague. To the young, ten years seems a great while, and during that period their reticent, rigid instructor had been quite out of touch with anything military other than their cadet battalion or the gun details of the institute battery of 6-pounders, with human teams, which it was his duty to put through their evolutions on the drill-ground.

The human side of this man has almost no record during these years, apart from what comes to us through the letters to his wife; he was not a man who wore his heart on his sleeve, and life seems to have always been to him as a trust, for which he held himself strictly accountable, and which was not to be squandered in trivialities of any sort. As we know now, he had much to do, and the time for it was to be all too brief for its full accomplishment; yet he seems to have been not quite devoid of some sense of humor, in spite of his habitual reserve and aloofness.

It is related that upon one occasion, at this stage of his career, he propounded to his class this question, "Young gentlemen, can any of you explain to me the reason why it has never been possible to send a telegraphic despatch from Lexington to Staunton?" Several theories were advanced, such as that the presence of iron ore in the surrounding mountains might have had the effect of deflecting the electric current. At last, one boy—the dullard of the class, usually—suggested,

"STONEWALL" AND THE MEN WHO BORE HIS ORDERS

Their honors came not easily to Jackson's staff officers. Tireless himself, regardless of all personal comforts, he seemed to consider others endowed with like qualities. After a day of marching and fighting it was no unusual thing for him to send a staff member on a thirty or forty mile ride. He was on terms of easy friendship and confidence with his aides off duty, but his orders were explicit and irrevocable. He had no confidants as to his military designs—quite the opposite: Before starting on his march to Harper's Ferry he called for a map of the Pennsylvania frontier, and made many inquiries as to roads and localities to the north of Frederick, whereas his route lay in the opposite direction. His staff, like his soldiers, first feared his apparent rashness, and then adored him for his success.

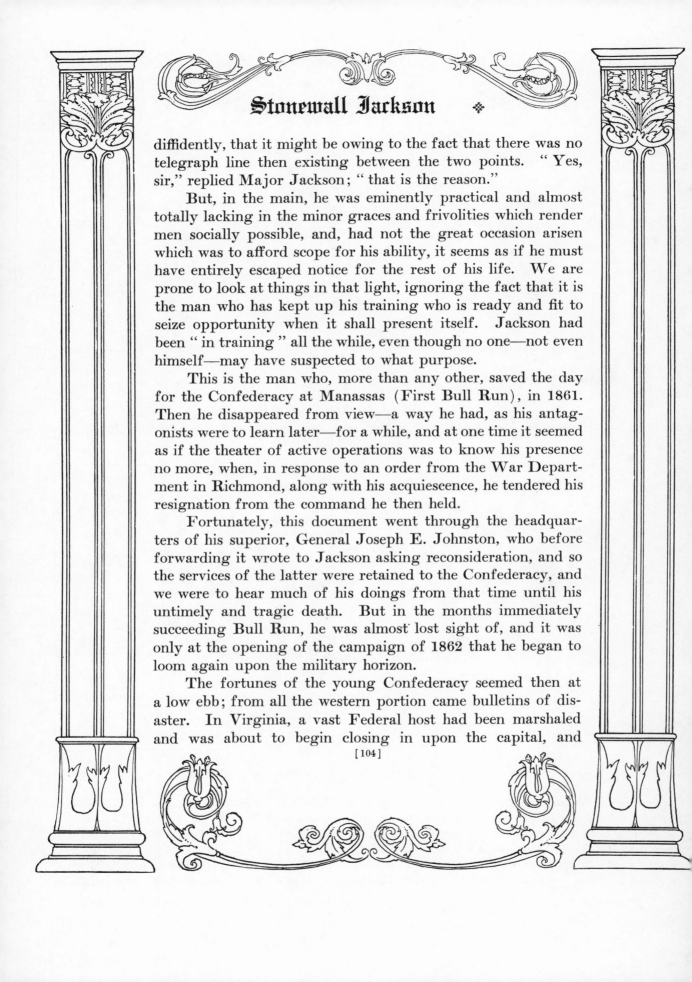

diffidently, that it might be owing to the fact that there was no telegraph line then existing between the two points. "Yes, sir," replied Major Jackson; "that is the reason."

But, in the main, he was eminently practical and almost totally lacking in the minor graces and frivolities which render men socially possible, and, had not the great occasion arisen which was to afford scope for his ability, it seems as if he must have entirely escaped notice for the rest of his life. We are prone to look at things in that light, ignoring the fact that it is the man who has kept up his training who is ready and fit to seize opportunity when it shall present itself. Jackson had been "in training" all the while, even though no one—not even himself—may have suspected to what purpose.

This is the man who, more than any other, saved the day for the Confederacy at Manassas (First Bull Run), in 1861. Then he disappeared from view—a way he had, as his antagonists were to learn later—for a while, and at one time it seemed as if the theater of active operations was to know his presence no more, when, in response to an order from the War Department in Richmond, along with his acquiescence, he tendered his resignation from the command he then held.

Fortunately, this document went through the headquarters of his superior, General Joseph E. Johnston, who before forwarding it wrote to Jackson asking reconsideration, and so the services of the latter were retained to the Confederacy, and we were to hear much of his doings from that time until his untimely and tragic death. But in the months immediately succeeding Bull Run, he was almost lost sight of, and it was only at the opening of the campaign of 1862 that he began to loom again upon the military horizon.

The fortunes of the young Confederacy seemed then at a low ebb; from all the western portion came bulletins of disaster. In Virginia, a vast Federal host had been marshaled and was about to begin closing in upon the capital, and

John Echols, Colonel of a "Stonewall" Regiment at Bull Run; Later Led a Brigade in Lee's Army.

J. D. Imboden, at Bull Run and always with Jackson; Later Commanded a Cavalry Brigade.

W. B. Taliaferro, with Jackson throughout 1862; Last, at Fredericksburg.

Arnold Elzey, a Brigade and Division Commander under Jackson and later.

CONFEDERATE GENERALS WITH JACKSON

AT THE DAWN OF HIS BRILLIANT CAREER

Isaac R. Trimble. Where "Stonewall" was, There was Trimble also.

all the outlying posts of the Confederate line were being severally driven in. Johnston had retired from Manassas to the line of the Rappahannock, presently to proceed to York-town, and eventually to retire thence to the Chickahominy. It was while lying there, awaiting McClellan's attack, that we began to get news of very active proceedings in the Valley region, which came to have important bearing upon our fortunes, and in the final issue to determine the contest we were expecting and awaiting in our immediate front.

To those sultry, squalid camps, reeking with malaria and swarming with flies, came from beyond the far-away Blue Ridge stirring and encouraging tidings of rapid march and sudden swoop; of telling blows where least expected; of skilful maneuvering of a small force, resulting in the frustrating of all combinations of one numerically its superior, and paralyzing for the time being all the plans of the Federal War Department and the grand strategy of the " young Napoleon " at the head of its armies in the field.

It seemed as if the *sobriquet* conferred upon Manassas field had become the veriest of misnomers; the " Stonewall " had acquired a marvelous mobility since that July day not yet a year old and had become a catapult instead. And what, perhaps, appealed to our personal interest more forcibly was the story of the capture of the rich spoil of war, the supplies, of which we were already beginning to feel the need. Our daily diet of unrelieved bread and bacon grew fairly nauseating at the thought of the bounty so generously provided by " Commissary-General " Banks, and of the extra dainties inviting pillage in the tents of Israel—but we were to get our share, with accrued interest, later on.

We had not yet ceased to marvel over these exploits when Jackson executed one of his mysterious disappearances, puzzling alike to friend and foe, and he next announced himself by the salvo of his guns, driving in McClellan's exposed right.

Edward Johnson Led an Independent Command under
Jackson in 1862.

George H. Steuart, Later
a Brigade Commander
in Lee's Army.

James A. Walker Led a
Brigade under Jack-
son at Antietam.

E. M. Law, Conspicuous at South Mountain
and Maryland Heights.

Charles W. Field, Later in Command of
one of Longstreet's Divisions.

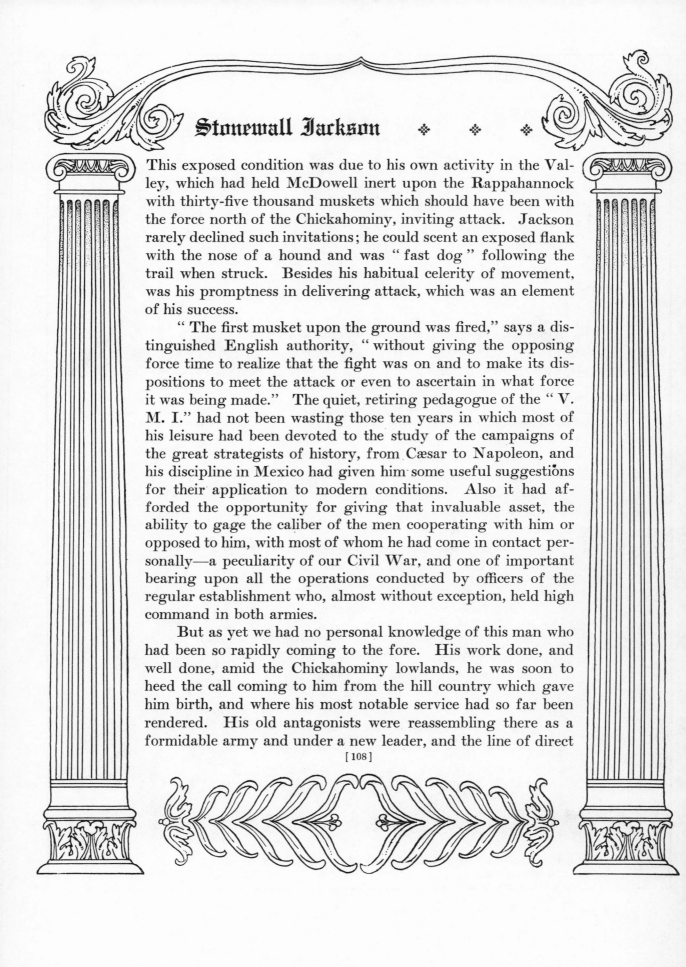

Stonewall Jackson ✦ ✦ ✦

This exposed condition was due to his own activity in the Valley, which had held McDowell inert upon the Rappahannock with thirty-five thousand muskets which should have been with the force north of the Chickahominy, inviting attack. Jackson rarely declined such invitations; he could scent an exposed flank with the nose of a hound and was "fast dog" following the trail when struck. Besides his habitual celerity of movement, was his promptness in delivering attack, which was an element of his success.

"The first musket upon the ground was fired," says a distinguished English authority, "without giving the opposing force time to realize that the fight was on and to make its dispositions to meet the attack or even to ascertain in what force it was being made." The quiet, retiring pedagogue of the "V. M. I." had not been wasting those ten years in which most of his leisure had been devoted to the study of the campaigns of the great strategists of history, from Cæsar to Napoleon, and his discipline in Mexico had given him some useful suggestions for their application to modern conditions. Also it had afforded the opportunity for giving that invaluable asset, the ability to gage the caliber of the men cooperating with him or opposed to him, with most of whom he had come in contact personally—a peculiarity of our Civil War, and one of important bearing upon all the operations conducted by officers of the regular establishment who, almost without exception, held high command in both armies.

But as yet we had no personal knowledge of this man who had been so rapidly coming to the fore. His work done, and well done, amid the Chickahominy lowlands, he was soon to heed the call coming to him from the hill country which gave him birth, and where his most notable service had so far been rendered. His old antagonists were reassembling there as a formidable army and under a new leader, and the line of direct

A. R. Lawton Led
Ewell's Old Di-
vision at the
Battle of
Antie-
tam.

Roswell S. Ripley,
Wounded at
Antietam in
Defense of
Lee's Left
Flank.

R. E. Colston Commanded Trimble's
Division at Chancellorsville.

Henry Heth Commanded the Light
Division at Chancellorsville.

CONFEDERATE

GENERALS

WITH

JACKSON

Jas. T. Archer Commanded a Brigade
at Chancellorsville.

AT ANTIETAM

AND

CHANCELLORS–

VILLE

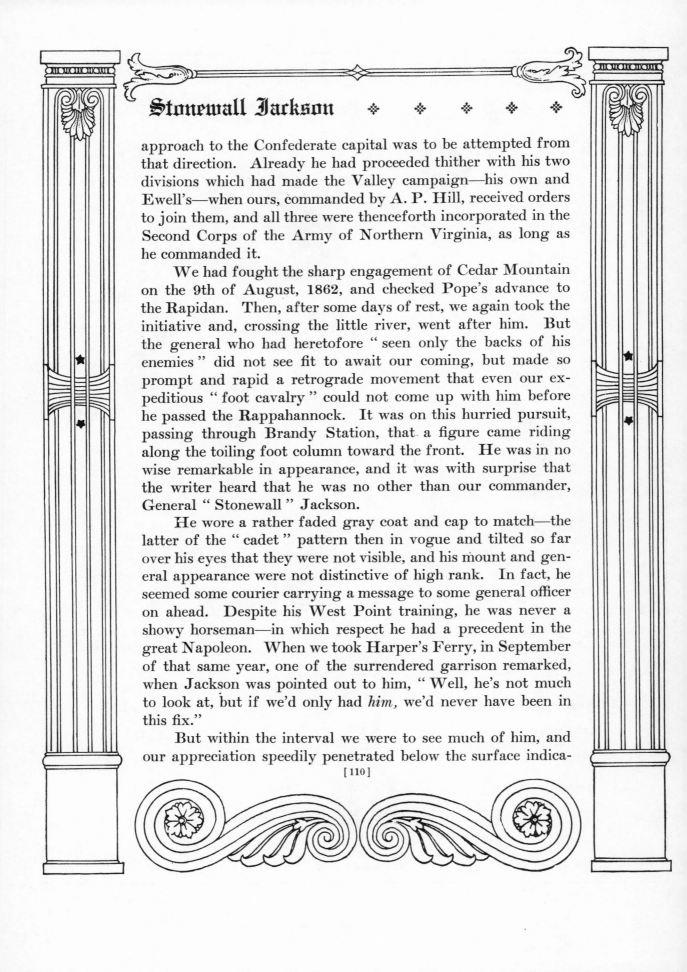

approach to the Confederate capital was to be attempted from that direction. Already he had proceeded thither with his two divisions which had made the Valley campaign—his own and Ewell's—when ours, commanded by A. P. Hill, received orders to join them, and all three were thenceforth incorporated in the Second Corps of the Army of Northern Virginia, as long as he commanded it.

We had fought the sharp engagement of Cedar Mountain on the 9th of August, 1862, and checked Pope's advance to the Rapidan. Then, after some days of rest, we again took the initiative and, crossing the little river, went after him. But the general who had heretofore " seen only the backs of his enemies " did not see fit to await our coming, but made so prompt and rapid a retrograde movement that even our expeditious " foot cavalry " could not come up with him before he passed the Rappahannock. It was on this hurried pursuit, passing through Brandy Station, that a figure came riding along the toiling foot column toward the front. He was in no wise remarkable in appearance, and it was with surprise that the writer heard that he was no other than our commander, General " Stonewall " Jackson.

He wore a rather faded gray coat and cap to match—the latter of the " cadet " pattern then in vogue and tilted so far over his eyes that they were not visible, and his mount and general appearance were not distinctive of high rank. In fact, he seemed some courier carrying a message to some general officer on ahead. Despite his West Point training, he was never a showy horseman—in which respect he had a precedent in the great Napoleon. When we took Harper's Ferry, in September of that same year, one of the surrendered garrison remarked, when Jackson was pointed out to him, " Well, he's not much to look at, but if we'd only had *him,* we'd never have been in this fix."

But within the interval we were to see much of him, and our appreciation speedily penetrated below the surface indica-

B. D. Fry, Colonel of the 13th Alabama; Later led a Brigade
in Pickett's Charge.

F. T. Nichols, Wounded in the Flank
Attack on Howard's Corps,
May 2, 1863.

Harry T. Hays, Later Charged the
Batteries at Gettysburg.

Robert F. Hoke, Later Defender of Petersburg, Richmond and Wilmington.

William Smith, Colonel of the 49th
Virginia; Later at Gettysburg

CONFEDERATE

GENERALS

WITH

JACKSON

J. R. Jones Commanded a Brigade
of Virginians in Trimble's
Division.

F. L. Thomas Commanded a
Brigade in A. P. Hill's
Division.

AT THE

LAST—

CHANCEL–

LORSVILLE

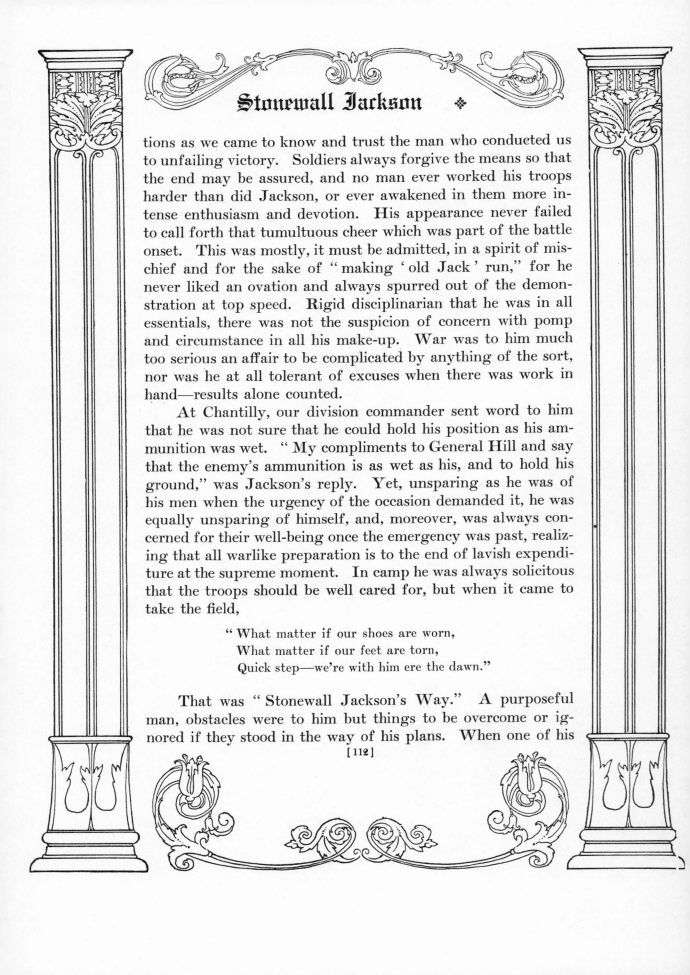

tions as we came to know and trust the man who conducted us to unfailing victory. Soldiers always forgive the means so that the end may be assured, and no man ever worked his troops harder than did Jackson, or ever awakened in them more intense enthusiasm and devotion. His appearance never failed to call forth that tumultuous cheer which was part of the battle onset. This was mostly, it must be admitted, in a spirit of mischief and for the sake of "making 'old Jack' run," for he never liked an ovation and always spurred out of the demonstration at top speed. Rigid disciplinarian that he was in all essentials, there was not the suspicion of concern with pomp and circumstance in all his make-up. War was to him much too serious an affair to be complicated by anything of the sort, nor was he at all tolerant of excuses when there was work in hand—results alone counted.

At Chantilly, our division commander sent word to him that he was not sure that he could hold his position as his ammunition was wet. "My compliments to General Hill and say that the enemy's ammunition is as wet as his, and to hold his ground," was Jackson's reply. Yet, unsparing as he was of his men when the urgency of the occasion demanded it, he was equally unsparing of himself, and, moreover, was always concerned for their well-being once the emergency was past, realizing that all warlike preparation is to the end of lavish expenditure at the supreme moment. In camp he was always solicitous that the troops should be well cared for, but when it came to take the field,

> "What matter if our shoes are worn,
>   What matter if our feet are torn,
>   Quick step—we're with him ere the dawn."

That was "Stonewall Jackson's Way." A purposeful man, obstacles were to him but things to be overcome or ignored if they stood in the way of his plans. When one of his

A. H. Colquitt, Later Conspicuous in the Defense of Petersburg.

R. L. Walker, Commander of a Light Artillery Brigade.

CONFEDERATE
GENERALS
WITH
JACKSON

IN HIS
MASTERLY
1863
CAMPAIGN

S. McGowan, Later Commanded the South Carolina Brigade which Immortalized His Name.

Alfred Iverson, Later at Gettysburg and with Hood at Atlanta.

E. A. O'Neal Charged with His Brigade in Rodes' First Line at Chancellorsville.

subordinates, after the three days' hard fighting of the Second Manassas, preceded by a march of almost a hundred miles within a little more than a like period of time, objected that his men could not march further until they should have received rations, he was promptly put under arrest by Jackson, bent as he was upon following up his advantage and overwhelming Pope's defeated army before it could reach the protection of its entrenched lines at Alexandria, some thirty miles distant.

A master of men, Jackson infused those of his command with much of his own indomitable spirit, as expressed in the lines quoted from the old song of the corps, until they came to take pride in their hardships and privations and to profess a Spartan-like contempt for the sybaritic softness, as they considered it, of the other corps of the army. As to their confidence in his ability to meet and to dominate any situation, it simply had no bounds. In the movement on Manassas and during the engagement, with hostile forces coming from almost every direction, and while as yet we had no tidings of Longstreet, we were remote from our base and the foe was in superior force between; we were footsore and fagged nearly to the limit of human endurance, but there was no faltering in the belief that Jackson saw his way out of the toils which seemed to compass him about, as he had aforetime in the Valley campaign. Those thin lines never held their ground more tenaciously nor charged with more *élan* than during those eventful August days.

The last time my eyes were to behold him—how well it comes to mind!—was upon the morning of the fateful May 2, 1863, before the close of which day was to be ended his career as a soldier. We were moving out by the flank on a little woodland road, where we had been in bivouac the night before; it was a gloomy, overcast morning, as if giving premonition of the calamity to come to us before the next rising of the sun. Before we reached the plank road, in a small opening among

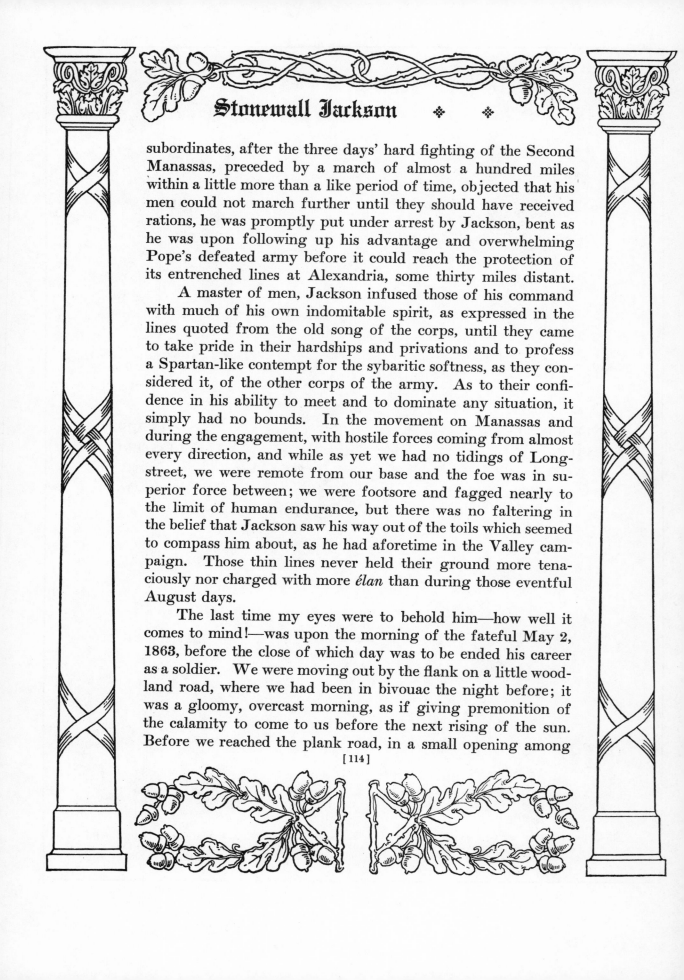

CONFEDERATE GENERALS OF LONGSTREET'S CORPS

WHO COÖPERATED WITH JACKSON IN '62 AND '63

Lafayette McLaws With His Division Supported Jackson's
Attacks at Harper's Ferry and Chancellorsville;
Later Conspicuous at Gettysburg and
Chickamauga.

Joseph Brevard Kershaw Captured Maryland Heights, Opposite Jackson's Position at Harper's Ferry.

James L. Kemper Commanded a Brigade on Jackson's Right at the Second Battle of Manassas.

Ambrose R. Wright With His Brigade Closed the Pass Along the Canal at Harper's Ferry.

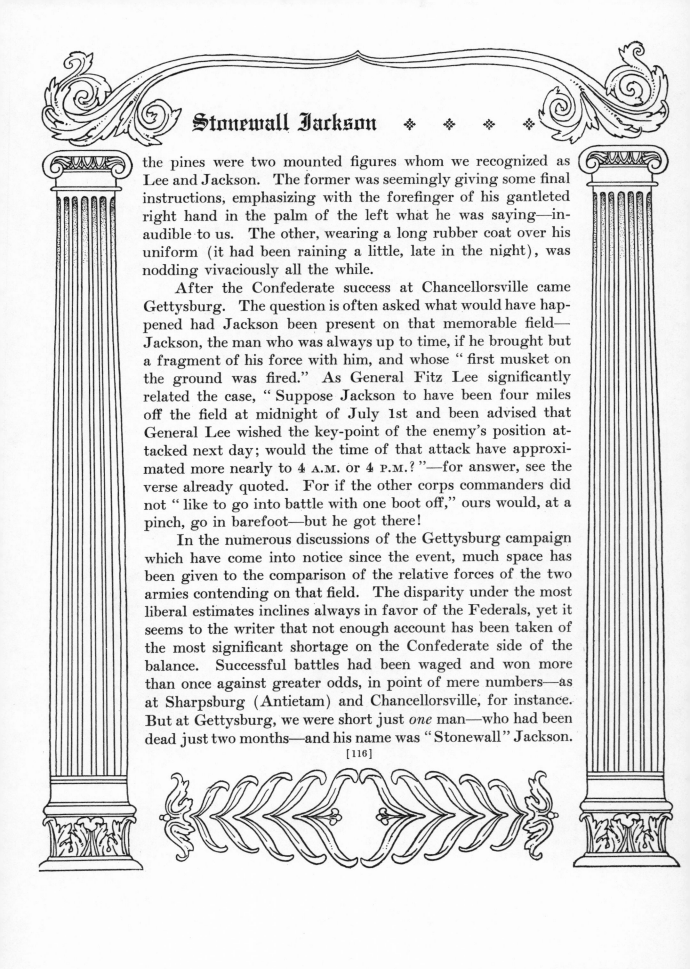

the pines were two mounted figures whom we recognized as Lee and Jackson. The former was seemingly giving some final instructions, emphasizing with the forefinger of his gantleted right hand in the palm of the left what he was saying—inaudible to us. The other, wearing a long rubber coat over his uniform (it had been raining a little, late in the night), was nodding vivaciously all the while.

After the Confederate success at Chancellorsville came Gettysburg. The question is often asked what would have happened had Jackson been present on that memorable field—Jackson, the man who was always up to time, if he brought but a fragment of his force with him, and whose " first musket on the ground was fired." As General Fitz Lee significantly related the case, " Suppose Jackson to have been four miles off the field at midnight of July 1st and been advised that General Lee wished the key-point of the enemy's position attacked next day; would the time of that attack have approximated more nearly to 4 A.M. or 4 P.M.? "—for answer, see the verse already quoted. For if the other corps commanders did not " like to go into battle with one boot off," ours would, at a pinch, go in barefoot—but he got there!

In the numerous discussions of the Gettysburg campaign which have come into notice since the event, much space has been given to the comparison of the relative forces of the two armies contending on that field. The disparity under the most liberal estimates inclines always in favor of the Federals, yet it seems to the writer that not enough account has been taken of the most significant shortage on the Confederate side of the balance. Successful battles had been waged and won more than once against greater odds, in point of mere numbers—as at Sharpsburg (Antietam) and Chancellorsville, for instance. But at Gettysburg, we were short just *one* man—who had been dead just two months—and his name was "Stonewall" Jackson.

V

THE MEANING OF
LOSSES
IN WARFARE

MEN OF THE FAMOUS ' VERMONT BRIGADE,'' ALL FROM THE ONE
STATE, WHICH SUFFERED MORE HEAVILY THAN ANY OTHER FEDERAL
BRIGADE DURING THE WAR—WITHIN A WEEK AT THE WILDERNESS
AND SPOTSYLVANIA, IT LOST 1,645 OUT OF 2,100 EFFECTIVE MEN

THE REGIMENT THAT SUSTAINED THE GREATEST LOSS OF ANY IN THE UNION ARMY

In the assault on Petersburg, June 18, 1864, these boys from Maine, serving as infantry, sustained the greatest loss of any one regiment in any one action of the war. Before the site where Fort Stedman was subsequently built 635 men were killed and wounded out of nine hundred engaged, a loss of over seventy per cent. in seven minutes. Such slaughter has never been paralleled in any warfare, ancient or modern. Of all the regiments in the Union armies this regiment lost most during the four years. Twenty-three officers and 400 enlisted men were killed and mortally wounded, and two hundred and sixty died of disease. The First Maine Heavy Artillery was organized at Bangor, and mustered in August 21, 1862. It left the State for Washington on August 24th. This section of the tremendous regimental quota—eighteen hundred men—is drilling at Fort Sumner in the winter of 1863. The men little imagine, as they go skilfully through their evo-

THE FIRST MAINE HEAVY ARTILLERY DRILLING IN FORT SUMNER,
ON A WINTER'S DAY OF '63

lutions in the snow, that the hand of death is to fall so ruthlessly on their ranks.   From the defenses of Washington they went to Belle Plain, Virginia, on May 15, 1864, as a part of Tyler's Heavy Artillery Division. Four days later, at Harris's Farm on the Fredericksburg Road, the first of their great disasters fell upon them. In this engagement their killed numbered eighty-two, their wounded 394, and their missing five.   Less than a month later came the awful slaughter at Petersburg.   The remnant of the regiment served until its fall, April 2, 1865.   After taking part in the Grand Review at Washington and remaining in its defenses till September 11th, the organization was mustered out, and ordered to Bangor, Maine.   On September 20, 1865, the survivors of this "fighting regiment" were mustered out.   The Second Wisconsin Infantry lost a greater percentage in killed during its whole term—19.7 per cent. as against 19.2 per cent. in the First Maine.

LOSSES IN THE BATTLES OF THE CIVIL WAR, AND WHAT THEY MEAN

By Hilary A. Herbert

*Late Colonel, Eighth Alabama Infantry, Confederate States Army,
and late Secretary of the Navy of the United States*

STATISTICS of losses in battles do not furnish an unfailing test of courage. Mistakes of officers, unavoidable surprises—these, now and then, occasion losses that soldiers did not knowingly face, and there are sometimes other reasons why the carnage in a particular command in this battle or that does not with accuracy indicate steadfast bravery. Such statistics, however, as all military experts agree, do tell a graphic story, when exceptional instances are not selected.

Colonel Dodge, in his "Bird's-Eye View of Our Civil War," exhibits statistics showing the percentage of losses in the most notable battles fought since 1745, and from them deduces this conclusion, "It thus appears that in ability to stand heavy pounding, since Napoleon's Waterloo campaign, the American has shown himself preeminent."

Colonel Dodge would have been justified in going much further. Waterloo itself, the most famous of the world's battles, does not show such fighting as Americans did at Sharpsburg (Antietam), Gettysburg, or Chickamauga.

In "Stonewall Jackson and the American Civil War," by Lieutenant-Colonel G. F. R. Henderson, a British military expert, is a complete list of killed and wounded in great battles from 1704 to 1882, inclusive. Since Eylau, 1807, there has been no great battle in which the losses of the victor—the punishment he withstood to gain his victory—equal the twenty-seven per cent. of the Confederates in their victory at Chickamauga.

The Henderson tables give the losses of both sides in each

MEN OF THE FIFTH GEORGIA

MORE THAN HALF THIS REGIMENT WAS KILLED AND WOUNDED AT THE BATTLE OF CHICKAMAUGA

Lounging beneath the Stars and Bars are eight members of an Augusta, Georgia, company—The "Clinch Rifles." Their new paraphernalia is beautifully marked "C. R." They have a negro servant. In a word, they are inexperienced Confederate volunteers of May, 1861, on the day before their company became a part of the Fifth Georgia Regiment. Pass to November, 1863; imagine six of the soldiers in the group lying dead or groaning with wounds, and but three unhurt,—and you have figured the state of the regiment after it was torn to shreds at the battle of Chickamauga. It was mustered in for twelve months at Macon, Georgia, May 11, 1861, being the last regiment taken for this short term. The Sixth Georgia and those following were mustered in for three years or the war. The Clinch Rifles were sent to garrison Pensacola, Florida, where General Braxton Bragg would occasionally come from his headquarters, eight miles away, to drill them. The ten companies were all from towns, or cities, and nicely uniformed, though each in a different style. This led Bragg to name them his "Pound Cake Regiment." In July and August, 1862, the Fifth marched from Chattanooga, Tennessee, to Bardstown, Kentucky, thence to the eastern part of the State, and down through Cumberland Gap to Knoxville, 800 miles in all. It lost heavily in the battle of Murfreesboro. At bloody Chickamauga, September 19 and 20, 1863, its killed and wounded were more than 54 per cent. of the regiment—surpassed by few organizations in history. It suffered again at Missionary Ridge, and in the spring of 1864, when it stood against Sherman through the Atlanta campaign. The regiment fought on through the campaigns from Savannah, Georgia, up to North Carolina, and in the last combat at Bentonville, North Carolina. It surrendered at Greensboro, April, 26, 1865.

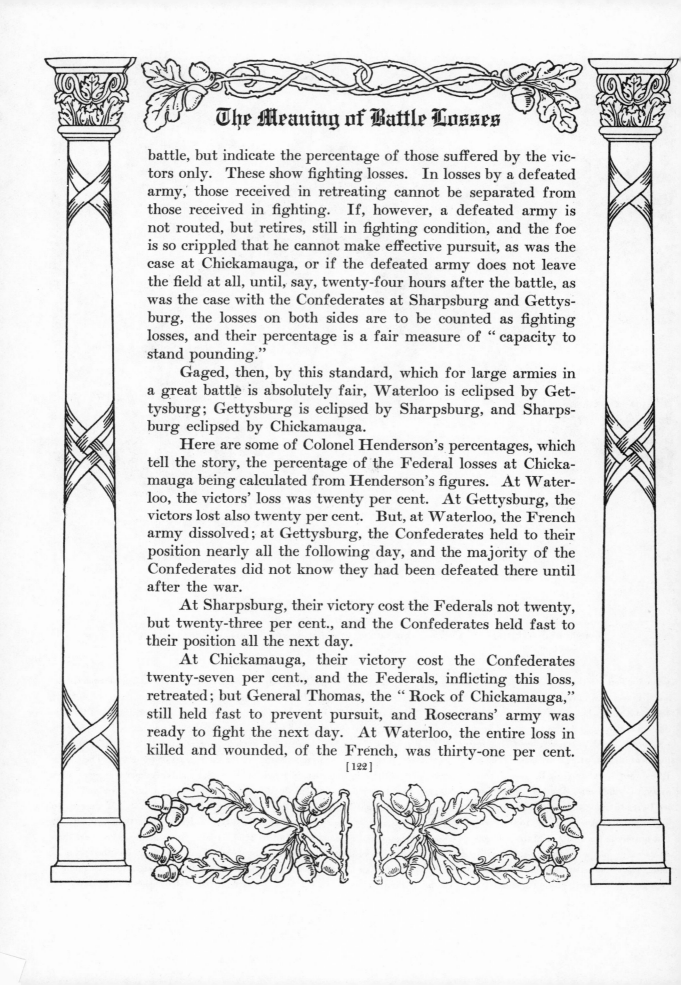

battle, but indicate the percentage of those suffered by the victors only. These show fighting losses. In losses by a defeated army, those received in retreating cannot be separated from those received in fighting. If, however, a defeated army is not routed, but retires, still in fighting condition, and the foe is so crippled that he cannot make effective pursuit, as was the case at Chickamauga, or if the defeated army does not leave the field at all, until, say, twenty-four hours after the battle, as was the case with the Confederates at Sharpsburg and Gettysburg, the losses on both sides are to be counted as fighting losses, and their percentage is a fair measure of "capacity to stand pounding."

Gaged, then, by this standard, which for large armies in a great battle is absolutely fair, Waterloo is eclipsed by Gettysburg; Gettysburg is eclipsed by Sharpsburg, and Sharpsburg eclipsed by Chickamauga.

Here are some of Colonel Henderson's percentages, which tell the story, the percentage of the Federal losses at Chickamauga being calculated from Henderson's figures. At Waterloo, the victors' loss was twenty per cent. At Gettysburg, the victors lost also twenty per cent. But, at Waterloo, the French army dissolved; at Gettysburg, the Confederates held to their position nearly all the following day, and the majority of the Confederates did not know they had been defeated there until after the war.

At Sharpsburg, their victory cost the Federals not twenty, but twenty-three per cent., and the Confederates held fast to their position all the next day.

At Chickamauga, their victory cost the Confederates twenty-seven per cent., and the Federals, inflicting this loss, retreated; but General Thomas, the "Rock of Chickamauga," still held fast to prevent pursuit, and Rosecrans' army was ready to fight the next day. At Waterloo, the entire loss in killed and wounded, of the French, was thirty-one per cent.

OFFICERS OF A WESTERN FIGHTING REGIMENT—THE 36TH ILLINOIS

Of the Illinois regiments the Thirty-sixth fought in every important battle of the entire war in Western territory, and suffered in killed alone a loss of no less than 14.8 per cent., a figure exceeded among Illinois organizations only by the 14.9 per cent. of the Ninety-third. No Federal regiment lost as much as 20 per cent. killed and only 200 out of the 3,559 organizations as much as ten per cent. The Thirty-sixth Illinois lost 204 men out of a total enrollment of 1,376. These figures refer to deaths alone, excluding wounded and missing. At the battle of Stone's River, Tennessee, the regiment lost forty-six killed, 151 wounded, and fifteen missing, a total of 212. This was its heaviest blow in any one battle. It fought at Pea Ridge, an early engagement in the West, at Chaplin Hills, at the bloody battle of Chickamauga, and on the corpse-strewn slopes of Missionary Ridge. It fought under Sherman from Resaca to Atlanta, and when that general marched away on his expedition to the coast, the Thirty-sixth turned back to suffer its fourth largest loss in killed at the battle of Franklin, and to help Thomas crush Hood at the battle of Nashville. Such were the Western fighting regiments.

A REGIMENT
THAT LOST
14.8% IN
KILLED ALONE

ILLINOIS
INFANTRY
IN THE
WEST

OFFICERS OF THE 36TH ILLINOIS

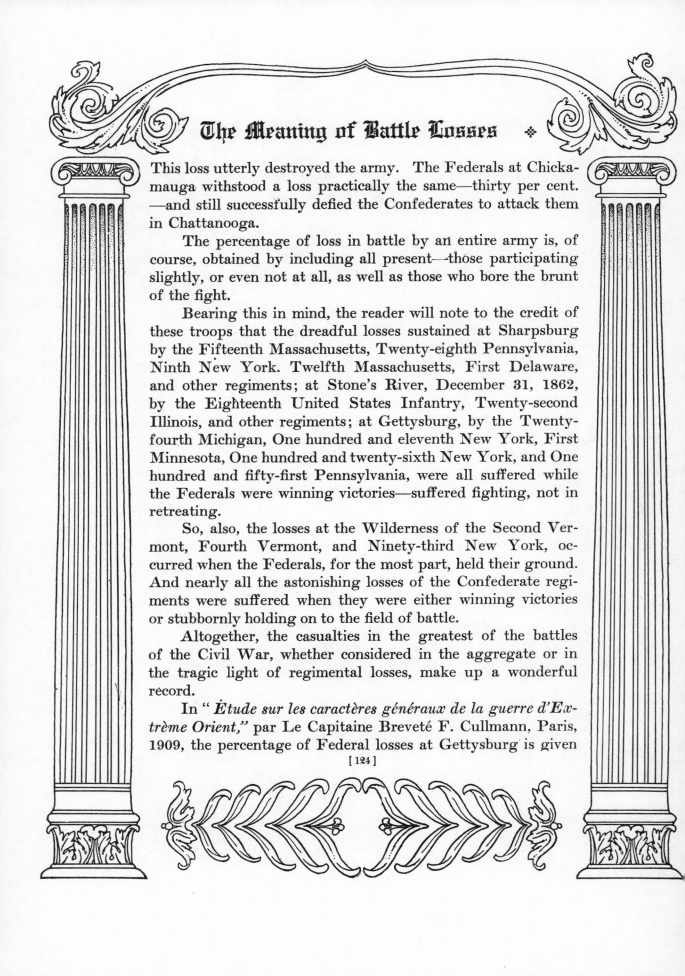

The Meaning of Battle Losses ❖

This loss utterly destroyed the army. The Federals at Chicka-mauga withstood a loss practically the same—thirty per cent.—and still successfully defied the Confederates to attack them in Chattanooga.

The percentage of loss in battle by an entire army is, of course, obtained by including all present—those participating slightly, or even not at all, as well as those who bore the brunt of the fight.

Bearing this in mind, the reader will note to the credit of these troops that the dreadful losses sustained at Sharpsburg by the Fifteenth Massachusetts, Twenty-eighth Pennsylvania, Ninth New York. Twelfth Massachusetts, First Delaware, and other regiments; at Stone's River, December 31, 1862, by the Eighteenth United States Infantry, Twenty-second Illinois, and other regiments; at Gettysburg, by the Twenty-fourth Michigan, One hundred and eleventh New York, First Minnesota, One hundred and twenty-sixth New York, and One hundred and fifty-first Pennsylvania, were all suffered while the Federals were winning victories—suffered fighting, not in retreating.

So, also, the losses at the Wilderness of the Second Vermont, Fourth Vermont, and Ninety-third New York, occurred when the Federals, for the most part, held their ground. And nearly all the astonishing losses of the Confederate regiments were suffered when they were either winning victories or stubbornly holding on to the field of battle.

Altogether, the casualties in the greatest of the battles of the Civil War, whether considered in the aggregate or in the tragic light of regimental losses, make up a wonderful record.

In "*Étude sur les caractères généraux de la guerre d'Extrème Orient,*" par Le Capitaine Breveté F. Cullmann, Paris, 1909, the percentage of Federal losses at Gettysburg is given

COMMANDERS OF UNION BRIGADES CONSPICUOUS FOR LOSSES

These brigades from the Armies of the Potomac, the Cumberland, and the Tennessee, are mentioned specifically by Colonel William F. Fox, on account of their notable losses in action.

Iron Brigade
SOLOMON MEREDITH
Originally Colonel of the 19th
Indiana.

Michigan Cavalry Brigade
PETER STAGG
Originally Colonel of the 1st
Michigan Cavalry.

Harker's Brigade
LUTHER P. BRADLEY
Originally Colonel of the
51st Illinois.

Vermont Brigade
LEWIS A. GRANT
Originally Colonel of the 5th
Vermont.

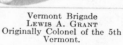

First New Jersey Brigade
WILLIAM H. PENROSE
Originally Colonel of the
15th New Jersey.

Iowa Brigade
WILLIAM W. BELKNAP
Originally Colonel of the
15th Iowa.

Willich's Brigade
AUGUST WILLICH
Originally Colonel of the 32d
Indiana.

Opdycke's Brigade
EMERSON OPDYCKE
Originally Colonel of the
125th Ohio.

Excelsior Brigade
JOSEPH B. CARR
Originally Colonel of the 2d
New York.

Philadelphia Brigade
DE WITT CLINTON BAXTER
Originally Colonel of the 72d
Pennsylvania.

Irish Brigade
THOMAS FRANCIS MEAGHER
Commanded the Brigade
in 1862.

Steedman's Brigade
JAMES B. STEEDMAN
Originally Colonel of the
14th Ohio.

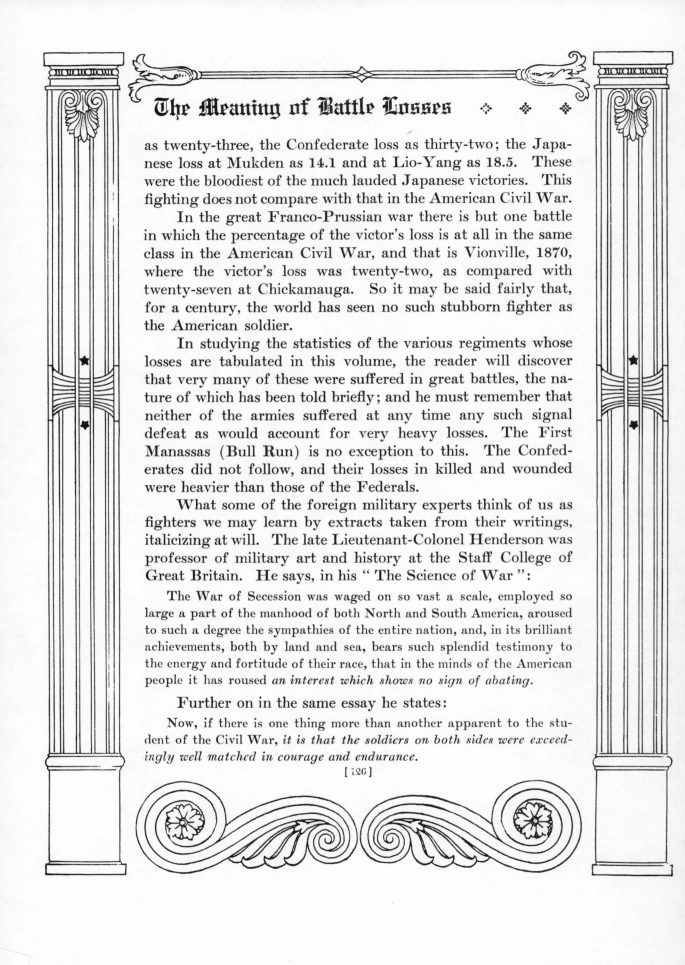

as twenty-three, the Confederate loss as thirty-two; the Japanese loss at Mukden as 14.1 and at Lio-Yang as 18.5. These were the bloodiest of the much lauded Japanese victories. This fighting does not compare with that in the American Civil War.

In the great Franco-Prussian war there is but one battle in which the percentage of the victor's loss is at all in the same class in the American Civil War, and that is Vionville, 1870, where the victor's loss was twenty-two, as compared with twenty-seven at Chickamauga. So it may be said fairly that, for a century, the world has seen no such stubborn fighter as the American soldier.

In studying the statistics of the various regiments whose losses are tabulated in this volume, the reader will discover that very many of these were suffered in great battles, the nature of which has been told briefly; and he must remember that neither of the armies suffered at any time any such signal defeat as would account for very heavy losses. The First Manassas (Bull Run) is no exception to this. The Confederates did not follow, and their losses in killed and wounded were heavier than those of the Federals.

What some of the foreign military experts think of us as fighters we may learn by extracts taken from their writings, italicizing at will. The late Lieutenant-Colonel Henderson was professor of military art and history at the Staff College of Great Britain. He says, in his " The Science of War ":

The War of Secession was waged on so vast a scale, employed so large a part of the manhood of both North and South America, aroused to such a degree the sympathies of the entire nation, and, in its brilliant achievements, both by land and sea, bears such splendid testimony to the energy and fortitude of their race, that in the minds of the American people it has roused *an interest which shows no sign of abating.*

Further on in the same essay he states:

Now, if there is one thing more than another apparent to the student of the Civil War, *it is that the soldiers on both sides were exceedingly well matched in courage and endurance.*

WILLIAM T. WOFFORD
Led his Brigade in the Maryland, Gettysburg, Wilderness and Shenandoah Campaigns.

DANIEL S. DONELSON
Led his Brigade in the Tennessee Campaign, notably at Murfreesboro.

ROBERT H. ANDERSON
Colonel of the 5th Georgia Cavalry; Promoted Brigadier-General July 26, 1864.

JAMES H. LANE
Led his Brigade at Fredericksburg, Gettysburg and in the Wilderness Campaign.

WILLIAM B. BATE
Led his Brigade in Bragg's Tennessee Campaigns, notably at Chickamauga.

ROGER ATKINSON PRYOR
Fought his Brigade on the Peninsula, where it bore a conspicuous part at Seven Pines.

CADMUS M. WILCOX
Led his Brigade at Manassas, Fredericksburg, Chancellorsville and Gettysburg.

WINFIELD SCOTT FEATHERSON
Originally Colonel of the 17th Mississippi; Promoted for Gallantry at Ball's Bluff; Led his Brigade on the Peninsula.

HENRY L. BENNING
Led his Brigade in the Principal Battles of Longstreet's Corps, including Gettysburg, Chickamauga and the Wilderness.

EDWARD AYLESWORTH PERRY
Commanded a Regiment on the Peninsula; was wounded at Frayser's Farm; Led his Brigade at Gettysburg and the Wilderness.

COMMANDERS OF
CONFEDERATE BRIGADES WHICH SUFFERED HEAVILY IN BATTLE

The Meaning of Battle Losses

The forces here credited with these "brilliant achievements" in 1861–65 are now thoroughly united, and would stand shoulder to shoulder against a foreign foe. Our population has increased threefold, while our military resources, our capacity to equip and to convey food to armies, to manufacture arms, and to build ships, even in the interior if need be, has increased tenfold. Our rivers still traverse the land, but the art of mining waters, practised with some success by the Confederates, has developed until no foe would think of exploiting these rivers with vessels in advance of troops.

Aye, but the spirit of our people, say the alarmists—we have lost patriotism, become commercialized, money-mad, and have now no militant instinct. To an old Confederate this prattle about our people being "commercialized" is especially amusing. It carries him back to 1860–61. In the hot sectional animosities that brought on the war he had imbibed that same idea about the North—the "Yankee" now worshiped "the Almighty Dollar,". and in his all-absorbing struggle for it had lost the spirit that animated his forefathers at Lexington, Bunker Hill, and Saratoga. When the news of Manassas came, many an ambitious Confederate who was so unfortunate as not to have been there, felt like going into mourning. He was never to have a chance to "flesh his maiden sword." But the young Confederate was miscalculating. The exasperated North roused itself, after Manassas, like an angry lion pricked by the spear of the hunter, and soon we were to hear its roar.

In reference to inexperienced volunteers, it must be said, as every veteran of the Civil War knows, that it was not always the oldest regiments that were the bravest. In the gallant, though finally unsuccessful, assault that was made by the Federals at Salem Church, May 3, 1863, just where the Confederate line was broken for a time, the official reports show that the One hundred and twenty-first New York was in the fore-

MAJ.-GEN. JAMES B. McPHERSON
Atlanta, July 22, 1864.

MAJ.-GEN. JOS. K. MANSFIELD
Antietam, September 18, 1864.

MAJ.-GEN. JOHN SEDGWICK
Spotsylvania, May 9, 1864.

MAJ.-GEN. JOHN F. REYNOLDS
Gettysburg, July 1, 1863.

FEDERAL GENERALS KILLED IN BATTLE—GROUP No. 1—ARMY AND CORPS COMMANDERS

On this and the following six pages are portraits of the fifty-one Union generals killed in battle. Beneath each portrait is the date and place of death, or mortal wounding. Since no such pictorial necrology existed to aid the editors of this History, many questions arose—such as the determination of the actual rank of an officer at a given date, or the precise circumstances of death in certain instances. The list of Colonel W. F. Fox, presented in his work on "Regimental Losses in the Civil War," has been followed.

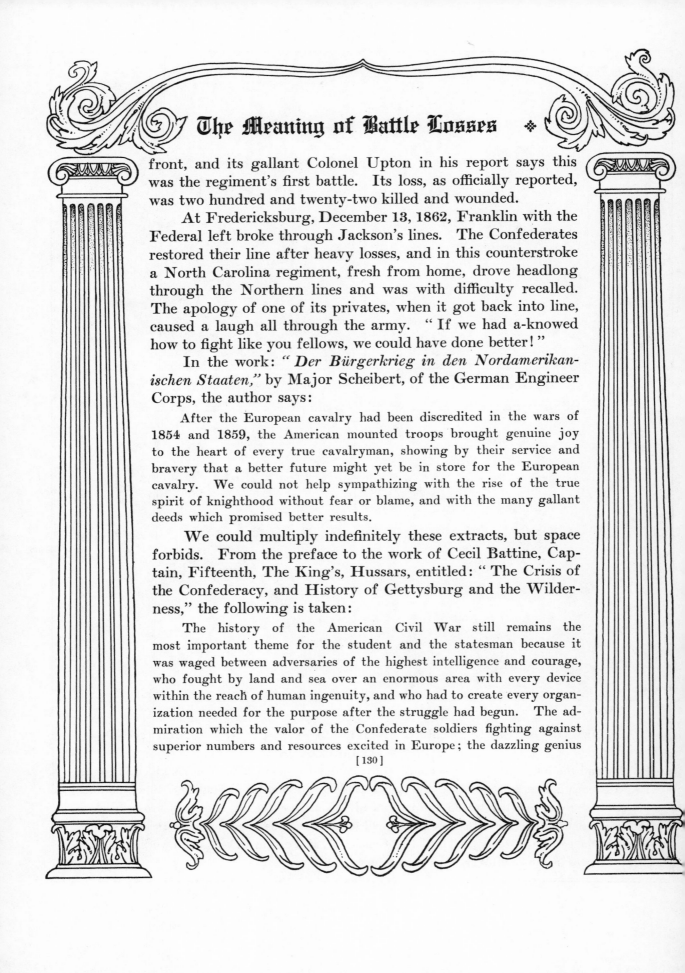

front, and its gallant Colonel Upton in his report says this was the regiment's first battle. Its loss, as officially reported, was two hundred and twenty-two killed and wounded.

At Fredericksburg, December 13, 1862, Franklin with the Federal left broke through Jackson's lines. The Confederates restored their line after heavy losses, and in this counterstroke a North Carolina regiment, fresh from home, drove headlong through the Northern lines and was with difficulty recalled. The apology of one of its privates, when it got back into line, caused a laugh all through the army. " If we had a-knowed how to fight like you fellows, we could have done better! "

In the work: *" Der Bürgerkrieg in den Nordamerikanischen Staaten,"* by Major Scheibert, of the German Engineer Corps, the author says:

After the European cavalry had been discredited in the wars of 1854 and 1859, the American mounted troops brought genuine joy to the heart of every true cavalryman, showing by their service and bravery that a better future might yet be in store for the European cavalry. We could not help sympathizing with the rise of the true spirit of knighthood without fear or blame, and with the many gallant deeds which promised better results.

We could multiply indefinitely these extracts, but space forbids. From the preface to the work of Cecil Battine, Captain, Fifteenth, The King's, Hussars, entitled: " The Crisis of the Confederacy, and History of Gettysburg and the Wilderness," the following is taken:

The history of the American Civil War still remains the most important theme for the student and the statesman because it was waged between adversaries of the highest intelligence and courage, who fought by land and sea over an enormous area with every device within the reach of human ingenuity, and who had to create every organization needed for the purpose after the struggle had begun. The admiration which the valor of the Confederate soldiers fighting against superior numbers and resources excited in Europe; the dazzling genius

PHILIP KEARNY
Chantilly
September 1, 1862.

ISRAEL B. RICHARDSON
Antietam
November 3, 1862.

FEDERAL GENERALS KILLED IN BATTLE

GROUP No. 2

ISAAC I. STEVENS
Chantilly
September 1, 1862.

MAJOR–GENERALS COMMANDING DIVISIONS AND CORPS

AMIEL W. WHIPPLE
Chancellorsville
May, 7, 1863.

HIRAM G. BERRY
Chancellorsville
May 3, 1863.

JESSE L. RENO
South Mountain
September 14, 1862.

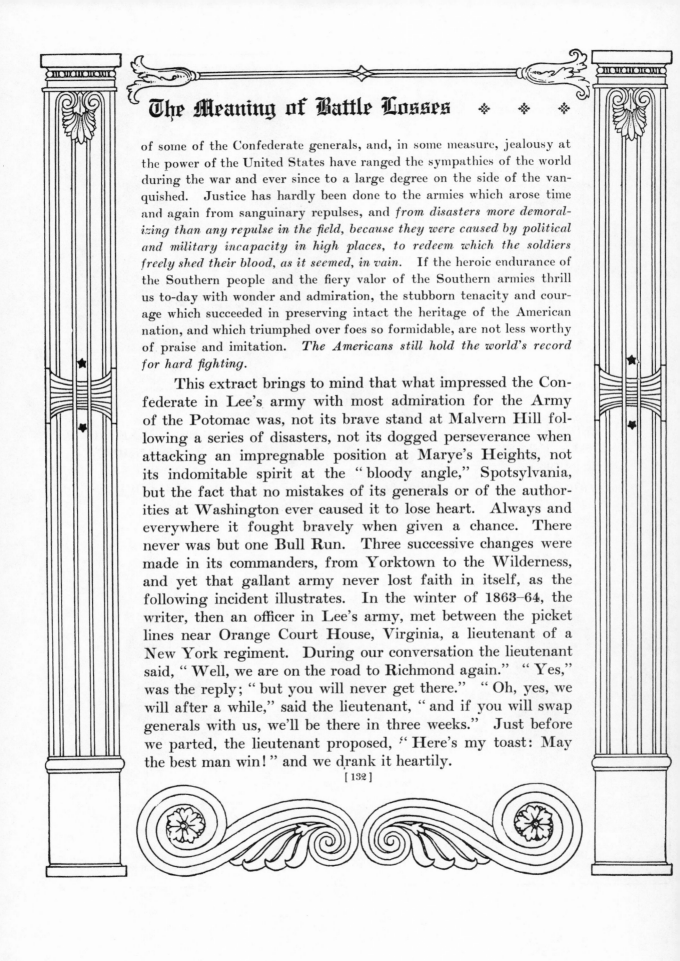

of some of the Confederate generals, and, in some measure, jealousy at the power of the United States have ranged the sympathies of the world during the war and ever since to a large degree on the side of the vanquished. Justice has hardly been done to the armies which arose time and again from sanguinary repulses, and *from disasters more demoralizing than any repulse in the field, because they were caused by political and military incapacity in high places, to redeem which the soldiers freely shed their blood, as it seemed, in vain.* If the heroic endurance of the Southern people and the fiery valor of the Southern armies thrill us to-day with wonder and admiration, the stubborn tenacity and courage which succeeded in preserving intact the heritage of the American nation, and which triumphed over foes so formidable, are not less worthy of praise and imitation. *The Americans still hold the world's record for hard fighting.*

This extract brings to mind that what impressed the Confederate in Lee's army with most admiration for the Army of the Potomac was, not its brave stand at Malvern Hill following a series of disasters, not its dogged perseverance when attacking an impregnable position at Marye's Heights, not its indomitable spirit at the "bloody angle," Spotsylvania, but the fact that no mistakes of its generals or of the authorities at Washington ever caused it to lose heart. Always and everywhere it fought bravely when given a chance. There never was but one Bull Run. Three successive changes were made in its commanders, from Yorktown to the Wilderness, and yet that gallant army never lost faith in itself, as the following incident illustrates. In the winter of 1863–64, the writer, then an officer in Lee's army, met between the picket lines near Orange Court House, Virginia, a lieutenant of a New York regiment. During our conversation the lieutenant said, "Well, we are on the road to Richmond again." "Yes," was the reply; "but you will never get there." "Oh, yes, we will after a while," said the lieutenant, "and if you will swap generals with us, we'll be there in three weeks." Just before we parted, the lieutenant proposed, "Here's my toast: May the best man win!" and we drank it heartily.

BRIG.-GEN.
THOMAS WILLIAMS
Baton Rouge, August 5, 1862.

BRIG.-GEN. ISAAC P. RODMAN
Antietam, September 30, 1862.

BRIG.-GEN.
WILLIAM H. L. WALLACE
Shiloh, April 10, 1862.

FEDERAL GENERALS KILLED IN BATTLE, GROUP No. 3

BRIG.-GEN.
JAMES E. JACKSON
Chaplin Hills, October 8, 1862.

BREVET MAJ.-GEN. JAMES S. WADSWORTH
Wilderness, May 8, 1864.

BREVET MAJ.-GEN.
DAVID A. RUSSELL
Opequon, September 19, 1864.

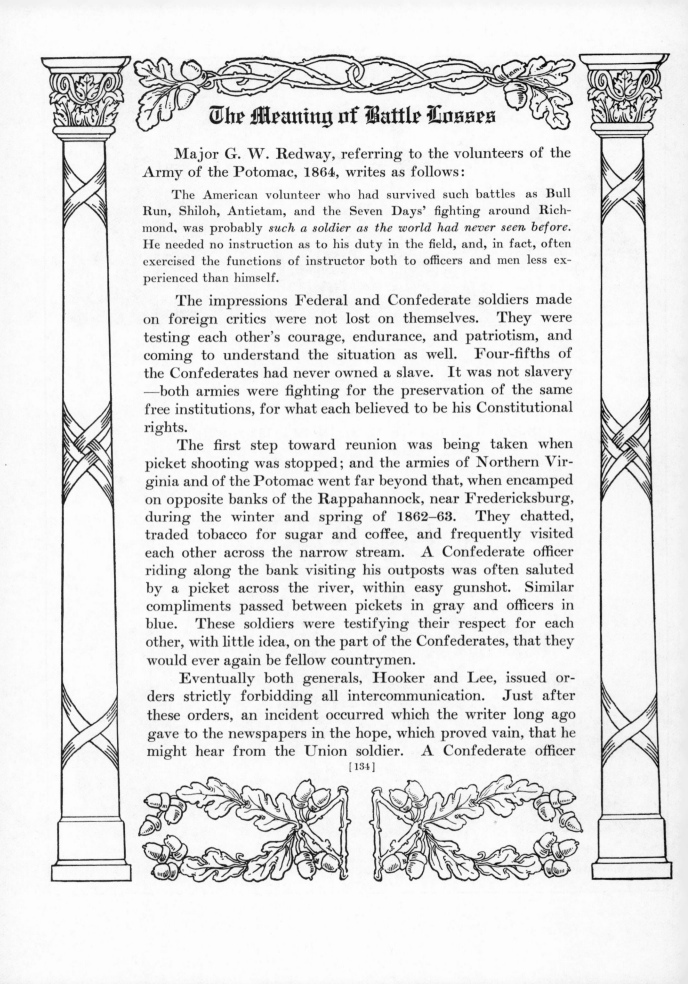

The Meaning of Battle Losses

Major G. W. Redway, referring to the volunteers of the Army of the Potomac, 1864, writes as follows:

The American volunteer who had survived such battles as Bull Run, Shiloh, Antietam, and the Seven Days' fighting around Richmond, was probably *such a soldier as the world had never seen before.* He needed no instruction as to his duty in the field, and, in fact, often exercised the functions of instructor both to officers and men less experienced than himself.

The impressions Federal and Confederate soldiers made on foreign critics were not lost on themselves. They were testing each other's courage, endurance, and patriotism, and coming to understand the situation as well. Four-fifths of the Confederates had never owned a slave. It was not slavery —both armies were fighting for the preservation of the same free institutions, for what each believed to be his Constitutional rights.

The first step toward reunion was being taken when picket shooting was stopped; and the armies of Northern Virginia and of the Potomac went far beyond that, when encamped on opposite banks of the Rappahannock, near Fredericksburg, during the winter and spring of 1862–63. They chatted, traded tobacco for sugar and coffee, and frequently visited each other across the narrow stream. A Confederate officer riding along the bank visiting his outposts was often saluted by a picket across the river, within easy gunshot. Similar compliments passed between pickets in gray and officers in blue. These soldiers were testifying their respect for each other, with little idea, on the part of the Confederates, that they would ever again be fellow countrymen.

Eventually both generals, Hooker and Lee, issued orders strictly forbidding all intercommunication. Just after these orders, an incident occurred which the writer long ago gave to the newspapers in the hope, which proved vain, that he might hear from the Union soldier. A Confederate officer

BREVET BRIG.-GEN.
JAMES A. MULLIGAN
Winchester, July 26, 1864.

BRIG.-GEN.
THOS. G. STEVENSON
Spotsylvania, May 10, 1864.

BREVET MAJ.-GEN.
THOMAS A. SMYTH
Farmville, April 9, 1865

BRIG.-GEN.
ROBT. L. McCOOK
Decherd, Tenn., August 6, 1862.

FEDERAL

GENERALS

KILLED

IN BATTLE

GROUP No. 4

BRIG.-GEN.
NATHANIEL LYON
Wilson's Creek, August 10, 1861.

BRIG.-GEN.
HENRY BOHLEN
Freeman's Ford, August 22, 1865.

MAJ.-GEN.
GEO. C. STRONG
Fort Wagner, July 30, 1863.

BREVET MAJ.-GEN.
S. K. ZOOK
Gettysburg, July 3, 1863.

BREVET MAJ.-GEN.
FREDERICK WINTHROP
Five Forks, April 1, 1865.

BREVET MAJ.-GEN.
ALEXANDER HAYS
Wilderness, May 5, 1864.

rode suddenly out of the woods on to his picket-post at Scott's dam, just above Banks' Ford. A Federal soldier was nearing the south bank of the river, newspaper in hand. The soldier reluctantly came ashore, insisting that he should be allowed to return; the Confederate pickets had promised it. "Yes," was the reply, "but they violated orders, and you violated orders on your side when you came over, and I happen to know it. Orders must be obeyed. You are my prisoner." The soldier, who was a big, manly fellow, stood straight as an arrow, looked the officer in the face, and with tears in his eyes, said: "Colonel, shoot me, if you want to, but for God's sake don't take me prisoner. I have been in the army only six weeks. I have never been in battle, and if I am taken prisoner under these circumstances, I will never get over it—it will always be believed that I deserted."

The officer hesitated for a moment, and then said, "Give me that paper and go, and tell your people you are the last man that will ever come over here and get back." Such an incident at the outset of the war would have been inconceivable.

It was in this spirit of kindly regard for each other that the war between the two armies went on, from Fredericksburg to Appomattox. It manifested itself with increasing tenderness after every bloody battle. It inspired Grant when he said to Lee, "Your men will need their horses to make a crop." It animated Grant's soldiers when they gave no cheer at the surrender, and when they divided their rations with the men who, in tears, laid down their arms. It did not die when the Confederates accepted the results of the war.

Time has only hallowed the memory of the glorious manhood displayed in those days by the men of both armies. The soldiers, had their sentiments prevailed, would soon have bound up the wounds of war, as they did those received in battle. But politicians, for a time, interfered.

ELON J. FARNSWORTH
Gettysburg
July 3, 1863.

STEPHEN H. WEED
Gettysburg
July 2, 1863.

EDW. P. CHAPIN
Port Hudson
May 27, 1863.

VINCENT STRONG
Gettysburg
July 7, 1863.

CONRAD F. JACKSON
Fredericksburg
December 13, 1862.

PLEASANT A. HACKLEMAN
Corinth
October 3, 1862.

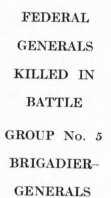

FEDERAL

GENERALS

KILLED IN

BATTLE

GROUP No. 5

BRIGADIER–

GENERALS

JOSHUA W. SILL
Stone's River
December 31, 1862.

GEO. D. BAYARD
Fredericksburg
December 14, 1862.

WM. R. TERRILL
Perryville
October 8, 1862.

GEO. W. TAYLOR
Manassas (Second Bull Run)
August 31, 1862.

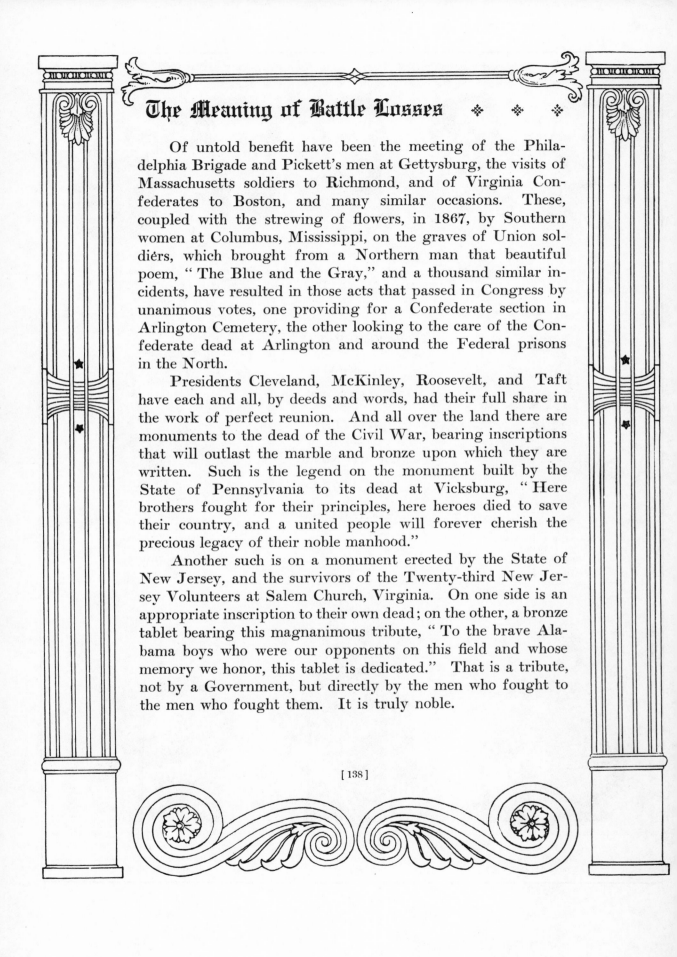

The Meaning of Battle Losses ❖ ❖ ❖

Of untold benefit have been the meeting of the Philadelphia Brigade and Pickett's men at Gettysburg, the visits of Massachusetts soldiers to Richmond, and of Virginia Confederates to Boston, and many similar occasions. These, coupled with the strewing of flowers, in 1867, by Southern women at Columbus, Mississippi, on the graves of Union soldiers, which brought from a Northern man that beautiful poem, " The Blue and the Gray," and a thousand similar incidents, have resulted in those acts that passed in Congress by unanimous votes, one providing for a Confederate section in Arlington Cemetery, the other looking to the care of the Confederate dead at Arlington and around the Federal prisons in the North.

Presidents Cleveland, McKinley, Roosevelt, and Taft have each and all, by deeds and words, had their full share in the work of perfect reunion. And all over the land there are monuments to the dead of the Civil War, bearing inscriptions that will outlast the marble and bronze upon which they are written. Such is the legend on the monument built by the State of Pennsylvania to its dead at Vicksburg, " Here brothers fought for their principles, here heroes died to save their country, and a united people will forever cherish the precious legacy of their noble manhood."

Another such is on a monument erected by the State of New Jersey, and the survivors of the Twenty-third New Jersey Volunteers at Salem Church, Virginia. On one side is an appropriate inscription to their own dead; on the other, a bronze tablet bearing this magnanimous tribute, " To the brave Alabama boys who were our opponents on this field and whose memory we honor, this tablet is dedicated." That is a tribute, not by a Government, but directly by the men who fought to the men who fought them. It is truly noble.

WILLIAM P. SANDERS
Knoxville
November 19, 1863.

WILLIAM H. LYTLE
Chickamauga
September 20, 1863.

JAMES C. RICE
Spotsylvania
May 10, 1864.

CHARLES G. HARKER
Kenesaw Mountain
June 27, 1864.

FEDERAL GENERALS

KILLED IN BATTLE

GROUP No. 6

BRIGADIER-GENERALS

HIRAM BURNHAM
Fort Harrison
September 30, 1864.

SAMUEL A. RICE
Jenkins' Ferry
July 6, 1864.

DANIEL McCOOK
Kenesaw Mountain
July 17, 1864.

J. H. KITCHING
Cedar Creek
Died January 10, 1865.

DANIEL D. BIDWELL
Cedar Creek
October 19, 1864.

Casualties in Great European Battles

COMPILED FROM HENDERSON'S "STONEWALL JACKSON AND THE AMERICAN CIVIL WAR"

LIST OF KILLED AND WOUNDED (EXCLUDING PRISONERS)

THE VICTORIOUS SIDE IS GIVEN FIRST IN EACH CASE

BATTLE	NUMBER OF TROOPS		KILLED AND WOUNDED	TOTAL	TOTAL PERCENTAGE	PERCENTAGE OF VICTOR
Blenheim, 1704	Allies,	56,000	11,000 ⎱	31,000	26	19
	French,	60,000	20,000 ⎰			
Oudenarde, 1708	Allies,	85,000	10,000 ⎱	20,000	11	11
	French,	85,000	10,000 ⎰			
Malplaquet, 1709	Allies,	100,000	14,000 ⎱	34,000	17	14
	French,	100,000	20,000 ⎰			
Prague, 1757	Prussians,	64,000	12,000 ⎱	22,000	17	18
	Austrians,	60,000	10,000 ⎰			
Zorndorf, 1758	Prussians,	32,760	12,000 ⎱	32,000	38	37
	Russians,	52,000	20,000 ⎰			
Kunnersdorf, 1759	Allies,	70,000	14,000 ⎱	31,000	27	20
	Prussians,	43,000	17,000 ⎰			
Torgau, 1760	Prussians,	46,000	12,000 ⎱	24,000	22	26
	Austrians,	60,000	12,000 ⎰			
Austerlitz, 1805	French,	65,000	9,000 ⎱	25,000	16	13
	Allies,	83,000	16,000 ⎰			
Eylau, 1807	French,	70,000	20,000 ⎱	42,000	33	28
	Russians,	63,500	22,000 ⎰			
Heilsberg, 1807	Russians,	84,000	10,000 ⎱	22,000	13	11
	French,	85,000	12,000 ⎰			
Friedland, 1807	French,	75,000	10,000 ⎱	34,000	23	13
	Russians,	67,000	24,000 ⎰			
Aspern, 1809	Austrians,	75,000	20,000 ⎱	45,000	26	26
	French,	95,000	25,000 ⎰			
Wagram, 1809	French,	220,000	22,000 ⎱	44,000	11	10
	Austrians,	150,000	22,000 ⎰			
Borodino, 1812	French,	125,000	30,000 ⎱	75,000	28	24
	Russians,	138,000	45,000 ⎰			
Bautzen, 1813	French,	190,000	12,000 ⎱	24,000	8	6
	Allies,	110,000	12,000 ⎰			
Leipsic, 1813	Allies,	290,000	42,000 ⎱	92,000	20	14
	French,	150,000	50,000 ⎰			
Ligny, 1815	French,	73,000	12,000 ⎱	24,000	15	16
	Prussians,	86,000	12,000 ⎰			
Waterloo, 1815	Allies,	100,000	20,000 ⎱	42,000	24	20
	French,	70,000	22,000 ⎰			
Solferino, 1859	Allies,	135,000	16,500 ⎱	31,500	10	11
	Austrians,	160,000	15,000 ⎰			
Königgrätz, 1866	Prussians,	211,000	8,894 ⎱	26,894	6	4
	Austrians,	206,000	18,000 ⎰			
Vionville, 1870	Germans,	70,000	15,800 ⎱	32,800	19	22
	French,	98,000	17,000 ⎰			
Gravelotte, 1870	Germans,	200,000	20,000 ⎱	30,000	9	10
	French,	120,000	10,000 ⎰			
Plevna, September 11, 1877	Turks,	35,000	16,000 ⎱	19,000	16	8
	Russians,	80,000	3,000 ⎰			

GRIFFIN A. STEDMAN, JR.
Petersburg
Died August 5, 1864.

GEO. D. WELLS
Cedar Creek
October 13, 1864.

SYLVESTER G. HILL
Nashville
December 15, 1864.

FEDERAL GENERALS KILLED IN BATTLE—GROUP No. 7

ARTHUR H. DUTTON
Bermuda Hundred
Died June 5, 1864.

CHARLES R. LOWELL
Cedar Creek
October 20, 1864.

THEODORE READ
High Bridge
April 6, 1865.

TABULAR STATEMENT OF LOSSES IN BOTH THE UNION AND CONFEDERATE ARMIES IN THE PRINCIPAL BATTLES OF THE CIVIL WAR, 1861-1865, COMPILED FROM OFFICIAL REPORTS BY MARCUS J. WRIGHT, CHIEF OF THE DIVISION OF CONFEDERATE RECORDS, U. S. WAR DEPARTMENT

	Union Army				Confederate Army			
	Killed	Wounded	Missing	Total	Killed	Wounded	Missing	Total
Bull Run, Va., July 21, 1861	481	1,011	1,216	2,708	387	1,582	12	1,981
Wilson's Creek, Mo., Aug. 10, 1861	223	721	291	1,235	257	900	27	1,184
Fort Donelson, Tenn., Feb. 12–16, 1862	500	2,108	224	2,832	2,000	....	14,623	16,623
Pea Ridge, Ark., Mar. 7, 1862	203	980	201	1,384	600	....	200	800
Shiloh, Tenn., Apr. 6–7, 1862	1,754	8,408	2,885	13,047	1,723	8,012	959	10,694
Williamsburg, Va., May 4–5, 1862	456	1,410	373	2,249	1,570	....	133	1,703
Fair Oaks, Va., May 31,–June 1, 1862	790	3,594	647	5,031	980	4,749	405	6,134
Mechanicsville, Va., June 26, 1862	49	207	105	361	1,484	....	....	....
Gaines' Mill, Va., June 27, 1862	894	3,107	2,836	6,837	8,751	....	....	....
Peach Orchard, Savage Station, Va., June 29, 1862								
White Oak Swamp, Glendale, Va., June 30, 1862	724	4,245	3,067	8,036	8,602	....	875	9,477
Malvern Hill, Va., July 1, 1862								
Seven Days, Va., June 25–July 1, 1862	1,734	8,062	6,075	15,849	3,478	16,261	875	20,614
Cedar Mountain, Va., Aug. 9, 1862	314	1,445	594	2,353	231	1,107	....	1,338
Manassas and Chantilly, Va., Aug. 27–Sept. 2, 1862	1,724	8,372	5,958	16,054	1,481	7,627	89	9,197
Richmond, Ky., Aug. 29–30, 1862	206	844	4,303	5,353	78	372	1	451
South Mountain, Md., Sept. 14, 1862	325	1,403	85	1,813	325	1,560	800	2,685
Antietam, or Sharpsburg, Md., Sept. 16–17, 1862	2,108	9,549	753	12,390	2,700	9,024	1,800	13,524
Corinth, Miss., Oct. 3–4, 1862	355	1,841	324	2,520	473	1,997	1,763	4,233
Perryville, Ky., Oct. 8, 1862	845	2,851	515	4,211	510	2,635	251	3,396
Prairie Grove, Ark., Dec. 7, 1862	175	813	263	1,251	164	817	336	1,317
Fredericksburg, Va., Dec. 13, 1862	1,284	9,600	1,769	12,653	595	4,061	653	5,309
Stone's River, or Murfreesboro, Tenn., Dec. 31, 1862, and Jan. 2, 1863	1,677	7,543	3,686	12,906	1,294	7,945	2,476	11,715
Arkansas Post, Ark., Jan. 11, 1863	134	898	29	1,061	28	81	4,791	4,900
Chancellorsville and Fredericksburg, Va., May 1–4, 1863	1,575	9,594	5,676	16,792	1,665	9,081	2,018	12,764

CONFEDERATE

GENERALS

KILLED

IN

BATTLE

GENERAL ALBERT SIDNEY JOHNSTON
Shiloh
April 6, 1862.

LIEUT.-GENERAL LEONIDAS POLK
Pine Mountain
June 14, 1864.

LIEUT.-GENERAL AMBROSE POWELL HILL
Petersburg
April 2, 1865.

Continued from page 142

Engagement								
Champion's Hill, Miss., May 16, 1863	410	1,844	187	2,441	381	1,769	1,670	3,851
Assault on Vicksburg, Miss., May 22, 1863	502	2,550	147	3,199	Full reports not available			
Port Hudson, La., May 27, 1863	293	1,545	157	1,995		235		
Port Hudson, La., June 14, 1863	203	1,401	188	1,792	22	25		47
Gettysburg, Pa., July 1–3, 1863	3,155	14,529	5,365	23,049	3,903	18,735	5,425	28,063
Fort Wagner, S.C., July 18, 1863	246	880	389	1,515	36	133	5	174
Chickamauga, Ga., Sept. 19–20, 1863	1,657	9,756	4,757	16,170	2,312	14,674	1,468	18,484
Chattanooga, Tenn., Nov. 23–25, 1863	753	4,722	349	5,824	361	2,160	4,146	6,667
Mine Run, Va., Nov. 27–Dec. 1, 1863	173	1,099	381	1,653	110	570	65	745
Pleasant Hill, La., Apr. 9, 1864	150	844	375	1,369		987	4,720	5,707
Wilderness, Va., May 5–7, 1864	2,246	12,137	3,383	17,666	Reports of losses not complete			
Spotsylvania, Va., May 10, 1864	753	3,347		4,100	Reports incomplete			
Spotsylvania, Va., May 12, 1864		6,020	800	6,820	Records of losses not shown			
Drewry's Bluff, Va., May 12–16, 1864	390	2,380	1,390	4,160	Reports incomplete			
Cold Harbor, Va., June 1–3, 1864				12,000	Reports incomplete			
Petersburg, Va., June 15–30, 1864	2,013	9,935	4,621	16,569	Estimated loss in Hill's Corps and Field and Kershaw's divisions, 2,970			
Atlanta Campaign, Ga., May, 1864 (including Buzzard's Roost, Snake Creek Gap and New Hope Church)	1,058		1,240	2,298	Killed and wounded, 9,187			
Assault on Kenesaw Mt., Ga., June 27, 1864		1,999	52	2,051	270		172	342
Tupelo, Miss., July 13–15, 1864	77	559	38	674	210	1,116		1,326
Atlanta, Ga., July 22, 1864 (Hood's attack)	430	1,599	1,733	3,722	2,890		851	3,741
Jonesboro, Ga., Aug. 31, 1864		179			1,640 — No full return of losses			
Jonesboro, Ga., Sept. 1, 1864	233	946	105	1,274	276	1,827	1,818	3,921
Winchester, Va., Sept. 19, 1864	697	3,983	338	5,018	No full report of losses			
Chaffin's Farm and Forts Harrison and Gilmer, Va., Sept. 29–30, 1864	383	2,299	645	3,327				
Cedar Creek, Va., Oct. 19, 1864	644	3,430	1,591	5,665	320	1,540	1,050	2,910
Franklin, Tenn., Nov. 30, 1864	189	1,033	1,104	2,336	1,750	3,800	702	6,252
Nashville, Tenn., Dec. 15–16, 1864	387	2,562	112	3,061	No report of killed and wounded			
Bentonville, N.C., Mar. 19, 1865	139	794	170	1,103	195	1,313	610	2,118
Appomattox, Va., Mar. 29–Apr. 9, 1865	1,316	7,750	1,714	10,780	No report of losses			
Petersburg, Va., Apr. 2, 1865	625	3,189	326	4,140	No report of losses			

WILLIAM D. PENDER
Gettysburg
July 18, 1863.

STEPHEN D. RAMSEUR
Cedar Creek
October 19, 1864.

CONFEDERATE

GENERALS

KILLED

IN BATTLE

J. E. B. STUART
Yellow Tavern
May 12, 1864.

GROUP

No. 2

MAJOR–

GENERALS

W. H. T. WALKER
Atlanta
July 22, 1864.

PATRICK R. CLEBURNE
Franklin
November 30, 1864.

ROBERT E. RODES
Opequon
September 19, 1864.

Summary of Union Troops Furnished by the Several States and Territories

STATES AND TERRITORIES	White Troops	Sailors and Marines	Colored Troops	Indian Nations	Aggregate	Total Deaths, All Causes
Alabama	2,578	....	....	....	2,578	345
Arkansas	8,289	....	....	....	8,289	1,713
California	15,725	....	....	....	15,725	573
Colorado	4,903	....	....	....	4,903	323
Connecticut	51,937	2,163	1,784	....	55,864	5,354
Dakota	206	....	....	....	206	6
Delaware	11,236	94	954	....	12,284	882
District of Columbia	11,912	1,353	3,269	....	16,534	290
Florida	1,290	....	....	....	1,990	215
Georgia	....	....	....	....	....	15
Illinois	255,057	2,224	1,811	....	259,092	34,834
Indiana	193,748	1,078	1,537	....	196,363	26,672
Iowa	75,797	5	440	....	76,242	13,001
Kansas	18,069	....	2,080	....	20,149	2,630
Kentucky	51,743	314	23,703	....	75,760	10,774
Louisiana	5,224	....	....	....	5,224	945
Maine	64,973	5,030	104	....	70,107	9,398
Maryland	33,995	3,925	8,718	....	46,638	2,982
Massachusetts	122,781	19,983	2,966	....	146,730	13,942
Michigan	85,479	498	1,387	....	87,364	14,753
Minnesota	23,913	3	104	....	24,020	2,584
Mississippi	545	....	....	....	545	78
Missouri	100,616	151	8,344	....	109,111	13,885
Nebraska	3,157	....	....	....	3,157	239
Nevada	1,080	....	....	....	1,080	33
New Hampshire	32,930	882	125	....	33,937	4,882
New Jersey	67,500	8,129	1,185	....	76,814	5,754
New Mexico	6,561	....	....	....	6,561	277
New York	409,561	35,164	4,125	....	448,850	46,534
North Carolina	3,156	....	....	....	3,156	360
Ohio	304,814	3,274	5,092	....	313,180	35,475
Oregon	1,810	....	....	....	1,810	45
Pennsylvania	315,017	14,307	8,612	....	337,936	33,183
Rhode Island	19,521	1,878	1,837	....	23,236	1,321
Tennessee	31,092	....	....	....	31,092	8,777
Texas	1,965	....	....	....	1,965	151
Vermont	32,549	619	120	....	33,288	5,224
Virginia	....	....	....	....	....	42
Washington Territory	964	....	....	....	964	22
West Virginia	31,872	133	196	....	32,068	4,017
Wisconsin	91,029	....	165	....	91,327	12,301
Indian Nations	....	....	....	3,530	3,530	1,018
Regular Army	....	....	....	....	....	5,798
Colored Troops	....	....	*99,337	....	99,337	**36,847
Veteran Volunteers	....	....	....	....	....	106
U. S. Volunteers***	....	....	....	....	....	243
U. S. Sharpshooters and Engineers	....	....	....	....	....	552
Veteran Reserves	....	....	....	....	....	1,672
Generals and Staffs	....	....	....	....	....	239
Miscellaneous—Bands, etc	....	....	....	....	....	232
	2,494,592	101,207	178,975	3,530	2,778,304	359,528

* Colored troops recruited in the Southern States.
** Includes all the deaths in the 178,975 Colored Troops.
*** Ex-Confederate Soldiers.
Eighty-six thousand seven hundred and twenty-four drafted men paid commutation and were exempted from service.

BRIG.-GEN.
BENJAMIN McCULLOCH
Pea Ridge, March 7, 1862.

BRIG.-GEN.
BERNARD E. BEE
First Bull Run, July 21, 1861.

CONFEDERATE GENERALS
KILLED IN BATTLE

MAJ.-GEN.
JOHN PEGRAM
Hatcher's Run, February 6, 1865.

GROUP No. 3

BRIG.-GEN.
FELIX K. ZOLLICOFFER
Mill Springs, January 19, 1862.

BRIG.-GEN.
FRANCIS S. BARTOW
First Bull Run, July 21, 1861.

BRIG.-GEN.
ROBERT SELDEN GARNETT
Rich Mountain, July 13, 1861.

DEATHS FROM ALL CAUSES IN UNION ARMIES

Cause	Officers	Enlisted Men	Total
Killed and died of wounds....................	6,365	103,705	110,070
Died of disease........................	2,712	197,008	199,720
In prison............................	83	24,873	24,866
Accidents............................	142	3,972	4,114
Drowning............................	106	4,838	4,944
Sunstroke...........................	5	308	313
Murdered............................	37	483	520
Killed after capture.................	14	90	104
Suicide.............................	26	365	391
Military execution...................	....	267	267
Executed by enemy...................	4	60	64
Causes unclassified.................	62	1,972	2,034
Cause not stated...................	28	12,093	12,121
Totals........................	9,584	349,944	359,528

DEATHS IN CONFEDERATE ARMIES

A tabulation of Confederate losses as compiled from the muster-rolls on file in the Bureau of Confederate Archives. (In the report for 1865–66, made by General James B. Fry, United States Provost Marshal-General.) These returns are incomplete, and nearly all the Alabama rolls are missing. Still the figures show that at least 74,524 Confederate soldiers were killed or died of wounds, and that 59,297 died of disease.

STATE	KILLED			DIED OF WOUNDS			DIED OF DISEASE		
	Officers	Enlisted Men	Total	Officers	Enlisted Men	Total	Officers	Enlisted Men	Total
Virginia..........	266	5,062	5,328	200	2,319	2,519	168	6,779	6,947
North Carolina.....	677	13,845	14,522	330	4,821	5,151	541	20,061	20,602
South Carolina.....	360	8,827	9,187	257	3,478	3,735	79	4,681	4,760
Georgia...........	172	5,381	5,553	140	1,579	1,719	107	3,595	3,702
Florida...........	47	746	793	16	490	506	17	1,030	1,047
Alabama..........	14	538	552	9	181	190	8	716	724
Mississippi........	122	5,685	5,807	75	2,576	2,651	103	6,704	6,807
Louisiana..........	70	2,548	2,618	42	826	868	32	3,027	3,059
Texas............	28	1,320	1,348	13	1,228	1,241	10	1,250	1,260
Arkansas.........	104	2,061	2,165	27	888	915	74	3,708	3,782
Tennessee........	99	2,016	2,115	49	825	874	72	3,353	3,425
Regular C. S. Army.	35	972	1,007	27	441	468	25	1,015	1,040
Border States......	92	1,867	1,959	61	672	733	58	2,084	2,142
Totals........	2,086	50,868	52,954	1,246	20,324	21,570	1,294	58,003	59,297

Colonel W. F. Fox, the authority on Civil War Statistics, states: "If the Confederate rolls could have been completed, and then revised—as has been done with the rolls of the Union regiments—the number of killed, as shown above (74,524), would be largely increased. As it is, the extent of such increase must remain a matter of conjecture. The Union rolls were examined at the same time, and a similar tabulation of the number killed appears, also, in General Fry's report. But this latter number was increased 15,000 by a subsequent revision based upon the papers known as "final statements" and upon newly-acquired information received through affidavits filed at the Pension Bureau."

WM. Y. SLACK
Pea Ridge
March 8, 1862.

ADLEY H. GLADDEN
Shiloh
April 11, 1862.

ROBERT HATTON
Fair Oaks
June 1, 1862.

RICHARD GRIFFITH
Savage Station
June 30, 1862.

GEORGE B. ANDERSON
Antietam
October 6, 1862.

CONFEDERATE

GENERALS KILLED

IN BATTLE

GROUP No. 4

TWELVE BRIGADIER–

GENERALS

LEWIS HENRY LITTLE
Iuka
September 19, 1862.

O. B. BRANCH
Antietam
September 17, 1862.

TURNER ASHBY
Harrisburg
June 6, 1862.

WILLIAM E. STARKE
Antietam
September 17, 1862.

JAMES McINTOSH
Pea Ridge
March 17, 1862.

CHARLES S. WINDER
Cedar Mountain,
August 9, 1862.

SAMUEL GARLAND, JR.
South Mountain
September 14, 1862.

TABULAR STATEMENT OF ORGANIZATIONS IN THE UNION SERVICE

	REGIMENTS	BATTALIONS	COMPANIES	BATTERIES
Cavalry	272	45	78	...
Heavy artillery	61	8	36	...
Light artillery	...	9	...	432
Engineers	13	1	7	...
Sharpshooters	4	3	35	...
Infantry	2,144	60	351	...
Totals	2,494	126	507	432

SUMMARY OF ORGANIZATIONS IN THE CONFEDERATE ARMY

Any attempt to present in statistical form the strength of the Confederate armies is manifestly impossible, as was explained by General Marcus J. Wright in his introductory chapter in Volume I of the PHOTOGRAPHIC HISTORY. The same conditions also render futile any accurate comparison of the troops furnished to the Confederate armies by the various states of the South. Nevertheless, by tabulating the various organizations and bearing in mind the limitations of the method as well as the original data, a slight basis is afforded to gain some idea of the relative numbers contributed by the different States. Furthermore, the numbers of the organizations when summarized are of interest in comparison with those given above.

No complete official roll of regiments and other organizations in the Confederate army is to be found either in the archives of the United States War Department or published in the War Records, and it is difficult, if not impossible, to give either an accurate list or the total number. Various lists have been compiled by private individuals, but none of these show absolute accuracy, and all differ among themselves. A list prepared by Colonel Henry Stone, a member of the Military Historical Society of Massachusetts, was made the basis of the following table by Colonel Thomas L. Livermore, which is published in his volume "Numbers and Losses in the Civil War." This list General Wright states is as accurate as can be found.

TABLE MADE BY COLONEL LIVERMORE FROM COLONEL STONE'S LIST

	INFANTRY				CAVALRY				ARTILLERY		
	Regiments	Legions	Battalions	Companies	Regiments	Legions	Battalions	Companies	Regiments	Battalions	Companies
Alabama	55	..	18	4	6	..	18	10	..	2	17
Arkansas	42	..	14	2	4	..	5	4	..	2	16
Florida	9	..	1	16	2	..	3	6	..	1	15
Georgia	67	3	14	9	7	..	21	...	..	..	...
Kentucky	9	..	...	..	11	..	1	...	..	..	...
Louisiana	33	..	22	..	3	..	13	8	5	3	19
Mississippi	53	..	21	..	25	1	4	...	..	1	9
Missouri	30	..	...	..	7	..	...	...	..	..	...
North Carolina	74	1	12	4	6	..	12	2	2	..	9
South Carolina	53	3	14	8	7	..	7	13	3	3	25
Tennessee	78	..	24	..	10	..	11	17	..	1	35
Texas	35	1	4	14	33	..	8	15	2	..	24
Virginia	99	1	19	5	16	..	40	26	4	12	58
Confederate or Prov. Army	5	..	...	..	...	..	...	...	..	..	...
Total	642	9	163	62	137	1	143	101	16	25	227

MAXCY GREGG
Fredericksburg,
December 13. 1862.

E. D. TRACY
Fort Gibson
May 1, 1863.

THOMAS R. R. COBB
Fredericksburg
December 13. 1862.

GROUP No. 5

CONFEDERATE GENERALS

KILLED IN BATTLE

LLOYD TILGHMAN
Champion's Hill
May 16, 1863.

ROGER W. HANSON
Stone's River
December 30, 1862.

E. F. PAXTON
Chancellorsville
May 3, 1863.

JAMES E. RAINS
Stone's River,
Dec. 31, 1862.

LEWIS A. ARMISTEAD
Gettysburg
July 3, 1863.

WILLIAM BARKSDALE
Gettysburg
July 2, 1863.

MARTIN E. GREEN
Vicksburg
June 27, 1863.

Regimental Casualties in the Union Army

IN any discussion of the total or relative casualties suffered by a military organization in a war, or in any particular engagement, it must be borne in mind that the entire subject is one around which many questions center. The general consideration has been discussed by Colonel Hilary A. Herbert in the preceding chapter. It now remains to give the readers of the PHOTOGRAPHIC HISTORY some few exact statistics of the losses suffered in both great armies.

In the official records there are summarized with considerable completeness the enlistments and casualties for the various regiments and other organizations of the Union army. The reports for the most part are complete and comprehensive, admitting of full discussion, yet often there is great difficulty in reducing the vast amount of material to a common denominator for purposes of comparison. The problem is to consider the various elements in their relations one to another. Thus, it is possible to take those regiments where the number killed or died of wounds during the entire period of service stood at a maximum in comparison with other organizations. Furthermore, it is possible to consider such casualties relatively, depending upon the strength of the organization, and this latter method gives a clear indication of the efficiency of the regiment during its entire period of service. Large total losses mean that the regiment was at the fore-front of the fighting in many battles and not necessarily unduly exposed at one particular action.

Such is the list to be found on page 154, compiled from the authoritative work of Lieutenant-Colonel William F. Fox, U. S. V.—" Regimental Losses in the Civil War." It is, indeed, a record of valor; the fifty regiments here listed are entitled to places of high honor on the scroll of history. It is, all things considered, the most useful basis of making a comparison of the services of the different regiments, and it is one which unfortunately cannot be made for the regiments comprising the Confederate army, on account of the absence of suitable rosters and reports.

Now, if we should consider the maximum percentage of casualties based on the total of killed, wounded, and missing, a similar roll could be constructed. It would be headed by the First Minnesota Infantry, which, at the battle of Gettysburg, with 262 men engaged on the second day, lost 168 wounded and 47 killed, or a percentage of 82. In fact, other regiments standing at the top of such a list are worthy of note, and a few such, as listed by Colonel Fox, are given in the table at the bottom of this page.

The tabular statement on page 154 must be considered, therefore, as suggestive rather than complete. The selection of fifty regiments is an arbitrary one; for, of over two thousand regiments in the Union army, 45 infantry regiments lost over 200 men killed or mortally wounded in action during the war. In fact, Colonel Fox has compiled a list of 300 fighting regiments, which lost over 130 who were killed and died of wounds during the war, or which, with a smaller enrollment, suffered an equivalent percentage of casualties.

REGIMENT	BATTLE	Killed	Wounded	Missing	Total	Engaged	Per Cent.
1st Minnesota	Gettysburg	47	168	—	215*	262	82.0
141st Pennsylvania	Gettysburg	25	103	21	149	198	75.7
101st New York	Bull Run	6	101	17	124	168	73.8
25th Massachusetts	Cold Harbor	53	139	28	220	310	70.0
36th Wisconsin (4 Cos.)	Bethesda Church	20	108	38	166	240	69.0
20th Massachusetts	Fredericksburg	25	138	—	163	238	68.4
8th Vermont	Cedar Creek	17	66	23	106	156	67.9
81st Pennsylvania	Fredericksburg	15	141	20	176	261	67.4
12th Massachusetts	Antietam	49	165	10	224	334	67.0
1st Maine H. A.	Petersburg	115	489	28	632	950	66.5
9th Louisiana Colored	Milliken's Bend	62	130	—	192	300	64.0
5th New Hampshire	Fredericksburg	20	154	19	193	303	63.6

*Action of July 2d,—8 companies engaged; total casualties at Gettysburg were 224.

RICHARD B. GARNETT
Gettysburg
July 3, 1863.

W. R. SCURRY
Jenkins Ferry
April 30, 1864.

PAUL J. SEMMES
Gettysburg
July 10, 1863.

CARNOT POSEY
Bristoe Station
November 13, 1863.

KILLED

IN

BATTLE

JAMES DESHLER
Chickamauga
September 20, 1863.

BENJAMIN H. HELM
Chickamauga
September 20, 1863.

JOHN M. JONES
Wilderness
May 2, 1864.

L. A. STAFFORD
Wilderness
May 11, 1864.

GROUP

No.

6

J. J. PETTIGREW
Falling Waters
July 17, 1863.

THOMAS GREEN
Pleasant Hill
April 12, 1864.

ALFRED MOUTON
Sabine Cross Roads
April 8, 1864.

PRESTON SMITH
Chickamauga
September 20, 1863.

Casualties of Fifty Union Regiments During Entire Term of Service

KILLED AND DIED OF WOUNDS—MAXIMUM PERCENTAGES OF ENROLLMENT

COMPILED FROM FOX'S "REGIMENTAL LOSSES IN THE CIVIL WAR"

REGIMENT	DIVISION	CORPS	Enrolled	Killed	Per Cent.
2d Wisconsin	Wadsworth's	First	1,203	238	19.7
1st Maine H. A.	Birney's	Second	2,202	423	19.2
57th Massachusetts	Stevenson's	Ninth	1,052	201	19.1
140th Pennsylvania	Barlow's	Second	1,132	198	17.4
26th Wisconsin	Schurz's	Eleventh	1,089	188	17.2
7th Wisconsin	Wadsworth's	First	1,630	281	17.2
69th New York	Hancock's	Second	1,513	259	17.1
11th Penn. Reserves	Crawford's	Fifth	1,179	196	16.6
142d Pennsylvania	Doubleday's	First	935	155	16.5
141st Pennsylvania	Birney's	Third	1,037	167	16.1
19th Indiana	Wadsworth's	First	1,246	199	15.9
121st New York	Wright's	Sixth	1,426	226	15.8
7th Michigan	Gibbon's	Second	1,315	208	15.8
148th Pennsylvania	Barlow's	Second	1,339	210	15.6
83d Pennsylvania	Griffin's	Fifth	1,808	282	15.5
22d Massachusetts	Griffin's	Fifth	1,393	216	15.5
36th Wisconsin	Gibbon's	Second	1,014	157	15.4
27th Indiana	Williams'	Twelfth	1,101	169	15.3
5th Kentucky	T. J. Wood's	Fourth	1,020	157	15.3
27th Michigan	Willcox's	Ninth	1,485	225	15.1
79th U. S. Colored	Thayer's	Seventh	1,249	188	15.0
17th Maine	Birney's	Third	1,371	207	15.0
1st Minnesota	Gibbon's	Second	1,242	187	15.0
93d Illinois	Quinby's	Seventeenth	1,011	151	14.9
36th Illinois	Sheridan's	Fourth	1,376	204	14.8
8th Penn. Reserves	Crawford's	Fifth	1,062	158	14.8
126th New York	Barlow's	Second	1,036	153	14.7
49th Pennsylvania	Wright's	Sixth	1,313	193	14.6
9th Illinois	Dodge's	Sixteenth	1,493	216	14.4
20th Indiana	Birney's	Third	1,403	201	14.3
15th Kentucky	Johnson's	Fourteenth	956	137	14.3
2d Massachusetts	Williams'	Twelfth	1,305	187	14.3
55th Illinois	Blair's	Fifteenth	1,099	157	14.2
4th Michigan	Griffin's	Fifth	1,325	189	14.2
15th Massachusetts	Gibbon's	Second	1,701	241	14.1
15th New Jersey	Wright's	Sixth	1,702	240	14.1
145th Pennsylvania	Barlow's	Second	1,456	205	14.1
28th Massachusetts	Barlow's	Second	1,778	250	14.0
1st Michigan	Morell's	Fifth	1,329	187	14.0
8th New York H. A.	Gibbon's	Second	2,575	361	14.0
7th West Virginia	Gibbon's	Second	1,008	142	14.0
37th Wisconsin	Willcox's	Ninth	1,110	156	14.0
5th Michigan	Birney's	Third	1,883	263	13.9
10th Penn. Reserves	Crawford's	Fifth	1,150	160	13.9
13th Penn. Reserves	Crawford's	Fifth	1,165	162	13.9
63d Pennsylvania	Birney's	Third	1,341	186	13.8
5th Vermont	Getty's	Sixth	1,533	213	13.8
6th Iowa	Corse's	Sixteenth	1,102	152	13.7
155th New York	Gibbon's	Second	830	114	13.7
49th Ohio	T. J. Wood's	Fourth	1,468	202	13.7

ABNER PERRIN
Spotsylvania
May 12, 1864.

W. E. JONES
Piedmont
June 5, 1864.

GEORGE DOLES
Bethesda Church
May 30, 1864.

ROBERT H. ANDERSON
Antietam
October 6, 1862

CONFEDERATE

GENERALS

KILLED

IN BATTLE

GROUP No. 7

BRIGADIER-

GENERALS

JOHN H. MORGAN
Greenville
September 4, 1864.

JOHN R. CHAMBLISS, JR.
Deep Bottom
August 16, 1864.

JUNIUS DANIEL
Spotsylvania
Died May 13, 1864.

JAMES B. GORDON
Yellow Tavern
May 11, 1864.

J. C. SAUNDERS
Weldon Railroad
August 21, 1864.

MICAH JENKINS
Wilderness
May 6, 1864.

C. H. STEVENS
Peach Tree Creek
July 20, 1864.

SAMUEL BENTON
Ezra Church
July 29, 1864.

Some Casualties of Confederate Regiments

By General Marcus J. Wright, Confederate States Army

AT the time when Lieutenant-Colonel William F. Fox, U. S. V., published his valuable and exceedingly accurate work, entitled " Regimental Losses of the American Civil War, 1861–1865," many regimental reports were missing or inaccessible, so that this work, in many respects a standard as far as Confederate material was concerned, necessarily is incomplete.

No compilation of statistics exists corresponding to that given for the Union armies on a preceding page, and but little exact statistical information of a broad character is available. Therefore, it seems desirable here to give on a following page a table from Colonel Fox's book, which shows remarkable percentages of losses in Confederate regiments at particular engagements. This list contains only a few of the many instances of regiments suffering a heavy percentage of loss. The list is compiled from the few cases in which the official Confederate reports on file in the United States War Department mention the number of effectives taken into action as well as the actual losses.

Because of these statistical deficiencies, no complete catalogue of distinguished Confederate regiments based on the records of battlefield casualties is possible. This is especially regrettable to those who recall the conspicuous services of many organizations from the very outset.

In addition to Colonel Fox's table we give a few other notable instances. At the first battle of Bull Run, the 33d Virginia lost 45 killed and 101 wounded, and the 27th Virginia lost 19 killed and 122 wounded. Hampton's Legion lost 19 killed and 100 wounded.

The 2d Georgia had the longest service of any infantry regiment from that State. In the Seven Days' around Richmond, with 271 men in the field, it lost 120. At Malvern Hill, it lost 81 men and about the same number at Gettysburg.

At Mills Springs, Ky., the 15th Mississippi Regiment lost 46 killed and 153 wounded. The 8th Kentucky regiment at Fort Donelson, Tenn., lost 27 killed and 72 wounded. The 4th Tennessee, at Shiloh, lost 36 killed and 183 wounded, while the 4th Kentucky lost 30 killed and 183 wounded. The 12th Mississippi, at Fair Oaks,

Va., lost 41 killed and 152 wounded. Hampton's Legion, a South Carolina organization, at Fair Oaks lost 21 killed and 122 wounded. The 20th North Carolina lost, at Gaines' Mill, 70 killed and 202 wounded. At Gaines' Mill and Glendale the 14th Alabama lost 71 killed and 253 wounded, the 19th Mississippi 58 killed and 264 wounded, the 14th Louisiana 51 killed and 192 wounded, and the 12th Mississippi 34 killed and 186 wounded. At Malvern Hill, the 2d Louisiana lost 30 killed and 152 wounded. The 21st Virginia lost, at Cedar Mountain, Va., 37 killed and 85 wounded.

At Manassas (Second Bull Run), Va., the 5th Texas lost 15 killed and 224 wounded; the 2d Louisiana lost 25 killed and 86 wounded. At Richmond, Ky., the 2d Tennessee lost 17 killed and 95 wounded. At Antietam, or Sharpsburg, the 13th Georgia lost 48 killed and 169 wounded; the 48th North Carolina lost 31 killed and 186 wounded. At Iuka, Miss., the 3d Texas, dismounted cavalry, lost 22 killed and 74 wounded. At Corinth, Miss., the casualties of the 35th Mississippi were 32 killed and 110 wounded, and of the 6th Missouri, 31 were killed and 130 wounded. At Chaplin Hills, Ky., from the 1st Tennessee regiment, 49 were killed and 129 wounded.

At Fredericksburg, Va., the 57th North Carolina lost 32 killed, 192 wounded, and the 48th North Carolina 17 killed and 161 wounded. At Stone's River, the 29th Mississippi lost 34 killed and 202 wounded.

At Chancellorsville, Va., the losses of the 37th North Carolina were 34 killed and 193 wounded; the 2d North Carolina, 47 killed and 167 wounded. At Vicksburg, Miss., the 3d Louisiana lost 49 killed, 119 wounded, and the 6th Missouri lost 33 killed and 134 wounded. At Helena, Ark., the 7th Missouri lost 16 killed and 125 wounded. At Gettysburg, the 42d Mississippi lost 60 killed and 205 wounded, and the 1st Maryland, with 400 present for duty, had 52 killed and 140 wounded.

At Charleston Harbor, the 21st South Carolina lost 14 killed and 112 wounded, and the 25th South Carolina 16 killed and 124 wounded. At the bloody battle of Chickamauga, Alabama regiments suffered great losses.

ARCHIBALD GRACIE, JR.
Petersburg Trenches
December 2, 1864.

JOHN ADAMS
Franklin
November 30, 1864.

H. B. GRANBURY
Franklin
November 30, 1864.

JAMES DEARING
High Bridge
April 6, 1865.

CONFEDERATE

GENERALS

KILLED

IN

BATTLE—

GROUP No. 8—

BRIGADIER-

GENERALS

JOHN DUNOVANT
Vaughn Road,
October 1, 1864.

JOHN GREGG
Darbytown Road,
October 7, 1864.

STEPHEN ELLIOTT, JR.
Petersburg
Died in 1864.

OSCAR F. STRAHL
Franklin
November 30, 1864.

ARCHIBALD C. GODWIN
Opequon
September 19, 1864.

S. R. GIST
Franklin
November 30, 1864.

VICTOR J. GIRARDEY
Petersburg
August 16, 1864.

Casualties of Fifty Confederate Regiments

From Fox's "Regimental Losses in the Civil War"

Showing Remarkable Percentages of Losses at Particular Engagements Based on Official Reports

NOTE—This list does not aim to include all the notable instances of remarkable casualties of regiments in the Confederate Army. It was based by Colonel Fox on available records where the numbers taken into action as well as the casualties were specified in official reports. The list is suggestive rather than complete, as many regiments omitted might with propriety claim to be included in any roll of "Fifty Fighting Regiments."

REGIMENT	BATTLE	DIVISION	Present	Killed	Wounded	Missing	Per Cent.
1st Texas	Antietam	Hood's	226	45	141	..	82.3
21st Georgia	Manassas	Ewell's	242	38	146	..	76.0
26th North Carolina	Gettysburg	Heth's	820	86	502	..	71.7
6th Mississippi	Shiloh	Hardee's	425	61	239	..	70.5
8th Tennessee	Stone's River	Cheatham's	444	41	265	..	68.2
10th Tennessee	Chickamauga	Johnson's	328	44	180	..	68.0
Palmetto Sharpshooters	Glendale	Longstreet's	375	39	215	..	67.7
17th South Carolina	Manassas	Evans'	284	25	164	1	66.9
23d South Carolina	Manassas	Evans'	225	27	122	..	66.2
44th Georgia	Mechanicsville	D. H. Hill's	514	71	264	..	65.1
2d N. C. Battalion	Gettysburg	Rodes'	240	29	124	..	63.7
16th Mississippi	Antietam	Anderson's	228	27	117	..	63.1
27th North Carolina	Antietam	Walker's	325	31	168	..	61.2
6th Alabama	Seven Pines	D. H. Hill's	632	91	277	5	59.0
15th Virginia	Antietam	McLaws'	128	11	64	..	58.5
8th Georgia	Antietam	Hood's	176	13	72	16	57.3
1st S. C. Rifles	Gaines' Mill	A. P. Hill's	537	81	225	..	56.9
10th Georgia	Antietam	McLaws'	148	15	69	..	56.7
18th North Carolina	Seven Days	A. P. Hill's	396	45	179	..	56.5
3d Alabama	Malvern Hill	D. H. Hill's	354	37	163	..	56.4
17th Virginia	Antietam	Pickett's	55	7	24	..	56.3
7th North Carolina	Seven Days	A. P. Hill's	450	35	218	..	56.2
12th Tennessee	Stone's River	Cheatham's	292	18	137	9	56.1
9th Georgia	Gettysburg	Hood's	340	27	162	..	55.0
5th Georgia	Chickamauga	Cheatham's	353	27	167	..	54.9
16th Tennessee	Stone's River	Cheatham's	377	36	155	16	54.9
4th North Carolina	Seven Pines	D. H. Hill's	678	77	286	6	54.4
27th Tennessee	Shiloh	Hardee's	350	27	115	48	54.2
12th South Carolina	Manassas	A. P. Hill's	270	23	121	2	54.0
4th Virginia	Manassas	Jackson's	180	18	79	..	53.8
4th Texas	Antietam	Hood's	200	10	97	..	53.5
27th Tennessee	Perryville	Cleburne's	210	16	84	12	53.3
1st South Carolina	Manassas	A. P. Hill's	283	25	126	..	53.3
49th Virginia	Fair Oaks	D. H. Hill's	424	32	170	22	52.8
12th Alabama	Fair Oaks	D. H. Hill's	408	59	156	..	52.6
7th South Carolina	Antietam	McLaws'	268	23	117	..	52.2
7th Texas	Raymond	John Gregg's	306	22	136	..	51.6
6th South Carolina	Fair Oaks	D. H. Hill's	521	88	181	..	51.6
15th Georgia	Gettysburg	Hood's	335	19	152	..	51.0
11th Alabama	Glendale	Longstreet's	357	49	121	11	50.7
17th Georgia	Manassas	Hood's	200	10	91	..	50.5
3d North Carolina	Gettysburg	Johnson's	312	29	127	..	50.0
4th Virginia	Chancellorsville	Trimble's	355	14	155	3	48.4
1st Maryland	Gettysburg	Johnson's	400	52	140	..	48.0
8th Mississippi	Stone's River	Jackson's	282	20	113	..	47.1
32d Virginia	Antietam	McLaws'	158	15	57	..	45.5
18th Mississippi	Antietam	McLaws'	186	10	73	..	44.6
14th South Carolina	Gaines' Mill	A. P. Hill's	500	18	197	..	43.0
33d North Carolina	Chancellorsville	A. P. Hill's	480	32	167	..	41.4
5th Alabama	Malvern Hill	D. H. Hill's	225	26	66	..	40.8

FEDERAL ARMIES, CORPS AND LEADERS

THE SECOND CORPS, ARMY OF THE POTOMAC

MARCHING DOWN PENNSYLVANIA AVENUE IN 1865—THE SECOND CORPS HAD A RECORD OF LONGER CONTINUOUS SERVICE, A LARGER ORGANIZATION, HARDEST FIGHTING, AND GREATEST NUMBER OF CASUALTIES, THAN ANY OTHER IN THE EASTERN ARMIES—IT CONTAINED THE REGIMENT WHICH SUSTAINED THE LARGEST PERCENTAGE OF LOSS IN ANY ONE ACTION; THE REGIMENT WHICH SUSTAINED THE GREATEST NUMERICAL LOSS IN ANY ONE ACTION; AND THE REGIMENT WHICH SUSTAINED THE GREATEST NUMERICAL LOSS DURING ITS TERM OF SERVICE—OF THE HUNDRED UNION REGIMENTS WHICH LOST THE MOST MEN IN BATTLE, THIRTY-FIVE BELONGED TO THE SECOND CORPS

| ORDERLY | | ORDERLY | COLONEL JOSEPH J. REYNOLDS | COLONEL WILLIAM G. LE DUC | CAPTAIN H. W. PERKINS |

"FIGHTING JOE HOOKER" WITH HIS STAFF

"Fighting Joe Hooker" was a man of handsome physique and intense personal magnetism. He graduated at West Point in 1837 in the same class with Jubal A. Early and Braxton Bragg. Having fought through the Mexican War, he resigned from the army in 1853. On May 17, 1861, he was appointed brigadier-general of volunteers, and on May 5, 1862, major-general of volunteers. He was active throughout the Peninsular campaign, and at Bristoe Station, Second Bull Run, Chantilly, South Mountain and Antietam. He commanded the center grand division of the Army of the Potomac at Fredericksburg. At last, on January 26, 1863, he was assigned by President Lincoln to the command of the Army of the Potomac. On the 4th of May, 1863, his right flank was surprised by Jackson at Chancellorsville, and his 90,000 soldiers were forced to recross the Rappahannock. While fighting in the East he was wounded at

WALKER, THE ARTIST   CAPTAIN R. H. HALL   GENERAL   GENERAL   COLONEL
    LIEUTENANT`   MAJOR WILLIAM   JOSEPH   DANIEL   JAMES D.
SAMUEL W. TAYLOR   H. LAWRENCE   HOOKER   BUTTERFIELD   FESSENDEN

ON THE SPOT WHENCE HE DIRECTED HIS "BATTLE ABOVE THE CLOUDS"

Antietam, and stunned at Chancellorsville by a cannon-ball which struck a pillar against which he was leaning.   In September, 1863, he was sent with the Eleventh and Twelfth Corps to reënforce Rosecrans at Chattanooga.   On November 24th, in the "battle among the clouds" at the head of his new command, he led a charge against the Confederate artillery and infantry posted on Lookout Mountain.   For his conduct on this occasion he was brevetted major-general in the regular army.   He further distinguished himself under Sherman at Dalton and Resaca, and in the attack on Atlanta.   At his own request (July 30, 1864) he was placed on waiting orders September 28th, when he was put in command of the Northern Department.   He retired from active service October 15, 1868, with the full rank of major-general in the regular army.   General Hooker died at Garden City, Long Island, New York, October 31, 1879.

THE ARMY OF GEORGIA—ON PARADE, GENERAL SLOCUM AT THE HEAD

Very different from the march through Georgia and the Carolinas was this magnificent parade of the Army of Georgia down Pennsylvania Avenue. In front ride General Slocum and his staff. Behind come the long straight lines of men who proved the Confederacy a hollow shell with all of its fighting men at the front. Eagerly crowding close to the line of march are the citizens of Washington who had alternately clamored for action, and shaken in their boots when the daring Confederate leaders pressed close to the Northern capital. Many a heartfelt prayer of thanks and relief was offered when mothers saw their boys march past, unscathed by the war and about to reënter civil life. Many a tear fell for those who could not be there to share the glory.

[162]

At Gaines' Mill, Slocum's Division of the Sixth Corps was sent to the support of General Porter, and lost 2,021 out of less than 8,000 present in the hot engagement. It was in front of Fredericksburg May 3, 1863, under General Sedgwick, that the Corps made its most brilliant display of dash and daring. It carried at the point of the bayonet Marye's Heights, the strong position before which there had fallen, gloriously but in vain, nearly 13,000 men the previous December. Most of the Corps was held in reserve at Gettysburg, and its casualties there were slight, but it added again to its laurels at Rappahannock Sta-

THE NINETEENTH ARMY CORPS

THE SIXTH ARMY CORPS IN THE GRAND
REVIEW—THE CORPS THAT SAVED
WASHINGTON FROM CAPTURE

tion. In the battles of the Wilderness and Spotsylvania it encountered its hardest fighting, the percentage of killed of the Fifteenth New Jersey in the latter battle being equaled in only one instance during the whole war. At Cold Harbor it suffered heavily again, and the appearance of two of its divisions at Fort Stevens checked Early's advance on Washington. It pursued Early up the Shenandoah, and fought at Opequon and Cedar Creek. In the final assault on Petersburg it played an important part. It was no less prominent in its final appearance at the Grand Review in Washington.

THE TWENTIETH ARMY CORPS

The Armies of the United States in the Civil War

BY THE PROVISIONS of the Constitution, the President of the United States is commander-in-chief of the army and navy. During the Civil War, this function was exercised in no small degree by President Lincoln. As Secretaries of War, he had in his cabinet Simon Cameron, from March 4, 1861, to January 14, 1862; and Edward M. Stanton, who served from January 15, 1862, throughout Lincoln's administration, and also under Johnson until May 28, 1868, except for a short interval during which he was suspended. There were four generals-in-chief of the armies: Brevet Lieutenant-General Scott, Major-Generals McClellan and Halleck, and Lieutenant-General Grant. The last named has been considered in previous pages of this volume, but the lives and services of the other three are summarized below, in addition to the treatment received in other volumes. (CONSULT INDEX.) This is true of all the army leaders not separately described in the pages that follow. The Index will refer to treatment in other volumes.

LIEUTENANT-GENERAL WINFIELD SCOTT was born near Petersburg, Virginia, June 13, 1786. After being graduated from William and Mary College, he studied law, was admitted to the bar, and then entered the army at the age of twenty-two. His career was one of bravery and incident. He was captured by the British, but exchanged in 1813, fought in the battle of Lundy's Lane, and was severely wounded. After the close of the war he was raised to the rank of major-general, and in 1841 succeeded General Macomb as commander of the United States army. In the war with Mexico, he won great fame and was nominated by the Whigs for President in 1852; but he carried only four States. In 1855, Congress revived the rank of lieutenant-general and conferred it by brevet upon Scott, the appointment being dated March 29, 1847, the day of his brilliant capture of Vera Cruz. It was evident that his age and infirmities would prevent his taking any active part in the Civil War, and on November 1, 1861, he was retired from the chief command of the army of the United States. He wrote an autobiography, and made a European trip in 1864, dying May 29, 1866, at West Point, New York.

MAJOR-GENERAL HENRY WAGER HALLECK (U.S.M.A. 1839) was born in Westernville, New York, January 16, 1815. He served in California and on the Pacific coast during the Mexican War. He retired from the army with the rank of captain in 1854 to practise law, but after the outbreak of the Civil War reentered the regular service, with the grade of major-general. He was in command of the Department of Missouri (afterward Department of Mississippi) from November 19, 1861, to July 11, 1862, when he became general-in-chief of all the armies. Grant succeeded him, March 9, 1864, and Halleck was his chief-of-staff until the close of the war. He continued in the army as head, successively, of the Military Division of the James, the Department of the Pacific, and Department of the South until his death at Louisville, Kentucky, January 9, 1872.

MAJOR-GENERAL GEORGE BRINTON McCLELLAN (U.S.M.A. 1846) was born in Philadelphia, December 3, 1826. He served in the Engineer Corps during the Mexican War, distinguished himself by gallant service, and reached the rank of captain in 1855, having been so brevetted in 1847. He became assistant instructor in practical engineering at West Point, later accompanied the Red River exploring expedition, and was sent on a secret mission to Santo Domingo. During the Crimean War, he was one of a commission of three appointed by Congress to study and report upon the whole art of European warfare. He remained some time with the British forces. McClellan's report was a model of comprehensive accuracy and conciseness, and showed him to be a master of siege-tactics. In 1857, McClellan resigned his army commission to devote himself to the practice of engineering. He became vice-president of the Illinois Central Railroad Company, and later president of the Eastern Division of the Ohio and Missouri Railroad. He made his home in Cincinnati until the outbreak of the Civil War, when he tendered his services to his country and was made major-general of volunteers, April 21, 1861. The Department of the Ohio was constituted, and McClellan took command, May 13th, his appointment as major-general dating from the following day. He drove the Confederates from northwestern Virginia and saved that section to the Union, an accomplishment of the most vital importance, since, in the event of the establishment of the Confederacy, the Union territory would have been contracted at

The upper photograph, as beautifully "composed" as a classic painting, shows General and Mrs. Scott at their home, Elizabeth, New Jersey, in 1862. A closer portrait study of the general appears below. Winfield Scott became the first general-in-chief of the United States Army during the Civil War, being already in that position when the war broke out. He was then nearly seventy-five years old. The aged hero owed his exalted rank and his military fame to his dashing and vigorous achievements as commander in the Mexican War. He directed until retired by his own request in November, 1861. Scott possessed an imposing figure and courage equal to every danger. He was exacting in discipline—that power which the French call "the glory of the soldier and the strength of armies.

Major-General Henry Wager Halleck assumed command of the Army and Department of Missouri in 1861, and from his headquarters at St. Louis directed the operations of the forces which early in 1862 compelled the Confederates to evacuate Kentucky and Central and West Tennessee. After he assumed control of all the armies as successor to McClellan in July, 1862, he made his headquarters in Washington, performing duties similar to those of a chief-of-staff in a modern army. His military decisions in particular crises as Fredericksburg, Chancellorsville and Gettysburg were not always approved by critics; nevertheless, he bore a reputation for genius as a commander. He was succeeded in the duties of general-in-chief in February, 1864, by Lieutenant-General Ulysses S. Grant.

SCOTT AND HALLECK—TWO GENERALS-IN-CHIEF OF THE UNITED STATES ARMY

this point into a neck but little more than one hundred miles in width. After this success, McClellan was placed, July 25, 1861, at the head of the newly created District (afterward Department) of the Potomac, and began the organization and training of the army of that name. From November 5, 1861 to March 11th of the following year, he was general-in-chief of the armies of the United States, and after the latter date continued in command of the Army of the Potomac until November 9, 1862, when he was replaced by Major-General A. E. Burnside. He took no further part in the war. His removal was due to dissatisfaction with his methods that gradually developed among President Lincoln and his advisers. The

failure of the army to capture Richmond in the Peninsula campaign, and the non-pursuit of Lee immediately after Antietam were the chief reasons. As the nominee of the Democratic party, he was defeated for the presidency in 1864, and his resignation from the army was accepted on November 8th. He now spent several years abroad, returning to live in New Jersey, of which State he became governor in 1877. Aside from his military abilities, McClellan was a man of fine tastes in literature and art, and also took an active interest in promoting the manufacturing industries of the State. He wrote his autobiography, and several works of a military nature. His death occurred October 29, 1885, at Orange.

Army of the Potomac

BY THE CONSOLIDATION of the Department of Washington and the Department of Northeastern Virginia, July 25, 1861, the Military District of the Potomac was constituted and placed under command of Major-General George B. McClellan. On August 15, 1861, the Department, or Army of the Potomac was created from it, and as such it was known thereafter. Major-General McClellan assumed command of this army August 20, 1861. As then constituted, it was organized in fourteen brigades composed largely of the troops (regular army and volunteer) of the Department of Northeastern Virginia, under Brigadier-General Irvin McDowell, and new organizations. Most of these brigades had artillery and some of them cavalry. McClellan immediately applied his military knowledge to remodeling the army, and in October a new organization was announced. The division was now the unit, and there were fourteen, including one stationed at Baltimore. There were also one provisional brigade, a provost-guard, a cavalry command, and a cavalry reserve. During the winter of 1861–62, the Army of the Potomac was thoroughly drilled. A new organization was announced in March, 1862, and this the army retained, except while Burnside created the grand division, until it was discontinued, June 28, 1865. The corps were the units, and their number varied from time to time. There were also the provost-guard, the guard for general headquarters, a full artillery, and cavalry reserve. A cavalry division was formed in July, 1862, and reorganized as a cavalry corps in February, 1863. The successive commanders of the Army of the Potomac were:

Major-General George B. McClellan to November 9, 1862; Major-General A. E. Burnside to January 26, 1863; Major-General Joseph Hooker to June 28, 1863, being succeeded by Major-General George G. Meade, who remained at its head until it was discontinued, June 28, 1865, except for a short interval in January, 1865, when Major-General John G. Parke was in temporary command.

MAJOR-GENERAL AMBROSE EVERETT BURNSIDE (U.S.M.A. 1847) was born in Liberty, Indiana, May 23, 1824. He served in the artillery with the rank of first lieutenant, resigned his commission, in 1853, to take up the manufacture of a breech-loading rifle which he had invented. At the outbreak of the Civil War he was an officer of the Illinois Central Railroad Company. For gallant service at Bull Run he was made brigadier-general of volunteers, and in March, 1862, major-general of volunteers. He organized an expeditionary corps in December, 1861, and this was merged in the Department of North Carolina, of which Burnside was the head from January to July, 1862. He captured Roanoke Island and occupied New Berne. From these troops and others was organized, July 22, 1862, the Ninth Corps, with Burnside at its head. He served under McClellan at South Mountain, and at Antietam, where he commanded the left wing, and succeeded him in the command of the Army of the Potomac. Later, Major-General Burnside was assigned to command of the Department of the Ohio. Burnside and the Ninth Corps were with Grant in the

Major-General George Brinton McClellan began his war career as commander of the Department of Ohio. After he had defeated and scattered the Confederate forces commanded by General Robert E. Lee, securing West Virginia to the Union, he was appointed general-in-chief of the United States Armies as successor to General Scott, in November, 1861. He planned and directed the expeditions which, under General A. E. Burnside captured the coast of North Carolina, under Butler and Farragut opened up the lower Mississippi, and in Kentucky and Tennessee resulted in the capture of Fort Donelson. He led the Army of the Potomac in the Peninsula and Antietam campaigns. Meade, its last commander, said: "Had there been no McClellan there could have been no Grant."

Virginia campaign of 1864. Major-General Burnside resigned his commission at the close of the war and resumed his career as a railroad projector and manager. He was governor of Rhode Island from 1866 to 1869, and senator from 1875 until his death, which occurred September 3, 1881, at Bristol, Rhode Island.

MAJOR-GENERAL JOSEPH HOOKER (U.S.M.A. 1837) was born in Hadley, Massachusetts, November 13, 1814. He entered the artillery and was brevetted lieutenant-colonel for distinguished services in the Mexican War. He resigned his commission in 1853. At the outbreak of the Civil War he was living in California as a farmer and civil engineer. He tendered his services to the Government and was appointed brigadier-general of volunteers. In March, 1862, he was made a division commander in the Army of the Potomac, with a promotion to major-general of volunteers in May. An appointment as brigadier-general of the regular army followed the battle of Antietam, in which he was wounded. In September, 1862, he rose to corps commander, and was at the head of the Center Grand Division in Burnside's organization. He was commander of the Army of the Potomac from January 26, 1863, to June 28th. Later, he exhibited great gallantry as corps commander at Lookout Mountain, and

in the Atlanta campaign. On October 1, 1864, he was placed at the head of the Northern Department, and served at the head of other departments until he was retired, as the result of a paralytic stroke, with full rank of major-general, in October, 1868. His death occurred at Garden City, New York, October 31, 1879.

MAJOR-GENERAL GEORGE GORDON MEADE (U. S.M.A. 1835) was born in Cadiz, Spain, December 31, 1815, while his father was American naval agent at that city. He saw service in the Seminole War, and then resigned in 1836 to take up the practice of civil engineering. He reentered the army and served with the Topographical Engineer Corps during the Mexican War. He was afterward employed on river and harbor improvements, lighthouse construction, and the survey of the Great Lakes, until the Civil War broke out, when he was commissioned brigadier-general of volunteers and put in command of a brigade in the Pennsylvania Reserve in the Army of the Potomac. Later, he commanded the First and Fifth corps and was made general commanding of the army, June 28, 1863. He was in chief command at Gettysburg. On August 18, 1864, he received a commission as major-general in the regular army, and served therein until his death, in Philadelphia, November 6, 1872.

Army of the Tennessee

THE TROOPS in the Military District of Cairo were under the command of Brigadier-General U. S. Grant from August 1, 1861, until February, 1862. The District of West Tennessee was organized February 17, 1862, and Grant was at its head until October 16th. His forces were known as the Army of West Tennessee, and were included in those of the Department of Mississippi, under Major-General Halleck. With this force, consisting of six divisions and some unassigned troops, Grant fought the battle of Shiloh. On October 16, 1862, the Department of Tennessee was created to include Cairo, western Kentucky and Tennessee, and northern Mississippi. Grant was commander until October 24, 1863, when the Military Division of the Mississippi was organized to include the Departments of the Ohio, Tennessee, Cumberland, and of Arkansas. The troops in the Department of Tennessee were designated the Thirteenth Army Corps until December 18, 1862,

when they were reorganized into the Thirteenth, Fifteenth, Sixteenth, and Seventeenth corps. Succeeding Grant, this force, usually called the Army of the Tennessee, was successively commanded by Major-Generals W. T. Sherman, James B. McPherson, John A. Logan, and O. O. Howard. This army took part in the capture of Vicksburg, battle of Chattanooga, Atlanta campaign, and Sherman's campaigns in Georgia and the Carolinas. A detachment of it was with the Red River expedition, in 1864.

MAJOR-GENERAL JAMES BIRDSEYE MCPHERSON (U.S.M.A. 1853) was born in Sandusky, Ohio, November 14, 1828. He practised engineering in the Government employ and also taught it at West Point. When the war broke out, he raised a force of engineers, and later he was aide to Major-General Halleck. In December, 1862, he was given command of the Seventeenth Corps. His services

AMBROSE EVERETT BURNSIDE

Commander of the Army of the Potomac During the Fredericksburg Campaign, November, 1862, to January, 1863.

GEORGE GORDCN MEADE

Commander of the Army of the Potomac in the Gettysburg Campaign, also in the Wilderness Campaign and Siege of Petersburg.

MAJOR–GENERALS

BURNSIDE,

HOOKER,

MEADE

COMMANDERS

OF

THE ARMY OF

THE POTOMAC

JOSEPH HOOKER

Commander of the Army of the Potomac During the Chancellorsville Campaign and the Opening of the Gettysburg Campaign.

in reenforcing Rosecrans after Corinth, October, 1862, won him the rank of major-general of volunteers, and after the fall of Vicksburg he received the commission of brigadier-general of the regular army. He succeeded Major-General William T. Sherman in the command of the Army of the Tennessee, March 12, 1864, and was killed at the battle of Atlanta, July 22, 1864.

MAJOR-GENERAL JOHN A. LOGAN was born in Jackson County, Illinois, February 9, 1826. He served in the Mexican War, rising from a private to the rank of second lieutenant. He was afterward admitted to the bar and finally reached Congress. During his term here the Civil War broke out and he enlisted and fought at Bull Run. Returning to the West, he raised the Thirty-first Illinois Infantry, afterward becoming its colonel. He was wounded at Fort Donelson and shortly afterward was made major-general of volunteers. In the Vicksburg campaigns he commanded a division of the Seventeenth Corps. In 1863, he took command of the Fifteenth Corps and served in the Atlanta campaign and led his troops through the Carolinas. He was made head of the Department of the Tennessee May 19, 1865. He was elected to the United States Senate in 1871, and was defeated for the vice-presidency of the United States on the Republican ticket of 1884. He died in Washington, December 26, 1886.

MAJOR-GENERAL OLIVER OTIS HOWARD (U.S. M.A. 1854) was born in Leeds, Maine, November 8, 1830. He served as chief of ordnance, and as first lieutenant taught mathematics at West Point until the Civil War broke out, when he left the regular army to command the Third Maine Volunteers. He headed a brigade in the first battle of Bull Run and was promoted to brigadier-general of volunteers in September, 1861. At Fair Oaks, where he lost his right arm, he achieved distinction as an able fighter. After Antietam, he commanded a division of the Second Corps, and later, as major-general of volunteers, the corps itself for a short time. On April 2, 1863, the Eleventh Corps was given him, and it was these troops that were so badly routed by " Stonewall " Jackson at Chancellorsville. In September, 1863, Howard and his corps were transferred to the Army of the Cumberland, in which he became leader of the Fourth Corps, April, 1864. Howard's services at Gettysburg, Lookout Mountain, and Missionary Ridge were conspicuous. He accompanied Sherman to the relief of Knoxville, and fought in all the battles of the Atlanta campaign, succeeding Major-General McPherson to the command of the Army of the Tennessee, and marching with Sherman through Georgia and the Carolinas. After the close of the war he commanded the Nez Percé Indian expedition of 1877, the Bannock, and Piute campaigns, and from 1880 to 1882, was superintendent of the Military Academy, West Point. He was (1865–74) commissioner of the Bureau of Refugees, Freedmen, and Abandoned Lands, and in 1895 founded the Lincoln Memorial University and the industrial school at Cumberland Gap, Tennessee. Major-General Howard was a noted total-abstinence advocate and was much interested in Sunday-school work. He was retired with full rank in 1894, and he died at Burlington, Vermont, October, 26, 1909.

Army of the Ohio and Army of the Cumberland

THE DEPARTMENT OF KENTUCKY, which constituted the whole of that State within a hundred miles of the Ohio River, was merged in the Department of the Cumberland, comprising the States of Kentucky and Tennessee, August 15, 1861. On November 9th, it was renamed the Department of the Ohio, the States of Ohio, Michigan, and Indiana being added. The troops in this region (over whom McClellan, Rosecrans, O. M. Mitchel, Robert Anderson, and W. T. Sherman had, at different times and places, control) were now organized into the Army of the Ohio, with Major-General Don Carlos Buell in command. Although the department was merged into that of Mississippi in March, 1862, the Army of the Ohio retained its name. This was the body that brought such timely assistance to Grant at Shiloh and drove Bragg out of Kentucky. The army was organized into three corps in September, 1862, but the following month (October 24th) the Department of the Cumberland was recreated to consist of eastern Tennessee, Alabama, and Georgia, and the Army of the Ohio, which had operated chiefly in that region, now became officially the Fourteenth Army Corps, but better known as the Army of the Cumberland. On October 30th, Buell was

GEORGE HENRY THOMAS
Commander of the Army of the Cumberland in the Tennessee and Georgia Campaigns, including Stone's River, Chickamauga, Chattanooga and Atlanta.

JOHN ALEXANDER LOGAN
Commander of the Army of the Tennessee in Front of Atlanta. He subsequently resumed Command of a Corps and Led it Through the Carolinas.

MAJOR–GENERALS

THOMAS

LOGAN

HOWARD

ARMY OF THE

CUMBERLAND

AND ARMY OF

THE TENNESSEE

OLIVER OTIS HOWARD
Commander of the Army of the Tennessee in Part of the Atlanta Campaign and in the March Through Georgia and the Carolinas.

replaced by Major-General W. S. Rosecrans, and the Fourteenth Corps was reorganized into the Right Wing, Center, and Left Wing, later the Fourteenth, Twentieth, and Twenty-first Army corps. The last two were afterward consolidated as the Fourth Corps. With this army, Rosecrans fought the battle of Stone's River, drove Bragg across the Tennessee, and was defeated at Chickamauga. Major-General George H. Thomas succeeded to the command October 20, 1863. The army distinguished itself on Missionary Ridge and through the Atlanta campaign (as a part of the Military Division of the Mississippi), and in the campaign against Hood in Tennessee. The army had four divisions of cavalry. It had a reserve corps for a short time, and received two corps from the Army of the Potomac, which were finally consolidated into the reorganized Twentieth Corps.

MAJOR-GENERAL DON CARLOS BUELL (U.S. M.A. 1841) was born March 23, 1818, near Marietta, Ohio, and served in the Mexican War. When the Civil War broke out he assisted in the organization of volunteers, and in November, 1861, took charge of the Department and Army of the Ohio. He was soon raised to the rank of major-general of volunteers. His last service in this army was the driving of Bragg out of Kentucky, for this, with the preceding Tennessee campaign during the summer of 1862, aroused such criticism that he was replaced, October 30th, by Major-General Rosecrans and tried before a military commission. An adverse report was handed in, and Buell resigned from the army June 1, 1864. He then became president of the Green River Iron Company, and, 1885–89, was pension-agent at Louisville. He died near Rockport, Kentucky, November 19, 1898.

MAJOR-GENERAL WILLIAM STARKE ROSECRANS (U.S.M.A. 1842) was born at Kingston, Ohio, September 6, 1818. He served in the Engineer Corps and as assistant professor at West Point. In 1854, he resigned from the army to practise architecture and civil engineering, but at the outbreak of the Civil War he tendered his services to the Government and was made brigadier-general of the regular army, and major-general of volunteers in March, 1862. He succeeded McClellan at the head of the army of occupation in western Virginia after his victory at Rich Mountain, and held it until Major-General Fremont took charge of the Mountain Department, March 29, 1862. From June 26th until the end of October, Rose-

crans was Pope's successor in the Army of the Mississippi and, taking command of the District of Corinth, he defeated the Confederate forces at Iuka and Corinth. He now replaced Buell in the Army of the Cumberland. As general commanding he won the battle of Stone's River, but was defeated at Chickamauga, and was succeeded by Major-General George H. Thomas. He then spent a year in command of the Department of Missouri, during which he drove Price out of the State, and on December 9, 1864, was relieved of active command. After resigning his commission, in 1866, he was United States minister to Mexico, and was in Congress from 1881 to 1885. In 1889, Congress restored him to the rank and pay of brigadier-general. He died at Redondo, California, March 11, 1898.

MAJOR-GENERAL GEORGE HENRY THOMAS (U. S.M.A. 1840) was born in Southampton County, Virginia, July 31, 1816. He served in the Seminole and Mexican wars, and had risen to the grade of lieutenant-colonel when the Civil War broke out. In August, 1861, he was made brigadier-general of volunteers. His first services in the war were rendered in the Departments of Pennsylvania and of the Shenandoah. His division of the Army of the Ohio defeated the Confederate forces at Mill Springs, Kentucky, January 19, 1862. This victory first brought him into notice, and shortly afterward he was made major-general of volunteers. He was put at the head of the Center (Fourteenth Corps) of the reorganized Army of the Cumberland, and in October, 1863, he assumed the chief command, distinguishing himself at Missionary Ridge, in the Atlanta campaign, and in the crushing defeat of Bragg at Nashville. He was promoted to major-general in the regular army for his services at Nashville, December 15, 1864. He narrowly escaped this honor, for, impatient at his delay in attacking Hood—a delay occasioned by the very inclement weather—Grant had sent Major-General Logan to relieve him, and the latter was on the way. He had also shown himself a gallant fighter in the earlier battles of Stone's River, and Chickamauga, where he held the left wing of the army against tremendous odds. This feat is considered one of the most glorious of the whole war. With the right wing of the army routed and in utter confusion, Thomas kept his position against the whole of Bragg's army until ordered to withdraw. He declined the brevet of lieutenant-general, which President Johnson offered him in 1868. Two years later he died in San Francisco, March 28, 1870.

JOHN McALLISTER SCHOFIELD

Commander of the Army of the Frontier and of the
Department and Army of the Ohio.

DON CARLOS BUELL

Commander of the Army of the Ohio in the Shiloh
Campaign and Afterward of a Department.

JOHN POPE

Commander of the Army of Virginia, June to September, 1862, Including Second Bull Run.

WILLIAM STARKE ROSECRANS

Commander of the Army of the Ohio (Cumberland) in
the Campaign of Stone's River and Chickamauga.

COMMANDERS OF THE ARMIES OF THE OHIO AND VIRGINIA

Army of the Ohio

THE DEPARTMENT OF THE OHIO having been merged in that of Mississippi, March, 1862, it was recreated on August 19th, to consist of the States of Ohio, Michigan, Indiana, Illinois, Wisconsin, and Kentucky, east of the Tennessee River, and Major-General H. G. Wright was placed at the head. The troops of the department were scattered through many districts. Some of the brigades constituted the Army of Kentucky, of which Major-General Gordon Granger was in command. Wright was replaced March 25, 1863, by Major-General A. E. Burnside, and shortly afterward the troops in the department were reorganized into the Twenty-third Army Corps, and this force is the Army of the Ohio associated with the Knoxville, Atlanta, and Nashville campaigns. The Ninth Corps was attached to the department from March, 1863, to March, 1864. Burnside was succeeded in turn by Major-Generals J. G. Foster, J. M. Schofield, and George Stoneman. A cavalry division organized in April, 1864, was headed by Major-General Stoneman, and afterward by Colonels Capron and Garrard. On January 17, 1865, the troops still in the department (the Twenty-third Corps having gone to North Carolina) were annexed to the Department of the Cumberland.

MAJOR-GENERAL JOHN MCALLISTER SCHOFIELD (U.S.M.A. 1853) was born in Chautauqua County, New York, September 29, 1831. After garrison duty in Florida and South Carolina, he held the chair of natural philosophy at West Point and later at Washington University, St. Louis, where the outbreak of the Civil War found him. He had command of the District of St. Louis, Department of Missouri; Army of the Frontier; of a division in the Fourteenth Corps; the Department and Army of the Ohio, and of the Twenty-third Corps, which was transferred to North Carolina late in the war. He was made major-general of volunteers in November, 1862. His most noteworthy active services were rendered during the Atlanta campaign and at the battle of Franklin. After the Civil War he was Secretary of War *ad interim*, after the resignation of General Grant. He was commander of the United States army from 1888 to 1895, rising to the rank of lieutenant-general, at which he was retired in September, 1895. He died at St. Augustine, Florida, March 4, 1906.

Army of the Mississippi

THE ARMY OF THE MISSISSIPPI had a short existence, being organized February 23d, and discontinued October 26, 1862. Its first commander was Major-General John Pope, who was succeeded, June 26th, by Major-General W. S. Rosecrans. This army consisted of five divisions, a flotilla brigade, and several brigades of cavalry, and operated on the Mississippi in the spring of 1862, capturing Island No. 10; before Corinth in May, 1862, and at Iuka and Corinth in September and October, 1862. Most of the troops went into the Thirteenth Army Corps.

Army of Virginia

TO OBTAIN CLOSER ORGANIZATION in the various commands operating in Virginia, President Lincoln, on June 26, 1862, constituted the Army of Virginia out of Major-General Fremont's forces (Mountain Department), those of Major-General McDowell (Department of the Rappahannock), those of Major-General Banks (Department of the Shenandoah), and Brigadier-General Sturgis' brigade from the Military District of Washington. This last, an unorganized body of troops, did not join the army at once. Major-General John Pope was placed at the head of the new organization, which was divided into three corps. Exclusive of Sturgis' troops it numbered between forty and fifty thousand men, and was augmented later by troops from three corps of the Army of the Potomac. A corps of the Army of Virginia checked " Stonewall " Jackson's advance

Eugene A. Carr, Commander of the Army
of the Southwest; Led Troops at
Wilson's Creek and Pea Ridge.

FEDERAL

MAJOR–GENERALS

COMMANDING

ARMIES

Quincy Adams Gillmore, Commander of the
Department and Army of the South
at the Siege of Charleston.

Frederick Steele, Commander of the Army
of Arkansas; Engaged at Little
Rock.

Benjamin Franklin Butler, Commander of the Department and
Army of the Gulf in 1862, and
of the Army of the James
in 1864. With this Army
he Operated Against Rich-
mond in May and June.

Gordon Granger, Commander of the Army
of Kentucky in 1862; Noted at
Chickamauga.

James G. Blunt, Commander in Kansas
and of the Army of the Frontier; at
Prairie Grove.

OPERATING

ON THE GULF

AND ALONG THE

WESTERN FRONTIER

David Hunter, Head of a Division at Bull
Run and later of the Department
of the South.

at Cedar Mountain, on August 9th, but the entire organization was defeated at Manassas by Jackson and Longstreet, August 29th and 30th, and withdrew to the lines of Washington. On September 12th, the Army of Virginia was merged in the Army of the Potomac.

MAJOR-GENERAL JOHN POPE (U.S.M.A. 1842) was born in Louisville, Kentucky, March 16, 1822. He served in the Mexican War, rising to the rank of captain. After this he did much work on engineering service in connection with the development of the West. When the Civil War broke out, Pope was sent to Cairo, Illinois, and later to command the troops in northern Missouri. From February to June, 1862, he headed the newly created Army of the Mississippi, during which time he was made major-general of volunteers and brigadier-general of the regular army. His most notable achievement was the capture of Island No. 10, as a result of which he was put in command of the Army of Virginia, June 26, 1862. The reverse of Second Bull Run caused him to ask to be relieved of this command, and he was sent to the Department of the Northwest, to carry on the war against the Sioux Indians. He headed other departments in the West until he was retired, in 1886. His last command was the Department of the Pacific. He was brevetted major-general in March, 1865, for his services at Island No. 10, and received the full rank in 1882. Major-General Pope died at Sandusky, Ohio, September 23, 1892.

Army of the Southwest

CREATED December 25, 1861, from troops in portions of the Department of Missouri. It was merged in the District of Eastern Arkansas, Department of Tennessee, December 13, 1862, and was commanded during its existence by Brigadier-Generals S. R. Curtis, Frederick Steele, E. A. Carr, and W. A. Gorman. This army fought many minor but important engagements in Missouri and Arkansas, including Bentonville, Sugar Creek, and Pea Ridge.

MAJOR-GENERAL SAMUEL RYAN CURTIS (U.S. M.A. 1831) was born near Champlain, New York, February, 1807, and resigned from the army to become a civil engineer and, later, a lawyer. He served as colonel of volunteers in the Mexican War, and afterward went to Congress. He was made brigadier-general of volunteers in May, 1861, and was commander of the Army of the Southwest from December, 1861, to August, 1862. He conducted an active campaign against Van Dorn and Price, during which he won the battle of Pea Ridge, March 7-8, 1862, and was made major-general of volunteers that same month. Later, he was unable to hold Arkansas and was compelled to march to the Mississippi River. He was in command of the Department of Missouri, September, 1862, to May, 1863, and of Kansas, January, 1864, to January, 1865, after which he was at the head of that of the Northwest. He negotiated treaties with several Indian tribes, and was mustered out of the volunteer service April 30, 1866. He died at Council Bluffs, Iowa, December 26, 1866.

MAJOR-GENERAL FREDERICK STEELE (U.S.M. A. 1843) was born in Delhi, New York, January 14, 1819, and served in the Mexican War. He was a major when the Civil War broke out and rose to be major-general of volunteers in November, 1862. Steele served with distinction in Missouri, and was given a division in the Army of the Southwest in May, 1862. For a short time, he had command of the army itself. When it was broken up, he was finally transferred into the Department of the Tennessee, having a division on Sherman's Yazoo Expedition, McClernand's Army of the Mississippi, and the new Fifteenth Army Corps, with which he took part in the Vicksburg campaign. In August, 1863, he was given charge of the Arkansas Expedition, which developed into the Seventh Army Corps, at the head of which he remained until December, 1864. He was given a separate command in the district of West Florida, and assisted Major-General Gordon Granger at the final operations around Mobile. After muster-out from the volunteer service, he returned to the regular army as colonel, having already received the brevet of major-general for the capture of Little Rock. He died at San Mateo, California, January 12, 1868.

MAJOR-GENERAL EUGENE ASA CARR (U.S.M. A. 1850) was born in Erie County, New York, in

[176]

GEORGE CROOK

Commander of the Army of West Virginia in 1864. Later Crook led a Cavalry Division under Sheridan in the Appomattox Campaign at Five Forks and during the pursuit of Lee.

JOHN C. FREMONT

Commander of the Mountain Department and Army in West Virginia in 1862. Fremont was in Command in Missouri in 1861 and at one time gave orders to Brigadier-General Grant.

NATHANIEL PRENTISS BANKS

Commander of the Department and Army of the Shenandoah in 1862 and of the Army of the Gulf in 1863–4. With this Army Banks captured Port Hudson in 1863.

PHILIP HENRY SHERIDAN

Commander of the Army of Shenandoah in 1864. Sheridan Led a Division at Chickamauga and Chattanooga and Commanded the Cavalry Corps of the Army of the Potomac in the Wilderness Campaign.

HENRY WARNER SLOCUM

Commander of the Army of Georgia in the Carolinas. Slocum Commanded the Twelfth Corps, Army of the Potomac, at Chancellorsville and Gettysburg and the Twentieth Corps in Front of Atlanta.

JOHN A. McCLERNAND

Commander of the Army of the Mississippi in 1862–3. McClernand Led Troops at Shiloh and later Commanded the Army of the Mississippi operating against Vicksburg; Head of a Corps in Grant's Siege.

COMMANDERS OF THE ARMIES OF WEST VIRGINIA, SHENANDOAH, GEORGIA AND MISSISSIPPI

1830, and served in the mounted rifles in Indian warfare until the opening of the Civil War, when he became colonel in the Illinois cavalry. His appointment of brigadier-general of volunteers was dated March 7, 1862. His service was chiefly in the Southwest, in the Army of the Southwest, the Thirteenth, Sixteenth, and Seventeenth corps, the Districts of Arkansas, and of Little Rock. For short periods he was at the head of the Army of the Southwest and of the left wing of the Sixteenth Corps. His gallant and meritorious service in the field won him a medal of honor and successive brevets in the regular army, and he showed especial bravery and military ability at Wilson's Creek, Pea Ridge, Black River Bridge, and the capture of Little Rock. He was mustered out of the volunteer service in January, 1866, with the brevet of major-general in the regular army. He returned to the army, and consinued in service on the frontier. In 1892, he was made brigadier-general and was retired February 15, 1893. He died in Washington, D. C., December 2, 1910.

Army of West Virginia

THE TROOPS in the Department of West Virginia were taken from the Eighth Army Corps when the department was reorganized, June 28, 1863. The department commanders were Brigadier-General B. F. Kelley, Major-Generals Franz Sigel, David Hunter, George Crook, Brigadier-General J. D. Stevenson, Brevet Major-General S. S. Carroll, and Major-Generals W. S. Hancock and W. H. Emory. In the campaign against Lieutenant-General Early (June-October, 1864), the two divisions (about seventy-five hundred men) under Crook were called the Army of West Virginia. This force was prominent at the Opequon, Fisher's Hill, Cedar Creek, and other engagements. After the campaign, the troops returned to the various districts in the department.

MAJOR-GENERAL DAVID HUNTER (U.S.M.A. 1822) was born in Washington, July 21, 1802, and rose to rank of major in the Mexican War. As brigadier-general of volunteers, he commanded the Second Division at Bull Run, where he was severely wounded. Shortly afterward, he was made major-general of volunteers. He succeeded Fremont in the Western Department, and was at the head of the Department of Kansas, November, 1861, to March, 1862, then of the South, until September, and of the Tenth Corps from January to June, 1863, and in May, 1864, he succeeded Major-General Sigel in the command of the Department of West Virginia. Hunter was the first general to enlist colored troops, and presided at the court which tried the Lincoln conspirators. He was retired in 1866, having been brevetted major-general, and died in Washington, February 2, 1886.

MAJOR-GENERAL GEORGE CROOK (U.S.M.A. 1852) was born near Dayton, Ohio, September 8, 1828. He spent the nine years before the opening of the Civil War in California. As brigadier-general of volunteers in the Army of the Cumberland, he commanded a division of cavalry. He succeeded Major-General David Hunter in the command of the Department of West Virginia in August, 1864, and shortly afterward was made major-general of volunteers. He was active in the Shenandoah campaign under Sheridan; also at Five Forks and Appomattox. In 1866, as lieutenant-colonel of the regular army, he was sent to the West, where he remained in constant warfare with the Indians for many years. He obtained charge of all the tribes and did much for their advancement. In 1888, he attained the rank of major-general, and died in Chicago, March 21, 1890.

Department of Virginia and North Carolina, Army of the James

THE DEPARTMENT OF VIRGINIA was created in May, 1861, and the troops therein were organized into the Seventh Army Corps on July 22, 1862. This corps was divided between Fort Monroe, Norfolk, Portsmouth, Yorktown, and other places. The Eighteenth Army Corps, created December 24, 1862, from troops in the Department of North Carolina was transferred to the Department of Virginia and North Carolina July 15, 1863, when the two departments were united, and the troops

Irvin McDowell Commanded the 1st
Corps in Front of Washington.

A. A. Humphreys Commanded the
2d Corps at Petersburg.

John Newton Commanded the 1st
Corps at Gettysburg and After.

Darius N. Couch Commanded the
2d Corps at Fredericksburg and
Chancellorsville.

Edwin Vose Sumner Commanded the
2d Corps on the Peninsula
and in Maryland.

Winfield Scott Hancock; Under Him
the Second Corps Earned the
Name "Old Guard."

FEDERAL MAJOR–GENERALS COMMANDING THE FIRST AND SECOND
ARMY CORPS

therein were all merged in the Eighteenth Corps. This was reorganized in April, 1864, and the Tenth Corps being transferred from the Department of the South, the whole force was called the Army of the James. Its principal commander was Major-General Benjamin F. Butler, although Major-Generals E. O. C. Ord and D. B. Birney held command for short periods. On December 3, 1864, the two corps were discontinued, the white troops being formed into the Twenty-fourth Army Corps and the colored into the Twenty-fifth. On January 31, 1865, the two departments were again separated.

MAJOR-GENERAL BENJAMIN FRANKLIN BUTLER was born in Deerfield, New Hampshire, November 5, 1818, and was graduated from Waterville College in 1838. He practised law and entered political life. As a brigadier-general of the Massachusetts State Militia, he answered President Lincoln's call and was placed in command of the Department of Annapolis. In May, 1861, he was made major-general of volunteers and given the Department of Virginia, and in August led the troops that assisted in the capture of Forts Hatteras and Clark. On March 20, 1862, he was put in command of the Department of the Gulf and his troops occupied New Orleans on May 1st. His army gained possession of most of the lower Mississippi, and in December he was relieved by Major-General Banks. On November 1st, he assumed command of the Department of Virginia and North Carolina and personally led the Eighteenth Corps (Army of the James) until May 2, 1864. He was sent to New York city in October to cope with the anticipated disturbance during the presidential election. Following an unsuccessful expedition (December 1864) against Fort Fisher, he was removed by Lieutenant-General Grant. He was elected to Congress as a Republican, in 1866. In 1883, he was Democratic governor of Massachusetts, and in the following year was the unsuccessful presidential candidate of the Greenback-Labor and Anti-Monopolist parties. He died in Washington, January 11, 1893.

Army and Department of the Gulf

CONSTITUTED February 23, 1862, comprising, in a general way, the territory of the Gulf States occupied by the Federal troops. Major-General Benjamin F. Butler was the first commander. He was followed by Major-Generals N. P. Banks, S. A. Hurlbut, and E. R. S. Canby, who commanded after the close of the war. There were, at first, many separate bodies of troops scattered over the department. One of these, the Nineteenth Army Corps, was organized in January, 1863, and was discontinued as a corps in this department November 7, 1864. The Thirteenth Army Corps joined this army from that of the Tennessee in August, 1863, and remained until June, 1864. A detachment of the Sixteenth Corps, also from the Army of the Tennessee, joined for the Red River expedition, in March, 1864. On May 7, 1864, the Department of the Gulf was merged in the Military Division of West Mississippi, but retained a separate existence.

MAJOR-GENERAL NATHANIEL PRENTISS BANKS was born in Waltham, Massachusetts, January 30, 1816. He received a common-school education, practised law, and was a prominent member of Congress from 1853 to 1857. He was governor of Massachusetts from 1858 until 1861, and when the Civil War broke out he was president of the Illinois Central Railroad Company, but immediately offered his services to the Government. He was made major-general of volunteers, and was appointed to the command of the Department of Annapolis, and then to the Department of the Shenandoah. In the organization of the Army of the Potomac in March, 1862, he was assigned to the Fifth Corps, but his force was detached April 4, 1862, and remained in the Shenandoah Valley, where Banks had command until that corps was merged in the Army of Virginia, June 26, 1862. After the Army of Virginia was discontinued, Banks was at the head of the Military District of Washington until October 27, 1862. He succeeded Major-General B. F. Butler in command of the Department of the Gulf, and was actively engaged along the lower Mississippi and Red rivers. He resigned his commission after the disastrous Red River expedition of 1864, and was reelected to Congress. In 1890, owing to an increasing mental disorder, he was obliged to retire from public life. He died at his home in Waltham, September 1, 1894.

TWO COMMANDERS
OF THE
THIRD ARMY CORPS,
SICKLES
AND
HEINTZLEMAN

Daniel E. Sickles Commanded the Third Corps at Chancellorsville and Gettysburg.

S. P. Heintzelman Led the Third Corps at Fair Oaks and Second Bull Run.

FEDERAL

MAJOR–

GENERALS

COMMANDERS OF THE

THIRD AND FOURTH

ARMY CORPS

W. H. French Commanded the
Third Corps in the Mine
Run Campaign.

T. J. Wood Commanded the Fourth Corps
(West) at Nashville, 1864.

Erasmus D. Keyes Commanded the Fourth
Corps (East) on the Peninsula.

Army of Georgia

MAJOR-GENERAL EDWARD RICHARD SPRIGG CANBY (U.S.M.A. 1839) was born in Kentucky in 1819. Entering the army, he served in the Seminole and Mexican wars. When the Civil War broke out, he served first as colonel in New Mexico, held that territory for the Union, and prevented a Confederate invasion of California. Then, for some time, he was on special duty in the North and East. In May, 1864, with the rank of major-general of volunteers, he assumed command of the Military Division of West Mississippi. He captured Mobile, April 12, 1865, and the following month arranged for the surrender of the Confederate forces in the Trans-Mississippi Department. June 3, 1865, he succeeded to the command of the Army and Department of the Gulf. After the close of the war he was made brigadier-general in the regular army, and was put in command of the Department of the Columbia. While engaged in attempting to settle difficulties between the Government and the Modoc Indians, he was treacherously murdered by their chief, April 11, 1873.

MAJOR-GENERAL GORDON GRANGER (U.S.M.A. 1845) was born in New York city in 1821, and served in the Mexican War and on the Southwestern frontier. When the Civil War broke out,

he was made captain and rose through successive grades until his appointment of major-general of volunteers was dated September 17, 1862. He fought at Wilson's Creek, and later commanded the cavalry and had a brigade in the Army of the Mississippi. Then he had charge of the so-called Army of Kentucky, from August to October, 1862, and served in the Department of the Ohio until put in charge of the newly organized Reserve Corps of the Army of the Cumberland. At Chickamauga, he rendered most timely assistance to Thomas and won a brevet of lieutenant-colonel in the regular army. He was the first commander of the new Fourth Corps until April, 1864, when he was sent to command the district of South Alabama, the troops of which were merged in the Reserve Corps, Department of the Gulf (afterward called New Thirteenth Army Corps) of which Granger took command in January, 1865. He commanded the land forces at the fall of Forts Morgan and Gaines (August, 1864), and in the operations around Mobile that resulted in its capture, April, 1865. After the war, Major-General Granger was mustered out of the volunteer service and received the commission of colonel in the regular army. He was brevetted major-general in March, 1865. He died in Santa Fé, New Mexico, January 10, 1876.

Army of Georgia

THE FOURTEENTH AND TWENTIETH ARMY CORPS on the march to the sea and through the Carolinas (November 1864–April 1865) were so known. This force was commanded by Major-General Henry W. Slocum, and constituted the left wing of Sherman's army.

MAJOR-GENERAL HENRY WARNER SLOCUM (U.S.M.A. 1852) was born in Delphi, New York, September 24, 1827, and, beginning the practice of law at Syracuse, New York, he resigned his commission as first lieutenant in 1855. At the outbreak of the Civil War, he joined McDowell's troops as colonel of the Twenty-seventh New York Volunteers, and at Bull Run was severely wounded. In August, 1861, as brigadier-general of volunteers, he commanded a brigade of Franklin's Division of the Army of the Potomac, and later had a division in the Sixth Corps. At Gaines' Mill and Glendale, General Slocum took a prominent part, and after the battle of Malvern Hill he was pro-

moted. As major-general of volunteers, he was given the Twelfth Corps in October, 1862. He fought with the armies of the Potomac and of Virginia, and was sent by Major-General Meade to command the army on the first day of Gettysburg. He went West with his corps, and was commanding at Tullahoma during the battle of Chattanooga. For short periods, in 1864 and 1865, he had charge of the District of Vicksburg. In the Atlanta campaign, he was in command of the Twentieth Corps and during the march to the sea and the Georgia and Carolina campaigns, he was at the head of the Army of Georgia, which formed the left wing of General Sherman's army. At the battle of Bentonville, North Carolina, General Slocum repulsed Johnston's attack, and later was present at the surrender of the Confederate Army. He resigned his commission in 1865, and devoted himself to the law. He died in Brooklyn, New York, April 14, 1894.

Fitz John Porter Commanded the
Fifth Corps on the Peninsula.

George Sykes Commanded the Fifth
Corps at Gettysburg.

William Farrar Smith Led the
Sixth Corps at Fredericksburg.

FEDERAL MAJOR–GENERALS
COMMANDERS OF THE FIFTH AND SIXTH ARMY CORPS

Horatio G. Wright Commanded the
Sixth Corps in the Shenandoah
and Petersburg Campaigns.

William Buel Franklin Commanded
the Sixth Corps on the Peninsula
and at Antietam under McClellan.

Gouverneur Kemble Warren, Long
Associated with the Fifth Corps,
finally as Corps Commander.

Army of the Shenandoah

A FORCE belonging to the Middle Military Division, organized for Major-General P. H. Sheridan, in August, 1864, in order to drive Lieutenant-General Early from the Shenandoah valley. It consisted of the Sixth Corps from the Army of the Potomac, and a detachment of the Nineteenth Corps, Army of the Gulf. There was also a cavalry corps made up of two divisions of the cavalry of the Army of the Potomac. With it acted the troops of the Department of West Virginia, a force created from the Eighth Corps (Middle Department), and sometimes called the Army of West Virginia, under the command of Major-General George Crook. Major-General Wright of the Sixth Corps had charge of the Army of the Shenandoah for a few days in October, 1864, and Major-General A. T. A. Torbert assumed the command in February, 1865, when Sheridan rejoined the Army of the Potomac with the cavalry.

Army of the Frontier

THE FIELD FORCES in Missouri and Kansas were organized into the Army of the Frontier on October 12, 1862. It was commanded by Major-Generals J. M. Schofield and F. J. Herron, and by Major-General James G. Blunt temporarily. It was very active during its existence, and fought many minor engagements in the Southwest, including Clark's Mill, Missouri, and Prairie Grove, Arkansas, and the capture of Van Buren, Arkansas. The army went out of existence June 5, 1863, and its troops were scattered among the districts in Tennessee and Missouri.

MAJOR-GENERAL FRANCIS JAY HERRON was born in Pittsburgh, Pennsylvania, in 1837, and gave up his business career in Iowa to go to the front as lieutenant-colonel of an Iowa regiment. He served in the Army of the Southwest, and was captured at Pea Ridge after conduct that brought him great praise and a medal of honor. He was given a division of the Army of the Frontier, which he commanded at Prairie Grove. From March to June, 1863, he was, as major-general of volunteers, at the head of the army itself. Later, as division commander of the Thirteenth Corps, he was present at the fall of Vicksburg, and also held command in Texas and at Port Hudson. He received the surrender of the Confederate forces west of the Mississippi in May, 1865. He resigned from the service in June, 1865, and practised law in New Orleans and New York. He died January 8, 1902.

MAJOR-GENERAL JAMES G. BLUNT was born in Trenton, Maine, in 1826, and became a physician. He settled in Kansas, where he became prominent for his work in the anti-slavery movement. He went to the Civil War as lieutenant-colonel and was made brigadier-general of volunteers in April, 1862. He was placed at the head of the Department of Kansas on May 5, 1862, and when that department was merged in that of Missouri, on September 19th, he was given a division in the Army of the Frontier. On December 7th, his division and that of Brigadier-General F. J. Herron checked, at Prairie Grove, Arkansas, the advance of Major-General Hindman into Missouri. Blunt was senior officer in command of both divisions in the battle. From June, 1863 to January, 1864, he was at the head of the District of the Frontier, that army having been broken up. From October, 1864, to the end of the war he commanded the District of South Kansas. He died in Washington, D. C., July 25, 1881.

Army of the Mountain Department

CREATED March 11, 1862, from the Department of Western Virginia. On March 29th, Brigadier-General Rosecrans turned over the troops therein to Major-General John C. Fremont. This force co-operated with Banks and McDowell against "Stonewall" Jackson in the Shenandoah valley, and its principal engagements were those at McDowell and Cross Keys. On June 26, 1862, the Mountain Department became the First Corps, Army of Virginia.

John A. Dix Commanded the Seventh Corps
(East) in 1862.

J. J. Reynolds Commanded the Seventh
Corps (West) in 1864.

FEDERAL
MAJOR–
GENERALS
COMMANDERS
OF THE
SEVENTH,
EIGHTH
AND NINTH
ARMY
CORPS

Robert C. Schenck Commanded the Eighth
Corps in 1863.

John E. Wool Commanded the Eighth Corps
in 1862.

John G. Parke Commanded the Ninth Corps
at Petersburg.

Orlando B. Willcox Commanded the Ninth
Army Corps in 1863–4.

First Army Corps

MAJOR-GENERAL JOHN CHARLES FREMONT was born in Savannah, Georgia, January 21, 1813. He became professor of mathematics in the United States navy, and was commissioned second lieutenant in the Corps of Topographical Engineers, in 1838. He conducted several exploring expeditions to the Far West, during one of which he fomented a revolt against Mexican rule in California and raised the Bear Flag in that region. Later, he assisted in the Mexican War and was made civil governor of California by Commodore Stockton. Trouble arose between him and General Kearny, who had been charged with the establishment of the Government, which resulted in a court martial and Fremont's resignation from the army. He settled in California, represented that State in the Senate, and was the unsuccessful Republican candidate for President, in 1856. At the outbreak of the Civil War, he was appointed major-general, and on July 25, 1861, put at the head of the Western Department, with headquarters at St. Louis, where he made an attempt to free the slaves of Southern sympathizers. This act led to his removal in November, and the following March he was given command of the newly created Mountain Department. He refused to serve as corps commander under Major-General Pope when his troops were merged in the Army of Virginia. He resigned from the army in June, 1864. He became interested in railroad building and was governor of Arizona (1878–1882). In 1890, he was reappointed major-general and was retired with that rank on April 28th. He died July 13, 1890.

First Army Corps

THE FIRST ARMY CORPS was originally planned to consist of the troops of the Mountain Department, earlier known as the Department of Western Virginia, under command of Brigadier-General W. S. Rosecrans, but by order of the President, the First Corps, from troops of the Army of the Potomac, was placed under command of Major-General Irvin McDowell, March 13, 1862. On April 4th, the First Corps was discontinued and the troops sent to the Department of the Rappahannock, and then in turn merged in the Army of Virginia, as the Third Corps, on June 26, 1862. The First Corps, Army of the Potomac, was re-created September 12, 1862, from the troops of the Third Corps, Army of Virginia, coming successively under command of Major-General Joseph Hooker, Brigadier-General George G. Meade, Brigadier-General J. S. Wadsworth, Major-Generals J. F. Reynolds, Abner Doubleday, and John Newton. This corps rendered gallant service at South Mountain, Antietam, Fredericksburg, Chancellorsville, and Gettysburg, among the more important engagements. It was discontinued March 24, 1864, when it became merged in the Fifth Corps, Army of the Potomac.

MAJOR-GENERAL IRVIN McDOWELL (U.S.M.A. 1838) was born in Columbus, Ohio, October 15, 1818. He rendered distinguished service in the Mexican War. As brigadier-general at the head of the Department of Northeastern Virginia, he had command of the Union army at First Bull Run. Afterward, with a commission of major-general of volunteers, he had a division in the Army of the Potomac. In further reorganizations and changes he headed his troops as commander of the First Corps, Army of the Potomac; Department of the Rappahannock, and Third Corps, Army of Virginia. His conspicuous services at Cedar Mountain won him the brevet of major-general, which full rank he attained in 1872. Immediately after Second Bull Run he was relieved from field service, and was president of several army boards. In July, 1864, he was placed at the head of the Department of the Pacific, and after the war held various commands. He was retired in 1882, and died in San Francisco, May 4, 1885.

MAJOR-GENERAL ABNER DOUBLEDAY (U.S. M.A. 1842) was born at Ballston Spa, New York, June 26, 1819, and served in the Mexican and Seminole wars. As captain of the artillery he was at Fort Sumter under Major Anderson, and fired upon the Confederates the first Federal gun of the Civil War. He served under Major-General Patterson in the Valley, and on February 3, 1862, was made brigadier-general of volunteers and placed in charge of the defenses of Washington. He had a brigade in the Third Corps, Army of Virginia, and afterward a division, which he retained when the corps again became the First

J. M. Brannan Commanded the
Tenth Corps in 1862–63.

FEDERAL

MAJOR–

GENERALS

COMMANDERS

OF   THE

TENTH ARMY CORPS

W. T. H. Brooks Commanded
the Tenth Corps in 1864.

David B. Birney Commanded
the Tenth Corps in 1864.

Ormsby M. Mitchel Commanded the
Tenth Corps in 1862.

Alfred H. Terry Commanded the Tenth
Corps in 1864–65.

Second Army Corps

Corps, Army of the Potomac. In November, 1862, he became major-general of volunteers. He fought at Fredericksburg and Chancellorsville. When Reynolds was killed on the field of Gettysburg, the command of the First Corps fell upon him for the day, July 1, 1863, until he was succeeded by Major-General John Newton. After being mustered out of the volunteer service, he served as colonel in the regular army until he was retired in 1873. He had been brevetted brigadier and major-general in 1865. Major-General Doubleday was the author of several important military works. He died January 27, 1893, at Mendham, New Jersey.

Major-General John Newton (U.S.M.A. 1842) was born in Norfolk, Virginia, August 24, 1823. After graduation he taught engineering at West Point for three years, and then devoted himself to the construction of fortifications. The outbreak of the Civil War found him chief engineer of the Department of Pennsylvania, and he assisted in preparing the defenses of the national capital. The rank of brigadier-general of volunteers was given him in September, 1861, and he remained with the organization which was eventually the First Corps, Army of the Potomac, as brigade and division commander, being made major-general of volunteers in March, 1863. He succeeded to the command of the corps after Reynolds' death at Gettysburg, July 1, 1863, and led it until it was discontinued, March 24, 1864. His appointment as major-general of volunteers expired in April, 1864, and with his former title he succeeded Sheridan in a division of the Fourth Corps,

Army of the Cumberland. After the war, he continued in the regular army and reached the grade of brigadier-general in 1884, being retired in 1886. His most renowned achievement was the removal of the reefs at Hell Gate in the harbor of New York. General Newton was commissioner of public works, New York city, from 1887 to 1888, and then president of the Panama Railroad Company. He died, May 1, 1895.

Major-General John Fulton Reynolds (U. S.M.A. 1841) was born in Lancaster, Pennsylvania, September 20, 1820, and served in the Mexican War, and in the Rogue River Indian and Utah expeditions. At the outbreak of the Civil War, he was commandant at West Point, but with the rank of brigadier-general of volunteers took active part in the operations of the Army of the Potomac from August, 1861. He commanded a brigade of the Pennsylvania Reserves which was merged in the First Corps, Army of the Potomac. He went with McDowell to the Department of the Rappahannock but returned to the Army of the Potomac at the head of a brigade in the Fifth Corps, for the move to the James. He was taken prisoner at Glendale but was exchanged. The brigade joined the Third Corps, Army of Virginia, in which Reynolds commanded a division. Again with the Army of the Potomac, Reynolds was given the First Corps on September 29, 1862, and later was made major-general of volunteers. On the first day of Gettysburg, July 1, 1863, he was killed by a Confederate sharpshooter. Reynolds' loss was most keenly felt in the Federal army.

Second Army Corps

Created by the general order of March 3, 1862, chiefly from Sumner's and Blenker's divisions of the Army of the Potomac as constituted in October, 1861. Major-General Sumner was its first commander, and his successors were Major-Generals D. N. Couch, John Sedgwick, O. O. Howard, W. S. Hancock, G. K. Warren, D. B. Birney, A. A. Humphreys, Brevet Major-Generals Gershom Mott, N. A. Miles, and F. C. Barlow, and Brigadier-Generals John Gibbon, William Hays, and J. C. Caldwell. The Second Corps was with the Army of the Potomac all through the war and took part in all its great engagements. It suffered most severely at Antietam. It was discon-

tinued June 28, 1865. The Second Corps made a notable record for itself. One interesting fact is that until the battle of Spotsylvania, on May 10, 1864, it never lost a gun or a color.

Major-General Edwin Vose Sumner was born in Boston, January 30, 1797, enlisting in the army in 1819. He rendered distinguished service in the Black Hawk and Mexican wars, and was military governor of New Mexico from 1851 to 1853. As brigadier-general, he superseded Brevet Brigadier-General Albert Sidney Johnston in the command of the Department of the Pacific in April, 1861. He came East to participate in

FEDERAL

MAJOR-GENERALS

Franz Sigel Commanded the 11th Corps.

John M. Palmer Commanded the 14th Corps.

COMMANDERS

OF THE

ELEVENTH

TWELFTH

THIRTEENTH

AND

FOURTEENTH

ARMY CORPS

Jeff C. Davis Commanded the 14th Corps.

C. C. Washburn Commanded the 13th Corps.

George W. Morgan Commanded the 13th Corps.

Alpheus S. Williams Commanded the 12th Corps.

the Civil War, and became the first commander of the Second Army Corps. He was made major-general of volunteers, July 4, 1862. He was wounded in the Peninsula campaign and also at Antietam. Upon Burnside's reorganization of the army, he commanded the Right Grand Division. When Hooker was put at the head, Major-General Sumner was relieved at his own request, and sent to the Department of Missouri. But he died on the way there, at Syracuse, New York, March 21, 1863.

MAJOR-GENERAL DARIUS NASH COUCH (U.S. M.A. 1846) was born in Putnam County, New York, July 23, 1822, and served in the Mexican and the Seminole wars, being brevetted first lieutenant in the former. In 1855, he resigned from the army and entered mercantile life in New York city, but returned to his profession at the opening of the Civil War as colonel of volunteers. He was identified with the Department and Army of the Potomac, first as brigade commander (August, 1861–March, 1862), then as division commander in the Fourth Army Corps to September, 1862, when he was made major-general of volunteers and his division was transferred to the Sixth Corps. In October, 1862, Couch was placed at the head of the Second Corps, which he led at Fredericksburg and at Chancellorsville. From June, 1863, to December, 1864, he was at the head of the Department of the Susquehanna, when he was given a division of the Twenty-third Army Corps, and fought at the battle of Nashville. He resigned from the army in 1865, and was defeated for governor of Massachusetts on the Democratic ticket in the same year. Subsequently, he was collector of the port of Boston, and quartermaster-general and adjutant-general of Connecticut. He died in Norwalk, Connecticut, February 12, 1897.

BRIGADIER-GENERAL WILLIAM HAYS (U.S.M.A. 1840) was born in Richmond, Virginia, in 1819, and served in the Mexican War. As lieutenant-colonel he had a brigade of horse artillery in the Army of the Potomac through the Peninsula campaign, the artillery reserve at Antietam, and the artillery of the Right Grand Division at Fredericksburg. In November, 1862, he was made brigadier-general of volunteers, and at Chancellorsville, in command of a brigade in the Second Army Corps he was wounded and captured. He was exchanged, and after the wounding of Hancock at Gettysburg, he had command

of the corps for a short time. Then he spent some time in the Department of the East and later had a brigade in the Second Corps. He died in Fort Independence, Boston Harbor, February 7, 1875.

MAJOR-GENERAL GERSHOM MOTT was born in Trenton, New Jersey, April 7, 1822, and served in the Mexican War. He went to the front in the Civil War as lieutenant-colonel of the Fifth New Jersey Infantry, and later became colonel of the Sixth New Jersey. In September, 1862, he was promoted to brigadier-general of volunteers, and had a brigade in the Third Corps from December, 1862, to March, 1864, and then had consecutively two divisions of the Second Corps. Several times he took command of the corps during the absence of Major-General Humphreys. Mott was brevetted major-general of volunteers in August, 1864, and received the title May 28, 1865, shortly before being mustered out. After the war, he was at one time treasurer of the State of New Jersey, and died in New York city, November 29, 1884.

MAJOR-GENERAL NELSON APPLETON MILES was born in Westminster, Massachusetts, August 8, 1839. He entered mercantile life, but went to the front in the Civil War as first lieutenant in the Twenty-second Massachusetts Infantry, and in May, 1862, he was made lieutenant-colonel of the Sixty-first New York Infantry. By September he had risen to a colonelcy of volunteers. He fought with the Army of the Potomac in all its battles and was wounded at Chancellorsville. From March to July, 1864, he had a brigade in the Second Corps and was made brigadier-general in May. The rank of major-general of volunteers was given him in October, 1865. After the war he entered the regular army as colonel, and his chief service was against the Indians in the West. In the Spanish-American War he commanded the United States army, and personally led the Porto Rico expedition, and upon the reorganization of the Army of the United States he was appointed lieutenant-general (1900), being retired with that rank three years later.

MAJOR-GENERAL WINFIELD SCOTT HANCOCK (U.S.M.A. 1844) was born in Montgomery Square, Pennsylvania, February 14, 1824. He served in the Mexican War and in the border troubles in Kansas, and had risen to the rank of captain when the Civil War broke out. He was

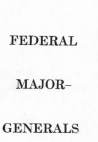

FEDERAL

MAJOR–

GENERALS

P. J. Osterhaus Commanded the Fifteenth
Corps in 1864.

S. A. Hurlbut Commanded the Sixteenth
Corps in 1863.

J. A. Mower Commanded the Seventeenth
Corps in the Carolinas.

J. G. Foster Commanded the Eighteenth
Army Corps in 1864.

COMMANDERS

OF THE

FIFTEENTH

SIXTEENTH

SEVENTEENTH

EIGHTEENTH

AND

NINETEENTH

ARMY CORPS

John H. Martindale Commanded the Eighteenth Corps in Front of Richmond.

William H. Emory Commanded the Nineteenth Corps in the Shenandoah Valley.

made brigadier-general of volunteers in September, 1861, and had a brigade in the Fourth Army Corps at Williamsburg, where McClellan called him "Hancock the Superb." At Antietam, he distinguished himself, and succeeded Richardson at the head of a division of the Second Corps. In November, 1862, he was made major-general of volunteers. His troops did noteworthy work at Fredericksburg and Chancellorsville, and Hancock received the Second Corps, in May, 1863. At Gettysburg, Meade sent him to take charge on the first day, after Reynolds' death, and on the third day he himself was severely wounded. In March, 1864, he resumed command of the Second Corps. He took charge of the Department of West Virginia and Middle Military Division in March, 1865. After the war, he became major-general in 1866, and commanded various departments. He was an unsuccessful candidate for the presidency against Garfield. Of Hancock, General Grant once said: " Hancock stands the most conspicuous figure of all the general officers who did not exercise a separate command. He commanded a corps longer than any other one, and his name was never mentioned as having committed in battle a blunder for which he was responsible." He died on Governor's Island, New York, February 9, 1886.

MAJOR-GENERAL ANDREW ATKINSON HUMPHREYS (U.S.M.A. 1831) was born in Philadelphia, November 2, 1810. He was closely associated with engineering and coast-survey work until the outbreak of the Civil War, when, as major, he became a member of Major-General McClellan's staff. In April, 1862, he was made brigadier-general of volunteers and was chief topographical engineer of the Army of the Potomac during the Peninsula campaign. He had a division of the Fifth Corps from September, 1862, to May, 1863, and fought at Fredericksburg and Chancellorsville. He was then given a division of the Third Corps, and after Gettysburg was promoted to major-general of volunteers and made General Meade's chief of staff. In the final campaign against Lee, he had the Second Corps (November, 1864, to June, 1865). After being mustered out of the volunteer service, September 1, 1866, he was made brigadier-general and placed at the head of the Engineer Corps of the United States army. He was retired in July, 1879, and died in Washington, December 27, 1883. He received brevets for gallant and meritorious services at the battles of Fredericksburg, Va., Gettysburg, Pa., and Sailors Creek, Va.

MAJOR-GENERAL JOHN GIBBON (U.S.M.A. 1847) was born in Holmesburg, Pennsylvania, April 27, 1827, and served in the Mexican War. Later, he was instructor in artillery practice and quartermaster at West Point. He had reached the grade of captain when the Civil War broke out, and became McDowell's chief of artillery. He was promoted to brigadier-general of volunteers in May, 1862. He had a brigade in the Third Corps, Army of Virginia, and a brigade and division in the First Corps, Army of the Potomac. He was given a division in the Second Army Corps, which he held for the most part until August, 1864. When Hancock was sent by Meade to take charge at Gettysburg on the first day, Gibbon was given temporary command of the corps and was seriously wounded. As major-general of volunteers, he had command of the Eighteenth and Twenty-fourth army corps for short periods. When mustered out of the volunteer service, he continued in the regular army as colonel, and rose to be brigadier-general in 1885. He did much Indian fighting, and in 1891 was retired from active service. He died in Baltimore, February 6, 1896.

MAJOR-GENERAL FRANCIS CHANNING BARLOW was born in Brooklyn, New York, October 19, 1834, and was a Harvard graduate of 1855. He enlisted as a private in the Twelfth New York Militia, and after the three months' service had expired, he returned to the field as lieutenant-colonel of the Sixty-first New York. His rise was rapid, due to ability displayed in the Army of the Potomac, and he was made brigadier-general of volunteers after the battle of Antietam (September, 1862), where he was badly wounded. He had a brigade in the Eleventh Corps at Chancellorsville, and a division at Gettysburg, when he was again badly wounded. On recovery, he was assigned to duty in the Department of the South and afterward given a division in the Second Army Corps, March 1864, and served until the Army of the Potomac was discontinued. He was made major-general of volunteers in May, 1865, for his conspicuous gallantry at the battle of Spotsylvania. In April and May, 1865, he had command of the Second Corps. General Barlow resigned from the army November 16, 1865, and returned to New York, where he entered political life and resumed the practice of law. He was secretary of state of New York 1865–1868, and attorney-general for New York from 1871 to 1873, in which capacity he conducted the prosecution of "Boss" Tweed and other municipal officials. He died in New York city, January 11, 1896.

FEDERAL
MAJOR–GENERALS
COMMANDERS
OF
ARMY
CORPS

TWENTIETH

TWENTY-FIRST

TWENTY-SECOND

TWENTY-THIRD

TWENTY-FOURTH

AND

TWENTY-FIFTH

CORPS

A. McD. McCook Commanded the
Twentieth Corps at Chickamauga.

Thos. L. Crittenden Commanded the
Twenty-first Corps in 1863.

C. C. Augur Commanded the Twenty-
second Corps at Port Hudson.

G. L. Hartsuff Commanded the Twenty-
third Corps in 1863.

E. O. C. Ord Commanded the Twenty-
fourth Corps in 1865.

Godfrey Weitzel Commanded the
Twenty-fifth Corps in 1864-5.

Third Army Corps

On the reorganization of the Army of the Potomac in March, 1862, a body of troops, chiefly from Heintzelman's, Porter's and Hooker's divisions of the earlier organization, was constituted the Third Army Corps. In May, Porter's men were transferred to the new provisional Fifth Army Corps. The future additions to the corps were chiefly from the Eighth and Twenty-second corps. The corps fought in the battles of the Army of the Potomac, and two divisions were sent to the assistance of the Army of Virginia at Second Bull Run and Chantilly. On March 24, 1864, it was merged in the Second Corps. Its commanders were Brigadier-Generals S. P. Heintzelman and George Stoneman, and Major-Generals D. E. Sickles, D. B. Birney, and W. H. French.

Major-General Samuel Peter Heintzelman (U.S.M.A. 1826) was born in Manheim, Pennsylvania, September 30, 1805, and served on the frontier, in Florida, in the Mexican War, and in California and Texas. At the opening of the Civil War he was promoted to a colonelcy, and became inspector-general of the defenses of Washington. In May, 1861, he was placed in command at Alexandria, Virginia. He headed the Third Division at Bull Run, and in subsequent organizations of the Army of the Potomac he had a brigade, a division, and afterward the Third Corps, which he commanded until November, 1862. His conduct at Fair Oaks won him a brevet of brigadier-general, for he was now major-general of volunteers. He fought through the Peninsula campaign, and was sent to assist Pope at Second Bull Run and Chantilly. He was in command of the defenses and later of the Department of Washington (Twenty-second Army Corps) from September, 1862, to October, 1863. After this, he took no active part in the war, but was commander of the Northern Department from January to October, 1864, and then served on court martials. He was mustered out of the volunteer service August, 1865, and was retired from the army with the rank of major-general, February 22, 1869. He died in Washington, May 3, 1880.

Major-General George Stoneman (U.S.M.A. 1846) was born in Busti, New York, August 8, 1822, and was captain in command at Fort Brown, Texas, when the Civil War broke out. He refused to obey the order of General Twiggs to surrender the property of the United States Government to the State of Texas, and escaped by steamer to New York. His first active service in the Civil War was as major in the West Virginia campaign, and as brigadier-general of volunteers he had the cavalry command in the Army of the Potomac. It was his troops that brought on the action at Williamsburg in May, 1862. After the death of Major-General Kearny, at Chantilly, he succeeded eventually to the command of his division, and later succeeded Major-General Heintzelman in the command of the Third Army Corps, which he led at Fredericksburg. He was promoted to major-general of volunteers in command of the Cavalry Corps, Army of the Potomac, and led a famous raid toward Richmond during the Chancellorsville campaign. From January to April, 1864, he was in command of the Twenty-third Army Corps, and then received the cavalry division of the same organization. After a raid in the Atlanta campaign, in which he was captured and held prisoner for three months, he assumed command of the Department of the Ohio, and later the District of East Tennessee, where his operations were very successful, especially his raid into North Carolina, in April, 1865. He was retired from the regular army with the rank of colonel, in 1871, and went to California, of which State he was governor from 1883 to 1887. He died in Buffalo, New York, September 5, 1894.

Major-General Daniel Edgar Sickles was born in New York city, October 20, 1825. Admitted to the bar in 1846, he afterward served in the State legislature, the diplomatic service, and in Congress, where he was when the Civil War broke out. He raised the Excelsior Brigade of five New York regiments, which served in the Army of the Potomac with Sickles as brigadier-general of volunteers at its head. In March, 1862, it was incorporated in the Third Army Corps. He led his brigade through the Peninsula campaign, commanded a division at Fredericksburg and, as major-general of volunteers, the Third Corps at Chancellorsville and Gettysburg. In the latter battle he lost a leg on the second day. He continued in the army after the close of the war, and was retired with rank of major-general in 1869. He went on a secret diplomatic mission to South America in 1867, and was minister to Spain, 1869–1873. He was sheriff of New York County, in 1890, and Democratic member of Congress, 1892–94, as well as president of the New

John E. Phelps, of Arkansas—
Colonel of the 2d Cavalry.

Marcus La Rue, of Arkansas—
Promoted for Gallantry.

John B. Slough, of Colorado—
Engaged in New Mexico.

Patrick E. Connor, of California—Colonel of the 3d Infantry.

FEDERAL GENERALS—No. 1—ARKANSAS (first two above). COLORADO (third above).
CALIFORNIA (fourth above and six below).

James Shields, Brave Irish Soldier,
A Friend of Lincoln.

George S. Evans, Originally Colonel
of the 2d Cavalry.

George W. Bowie, Originally Colonel
of the 5th Infantry.

Edward McGarry, Brevetted for
Conspicuous Gallantry.

James W. Denver; Denver, Colo.,
Named After Him.

J. H. Carleton Commanded a Column
in March Across Arizona.

This is the first of 29 groups embracing representative general officers of 34 states and territories. On preceding pages portraits appear of many leaders, including all the commanders of armies and army corps, and all generals killed in battle. Many others appear in preceding volumes, as identified with particular events or special branches, such as cavalry and artillery and the signal and medical corps. Information of every general officer can be found through the index and the roster concluding this volume.

Fourth Army Corps (Potomac)

York State Board of Civil Service Commissioners for several years.

MAJOR-GENERAL WILLIAM HENRY FRENCH (U.S.M.A. 1837) was born in Baltimore, January 13, 1815, and served in the Seminole and Mexican wars. In September, 1861, he was appointed brigadier-general of volunteers and major-general of volunteers the following year. He had a brigade in Sumner's Division, a division in the Second Corps, Army of the Potomac, and for a short time a command in the Eighth Corps, that joined the Third Corps after the battle of Gettysburg. He was in command of the Third Corps, from July 7, 1863, to January 28, 1864, and again from February 17th to March 24, 1864. In May, 1864, he was mustered out of the volunteer service, and was brevetted major-general the following year. In the regular army he rose to the rank of colonel in 1877, and, in 1880, was retired from active service. He died in Baltimore, May 20, 1881.

Fourth Army Corps (Potomac)

CREATED March 3, 1862, chiefly from troops in Couch's, W. F. Smith's, and Casey's divisions of the earlier Army of the Potomac, together with some new organizations. It was commanded by Major-General E. D. Keyes. The corps fought through the Peninsula campaign and remained in that region when the rest of the Army of the Potomac withdrew. The troops were gradually sent to other corps of the army—to North Carolina, Washington, and other places, and the corps was discontinued on August 1, 1863.

MAJOR-GENERAL ERASMUS DARWIN KEYES (U. S.M.A. 1832) was born in Brimfield, Massachusetts, May 29, 1810. He did duty on the Western frontier until the Civil War began, when he was raised to a colonelcy and made brigadier-general of volunteers in May, 1861. He commanded a brigade at Bull Run, and eventually was put in command of the Fourth Army Corps when it was created. His appointment as major-general of volunteers was dated from the battle of Williamsburg, and he received a brevet of brigadier-general in the regular army for his gallant and meritorious service at Fair Oaks. He resigned from the army in May, 1864, and went to California. He died in Nice, France, October 11, 1895.

Fourth Army Corps (Cumberland)

THE TWENTIETH AND TWENTY-FIRST army corps were consolidated on September 28, 1863, and the new organization was designated the Fourth Army Corps—the first one of that name, in the Army of the Potomac, having passed out of existence. It was commanded by Major-Generals Gordon Granger, O. O. Howard, D. S. Stanley, and Brigadier-General T. J. Wood. The corps fought in the battle of Chattanooga, was sent to the relief of Knoxville, and took part in the Atlanta campaign. When Sherman turned back toward Atlanta from Gaylesville, Alabama, the Fourth Corps went into Tennessee for the campaign against Hood. It fought at Franklin and Nashville, and was discontinued April 1, 1865.

MAJOR-GENERAL DAVID SLOAN STANLEY (U.S. M.A. 1852) was born in Cedar Valley, Ohio, June 1, 1828. He distinguished himself by his services, at the beginning of the Civil War, in the Southwest, at Dug Springs and Wilson's Creek. As brigadier-general of volunteers he had a division in the Army of the Mississippi and fought at Island No. 10, Iuka, and Corinth. In November, 1862, he became chief of cavalry in the Army of the Cumberland, and soon afterward was made major-general of volunteers. In November, 1863, he received a division of the Fourth Corps and became its head in July, 1864, when Major-General Howard took command of the Army of the Tennessee. Major-General Stanley was wounded at Franklin, November 30, 1864, and this ended his active service in the war, although he again headed the corps from February to August, 1865. Later on, he was given a colonelcy in the regular army and fought against the Indians in the

Orris S. Ferry, of Connecticut, Colonel of the 5th Regiment, Later U. S. Senator.

Joseph R. Hawley, of Connecticut, Distinguished at the Battle of Olustee.

Henry W. Birge, of Connecticut, Commander of a Division in the 19th Corps.

Henry W. Wessells, of Connecticut, Led Troops on the Peninsula in 1862.

H. H. Lockwood, of Delaware, Commander of a Brigade at Gettysburg.

Robert O. Tyler, of Connecticut, Commanded Artillery at Fredericksburg.

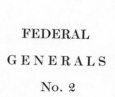

Lorenzo Thomas, of Delaware, Adjutant-General of the United States Army.

Daniel Tyler, of Connecticut, Led the Advance at Bull Run, 1861.

FEDERAL

GENERALS

No. 2

John B. S. Todd, of Dakota Territory, Appointed Brigadier-General to Date from September 19, 1861.

CONNECTICUT

DAKOTA

DELAWARE

Northwest. He was made brigadier-general in 1884, and was retired in 1892. He died in Washington, D. C., March 13, 1902.

MAJOR-GENERAL THOMAS JOHN WOOD (U.S. M.A. 1845) was born in Mumfordville, Kentucky, September 25, 1823, and served in the Mexican War. As brigadier-general of volunteers he had a brigade and then a division in the Army of the Ohio, a division of the Left Wing (Fourteenth Corps), Army of the Cumberland, which was continued in the Twenty-first Corps when the Left Wing was reorganized, and likewise in the Fourth Corps until it was discontinued. He had command of the Twenty-first and Fourth corps for short periods, succeeding Stanley in the latter at Franklin and leading it at Nashville. He was wounded at Stone's River and in the Atlanta campaign. He was made major-general of volunteers in January, 1865, and was mustered out of the volunteer service in 1866, having been brevetted major-general in 1865. He was retired in 1868, and died in Dayton, Ohio, February 25, 1906.

Fifth Army Corps

ON THE ORGANIZATION of the Army of the Potomac into corps, March 3, 1862, the Fifth Army Corps was created and given to Major-General N. P. Banks. But this corps was detached, April 4th, from the Army of the Potomac and assigned, with its commander, to the Department of the Shenandoah, and was made the Second Corps of the Army of Virginia, in June. On May 18th, a new Fifth Corps was created and existed provisionally until confirmed by the War Department. It was composed, at first, of Brigadier-General Porter's division of the Third Corps, and Brigadier-General Sykes' troops of the regular army. Other bodies of troops were added from time to time, and the First Corps was merged in it, when the Army of the Potomac was reorganized in March, 1864. It was commanded from time to time by Brigadier-General F. J. Porter, Major-General Joseph Hooker, Brigadier-General Daniel Butterfield, Major-Generals George G. Meade, Charles Griffin, George Sykes, and A. A. Humphreys, Brevet Major-General S. K. Crawford, and Major-General G. K. Warren. The corps fought in whole or in part through all the battles of the Army of the Potomac.

MAJOR-GENERAL FITZ JOHN PORTER (U.S.M.A. 1845) was born in Portsmouth, New Hampshire, June 13, 1822, served in the Mexican War, and afterward taught at West Point. He was assistant adjutant-general in Albert Sidney Johnston's Utah expedition, in 1857. When the Civil War broke out, he was appointed brigadier-general of volunteers and served as chief of staff to Patterson and Banks. He was given a division in the Army of the Potomac, and after it had been assigned to the Third Corps it was made the basis of the Fifth Corps, of which Porter was given command on May 18, 1862, just before McClellan's advance to the Chickahominy. After fighting through the Peninsula campaign, Porter was made major-general of volunteers, and went with his corps to the assistance of Pope and the Army of Virginia. At Second Bull Run, his action on an order from Major-General Pope led to his dismissal from the army. After long years of struggle, in 1886 he succeeded in being restored to the army with the rank of colonel, and shortly afterward was retired. He was engaged in business in New York and held several municipal offices. He died in Morristown, New Jersey, May 21, 1901.

MAJOR-GENERAL DANIEL BUTTERFIELD was born in Utica, New York, October 31, 1831, and was graduated from Union College. Early in the Civil War he became colonel of the Twelfth New York Volunteers, and brigadier-general of volunteers, taking part in the campaigns of McClellan, Burnside, Hooker, and Pope. At Fredericksburg, he had command of the Fifth Army Corps, and afterward became chief-of-staff to the commanding general. He went with Hooker to Chattanooga in October, 1863, and was his chief-of-staff until given a division in the Twentieth Army Corps, which he commanded until July, 1864. At the close of the war he was mustered out of the volunteer service and was brevetted major-general in the United States Army. He resigned from the army in 1869, and was United States treasurer in New York city, 1869–1870. He died at Cold Spring, New York, July 17, 1901.

FEDERAL
GENERALS
No. 3

DISTRICT OF
COLUMBIA
(UPPER TWO)

ILLINOIS
(NINE BELOW)

George W. Getty Led a Division
in the Army of the Potomac.

Samuel Sprigg Carroll, Brevetted
for Gallantry at Spotsylvania.

Isham Nichols
Haynie, Orig-
inally Colonel
of the 48th Reg-
iment.

Joseph Adal-
mon Maltby,
Originally Col-
onel of the 45th
Regiment.

Thomas E. G. Ranson Commanded
the 16th Army Corps.

E. N. Kirk, Severely Wounded in Re-
sisting the Attack on Johnson's
Division at Stone's River.

John F. Farnsworth, Originally
Colonel of the 8th Cavalry.

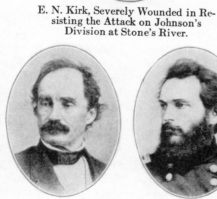

Alexander C. McClurg, Chief of
Staff, 14th Army Corps.

Abner Clark Hardin,
Promoted for Gallan-
try at Donelson.

Charles E. Hovey, a
Gallant Division
Commander.

John McArthur, Conspicuous
as a Division Commander.

Sixth Army Corps

MAJOR-GENERAL GOUVERNEUR KEMBLE WARREN (U.S.M.A. 1850) was born at Cold Spring, New York, January 8, 1830. He made a specialty of topographical engineering, and was assistant professor of mathematics at West Point until the beginning of the Civil War, when he came into active service as lieutenant-colonel of the Fifth New York Volunteers. His promotion was rapid, and he reached the rank of major-general of volunteers in May, 1863. He served as brigade and division commander in the Fifth Army Corps, and in January, 1863, became chief topographical engineer, and, later, chief engineer of the Army of the Potomac. His service to the Union cause in defending Little Round Top at Gettysburg won him a brevet of colonel in the regular army. For a short time after Gettysburg he was in command of the Second Corps, and from March, 1864, to April, 1865, of the Fifth Corps, Army of the Potomac; after which he served for a short time in the Department of Mississippi. He left the volunteer service in May, 1865, having received the brevet of major-general in the regular army, in which he remained until February 13, 1866, when he resigned. His last years were spent on surveys and harbor improvements, and he died at Newport, Rhode Island, August 8, 1882.

MAJOR-GENERAL GEORGE SYKES (U.S.M.A. 1842) was born in Dover, Delaware, October 9, 1822, and served in the Mexican and Seminole wars. As major, he entered the Civil War, and was commissioned brigadier-general of volunteers in September, 1861. He led a division of the Fifth Army Corps and was commander for several short periods, notably at the battle of Gettysburg. His commission of major-general of volunteers was dated November 29, 1862. In September–October, 1864, he was in command of the District of South Kansas. After leaving the volunteer service he was made colonel in the regular army, where he remained until he died in Brownsville, Texas, February 9, 1880.

MAJOR-GENERAL CHARLES GRIFFIN (U.S.M.A. 1847) was born in Licking County, Ohio, in 1826, and served in the Mexican War and on the frontier. He was captain when the Civil War broke out, at the head of the Fifth Artillery. His battery fought with great bravery at Bull Run. As brigadier-general of volunteers, he had a brigade and then a division in the Fifth Army Corps, and took part in most of its important battles. He was given command of the corps on April 1, 1865, from which dated his appointment as major-general of volunteers. He led his corps in the final operations against Petersburg, and at Lee's surrender he received the arms and colors of the Army of Northern Virginia. He was one of the commission to carry out the terms of the surrender. After the close of the war, as colonel in the regular army, he was in command of the Department of Texas, where, during an outbreak of yellow fever, he refused to leave his post. Contracting the disease, he died in Galveston, September 15, 1867.

Sixth Army Corps

THE CREATION of this corps was similar to that of the Fifth, on May 18, 1862. Its basis was Brigadier-General W. B. Franklin's division, which was transferred from the Department of the Rappahannock (McDowell's command) and Brigadier-General W. F. Smith's division of the Fourth Army Corps. Franklin was the first commander, and he was followed by Major-Generals W. F. Smith, John Sedgwick, Brigadier-General J. B. Ricketts, Major-General H. G. Wright, and Brevet Major-General G. W. Getty. One division of the corps was prominent at Gaines' Mill, where there were about twenty thousand men present for duty, and it was partially engaged at Second Bull Run, South Mountain, Antietam, and Fredericksburg. In the last battle it was in the Left Grand Division. The corps carried Marye's Heights in the Chancellorsville campaign, but, excepting one brigade, it was held in reserve at Gettysburg. Several changes were made in the reorganization of March, 1864, and with about twenty-five thousand men at the opening of the Wilderness campaign, it fought with the Army of the Potomac as far as Petersburg, when it was sent to the defense of Washington. Afterward it joined the Army of the Shenandoah and was prominent at the Opequon, Fisher's Hill, and Cedar Creek. In December, 1864, the corps returned to Petersburg and continued with the Army of the Potomac until it was discontinued, June 28, 1865.

P. S. Post. Originally Colonel of the 59th Regiment, Led a Brigade at Stone's River and Nashville.

Julius White, Originally Colonel of the 37th Regiment.

James Grant Wilson, Originally Colonel of the 4th U. S. Cavalry.

John W. Turner, Commander of a Division at Drewry's Bluff and in the Siege of Petersburg.

August Mersy, Originally Colonel of the 9th Infantry.

Benjamin M. Prentiss, Noted for His Heroic Defense at Shiloh.

John Eugene Smith, Originally Colonel of the 45th Regiment.

Leonard F. Ross, Originally Colonel of the 17th Regiment.

Richard J. Oglesby, Conspicuous at Corinth, where He was Wounded.

Hasbrouck Davis Led his Command out of the Net at Harper's Ferry.

Elias S. Dennis, Originally Colonel of the 30th Regiment; Conspicuous at Mobile.

John C. Black, Originally Colonel of the 37th Regiment.

Michael K. Lawler Promoted for Gallant Service Throughout the War.

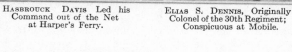

Giles A. Smith Commander of a Division in Georgia and the Carolinas.

FEDERAL GENERALS—No. 4—ILLINOIS

MAJOR-GENERAL WILLIAM BUEL FRANKLIN (U.S.M.A. 1843) was born in York, Pennsylvania, February 27, 1823, and served in the Mexican War. He was also an engineer, and taught at West Point. At the opening of the Civil War, as colonel, he had a brigade at Bull Run, and subsequently a division in the First Corps, Army of the Potomac, which formed the nucleus of the Sixth when it was ordered to McClellan on the Peninsula, after having gone with McDowell to the Department of the Rappahannock. Franklin rose to be major-general of volunteers, his commission being dated July 4, 1862. In Burnside's reorganization of the Army of the Potomac, he commanded the Left Grand Division at Fredericksburg. His conduct in this battle was unsatisfactory to Burnside, and Franklin was relieved from duty in the service. In August, 1863, he was put in command of the Nineteenth Army Corps, serving until May, 1864, and was wounded at Sabine Cross Roads on the Red River expedition. From December, 1864, to November, 1865, he was at the head of a board for retiring disabled officers. On the latter date he resigned from the volunteer service, and gave up the regular army, in which he had been brevetted major-general on March 15, 1866. He then became vice-president of the Colt Firearms Company, and was American commissioner-general to the Paris Exposition of 1889. He died in Hartford, Connecticut, March 8, 1903.

MAJOR-GENERAL JOHN SEDGWICK (U.S.M.A. 1837) was born in Cornwall, Connecticut, September 13, 1813. He served with great distinction in the Mexican and Seminole wars. At the outbreak of the Civil War, he was lieutenant-colonel in the cavalry, and he rose to major-general of volunteers by July, 1862. After having a brigade in the Army of the Potomac, he was given a division of the Second Corps, and it met with frightful loss at Antietam, where Sedgwick was twice wounded. After recovery he took command of the Second and Ninth corps for short periods, and in February, 1863, he became head of the Sixth Army Corps, with which his name is so nobly associated. His brave attack upon the heights of Fredericksburg in May, 1863, won him renown. At Gettysburg, which he reached by a forced march on the second day, the left wing of the army was under his command. He was killed by a Confederate sharpshooter near Spotsylvania Court House, May 9, 1864.

MAJOR-GENERAL HORATIO GOUVERNEUR WRIGHT (U.S.M.A. 1841) was born in Clinton, Connecticut, March 6, 1820. At the beginning of the Civil War he had the rank of captain, having been in the Engineers Corps since his graduation. He was chief engineer of the expedition that destroyed the Norfolk Navy-Yard and occupied the same position in the Port Royal expedition. He was division commander in the Department of the South, and was then placed at the head of the re-created Department of the Ohio in August, 1862. Later, he was division and corps commander of the Sixth Army Corps. Being sent by Grant to defend Washington, he took part in the Shenandoah campaign and rejoined the Army of the Potomac before Petersburg. He led the assault on April 2, 1865, which ended the siege. He was promoted to major-general of volunteers in May, 1864. He served on several important commissions after the war, being made brigadier-general in 1879, and was retired from the army in 1884. He died in Washington, July 2, 1899.

Seventh Army Corps

THE TROOPS in the Department of Virginia at Fort Monroe, Norfolk, Portsmouth, and elsewhere, were organized into the Seventh Army Corps, on July 22, 1862, which existed until discontinued on August 1, 1863, when the troops were merged in the Eighteenth Army Corps. It was commanded in turn by Major-General John A. Dix and Brigadier-Generals H. M. Naglee and G. W. Getty. Its principal engagements were the affair at Deserted House, Virginia, and the defense of Suffolk, when besieged by Longstreet in 1863. Its greatest strength, present for duty, was about thirty-three thousand.

MAJOR-GENERAL JOHN ADAMS DIX was born in Boscawen, New Hampshire, July 24, 1798. In 1812, he entered the United States army as a cadet, and continued in military service until 1828, when he settled in Cooperstown, New York, to practise law. He served one term in the United States Senate, and became Secretary of the Treasury under President Buchanan. On the outbreak of the Civil

Robert Francis Catterson, Originally Colonel of the 97th Regiment.

Silas Colgrove Forwarded Lee's "Lost Order" Before Antietam to McClellan.

Thomas T. Crittenden, Originally Colonel of the 6th Infantry.

Robert Sanford Foster, Brevetted for Gallantry.

Alvin P. Hovey, Gallant Division Commander.

Thomas John Lucas, Originally Colonel of the 16th Infantry.

George F. McGinnis, Originally Colonel of the 11th Infantry.

James W. McMillan, Originally Colonel 1st Artillery.

John F. Miller, Colonel of the 29th Regiment; wounded at Stone's River.

Charles Cruft, Conspicuous at Stone's River and Chattanooga.

Jeremiah C. Sullivan Fought in the Shenandoah and Vicksburg Campaigns.

Robert A. Cameron, Originally Colonel of the 34th Regiment.

W. P. Benton Commanded a Brigade at Pea Ridge.

F. Knefler, Originally Colonel of the 79th Regiment.

Walter Q. Gresham, Engaged in the Nashville Campaign.

William Grose Led a Brigade under Thomas.

FEDERAL GENERALS—No. 5—INDIANA

War, Dix was appointed major-general of volunteers, and was given command of the Department of Annapolis (afterward Maryland, and finally merged in the Department of Pennsylvania, July, 1861). Then he was given a division at Baltimore, which became part of the Army of the Potomac, when it was organized. On March 22, 1862, Dix's Division was organized with other troops into the Middle Department, which he headed until June, when he was transferred to the Department of Virginia, the troops of which were organized into the Seventh Army Corps, in July. In July, 1863, Dix was transferred to the Department of the East with headquarters at New York, and remained there until the end of the war. He was twice minister to France (1866-69) and was governor of New York, 1873-75. He died in New York city, April 21, 1879.

Seventh Army Corps (Department of Arkansas)

ANOTHER CORPS designated the Seventh was created on January 6, 1864, to consist of the troops in the Department of Arkansas. The command was given to Major-General Frederick Steele, who was succeeded by Major-General J. J. Reynolds in December, 1864. For a year from May, 1864, the corps was a unit of the Military Division of West Mississippi and was discontinued August 1, 1865. The principal fighting done by the Seventh Corps was in Steele's Arkansas Expedition, especially at Jenkins' Ferry.

MAJOR-GENERAL JOSEPH JONES REYNOLDS (U. S.M.A. 1843) was born in Flemingsburg, Kentucky, January 4, 1822. He taught at West Point and, after resigning, at Washington University, St. Louis, and finally engaged in business in Lafayette, Indiana. He entered the Civil War as colonel of the Tenth Indiana Volunteers, and reached the rank of major-general of volunteers in November, 1862. After active service in Western Virginia, he had a division in the Army of the Cumberland, and was chief-of-staff to Rosecrans in October, 1863. In December, he was put in command of the defenses of New Orleans, and on July 7, 1864, he took command of that portion of the Nineteenth Army Corps which remained in Louisiana, going from there to the head of the Gulf Reserve Corps. On December 22, 1864, he took command of the Seventh Army Corps (Arkansas) until it was discontinued, August 1, 1865. Mustered out of the volunteer service, he returned to the regular army as colonel in the cavalry and received the brevet of major-general. He was retired June 25, 1877, and died in Washington, February 25, 1899.

Eighth Army Corps

THE TROOPS in the Middle Department were organized into the Eighth Army Corps on July 22, 1862. The forces were stationed at various points in Maryland. Its first commander was Major-General John E. Wool, and he was succeeded by Major-Generals R. C. Schenck, Brevet Brigadier-General W. W. Morris, Brigadier-Generals E. B. Tyler, H. H. Lockwood, and Major-General Lewis Wallace. The Eighth Corps saw little active fighting except in West Virginia. Wallace was in command at the Monocacy (July 9, 1864), and the First Separate Brigade under Brigadier-General E. B. Tyler took part, but that battle was fought chiefly by a division of the Sixth Corps. The Eighth Corps was discontinued, August 1, 1865.

MAJOR-GENERAL JOHN ELLIS WOOL was born in Newburg, New York, February 20, 1787. He became a lawyer, but raised an infantry company at Troy and entered the War of 1812. He remained in the army, and in 1841 was raised to the rank of brigadier-general. He selected the American position at Buena Vista in the Mexican War, and for his skill and courage received a vote of thanks and a sword from Congress. He was in command of the Department of the East when the Civil War broke out, and was transferred, in August, 1861, to the Department of Virginia, where he succeeded in saving Fort Monroe to the Federal Government. In May, 1862, his troops occupied Norfolk and Portsmouth

JOHN EDWARDS
Colonel of the 18th Infantry.

ALEXANDER CHAMBERS
Promoted for Gallantry.

WILLIAM T. CLARK
Promoted at Atlanta.

FITZ-HENRY WARREN
Colonel of the 1st Infantry.

CYRUS BUSSEY
Daring Leader of Cavalry.

JAMES B. WEAVER
Brevetted for Gallantry.

JAMES MADISON TUTTLE
Colonel of the 2d Infantry.

JAMES A. WILLIAMSON
Colonel of the 4th Infantry.

EDWARD HATCH
Brilliant Cavalry Commander.

JACOB G. LAUMAN
Conspicuous at Belmont.

MARCELLUS M. CROCKER
At Corinth and Vicksburg.

E. W. RICE
Colonel of the 19th Regiment.

FEDERAL GENERALS

No. 6

IOWA

JAMES I. GILBERT
Colonel of the 27th Infantry.

after the Confederate evacuation, and at this time he was made major-general. He was given command of the Middle Department in June, and headed the Eighth Army Corps when it was organized in July. In January, 1863, he went back to the Department of the East, which had been recreated, and remained there until July 18th. He was retired from the army on August 1, 1865, and died in Troy, New York, November 10, 1869.

MAJOR-GENERAL ROBERT CUMMING SCHENCK was born in Franklin, Ohio, October 4, 1809. He became a lawyer, and was minister to Brazil, 1851–53. When the Civil War broke out he was made brigadier-general of volunteers, and commanded a brigade at the battle of Bull Run. His force was transferred to the Department of Western Virginia, and he aided in saving that valuable region to the Union. In the new Mountain Department, Schenck had an independent brigade, and he commanded the Federal right at the battle of Cross Keys. He was given a division of the First Corps, Army of Virginia, when the Mountain troops were merged in that army. He was severely wounded at Second Bull Run, where his gallantry won him promotion to major-general of volunteers. After recovery, he was given the Eighth Army Corps (troops of the Middle Department), December 22, 1862. He resigned from

the army December 3, 1863, having been elected member of Congress, where he served until 1870. In 1871, he was a member of the commission which drew up the treaty of Washington, and from 1871 to 1876 was United States minister to Great Britain. He died in Washington, March 23, 1890.

MAJOR-GENERAL LEWIS WALLACE was born in Brookville, Indiana, April 10, 1827. He became a lawyer and served in the Mexican War. At the commencement of the Civil War he headed the Eleventh Indiana Infantry, and was made brigadier-general of volunteers in September, 1861. At Fort Donelson and Shiloh he was in command of a division, and after the former battle he was promoted to major-general of volunteers. In 1863, he superintended the construction of the defenses of Cincinnati. In March, 1864, he took command of the Eighth Army Corps and was defeated by Lieutenant-General Early at the Monocacy. He resigned from the army in November, 1865. After the war he was appointed Governor of New Mexico, and from 1881 to 1885 was United States minister to Turkey. Major-General Wallace was the author of " Ben-Hur," the " Prince of India," and other well-known books, in addition to enjoying great popularity as a lecturer. He died at Crawfordsville Indiana, February 15, 1905.

Ninth Army Corps

THE TROOPS that Major-General Burnside took with him to North Carolina in December, 1861, which were then known as Burnside's Expeditionary Corps and which made a record for themselves at Roanoke Island, New Berne, and elsewhere, were merged in the Department of North Carolina in April, 1862. They and some others from the Department of the South were transferred to the Army of the Potomac in July, and on the 22d, the Ninth Army Corps came into existence. At first, it contained less than five thousand men. Its commanders were Major-Generals Burnside, J. L. Reno, Brigadier-General J. D. Cox, Major-Generals John Sedgwick, W. F. Smith, J. G. Parke, Brigadier-General R. B. Potter, and Brevet Major-General O. B. Willcox. Two divisions went to the assistance of Pope, and fought at Second Bull Run and Chantilly. Afterward,

the corps distinguished itself at South Mountain, Antietam, and Fredericksburg. After the latter battle, Burnside was transferred to the Department of the Ohio (March, 1863) and two divisions of the corps (one having gone to the Seventh) went West with him. The corps took part in the siege of Vicksburg, and was itself besieged in Knoxville, where it suffered great hardships. Early in 1864, the corps was ordered East for reorganization, with Burnside at the head. At the end of May, it became part of the Army of the Potomac, having acted as a separate command through the earlier battles of Grant's campaign. It was very prominent in the siege of Petersburg, and the famous mine was constructed and exploded in front of its lines. The flags of the Ninth Corps were the first that were shown on the public buildings of Petersburg. In June, 1865, the corps was

FEDERAL
GENERALS
No. 7

KANSAS
(THREE TO LEFT AND
EXTREME RIGHT
SECOND ROW)

LOUISIANA
(EXTREME RIGHT
THIRD ROW)

KENTUCKY
(TEN REMAINING)

GEORGE W. DITZLER
Originally Colonel of the 1st Infantry.

THOMAS EWING, JR.
Originally Colonel of the 11th Cavalry.

THOMAS MOONLIGHT
Originally Colonel of the 11th Cavalry.

SPEED S. FRY
Noted for his Encounter at
Mill Springs.

STEPHEN G. BURBRIDGE
Cavalry Leader in the Morgan
Campaigns.

JOHN T. CROXTON
Led a Brigade in Tennessee and
Georgia.

POWELL CLAYTON
Of Kansas—Later Governor of
Arkansas.

EDWARD H. HOBSON
Noted for the Pursuit of Morgan's
Raiders.

WALTER C. WHITTAKER
Commander of a Brigade at
Chickamauga.

THEOPHILUS T. GARRARD
Defender of Kentucky and East
Tennessee.

D. J. KEILY
Of Louisiana—Colonel of the
Second Cavalry.

JAMES M. SCHACKLEFORD
Prominent in the Pursuit of Morgan's Raiders.

WILLIAM NELSON
Commanded a Division in Buell's
Army at Shiloh.

JEREMIAH T. BOYLE
Defender of Kentucky and
Tennessee.

N. B. BUFORD
Leader of Cavalry in Kentucky
and Tennessee.

Ninth Army Corps

transferred to the Department of Washington and was discontinued on August 1st. This organization is often referred to as the "wandering corps," for it fought in seven States.

MAJOR-GENERAL JESSE LEE RENO (U.S.M.A. 1846) was born in Wheeling, West Virginia, June 20, 1823, and served in the Mexican War, where he was severely wounded at Chapultepec. He was a captain when the Civil War broke out, but was commissioned brigadier-general of volunteers and commanded a brigade in Burnside's Expeditionary Corps, a division in the Department of North Carolina, and the same in the Ninth Army Corps, when it was created. He fought at Roanoke Island, New Berne, Camden, Manassas, and Chantilly and was placed in command of the Ninth Corps, September 3, 1862. He was killed at South Mountain on the 14th. His commission of major-general of volunteers was dated July 18, 1862.

MAJOR-GENERAL JOHN GRUBB PARKE (U.S. M.A. 1849) was born in Chester County, Pennsylvania, September 22, 1827, and entered the Corps of Topographical Engineers. He was first lieutenant when the Civil War broke out, and his commission of brigadier-general of volunteers was dated November 23, 1861. He commanded a brigade in Burnside's expedition to North Carolina, and later had a division in the Ninth Corps. As major-general of volunteers he was Burnside's chief-of-staff at Antietam and Fredericksburg. He went with the corps to the West as its commander, fought through the Vicksburg campaign, and was at the siege of Knoxville. He also commanded the corps after August, 1864, in the operations around Petersburg. He was in command of the Twenty-second Army Corps and at Alexandria, in 1865. After the war he rose to the rank of colonel in the regular army, with the brevet of major-general. He was engaged in engineering, and as superintendent of West Point until he was retired in July, 1889. He died in Washington, December 16, 1900.

BREVET MAJOR-GENERAL ORLANDO BOLIVAR WILLCOX (U.S.M.A. 1847) was born in Detroit, Michigan, April 16, 1823. He served in Texas, in Florida, and in the Mexican War, resigning his commission of first lieutenant in 1857 and taking up the practice of law. He hastened to the front at the outbreak of the war, as colonel of the First Michigan Infantry, and was present at the occupation of Alexandria (May 24, 1861). He commanded a brigade at the battle of Bull Run, where he was severely wounded and captured. For his services here he was made brigadier-general of volunteers. He was exchanged (February, 1862), and later had a division of the Ninth Army Corps, and headed the corps itself at the battle of Fredericksburg. For a short time he was stationed in Indiana and Michigan, and had charge of the district of East Tennessee. He served again with the Ninth Corps in the Knoxville campaign and was at its head for a short period. As division commander he fought through the Wilderness campaign and in the last operations of the Army of the Potomac until July, 1865, except for short periods when he was at the head of the corps. He received the surrender of Petersburg. In August, 1864, he was brevetted major-general of volunteers. After being mustered out of the volunteer service, he became a colonel in the regular army and brigadier-general in 1886. The following year he was retired, and he died at Coburg, Ontario, May 10, 1907.

MAJOR-GENERAL JACOB DOLSON COX was born in Montreal, Canada, October 27, 1828. He became a lawyer and a member of the Ohio State Senate. He entered the Civil War as brigadier-general in the Ohio militia, and was made brigadier-general of volunteers in May, 1861. After distinguished service in western Virginia and under Pope, he succeeded to the command of the Ninth Army Corps upon the death of Major-General Reno, at South Mountain. He was in command of forces in West Virginia and of the Military District of Ohio in 1862-63. On March 4, 1863, his appointment of major-general of volunteers, which dated from October 6, 1862, expired, and it was renewed December 7, 1864. He received a division of the Twenty-third Army Corps in April, 1864, and during the Atlanta and Tennessee campaigns was several times in command of the corps itself. After the battle of Nashville, the corps was moved to North Carolina, where Major-General Cox served in various capacities, and finally as head of the corps from April to June, 1865. In 1866, he resigned from the volunteer service. From 1866 to 1868, he was governor of Ohio, and President Grant's Secretary of the Interior in 1869. He was prominent in politics, finance, and the law until his death, which occurred at Magnolia, Massachusetts, August 4, 1900.

Jonathan P. Cilley, Gallant Cavalry Leader.

Seldon Connor, Colonel of the 19th Regiment.

Joshua L. Chamberlain, Active at Round Top.

L. G. Estes, Promoted at the Close of the War.

Cyrus Hamlin, Colonel of the 80th U. S. Colored Infantry.

James D. Fessenden, Brevetted for Meritorious Service.

Francis Fessenden, Active in the Red River Campaign.

George L. Beal, Brevetted for Conspicuous Gallantry.

Albion P. Howe, Leader of the Light Division at the Storming of Marye's Heights, May 3, 1863.

Joseph Dickinson, Brevetted for Gallantry on Staff Duty at Gettysburg.

FEDERAL GENERALS

Neal Dow, Captured and Exchanged for a Son of Gen. R. E. Lee.

No. 8—MAINE

Tenth Army Corps

CREATED September 3, 1863, to consist of the troops in the Department of the South. Its commanders were Brigadier-General John M. Brannan, and Major-Generals O. M. Mitchel, David Hunter, and Q. A. Gillmore. It took part in the various operations around Charleston Harbor, and in February, 1864, one division went to Florida, where it suffered severely in the battle of Olustee. In April, 1864, the corps entered the Army of the James, in which its commanders were Brigadier-General A. H. Terry, Major-General Q. A. Gillmore, Brigadier-General W. H. T. Brooks, Major-General D. B. Birney, and Brigadier-General Adelbert Ames. It fought around Drewry's Bluff, and two divisions went to Cold Harbor, forming a third division of the Eighteenth Corps. After this, the corps fought at Deep Bottom, Darbytown Road, and Fair Oaks. It was discontinued December 3, 1864 and merged in the new Twenty-fourth Corps. One division and a brigade of the Twenty-fourth, under Major-General Terry, went to Fort Fisher, and, after its capture, the Tenth Corps was reorganized March 27, 1865, in the Department of North Carolina, from Terry's troops. Besides Major-General Terry, Brevet Major-General Adelbert Ames had command from May 13 to August 1, 1865, when the corps was discontinued.

MAJOR-GENERAL ORMSBY McKNIGHT MITCHEL (U.S.M.A. 1829) was born in Union County, Kentucky, August 28, 1810, and served as assistant professor of mathematics at West Point until 1831, later becoming professor of mathematics, philosophy, and astronomy at Cincinnati College. For a time he practised law. He was director of the Dudley Observatory at Albany, New York, when the Civil War broke out, and entered the army, receiving a commission of brigadier-general of volunteers. From September to November, 1861, he was at the head of the Department of the Ohio, and had a division in the Army of the Ohio, December, 1861, to July, 1862, during which he made a brilliant expedition into Alabama, and won promotion to major-general of volunteers. In September, he was placed at the head of the Tenth Army Corps and died at Hilton Head, South Carolina, of yellow fever, October 27, 1862. He made several important astronomical discoveries.

BREVET MAJOR-GENERAL JOHN MILTON BRANNAN (U.S.M.A. 1841) was born in the District of Columbia in 1819, and served in the Mexican War. He had reached the rank of captain when the Civil War broke out, and was promoted to brigadier-general of volunteers in September, 1861. He was commander of the Department of Key West from February, 1862, until it was merged, the following month, in the Department of the South, of which he was twice in command, as well as temporarily at the head of the Tenth Army Corps between September, 1862, and January, 1863. During this period he led the St. John's River expedition and took part in the battle of Pocotaligo. After this, he commanded divisions in the Twenty-first and Fourteenth corps. He reorganized the artillery in the Army of the Cumberland, and placed the artillery for the defense of Atlanta. He was mustered out of the volunteer service, having been brevetted major-general of volunteers, in May, 1866, and continued in the regular army as lieutenant-colonel and colonel, but with the brevet of major-general, serving at various posts until he was retired in April, 1882. He died in New York city, December 16, 1892.

MAJOR-GENERAL QUINCY ADAMS GILLMORE (U.S.M.A. 1849) was born at Black River, Ohio, February 28, 1825. He entered the Engineer Corps, and served as assistant instructor in engineering at West Point. Before the Civil War broke out he had done much work on fortifications and other engineering projects connected with the army. As captain and chief engineer, he accompanied Burnside to North Carolina, and later planned the details of the successful attack on Fort Pulaski, which feat won him the rank of brigadier-general of volunteers. After this, he held a command in West Virginia and also served in the Department of the Ohio. In June, 1863, he took command of the Tenth Army Corps and held it for a year, participating in the operations around Charleston Harbor, Bermuda Hundred, and the battle of Drewry's Bluff. His commission of major-general of volunteers was dated July 10, 1863. He went to the defense of Washington against Early with the Nineteenth Corps in July, 1864. Resigning from the volunteer service after the war, he rose to rank of colonel in the regular army and was connected with many great engineering projects until his death, which occurred at Brooklyn, New York, April 7, 1888.

MAJOR-GENERAL ALFRED HOWE TERRY was born in Hartford, Connecticut, November 10, 1827. He was colonel of the Second Connecticut

Charles H. Smith, Conspicuous as a Cavalry Leader.

George F. Shepley, Originally Colonel of the 20th Regiment.

Elias Spear, Colonel of the 20th Regiment.

FEDERAL GENERALS—No. 9—MAINE (ABOVE) MARYLAND (BELOW)

Frank Nickerson, Originally Colonel of the 4th Regiment.

Daniel White, Brevetted for Gallantry at the Wilderness.

Nathaniel J. Jackson, Originally Colonel of the 1st and 5th Infantry.

Cuvier Grover, Division Leader in the East and in the West.

James M. Deems, Brevetted for Gallantry.

John R. Kenly, Originally Colonel of the 1st Regiment.

James Cooper, In Command of Maryland Volunteers in 1861.

Volunteers at Bull Run. He returned home to raise the Seventh Connecticut Volunteers, and with this regiment served under Brigadier-General T. W. Sherman at the capture of Port Royal and under Major-General Hunter at Fort Pulaski, which he then commanded. Being raised to brigadier-general of volunteers in April, 1862, he commanded several districts in the Department of the South (Tenth Army Corps), and took command of this corps when it was transferred to the Army of the James, in April, 1864. As brevet major-general of volunteers he headed the Twenty-fourth Army Corps which was organized out of the Tenth, December, 1864, to January, 1865. On the latter date, he was put in command of the provisional corps organized for the capture of Fort Fisher and Wilmington. After these events had taken place, his corps became the reorganized Tenth Corps, and Major-General Terry was in command until May 13, 1865, when he took charge of Richmond. After leaving the volunteer service, he rose to the rank of major-general in the regular army (1886) and was retired in April, 1888. He died in New Haven, Connecticut, December 16, 1890. For the capture of Fort Fisher he was tendered the thanks of Congress.

MAJOR-GENERAL WILLIAM THOMAS HARBAUGH BROOKS (U.S.M.A. 1841) was born in New Lisbon, Ohio, January 28, 1821, and served in the Seminole and Mexican wars, and in Texas and New Mexico. He had reached the rank of captain when the Civil War broke out, and was made brigadier-general of volunteers in September, 1861. He commanded a brigade in the Sixth Army Corps until October, 1862, and a division until after the Chancellorsville campaign, when, as major-general of volunteers, he was at the head of the Department of the Monongahela until Grant's operations against Lee and Richmond began. His commission of major-general of volunteers having expired, Brigadier-General Brooks was then in command of a division of the Eighteenth Army Corps, and on June 21, 1864, was put at the head of the Tenth Corps. He resigned from the volunteer service the following month, and died in Huntsville, Alabama, July 19, 1870.

MAJOR-GENERAL DAVID BELL BIRNEY was born in Huntsville, Alabama, May 29, 1825. He practised law in Philadelphia until 1861, when he entered the Federal army as lieutenant-colonel of a Pennsylvania regiment and reached the rank of brigadier-general of volunteers, in February, 1862. He had a brigade in the Third Army Corps through the Peninsula campaign and was with Pope at Second Bull Run and Chantilly, taking the division temporarily after Brigadier-General Kearny was killed. As major-general of volunteers, he had a division at Fredericksburg and Chancellorsville and commanded the Third Corps at Gettysburg after Major-General Sickles was wounded, holding it from time to time until February, 1864. In the new organization of the Army of the Potomac (March, 1864), he had a division in the Second Corps until July, when he was given command of the Tenth Corps, Army of the James. While in this position he contracted a fever, and died in Philadelphia, October 18, 1864.

Eleventh Army Corps

WHEN THE ARMY OF VIRGINIA was discontinued, September 12, 1862, its First Corps, which had been the troops of the Mountain Department under Rosecrans and Fremont, and had been led by Sigel in the Pope campaign, was merged in the Army of the Potomac as the Eleventh Corps. It remained on the line of Manassas during the Antietam campaign, did not reach Fredericksburg in time for the battle, and at Chancellorsville was badly routed by "Stonewall" Jackson, because its commander allowed himself to be surprised. In this battle about twelve thousand troops were present. It was one of the two corps heavily engaged on the first day at Gettysburg. After that battle, one division was sent to Charleston Harbor, and the other two went with Hooker to Tennessee to assist Grant in the Chattanooga campaign. These two divisions then went with Sherman to the relief of Knoxville, and shared all the great hardships of the march. In April, 1864, these troops were merged in the new Twentieth Army Corps, for the Atlanta campaign. The leaders of the Eleventh Corps were Major-General Franz Sigel, Brigadier-General J. H. Stahel, Major-General Carl Schurz, Brigadier-General A. von Steinwehr, and Major-General O. O. Howard.

Stephen M. Weld, Jr., Leader of Colored Troops at the Crater Battle.

William F. Bartlett Led His Brigade at the Crater and Was Captured.

Oliver Edwards Led a Brigade at the "Bloody Angle," Spotsylvania; Brevetted for Gallantry at Sailor's Creek.

Edward F. Jones, Commander of the 6th Massachusetts on Its Memorable March Through Baltimore, April, '61.

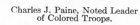

Frederick W. Lander, One of the Early Heroes of the War.

Charles J. Paine, Noted Leader of Colored Troops.

George H. Gordon Led a Charge at Cedar Mountain.

Charles P. Stone, Later Distinguished in the Service of Egypt.

Albert Ordway, Promoted at the Close of the War.

N. A. Miles Commanded a Brigade at Chancellorsville and Later Led a Division in the Army of the Potomac.

Henry L. Eustis, Originally Colonel of the 10th Regiment.

FEDERAL GENERALS—No. 10—MASSACHUSETTS

MAJOR-GENERAL FRANZ SIGEL was born in Sinsheim, Baden, November 18, 1824, and was graduated from the Military School at Carlsruhe, becoming a champion of German unity and minister of war to the revolutionary Government of 1848, which was overthrown by Prussia. Later, having withdrawn to Switzerland, the Government expelled him, and he emigrated to America in 1852. He taught in a military institute in St. Louis and edited a military periodical. When the Civil War broke out, he organized the Third Missouri Infantry and an artillery battery, and after assisting Captain Lyon in the capture of Camp Jackson, he served in Missouri, at Carthage and at Springfield. As brigadier-general of volunteers, he was conspicuous for his bravery at Pea Ridge, and as major-general of volunteers was placed in command of Harper's Ferry in June, 1862. Then he served in the Army of Virginia, in command of its First Corps, out of which the Eleventh Corps, Army of the Potomac, was created. He relinquished the latter in January, 1863. On March 10, 1864, he succeeded Brigadier-General B. F. Kelley in the command of the Department of West Virginia, but after the defeat at New Market, May 15th, he was relieved by Major-General Hunter and given the division at Harper's Ferry, where he successfully held out against Lieutenant-General Early. In July, 1864, he was relieved from his command, and he resigned from the army in May, 1865. After the war, he edited a German paper in Baltimore, and later was register and United States pension-agent in New York city. He was well known as a lecturer and editor of the "New York Monthly," a German periodical. He died in New York city, August 21, 1902.

MAJOR-GENERAL CARL SCHURZ was born in Cologne, Prussia, March 2, 1829, studying there in the gymnasium and later at the University of Bonn. He was engaged in the revolutionary movement in 1848, and was compelled to seek refuge in Switzerland. In 1852, he came to the United States and settled in Philadelphia, later going to Milwaukee, Wisconsin, where he began the practice of law. Lincoln appointed him United States minister to Spain, but he resigned to take part in the Civil War. As brigadier-general of volunteers, he commanded a division of the First Corps, Army of Virginia, at Second Bull Run, and at Chancellorsville a division of the Eleventh Corps. At Gettysburg he had command, as major-general of volunteers, of the Eleventh Corps, temporarily, and again in January and February, 1864. At Chattanooga, he took an active part. In March, 1864, he was put in charge of a corps of instruction near Nashville, and at the close of the war was chief-of-staff to Major-General Slocum in the Army of Georgia. He resigned from the volunteer service in May, 1865, and became a newspaper correspondent in Washington, and, in 1866, founded the *Detroit Post*. He was senator from Missouri (1869-1875), and Secretary of the Interior from 1877 to 1881, and editor of the New York *Evening Post* from 1881 to 1884. He was an enthusiastic advocate of civil-service reform and other political movements. He was a writer and speaker of note, and died in New York city, May 14, 1906.

Twelfth Army Corps

CREATED September 12, 1862, from the Second Corps, Army of Virginia, the troops of which, under Major-General N. P. Banks, had been in the Department of the Shenandoah, and in earlier organizations of the Army of the Potomac. It was the smallest corps in the army, and in the early days contained about twelve thousand men. The command was given to Major-General J. F. K. Mansfield, who was killed at Antietam, the first battle of the new corps. Its next battle was that of Chancellorsville where, with the Third, it bore the real brunt of the fight. After Gettysburg, in which we remember the Twelfth by its gallant defense of Culps' Hill, it went with Hooker to Tennessee where one division opened the line of supplies to the starving Army of the Cumberland and fought "the battle in the clouds" on Lookout Mountain. In April, 1864, the Twelfth Corps was merged in the newly formed Twentieth, for the Atlanta campaign. After Mansfield's death, the command of the Twelfth Corps was held by Major-General H. W. Slocum except for very brief periods, when it was headed by Brigadier-General A. S. Williams, the senior division commander. In its short career, the corps is said to have never lost a gun or a color.

JOHN C. PALFREY
Chief Engineer of the 13th
Army Corps.

EDWARD W. HINKS
Originally Colonel of the 8th
Infantry.

MASSACHUSETTS

(ABOVE)

CHARLES DEVENS
Colonel of the 15th Regiment.
Later Commanded Division.

GEORGE L. ANDREWS
Engaged in the Siege and Capture
of Port Hudson.

MICHIGAN

(BELOW)

J. M. OLIVER
Originally Colonel of the
15th Regiment.

HENRY BAXTER
Promoted for Gallantry at
the Wilderness.

JOSEPH T. COPELAND
Originally Colonel of the
5th Cavalry.

FEDERAL

GENERALS

No. 11

WM. R. SHAFTER
Later Commander at Santiago, Cuba.

CHARLES C. DOOLITTLE
Originally Colonel of the 18th Infantry;
Promoted for Merit.

BYRON R. PIERCE
Originally Colonel of the
3d Infantry.

HENRY A. MORROW
"Here to fight, not to surrender"—Gettysburg, July 1.

RALPH ELY
Leader of the Brigade which
was first in Petersburg.

Thirteenth Army Corps

MAJOR-GENERAL JOSEPH KING FENNO MANS-FIELD (U.S.M.A. 1822) was born in New Haven, Connecticut, December 22, 1803, and served in the Mexican War and in the Engineer Corps. From May, 1861, to March, 1862, he had charge of the Department of Washington, and as brigadier-general of volunteers commanded the District of Suffolk of the Seventh Army Corps, and captured the town of Norfolk in May. As major-general of volunteers, he was put at the head of the newly formed Twelfth Army Corps on September 12, 1862, and was mortally wounded at Antietam, on the 17th.

BREVET MAJOR-GENERAL ALPHEUS STARKEY WILLIAMS was born in Saybrook, Connecticut, September 10, 1810, was graduated from Yale College, and held various political positions in Detroit where he also practised law. As colonel of a Michigan regiment, when the Civil War broke out, he was made brigadier-general of volunteers and headed a brigade in the Department of Pennsylvania. Passing through the various organizations of the Army of the Potomac, he was given a division in the Fifth Corps, which became the Second Corps, Army of Virginia, and the Twelfth Corps, Army of the Potomac, and finally was merged in the Twentieth Corps, Army of the Cumberland. Williams was the only general to lead the same division through the whole of the war, although at various times he temporarily headed the corps in which he was placed. He was corps commander at Antietam, after Mansfield fell; at Gettysburg, and also on the march to the sea and in the campaign through the Carolinas. His brevet of major-general of volunteers for marked ability and energy, was dated January 12, 1865, and a year later he was mustered out of the service. After the war, he was United States minister to San Salvador (1866–69), and member of Congress from 1874 until his death, which occurred in Washington, December 21, 1878.

Thirteenth Army Corps

ON OCTOBER 24, 1862, the troops in the newly created Department of the Tennessee, under Major-General Grant, were designated the Thirteenth Army Corps, and Major-General W. T. Sherman was put in command. The troops were scattered in many districts. Sherman organized four of the divisions into the Yazoo Expedition, and started on the campaign that ended in failure at Chickasaw Bluffs, December 29, 1862. On December 18th, the corps was subdivided, and the Army of the Tennessee now consisted of the Thirteenth, Fifteenth, Sixteenth, and Seventeenth corps. Brigadier-General Morgan succeeded Sherman, who commanded the whole department, at the head of the new Thirteenth Army Corps. The corps went with Major-General McClernand (January 4-12, 1863) on the expedition to Arkansas Post, the expedition being known as McClernand's Army of the Mississippi, in which the Thirteenth Corps became the First Corps for that period. Following Morgan, the commanders of the Thirteenth Corps were Major-Generals J. A. McClernand, E. O. C. Ord (who succeeded when McClernand was relieved at Vicksburg), and C. C. Washburn. One division fought the battle of Helena (July 4, 1863), and the battle of Port Gibson (May 1, 1863) was fought almost entirely by it.

After Vicksburg, the corps invested Jackson, and on August 7th it was transferred to the Army of the Gulf, where its chief active service (two divisions) took place in the Red River campaign of 1864. New commanders of the corps while in the Army of the Gulf were Major-General N. J. T. Dana, and Brigadier-Generals T. E. G. Ransom, R. A. Cameron, M. K. Lawler, and W. P. Benton. On June 11, 1864, the troops of the corps were transferred to other commands, but they were largely brought together again for the Reserve Corps, Army of the Gulf, in December, 1864, out of which on February 18, 1865, a new Thirteenth Army Corps was created, which, under command of General Gordon Granger, took part in the capture of Mobile, in April, 1865. The corps was discontinued at Galveston, Texas, July 20, 1865.

BRIGADIER - GENERAL GEORGE WASHINGTON MORGAN was born in Washington County, Pennsylvania, September 20, 1820. He did not graduate from West Point, which he entered in 1841, but took up the practice of law in Mount Vernon, Ohio. But he went to the Mexican War and was brevetted brigadier-general. Entering the diplomatic service, he was consul at Marseilles and minister to Portugal. When the Civil War broke

EGBERT B. BROWN
Originally of the 7th
Regiment.

JOHN D. STEVENSON
Originally Colonel of the
7th Regiment.

ISAAC F. SHEPHARD
Originally Colonel of the
3d Regiment.

JOSEPH CONRAD
Noted Brigade Commander.

GABRIEL R. PAUL
Gallant Figure at Gettysburg.

JOHN ELISHA PHELPS
Originally Colonel of the
2d Kansas Cavalry.

CLINTON B. FISK
Originally Colonel of
the 33d Regiment.

LEWIS B. PARSONS
Promoted at the Close
of the War.

JOHN McNEIL
Originally Colonel of the 3d
Infantry

ALEXANDER ASBOTH
Promoted at the End of
the War.

FEDERAL GENERALS—No. 12

MISSOURI (ABOVE)

MICHIGAN (MIDDLE ONE BELOW)

MINNESOTA (FOUR REMAINING BELOW)

NAPOLEON T. J. DANA
Commander of a Brigade
in the Peninsula.

C. C. ANDREWS
Organizer and Division
Commander.

WILLIAM SANBORN
Promoted for Conspicuous
Gallantry.

STEPHEN MILLER
Colonel of the 7th Regiment;
Governor in 1863.

WILLIS A. GORMAN
First Commander of
the 1st Minnesota.

out he returned, and was made brigadier-general of volunteers in November, 1861. He served first under Buell and then as division commander in the Department of the Tennessee (Thirteenth Army Corps). He commanded a division in the Yazoo Expedition, and was the first commander of the reorganized Thirteenth Corps which he led at the capture of Arkansas Post (January, 1863). Ill-health compelled him to resign from the service in June, 1863. In 1868 and 1870, he was a member of Congress. He died at Old Point Comfort, Virginia, July 26, 1893.

MAJOR-GENERAL JOHN ALEXANDER McCLERNAND was born in Breckinridge County, Kentucky, May 30, 1812. He became a lawyer and served in the Black Hawk War as private. He was a member of Congress when the Civil War broke out and resigned to enter it, being made brigadier-general of volunteers in May, 1861. He first distinguished himself at Belmont, November 7, 1861. After Fort Donelson, he was made major-general of volunteers in the Army of West Tennessee, and commanded a division at Shiloh. On January 4, 1863, he replaced Sherman in command of the Yazoo Expedition which, under the name of McClernand's Army of the Mississippi, together with the Mississippi Squadron, captured Arkansas Post, January 11th. Grant removed McClernand from the command, and he was placed at the head of the Thirteenth Army Corps, of which he was in turn relieved on June 19th, during the siege of Vicksburg. He commanded this corps again for a short time in 1864, while it was serving in the Army of the Gulf. He resigned his commission on November 30, 1864, and resumed the practice of law. He died at Springfield, Illinois, September 20, 1900.

MAJOR-GENERAL CADWALLADER COLDEN WASHBURN was born in Livermore, Maine, April 22, 1818. He settled in Wisconsin as a lawyer and financier. At the outbreak of the war he raised the Second Wisconsin Cavalry, and as its colonel was successful under Major-General Curtis in Arkansas. He rose to the rank of major-general of volunteers in November, 1862, and later headed divisions in the Army of the Tennessee. He was the first commander of the reorganized Thirteenth Army Corps, and went with it from the Army of the Tennessee to that of the Gulf. After that, he was at the head of the District of West Tennessee, and resigned from the volunteer service in May, 1865. Later on, he was member of Congress and governor of Wisconsin. He died at Eureka Springs, Arkansas, May 14, 1882.

BREVET MAJOR-GENERAL THOMAS EDWARD GREENFIELD RANSOM was born in Norwich, Vermont, November 29, 1834. He became a captain in an Illinois regiment in April, 1861, and was made brigadier-general of volunteers in November, 1862. He fought at Fort Donelson and Shiloh, and was for a time on Grant's staff. He commanded a brigade in the Seventeenth Army Corps during the Vicksburg campaign, and a detachment of the Thirteenth Army Corps on the Red River expedition, in 1864. He was wounded at Sabine Cross Roads. In the Atlanta campaign, he commanded a division of the Sixteenth Army Corps and headed that and the Seventeenth for short periods. On October 10th, he was obliged to give up the Seventeenth Corps on account of illness, and he died, October 29th, near Rome, Georgia. The brevet of major-general of volunteers had been conferred on him in September, a few weeks before his death.

Fourteenth Army Corps

THE ORGANIZATION of the Army of the Ohio into three corps, in September, 1862, was changed on October 24th, when this force became the Army of the Cumberland, and consisted of the Fourteenth Army Corps, with Major-General Rosecrans at its head. In November, the Fourteenth Corps was divided into the Right Wing, Center, and Left Wing, and on January 9, 1863, the Center was designated the Fourteenth Army Corps, with Major-General George H. Thomas in command.

The corps fought at Stone's River and won its greatest fame at Chickamauga. It also distinguished itself at Missionary Ridge. It was prominent in the Atlanta campaign, and was one of the two corps of the Army of Georgia in the march to the sea and the campaign through the Carolinas. It was discontinued August 1, 1865. Besides Thomas, it was commanded by Major-Generals John M. Palmer, Jeff. C. Davis, and Brigadier-General R. W. Johnson.

Gilman Marston, Colonel of the 10th Regiment.

Simon G. Griffin, Leader at the Crater Battle.

Joab N. Patterson, Colonel of the 2d Regiment.

Joseph H. Potter, Promoted for Gallantry.

John L. Thompson, Colonel of the 1st Cavalry.

FEDERAL GENERALS—No. 13—NEW HAMPSHIRE (ABOVE) NEW JERSEY (BELOW)

Joseph W. Revere, Originally Colonel of the 7th Regiment. Promoted in 1862.

Gershom Mott, Active as a Division Commander in the Wilderness Campaign.

Ranald S. Mackenzie, Dashing Cavalry Leader in the Army of the Potomac.

Horatio P. VanCleve, Division Leader at Stone's River and Chickamauga.

Geo. W. Mindil, Originally Colonel of the 33d New Jersey.

Lewis C. Arnold, Active Commander in Florida.

William Birney, Brevetted for Gallantry in Action.

Edward Burd Grubb, Brevetted at the Close of the War.

Fifteenth Army Corps

MAJOR-GENERAL JOHN McAULEY PALMER was born at Eagle Creek, Kentucky, September 13, 1817, and became a lawyer and politician. He entered the Civil War as colonel of volunteers and was major-general of volunteers before the end of 1862. His first service was with Fremont and Pope in Missouri, and later he was given a division of the Army of the Cumberland. For a short time during the Tullahoma campaign he headed the Twenty-first Corps. During the Atlanta campaign he was in command of the Fourteenth Corps until August, 1864. Later, he was in charge of the Department of Kentucky. After the war, he was governor of Illinois, United States senator, and candidate of the Gold Democrats for President, in 1896. He died in Springfield, Illinois, September 25, 1900.

BREVET MAJOR-GENERAL JEFFERSON COLUMBUS DAVIS was born in Clarke County, Indiana, March 2, 1828, and served as a volunteer in the Mexican War. After this he entered the regular army. He was a lieutenant at Fort Sumter when the Civil War broke out. Later on, he became captain and then colonel of an Indiana Regiment, and led a division in the Army of the Southwest at Pea Ridge. As brigadier-general of volunteers, he served as division commander in Pope's Army of the Mississippi and also in that of the Cumberland, and took command of the Fourteenth Army Corps, August 22, 1864, and led it through Georgia and the Carolinas until the close of the war. He remained in the regular army as colonel,

and was at one time commander of the United States troops in Alaska, and also was at the head of the troops that quelled the Modoc uprising of 1873, after the murder of Canby. He received the brevet of major-general in 1865. He died in Chicago, November 30, 1879.

BREVET MAJOR-GENERAL RICHARD W. JOHNSON (U.S.M.A. 1849) was born in Livingston County, Kentucky, February 7, 1827, and saw his first service on the frontier. He entered the Civil War as captain of cavalry, becoming colonel of a Kentucky regiment. He served in the Army of the Cumberland and its prior organizations. His commission as brigadier-general of volunteers was dated October 19, 1861. As cavalry commander, he was captured by Morgan in August, 1862. He commanded a division at Stone's River, Chickamauga, and Chattanooga, and was severely wounded at New Hope Church. For a short time in August, 1864, he headed the Fourteenth Army Corps. Then he took charge of the cavalry forces in the Army of the Cumberland, and headed a division at Nashville, for which service he received a brevet of major-general in the regular army. After the war he entered the regular army as major in the Fourth Cavalry, also serving as provost-marshal-general and judge advocate in several departments. He was professor of military science in the University of Minnesota, 1869-71. He retired as major-general in 1867, and after 1875 had the rank of brigadier-general. He died in St. Paul, Minnesota, April 21, 1897.

Fifteenth Army Corps

Two DIVISIONS and some district troops of the Thirteenth Corps, Army of the Tennessee, were constituted the Fifteenth, on December 18, 1862. In two divisions, it was on Sherman's Yazoo Expedition and was also known as the Second Corps, McClernand's Army of the Mississippi, from January 4 to January 12, 1863. The commanders of the Fifteenth Corps were Major-Generals W. T. Sherman, F. P. Blair, Jr., John A. Logan, Brigadier-General M. L. Smith, and Major-Generals P. J. Osterhaus and W. B. Hazen. The corps took part in the Vicksburg campaign, the battle of Chattanooga, the relief of Knoxville, the Atlanta campaign, and the last campaigns of Sherman. After the Grand Review of May 24, 1865, the corps

went to Louisville, Kentucky, and one division served with the army of occupation at Little Rock, Arkansas. The corps was discontinued August 1, 1865.

MAJOR-GENERAL PETER JOSEPH OSTERHAUS was born in Coblenz, Germany, in 1823, and served as an officer in the Prussian army. He came to St. Louis, and in 1861 entered the Union army as major of volunteers. Later, as colonel, he had a brigade in the Army of the Southwest, and at Pea Ridge he commanded a division. Passing into the Army of the Tennessee as brigadier-general of volunteers, he commanded divisions in the Thirteenth and Fifteenth corps, taking part in the

FEDERAL GENERALS

No. 14

NEW MEXICO
(LEFT)

NEBRASKA
(RIGHT)

NEW YORK
(BELOW)

Christopher Carson (Kit Carson), of New Mexico, Famous Rocky Mountain Scout.

John M. Thayer, of Nebraska, an Important Division Commander.

Henry M. Judah, Conspicuous During Morgan's Raid of 1863.

J. J. Bartlett Received the Arms of Lee's Troops at Appomattox.

Gustavus A. De Russy, who was Brevetted for Gallantry.

Charles K. Graham Led a Brigade at Chancellorsville.

N. Martin Curtis, Promoted for Gallantry at Fort Fisher.

Romeyn B. Ayres, Active as a Division Commander.

Abram Duryee, First Colonel of Duryee's Zouaves.

John P. Hatch, Dashing Leader of Cavalry.

Henry A. Barnum, Conspicuous Brigade Leader.

Vicksburg campaign and assisting Hooker in the capture of Lookout Mountain. During the Atlanta campaign, he was made major-general of volunteers (July, 1864), and he commanded the Fifteenth Army Corps on the march to the sea. He was Major-General Canby's chief-of-staff in 1865. After the war he resigned from the service, and was American consul at Lyons, France. Thereafter, remaining in Europe, he made his home in Mannheim, Germany.

Sixteenth Army Corps

CREATED from three divisions and troops of several districts of the Thirteenth Army Corps on December 18, 1862, with Major-General S. A. Hurlbut in command. The corps was much divided during its existence, and divisions were several times exchanged for others in the Seventeenth Corps. Some of it saw service at Vicksburg, but little active fighting at that place. A division went with Sherman to Chattanooga. Two divisions were in the Atlanta campaign, and two on the Red River expedition of 1864. Some troops were sent to the Seventh Corps in Arkansas. The corps was officially discontinued on November 1, 1864, but the right wing, under Major-General A. J. Smith, known as "Detachment, Army of the Tennessee," assisted Thomas at Nashville. Besides Hurlbut, the command was held by Brigadier-General C. S. Hamilton and Major-General N. J. T. Dana. The left wing was commanded from time to time by Major-Generals C. S. Hamilton, R. J. Oglesby, Brigadier-General G. M. Dodge, Colonel A. Mersey, and Brigadier-Generals E. A. Carr and T. E. G. Ransom. The "Detachment," which included a division of the Seventeenth Army Corps, was, on February 18, 1865, designated the Sixteenth Corps, with Smith in command. The corps was now in the Military Division of West Mississippi and assisted in the last operations around Mobile. It was discontinued July 20, 1865.

MAJOR-GENERAL STEPHEN AUGUSTUS HURLBUT was born in Charleston, South Carolina, November 29, 1815, and was admitted to the bar in 1837. In 1845, he removed to Illinois and attained considerable prominence in politics. At the opening of the Civil War he was appointed a brigadier-general of volunteers, and commanded a division at Shiloh. Later, he was at the head of several districts in the department and was given command of the reorganized Sixteenth Corps, Army of the Tennessee, in December, 1862. In September, 1862, he was promoted to major-general of volunteers. He succeeded Major-General N. P. Banks in command of the Army and Department of the Gulf. He left the volunteer service at the end of the war, and at the time of his death, March 27, 1882, was United States minister to Peru.

MAJOR-GENERAL GRENVILLE MELLEN DODGE was born in Danvers, Massachusetts, April 12, 1831. He was a member of the Government survey in the West until the Civil War broke out, when he went to the front as colonel of the Fourth Iowa Infantry, in July, 1861. He fought with the Army of the Southwest, and, being transferred to the Department of Tennessee, he commanded the troops in several districts thereof, as well as divisions of the Thirteenth and Sixteenth corps, having been made brigadier-general of volunteers in March, 1862. In the summer of 1863, he was put in command of the left wing of the Sixteenth Army Corps as major-general of volunteers, and was wounded on August 19, 1864, at Jonesboro, Georgia, in the Atlanta campaign. In December, 1864, he succeeded Major-General Rosecrans in the Department of Missouri, and remained there until the close of the war. He resigned from the service in May, 1866, and became chief engineer of the Union Pacific and Texas Pacific railways. In 1866-67, he was member of Congress from Iowa. In 1898, he was at the head of the commission appointed to investigate the conduct of the Spanish-American war.

MAJOR-GENERAL ANDREW JACKSON SMITH (U. S.M.A. 1838) was born in Berks County, Pennsylvania, April 28, 1815, and served in the Mexican War and in the West. He was made major in the cavalry when the Civil War broke out. His appointment of brigadier-general of volunteers was dated March 17, 1862. He had a division in the Army of the Ohio, but his name is chiefly associated with the Army of the Tennessee. He commanded a division in the Thirteenth Corps and was with the Yazoo Expedition and McClernand's Army of the Mississippi, and took part in

William Dwight, Originally Colonel of the 70th Regiment.

Morgan H. Chrysler, Brevetted for Meritorious Services.

Hiram Berdan, Celebrated Commander of Sharpshooters.

Schuyler Hamilton, Conspicuous at Island No. 10.

Wladimir Krzyzanowski, Originally Colonel of the 58th Regiment.

Henry E. Davies, Daring Cavalry Leader in the East.

Joseph E. Hamblin, Originally Colonel of the 65th Volunteers.

John Cochrane, Originally Colonel of the 65th Regiment.

Philip Regis De Trobriand, Prominent Brigade Commander.

FEDERAL GENERALS

No. 15

NEW YORK

(CONTINUED)

Thomas W. Egan, Prominent Brigade Commander in the East.

the siege of Vicksburg. He commanded the right wing of the Sixteenth Army Corps on the Red River expedition, and, as major-general of volunteers, in various operations in Tennessee and Mississippi during the Atlanta campaign. He took part in the battle of Nashville, and became commander of the reorganized Sixteenth Corps on February 18, 1865, participating in the closing operations around Mobile. He reentered the regular army as colonel in 1866, and was retired in 1899. For a time he was postmaster of St. Louis. He died in St Louis, January 30, 1897.

Seventeenth Army Corps

CREATED December 18, 1862, from troops in the Thirteenth Corps, Army of the Tennessee, and the command given to Major-General J. B. McPherson, with whose name it is closely linked. Divisions were exchanged with the Sixteenth Corps. It was prominent in the operations on the Mississippi before and after the fall of Vicksburg, and was a member of Sherman's Meridian expedition. After this the corps was divided: half remained in the Mississippi valley; the other two divisions went with Sherman to Atlanta. The Mississippi section was on the Red River expedition with Brigadier-General A. J. Smith and formed part of the detachment that fought at Nashville. It never rejoined the rest of the corps, which followed Sherman through Georgia and the Carolinas. On August 1, 1865, the corps was discontinued. Besides McPherson, it was commanded by Major-Generals F. P. Blair, Jr., J. A. Mower, Brigadier-Generals T. E. G. Ransom, M. D. Leggett, and W. W. Belknap.

MAJOR-GENERAL FRANCIS PRESTON BLAIR, JR., was born in Lexington, Kentucky, February 19, 1821, and became a lawyer and editor in St. Louis. He was a member of Congress for several years, and at the outbreak of the Civil War he was instrumental in saving Missouri to the Union. Entering the army as colonel, his commission of major-general of volunteers was dated November 29, 1862. He commanded a brigade on the Yazoo expedition, and afterward was division commander in the Fifteenth Army Corps, and headed it for a short time. In Sherman's campaigns to Atlanta and through Georgia and the Carolinas, he commanded the Seventeenth Army Corps. Resigning from the volunteer service in November, 1865, he was Democratic nominee for vice-president in 1868, and senator from Missouri, 1871-73. He died in St. Louis, July 8, 1875.

MAJOR-GENERAL JOSEPH ANTHONY MOWER was born in Woodstock, Vermont, August 22, 1827. He served as a private in the Mexican War and reentered the army as second lieutenant in 1855. After the Civil War broke out, he was promoted to a captaincy, became colonel of a Missouri regiment in May, 1862, and brigadier-general of volunteers in November of that year. He led his regiment in the attacks on Island No. 10, in other activities in Kentucky and Tennessee, and headed a brigade in the Army of the Mississippi at the time it was discontinued, passing thence to brigades in the Thirteenth, Sixteenth, and Fifteenth corps (Army of the Tennessee). With the latter, he served at the siege of Vicksburg. From December, 1863, to October, 1864, he commanded a brigade and then a division in the right wing of the Sixteenth Corps, and took part in the Red River expedition and in the operations in Mississippi and Tennessee while Sherman was fighting his way to Atlanta. In October, he joined Sherman's army at the head of a division of the Seventeenth Army Corps, and was its commander for a short time. In the closing days of the Carolina campaign he had command of the Twentieth Army Corps. Mower was appointed major-general of volunteers in August, 1864. After leaving the volunteer service he continued as colonel in the regular army, serving with the Thirty-ninth and Twenty-fifth infantry. He commanded the Department of Louisiana. He died in New Orleans, January 6, 1870.

Eighteenth Army Corps

ON DECEMBER 24, 1862, the troops in the Department of North Carolina were designated the Eighteenth Army Corps, and Major-General J. G. Foster was placed at its head. There were five divisions, at first. Two divisions were detached in February, 1863, and sent to the Tenth Corps,

John J. Peck, Commander on the Peninsula.

Charles H. Tompkins, Promoted in 1865.

Edward E. Potter, Brevetted for Gallantry.

William H. Morris, Colonel of the 6th Artillery.

Elisha G. Marshall Led a Brigade in the Crater Battle.

Robert Nugent, Originally Colonel of the 69th Regiment.

John C. Robinson Commanded a Division at Gettysburg.

James R. O'Beirne, Promoted from Major for Gallantry.

Rush C. Hawkins, Colonel of "Hawkins' Zouaves," 9th Infantry.

FEDERAL GENERALS

No. 16

NEW YORK (CONTINUED)

R. B. Potter, Commander of a Division at Crater Battle.

operating around Charleston Harbor. On July 15th, the Departments of Virginia and North Carolina were united, and on August 1st, the Seventh Corps, including Getty's division of the Ninth, was merged in the Eighteenth. The other commanders of the corps were Brigadier-General I. N. Palmer, Major-Generals B. F. Butler, W. F. Smith, Brigadier-General J. H. Martindale, Major-Generals E. O. C. Ord, John Gibbon, Brigadier-General C. A. Heckman, and Brevet Major-General Godfrey Weitzel. In April, 1864, this corps, with the Tenth, formed the Army of the James. It fought a series of battles after reaching Bermuda Hundred—especially that at Drewry's Bluff. Later in May, the corps joined the Army of the Potomac at Cold Harbor, in which battle it was very prominent. Then it returned to Bermuda Hundred and was very active in numerous engagements around Petersburg until December 3, 1864, when it was discontinued. The white troops were merged in the Twenty-fourth and the colored ones in the Twenty-fifth Corps.

MAJOR-GENERAL JOHN GRAY FOSTER (U.S. M.A. 1846) was born in Whitefield, New Hampshire, May 27, 1823. He rendered able service in the Mexican War, taught engineering at West Point, superintended Government works, and was one of the officers garrisoned at Fort Sumter during the siege. He distinguished himself at the capture of Roanoke Island and at New Berne; assumed chief command of the Department of North Carolina, the Department of Virginia and North Carolina, the Department and Army of the Ohio, and the Department of the South. He became major-general of volunteers in July, 1862. Being mustered out of the volunteer service in 1866, he, with the rank of lieutenant-colonel of engineers, continued his work on important engineering projects of the Government. He died in Nashua, New Hampshire, September 2, 1874.

BREVET MAJOR-GENERAL JOHN HENRY MARTINDALE (U.S.M.A. 1835) was born at Sandy Hill, New York, March 20, 1815. He resigned from the army the year after leaving West Point, but, offering his services at the outbreak of the Civil War, he was made brigadier-general of volunteers in August, 1861. He was brigade commander in several corps of the Army of the Potomac, and in February, 1863, took charge of the troops in the District of Washington—a portion of the Twenty-second Army Corps. In May, 1864, he was assigned to a division in the Eighteenth Army Corps, and for a short period in July, during the early operations against Petersburg, he had command of the corps itself. On September 13th, he resigned from the service. The brevet of major-general of volunteers was conferred upon him on March 13, 1865, in recognition of his services at the battle of Malvern Hill (1862). He became attorney-general of the State of New York, and died at Nice, France, December 13, 1881.

MAJOR-GENERAL WILLIAM FARRAR SMITH (U. S.M.A. 1845) was born in St. Albans, Vermont, February 17, 1824, and taught mathematics at West Point. In the early days of the Civil War he served on the staffs of Major-Generals Butler and McDowell. His commission as major-general of volunteers was dated July 4, 1862, to which rank he was recommissioned March 9, 1864. After leading a brigade and division in the early organization of the Army of the Potomac, he had divisions in the Fourth and Sixth corps, and commanded the latter in the battle of Fredericksburg. After heading the Ninth Corps for a short time, he went to the Department of the Susquehanna and later—in 1863—became chief engineer of the Army of the Cumberland, where he rendered valuable assistance in the relief of Chattanooga. In May, 1864, he took command of the Eighteenth Corps in the Army of the James and led it at the battle of Cold Harbor, where it had joined the Army of the Potomac. He resigned from the volunteer service in 1865, and from the regular army in 1867, with the brevet of major-general. He became president of the International Telegraph Company, and was president of the board of Police Commissioners in New York City, 1877. After that, he practised civil engineering. He died in Philadelphia, February 28, 1903.

BRIGADIER-GENERAL CHARLES ADAMS HECKMAN was born in Easton, Pennsylvania, December 3, 1822. He served in the Mexican War, and went to the Civil War as lieutenant-colonel of the Ninth New Jersey Infantry. He became a colonel and had a brigade in the Department of North Carolina, where, after being made brigadier-general of volunteers, he had a division in the Eighteenth Army Corps. Later, he had charge of the District of Beaufort and the defenses of New Berne and at Newport News. On May 16, 1864, at the head of a brigade he was captured at Drewry's Bluff. He had temporary command of the Eighteenth Corps in September, 1864, and was temporary commander of the Twenty-fifth Army Corps, January-February, 1865. He resigned from the service in May, 1865, and died in Philadelphia, January 14, 1896.

Nelson Taylor, Originally Colonel
of the 72d Regiment.

John H. H. Ward, Originally Colonel
of the 38th Regiment.

Daniel Ullmann, Originally Colonel
of the 78th Regiment.

Adolph Von Steinwehr, Originally
Colonel of the 29th Infantry.

FEDERAL

GENERALS

No. 17

NEW YORK

(CONTINUED)

Emory Upton Led a Storming Column
at Spotsylvania.

Egbert L. Viele, Engaged at Fort
Pulaski and Norfolk.

Alexander Shaler Commanded a Brigade at Spotsylvania.

Nineteenth Army Corps

ON JANUARY 5, 1863, the troops in the Department of the Gulf were constituted the Nineteenth Army Corps, with Major-General N. P. Banks in command. Its other leaders were Major-General W. B. Franklin, Brigadier-Generals W. H. Emory, B. S. Roberts, M. K. Lawler, and Major-General J. J. Reynolds. It operated in Louisiana, took part in the investment of Port Hudson, and did garrison duty until it went on the Red River expedition in March, 1864, where it was prominent at Sabine Cross Roads and in other engagements. In July, the First and Second divisions, under Emory, went to Virginia, and entered the Army of the Shenandoah and fought at the Opequon, Fisher's Hill, and Cedar Creek. This "detachment," as it was called until November 7th, was commanded by Brigadier-Generals W. H. Emory and Cuvier Grover, and after the campaign in the Shenandoah, it went, in different sections, to Savannah. Some of the troops were afterward attached to the Tenth Corps; others remained in Savannah until the corps was discontinued on March 20, 1865, and even longer. On November 7, 1864, the portion of the corps that had remained in Louisiana was discontinued, and the designation, Nineteenth Army Corps, passed to the divisions operating in the Shenandoah valley. Most of the troops in Louisiana were put in the Gulf Reserve Corps, which, in February, 1865, became the new Thirteenth Corps, and assisted at the capture of Mobile.

MAJOR-GENERAL WILLIAM HEMSLEY EMORY (U.S.M.A. 1831) was born in Queen Anne's County, Maryland, September 9, 1811. He served in the Mexican War, and later was appointed astronomer to the commission which determined the boundary between Mexico and the United States. As colonel, he entered the Civil War in the cavalry of the Army of the Potomac, and, as brigadier-general of volunteers, had a brigade in the Fourth Army Corps after the Peninsula campaign. In 1863, he was sent to the Department of the Gulf, where, for a time, he was in charge of the defenses of New Orleans, and in May, 1864, he assumed command of the Nineteenth Army Corps. In July, with two divisions, he went to Washington and the Shenandoah valley to assist in the campaign against Early. He received the rank of major-general of volunteers in September, 1865, and commanded several departments after the war, being retired in 1876, as brigadier-general. He died in Washington, December 1, 1887.

Twentieth Army Corps

THE RIGHT WING of the Army of the Cumberland was made the Twentieth Army Corps on January 9, 1863, under Brigadier-General A. McD. McCook, who held it until October 9, 1863, when it was merged in the Fourth Corps, which had been created on September 28th. It was prominent in the engagement at Liberty Gap, Tennessee, June 25th, during the advance of the army to Tullahoma, and eight of its brigades were in the battle of Chickamauga.

MAJOR-GENERAL ALEXANDER McDOWELL McCOOK (U.S.M.A. 1863) was born in Columbiana County, Ohio, April 22, 1831, and was the son of Major Daniel McCook, whose eight other sons also served in the Civil War. He did garrison duty in the West and was an instructor at West Point. He was colonel of the First Ohio at Bull Run, and then, as brigadier-general of volunteers, went to the Department of the Ohio, where he had a command, and, later, a division at Shiloh and elsewhere, until he headed the First Corps, Army of the Ohio, in the Kentucky campaign against Bragg. He had been made major-general of volunteers in July. He had command of the right wing (Army of the Cumberland), which bore the brunt of the attack at Stone's River. In the new organization of the army, he commanded the Twentieth Corps until after the battle of Chickamauga. Later, he had command of the northern defenses of Washington, and the District of Eastern Kansas. Retiring from the volunteer service, he resumed his rank of lieutenant-colonel in the regular army, serving with the Twenty-sixth and other infantry regiments. He was aide-de-camp to General Sherman from 1875 to 1880. In 1890 he was made brigadier-general, and became major-general, in 1894. He held several public positions of honor, and was retired in 1895. General McCook served on a commission to investigate the administration of the War Department during the Spanish war. He died in Dayton, Ohio, June 12, 1903.

John H. Ketcham, Promoted for Gallantry During the War.

George W. Von Schaack Led the Seventh New York in the Charge against the Stonewall at Fredericksburg.

Max Weber, in Command at Harper's Ferry in 1864.

Charles G. Halpine (Miles O'Reilly), Poet and Author; Assistant Adjutant-General.

Charles H. Morgan, Promoted to Regular Rank for Gallantry in the Field.

Patrick H. Jones, Originally Colonel of the 154th Regiment.

Charles H. Van Wyck, Originally Colonel of the 56th Regiment.

Hiram C. Rogers, Chief of Staff to General H. W. Slocum.

FEDERAL GENERALS
No. 18

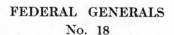

NEW YORK
(Continued)

Guy V. Henry, Originally Colonel of the 40th Regiment.

Twentieth Army Corps

A corps with the designation of Twentieth was created on April 4, 1864, from the troops of the Eleventh and Twelfth corps which, under Hooker, had joined the Army of the Cumberland in October, 1863. One division never joined the main body and finally engaged in Thomas' campaign against Hood in Tennessee, but the remainder followed the fortunes of the Atlanta campaign, and one of its brigades was the first to enter that city. On the march to the sea and the campaign through the Carolinas, the Twentieth Corps was part of Slocum's Army of Georgia. The corps commanders were Major-Generals Joseph Hooker, Henry W. Slocum, Joseph A. Mower, and Brigadier-General Alpheus S. Williams. The corps was discontinued on June 1, 1865.

Twenty-first Army Corps

THE LEFT WING of the Army of the Cumberland was made the Twenty-first Army Corps on January 9, 1863, and the command was given to Major-General T. L. Crittenden. Its other commanders were Brigadier-Generals T. J. Wood and Major-General J. M. Palmer. On October 9th, it was consolidated with the original Twentieth Corps and merged in the new Fourth Corps. The only battle the Twenty-first Corps participated in as an organization was Chickamauga, where one division fought with Thomas throughout the entire battle.

MAJOR-GENERAL THOMAS LEONIDAS CRITTENDEN was born in Russellville, Kentucky, May 15, 1815, and became a lawyer. He served in the Mexican War and later was United States consul at Liverpool, until 1853. In September, 1861, he was given a division in the Army of the Ohio under Buell, and was made major-general of volunteers for his conduct at Shiloh. In the campaign against Bragg, in Kentucky, he commanded the Second Corps, Army of the Ohio; the Left Wing, Army of the Cumberland, at Stone's River and the Twenty-first Army Corps at Chickamauga. For a short period, May–June, 1864, he led a division in the Ninth Corps. He resigned from the volunteer service in December, 1864, and after the war reentered the regular army as colonel. He received the brevet of brigadier-general in 1867, was retired in 1881, and died on Staten Island, New York, October 23, 1893.

Twenty-second Army Corps

CREATED February 2, 1863, and consisted of the troops occuping the defenses of Washington. It was first headed by Major-General S. P. Heintzelman, and he was succeeded by Major-Generals C. C. Augur and J. G. Parke. This corps saw active service only when it held the outer line of works during Lieutenant-General Early's attack on Washington, July 12, 1864. The roster of this corps was constantly changing as the troops were sent to reenforce other corps, so that it had no strong organization.

MAJOR-GENERAL CHRISTOPHER COLON AUGUR (U.S.M.A. 1843) was born in New York, July 10, 1821. He served in the Mexican War, and the campaign against the Oregon Indians. He entered the Civil War as major in the infantry, and was made brigadier of volunteers in November, 1861. He was severely wounded at Cedar Mountain, August 9, 1862, where he commanded a division in the Second Corps, Army of Virginia. He subsequently, as major-general of volunteers, had a division in the Nineteenth Corps, Army of the Gulf, from January to July, 1863, and in October was put in command of the Twenty-second Army Corps (Department of Washington) where he remained until the close of the war. He returned to the regular army in 1866, as colonel, and was made brigadier-general in 1869. He commanded several departments in the West and South and was retired in July, 1885. He died in Washington, D. C., January 16, 1898.

Samuel H. Hurst, Colonel of the 73d
Regiment.

John W. Sprague, Originally Colonel
of the 63d Regiment.

Charles F. Manderson, Originally
Colonel of the 19th Infantry.

Eliakim P. Scammon, Colonel of the
23d Regiment.

Americus V. Rice, Originally Colonel
of the 57th Regiment.

Thomas C. H. Smith, Promoted from
the 1st Cavalry in 1862.

FEDERAL

GENERALS

No. 19—OHIO

Nathaniel C. McLean, Originally
Colonel of the 7th Infantry.

E. B. Tyler, Originally Colonel of
the 7th Infantry.

Twenty-third Army Corps

CREATED April 27, 1863, out of troops in the Department of the Ohio, then headed by Major-General A. E. Burnside. The regiments forming it had been stationed in Kentucky, and Major-General G. L. Hartsuff was placed in command. He was succeeded by Brigadier-Generals M. D. Manson, J. D. Cox, Major-Generals George Stoneman, and J. M. Schofield. The corps fought in Eastern Tennessee and was besieged in Knoxville. As the Army of the Ohio, it went on the Atlanta campaign and after the capture of that city, it returned to Tennessee and was prominent at Franklin and Nashville. The corps was then (except two divisions) moved to North Carolina and captured Wilmington in February, 1865. It joined Sherman's army at Goldsboro and marched with it to Washington. The corps was discontinued, August 1, 1865.

MAJOR-GENERAL GEORGE LUCAS HARTSUFF (U. S.M.A. 1852) was born in Tyre, New York, May 28, 1830, and served in Texas and Florida. He was at Fort Pickens from April to July, 1861, and then under Rosecrans. At Cedar Mountain, Manassas, and Antietam, he commanded a brigade, and in the last battle was severely wounded. In November, he was made major-general of volunteers, and after May, 1863, he was in command of the new Twenty-third Army Corps until September 24, 1863. Toward the end of the siege of Petersburg, he commanded the works at Bermuda Hundred. After leaving the volunteer service at the conclusion of the war he continued in the regular army, and was retired with the rank of major-general in June, 1871, on account of his wounds. He died in New York, May 16, 1874.

Twenty-fourth Army Corps

CREATED December 3, 1864, to consist of white troops of the Tenth and Eighteenth corps, Army of the James. Its first commander, Major-General E. O. C. Ord, headed it for only three days, and he was followed by Brevet Major-General A. H. Terry, Brigadier-General Charles Devens, Jr., Major-General John Gibbon, and Brevet Major-General John W. Turner. One division was sent to the operations against Fort Fisher, and its place was taken by one from the Eighth Army Corps. It was present at the final operations around Petersburg, and the pursuit of Lee. The corps was discontinued August 1, 1865.

MAJOR-GENERAL EDWARD OTHO CRESAP ORD (U.S.M.A. 1839) was born in Cumberland, Maryland, October 18, 1818. He served in the Seminole War and in various Indian expeditions in the far West. In 1859, he took part in the capture of John Brown at Harper's Ferry. As brigadier-general of volunteers, he commanded a brigade in Buell's Division and the First Corps of the Army of the Potomac from October, 1861, to April, 1862, and had a division in the Department of the Rappahannock until June 10th. As major-general of volunteers, he commanded a division in the Army of West Tennessee. Then he assumed command of the Thirteenth Army Corps in the Armies of the Tennessee, and of the Gulf; of the Eighteenth Army Corps in the Department of Virginia and North Carolina, and of the Twenty-fourth Army Corps in the Army of the James, to the command of which army he succeeded Major-General B. F. Butler in January, 1865. He was wounded in the assault on Fort Harrison, but did not give up his command. Ord was retired with full rank of major-general in 1880, and died July 22, 1883, in Havana, Cuba.

Twenty-fifth Army Corps

CREATED December 3, 1864, to consist of the colored troops of the Tenth and Eighteenth corps, Army of the James. Its commanders were Major-General Godfrey Weitzel and Brigadier-General C. A. Heckman. One division went with Terry to Fort Fisher; the others remained in Virginia, taking part in the final operations around Petersburg, and then formed the army of occupation in Texas.

James S. Robinson, Originally
Colonel of the 82d Regiment.

John G. Mitchell, Originally Colonel
of the 113th Regiment.

George W. Morgan, Commander of a
Division at Chickasaw Bluffs.

James W. Forsyth, Originally Colonel of the
18th U. S. Infantry.

FEDERAL GENERALS—

No. 20

OHIO

Ralph P. Buckland, Originally Colonel of the 72d
Regiment.

Benjamin Potts, Originally
Colonel of the 32d
Regiment.

Charles G. Gilbert, Corps
Commander at Perry-
ville under Gen. Buell.

Jacob Ammen, Originally
Colonel of the 24th Ohio;
Led a Brigade at Shiloh.

Thomas Smith, Originally
Colonel of the 54th
Regiment.

Its last regiments were mustered out on January 8, 1866. In February, 1865, it numbered about fourteen thousand troops.

MAJOR-GENERAL GODFREY WEITZEL (U.S.M.A. 1855) was born in Cincinnati, Ohio, November 1, 1835, and entered the Engineer Corps. At the opening of the Civil War, as first lieutenant, he served at the defense of Fort Pickens and was chief engineer of Butler's expedition to New Orleans, the capture of which city he planned and the acting mayor of which he became. As brigadier-general of volunteers, he had a brigade in the Department of the Gulf, and a brigade and division in the Nineteenth Army Corps at the siege of Port Hudson, where he commanded the right wing of Major-General Banks' forces. In May, 1864, he was given a division in the Eighteenth Army Corps, and later was chief engineer of the Army of the James, and constructed the fortifications at Bermuda Hundred and Deep Bottom. He was in command of the Eighteenth Army Corps from October to December, 1864, having been made major-general of volunteers. On the formation of the Twenty-fifth Army Corps (December, 1864) he was placed at its head and remained so, except for one short interval, until it was discontinued in January, 1866. He occupied Richmond, in April, 1865. After commanding a district in Texas, he was mustered out of the service, and returned to engineering work in the army. He became lieutenant-colonel of engineers in 1882. He had been brevetted major-general in the regular army in 1865. He died in Philadelphia, March 19, 1884.

First Corps—Army of the Ohio

THE ARMY OF THE OHIO was organized into three corps on September 29, 1862. The First was commanded by Major-General A. McDowell McCook. It bore the chief part in the battle of Perryville, Kentucky (October 8, 1862), and the campaign against Bragg in Kentucky. On October 24th, it was merged in the Fourteenth Corps, known as the Army of the Cumberland.

Second Corps—Army of the Ohio

THIS CORPS fought at Bardstown in the campaign against Bragg. It was headed by Major-General T. L. Crittenden. It constituted the right wing of the army, and was accompanied by Major-General George H. Thomas, who was second in command in the Army of the Ohio. Like the First Corps it had a brief existence, and it was merged in the Fourteenth Corps, October 24, 1862.

Third Corps—Army of the Ohio

THIS CORPS was commanded by Major-General C. C. Gilbert. It took part in the Kentucky campaign, but was only slightly engaged in Perryville. Its three divisions were commanded by Brigadier-Generals Schoepff, Mitchell, and Sheridan and Colonel Kennett. It was merged in the Fourteenth Corps, October 24, 1862.

Cavalry Corps—Military Division of the Mississippi

THE FIRST CAVALRY CORPS in the West was organized in October, 1864, with Brevet Major-General J. H. Wilson at its head. There were seven divisions, of which four took part in the battle of Nashville, December 15th and 16th. Wilson entered Alabama in March, 1865, and the corps fought its last engagement with Forrest at Columbus, Georgia, on April 16th. One division of this corps, under Brigadier-General Judson Kilpatrick, consisting of four brigades, accompanied Sherman's army through Georgia and the Carolinas, and was present at Bentonville and Johnston's surrender.

Emerson Opdycke, Brevetted for Gallantry at the Battle of Franklin.

Henry Van Ness Boynton, Decorated for Gallantry in Action.

Joseph Warren Keifer, Originally Colonel of the 110th Regiment.

FEDERAL GENERALS

No. 21

OHIO (CONTINUED)

John Beatty, Originally Colonel of the 3d Regiment of Infantry.

Joel A. Dewey, Originally Colonel of the 111th U. S. Colored Troops.

Hugh Ewing, Brevetted for Gallantry in 1865.

George P. Este, Originally Colonel of the 14th Infantry.

Catherinus P. Buckingham, Appointed in 1862.

Cavalry Forces—Department of the Cumberland

THE CAVALRY was a separate command in the Army of the Cumberland after the reorganization of January 9, 1863. It was headed in turn by Major-General D. S. Stanley and Brigadier-Generals R. B. Mitchell, W. L. Elliott, and R. W. Johnson. In October, 1864, this force was included in the newly formed Cavalry Corps of the Military Division of the Mississippi.

Reserve Corps—Army of the Cumberland

ORGANIZED June 8, 1863, and discontinued October 9th, when the troops were merged in the reorganized Fourth and Fourteenth corps. Major-General Gordon Granger was its commander. It served through the Tullahoma campaign, and went to the assistance of Thomas at Chickamauga.

Reserve Corps—Army of the Gulf

THE TROOPS of the Nineteenth Corps that were not sent to Washington and the Shenandoah valley were organized into the Reserve Corps of the Army of the Gulf, on December 5, 1864. It was commanded by Major-Generals J. J. Reynolds and Gordon Granger, and was merged in the reorganized Thirteenth Army Corps, February 18, 1865.

South Carolina Expeditional Corps

ORGANIZED under the command of Brigadier-General T. W. Sherman in September and October, 1861. It consisted of three brigades. This was the force that assisted the navy at the capture of Port Royal, occupying the abandoned works and garrisoning the base thus secured. It formed the nucleus of the Department of the South and the Tenth Army Corps.

BRIGADIER-GENERAL THOMAS WEST SHERMAN (U.S.M.A. 1836) was born at Newport, Rhode Island, March 26, 1813. He served in the Seminole War and as captain in the War with Mexico. At the opening of the Civil War, he was lieutenant in the artillery, and was promoted to brigadier-general of volunteers, May 17, 1861. He was placed at the head of the South Carolina Expeditional Corps and commanded the land forces in the operations around Port Royal. After that, he commanded a division in Grant's Army of West Tennessee. In September, 1862, he was put at the head of the Federal troops at Carrollton, Louisiana, in the Department of the Gulf, and in January, 1863, took charge of the defenses of New Orleans. He went with Banks to Port Hudson, in May, 1863, as division commander in the Nineteenth Army Corps. After that, he was again stationed at New Orleans with the reserve artillery and at the defenses of the city. After leaving the volunteer service at the close of the war, he was colonel of the Third Artillery, at Fort Adams, Rhode Island. On December 31, 1870, he was retired with full rank, of major-general. He died in Newport, March 16, 1879.

First Corps—Army of Virginia

CREATED June 26, 1862, from troops in the Mountain Department under Major-General Fremont, who, refusing to serve under Major-General Pope, was replaced by Major-General Franz Sigel. Brigadier-General R. C. Schenck headed the corps for short periods. After the close of Pope's Virginia campaign, it was merged in the Eleventh Corps, Army of the Potomac, September 12, 1862.

Franklin Sawyer, Originally Colonel of the 8th Regiment.

Anson G. McCook, Colonel of the 194th Regiment.

Henry M. Cist, Promoted for Gallantry at Stone's River.

Charles H. Grosvenor, Colonel of the 18th Veteran.

Timothy Stanley, Originally Colonel of the 18th Regiment.

Anson Stager, Conspicuous in the Telegraph Corps.

Henry C. Corbin, Colonel of Colored Infantry; Later Lieutenant-General of the United States Army.

William S. Smith, Originally Colonel of the 13th Regiment.

FEDERAL

GENERALS

—No. 22—

OHIO

William B. Woods, Originally Colonel of the 76th Regiment.

Robert K. Scott, Originally Colonel of the 68th Regiment.

Second Corps—Army of Virginia

CREATED June 26, 1862, from the troops in the Department of the Shenandoah. It was commanded by Major-General N. P. Banks, and later by Brigadier-General A. S. Williams. It defeated Jackson at Cedar Mountain and fought in the other battles of the campaign. When the Army of Virginia was discontinued it was merged in the Twelfth Corps, Army of the Potomac.

Third Corps—Army of Virginia

CREATED June 26, 1862, from the troops in the Department of the Rappahannock, previously the First Corps of the Army of the Potomac. It was commanded by Major-General Irvin McDowell and later by Brigadier-General J. B. Ricketts and Major-General Joseph Hooker. On the discontinuation of the Army of Virginia, it became again the First Corps of the Army of the Potomac.

Cavalry Corps—Army of the Potomac

A CAVALRY DIVISION under Brigadier-General A. Pleasonton was organized in July, 1862, and was with the Army of the Potomac, until February, 1863, when the Cavalry Corps was created with Major-General George Stoneman at its head. Its other commanders were Brigadier-Generals A. Pleasonton, D. McM. Gregg, Major-General P. H. Sheridan, Brigadier-General A. T. A. Torbert, Brevet Brigadier-General William Wells, Major-Generals Wesley Merritt and George Crook. Two divisions were transferred to the Army of the Shenandoah in August, 1864, and remained with it until til March, 1865. At first, the corps numbered over eleven thousand men. It saw constant active service; its most important battle being the one at Beverly Ford, Virginia, on June 9, 1863. Its hardest fighting took place in the Wilderness campaign of 1864. The corps was broken up in May, 1865.

MAJOR-GENERAL PHILIP HENRY SHERIDAN (U.S.M.A. 1853) was born in Albany, New York, March 6, 1831. After service in the West he became captain in May, 1861. He was on the staff of Halleck at Corinth, and in May, 1862, was made colonel of the Second Michigan Cavalry. Defeating Forrest's and repulsing Chalmer's superior force at Booneville, he was made brigadier-general of volunteers. In August, he defeated Falkner in Mississippi, and in September commanded a division in the Army of the Ohio, at Perryville and another in the Army of the Cumberland at Stone's River, for which service he was made major-general of volunteers and fought with great ability at Chickamauga and Missionary Ridge. In April, 1864, he was transferred to the command of the Cavalry Corps, Army of the Potomac, and in August he was put at the head of the Army of the Shenandoah and defeated Early at Cedar Creek. In December, 1864, he was made major-general in the regular army, lieutenant-general in March, 1869, and general June 1, 1888. He died in Nonquit, Massachusetts, August 5, 1888.

BREVET MAJOR-GENERAL ALFRED THOMAS ARCHIMEDES TORBERT (U.S.M.A. 1855) was born in Georgetown, Delaware, July 1, 1833. He entered the Civil War as colonel of the First New Jersey Volunteers, and commanded a brigade in the Sixth Army Corps. He had command of a division in the Sixth Corps, March–April, 1864, after which he had a division in the Cavalry Corps, and was given command of the Corps on August 6, 1864. He resigned in 1866, with the brevet of major-general of volunteers and served as United States consul-general at Havana in 1871. September 30, 1880, he was drowned in the wreck of the ill-fated steamer *Vera Cruz* off the Florida coast.

MAJOR-GENERAL WESLEY MERRITT (U.S.M.A. 1860) was born in New York, June 16, 1836. In 1861, he was at first, second and then first lieutenant of cavalry. He served throughout the Civil War, for the most part in the cavalry of the Army of the Potomac, where he rose to the command of the Cavalry Corps in the Shenandoah on January 26, 1865, and in the Army of the Potomac from March 25–May 22, 1865. After the war he served in various Indian campaigns, was superintendent of the United States Military Academy at West Point, and in May, 1898, was given command of the United States forces to be sent to the Philippines. He was first American military governor of those islands. He retired from the army in 1900 and died December 3, 1910.

VII

CONFEDERATE
ARMIES
AND
GENERALS

CONFEDERATES OF '61—AT THE BIRTH OF THE SOUTHERN ARMY, WHEN
"GUARDS," "GRAYS," AND "RIFLES" ABOUNDED—THESE ARE THE "PELICAN
RIFLES" OF BATON ROUGE, LOUISIANA, LATER MERGED INTO THE SEVENTH
LOUISIANA VOLUNTEERS WHICH SUFFERED THE HEAVIEST LOSS OF ANY CON-
FEDERATE REGIMENT ENGAGED IN THE FIGHT AT PORT REPUBLIC, JUNE 9, 1862

The Armies of the Confederate States

THE permanent Constitution of the Confederate States of America provided that the President should be commander-in-chief of the army and navy, and of the militia of the several States when called into actual service. Accordingly, in any consideration of the Confederate army, the part played by President Davis must be borne in mind; also the fact that he previously had seen service in the United States army and that he had been Secretary of War of the United States. As Secretaries of War in the Confederate States Government there were associated with President Davis, the following: LeRoy Pope Walker, of Alabama, February 21, 1861, to September 17, 1861; Judah P. Benjamin, of Louisiana, September 17, 1861, to March 17, 1862; George W. Randolph, of Virginia, March 17, 1862, to November 17, 1862: Major-General Gustavus W. Smith, of Kentucky, November 17, 1862, to November 21, 1862; James A. Seddon, of Virginia, from November 21, 1862, to February 6, 1865; and Major-General John C. Breckinridge, of Kentucky, February 6, 1865, to the close of the war.

Unlike the Union army there were generals, both regular and of the provisional army, as well as lieutenant-generals; it being the intention that every commander of an army should rank as general, and every commander of a corps should rank as lieutenant-general. Such was the case with the generals mentioned in the biographical matter following in connection with the various armies and other organizations. An exception to this statement was General Samuel Cooper, who served at Richmond as adjutant and inspector-general.

GENERAL SAMUEL COOPER (U.S.M.A. 1815) was born in Hackensack, New Jersey, June 12, 1798, and served in the army, receiving the brevet of colonel for his services in the Mexican War. He resigned in March, 1861, to enter the service of the Confederacy. He was appointed general on May 16th, but, owing to his age, took no active part in the field. He was adjutant and inspector-general of the Confederate States army throughout the entire war, performing his duties with great thoroughness and ability. He died at Cameron, Virginia, December 3, 1876.

Army of the Shenandoah

MAJOR-GENERAL KENTON HARPER, of the Virginia State forces, had collected about two thousand Virginia volunteers at Harper's Ferry as early as April 21, 1861. He was relieved on the 28th by Colonel Thomas J. Jackson, and the mustering in of volunteers went rapidly on. On May 24th, Brigadier-General Joseph E. Johnston assumed command of the troops, and on June 30th, there were 10,654 present for duty, in four brigades and cavalry. This was the force that opposed Major-General Patterson in the Valley, and it was known as the Army of the Shenandoah. It took part in the engagement at Falling Waters, July 2d, and the skirmishes near Bunker Hill and Charlestown. Strengthened with eight Southern regiments, this army started for Manassas, on July 18th, and took part in the first battle of Bull Run. After this, it formed a part of the Confederate Army of the Potomac.

GENERAL JOSEPH EGGLESTON JOHNSTON (U.S.M.A. 1829) was born in Cherry Grove, near Farmville, Virginia, February 3, 1807. He served in the Black Hawk, Seminole, and Mexican wars, in the last of which he was twice severely wounded. He resigned his rank of brigadier-general to enter the Confederate service on April 20, 1861, and was given the rank of general in August. He was in command at Harper's Ferry after May 24th, and headed the Army of the Shenandoah. He brought his troops to Manassas and superseded Beauregard in the command, at Bull Run, joining his force to the Army of the Potomac. In command of the Army of Northern Virginia, he was severely wounded at Fair Oaks. In November, 1862, he was assigned to the head of the Department of Tennessee, but outside of an attempt to relieve Pemberton at Vicksburg in May, 1863, he saw no active service until he assumed command of the Army of Tennessee in December, 1863. He opposed Sherman during the Atlanta campaign of 1864, being superseded by General Hood on July 18th. His strategy was much criticised at the time, but it is now recognized that he displayed great ability during the campaign. In February, 1865, he was again given command of the Army of Tennessee,

CONFEDERATE
GENERALS
FULL RANK
BEAUREGARD
AND
JOHNSTON

Pierre Gustave Tou-
tant Beauregard re-
ceived the Surrender
of the First Federal
Citadel — Fort Sum-
ter; Fought in De-
fense of the Last Con-
federate Citadel—the
City of Petersburg.

All the officers who
held the rank of Gen-
eral in the Confed-
erate States Army are
shown here, except-
ing Robert E. Lee,
whose portrait has
already appeared in
this volume, and
Albert Sidney John-
ston, whose portrait
appears among those
killed in battle.

Joseph Eggleston
Johnston commanded
the First and the Last
Great Aggressive
Movements of Con-
federate Armies—Bull
Run and Bentonville.

Army of the Peninsula

and attempted to prevent Sherman's advance through the Carolinas. Johnston's capitulation was agreed upon near Durham's Station, North Carolina, April 26, 1865. He was United States commissioner of railroads from 1885 to 1889. He died in Washington, March 21, 1891.

Army of the Peninsula

THE DEPARTMENT OF THE PENINSULA was established on May 26, 1861, and Colonel John B. Magruder was put in command. The troops therein were organized into divisions in November, and denominated the Army of the Peninsula. In December, the aggregate present was about sixteen thousand. On April 12, 1862, it was merged in the Army of Northern Virginia—constituting, under Major-General Magruder, the right wing of that army.

MAJOR-GENERAL JOHN BANKHEAD MAGRUDER (U.S.M.A. 1830) was born at Winchester, Virginia, August 15, 1810, and served in the Seminole and Mexican wars. He was stationed in Washington in 1861, and resigned in April to enter the Confederate service as colonel. He had charge of the artillery in and around Richmond, and after May 21st, a division in the Department of the Peninsula, the troops of which were later designated the Army of the Peninsula. On June 10th, his division repelled the attack of Major-General B. F. Butler at Big Bethel, for which feat he was made brigadier-general. In October, he was promoted to major-general. Having fortified the Peninsula, he kept McClellan's army in check in April, 1862. On April 18th, his forces became the Right Wing of the Army of Northern Virginia, and he commanded it during the Peninsula campaign. Magruder was then appointed to the Trans-Mississippi Department, in order to prosecute the war more vigorously in the West, but the assignment was changed, and in October, 1862, he was given the District of Texas, which was afterward enlarged to include New Mexico and Arizona. Magruder recaptured Galveston, January 1, 1863, and kept the port open. After the war he served in the army of Maximilian, and after the fall of the Mexican empire settled in Houston, Texas, where he died, February 19, 1871.

Army of the Northwest

THE TROOPS assigned to operate in northwestern Virginia were placed under the command of Brigadier-General R. S. Garnett on June 8, 1861, and were subsequently known as the Army of the Northwest. This was the force that opposed McClellan and Rosecrans in West Virginia, and was defeated at Rich Mountain and other places. On July 13th, Garnett was killed while retreating, and Brigadier-General Henry R. Jackson was put in command, to be superseded, within a week, by Brigadier-General W. W. Loring. Early in 1862, dissension arose between Loring and T. J. Jackson, commanding the Valley District (Department of Northern Virginia), which led to the latter preferring charges against the commander of the Army of the Northwest. As a result, the Secretary of War, on February 9, 1862, divided the army, sending some of the regiments to Knoxville, some to the Aquia District, and the remainder to the Army of the Potomac (Department of Northern Virginia). After this, the forces under Brigadier-General Edward Johnson stationed at Camp Alleghany, and sometimes called the Army of the Alleghany, continued to be called the Army of the Northwest. Its aggregate strength in March, 1862, was about four thousand. It finally came under Jackson in the Valley District and passed into the Army of Northern Virginia.

BRIGADIER-GENERAL ROBERT SELDEN GARNETT (U.S.M.A. 1841) was born in Essex County, Virginia, December 16, 1819, and served in the Mexican War as aide to General Taylor. At the outbreak of the Civil War he entered the Confederate service, and in June, 1861, was appointed brigadier-general, with command of the Army of the Northwest. In the action at Carrick's Ford he was killed, June 13, 1861.

BRIGADIER-GENERAL HENRY ROOTES JACKSON was born in Athens, Georgia, June 24, 1820, and became a lawyer. He served in the Mexican War as colonel of the First Georgia Volunteers, and was *chargé d'affaires* at Vienna, in 1863. As United States district attorney for Georgia he aided in trying slave-trading cases. At the outbreak of the

JOHN BELL HOOD

To Paraphrase a Classic Eulogy, "None Led with More Glory than Hood, yet Many Led and There Was Much Glory."

EDMUND KIRBY SMITH

Skilful and Persistent Fighter Against Odds and Ever Indomitable in the Face of Reverses in the Field.

BRAXTON BRAGG

Leader in Three of the Fiercest Battles of the War and Carried the Southern Battle Line to Its Farthest North in the West; A Record of Four Years in the Field.

SAMUEL COOPER

Ranking Officer of the Army. All Commanding Generals Reported to Cooper and Received All Orders from Him. His Post and Duties were those of a Modern Chief of Staff.

CONFEDERATE GENERALS—FULL RANK
HOOD, KIRBY SMITH, BRAGG AND COOPER

Civil War he entered the Confederate Army as a brigadier-general, succeeding to temporary command of the Army of the Northwest after Brigadier-General Garnett was killed. He resigned his commission because he could not obtain leave of absence to take charge of the Georgia coast defenses, to which post he was called by the Governor of Georgia, who made him a major-general in command of the State troops. After these became part of the Confederate army, in 1862, Jackson received no commission until July, 1864, when he was assigned a brigade in the Army of Tennessee. During the battle of Nashville he was made prisoner and not released until the close of the war, when he returned to Savannah to practise law. He was United States minister to Mexico in 1885, and died in Savannah, May 23, 1898.

MAJOR-GENERAL WILLIAM WING LORING was born in Wilmington, North Carolina, December 4, 1818, and served in the Seminole and Mexican wars. In the latter he lost an arm. Later, he was colonel of a regiment sent against the Indians in New Mexico. He resigned from the army to enter the Confederate service, and came into command of the Army of the Northwest, July 20, 1861. He was made major-general in February, 1862. His chief active service was in Kentucky, and in Mississippi, before and during the Vicksburg campaign; in that same State under Polk, and as division commander in the Army of Mississippi in the Atlanta campaign, and in the Army of Tennessee at Franklin and Nashville, and under Johnston in the Carolinas. After the war he went to Egypt, where he served as general in command of a division in the army of the Khedive. He died in New York city, December 30, 1886.

MAJOR-GENERAL EDWARD JOHNSON (U.S.M. A. 1838) was born in Chesterfield County, Virginia, April 16, 1816, and served in the Mexican War. He entered the Confederate army and was made a brigadier-general, commanding the Northwest forces directly under Major-General T. J. Jackson, in May, 1862. The next year (February, 1863), he was made major-general. He had a division in the Second Corps, Army of Northern Virginia, and in September, 1864, was assigned to the division of the Second Corps, Army of Tennessee. He died in Richmond, Virginia, March 2, 1873.

Army of the Potomac

ON MAY 24, 1861, Brigadier-General M. L. Bonham was placed in command of the troops on the line of Alexandria. On the 31st, he was relieved by Brigadier-General P. G. T. Beauregard. The forces here gathered were denominated the Army of the Potomac (afterward First Corps, Army of the Potomac) and consisted of six brigades, some unattached troops, and artillery, by the date of the battle of Bull Run. The Army of the Shenandoah joined this force on July 20th, when Johnston superseded Beauregard. The Department of Northern Virginia was created October 22, 1861, with Johnston at its head. It included the District of the Potomac (Beauregard); Valley District (T. J. Jackson), and Aquia District (T. H. Holmes.) In February, 1862, some of the troops in the Army of the Northwest came under Johnston's control, giving his entire command a strength of over eighty-two thousand. Beauregard had been sent to Kentucky on January 29th, and the troops in the Potomac district were now divided into four divisions with several separate detachments. On March 14th, the Army of the Potomac was denominated the Army of Northern Virginia. The total force then amounted to about fifty-five thousand.

GENERAL PIERRE GUSTAVE TOUTANT BEAUREGARD (U.S.M.A. 1838) was born near New Orleans, May 28, 1818, and entered the Engineer Corps. He served with distinction in the Mexican War, and at the outbreak of the Civil War resigned his commission (February 20, 1861), to enter the Confederate army as a brigadier-general, being given command of the Confederate forces bombarding Fort Sumter. He took command of the Army of the Potomac on June 20th. After Bull Run he was made general. He was given the command of the Army of the Mississippi in March, 1862, and was second in command after A. S. Johnston joined his forces with it. After the latter's death at Shiloh, Beauregard remained at the head of the army until after the withdrawal from Corinth at the end of May. In 1863, he defended Charleston, and after May, 1864, cooperated with Lee in the defense of Petersburg and Richmond. He commanded the Confederate forces in the Carolinas in 1865, merging them with those under General J. E. Johnston, and surrendered his army to Sherman. After the war, he was a railroad president, adjutant-general of Louisiana, and manager of the State lottery. He died in New Orleans, February 20, 1893.

RICHARD STODDERT EWELL
A Battle Record from July 21, 1861, to April 6, 1865.
Fought Nearly Three Years on a Wooden Leg.

JAMES LONGSTREET
None Knew Better than Longstreet's Opponents How and
Where He Earned the Sobriquet "Lee's Warhorse."

JUBAL ANDERSON EARLY
Modest in Victory, Undaunted by Defeat, He Defended the
Shenandoah Against Enormous Odds.

DANIEL HARVEY HILL
Had No Superior as the Marshal of a Division in
Assault or Defense.

LIEUTENANT–GENERALS OF THE CONFEDERACY—GROUP No. 1

On this and the two pages following appear portraits of all officers who held the rank of Lieutenant-
General in the Confederate States Army, with the exception of "Stonewall" Jackson and
A. P. Hill, whose portraits have appeared among the general officers killed in battle.

Army of Northern Virginia

GENERAL J. E. JOHNSTON was wounded at.Seven Pines, May 31, 1862, and Major-General G. W. Smith took command of the Army of Northern Virginia. On June 1st, General Robert E. Lee assumed command. In April, the forces on the Peninsula had been included in this army, and now the troops in eastern Virginia and North Carolina were made part of it. By the end of July, 1862, the division organization had been further concentrated into three commands, or corps, headed by Major-Generals T. J. Jackson, James Longstreet, and D. H. Hill, with cavalry under Brigadier-General J. E. B. Stuart, and artillery under Brigadier-General W. N. Pendleton. There was an aggregate present of about ninety-five thousand. Subsequently, the army took a more permanent form in two corps commanded by Jackson and Longstreet, with cavalry corps and artillery separate. Lieutenant-General A. P. Hill was given the Second Corps after Jackson's death, and on May 30, 1863, this was divided, with additions from the First Corps, into the Second and Third corps, commanded by Lieutenant-Generals R. S. Ewell and A. P. Hill respectively. The army numbered about seventy thousand in the Gettysburg campaign. This organization of the main body of the army continued throughout the war, although other generals, for various reasons, commanded the corps from time to time. A new corps of North Carolina and Virginia troops under Lieutenant-General R. H. Anderson was added at the end of 1864. Longstreet's corps, with the exception of Pickett's division, was with the Army of Tennessee, and in eastern Tennessee, for a short period in 1863 and 1864, at and after the battle of Chickamauga. The last report of the army, February, 1865, showed an aggregate present of over seventy-three thousand. The Army of Northern Virginia laid down its arms at Appomattox Court House, April 9, 1865.

First Corps—Army of Northern Virginia

THE ORGANIZATION of the volunteer Confederate forces under Brigadier-General Beauregard into the First Corps, Army of the Potomac, was announced on June 20, 1861. There were then six brigades, which number was increased later to eight. The strength of the corps was about thirty thousand. A division organization was afterward adopted, and one of these divisions, commanded by Major-General Longstreet, was denominated the Center of Position, Army of Northern Virginia, at the opening of the Peninsula campaign. It contained about fourteen thousand men. As the Second Division (or Corps) of the army, the troops fought from Fair Oaks, where they were known as the Right Wing, through the Seven Days' battles. Toward the end of July, the army was further concentrated into commands of which one, consisting of six divisions, was headed by Longstreet, and this, during the campaign against Pope, was called the Right Wing or Longstreet's Corps. After the battle of Antietam, the corps was designated the First Corps, Army of Northern Virginia. In September, 1863, Lee sent the corps, with the exception of Pickett's division, to assist Bragg, and, as Longstreet's Corps, fought in the Army of Tennessee at Chickamauga and remained in East Tennessee until April, 1864, when it rejoined the Army of Virginia. Major-General R. H. Anderson succeeded to the command of the corps after Longstreet was wounded at the battle of the Wilderness, May 6th. The latter returned to his corps, October 19th, and continued at the head until the surrender at Appomattox.

LIEUTENANT-GENERAL JAMES LONGSTREET (U. S.M.A. 1842) was born in Edgefield District, South Carolina, January 8, 1821, and served in the Mexican War, where he was severely wounded. In June, 1861, he resigned as major in the army and was appointed brigadier-general in the Confederate service. As major-general, he had a division, and, later, as lieutenant-general, the First Corps of the Army of Northern Virginia. In September, 1863, he was sent with part of his corps to Tennessee and took command of the left wing at the battle of Chickamauga. He was then placed at the head of the Department of East Tennessee and returned to Virginia in April, 1864. He was severely wounded at the battle of the Wilderness, May 6, 1864, but resumed command of the corps in October. After the war, he engaged in business in New Orleans and held several political offices. In 1880-81 he was American minister to Turkey, and in 1898 he was appointed United States railway commissioner. He died at Gainesville, Georgia, January 2, 1904.

Wade Hampton Fought from Bull Run to Bentonville. With J. E. B. Stuart's Cavalry he "Stood in the Way" of Sheridan at Trevilian Station in 1864.

Richard Henry Anderson Commanded a Brigade on the Peninsula; Later He Commanded a Division and, after the Wilderness, Longstreet's Corps.

John Brown Gordon. This Intrepid Leader of Forlorn Hope Assaults Rose from a Civilian Captain to the Second Highest Rank in the Army.

Leonidas Polk, Bishop and Soldier Both, to the End; He Fell on the Battlefield of Pine Mountain in the Defense of Atlanta.

William Joseph Hardee, On the Front Line for Four Years; Last Commander of the Defense of Charleston and Savannah.

Stephen Dill Lee Fought in Five States; with Beauregard at Charleston, April, 1861, and with Hood at Nashville, December, 1864.

LIEUTENANT-GENERALS OF THE CONFEDERACY—GROUP No. 2

Second Corps—Army of Northern Virginia

ON SEPTEMBER 25, 1861, Major-General G. W. Smith was assigned to the command of the Second Corps, Army of the Potomac, which was organized to consist of all the troops not hitherto assigned to the First Corps. After October 22d, the force was known as the Second Division and contained five brigades. It numbered almost twenty thousand men, and passed into the Reserve, Second Division, and D. H. Hill's Division of the Army of Northern Virginia. Most of these troops finally came under the command of Lieutenant-General T. J. Jackson and became known as the Second Corps of the Army of Northern Virginia, after the battle of Antietam. After Jackson's death, Lieutenant-General R. S. Ewell succeeded to the corps, after it had been temporarily headed by Stuart and A. P. Hill. On May 30, 1863, two divisions were detached to enter the Third Army Corps. The corps was commanded by Lieutenant-General J. A. Early in the Shenandoah campaign of 1864, and in the closing months of the war around Petersburg, by Lieutenant-General John B. Gordon.

MAJOR-GENERAL GUSTAVUS WOODSON SMITH (U.S.M.A. 1842) was born in Georgetown, Kentucky, January 1, 1822, and served in the Mexican War. He resigned from the army in 1854 to enter upon a Cuban expedition under Quitman, and afterward settled in New York City. At the outbreak of the Civil War he joined the Confederate forces at New Orleans, under Lovell. In September, 1861, he was appointed major-general and was given command of the Second Corps, Army of the Potomac, which was continued in the Army of Northern Virginia, until March 23, 1862, when he was put at the head of the Reserves. After Johnston was wounded at Fair Oaks, May 31st, Major-General Smith, who was leading the left wing, took command of the whole army, but was stricken by illness the following day and was succeeded by General Lee. In August, he took charge of the defenses of Richmond and was acting Secretary of War in November. In February, 1863, he resigned from the service, and on June 1, 1864, took command of the Georgia Militia. He was captured by Major-General J. H. Wilson at Marion in April, 1865. He died in New York, June 24, 1896.

LIEUTENANT-GENERAL RICHARD STODDERT EWELL (U.S.M.A. 1840) was born in Georgetown, District of Columbia, February 8, 1817, and served with distinction in the Mexican War. He joined the Confederate army in 1861, and was made major-general the following year. He fought as bri-gade and division commander with the Army of Northern Virginia, and was given command of the Second Corps after the death of Lieutenant-General T. J. Jackson, being made lieutenant-general in May, 1863. He was prominent in all its battles, and at Groveton he lost a leg. After June, 1864, when his corps was sent to the Shenandoah valley under Lieutenant-General J. A. Early, he was in command of the defenses of Richmond until the evacuation of that city. He died at Spring Hill, Tennessee, January 25, 1872.

LIEUTENANT-GENERAL JUBAL ANDERSON EARLY (U.S.M.A. 1837) was born in Franklin County, Virginia, November 3, 1816, and served in the Seminole War of 1837, after which he resigned to take up the practice of law. In the Mexican War, he served as major of Virginia volunteers, and at the outbreak of the Civil War he entered the Confederate army as colonel, rising to the rank of lieutenant-general in May, 1864. He commanded a brigade at Bull Run, was wounded at Williamsburg, and had a division at Antietam and afterward. He had temporary command of both the Second and Third corps, Army of Northern Virginia, during the Wilderness campaign, and in June, 1864, was sent with the Second Army Corps to the Shenandoah valley, whence he made his way to Washington and attacked the city on July 12th. His forces were finally routed at Cedar Creek, October 19th, by Sheridan. He was relieved of the command of the Trans-Alleghany Department in March, 1865, after a defeat by Custer. After the war he practised law. He refused to take the oath of allegiance to the United States, and died in Lynchburg, Virginia, March 2, 1894. He is recognized as one of the ablest of the Confederate generals.

LIEUTENANT-GENERAL JOHN BROWN GORDON was born in Upson County, Georgia, February 6, 1832. He became a lawyer, but entered the Confederate service as lieutenant-colonel of an Alabama regiment, and rose to the rank of lieutenant-general before the close of the war. He was brigade and division commander in the Army of Northern Virginia, and was prominent in the Second Army Corps during Early's campaign in the Shenandoah valley. He was at the head of the Second Corps after January 31, 1865, and was in command of the left wing at the time of Lee's surrender. After the war, he became prominent in Georgia politics and was United States senator from that State, 1873–1880, and in 1891–1897.

ALEXANDER PETER STEWART	NATHAN BEDFORD FORREST	JOSEPH WHEELER
A Leader in Every Great Campaign from Shiloh to Bentonville.	The American Murat and the King of Mounted Raiders.	Masterful as Well as Indefatigable and Indomitable Leader of Cavalry.

LIEUTENANT–GENERALS OF THE CONFEDERACY—GROUP No. 3

SIMON BOLIVAR BUCKNER	RICHARD TAYLOR	THEOPHILUS HUNTER HOLMES	JOHN CLIFFORD PEMBERTON
Defender of His Native Kentucky in 1861 and in 1865; Led a Corps to Victory at Chickamauga.	Skillful Defender of the Trans-Mississippi Territory.	Defender of the James River in 1862 and Arkansas in 1863.	Baffled the Assailants of Vicksburg Through Three Campaigns, Yielding to only Heavy Odds.

From 1887 to 1890, he was governor of Georgia. He was commander-in-chief of the United Confederate Veterans after 1900. He died at Miami, Florida, January 9, 1904.

Third Corps—Army of Northern Virginia

CREATED from three divisions of the First and Second corps, Army of Northern Virginia, on May 30, 1863, and put under the command of Lieutenant-General A. P. Hill. Its first battle was Gettysburg. Hill was killed in front of Petersburg, April 2, 1865, and the corps was united with the First until the surrender at Appomattox.

LIEUTENANT-GENERAL AMBROSE POWELL HILL (U.S.M.A. 1847) was born in Culpeper County, Virginia, November 9, 1825, and served in the Mexican and Seminole wars. In 1861, he resigned from the army to enter the Confederate volunteers. He was appointed brigadier-general February 26, 1862, major-general in the following May and was one of the most efficient officers in the Confederate army, and rose to the command of the Third Corps, Army of Northern Virginia, when it was created in May, 1863, being made lieutenant-general at the same time. He was killed April 2, 1865.

Anderson's Corps—Army of Northern Virginia

ORGANIZED late in 1864 to consist of the divisions of Major-Generals R. F. Hoke and Bushrod R. Johnson, and a battalion of artillery under Colonel H. P. Jones. It contained an aggregate strength of about fourteen thousand. Hoke's division served with the First Army Corps and was sent to Wilmington, North Carolina, on December, 20, 1864. Johnson's division remained with the Army of Northern Virginia until the surrender at Appomattox.

LIEUTENANT-GENERAL RICHARD HERRON ANDERSON (U.S.M.A. 1842) was born in South Carolina, October 27, 1821, and served with distinction in the Mexican War. He resigned from the army in March, 1861, to enter the Confederate service. As colonel, he commanded the First South Carolina Infantry in the attack on Fort Sumter, and became brigadier-general in July, 1861. He destroyed a Union camp near Pensacola, in October, and in February, 1862, was assigned to a brigade in Longstreet's Division in the Department of Northern Virginia. This he led with great distinction through the Peninsula campaign, being made major-general in July, 1862. He had a division in the First Corps, Army of Northern Virginia, at Second Bull Run and after. At Antietam, he was severely wounded, but he fought at Fredericksburg and Chancellorsville, and at Gettysburg he was in the Third Army Corps. After the wounding of Longstreet, in the battle of the Wilderness, Anderson was given command of the First Army Corps, receiving the appointment of lieutenant-general on June 1, 1864. In August, he was sent with an infantry division, one of cavalry, and a battalion of artillery to the assistance of Lieutenant-General Early in the Shenandoah, remaining there about a month. After the return of Longstreet to his corps, Anderson's Corps, consisting of two divisions, was organized, with Lieutenant-General Anderson at its head. He died at Beaufort, South Carolina, June 26, 1879.

Cavalry Corps—Army of Northern Virginia

THE VARIOUS TROOPS of cavalry in this army were finally gathered into a division of several brigades under the command of Brigadier-General J. E. B. Stuart. By the date of the battle of Gettysburg, July, 1863, the cavalry was organized in divisions and the organization was known as the Cavalry Corps. After the death of Major-General J. E. B. Stuart, May, 1864, Major-General (later Lieutenant-General) Wade Hampton took command. Major-General Fitzhugh Lee also

Gustavus Woodson Smith, Defender of Yorktown and Richmond.

John Bankhead Magruder, Defender of the Virginia Peninsula in 1861.

William Wing Loring, with Robert E. Lee in West Virginia in 1861.

Samuel Jones, Commander Florida, Georgia and South Carolina.

Sterling Price Fought on Both Sides of the Mississippi River.

Benjamin Franklin Cheatham, Brigade, Division and Corps Commander.

Dabney Herndon Maury, Defender of the Lower Mississippi in 1862-4.

John Cabel Breckinridge, Defender of the Mississippi in 1861.

CONFEDERATE MAJOR-GENERALS

Earl Van Dorn, a Daring and Resourceful Army Commander.

CONSPICUOUS AS COMMANDERS OF ARMIES OR ARMY CORPS

commanded several divisions at one time and was in command of the corps at Appomattox.

MAJOR-GENERAL JAMES EWELL BROWN STUART (U.S.M.A. 1854) was born in Patrick County, Virginia, February 6, 1833, and entered the Cavalry Corps of the United States army, serving in Kansas and against the Cheyenne Indians. He resigned his commission as captain in the army in May, 1861, to enter the Confederate service, as colonel of the First Virginia Cavalry, with which he fought under Johnston at Bull Run. He was made brigadier-general in September and major-general the following July. He had a brigade, and a division, and was placed at the head of the Cavalry Corps, Army of Northern Virginia, when it was organized, in the summer of 1863. Stuart proved himself to be a great cavalry leader, and his exploits won him much renown. Among his famous deeds were the ride around McClellan's army in June, 1862; the dash on Pope's headquarters at Catlett's Station, Virginia, and the raid on Manassas Junction in August; the expedition into Pennsylvania after Antietam, and the cooperation with Jackson at Chancellorsville. After the wounding of Jackson in that battle, he had temporary command of the Second Corps, Army of Northern Virginia. In the Wilderness campaign of 1864, he was very active, but was mortally wounded in an encounter with Sheridan's cavalry at Yellow Tavern. He died May 12, 1864.

LIEUTENANT-GENERAL WADE HAMPTON was born in Charleston, South Carolina, March 28, 1818. He was one of the largest slave-owners in the South. At the outbreak of the Civil War, he raised and equipped, in part, Hampton's South Carolina Legion, of which he was colonel. He was wounded at Fair Oaks, as brigadier-general at the head of a brigade, and thrice at Gettysburg, where he commanded a cavalry brigade. In August, 1863, he was made major-general with a division in the cavalry, and after the death of Stuart, he became head of the Cavalry Corps, Army of Northern Virginia. He made a famous raid on General Grant's commissariat, capturing some twenty-five hundred head of cattle. In February, 1865, he was made lieutenant-general, and commanded the cavalry in the Army of Tennessee, as well as a division of that of the Army of Northern Virginia. After the war, he strongly advocated the policy of conciliation. In 1876, he was governor of South Carolina; from 1878 to 1891, United States senator, and from 1893 to 1897, United States commissioner of railroads. He died in Columbia, South Carolina, April 11, 1902.

MAJOR-GENERAL FITZHUGH LEE (U.S.M.A. 1856) was born in Clermont, Virginia, November 19, 1835. He served against the Indians, and was cavalry instructor at West Point until he resigned his commission in May, 1861, to enter the Confederate service, becoming adjutant-general in Ewell's brigade. He was made major-general September 3, 1863. He had a brigade and division in the cavalry of the Army of Northern Virginia through all its campaigns, including that of Early in the Shenandoah in 1864, where he was wounded at the Opequon. He was in command of the Cavalry Corps, Army of Northern Virginia, from March, 1865, until the surrender, replacing Wade Hampton, who went to the Army of Tennessee. From 1886 to 1890 he was governor of Virginia, and, under appointment of President Cleveland, consul-general at Havana from 1896 to the outbreak of the Spanish-American War. President McKinley appointed him major-general of volunteers in 1898 and placed him at the head of the Seventh Army Corps. He was made military governor of Havana in 1899. Later, he commanded the Department of the Missouri. He received the rank of brigadier-general in February, 1901, and was retired the following month. He died in Washington, April 28, 1905.

Army of the Kanawha

THE CONFEDERATE FORCES assigned to operate in the Kanawha valley, West Virginia, were placed under the command of Brigadier-General John B. Floyd on August 11, 1861, and denominated the Army of the Kanawha. This force and one under Brigadier-General Henry A. Wise were its chief constituents. The troops took part in the engagement at Carnifex Ferry. The strength of the command was about thirty-five hundred. Some of the troops were sent with Floyd to the Central Army of Kentucky, early in 1862, and formed one of its divisions. Several of the regiments were captured at Fort Donelson when this post capitulated to General Grant.

James T. Holtzclaw Led a Brigade
of Alabamians.

John H. Kelly, a Gallant Boy
General.

Cullen A. Battle Led a Brigade in
Virginia.

CONFEDERATE GENERALS
No. 1—ALABAMA

This is the first of 25 groups
embracing representative general officers of 14 States. On
preceding pages of this volume
appear portraits of all generals
and lieutenant-generals, all
generals killed in battle, also
commanders of armies and
army corps. Many appear in
preceding volumes of this History as identified with particular events or special branches
of the service, as cavalry and
artillery. Information concerning every general officer may
be found through the roster and
index concluding this volume.

Jonas M. Withers, Originally Colonel
of the 3d Infantry.

Edmund W. Pettus Became a Noted
United States Senator.

James H. Clanton Led a Cavalry Brigade in Mississippi.

Charles M. Shelley Led
a Brigade with Stewart.

Philip D. Roddey, Conspicuous Cavalry Leader.

Henry De Lamar Clayton,
Originally Colonel of Infantry.

Army of Eastern Kentucky

BRIGADIER-GENERAL JOHN BUCHANAN FLOYD was born at Blacksburg, Virginia, June 1, 1807, and became a lawyer, practising in Arkansas and Virginia. He entered politics, and served in the Virginia legislature, and as governor of the State in 1850. He was Secretary of War in the Buchanan cabinet, where owing to his administrative methods he was requested to resign in 1860. At the opening of the Civil War he entered the Confederate army and was appointed brigadier-general in May, 1861.

He headed the force known as the Army of the Kanawha, and in February, 1862, was in command of Fort Donelson, Tennessee. He and Brigadier-General Gideon J. Pillow fled therefrom the night before the capitulation, leaving Brigadier-General Simon Bolivar Buckner to conduct the negotiations and surrender to General Grant. For this General Floyd was relieved of his command. In November, 1862, he was in command of the Virginia State Line, and died at Abingdon, Virginia, August 26, 1863.

Army of Eastern Kentucky

A TITLE applied to the troops under Brigadier-General Humphrey Marshall, consisting of the militia of Wise, Scott and Lee counties, in 1861. It was a small force of about fifteen hundred men, and was scattered by Federal troops under Brigadier-General James A. Garfield. Its chief action was at Pound Gap, March 16, 1862.

BRIGADIER - GENERAL HUMPHREY MARSHALL (U.S.M.A. 1832) was born in Frankfort, Kentucky, January 13, 1812. He resigned from the army the year after his graduation and became a lawyer. He went to the Mexican War as colonel of

cavalry, and led a charge at Buena Vista. In 1849, he became a member of Congress, and, after being commissioner to China in 1852, served again until 1859. He entered the Confederate service, being made brigadier-general in October, 1861. At the head of a small force, sometimes called the Army of Eastern Kentucky, he undertook the conquest of that region, but was driven from it by Brigadier-General James A. Garfield in March, 1862. After this, he had several commands in Virginia and resigned from the service in June, 1863. He resumed his practice of law and was elected member of the Confederate Congress from Kentucky. He died in Louisville, March 28, 1872.

Army of New Mexico

ORGANIZED December 14, 1861, to embrace all the forces on the Rio Grande above Fort Quitman, and those in the territories of New Mexico and Arizona. Its main object was the conquest of California. Brigadier-General H. H. Sibley was placed in command. He had about thirty-seven hundred men. His troops won the battle of Valverde, occupied Santa Fé and fought at Glorieta (or Apache Cañon). The army was forced to retreat into Texas, in April, 1862, by Federal troops under Colonel E. R. S. Canby. Sibley was relieved of the command in December, 1862.

BRIGADIER-GENERAL HENRY HOPKINS SIBLEY (U.S.M.A. 1838) was born at Natchitoches, Louis-

iana, May 23, 1816, and served in the Seminole and Mexican wars. He was the inventor of the famous Sibley tent. The outbreak of the Civil War found him on an Indian campaign in New Mexico, serving as a major of dragoons, but he accepted a commission as brigadier-general in the Confederate army and became commander of the Army of New Mexico. After his repulse at Glorieta, March 28, 1862, he was driven back into Texas. He continued his service at the head of various commands in Louisiana, south of the Red River. After the war he entered the service of the Khedive of Egypt, where he was, from 1869 to 1873, engaged in building coast and river defenses. He died at Fredericksburg, Virginia, August 23, 1886.

Army of Louisiana

AT THE BEGINNING of the war, the Louisiana State troops, commanded by Major-General Braxton Bragg and later by Colonel P. O. Hébert, were sometimes designated the Army of Louisiana.

BRIGADIER-GENERAL PAUL OCTAVE HÉBERT (U.S.M.A. 1840) was born in Bayou Goula, Herville Parish, Louisiana, November 12, 1818. He resigned from the army in 1845, reentering as

Young M. Moody, Commander of the District of Florida.

Isham W. Garrott, Original Colonel of 20th Regiment.

William F. Perry Led a Noted Brigade under Longstreet.

William H. Forney Led an Alabama Brigade in Hill's Corps.

CONFEDERATE

GENERALS

No. 2

ALABAMA

William W. Allen Led a Cavalry Division in Wheeler's Corps.

John H. Forney, One of the Defenders of Vicksburg in 1863.

LeRoy P. Walker, First Confederate Secretary of War.

Sterling A. M. Wood Led a Brigade at Chickamauga.

James Cantey Commanded the Garrison at Mobile.

Zachary C. Deas Led a Brigade of Alabamians in Tennessee.

lieutenant-colonel in the Mexican War, where he received the brevet of colonel for his gallant conduct at Molino del Rey. While governor of Louisiana, 1853 to 1856, he appointed his classmate, W. T. Sherman, to the head of the Louisiana Military Academy. When the Civil War broke out he succeeded Bragg in command of the Confederate forces in Louisiana, and was appointed brigadier-general August 17, 1861. He was in special command of the defenses of New Orleans. Later, he commanded in turn the Department and District of Texas in the Trans-Mississippi. After the war he became state engineer of Louisiana. He died in New Orleans, August 29, 1880.

Army of Pensacola

THE FORCES at or near Pensacola, Florida, under Major-General Braxton Bragg, were designated the Army of Pensacola on October 22, 1861. Brigadier-General A. H. Gladden had temporary command in December, and Brigadier-General Samuel Jones took charge on January 27, 1862. The force then numbered eighty-one hundred men, divided among regiments from Alabama, Florida, Georgia, Louisiana, and Mississippi. On March 13th, the army was discontinued, the regiments entering the Army of the Mississippi or assigned for duty elsewhere. Pensacola was evacuated by the Confederate troops on the 9th of May.

BRIGADIER-GENERAL ADLEY H. GLADDEN was born in South Carolina. He entered the Confederate army and was appointed a brigadier-general from Louisiana in September, 1861. He had a brigade at Pensacola, and was in temporary command of the Army of Pensacola in December, 1861, and was given command of a brigade in the Second Corps, Army of the Mississippi. He was mortally wounded at Shiloh April 6, 1862.

MAJOR-GENERAL SAMUEL JONES (U.S.M.A. 1841) was born in Virginia, in 1820, and resigned his commission of captain in April, 1861, to enter the Confederate service. He was made major of artillery. He was acting adjutant-general of the Virginia forces in May and chief of artillery and ordnance in the Army of the Potomac from May to July, 1861. Appointed brigadier-general after the battle of Bull Run, he was assigned to the Army of Pensacola, in January, 1862, and the following month to the head of the Department of Alabama and West Florida. In April, he was given a division in the Army of the West, and in June, after having been appointed major-general in May, he was put at the head of a division in the Second Corps, Army of the Mississippi. After September, 1862, he commanded various departments in Tennessee and Virginia, being placed at the head of the Department of South Carolina, Georgia, and Florida, in April, 1864. At the close of the war he was in charge of the Department of Florida and South Georgia. He died in Washington, D. C., April 1, 1887.

Army of Mobile

ON JANUARY 27, 1862, the command of Brigadier-General Jones M. Withers, consisting of Alabama troops in and around the city of Mobile, was designated the Army of Mobile. Its strength was about ten thousand. It was subsequently commanded by Colonel J. B. Villepigue, temporarily, and Brigadier-General Samuel Jones, after March 15th. Many of the regiments entered the Army of the Mississippi and fought at Shiloh under Withers. More regiments were sent to that army, and on June 27, the Army of Mobile was discontinued.

MAJOR-GENERAL JONES MITCHELL WITHERS (U.S.M.A. 1835) was born in Madison County, Alabama, January 12, 1814, and resigned from the army in 1848. He entered the Confederate service and received an appointment as brigadier-general in July, 1861. He was promoted to major-general after the battle of Shiloh. From January 27th to February 28, 1862, he was in command of the Army of Mobile. He then had a division in the Second Corps, Army of the Mississippi, and also the Reserve Corps for a time, and passed into the Right Wing and Polk's Corps, Army of Tennessee. He resigned his commission July 13, 1863, but his rank was restored within a few days, after which he assumed various commands in Alabama. He surrendered at Merid-

Thomas Churchill Commanded a Division in the Army of the West; Defender of Arkansas and Red River Region.

Thomas C. Hindman Commanded the Trans-Mississippi District in 1863; Led Troops at Shiloh and Chickamauga.

John F. Fagan, Originally Colonel of the 1st Arkansas Infantry; Conspicuous in the Attack on Helena, July 4, 1863.

CONFEDERATE

GENERALS

No. 3

ARKANSAS

Lucius E. Polk, Leader of a Charge at Murfreesboro.

Albert Pike, Commander of Indian Troops at Pea Ridge.

Albert Rust Led a Brigade in the Army of the West.

James C. Tappan Led a Brigade West of the Mississippi.

William L. Cabell Led a Brigade of Arkansas Cavalry.

John S. Roane, in Commission at Little Rock, Ark.

Central Army of Kentucky

ian, Mississippi, May 11, 1865, and died March 13, 1890.

BRIGADIER-GENERAL JOHN BORDENAVE VILLE-PIGUE (U.S.M.A. 1854) was born in Camden, South Carolina, July 2, 1830, and resigned from the army in March, 1861, to enter the Confederate service. As colonel, he was temporarily in command of the Army of Mobile. He was appointed brigadier-general, March 18, 1862. He was in command at Fort Pillow at the time of Flag-Officer Davis's attack, May-June, 1862, and commanded a brigade at the battle of Corinth, October 4th. He died at Port Hudson, Louisiana, November 9, 1862, as the result of illness. Villepigue was considered one of the most promising young officers in the Confederate service, and his untimely death was greatly deplored.

Central Army of Kentucky

BRIGADIER-GENERAL S. B. BUCKNER assumed command of the forces in central Kentucky, September, 1861, and he was followed October 28th, by General Albert Sidney Johnston. The troops were organized in two divisions with a reserve, and a third division, under Brigadier-General John B. Floyd, was added later on. Major-General Hardee had temporary command, December, 1861-February, 1862. On March 29, 1862, the Central Army of Kentucky, whose strength was about twenty-three thousand, was consolidated with the Army of the Mississippi, under the latter designation, with General Johnston in command and General P. G. T. Beauregard second.

LIEUTENANT-GENERAL SIMON BOLIVAR BUCK-NER (U.S.M.A. 1841) was born in Kentucky, April 1, 1823. He served in the Mexican War and taught at West Point. He resigned from the army in 1855, and returned to Kentucky to practise law. He entered the Confederate service in September, 1861, taking command in central Kentucky. He commanded a division of the Central Army of Kentucky at Bowling Green and at Fort Donelson. On February 16, 1862, he surrendered the fort and garrison of Fort Donelson and was sent to Fort Warren as a prisoner of war, being exchanged in August. He was then made major-general and had a division in Bragg's army and was given a temporary corps at Chickamauga. He was made lieutenant-general in September, 1864, and was commander in several districts of the Trans-Mississippi Department. He was elected governor of Kentucky in 1887, and in 1896 was the candidate of the Gold Democrats for Vice-President.

Army of East Tennessee—Army of Kentucky

IN FEBRUARY, 1862, Major-General E. Kirby Smith was sent to Knoxville to assume command of the troops in East Tennessee. With the army thus organized, it was intended to create a diversion in favor of General A. S. Johnston's operations with the Army of the Mississippi. The Army of East Tennessee was engaged in many minor engagements. On August 25th, the organization was designated the Army of Kentucky and was composed of three divisions. It led the advance in Bragg's invasion of Kentucky and was successful at the battle of Richmond, August 30th, raising great hopes for the Confederate conquest of Kentucky. On November 20, 1862, the Army of Kentucky was merged as Smith's Corps in the Army of Tennessee.

GENERAL EDMUND KIRBY SMITH (U.S.M.A. 1845) was born in St. Augustine, Florida, May 16, 1824, and served in the Mexican War, after which he was professor of mathematics at West Point. In April, 1861, he resigned his commission as captain to join the Confederates, becoming a brigadier-general in June. He was chief-of-staff to and had a brigade under General Joseph E. Johnston. He was seriously wounded at Bull Run. Early in 1862, as major-general, he was placed in command of the Army of East Tennessee (afterward Kentucky). In October of the same year he was made lieutenant-general and continued in the Department of East Tennessee. He was made general, and assumed command of the Trans-Mississippi Department in February, 1863. He surrendered his troops to Major-General Canby at Baton Rouge, May 26, 1865, having, the year before, defeated Major-General Banks in the Red

William N. R. Beall, District Commander in Mississippi and Louisiana.

Dandridge McRae Led a Brigade in Battles West of the Mississippi.

Alexander T. Hawthorne Led a Brigade in the Army of the Mississippi.

Daniel H. Reynolds Fought with Hood at Nashville.

Daniel C. Govan Commanded a Noted Brigade.

Evander McNair, Important Leader in the Army of Tennessee.

CONFEDERATE GENERALS

No. 4

ARKANSAS

Thomas P. Dockery Led a Cavalry Brigade.

Frank C. Armstrong, Brilliant Cavalry Commander.

River campaign. After the war, he devoted himself largely to education, becoming chancellor of the University of Nashville from 1870 to 1875, and later professor of mathematics at the University of the South. He died in Sewanee, Tennessee, March 28, 1893.

Army of the Mississippi

FROM TROOPS in the Western Department (Department No. 2) was created the Army of the Mississippi on March 5, 1862, and to General P. G. T. Beauregard was given the command. The army was divided into two corps headed by Major-Generals Leonidas Polk and Braxton Bragg. On March 29th, the army was joined to the Central Army of Kentucky with its three divisions, reserve corps, and cavalry. General A. S. Johnston, of the latter, took command of the Army of the Mississippi, that name having been preserved. Beauregard was second in command. The whole body was gathered at Corinth (except a force at Fort Pillow) in three corps, a reserve corps, and cavalry, and this was the organization that fought at Shiloh, when its strength was about forty thousand. The death of General Johnston placed the chief command upon General Beauregard, who was relieved June 27, 1862, by Major-General Hardee, and he, on August 15th, by Major-General Bragg. The army was transferred to Chattanooga in July. Major-General Polk had temporary command from September 28th to November 7, 1862, when, on the return of Bragg, the organization was called the Army of Tennessee.

GENERAL ALBERT SIDNEY JOHNSTON (U.S.M. A. 1826) was born in Washington, Mason County, Kentucky, February 3, 1803. He served in the Black Hawk War and resigned his commission in 1834. Two years later, he entered the army of the Texan Republic as a private, soon becoming a brigadier-general, and in 1838 was commander-in-chief of the army of Texas and Secretary of War. Later, he reentered the United States Army and served in the Mexican War with distinction. As colonel, he conducted an expedition against the Mormons in Utah in 1857, which won him a brevet of brigadier-general. He remained in command in Utah until February, 1860. At the outbreak of the Civil War, he was in command of the Department of the Pacific, but, by reason of his Southern sympathies, he resigned his commission to enter the Confederate service with the rank of general. He assumed command of Department No. 2, or Western Department, on September 15, 1861. In October he took immediate control of the Central Army of Kentucky, holding the line of Bowling Green, Kentucky, until February, 1862, against vastly superior numbers. On March 29, 1862, this army united with the Army of the Mississippi and Johnston took command of the new organization. He was killed on the battlefield of Shiloh, April 6, 1862, and his death was a stunning blow to the new Confederacy.

Third Corps—Army of the Mississippi

MAJOR-GENERAL W. J. HARDEE, who had been commander in northwestern Arkansas, was placed at the head of the Third Corps of the Army of the Mississippi on its reorganization, March 29, 1862. In August, the corps was merged in the Left Wing of the Army of the Mississippi.

Reserve Corps—Army of the Mississippi

COMMANDED by Major-General George B. Crittenden on March 29, 1862, and by Major-General J. C. Breckinridge after April 6th, and, later, by Brigadier-General Jones M. Withers. After Shiloh, and the siege of Corinth, the corps went to Louisiana and fought the battle of Baton Rouge, August 6, 1862, with the Federal troops under Brigadier-General Thomas Williams. Then it returned with Breckinridge to form the Army of Middle Tennessee and was merged in Hardee's (Second) Corps, Army of Tennessee, as the First Division, in November, 1862.

Jesse J. Finley Commanded a Brigade.

William G. M. Davis Led a Brigade of Cavalry.

Robert Bullock, Colonel of the 7th Regiment.

William Miller Commanded Reserve Forces in Florida.

CONFEDERATE GENERALS

No. 5

FLORIDA

J. Patton Anderson, Active Division Commander in the West.

Martin L. Smith, One of the Defenders of Vicksburg.

Francis A. Shaup, Chief of Artillery. Army of Tennessee.

William S. Walker Commanded a South Carolina Brigade.

Theodore W. Brevard, Colonel of the 11th Regiment.

Army of Tennessee

THE JOINING of the Army of Kentucky with the Army of the Mississippi, on November 20, 1862, was the origin of the Army of Tennessee—the great Confederate army of the West. There were three corps and a division of cavalry, with an effective total of forty-seven thousand. General Braxton Bragg was in command. This army fought the battle of Stone's River, went through the Tullahoma campaign, and fought the battle of Chickamauga, assisted by Longstreet's Corps from the Army of Northern Virginia. It was driven from Chattanooga in November, 1863, by Grant's forces. After the battle of Chickamauga, the corps were reorganized several times. Bragg was removed from the command on December 2, 1863, and until General Johnston assumed it, on December 27th, both Hardee and Polk were in temporary command. Polk was sent to the Department of Alabama, Mississippi and East Louisiana before the end of December. The army spent the winter around Dalton, Georgia, and faced Sherman's advance in May, 1864, in two infantry and one cavalry corps. Polk brought back his divisions, which he called the Army of Mississippi, and these forces were consolidated with the Army of Tennessee on July 26th, after Polk had been killed. On July 18th, Johnston was replaced by General John B. Hood. After the capture of Atlanta, the army returned to Tennessee, and, failing to cut off Major-General Schofield's command at Franklin, was routed by Major-General Thomas at Nashville (December 15-16, 1864). In February, 1865, General Johnston was again placed in command of the Army of Tennessee, as well as the troops in South Carolina, Georgia, and Florida. The army had greatly dwindled. Lieutenant-General A. P. Stewart was at the actual head of the Army of Tennessee after March 16th, and Johnston's enlarged command included troops from the far South under Hardee, which, in February, had been organized in a corps, and those in North Carolina under Bragg. The aggregate present of the old Army of Tennessee was about twenty thousand. The army surrendered to Sherman in North Carolina, April 26, 1865.

GENERAL BRAXTON BRAGG (U.S.M.A. 1837) was born in Warren County, North Carolina, March 22, 1817, and served in the Seminole and Mexican wars. He resigned from the army in 1859, and became an extensive planter in Louisiana. On the secession of Louisiana, he was made a brigadier-general in the Confederate provisional army, and was the first commander of the military forces of Louisiana. After being appointed major-general in September, he took command of the forces in Alabama and West Florida from October, 1861, to February, 1862. He commanded the right wing of the Army of the Mississippi at Shiloh, and was made general after the death of Albert Sidney Johnston. He succeeded Beauregard as commander of the Army of the Mississippi (or Tennessee), and led it into Kentucky in September, 1862, and after his retreat therefrom, was defeated by Rosecrans at Stone's River (January, 1863). He in turn defeated Rosecrans at Chickamauga, but was driven from Chattanooga by Grant in November, 1863. Bragg was now relieved of the Army of Tennessee, and, later, was given control of the Confederate army's military operations at Richmond. As commander of the Department of North Carolina, he failed in attempts to check Sherman and prevent the fall of Wilmington. After February, 1865, he cooperated with Johnston and surrendered with the latter. Later on, he was state engineer of Alabama, and died in Galveston, Texas, September 27, 1876.

GENERAL JOHN BELL HOOD (U.S.M.A. 1853) was born in Owingsville, Kentucky, June 1, 1831, and fought against the Comanche Indians in Texas. He resigned from the army in April, 1861, to enter the Confederate service. After serving as captain in the cavalry and colonel of a Texas regiment, he received the appointment of brigadier-general in March, 1862. He was made major-general in October, 1862, after taking a conspicuous part in the Virginia campaigns. At Gettysburg, he commanded the largest division in Longstreet's Corps. In September, he went to Tennessee with Longstreet's Corps, which he commanded at Chickamauga, where he lost a leg. After the battle, he was given the rank of lieutenant-general, and at the head of the Second Corps in the Army of Tennessee, took part in the Atlanta campaign from May to July 18, 1864, when he succeeded Johnston in the command of the army with the temporary rank of general. He lost Atlanta, and, returning to Tennessee, was driven into Alabama by Major-General Thomas in the middle of December. In January, 1865, he was relieved of his command and was ordered to Richmond. After the war, he went to New Orleans, where he died, August 30, 1879.

Howell Cobb, Leader of Cobb's Georgia Legion.

G. T. Anderson Commanded a Brigade in Longstreet's Corps.

David E. Twiggs, in Command in East Louisiana in 1861.

Pierce M. B. Young, Brilliant Cavalry Leader.

Goode Bryan Led a Georgia Brigade in Longstreet's Corps.

Hugh W. Mercer Led a Georgia Brigade in the Army of Tennessee.

David R. Jones, Active Leader at Second Manassas and Sharpsburg.

William M. Brown, Defender of Savannah, December, 1864.

CONFEDERATE

GENERALS

No. 6

GEORGIA

Clement A. Evans, Leader in the Army of Northern Virginia.

Robert Toombs, Defender of Lee's Right Flank at Antietam.

First Corps—Army of the Mississippi and of Tennessee

MAJOR-GENERAL LEONIDAS POLK commanded from June, 1861, to March, 1862, the First Division in the Western Department (No. 2), the troops of which were scattered along the Mississippi from Columbus, Kentucky, to Memphis, and in the interior of Tennessee and Mississippi. It numbered about twenty-five thousand men. On the organization of the Army of the Mississippi in March, 1862, this division was called the First Grand Division, and after the consolidation with the Central Army of Kentucky, on March 29th, the First Corps, Army of the Mississippi. On August 15th, Polk's Corps was reorganized as the Right Wing in ten divisions, with over fifteen thousand present for duty. In the Army of Tennessee, the Right Wing became the First, or Polk's Corps. After the battle of Chickamauga, Polk was relieved of the command, and both corps of the army underwent reorganization. The leading corps was thereafter known as Hardee's, or Cheatham's Corps, from the names of its commanders.

LIEUTENANT-GENERAL LEONIDAS POLK (U.S. M.A. 1827) was born in Raleigh, North Carolina, April 10, 1806. He left the army for the church, and eventually became the first Protestant Episcopal Bishop of Louisiana, in 1841. In 1861, he entered the Confederate army and was made major-general in June. He was assigned to the command of the Western Department (No. 2); and in September he was replaced by General A. S. Johnston and given the First Division, Army of the Mississippi, with which he won the battle of Belmont in November. He led the First Corps at Shiloh, and later had temporary command of the army itself. In October, 1862, he was given the rank of lieutenant-general, and accompanied the Western Confederate army until after Chickamauga, where he commanded the Right Wing when he was temporarily suspended, but the charge of delay on his part was dismissed by President Davis. In the winter of 1863–64, he was in command of the Department of Alabama, Mississippi, and East Louisiana, and brought his forces, which he called the Army of Mississippi, to Georgia in May, 1864, to assist Johnston in opposing Sherman's advance to Atlanta. On Pine Mountain, near Marietta, Georgia, he was killed by a cannon-ball, June 14, 1864.

MAJOR-GENERAL BENJAMIN FRANKLIN CHEATHAM was born in Nashville, Tennessee, October 20, 1820. He entered the Mexican War, rising to the rank of colonel after distinguished service at Monterey and elsewhere. At the close of this war he became major-general of the Tennessee militia, and when the Civil War broke out he attached himself to the Confederate cause and organized the entire supply department for the Western troops. As brigadier-general, he served under Polk at Belmont, and had a division of the First Corps, Army of the Mississippi, at Shiloh, and was commander of the Right Wing of the same army during Bragg's invasion of Kentucky in 1862. He led his division at Stone's River, through the Tullahoma campaign, and at Chickamauga, and after that battle was head of Cheatham's Corps, an organization formed upon the departure of Polk from the army, and of which Hardee shortly afterward took command. In the Atlanta campaign he led a division in Hardee's Corps, and assumed command of the corps, which later was known as Cheatham's Corps, after the departure of Hardee for Savannah in October, 1864, with which he continued until the surrender at Durham Station. After the war he became a farmer in Tennessee, and was appointed postmaster of Nashville in 1885. He died there September 4, 1886.

MAJOR-GENERAL PATRICK ROMAYNE CLEBURNE was born in County Cork, Ireland, March 17, 1828. He ran away from Trinity College, Dublin, and enlisted in the Forty-first Foot. In 1855 he came to America, settling in Helena, Arkansas, where he practised law until the opening of the war. He entered the Confederate service as private, and rose to the rank of major-general, in 1862. He planned the capture of the United States arsenal in Arkansas, March, 1861. He was colonel of an Arkansas regiment, and at Shiloh, as brigadier-general, he commanded a brigade in the Third Corps, Army of the Mississippi. He was wounded at Perryville. At Murfreesboro and Chickamauga he commanded a division, and his troops formed the rear guard at Missionary Ridge. For his defense of Ringgold Gap, in the Atlanta campaign, he received the thanks of the Confederate Congress. Cleburne covered Hood's retreat at Jonesboro, and had temporary command of Hardee's Corps. He continued to hold his division in Cheatham's Corps, and at the battle of Franklin was killed, November 30, 1864. A brilliant charge at Chickamauga earned him the title of "Stonewall of the West," and it was he who initiated the Order of the Southern Cross and was among the first to urge the advantages to the Confederates of colored troops.

PHILIP COOK
Leader in Gordon's Attack
on Fort Stedman.

WILLIAM M. GARDNER
Commander of the Post of
Richmond, Va., in 1865.

JOHN K. JACKSON
Commanded a Reserve Corps
Army of the Mississippi.

CLAUDIUS C. WILSON
Led a Brigade in the
Army of Tennessee.

ISAAC M. ST. JOHN
Commissary General,
1865,

CONFEDERATE

GENERALS

No. 7—GEORGIA

(CONTINUED)

BRYAN M. THOMAS
Led a Brigade of Alabamians.

G. MOXLEY SORRELL
Staff Officer with Longstreet.

DUDLEY M. DUBOIS
Led a Brigade in Longstreet's Corps.

MARCELLUS A. STOVALL
Led a Brigade in
Hood's Corps.

LUCIUS J. GARTRELL
Led a Brigade in
Georgia Reserves.

HENRY C. WAYNE
Adjutant-General and
Inspector-General of
Georgia.

ALFRED CUMMING
Led a Brigade of
Georgians in the West.

JAMES P. SIMMS
Led a Georgia Brigade in
Longstreet's Corps.

WILLIAM R. BOGGS
Chief of Staff to Gen.
E. Kirby Smith.

Second Corps—Army of the Mississippi and of Tennessee

Major-General Braxton Bragg was given command of the Second Corps of the Army of the Mississippi on its organization, March 29, 1862. There were ten divisions, composed chiefly of Alabama, Mississippi, and Louisiana troops. In July, Major-General Samuel Jones had command, and on August 15th, when General Bragg resumed command of the whole army, his former corps passed to the control of Major-General Hardee. There was an aggregate present of about sixteen thousand men. On November 7th, the Left Wing, in an organization that had a short existence after August 15th, again became the Second (or Hardee's) Corps. In July, 1863, Lieutenant-General Hardee was relieved by Lieutenant-General D. H. Hill, who commanded at Chickamauga, and the later commanders were Major-Generals J. C. Breckinridge, T. C. Hindman, Lieutenant-General J. B. Hood, Major-General C. L. Stevenson and Lieutenant-General S. D. Lee. After 1864, the corps was known as Hood's, or Lee's Corps, Hardee having assumed command of the other corps.

Lieutenant-General William Joseph Hardee (U.S.M.A. 1838) was born in Savannah, Georgia, October 10, 1815, and served in the Seminole and Mexican wars. He resigned his commission of lieutenant-colonel in January, 1861, to join the Confederate forces, in which he was appointed a brigadier-general in June. He was given command of Fort Morgan, Mobile Bay, in March, and later, as major-general, was transferred to the Central Army of Kentucky, of which he had command from December, 1861, to February, 1862. He was given the Second Corps in the Army of the Mississippi and led the advance at Shiloh. He took part with this army as corps or wing commander in Bragg's invasion of Kentucky, at Stone's River, and at Chattanooga, having been made lieutenant-general in October, 1862. In the summer of 1863 he had charge of the defenses of Mississippi and Alabama. He had temporary command of the Army of Tennessee after Bragg was removed in December, 1863. He had a corps during the Atlanta campaign, and in October, 1864, he was placed in command of the Department of South Carolina, Georgia, and Florida. He was unable to prevent the capture of Savannah, and, in February, 1865, joined Johnston, serving in the Army of Tennessee, at the head of a corps formed from the troops in his department, until its surrender. After the war, he lived at Selma, Alabama, and died at Wytheville, Virginia, November 6, 1873.

Lieutenant-General Daniel Harvey Hill (U.S.M.A. 1842) was born at Hill's Iron Works, York District, South Carolina, July 12, 1821. He resigned from the army after the Mexican War, in which he had received the brevet of major, and was engaged in teaching until he entered the Confederate army, in 1861. As colonel of the First North Carolina Infantry, he showed marked talent at Big Bethel, June 10th, and was made brigadier-general the following month. As major-general, he had a division and later a command, or corps, in the Army of Northern Virginia, and fought through the Peninsula campaign. He was assigned to the Department of North Carolina in July, but fought with his division at South Mountain, where he held the Federal forces in check, and at Antietam. In July, 1863, he was made lieutenant-general, and replaced Lieutenant-General Hardee in command of the Second Corps, Army of Tennessee, which he led at Chickamauga, and of which he was relieved in November. With the rank of major-general, he took command of a division in Lee's Corps, Army of Tennessee, in March, 1865, and at the battle of Bentonville he led the corps itself. After the war, he became an editor, and from 1877 to 1884 was president of the Arkansas Industrial University. He died at Charlotte, North Carolina, September 25, 1889.

Major-General Carter Littlepage Stevenson (U.S.M.A. 1838) was born near Fredericksburg, Virginia, September 21, 1817. He was dismissed from the army in June, 1861, having entered the Confederate service as lieutenant-colonel. He did duty at Cumberland Gap, from which he drove Brigadier-General G. W. Morgan away, and commanded a division in the Army of Tennessee. He rose to the rank of major-general in October, 1862. His division was with Pemberton's forces in the battle of Chickasaw Bayou, December 26, 1862. He fought at Chickamauga and in the Atlanta campaign onward with the Army of Tennessee, having on July, 1864, temporary command of Hood's Corps, before the appointment of Lieutenant-General S. D. Lee. He also assumed command of Lee's Corps, when the latter was wounded after the battle of Nashville, until the army had crossed the Tennessee. He died August 15, 1888.

Major-General Thomas Carmichael Hindman was born in Tennessee, November, 1818. He became a lawyer and served in Congress. He fought in the Mexican War, and in 1860 was a

John S. Williams Commanded
a Cavalry Brigade.

INDIAN

TERRITORY

(ONE TO RIGHT)

KENTUCKY

(FIVE REMAINING)

Stand Watie, Indian Leader of Troops
at Pea Ridge.

Thomas H. Taylor Led a
Brigade in the Army of
Tennessee.

William Preston Led a Division
at the Battle of
Chickamauga.

James M. Hawes Com-
manded a Brigade West
of the Mississippi.

CONFEDERATE

GENERALS

No. 8

Humphrey Marshall, Confederate
Defender of Kentucky.

member of the Charleston Convention. He went to the Civil War as colonel of an Arkansas regiment, and served in the armies of the West and of the Mississippi. For his conduct at Shiloh he was made major-general. He was, at different times, division commander in the Army of Tennessee, and a temporary commander of the Second Corps, and was also at the head of the Trans-Mississippi District and that of Arkansas. He was defeated at Prairie Grove and at Newtonia. After the war, he went to Mexico, but returned to Arkansas and was murdered by one of his former soldiers at Helena, September 28, 1868.

LIEUTENANT-GENERAL STEPHEN DILL LEE (U. S.M.A. 1854) was born in Charleston, South Carolina, September 22, 1833. He resigned from the army in February, 1861, to enter the Confederate service as captain in the artillery, and rose to the rank of lieutenant-general June, 1864. He was one of the three men who called on Major Anderson, April 12, 1861, and demanded the surrender of Fort Sumter. He had a battalion in the Washington Artillery, and was prominent at Second Bull Run and at Antietam. He was then sent to the West and commanded a division at the battle of Chickasaw Bayou, December 27, 1862, driving back the Federal troops with great slaughter. He was among those who surrendered at Vicksburg, July 4, 1863, and in August was put at the head of the cavalry in the Department of Alabama, Mississippi, and East Louisiana, and fought at Tupelo and other places. In May, 1864, he succeeded Lieutenant-General Polk at the head of this department, remaining there until July, when he was assigned to the command of Hood's Corps, Army of Tennessee, General Hood having been placed at the head of the whole army. Henceforth it was known as Lee's Corps. He was wounded December 17, 1864, while protecting the rear of the army in the retreat from Nashville. After the war he became a planter in Mississippi; a member of the State legislature; and in 1880 he became president of the Mississippi Agricultural and Mechanical College. He was also at the head of the Vicksburg National Park, and was commander-in-chief of the United Confederate Veterans, after the death of Lieutenant-General John B. Gordon, in 1904. He died at Vicksburg, Mississippi, May 28, 1908.

Wheeler's Cavalry Corps—Army of Tennessee

ON JANUARY 22, 1863, Major-General Joseph Wheeler was assigned to command all the cavalry in Middle Tennessee. On March 16th, the cavalry divisions in the Army of Tennessee were designated as corps, and were given the names of their respective commanders, Wheeler and Van Dorn. The corps were organized into divisions and brigades, and Wheeler's Corps, sometimes known as the Second Corps, had an aggregate present of nearly twelve thousand. It displayed great activity in Tennessee, making numerous raids and guarding the flanks of the army. After the battle of Chickamauga, it made a famous raid on Rosecrans' communications, October, 1863. It also operated on the flanks of the army during the Atlanta and other campaigns until the close of the war.

LIEUTENANT-GENERAL JOSEPH WHEELER (U. S.M.A. 1859) was born in Augusta, Georgia, September 10, 1836, and entered the mounted infantry, resigning, in 1861, to join the Confederate army, in which he reached the rank of major-general (January, 1863), and commander of the Second Cavalry Corps, Army of Tennessee. He was conspicuous as a raider, and was constantly employed in guarding the flanks of the army, cutting the Federal communications, covering retreats, and obtaining information for the army commanders. He was appointed lieutenant-general, February 28, 1865. After the war, he was a member of Congress from 1881 to 1899. He was commissioned major-general of volunteers in 1898, and went to the Spanish War, commanding the troops at Las Guasimas, and was senior field-officer at the battle of San Juan Hill. He was senior member of the commission which negotiated the surrender of Santiago. He served with the American troops during the insurrection in the Philippines from August, 1899, to January 24, 1900, and on June 13, 1900, was appointed brigadier-general of the United States army, being retired the following September. He died in Brooklyn, New York, January 25, 1906. General Wheeler made a unique reputation for himself as a cavalry leader, and in the Spanish war his services won universal acknowledgment as typical of the complete reunion of the North and South.

George B. Crosby Led a Brigade in
Mississippi and Louisiana.

Abraham Buford, Active Leader
of Cavalry.

Adam R. Johnson Led a Brigade of
Morgan's Cavalry.

CONFEDERATE GENERALS—No. 9—KENTUCKY (Continued)

Hyland B. Lyon Led a Brigade of
Cavalry in Forrest's Division.

Joseph H. Lewis Led a Brigade in
the Army of Tennessee.

George B. Hodge Commanded a
Brigade of Cavalry.

Van Dorn's Cavalry Corps—Army of Tennessee

On March 16, 1863, Major-General Van Dorn's Cavalry Division in the Army of Tennessee was called Van Dorn's, or the First Cavalry Corps. It had an average aggregate present of about eight thousand, and was a valuable adjunct to General Bragg's army.

Army of Middle Tennessee

When Major-General John C. Breckinridge assumed command of the forces around Murfreesboro on October 28, 1862, they were denominated the Army of Middle Tennessee. There were three brigades, with cavalry under Brigadier-General Forrest, who was shortly relieved by Brigadier-General Wheeler. When Bragg advanced from Chattanooga to oppose Rosecrans, the Army of Middle Tennessee became identified with a division of Hardee's Corps, Army of Tennessee.

Major-General John Cabell Breckinridge was born near Lexington, Kentucky, January 21, 1821, and became a lawyer. He served as major in the Mexican War. From 1857 to 1861, he was vice-president of the United States. In 1860, he was a candidate for the presidency, receiving the electoral votes of the Southern States, with the exception of Virginia, Kentucky, Tennessee, and Missouri. He was sent to the Senate, but left that body to join the Confederates. He was made brigadier-general in November, 1861, and major-general in April, 1862, after the battle of Shiloh. He had a command under General A. S. Johnston in the Central Army of Kentucky, and Army of the Mississippi, and led the reserve corps at Shiloh. After the siege of Corinth he took his force to Louisiana, and fought the battle of Baton Rouge, August 6, 1862. Later, he headed the Department and Army of Middle Tennessee. Rejoining the Army of Tennessee at the end of 1862, he fought at Stone's River, Chickamauga, and Chattanooga, at the head of a division in Hardee's Corps, and was its temporary commander for a period before the battle of Chattanooga. He was brought East after the opening of the Wilderness campaign, fought at Cold Harbor, and was second in command under Early in the Shenandoah. From February 6, 1865, to the downfall of the Confederacy, he was Secretary of War. He then went to Europe, but returned in 1868, and resumed the practice of law. He died in Lexington, Kentucky, May 17, 1875.

Missouri State Guard

On June 12, 1861, Governor C. F. Jackson of Missouri, in defiance of the United States military government, issued a call for fifty thousand of the State militia for active service. At the time of the flight of the governor and his followers to the extreme southwestern corner of the State, he was joined by Price. At that time, the whole Confederate State force amounted to about three thousand men. This Missouri State Guard was in command of Brigadier-Generals Sterling Price and M. M. Parsons from October 29, 1861, to March 17, 1862, when it merged in the Army of the West.

Army of the West

Major-General Earl Van Dorn assumed command of the troops in the Trans-Mississippi District of Western Department (No. 2), on January 29, 1862. Out of the force grew the Army of the West, so called after March 4th. It was largely composed of the Missouri State Guard. This army fought at Pea Ridge and elsewhere in Arkansas, and, being transferred across the Mississippi, was present at the siege of Corinth. The First Division was commanded by Major-General Sterling Price after March 22d, and the Second by Major-General Samuel Jones. It had three divisions after May, and a strength of over twenty thousand. On June 20th, Van Dorn was replaced by Major-General John P. McCown, who had commanded the Third Division, and he in turn by Major-General Price, on July 3d. The transfer of the Army of the Mississippi to Chattanooga at

Paul O. Hébert Commanded the Army of Louisiana Defending New Orleans.

Louis Hébert, Active Commander in the Southwest.

Thomas M. Scott, Originally Colonel of the 12th Regiment.

Franklin Gardner, Defender of Port Hudson against Banks in 1863.

CONFED—

ERATE

GENERALS

No. 10

LOUISI—

ANA

James P. Major Led a Cavalry Brigade in Louisiana.

Edward Higgins, Conspicuous at New Orleans in 1862.

Henry H. Sibley, Conspicuous Leader in New Mexico.

Albert G. Blanchard Led a Brigade in the Army of Northern Virginia.

Zebulon York Commanded a Brigade.

Allan Thomas Led a Brigade in the Army of Northern Virginia.

the end of July, left the Army of the West in control of western Tennessee, and northern Mississippi. One division of the army fought the battle of Iuka, September 10th. On September 28th, a junction was made with Van Dorn's new command of troops in Mississippi, and the new organization was denominated the Army of West Tennessee. To Price was assigned a corps, which continued to be called, sometimes, the Army of the West.

MAJOR-GENERAL EARL VAN DORN (U.S.M.A. 1842) was born near Port Gibson, Mississippi, September 17, 1820, and served in the Mexican War and in several Indian campaigns. He resigned from the army, and was commissioned a colonel in the Confederate States army in March, 1861. His first commands were at New Orleans, and in the Department of Texas, where he forced the surrender of United States troops under Major Sibley and Colonel Reeve. He was made brigadier-general in June and major-general in September. In October and November, 1861, he commanded a division in the Army of the Potomac, and was assigned, in January, 1862, to the Trans-Mississippi District (Department No. 2), in which he had command of the Army of the West. He was defeated at Pea Ridge in March, and, with the Army of West Tennessee, at Corinth in October. After Pemberton assumed control of this force in the department in which Van Dorn was operating, he continued to command a cavalry division, at the

head of which he made a brilliant raid in Mississippi in December, 1862. In March, 1863, Van Dorn's cavalry division was designated a corps in the Army of Tennessee. On May 8, 1863, he was shot and killed by Doctor Peters, at Spring Hill, Tennessee, the result of a private quarrel.

MAJOR-GENERAL JOHN PORTER McCOWN (U. S.M.A. 1840) was born in Tennessee, in 1815, and served in the Mexican war, being brevetted captain for gallant conduct at Cerro Gordo. He resigned from the service in May, 1861, and entered the Confederate army, taking charge of the artillery in the provisional army of the State of Tennessee. As brigadier-general, he commanded a division of Polk's army at the battle of Belmont, November 7, 1861. After commanding at New Madrid, he had a division in the Army of the West, and was temporarily at the head of that force in June, 1862. He was placed in command of the Department of East Tennessee in September. Subsequently, he commanded a division of the Army of Kentucky, which fought with the Second Corps, Army of Tennessee, at the battle of Stone's River. In February, 1863, he was arrested on charges of conduct prejudicial to good order and military discipline and sent to Chattanooga, but was released. At the end of the war he fought with the Army of Tennessee in North Carolina. He died, January 22, 1879.

Army of West Tennessee—Army of Mississippi

MAJOR-GENERAL VAN DORN was transferred June 20, 1862, from the Army of the West to the Department of Southern Mississippi and East Louisiana. His troops occupied Vicksburg, and a force from the Reserve Corps of the Army of the Mississippi, under Major-General Breckinridge, fought the battle of Baton Rouge, August 6th. On September 28th, Van Dorn's troops joined the Army of the West to oppose Rosecrans' activities in northern Mississippi, and the combined force was denominated the Army of West Tennessee, with Van Dorn at the head. It fought the battle of Corinth (October 4th), and on December 7th its name was changed to the Army of Mississippi. It consisted of two corps, headed by Van Dorn and Price, the chief control having passed to Lieutenant-General John C. Pemberton, at the head of the Department of Mississippi and East Louisiana. Van Dorn, with his cavalry, made a famous raid in

northern Mississippi in December, capturing the Federal supply depot at Holly Springs. In January, 1863, the corps were changed into divisions. The title, Army of Mississippi, ceased to be used shortly after this date. The chief force under Pemberton surrendered at Vicksburg. Meanwhile, Van Dorn had been killed in Tennessee, May 8, 1863, and Price had been ordered to the Trans-Mississippi Department, February 27, 1863.

LIEUTENANT-GENERAL JOHN CLIFFORD PEMBERTON (U.S.M.A. 1837) was born in Philadelphia, August 10, 1814, and served in the Seminole and Mexican wars, making a noteworthy record in the artillery service. He entered the Confederate army in April, 1861, as major and chief of the Virginia artillery, being made brigadier-general in June. In November, 1861, he was transferred to South Carolina, and appointed major-general in

Johnson K. Duncan Commanded the River Defenses below New Orleans.

Randall L. Gibson, Active Leader in many Western Battles.

William R. Peck Commanded 9th Louisiana; Led a Charge at Appomattox.

Daniel W. Adams, Noted Commander in the Southwest.

CONFEDERATE

GENERALS—No. 11

LOUISIANA AND

MARYLAND

(Two Below.)

St. John Lidell Led a Brigade in the Army of the Mississippi.

Mansfield Lovell, Defender of the Lower Mississippi in 1862.

William W. Mackall, Chief of Staff, Army of Tennessee.

January, 1862, when his command was enlarged to include Georgia and East Florida. In October, he was advanced to the rank of lieutenant-general and sent to the Department of Mississippi and East Louisiana, where he took chief command of all the troops therein, including the Army of West Tennessee (or Mississippi) under Van Dorn and Price. He surrendered Vicksburg to Major-General Grant, July 4, 1863, and after exchange resigned his commission on account of criticism resulting from the surrender. In May, 1864, with the rank of lieutenant-colonel, he was given command of the artillery defenses at Richmond where he served until the close of the war. He became a farmer in Virginia, and died in Penllyn, Pennsylvania, July 13, 1881.

Southern Army—Trans-Mississippi Army

THE FORCES in the Department of West Louisiana and Texas were constituted the Southwestern Army, January 14, 1863, and the command was given to Lieutenant-General E. Kirby Smith. On February 9th, the command was enlarged so as to embrace the whole Trans-Mississippi Department, which, on May 26, 1862, had been separated from the Western Department (Department No. 2). Major-General T. H. Holmes had previously commanded in the Trans-Mississippi. Smith had about thirty thousand men, widely scattered from Fort Smith, Arkansas, to the Rio Grande. Major-General Holmes was defeated at Helena, July 4, 1863. The various portions of the army were constantly occupied in small engagements. These forces opposed the Federal Red River expedition in 1864. At the latest returns, in 1865, the aggregate present of the force was about forty-three thousand. They were the last Confederate troops to surrender, May 26, 1865.

LIEUTENANT-GENERAL THEOPHILUS HUNTER HOLMES (U.S.M.A. 1829) was born in Sampson County, North Carolina, in 1804, and fought in the Florida and Mexican wars. He resigned his commission of major in April, 1861, and entered the Confederate service, rising to the rank of lieutenant-general on October 10, 1862. On account of his age he saw little active service, but was placed at the head of various districts and departments throughout the Confederacy. On July 4,

1863, while in command of the District of Arkansas, Trans-Mississippi Department, he led an unsuccessful attack on Helena. He died in Fayetteville, North Carolina, June 20, 1880.

LIEUTENANT-GENERAL RICHARD TAYLOR, son of Zachary Taylor, was born in New Orleans, Louisiana, January 27, 1826. He was a Yale graduate and went to the Mexican War with General Taylor. He joined the Confederate army in 1861, serving first as colonel of the Ninth Louisiana Volunteers in the Army of the Potomac. He was promoted to brigadier-general in October, and served under " Stonewall " Jackson in the Shenandoah valley and in the Peninsula campaign. He was made major-general in July, 1862, and the following month was assigned to the command of the District of West Louisiana (Trans-Mississippi Department), where he remained until June, 1864. It was hoped that he would recover New Orleans. He occupied the Teche country during the winter of 1862–63. In the following spring and summer he fought against Weitzel and captured Brashear City. He reached the west bank of the Mississippi near New Orleans in July, but was driven back by Weitzel and Franklin. The following year he was instrumental in defeating the Red River expedition. In September, 1864, he was sent to command the Department of Alabama, Mississippi and East Louisiana, and surrendered to Major-General Canby, May 4, 1865. He died in New York City, April 12, 1879.

Army of Missouri

IN AUGUST, 1864, General E. Kirby Smith ordered Major-General Sterling Price to move into Missouri. It was expected that the various independent bands could be organized and bring at least twenty thousand recruits into the Confederate army. Price's force, consisting of the divisions of Fagan, Marmaduke, and Shelby, amounted to nearly twelve thousand men, and is variously called the Army of the Missouri, Price's Expeditionary Corps, and the Army in the Field. After a

John W. Frazer Commanded
a Brigade.

Samuel J. Gholson Com-
manded a Brigade.

William F. Tucker Led a
Brigade under Hood.

Benjamin G. Humphries Led
a Brigade in Virginia.

CONFEDERATE

GENERALS

No. 12

MISSISSIPPI

William E. Baldwin, Commander of
a Brigade at Mobile.

Jacob H. Sharp Led a Brigade in
General Polk's Corps.

Claudius W. Sears, Originally
Colonel of the 46th Regt.

Robert Lowry, Commander
of a Brigade.

William F. Brantly Commanded a Brigade in Tennessee.

Douglas H. Cooper, Leader
of Indian Troops.

very active campaign, Price was driven into Arkansas at the end of November by Major-Generals Rosecrans and Pleasanton, and the Army of the Missouri again became identified with the forces in the Trans-Mississippi Department.

MAJOR-GENERAL STERLING PRICE was born in Prince Edward County, Virginia, September 14, 1809. He settled in Missouri in 1830, and was a member of Congress in 1845, when he went to the Mexican War, in which he was made brigadier-general of volunteers. From 1853 to 1857, he was governor of the State, and president of the State Convention of 1853. He was made major-general of the Missouri militia in May, and assumed command of the Missouri State Guard, July 30, 1861. As major-general of the Confederate Army he commanded the Army of the West from July 2 to September 28, 1862, and later a corps of Van Dorn's Army of Mississippi. In February, 1863, he was ordered to the Trans-Mississippi Department, where he held various commands in Arkansas and elsewhere. His most noteworthy effort was the expedition into Missouri, August-December, 1864, in an attempt to gather a large number of recruits from the independent bands in that State. But Rosecrans drove him back to Arkansas. After the war he became interested in a colonization scheme in Mexico, but returned to the United States in 1866, and died in St. Louis, September 29, 1867.

Army of Mississippi

IN DECEMBER, 1863, Lieutenant-General Leonidas Polk, succeeding Pemberton, was put in command of the force of the Department of Alabama, Mississippi and East Louisiana. It had two divisions of cavalry and a strength of about twenty thousand. This is the force that contended with Major-General Sherman in Mississippi during the winter of 1864. In May, Polk joined the Army of Tennessee to oppose Sherman's advance to Atlanta, and he then denominated his troops the Army of Mississippi. Polk was killed on Pine Mountain, Georgia, June 14th, and was succeeded by Lieutenant-General A. P. Stewart. On July 26th, the Army of Mississippi was joined to the Army of Tennessee as Stewart's Corps.

LIEUTENANT - GENERAL ALEXANDER PETER STEWART (U.S.M.A. 1842) was born in Rogersville, Tennessee, October 12, 1821. He resigned from the army in 1845. He entered the Confederate service from Tennessee, rising to the rank of lieutenant-general in June, 1864, which rank was confirmed the following year. He had a brigade in Polk's command in the Western Department, and later a division in the Army of Tennessee. He was wounded at Ezra Church in the Atlanta campaign, and after Polk's death, he succeeded to the command of the Army of Mississippi, which later became a corps of the Army of Tennessee. On March 16, 1865, he was assigned to the command of the infantry and artillery in that army. He died at Biloxi, Mississippi, August 30, 1908.

MAJOR-GENERAL EDWARD CARY WALTHALL was born in Richmond, Virginia, April 4, 1831. He became a lawyer, practising in Coffeyville, Mississippi. He entered the Confederate service, in 1861, as lieutenant of the Fifteenth Mississippi Infantry, and in December, 1862, became brigadier-general, and major-general in June, 1864. He fought gallantly at Missionary Ridge and covered Hood's retreat at Nashville, where he prevented the capture of the Army of Tennessee by Thomas. In March, 1865, he had command of Stewart's Corps, Army of Tennessee, until the reorganization of April 9th, when he returned to the head of his division. After the war he became United States senator from Mississippi. He died in Washington, April 21, 1898.

Confederate Generals

MAJOR-GENERAL WILLIAM DORSEY PENDER (U. S.M.A. 1854) was born in Edgecombe County, North Carolina, February 6, 1834. He resigned from the army in March, 1861, to enter the Confederate service as colonel of the Sixth North Carolina Infantry. In June, 1862, he became brigadier-general and was made major-general in May, 1863. He was brigade and division commander in

Mark B. Lowrey Led a
Brigade in Cleburne's
Division in the Army
of Tennessee.

Edward Cary Walthall,
Conspicuous at Frank-
lin; Later United
States Senator.

Charles Clark Com-
manded a Division
under General J. C.
Breckinridge.

CONFEDERATE GENERALS—
No. 13—MISSISSIPPI

Samuel G. French, Leader of the Assault on
Alatoona Pass in 1864.

William L. Brandon Com-
manded a Cavalry Brigade.

Nathaniel H. Harris, Colonel
of the 19th Regiment.

Peter B. Stark Led a Cavalry
Brigade in Forrest's Corps.

Samuel W. Ferguson Com-
manded a Cavalry Brigade.

George D. Johnston Led a
Brigade under Bragg.

Joseph R. Davis Led a Brigade
in R. E. Lee's Army.

Wirt Adams, a Conspicuous
Cavalry Commander.

the Army of Northern Virginia, receiving his division on the organization of the Third Army Corps. He died in Staunton, Virginia, July 18, 1863, from wounds received upon the field of Gettysburg.

MAJOR-GENERAL STEPHEN DODSON RAMSEUR (U.S.M.A. 1860) was born in Lincolnton, North Carolina, May 31, 1837, and was assigned to the artillery at Fort Monroe. He resigned in April, 1861, to enter the Confederate service. He was made major in the North Carolina State artillery. He was present at the siege of Yorktown, and was placed at the head of a North Carolina regiment in April. He was severely wounded at Malvern Hill, but returned to the army during the winter of 1862-63, having been made brigadier-general in October. He led a brigade with great ability in the Second Army Corps at Chancellorsville and at Gettysburg. In the latter battle he was prominent in the capture of the town. The following year he was again wounded at Spotsylvania, and as major-general he succeeded to Early's division, when the latter was placed at the head of the Second Army Corps. He went to the Shenandoah valley with Early, and after taking a prominent part in all the principal engagements, he was captured, mortally wounded, at Cedar Creek on October 19, 1864.

MAJOR-GENERAL WILLIAM HENRY TALBOT WALKER (U.S.M.A. 1837) was born in Georgia in October, 1816. While serving in Florida he was thrice wounded in the battle of Okeechobee, December 25, 1837. He fought with great distinction in the Mexican War. Early in 1861, he joined the Confederate army, in which he rose to the rank of major-general in May, 1863. He had a brigade in the Second Corps, Army of the Mississippi, and later a command in the District of Georgia, under Beauregard. He was sent with a brigade to the assistance of Johnston in the latter's attempt to keep Grant from Vicksburg, in May, 1863. In August, he was given a division in Hill's Corps, Army of Tennessee, and commanded the reserves at Chickamauga, after which he was in Hardee's Corps in the Chattanooga and Atlanta campaigns until he was killed at Decatur, near Atlanta, July 22, 1864.

LIEUTENANT-GENERAL NATHAN BEDFORD FORREST was born near the site of Chapel Hill, Tennessee, July 13, 1821, and became a slave-trader at Memphis. In the summer of 1861, he joined the Tennessee mounted rifles as private, and a

month later raised and equipped a force of Confederate cavalry. He escaped with his battalion from Fort Donelson, and by the middle of 1862 he had become brigadier-general and was one of the most important officers in the Confederate army. At the head of his independent cavalry organization, he was active during Bragg's invasion of Kentucky and remained there some time. He was with the Army of Tennessee at Chickamauga, and in November, 1863, was made major-general and assigned to the command of all the cavalry in western Tennessee and northern Mississippi. In March and April, 1864, he advanced from Mississippi with a large force. He captured Union City with its garrison, and attacked Paducah, Kentucky. He fought with Sooy Smith, and retreating to Fort Pillow, captured the garrison there, amid great slaughter on April 12th. He then returned to Mississippi and began to operate against Sherman's lines of communication. He defeated Sturgis, at Guntown, on June 10th, but was put to rout by A. J. Smith, at Tupelo, on July 14th. In January, 1865, he was placed in command of the District of Mississippi and East Louisiana, and on February 28th was made lieutenant-general. He was defeated at Selma, Alabama, by the Federal cavalry-leader, J. H. Wilson, and surrendered his forces with those of Lieutenant-General Richard Taylor in May. After the war he conducted several large plantations. He died in Memphis, Tennessee, October 29, 1877.

MAJOR-GENERAL DABNEY HERNDON MAURY (U.S.M.A. 1846) was born in Fredericksburg, Virginia, May 20, 1822, and served in the Mexican War with distinction. He taught at West Point, and served in the West, being assistant adjutant-general in New Mexico when the Civil War broke out. He was dismissed from the service in June, 1861, having enlisted as captain in the Confederate cavalry. He served with the forces that later became the Army of the West, and after the battle of Pea Ridge was made brigadier-general. He had a division in the Army of the West, and commanded the whole force temporarily in June, 1862. As major-general, he had a division with Pemberton's forces in the battle with Sherman at Chickasaw Bayou, December 26, 1862. In 1863, he was placed at the head of the Department of East Tennessee, and in 1864-65, he was in command of the Department of the Gulf, surrendering at Meridian, Mississippi, May 11, 1865. He was the founder of the Southern Historical Society, and from 1886 to 1889 was American minister to Colombia. He died in Peoria, Illinois, January 11, 1900.

John B. Clark Commanded a Cavalry Brigade; Engaged at Pea Ridge.

John G. Walker, a Daring Leader in the Army of Northern Virginia.

Joseph O. Shelby, Cavalry Commander in Arkansas and Missouri Battles.

M. M. Parsons Led a Brigade in Price's Division; Defender of Red River.

Joseph H. Cockrell, Distinguished in Missouri Campaigns; Later U. S. Senator.

CONFEDERATE

GENERALS—No. 14

MISSOURI

(ABOVE AND TO RIGHT)

NORTH CAROLINA

(BELOW)

John S. Marmaduke, Leader of Cavalry West of the Mississippi.

Daniel M. Frost Led a Brigade of State Guard under General Price.

John S. Bowen, Conspicuous at Port Gibson and Vicksburg in 1863.

James G. Martin Led a Brigade Defending Richmond in 1864–5.

Robert Ransom, Jr., One of the Defenders of Marye's Heights in 1862.

Richard C. Gatlin, Colonel of a Corps of Infantry, C. S. A., in 1861.

Bryan Grimes Led a Division in the Army of Northern Virginia.

Confederate Generals

BRIGADIER-GENERAL JOHN HUNT MORGAN was born in Huntsville, Alabama, June 1, 1826. He served in the Mexican War and joined the Confederate army in command of the Lexington Rifles, of Kentucky. He did scouting duty, and, as colonel, organized three cavalry companies known as Morgan's Squadron, which operated in Tennessee and Kentucky and fought at Shiloh. His invasion of Kentucky in July, 1862, prepared the way for Bragg. At Lexington, he routed a Union force and his frequent raids, especially the famous Christmas raid of 1862, were among the boldest Confederate exploits. His ability won him promotion to brigadier-general. In July, 1863, he made another raid into Kentucky. At Buffington Ford, about seven hundred of his men, hemmed in by Shackelton and Hobson, were forced to surrender, but Morgan escaped. At last he was captured by Shackelton at New Lisbon, July 26, 1863, but he and six fellow prisoners escaped from the Ohio State Penitentiary at Columbus, on November 27th, and joined the Confederate army in northern Georgia. In April, 1864, he was put at the head of the Department of Southwestern Virginia. Late in May, Morgan, with a few followers, went over into Kentucky, making a raid upon Lexington and dashing toward Frankfort, but Burbridge struck him a severe blow at Cynthiana, June 12th, and Morgan lost seven hundred men and one thousand horses. The early part of September found him in Greenville. While there the town was surprised and surrounded by Gillem's troops, and in attempting to escape Morgan was shot and killed September 4, 1864.

MAJOR-GENERAL LAFAYETTE McLAWS (U.S. M.A. 1842) was born in Augusta, Georgia, January 15, 1821. In March, 1861, he resigned from the army to enter the Confederate service, in which he reached the rank of major-general in May, 1862. He commanded a division in Magruder's command, Army of Northern Virginia, through the Seven Days' battle, and was then transferred to Longstreet's command, being identified as division commander with the First Army Corps through the Maryland campaign of 1862, and all the succeeding campaigns of the Army of Northern Virginia (including Chancellorsville) until September, 1863, when he went West with Longstreet and fought at Chickamauga and Knoxville. In May, 1864, he was sent to Georgia and South Carolina and being under Lieutenant-General Hardee eventually had a division in Hardee's Corps, when in February, 1865, the latter united his forces with the Army of Tennessee. After the war he

was collector of internal revenue and postmaster at Savannah, where he died, July 24, 1897.

BRIGADIER-GENERAL FELIX KIRK ZOLLICOFFER was born in Maury County, Tennessee, May 19, 1812. He became a printer and editor, interrupting the pursuit of this calling to serve in the Seminole War. In 1841, he was made associate editor of the Nashville *Banner*, was State comptroller from 1844 to 1849, and continued his political career in the State senate. He was a member of Congress from 1853 to 1859, and also a delegate to the Peace Conference held at Washington, 1861. In May of that year he was appointed major-general of the provisional army of Tennessee, and in July, after commanding an instruction camp, was made brigadier-general of the Confederate army and assigned to the District of East Tennessee. His forces were defeated by Brigadier-General Schoepf at Camp Wildcat, Kentucky, October 21st, and in an encounter with Brigadier-General Thomas at Logan's Cross Roads, or Mill Springs, Kentucky, January 19, 1862, he was killed.

MAJOR-GENERAL HENRY HETH (U.S.M.A. 1847) was born in Chesterfield County, Virginia, December 16, 1825. He rose to the rank of captain in the Tenth Infantry, from which he resigned, April 25, 1861, to enter the Confederate Army. He was made colonel of the Forty-fifth Virginia Infantry, June 17, 1861. He was commissioned brigadier-general, January 6, 1862, and major-general, May 24, 1863. After serving with his brigade in West Virginia under General Humphrey Marshall, and in the invasion of Kentucky under General Bragg, where he commanded a division of infantry and a brigade of cavalry, he came East, and commanded a division in the Gettysburg campaign. He was also in various campaigns with the Army of Northern Virginia, commanding a division in A. P. Hill's Third Army Corps. He surrendered at Appomattox, and died at Washington, D. C., September 26, 1899.

MAJOR-GENERAL JOSEPH B. KERSHAW was born at Camden, South Carolina, January 5, 1822. He was a member of the State Senate, 1852–57. He entered the Confederate service and was soon made colonel of the Second South Carolina regiment, and on February 15, 1862, he was appointed a brigadier-general. In that capacity he served on the Peninsula and in the Seven Days' battle. He also fought at Antietam, Fred-

Alfred M. Scales Led a North Carolina Brigade in Hill's Corps.

William P. Roberts Led a Brigade of Cavalry in Virginia.

John D. Barry, Colonel of the 18th North Carolina Regiment.

William McRae Led a North Carolina Brigade in Lee's Army.

William R. Cox Led a North Carolina Brigade in Ewell's Corps.

CONFED–ERATE GENERALS

No. 15 NORTH CAROLINA

R. Leventhorpe, Defender of Fort Fisher.

Lawrence S. Baker, Colonel of the 1st Cavalry.

Thomas F. Toon Led a North Carolina Brigade in Lee's Army.

John R. Cooke, Engaged in Repelling Burnside at Fredericksburg.

Rufus Barringer Led a Brigade of Cavalry in Virginia.

Thomas L. Clingman Led a North Carolina Brigade in Lee's Army.

ericksburg, and Gettysburg, and with General Longstreet's Corps. He was engaged at the battle of Chickamauga, commanding a brigade in McLaws' Division of the Left Wing. Returning to the East he was prominent in the Wilderness campaign, and in the Shenandoah he was with Ewell's Corps at Sailors' Creek, when his command was captured on April 6, 1865, and he was released from Fort Warren, Mass., July 24, of the same year. He was elected President of the State Senate and later became a judge of the Circuit Court of South Carolina. General Kershaw died at Camden, South Carolina, April 13, 1894.

MAJOR-GENERAL CHARLES WILLIAM FIELD (U.S.M.A. 1849) was born in Woodford County, Kentucky, in 1818. He served in the Second Dragoons until May, 1861, when he resigned to enter the Confederate service, and was appointed brigadier-general on March 14, 1862. On February 12, 1864, he was appointed major-general. He served at Gaines' Mill, the Second Bull Run, the Wilderness, Spotsylvania, Drewry's Bluff, and in the campaign around Petersburg; being in command of Field's Division of the First Army Corps. General Field died in Washington, D. C., April 9, 1892.

MAJOR-GENERAL CADMUS MARCELLUS WILCOX (U.S.M.A. 1846) was born in Wayne County, North Carolina, May 29, 1826. He served with distinguished bravery in the Mexican War and was brevetted for gallantry and meritorious conduct at Chapultepec, acting as assistant instructor at West Point (1852–57) and becoming a Captain in 1860. On June 8, 1861, he resigned to enter the Confederate service. He was made a brigadier-general October 21, 1861, and served at Seven Pines, the Second Bull Run, and in the Antietam campaign; his name being associated with a brigade that achieved notable reputation during the war. It was composed of the Eighth, Ninth, Tenth, and Eleventh Alabama regiments and Thomas' Artillery, and was in Longstreet's division of the Army of Northern Virginia. It made a striking record in the Seven Days' battles, where it sustained a loss of 1055, or 57 per cent. of its entire number. Later this brigade was in General R. H. Anderson's division, to the command of which General Wilcox succeeded. He also participated at the battle of Gettysburg and served through a number of campaigns in the Army of Northern Virginia until the final surrender at Ap-

pomattox. He was appointed a major-general in 1863. From 1886 until his death, on December 2, 1890, he was chief of the Railroad Division of the General Land Office at Washington, D. C. He wrote a " History of the Mexican War," which is regarded as the standard military work on the subject.

MAJOR-GENERAL ROBERT E. RODES was born at Lynchburg, Virginia, March 29, 1829. He was graduated at the Virginia Military Institute at Lexington in 1848, and was a professor there until appointed captain of the Mobile Cadets early in 1861. He was made colonel of the Fifth Alabama and in October, 1861, was appointed brigadier-general. He served at the First Battle of Bull Run and at the battles of Seven Pines and Gaines' Mills, and distinguished himself in command of Rodes' Brigade, which was composed of Alabama troops in Hill's Division of Jackson's Corps, Army of Northern Virginia. On May 7, 1863, General Rodes was appointed major-general and he commanded a division at Chancellorsville and Gettysburg in Ewell's Second Corps of the Army of Northern Virginia. He also participated in the Wilderness campaign and in the operations in the Shenandoah valley, where he was killed in action at Winchester, September 19, 1864.

MAJOR-GENERAL GEORGE EDWARD PICKETT (U.S.M.A. 1846) was born at Richmond, Virginia, June 28, 1828. He served in the Mexican War, receiving the brevet of first lieutenant for gallant service at Contreras and Churubusco, and also the brevet of lieutenant for distinguished service at Chapultepec. He served with the regular army in the Territory of Washington, and at various posts in the West until June 25, 1861, when he resigned. He was appointed a colonel in the Confederate army, on July 23, and on January 14, 1862, he was appointed as brigadier-general. He served in command of a brigade in Longstreet's division of General Joseph E. Johnston's Army, and on October 11 he was made major-general, commanding a division in the Army of Northern Virginia. General Pickett made a memorable charge against the Federal front at Cemetery Hill on the third day of Gettysburg, his division having reached the field on that day. In September, 1863, General Pickett commanded the Department of North Carolina and operated against Drewry's Bluff in the following year, after his return to Virginia. He was defeated at Lynchburg in an attempt to

James H. Trapier, Commander at Fort Moultrie and Sullivan's Island.

Benjamin Huger, Commander of a Division at Seven Pines.

William H. Wallace, Originally Colonel of the 18th Regiment.

CONFEDERATE

GENERALS

No. 16

SOUTH CAROLINA

Milledge L. Bonham Became Governor of South Carolina.

Thomas F. Drayton Commanded a Military District in South Carolina.

James Chestnut, Aide to Beauregard at Fort Sumter.

Johnson Hagood, Defender of Richmond and Petersburg.

Arthur M. Manigault, Colonel 10th Regiment.

oppose Sheridan's cavalry in March, 1865, and also at Dinwiddie Court House and Five Forks. He surrendered with the Army of Northern Virginia and at the conclusion of the war he settled in Richmond, where he died in 1875.

MAJOR-GENERAL WILLIAM HENRY FITZHUGH LEE was born at Arlington, Virginia, May 31, 1837, the second son of General Robert E. Lee. For two years he served as second lieutenant with the Sixth U. S. Infantry, resigning in May, 1859. At the outbreak of the Civil War he entered the Confederate Army in a Virginia cavalry regiment, was made a brigadier-general to rank from September 15, 1862, being promoted to major-general, April 23, 1864. During the Peninsula campaign General Lee, then colonel commanding the Ninth Virginia Cavalry, participated in Stuart's ride around McClellan's army. In the Chancellorsville campaign General Lee was in command of a body of cavalry which fought with the Union Cavalry of General Stoneman under the immediate command of General Averell. General Lee's brigade also participated in the Gettysburg campaign, forming one of the six brigades commanded by Major-General J. E. B. Stuart. General Lee with his cavalry opposed the advances of General Sheridan in his Trevilian raid when Wilson was sent out to cut the Weldon and South Side Road; and at the Petersburg campaign his cavalry participated actively, making many valiant assaults on the Federal lines. Before the surrender of Appomattox, General Lee with his cavalry aided General Gordon in keeping back the Union advances and protecting the wagon-trains of the Confederate army. He was paroled at Appomattox Court House, April 9, 1865, and died at Ravensworth, Fairfax County, Virginia, October 15, 1891.

MAJOR-GENERAL GEORGE WASHINGTON CUSTIS LEE (U.S.M.A. 1854) was born at Fortress Monroe, Virginia, September 16, 1832, and was the eldest son of General Robert E. Lee. Upon graduation from the United States Military Academy he joined the corps of engineers, in which he served until May 2, 1861, when he resigned to enter the Confederate Army. The greater part of his service was as aide to President Jefferson Davis. He was appointed major-general serving with the volunteer troops with temporary rank on February 7, 1865, the commission dating from October 20, 1864. On the same date he was also made full major-general. He was captured at Sailor's Creek, April 6, 1865, and was paroled six days later, which parole was extended until April 23, 1865.

In addition to serving as aide to President Davis, General Lee was in command of military forces in the city of Richmond. In the latter part of the war he commanded a division of Ewell's corps, and it was at this time that his division was captured along with that of General Kershaw. After the war he became professor of civil engineering at the Virginia Military Institute, and in 1871 he succeeded his father,—General Robert E. Lee,—as president of the Washington & Lee University. This position he held until 1897, when he became president emeritus.

MAJOR-GENERAL MATTHEW CALVIN BUTLER was born near Greenville, South Carolina, March 8, 1836. He was admitted to the South Carolina bar in 1856, and in addition to practising law was elected to the State legislature in 1859. At the outbreak of the Civil War he entered the Confederate Army as captain, and rose to the command of the Second South Carolina Cavalry, which fought a notable action at Brandy Station on June 10, 1863, in which Colonel Butler lost his right leg. He was appointed brigadier-general, September 2, 1863. In the following year General Butler had command of a brigade consisting of the Fourth, Fifth, and Sixth South Carolina Cavalry, which was included in General Wade Hampton's division and operated with the Army of Northern Virginia. General Butler participated in the battle of Trevilian Station on June 12, 1864, commanding General Hampton's division, where he was engaged with the cavalry of General Sheridan, and later broke through General J. H. Wilson's lines. General Butler was sent to resist the onward march of Sherman through North Carolina, and he participated in the battle of Bentonville. He had previously, December 7, 1864, been appointed major-general. After the surrender at Greensboro, General Butler was paroled, May 1, 1865. Entering politics again after the war, General Butler met with rapid advancement, and was United States Senator from South Carolina from 1877 to 1889. At the outbreak of the Spanish War he was made a major-general of volunteers, May 28, 1898, and served until honorably discharged, April 15, 1899. He was a member of the commission appointed by President McKinley to arrange for the evacuation of Cuba by the Spaniards. General Butler died at Columbus, S. C., April 14, 1909.

MAJOR-GENERAL WILLIAM MAHONE was born at Monroe, Southampton County, Virginia, December 1, 1826. Graduating from the Virginia Military Institute in 1847, he followed the profes-

John Bratton Led a Brigade in Longstreet's Corps.

Thomas M. Logan Led a Cavalry
Brigade in Lee's Army.

Nathan G. Evans, Commander of a
District on the Atlantic Coast.

CONFEDERATE

GENERALS

No. 17

SOUTH CAROLINA

Martin W. Gary, Originally Colonel
in Hampton's Legion.

James Connor Commanded a Brigade
in Lee's Army.

Ellison Capers Led a Brigade in the
Army of Tennessee.

John D. Kennedy Led a Brigade in
Longstreet's Corps.

John S. Preston, Chief of the Bureau
of Conscription.

sion of civil engineering until the outbreak of the Civil War, when he entered the Confederate Army. He participated in the capture of the Norfolk Navy Yard by the Virginia volunteers, raised and commanded the Sixth Virginia regiment and on November 16, 1861, he was appointed brigadier-general in the Confederate Army in March, 1864. In the battle of Seven Pines, General Mahone commanded a brigade in Huger's Division, while at Malvern Hill also his troops were engaged. General Mahone also fought in the Chancellorsville and Gettysburg campaigns, as well as in the Wilderness. At the North Anna on May 24th, General Mahone made a desperate attack on Warren's Corps, driving it back. On August 3, 1864, General Mahone was promoted to be major-general. He was active in the brilliant repulse of the Federal attack after the explosion of the mine at Petersburg and in the various operations about the Weldon Railroad. General Mahone was present at the last struggles of the war, and was paroled at Appomattox Court House, April 9, 1865. After the war he was made president of the Norfolk and Tennessee Railroad and became a leading figure in Virginia politics, being elected to the United States Senate in 1880, where he acted with the Republican party. He failed of re-election on the expiration of his term in 1887, and died at Washington, D. C., October 9, 1893.

VIII

THE ORGANIZATIONS
OF THE
VETERANS

THE GERM OF THE "G. A. R." IDEA

William W. Silkworth, of Long Branch, New Jersey, a veteran who had an opportunity to inspect some of the pictures reproduced in the PHOTOGRAPHIC HISTORY, recognized this group as Company B, 170th Regiment, New York Volunteers. "You cannot appreciate or understand fully my amazement and joy in the discovery," he wrote to the editors. "There right in the front of the picture sits my brother playing cards (You will note that he is left handed. We laid him away in front of Petersburg). With him is John Vandewater, Geo. Thomas and Wash. Keating. There is Charlie Thomas and all the rest as true as life. With the exception of two, I have not seen any of the boys for thirty years." It was at such moments as this, when the Federal soldiers played games and chatted and became

UNION RESERVES ON PICKET DUTY

acquainted, that the organization was being evolved which has grown into a leading national institution since its formation at Decatur, Illinois, on April 6, 1866. Between the men who had fought and marched and suffered together, who time out of mind had shared their last crust and saved each others' lives, who had nursed each other and cheered each other on when another step forward seemed to mean certain death, there arose a great love that extended to the widows and orphans of those whose dying words they had heard on the field of battle. Ever since that time the organization has lent assistance to those reduced to need by the inexorable war. It admits to membership any soldier or sailor of the United States Army, Navy or Marine Corps, who served between April 12, 1861, and April 9, 1865.

The Grand Army of the Republic

By John E. Gilman, Commander-in-Chief, Grand Army of the Republic

AT the close of the Civil War, there were over a million men in the Union armies. Nearly two and a half million had served under the Stars and Stripes during the four long years of warfare, of whom three hundred and fifty-nine thousand had died. It was essential that those still in the service should disband and retire to civilian life. This was effected after a grand parade of the armies of the Potomac, the Tennessee, and of Georgia, on May 23 and 24, 1865, when one hundred and fifty thousand men marched through the wide avenues of Washington in review before the President and the commanding generals. From the glare and glory, the power and prestige of the soldier's career, they went into the obscurity of the peaceful pursuits of American citizenship, and in a few short months the vast armies of the United States had disappeared.

The great war was ended, but it would have been strange indeed if the memories of those years of storm and stress, the sacrifices of those who had fallen, the experiences of the march, the battlefield, and the camp, and the needs of their disabled comrades, and of the widows and the orphans had been forgotten.

Even before the war had ended, organizations of veterans of the Union armies had begun to be formed. The first veteran society formed, The Third Army Corps Union, was organized at the headquarters of General D. B. Birney, commander of the Third Army Corps, at a meeting of the officers of the corps, September 2, 1863. The main object, at that time, was to secure funds for embalming and sending home for burial the bodies of officers killed in battle or dying in hospitals at the front. General D. A. Sickles was its first president.

In April, 1865, the Society of the Army of the Tennessee was formed at Raleigh, North Carolina, membership being restricted to officers who had served with the old Army of the Tennessee. The object was declared to be " to keep alive that kindly and cordial feeling which has been one of the characteristics of this army during its career in the service." General Sherman was elected president in 1869, and continued to hold the office for many years.

After the war, many other veteran societies

were formed, composed not only of officers but of enlisted men of the various armies, corps, and regiments, as well as many naval organizations. Among them, the Military Order of the Loyal Legion of the United States was the first society formed by officers honorably discharged from the service. It was first thought of at a meeting of a group of officers who had met the day after the assassination of President Lincoln for the purpose of passing resolutions on his death. These resolutions were subsequently adopted, and it was determined to effect a permanent organization. This was done May 3, 1865, and a constitution and by-laws were, in part, adopted the same month. The titles of officers, the constitution, and general plan, were, in part, afterward adopted by the Grand Army of the Republic. The essential difference was that first-class membership of the Loyal Legion was restricted to officers.

Besides the foregoing organizations of veterans, there were others formed of a political nature, such as the Boys in Blue and other similar societies, and there were held in September, 1866, two political conventions of veterans of the army and navy. These political soldiers' clubs were the result of the times, for the controversy between Congress and President Johnson was at its height. In the East, after the fall elections of 1866, most of these political clubs of veterans were ready to disband. The desire for a permanent organization of veterans became strong. No post of the Grand Army had been organized east of Ohio prior to October, 1866. Posts were started, and inasmuch as eligibility to membership in the Grand Army was possessed by those who composed the membership of these political clubs, the Boys in Blue and similar clubs formed, in many places, the nucleus of the Grand Army posts.

This fact gave, in good part, a political tinge to the Grand Army during the first year or two of its existence, and to it was due, chiefly, the severe losses in membership that the order sustained for a short period. But, eventually, the political character was wholly eradicated, and the order recovered its standing and its losses.

During the winter of 1865–66, Major B. F. Stephenson, surgeon of the Fourteenth Illinois regiment, discussed with friends the matter of the

Galusha Pennypacker, Colonel of the 97th Regiment.

Joshua T. Owens, Colonel
of the 69th Regiment.

James A. Beaver, Colonel
of the 148th Regiment.

Isaac J. Wistar, Originally
Colonel of the 71st Reg't.

FEDERAL GENERALS

No. 23

PENNSYLVANIA

Joshua K. Sigfried, Originally Colonel of the 48th Regiment.

David H. Williams, Originally Colonel of the 82d Infantry.

John B. McIntosh, Origi-
nally Colonel of the 3d
Cavalry.

Frederick· S. Stumbaugh,
Originally Colonel of
the 2d Infantry.

Thomas J. McKean Led
a Division at
Corinth.

Montgomery C. Meigs,
Quartermaster-General
of the Army.

formation of an organization of veteran soldiers. He had, previously, while the war was still continuing, talked over the formation of such an organization with his tent-mate, Chaplain William J. Rutledge of the same regiment, and both had agreed to undertake the work of starting such a project after the war was ended, if they survived.

At the national encampment in St. Louis, in 1887, it was stated by Fred. J. Dean, of Fort Scott, Arkansas, that in February, 1866, he, with Doctors Hamilton and George H. Allen, assisted Doctor Stephenson in compiling ritualistic work, constitution, and by-laws at Springfield, Illinois, and these four assumed the obligations of the Grand Army of the Republic at that time. It is conceded that the initiatory steps to constitute the order were taken in Illinois, and Doctor Stephenson's name is the first one connected with the systematic organization of the Grand Army. He and his coworkers were obligated in the work. Several other veterans joined with them, and a ritual was prepared.

The question of printing this ritual occasioned some anxiety on account of the desire to keep it secret, but this difficulty was solved by having it printed at the office of the Decatur (Illinois) *Tribune*, the proprietor of which, together with his compositors, were veterans. They were accordingly obligated, and the ritual was printed by them. Captain John S. Phelps, one of the active associates of Doctor Stephenson, who had gone to Decatur to supervise the work of printing the ritual, had met several of his comrades of the Forty-first Illinois and had sought their cooperation. One of them, Doctor J. W. Routh, who was acquainted with Doctor Stephenson, went to Springfield to consult the latter about organizing, and, with Captain M. F. Kanan, called upon Doctor Stephenson. They returned to Decatur to organize a post there, and at once set to work and secured a sufficient number of signatures to an application for a charter. They returned to Springfield to present the application in person. On April 6, 1866, Doctor Stephenson issued the charter, signing it as department commander of Illinois, thus creating the first post of the Grand Army of the Republic. The ritual was revised and a constitution written by a committee from this post, at the suggestion of Doctor Stephenson. The committee reported that the regulations and ritual had been presented to department headquarters and accepted. The plan of organization consisted of post, district, department, and national organizations, to be known as the Grand Army of the Republic.

The declaration of principles in the constitution, written by Adjutant-General Robert M. Woods, set forth that the soldiers of the volunteer army of the United States, during the war of 1861–65, actuated by patriotism and combined in fellowship, felt called upon to declare those principles and rules which should guide the patriotic freeman and Christian citizen, and to agree upon plans and laws which should govern them in a united and systematic working method to effect the preservation of the grand results of the war. These results included the preservation of fraternal feelings, the making of these ties advantageous to those in need of assistance, the providing for the support, care, and education of soldiers' orphans, and maintenance of their widows, the protection and assistance of disabled soldiers, and the " establishment and defense of the late soldiery of the United States, morally, socially, and politically, with a view to inculcate a proper appreciation of their services to the country, and to a recognition of such services and claims by the American people."

To this last section, the national encampment in Philadelphia, in 1868, added, " But this association does not design to make nominations for office or to use its influence as a secret organization for partisan purposes." The word " sailors " was added by the Indianapolis encampment. In May, 1869, the present form of rules and regulations was adopted.

Post No. 2 of the Department of Illinois was organized at Springfield, as stated by General Webber, in April, 1866.

In 1865, in Indiana, correspondence relating to the continuance of the Army Club, a society of veterans, had come to the hands of Governor Oliver P. Morton, of Indiana. He sent General R. S. Foster, of Indianapolis, to Springfield, to examine into Doctor Stephenson's plan of organization. General Foster met the latter, and was obligated by him. On his return, he obligated a number of his intimate comrades, and these he constituted as a department organization. The first post of this department was organized at Indianapolis, on the 22d of August, 1866.

Doctor Stephenson had issued, as department commander, General Orders No. 1, on April 1, 1866, at Springfield, in which he announced the following officers: General Jules C. Webber, aide-de-camp and chief of staff; Major Robert M. Woods, adjutant-general; Colonel John M. Snyder, quartermaster-general; Captain John S. Phelps, aide-de-camp, and Captain John A. Lightfoot, assistant adjutant-general, on duty at the de-

Charles T. Campbell, Originally
Colonel of the 1st Regiment
of Artillery.

Thomas R. Rowley, Originally Colonel of the 102d Regiment.

FEDERAL GENERALS–
No. 24

James Nagle, Originally Colonel of
the 48th Regiment.

PENNSYLVANIA
(CONTINUED)

Alexander Schimmelpfennig, Originally
Colonel of the 14th Infantry.

George A. McCall, Commander of the
Pennsylvania Reserves in
the Seven Days.

Albert L. Lee Led a Cavalry
Column in the Red River
Campaign.

Joshua B. Howell, Originally
Colonel of the 85th
Regiment.

partment headquarters. On June 26, 1866, a call had been issued for a convention, to be held at Springfield, Illinois, July 12, 1866. The convention was held on this date and the Department of Illinois organized, General John M. Palmer being elected department commander. Doctor Stephenson was recognized, however, in the adoption of a resolution which proclaimed him as " the head and front of the organization." He continued to act as commander-in-chief.

In October, 1866, departments had been formed in Illinois, Wisconsin, Indiana, Iowa, and Minnesota, and posts had been organized in Ohio, Missouri, Kentucky, Arkansas, District of Columbia, Massachusetts, New York, and Pennsylvania. On October 31, 1866, Doctor Stephenson issued General Orders No. 13, directing a national convention to be held at Indianapolis, November 20, 1866, signing this order as commander-in-chief. In accordance with this order, the First National Encampment of the Grand Army of the Republic convened at Indianapolis on the date appointed, and was called to order by Commander-in-Chief Stephenson. A committee on permanent organization was appointed and its report nominating the officers of the convention was adopted, and General John M. Palmer became the presiding officer of the convention. The committee on constitution submitted a revised form of the constitution which, with a few amendments, was adopted. Resolutions were adopted calling the attention of Congress to the laws in regard to bounties, recommending the passage of a law making it obligatory for every citizen to give actual service when called upon in time of war, instead of providing a substitute, and suggesting, for the consideration of those in authority, the bestowal of positions of honor and profit upon worthy and competent soldiers and sailors. General S. A. Hurlbut, of Illinois, was elected commander-in-chief and Doctor Stephenson, adjutant-general.

The national organization of the Grand Army of the Republic was thus fairly started. The Second National Encampment was held at Philadelphia, January 15, 16, and 17, 1868, when General John A. Logan was elected commander-in-chief. At the Third National Encampment at Cincinnati, May 12 and 13, 1869, General Logan was reelected commander-in-chief. It appears from Adjutant-General Chipman's report at this encampment that, at the Philadelphia encampment in 1868, there were represented twenty-one departments, which claimed a total membership of over two hundred thousand. But there had been very few records kept, either in departments or at national headquarters, and there seems to have been very little communication between posts and headquarters. At the Cincinnati encampment, the adjutant-general reported that the aggregate number of departments was thirty-seven, and that the number of posts, reported and estimated, was 2050. At the encampment at Cincinnati, in 1869, the grade system of membership was adopted, establishing three grades of recruit, soldier, and veteran. This system met with serious opposition and was finally abandoned at the encampment at Boston, in 1871. It was claimed that to this system much of the great falling-off in membership was due. It is a fact that, at this period, there had been a large decrease in the numbers in the order, particularly in the West. But the cause of this may be laid to a variety of reasons. The order, at first, seems to have had a rapid growth. Because of the incompleteness of the records, it is impossible even to estimate what the strength of the membership in those early days was. But the real solidity of the order was not established until some years had passed.

On May 5, 1868, Commander-in-Chief Logan, by General Orders No. 11, had assigned May 30, 1868, as a memorial day which was to be devoted to the strewing of flowers on the graves of deceased comrades who had died in the defense of their country during the Civil War. The idea of Memorial Day had been suggested to Adjutant-General Chipman in a letter from some comrade then living in Cincinnati, whose name has been lost. At the encampment at Washington, in 1870, Memorial Day was established by an amendment to the rules and regulations. It has been made a holiday in many of the States, and is now observed throughout the country, not only by the Grand Army but by the people generally, for the decoration of the graves of the soldiers.

The first badge of the order was adopted in 1866. A change was made in October, 1868, in its design, and a further change in October, 1869. At the national encampment of 1873, the badge was adopted which is substantially the one that exists to-day, a few minor changes being made in 1886. It is now made from captured cannon purchased from the Government. The bronze button worn on the lapel of the coat was adopted in 1884.

The matter of pensions has, in the nature of things, occupied much of the time of the Grand Army encampments, both national and departmental. The order has kept careful watch over pension legislation; its recommendations have been conservative, and of late years have been adopted by Congress to a very great extent. Aid

William A. Quarles, Wounded in Hood's Charge at Franklin.

George G. Dibrell, Leader of Cavalry Opposing Sherman's March.

Alfred E. Jackson Commanded a District of East Tennessee.

CONFEDERATE

GENERALS

No. 18

TENNESSEE

George Maney, Active Organizer and Leader of Tennessee.

Bushrod R. Johnson, Conspicuous in the West and in the East.

John P. McCown; At Belmont, in 1861. Later Led a Division.

John C. Brown Led a Division in the Army of Tennessee.

William H. Jackson Led a Brigade of Forrest's Cavalry.

has been given to veterans and widows entitled to pensions, by cooperation with the Pension Office in obtaining and furnishing information for the adjudication of claims.

The Grand Army has been assisted in carrying out its purposes by its allied orders, the Woman's Relief Corps, the Sons of Veterans, the Daughters of Veterans, and the Ladies of the G. A. R. These organizations have adopted the principles and purposes that have actuated the Grand Army and have given much valued aid in the achievement of the results obtained.

The Grand Army of the Republic before the end of the nineteenth century had passed the zenith of its career. Its membership remained about the same in numbers after its first great leap and subsequent subsidence, varying between 25,000 and 50,000 from 1870 to 1880. During the decade between 1880 and 1890 it rose to its highest number of 409,-489. Since then it has decreased, through death, in very great part, until, at the national encampment of 1910, at Atlantic City, it had diminished to 213,901. Its posts exist throughout the length and breadth of the country, and even outside, and nearly every State has a department organization. Its influence is felt in every city, town, and village, and it has earned the good-will and support of the entire American people. Among its leaders have been some of the most prominent men of the country. Its commanders-in-chief have been:

B. F. Stephenson,	Illinois,	1866
S. A. Hurlbut,	Illinois,	1866–67
John A. Logan,	Illinois,	1868–70
Ambrose E. Burnside,	Rhode Island,	1871–72
Charles Devens,	Massachusetts,	1873–74
John F. Hartranft,	Pennsylvania,	1875–76
John C. Robinson,	New York,	1877–78
William Earnshaw,	Ohio,	1879
Louis Wagner,	Pennsylvania,	1880
George S. Merrill,	Massachusetts,	1881
Paul Van Dervoort,	Nebraska,	1882
Robert B. Beath,	Pennsylvania,	1883
John S. Kountz,	Ohio,	1884
S. S. Burdett,	Dist. of Columbia,	1885
Lucius Fairchild,	Wisconsin,	1886
John P. Rea,	Minnesota,	1887
William Warner,	Missouri,	1888
Russell A. Alger,	Michigan,	1889
Wheelock G. Veazey,	Vermont,	1890
John Palmer,	New York,	1891
A. G. Weissert,	Wisconsin,	1892
John G. B. Adams,	Massachusetts,	1893
Thomas G. Lawler,	Illinois,	1894
Ivan N. Walker,	Indiana,	1895
T. S. Clarkson,	Nebraska,	1896
John P. S. Gobin,	Pennsylvania,	1897
James A. Sexton,	Illinois,	1898
W. C. Johnson,	Ohio,	1899
Albert D. Shaw,	New York,	1899
Leo Rassieur,	Missouri,	1900
Ell Torrence,	Minnesota,	1901
Thomas J. Stewart,	Pennsylvania,	1902
John C. Black,	Illinois,	1903
Wilmon W. Blackmar,	Massachusetts,	1904
John R. King,	Maryland,	1904
James Tanner,	Dist. of Columbia,	1905
Robert B. Brown,	Ohio,	1906
Charles G. Burton,	Missouri,	1907
Henry M. Nevius,	New Jersey,	1908
Samuel R. Van Sant,	Minnesota,	1909
John E. Gilman,	Massachusetts,	1910
Hiram M. Trimble,	Illinois,	1911

The United Confederate Veterans

By S. . . Cunningham, Late Sergeant-Major, Confederate States Army, and Founder and Editor of "The Confederate Veteran"

THE organization known as the United Confederate Veterans was formed in New Orleans, June 10, 1889. The inception of the idea for a large and united association is credited to Colonel J. F. Shipp, a gallant Confederate, commander of N. B. Forrest Camp, of Chattanooga, Tennessee—the third organized—who was in successful business for years with a Union veteran. Colonel Shipp had gone to New Orleans in the interest of the Chattanooga and Chickamauga Military Park, and there proposed a general organization of Confederates on the order of the Grand Army of the Republic, his idea being to bring into a general association the State organizations, one of which in Virginia, and another in Tennessee, had already been organized.

Following these suggestions, a circular was sent out from New Orleans in regard to the proposed organization, and the first meeting was held in that city on June 10, 1889, the organization being

ROBERT V. RICHARDSON
Commanded a Tennessee
Brigade.

SAMUEL R. ANDERSON
Commander of a Tennessee
Brigade.

BENJAMIN J. HILL
Provost-Marshal-General Army
of Tennessee.

JAMES A. SMITH
Led a Brigade in Cleburne's
Division.

ROBERT C. TYLER
Commander of the Garrison at West
Point, Georgia.

THOMAS B. SMITH
Led a Brigade in the Army of
Tennessee.

WILLIAM Y. C. HUMES
Commanded a Division of Wheeler's
Cavalry.

CONFEDERATE
GENERALS
No. 19
TENNESSEE

LUCIUS M. WALKER
Led a Calvary Brigade in the Army of the West.

ALEXANDER W. CAMPBELL
Led a Brigade of Forrest's Cavalry.

perfected under the name of United Confederate Veterans, with F. S. Washington, of New Orleans, as president, and J. A. Chalaron, secretary. A constitution was adopted, and Lieutenant-General John B. Gordon, of Georgia, was elected general and commander-in-chief. At this meeting there were representatives from the different Confederate organizations already in existence in the States of Louisiana, Mississippi and Tennessee.

While giving Colonel Shipp credit for suggesting the general organization of the United Confederate Veterans, the important part played by the Louisiana camps in furthering the association must be emphasized. The previously existing organizations became the first numbers in the larger association. The Army of Northern Virginia, of New Orleans, became Camp No. 1; Army of Tennessee, New Orleans, No. 2; and LeRoy Stafford Camp, Shreveport, No. 3. The N. B. Forrest Camp, of Chattanooga, Tennessee, became No. 4; while Fred. Ault Camp, of Knoxville, is No. 5. There are other camps, not among the first in the list, which are among the most prominent in the organization. For instance, Tennessee had an organization of bivouacs, the first and largest of which was Frank Cheatham, No. 1, of Nashville, but which is Camp No. 35, U. C. V. Then, Richmond, Virginia, had its R. E. Lee Camp, which has ever been of the most prominent, and was the leader in a great soldiers' home movement. In the U. C. V. camp-list, the R. E. Lee, of Richmond, is No. 181. The camps increased to a maximum of more than fifteen hundred, but with the passage of years many have ceased to be active.

While the organization was perfected in New Orleans, the first reunion of United Confederate Veterans was held in Chattanooga, Tennessee, July 3 to 5, 1890. To this reunion invitations were extended " to veterans of both armies and to citizens of the Republic," and the dates purposely included Independence Day.

The first comment both in the North and South was, " Why keep up the strife or the memory of it? " but it was realized that such utterances were from those who did not comprehend the scope of the organization of United Confederate Veterans, which, from the very outset, was clear in the minds of its founders. It was created on high lines, and its first commander was the gallant soldier, General John B. Gordon, at the time governor of Georgia, and later was United States senator. General Gordon was continued as commander-in-chief until his death.

The nature and object of the organization can-not be explained better than by quoting from its constitution.

The first article declares:

" The object and purpose of this organization will be strictly social, literary, historical, and benevolent. It will endeavor to unite in a general federation all associations of the Confederate veterans, soldiers and sailors, now in existence or hereafter to be formed; to gather authentic data for an impartial history of the War between the States; to preserve the relics or memories of the same; to cherish the ties of friendship that exist among the men who have shared common dangers, common suffering and privations; to care for the disabled and extend a helping hand to the needy; to protect the widow and orphan, and to make and preserve the record of the services of every member and, as far as possible, of those of our comrades who have preceded us in eternity."

Likewise, the last article provides that neither discussion of political or religious subjects nor any political action shall be permitted in the organization, and that any association violating that provision shall forfeit its membership.

The notes thus struck in the constitution of the United Confederate Veterans were reechoed in the opening speech of the first commander-in-chief. General Gordon, addressing the Veterans and the public, said:

" Comrades, no argument is needed to secure for those objects your enthusiastic endorsement. They have burdened your thoughts for many years. You have cherished them in sorrow, poverty, and humiliation. In the face of misconstruction, you have held them in your hearts with the strength of religious convictions. No misjudgments can defeat your peaceful purposes for the future. Your aspirations have been lifted by the mere force and urgency of surrounding conditions to a plane far above the paltry consideration of partisan triumphs. The honor of the American Government, the just powers of the Federal Government, the equal rights of States, the integrity of the Constitutional Union, the sanctions of law, and the enforcement of order have no class of defenders more true and devoted than the ex-soldiers of the South and their worthy descendants. But you realize the great truth that a people without the memories of heroic suffering or sacrifice are a people without a history.

" To cherish such memories and recall such a past, whether crowned with success or consecrated in defeat, is to idealize principle and strengthen character, intensify love of country, and convert defeat and disaster into pillars of support for

Gideon D. Pillow, Opponent of Grant
in Grant's First Battle—Belmont.

William H. Carroll
Led a Brigade in
East Tennessee.

John C. Carter, Orig-
inally Colonel of the
38th Regiment.

John C. Vaughen, Com-
mander of a Cav-
alry Brigade.

George W. Gordon
Led a Brigade in
Army of Tennessee.

Alfred J. Vaughn Led
a Brigade in Gen-
eral Polk's Corps.

Henry B. Davidson
Led a Brigade of
Wheeler's Cavalry.

CONFEDERATE GENERALS

No. 20—TENNESSEE

Tyree H. Bell Led a Cavalry Command under Forrest.

William McComb Led a Brigade
in R. E. Lee's Army.

Joseph B. Palmer Led a Brigade in
General Polk's Corps.

future manhood and noble womanhood. Whether the Southern people, under their changed conditions, may ever hope to witness another civilization which shall equal that which began with their Washington and ended with their Lee, it is certainly true that devotion to their glorious past is not only the surest guarantee of future progress and the holiest bond of unity, but is also the strongest claim they can present to the confidence and respect of the other sections of the Union."

Referring to the new organization, General Gordon said:

"It is political in no sense, except so far as the word 'political' is a synonym of the word 'patriotic.' It is a brotherhood over which the genius of philanthropy and patriotism, of truth and justice will preside; of philanthropy, because it will succor the disabled, help the needy, strengthen the weak, and cheer the disconsolate; of patriotism, because it will cherish the past glories of the dead Confederacy and transmute them into living inspirations for future service to the living Republic; of truth, because it will seek to gather and preserve, as witnesses for history, the unimpeachable facts which shall doom falsehood to die that truth may live; of justice, because it will cultivate national as well as Southern fraternity, and will condemn narrow-mindedness and prejudice and passion, and cultivate that broader and higher and nobler sentiment which would write on the grave of every soldier who fell on our side, 'Here lies an American hero, a martyr to the right as his conscience conceived it.'"

The reunions, thus happily inaugurated, became at once popular and have been held every year except the first appointment at Birmingham, Alabama, which was postponed from 1893 to 1894. No event in the South is comparable in widespread interest to these reunions. Only the large cities have been able to entertain the visitors, which range in number between fifty thousand and one hundred thousand.

The greatest of all gatherings was at Richmond, Virginia, June 30, 1907, when the superb monument to the only President of the Confederacy was unveiled. There were probably a hundred thousand people at the dedication. An idea of the magnitude of these reunion conventions and the interest in them may be had by reference to that held in Little Rock, Arkansas, in May, 1911, a city of a little more than thirty thousand inhabitants, wherein over a hundred thousand visitors were entertained during the three days.

No finer evidences of genuine patriotism can be found than in the proceedings of these conventions. In fact, there are no more faithful patriots. The Gray line of 1911 is not yet so thin as the press contributions make it. True, the veterans are growing feeble, but the joy of meeting comrades with whom they served in camp and battle for four years—many of whom had not seen one another in the interim—is insuppressible. It is not given to men in this life to become more attached to each other than are the Confederates. They had no pay-roll to look to, and often but scant rations, which they divided unstintedly. And their defeat increased their mutual sympathy.

Yet, on the other hand, there is a just appreciation of their adversaries. The great body of Confederate veterans esteem the men who fought them, far above the politician. They look confidently to the better class of Union veterans to cooperate with them in maintaining a truthful history. Maybe the time will come when the remnant of the soldiers, North and South, will confer together for the good of the country.

The Confederates have not pursued the excellent method of rotation in office in their organization, as have the Grand Army comrades. General John B. Gordon sought to retire repeatedly, but his comrades would not consent. At his death General Stephen D. Lee, next in rank, became commander-in-chief. It was a difficult place to fill, for there never was a more capable and charming man in any place than was General Gordon as commander-in-chief. However, General Lee was so loyal, so just, and so zealous a Christian that he grew rapidly in favor, and at his death there was widespread sorrow. He was succeeded by General Clement A. Evans, of Georgia, who possessed the same high qualities of Christian manhood, and he would have been continued through life, as were his predecessors, but a severe illness, which affected his throat, made a substitute necessary, so he and General W. L. Cabell, commander of the Trans-Mississippi Department from the beginning—their rank being about equal—were made honorary commanders-in-chief for life, and General George W. Gordon, a member of Congress from Tennessee, was chosen as active commander-in-chief in 1910. Generals Gordon, Cabell, and Evans died in 1911. Each had a military funeral in which U. S. Army officials took part.

Within a score of years there had developed a close and cordial cooperation between the veterans and such representative Southern organizations as the Confederated Southern Memorial Association, the United Sons of Confederate Veterans, and the United Daughters of the Confederacy. All are devoted to the highest patriotic ideals.

IX

ROSTER
OF
GENERAL OFFICERS

BOTH UNION
AND CONFEDERATE

THE GENERAL-IN-CHIEF OF THE ARMIES OF THE UNITED STATES   A
PICTURE OF GRANT WITH HIS FAVORITE CHARGER "CINCINNATI"
TAKEN AT COLD HARBOR ON JUNE 4, 1864, IN THE MIDST OF THE
"HAMMERING POLICY" THAT IN TEN MONTHS TERMINATED THE WAR

General Officers of the Union Army

This roster includes in alphabetical order under the various grades the names of all general officers either of full rank or by brevet in the United States (Regular) Army and in the United States Volunteers during the Civil War. The highest rank attained, whether full or by brevet, only is given, in order to avoid duplications. It is, of course, understood that in most cases the actual rank next below that conferred by brevet was held either in the United States Army or the Volunteers. In some cases for distinguished gallantry or marked efficiency brevet rank higher than the next grade above was given. The date is that of the appointment.

LIEUTENANT-GENERAL
UNITED STATES ARMY
(*Full Rank*)
Grant, Ulysses S., Mar. 2, '64.

LIEUTENANT-GENERAL
UNITED STATES ARMY
(*By Brevet*)
Scott, Winfield, Mar. 29, '47.

MAJOR-GENERALS
UNITED STATES ARMY
(*Full Rank*)
Fremont, J. C., May 14, '61.
Halleck, H. W., Aug. 19, '61.
Hancock, Winfield, July 26, '66.
McClellan, G. B., May 14, '61.
Meade, G. G., Aug. 18, '64.
Sheridan, P. H., Nov. 8, '64.
Sherman, Wm. T., Aug. 12, '64.
Thomas, Geo. H., Dec. 15, '64.
Wool, John E., May 16, '62.

MAJOR-GENERALS
UNITED STATES ARMY
(*By Brevet*)
Allen, Robert, Mar. 13, '65.
Ames, Adelbert, Mar. 13, '65.
Anderson, Robert, Feb. 3, '65.
Arnold, Richard, Mar. 13, '65.
Augur, Chris. C., Mar. 13, '65.
Ayres, R. B., Mar. 13, '65.
Baird, Absalom, Mar. 13, '65.
Barnard, John G., Mar. 13, '65.
Barnes, Joseph K., Mar. 13, '65.
Barry, Wm. F., Mar. 13, '65.
Beckwith, Amos, Mar. 13, '65.
Benham, H. W., Mar. 13, '65.
Brannan, J. M., Mar. 13, '65.
Brice, Benj. W., Mar. 13, '65.
Brown, Harvey, Aug. 2, '66.
Buchanan, R. C., Mar. 13, '65.
Butterfield, D., Mar. 13, '65.
Canby, Ed. S. R., Mar. 13, '65.
Carleton, J. H., Mar. 13, '65.
Carlin, Wm. P., Mar. 13, '65.
Carr, Eugene A., Mar. 13, '65.
Carroll, Sam. S., Mar. 13, '65.
Casey, Silas, Mar. 13, '65.

Clarke, Henry F., Mar. 13, '65.
Cook, P. St. G., Mar. 13, '65.
Cram, Thomas J., Jan 13, '66.
Crawford, S. W., Mar. 13, '65.
Crook, George, Mar. 13, '65.
Crossman, G. H., Mar. 13, '65.
Cullum, Geo. W., Mar. 13, '65.
Custer, Geo. A., Mar. 13, '65.
Davidson, J. W., Mar. 13, '65.
Davis, Jef. C., Mar. 13, '65.
Delafield, Rich., Mar. 13, '65.
Donaldson, J. L., Mar. 13, '65.
Doubleday, A., Mar. 13, '65.
Dyer, Alex. B., Mar. 13, '65.
Easton, L. E., Mar. 13, '65.
Eaton, Amos B., Mar. 13, '65.
Elliott, W. L., Nov. 13, '65.
Emory, Wm. H., Mar. 13, '65.
Fessenden, F., Mar. 13, '65.
Foster, John G., Mar. 13, '65.
Franklin, Wm. B., Mar. 13, '65.
French, Wm. H., Mar. 13, '65.
Fry, James B., Mar. 13, '65.
Garrard, Kenner, Mar. 13, '65.
Getty, Geo. W., Mar. 13, '65.
Gibbon, John, Mar. 13, '65.
Gibbs, Alfred, Mar. 13, '65.
Gibson, Geo., May 30, '48.
Gillem, Alvan G., April 12, '65.
Gilmore, Q. A., Mar. 13, '65.
Granger, Gordon, Mar. 13, '65.
Granger, Robt. S., Mar. 13, '65.
Grierson, B. H., Mar. 2, '67.
Griffin, Charles, Mar. 13, '65.
Grover, Cuvier, Mar. 13, '65.
Hardie, James A., Mar. 13, '65.
Harney, Wm. S., Mar. 13, '65.
Hartsuff, G. L., Mar. 13, '65
Hatch, Edward, Mar. 2, '67.
Hawkins, J. P., Mar. 13, '65.
Hazen, Wm. B., Mar. 13, '65.
Heintzelman, S. P., Mar. 13, '65.
Hoffman, Wm. Mar. 13, '65.
Holt, Joseph, Mar. 13, '65.
Hooker, Joseph, Mar. 13, '65.
Howard, O. O., Mar. 13, '65.
Howe, A. P., Mar. 13, '65.
Humphreys, A. A., Mar. 13, '65.
Hunt, Henry J., Mar. 13, '65.
Hunter, David, Mar. 13, '65.
Ingalls, Rufus, Mar. 13, '65.
Johnson, R. W., Mar. 13, '65.
Kautz, August V., Mar. 13, '65.
Ketchum, Wm. S., Mar. 13, '65.

Kilpatrick, Judson, Mar. 13, '65.
King, John H., Mar. 13, '65.
Long, Eli, Mar. 13, '65.
McCook, A. McD., Mar. 13, '65.
McDowell, Irvin, Mar. 13, '65.
McIntosh, John B., Aug. 5, '62.
Marcy, R. B., Mar. 13, '65.
Meigs, Mont. C., July 5, '64.
Merritt, Wesley, Mar. 13, '65.
Miles, Nelson A., Mar. 2, '67.
Morris, Wm. W., Mar. 13, '65.
Mower, J. A., Mar. 13, '65.
Newton, John, Mar. 13, '65.
Nichols, Wm. A., Mar. 13, '65.
Ord, Ed. O. C., Mar. 13, '65.
Parke, John G., Mar. 13, '65.
Pennypacker, G., Mar. 2, '67.
Pleasonton, A., Mar. 13, '65.
Pope, John, Mar. 13, '65.
Ramsey, Geo. D., Mar. 13, '65.
Rawlins, John A., April 9, '65.
Reynolds, J. J., Mar. 2, '67.
Ricketts, J. B., Mar. 13, '65.
Ripley, Jas. W., Mar. 13, '65.
Robinson, J. C., Mar. 13, '65.
Rosecrans, W. S., Mar. 13, '65.
Rousseau, L. H., Mar. 28, '67.
Rucker, D. H., Mar. 13, '65.
Russell, David A., Sept. 19, '64.
Sackett, Delos B., Mar. 13, '65.
Schofield, J. M., Mar. 13, '65.
Schriver, E., Mar. 13, '65.
Seymour, T., Mar. 13, '65.
Sherman, T. W., Mar. 13, '65.
Shiras, Alex., Mar. 13, '65.
Sickles, Daniel E., Mar. 2, '67.
Simpson, M. D. L., Mar. 13, '65.
Smith, Andrew J., Mar. 13, '65.
Smith, Chas., Mar. 21, '67.
Smith, John E., Mar. 2, '67.
Smith, W. F., Mar. 13, '65.
Stanley, David S., Mar. 13, '65.
Steele, Frederick, Mar. 13, '65.
Stoneman, G., Mar. 13, '65.
Sturgis, S. D., Mar. 13, '65.
Sumner, Edwin V., May 6, '64.
Swayne, Wager, Mar. 2, '67.
Swords, Thomas, Mar. 13, '65.
Sykes, George, Mar. 13, '65.
Terry, Alfred H., Mar. 13, '65.
Thomas, Charles, Mar. 13, '65.
Thomas, Lorenzo, Mar. 13, '65.

Torbert, A. T. A., Mar. 13, '65.
Totten, J. G., April 21, '64.
Tower, Z. B., Mar. 13, '65.
Townsend, E. D., Mar. 13, '65.
Turner, J. W., Mar. 13, '65.
Tyler, Robt. O., Mar. 13, '65.
Upton, Emory, Mar. 13, '65
Van Vliet, S., Mar. 13, '65.
Vinton, D. H., Mar. 13, '65.
Warren, G. K., Mar. 13, '65.
Webb, Alex. S., Mar. 13, '65.
Weitzel, G., Mar. 13, '65.
Wheaton, Frank, Mar. 13, '65.
Whipple, A. W., May 7, '63.
Whipple, Wm. D., Mar. 13, '65.
Willcox, O. B., Mar. 2, '67.
Williams, Seth, Mar. 13, '65.
Wilson, James H., Mar. 13, '65.
Wood, Thos. J., Mar. 13, '65.
Woodbury, D. P., Aug. 15, '64.
Woods, Chas. R., Mar. 13, '65.
Wright, H. G., Mar. 13, '65.

MAJOR-GENERALS
U. S. VOLUNTEERS
(*Full Rank*)
Banks, N. P., May 16, '61.
Barlow, F. C., May 25, '65.
Berry, H. G., Nov. 29, '62.
Birney, David D., May 3, '63.
Blair, Frank P., Nov. 29, '62.
Blunt, James G., Nov. 29, '62.
Brooks, W. T. H., June 10, '63.
Buell, Don Carlos, Mar. 21, '62.
Buford, John, July 1, '63.
Buford, N. B., Mar. 13, '65.
Burnside, A. E., Mar. 18, '62.
Butler, Benj. F., May 16, '61.
Cadwalader, G. B., Apr. 25, '62.
Clay, Cassius M., April 11, '62.
Couch, Darius N., July 4, '62.
Cox, Jacob Dolson, Oct. 6, '62.
Crittenden, T. L., July 17, '62.
Curtis, S. R., Nov. 21, '62.
Dana, N. J. T., Nov. 29, '62.
Davies, Henry E., May 4, '65.
Dix, John A., May 16, '61.
Dodge, G. M., June 7, '64.
Doubleday, A., Nov. 29, '62.
Garfield, J. A., Sept. 19, '63.
Hamilton, C. S., Sept. 18, '62.
Hamilton, S., Sept. 17, '62.
Herron, F. J., Nov. 29, '62.
Hitchcock, E. A., Feb. 10, '62.

Samuel P. Spear, Originally
Colonel of the 11th
Cavalry.

Roy Stone, Commander
of the "Bucktail
Brigade."

William A. Nichols, Promoted
for Faithful Services
in the War.

Israel Vogdes, Promoted
for Gallantry in the
Field.

S. B. M. Young, Originally
Colonel 4th Cavalry; Later
Commander of the U. S. Army.

John R. Brooke, Originally
Colonel of the 54th Reg't,
Army of the Potomac.

Pennock Huey, Originally
Colonel of the 8th Cavalry,
Army of the Potomac.

Henry J. Madill, Originally
Colonel of the 141st Reg't,
Noted at Gettysburg.

FEDERAL GENERALS---No. 25---PENNSYLVANIA

Andrew Porter, Commanded
a Brigade at First
Bull Run.

Thomas Welsh, Originally
Colonel of the 45th
Regiment.

Charles F. Smith, Originally
Colonel of the 3d
Infantry.

Thomas L. Kane, Organizer
and Leader of "Kane's
Bucktails."

Hurlbut, Stephen, Sept. 17, '62.
Kearny, Philip, July 4, '62.
Keyes, Erasmus D., May 5, '62.
Leggett, M. D., Aug. 21, '65.
Logan, John A., Nov. 29, '62.
McClernand, J. A., Mar. 21, '62.
McPherson, J. B., Oct. 8, '62.
Mansfield, J. K. F., July 18, '62.
Milroy, Robt. H., Nov. 29, '62.
Mitchell, Ormsby, April 11, '62.
Morell, Geo. W., July 4, '62.
Morgan, E. D., Sept. 28, '61.
Morris, Thos. A., Oct. 25, '62.
Mott, Gersham, May 26, '65.
Mower, Joseph A., Aug. 12, '64.
Negley, James S., Nov. 29, '62.
Nelson, William, July 17, '62.
Oglesby, R. J., Nov. 29, '62.
Osterhaus, P. J., July 23, '64.
Palmer, John M., Nov. 29, '62.
Peck, John J., July 4, '62.
Porter, Fitz John, July 4, '62.
Potter, Rbt. B., Sept. 29, '65.
Prentiss, B. M., Nov. 29, '62.
Reno, Jesse L., July 18, '62.
Reynolds, J. F., Nov. 29, '62.
Reynolds, Jos. J., Nov. 29, '62.
Richardson, I. B., July 4, '62.
Schenck, Robt. C. Aug. 30, '62.
Schurz, Carl, March 14, '63.
Sedgwick, John, July 4, '62.
Sigel, Franz, March 21, '62.
Slocum, Henry W., July 4, '62.
Smith, Chas. F., Mar. 21, '62.
Smith, Giles A., Nov. 24, '65.
Stahel, Julius H., Mar. 14, '63.
Steedman, Jas. B., April 30, '64.
Stevens, Isaac I., July 18, '62.
Strong, Geo. C., July 18, '63.
Wallace, Lewis, March 21, '62.
Washburn, C. C., Nov. 29, '62.

MAJOR–GENERALS

U. S. VOLUNTEERS

(By Brevet)

Abbott, Henry L., Mar. 13, '65.
Allen, Robert, Mar. 13, '65.
Alger, Russell A., June 11, '65.
Anderson, N. L., Mar. 13, '65.
Andrews, C. C., Mar. 9, '65.
Andrews, G. L., Mar. 26, '65.
Asboth, Alex., Mar. 13, '65.
Atkins, Smith D., Mar. 13, '65.
Avery, Robert, Mar. 13, '65.
Ayres, R. B., Aug. 1, '64.
Bailey, Joseph, Mar. 13, '65.
Baker, Benj. F., Mar. 13, '65.
Banning, H. B., Mar. 13, '65.
Barnes, James, Mar. 13, '65.
Barney, Lewis T., Mar. 13, '65.
Barnum, H. A., Mar. 13, '65.
Barry, H. W., Mar. 13, '65.
Bartlett, Jos. J., Aug. 1, '64.
Bartlett, Wm. F., Mar. 13, '65.
Baxter, Henry, April 1, '65.
Beal, Geo. L., Mar. 13, '65.
Beatty, Samuel, Mar. 13, '65.
Belknap, Wm. W., Mar. 13, '65.
Benton, Wm. P., Mar. 26, '65.
Birge, H. W., Feb. 25, '65.

Birney, Wm., Mar. 13, '65.
Bowen, James, Mar. 13, '65.
Brayman, Mason, Mar. 13, '65.
Brisbin, James, Mar. 13, '65.
Brooke, John R., Aug. 1, '64.
Buckland, R. P., Mar. 13, '64.
Bussey, Cyrus, Mar. 13, '65.
Byrne, James J., Mar. 13, '65.
Caldwell, John C., Aug. 19, '65.
Cameron, R. A., Mar. 13, '65.
Capehart, Henry, June 17, '65.
Carr, Joseph B., Mar. 13, '65.
Carter, Samuel P., Mar. 13, '65.
Catlin, Isaac S., Mar. 13, '65.
Chamberlain, J. L., Mar. 29, '65.
Chapin, Daniel, Aug. 17, '64.
Chapman, G. H., Mar. 13, '65.
Chetlain, A. L., June 18, '65.
Chrysler, M. H., Mar. 13, '65.
Clark, Wm. T., Nov. 24, '65.
Comstock, C. B., Nov. 26, '65.
Connor, P. E., Mar. 13, '65.
Cooke, John, Aug. 24, '65.
Cooper, Jos. A., Mar. 13, '65.
Cole, Geo. W., Mar. 13, '65.
Collis, C. H. T., Mar. 13, '65.
Corse, John M., Oct. 5, '64.
Coulter, Richard, April 6, '65.
Crawford, S. W., Aug. 1, '64.
Cross, Nelson, Mar. 13, '65.
Croxton, John T., April 27, '65.
Cruft, Charles, March 5, '65.
Curtis, N. M., Mar. 13, '65.
Cutler, Lys., Aug. 19, '64.
Davies, Thos. A., July 11, '65.
Dennis, Elias S., April 13, '65.
Dennison, A. W., Mar. 31, '65.
De Trobriand, P. R., Apr. 9, '65.
Devens, Chas., April 3, '65.
Devin, Thos. C., Mar. 13, '65.
Doolittle, C. C., June 13, '65.
Dornblazer, B., Mar. 13, '65.
Duncan, Sam'l A., Mar. 13, '65.
Duryee, Abram, Mar. 13, '65.
Duval, Isaac H., Mar. 13, '65.
Edwards, Oliver, April 5, '65.
Egan, Thos. W., Oct. 27. '64.
Ely, John, April 15, '65.
Ewing, Hugh, Mar. 13, 1865.
Ewing, Thos. Jr., Mar. 13, '65.
Ferrero, Edward, Dec. 2, '64.
Ferry, Orris S., May 23, '65.
Fessenden, J. D., Mar. 13, '65.
Fisk, Clinton B., Mar. 13, '65.
Force, M. F., Mar. 13, '65.
Foster, R. S., Mar. 31, '65.
Fuller, John W., Mar. 13, '65.
Geary, John W., Jan. 12, '65.
Gilbert, Jas. J., Mar. 26, '65.
Gleason, John H., Mar. 13, '65.
Gooding, O. P., Mar. 13, '65.
Gordon, Geo. H., April 9, '65.
Graham, C. K., Mar. 13, '65.
Grant, Lewis A., Oct. 19, '64.
Greene, George S., Mar. 13, '65.
Gregg, D. McM., Aug. 1, '64.
Gregg, John J., Mar. 13, '65.
Gregory, E. M., April 9, '66.
Gresham, W. Q., Mar. 13, '65.
Griffin, S. G., April 2, '65.
Grose, Wm., Aug. 15, '65.

Guss, Henry R., Mar. 13, '65.
Gwyn, James, April 1, '65.
Hamblin, J. E., April 5, '65.
Hamlin, Cyrus, Mar. 13, '65.
Harris, T. M., April 2, '65.
Hartranft, John F., Mar. 25, '65.
Hatch, John P., Mar. 13, '65.
Hawley, Jos. R., Sept. 28, '65.
Hayes, Joseph, Mar. 13, '65.
Hayes, Ruth. B., Mar. 13, '65.
Hays, Alex., May 5, '65.
Heath, H. H., Mar. 13, '65.
Hill, Chas. W., Mar. 13, '65.
Hinks, Edw. W., Mar. 13, '65.
Hovey, Chas. E., Mar. 13, '65.
Howe, Al. P., July 13, '65.
Jackson, N. J., Mar. 13, '65.
Jackson, R. H., Nov. 24, '65.
Jourdan, Jas., Mar. 13, '65.
Kane, Thos. L., Mar. 13, '65.
Keifer, J. W., April 9, '65.
Kelly, Benj. F., Mar. 13, '65.
Kenly, John R., Mar. 13, '65.
Ketcham, J. H., Mar. 13, '65.
Kiddoo, Jos. B., Sept. 4, '65.
Kimball, Nathan, Feb. 1, '65.
Kingsman, J. B., Mar. 13, '65.
Lanman, J. G., Mar. 13, '65.
Lawler, M. K., Mar. 13, '65.
Long, Eli, Mar. 13, '65.
Loring, Chas. G., July 17, '65.
Lucas, Thos. J., Mar. 26, '65.
Ludlow, Wm. H., Mar. 13, '65.
McAllister, Rbt., Mar. 13, '65.
McArthur, John, Dec. 15, '64.
McCallum, D. C., Mar. 13, '65.
McCook, E. M., Mar. 13, '65.
McCook, E. S., Mar. 13, '65.
McIvor, Jas. P., Mar. 13, '65.
McIntosh, J. B., Mar. 13, '65.
McKean, T. J., Mar. 13, '65.
McMahon, M. T., Mar. 13, '65.
McMillan, J. W., Mar. 5, '65.
McMillan, W. L., Mar. 13, '65.
McNeil, John, April 12, '65.
McQuade, Jas., Mar. 13, '65.
Mackenzie, R. S., Mar. 31, '65.
Macy, Geo. A., April 9, '65.
Madill, Henry J., Mar. 13, '65.
Marshall, E. G., Mar. 13, '65.
Martindale, J. H., Mar. 13, '65.
Maynadier, H. E., Mar. 13, '65.
Meredith, Sol., Aug. 14, '65.
Miller, John F., Mar. 13, '65.
Mindil, Geo. W., Mar. 13, '65.
Minty, R. H. G., Mar. 13, '65.
Mitchell, J. G., Mar. 13, '65.
Molineux, E. L., Mar. 13, '65.
Moore, M. F., Mar. 13, '63.
Morgan, Jas. D., Mar. 19, '65.
Morris, Wm. H., Mar. 13, '65.
Morrow, H. A., Mar. 13, '65.
Mulholland, St. C., Mar. 13, '65.
Neil, Thos. H., Mar. 13, '65.
Nye, Geo. H., Mar. 13, '65.
Oliver, John M., Mar. 13, '65.
Opdyke, Emer., Nov. 30, '64.
Osborn, Thos. O., Apr. 2, '65.
Paine, Chas. J., Jan. 15, '65.
Paine, Hal. E., Mar. 13, '65.
Palmer, I. M., Mar. 13, '65.
Parsons, L. B., Apr. 30, '65.

Patrick, M. R., Mar. 13, '65.
Pearson, A. L., May 1, '65.
Peck, Lewis M., Mar. 13, '65.
Pierce, B. R., Mar. 13, '65.
Pile, Wm. A., April 9, '65.
Plaisted, H. M., Mar. 13, '65.
Potter, Edw. E., Mar. 13, '65.
Potts, B. F., March 13, '65.
Powell, Wm. H., Mar. 13, '65.
Powers, Chas. J., Mar. 13, '65.
Ramsey, John, Mar. 13, '65.
Ransom, T. E. S., Sept. 1, '64.
Rice, Eliot W., Mar. 13, '65.
Runkle, Benj. P., Nov. 9, '65.
Roberts, Benj. S., Mar. 13, '65.
Robinson, J. C., June 27, '64.
Robinson, J. S., Mar. 13, '65.
Root, Adrian R., Mar. 13, '65.
Ruger, Thos. H., Nov. 30, '64.
Salomon, Fred'k, Mar. 13, '65.
Sanborn, John B., Feb. 10, '65.
Saxton, Rufus, Jan. 12, '65.
Scott, R. K., Dec. 5, '65.
Sewell, Wm. J., Mar. 13, '65.
Shaler, Alex., July 27, '65.
Shanks, J. P. C., Mar. 13, '65.
Sharpe, Geo. H., Mar. 13, '65.
Sibley, Henry H., Nov. 29, '65.
Sickle, H. G., Mar. 31, '65.
Slack, Jas. R., Mar. 13, '65.
Smith, G. C., Mar. 13, '65.
Smith, T. K., Mar. 13, '65.
Smyth, T. A., April 7, '65.
Spooner, B. U., Mar. 13, '65.
Sprague, J. W., Mar. 13, '65.
Stannard, Geo. J., Oct. 28, '64.
Stevenson, J. D., Mar. 13, '65.
Stoughton, W. L., Mar. 13, '65.
Sully, Alfred, Mar. 8, '65.
Thayer, John M., Mar. 13, '65.
Thomas, H. G., Mar. 13, '65.
Tibbetts, Wm. B., Mar. 13, '65.
Tidball, John C., April 2, '65.
Tillison, Davis, Mar. 13, '65.
Trowbridge, L. S., Mar. 13, '65.
Tyler, E. B., Mar. 13, '65.
Tyler, Robt. O., Aug. 1, '64.
Tyndale, Hector, Mar. 13, '65.
Ullman, Daniel, Mar. 13, '65.
Underwood, A. B., Aug. 15, '65.
Van Cleve, H. P., Mar. 13, '65.
Vandever, Wm., June 7, '65.
Veatch, Jas. C., Mar. 26, '65.
Voris, Alvin C., Nov. 15, '65.
Wadsworth, Jas. S., May 6, '64.
Walcutt, C. C., Mar. 13, '65.
Ward, Wm. T., Feb. 24, '65.
Warner Willard, Mar. 13, '65.
Warren, FitzH., Aug. 24, '65.
Washburn, H. D., July 26, '65.
Webster, Jos. D., Mar. 13, '65.
Wells, Wm., Mar. 13, '65.
West, Jas. R., Jan. 4, '66.
Wheaton, Frank, Oct. 19, '64.
Whitaker, W. C., Mar. 13, '65.
White, Julius, Mar. 13, '65.
Williams, A. S., Jan. 12, '65.
Williamson, J. A., Mar. 13, '65.
Willich, Aug., Oct. 21, '65.
Winthrop, Fred., April 1, '65.
Wood, Jas., Jr., Mar. 13, '65.
Woods, Wm. B., Mar. 13, '65.
Zook, S. K., July 2, '64.

Frank Wheaten, Brigade and
Division Commander in the
Army of the Potomac.

Richard Arnold, Originally
Colonel of the 5th Regi-
ment, U. S. Artillery.

George S. Greene Commanded
a Brigade at Antietam
and Gettysburg.

John G. Hazard, Originally
Major of the 1st Regi-
ment of Light Artillery.

FEDERAL GENERALS
No. 26

RHODE ISLAND
(ABOVE AND TO LEFT)

TENNESSEE
(BELOW AND TO RIGHT)

William Hays, Brevetted for
Gallantry on the Field.

Samuel P. Carter, Originally
Colonel 2d Regiment.

James A. Cooper, Originally
Colonel of the 6th
Regiment.

James G. Spears, Brevetted
Brigadier-General in
1862.

Robert Johnson, Originally
Colonel of the 1st
Cavalry.

William B. Campbell, Com-
missioned in 1862; Re-
signed in 1863.

BRIGADIER-GENERALS
U. S. Army
(Full Rank)

Hammond, W. A., April 25, '62.
Taylor, Jos. P., Feb. 9, '63.

BRIGADIER-GENERALS
U. S. Army
(By Brevet)

Abercrombie, J. J., Mar. 13, '65.
Alexander, A. J., April 16, '65.
Alexander, B. S., Mar. 13, '65.
Alexander, E. B., Oct. '65.
Alvord, Ben., April 9, '65.
Arnold, Lewis G., Mar. 13, '65.
Babbitt, E. B., Mar. 13, '65.
Babcock, O. E., Mar. 13, '65.
Bache, H., Mar. 13, '65.
Badeau, Adam, Mar. 2, '67.
Barriger, J. W., Mar. 13, '65.
Beckwith, E. G., Mar. 13, '65.
Bell, George, April 9, '65.
Bingham, J. D., April 9, '65.
Blake, Geo. A. H., Mar. 13, '65.
Bomford, Jas. V., Mar. 13, '65.
Bonneville, B. L. E., Mar. 13, '65.
Bowers, Theo. S., April 9, '65.
Bradley, L. P., Mar. 2. '67.
Breck, Samuel, Mar. 13, '65.
Brewerton, H., Mar. 13, '65.
Brooks, Horace, Mar. 13, '65.
Brown, N. W., Oct. 15, '67.
Buell, Geo. P., Mar. 2, '67.
Burbank, Sid., Mar. 13, '65.
Burke, Martin, Mar. 13, '65.
Burns, Wm. W., Mar. 13, '65.
Burton, H. S., Mar. 13, '65.
Cady, Al., Mar. 13, '65.
Callender, F. D., April 9, '65.
Card, Benj. C., Mar. 13, '65.
Carrington, H. B., April 9, '65.
Churchill, Syl., Feb. 23, '47.
Clary, Rbt. E., Mar. 13, '65.
Clitz, Henry B., Mar. 13, '65.
Craig, Henry K., Mar. 13, '65.
Crane, Chas. H., Mar. 13, '65.
Crawford, S. W., Mar. 13, 65.
Cross, Osborn, Mar. 13, '65.
Cuyler, John M., April 9, '65.
Dana, James J., Mar. 13, '65.
Dandy, Geo. B., Mar. 13, '65.
Davis, N. H., Mar. 13, '65.
Dawson, Sam. K., Mar. 13, '65.
Day, Hannibal, Mar. 13, '65.
Dent, Fred. T., Mar. 13, '65.
DeRussey, R. E., Mar. 13, '65.
De Russy, G. A., Mar. 13, '65.
Dimick, Justin, Mar. 13, '65.
Drum, Rich. C., Mar. 13, ' 65.
Duane, Jas. C., Mar. 13, '65.
Duncan, Thos., Mar. 13, '65.
Dunn, W. McK., Mar. 13, '65.
Eastman, Seth, Aug. 9, '66.
Eaton, Joseph H., Mar. 13, '65.
Ekin, James A., Mar. 13, '65.
Finley, Clement, Mar. 13, '65.
Fitzhugh, C. L., Mar. 13, '65.
Forsyth, Jas. W., April 9, '65.
Fry, Cary H., Oct. 15, '67.

Gardner, John L., Mar. 13, '65.
Garland, John, Aug. 20, '47.
Gates, Wm., Mar. 13, '65.
Graham, L. P., Mar. 13, '65.
Graham, W. M., Mar. 13, '65.
Greene, James D., Mar. 13, '65.
Greene, Oliver D., Mar. 13, '65.
Grier, Wm. N., Mar. 13, '65.
Hagner, Peter V., Mar. 13, '65.
Haines, Thos. J., Mar. 13, '65.
Hardin, M. D., Mar. 13, '65.
Haskin, Jos. A., Mar. 13, '65.
Hayden, Julius, Mar. 13, '65.
Hays, William, Mar. 13, '65.
Hill, Bennett H., Jan. 31, '65.
Holabird, S. B., Mar. 13, '65.
Hunt, Lewis C., Mar. 13, '65.
Ibrie, George P., Mar. 2, '65.
Kelton, John C., Mar. 13, '65.
Kilburn, C. L., Mar. 13, '65.
Kingsbury, C. P., Mar. 13, '65.
Kirkham, R. W., Mar. 13, '65.
Leonard, H., Mar. 13, '65.
Leslie, Thos. J., Mar. 13, '65.
Loomis, Gus., Mar. 13, '65.
Lovell, Chas. S., Mar. 13, '65.
Lowe, Wm. W., Mar. 13, '65.
McAlester, M. D., April 9, '65.
McDougall, C., Mar. 13, '65.
McFerran, J. C., Mar. 13, '65.
McKeever, C., Mar. 13, '65.
McKibbin, D. B., Mar. 13, '65.
McLaughlin, N. B., Mar. 13, '65.
Mason, John S., Mar. 13, '65.
Maynadier, W., Mar. 13, '65.
Merchant, C. S., Mar. 13, '65.
Meyer, Albert J., Mar. 13, '65.
Michler, Nat., April 2, '65.
Miller, M. S., Mar. 13, '65.
Mills, Madison, Mar. 13, '65.
Moore, Tred., Mar. 13, '65.
Morgan, Chas. H., Mar. 13, '65.
Morgan, M. R., April 3, '65.
Morrison, P., Mar. 13, '65.
Morton, J. St. C., June, 17, '64.
Myers, Fred., Mar. 13, '65.
Myers, William, Mar. 13, '65.
Oakes, James, Mar. 30, '65.
Palfrey, John C., Mar. 26, '65.
Parker, Ely S., Mar. 2, '67.
Paul, G. R., Feb. 23, '65.
Pelouze, L. H., Mar. 13, '65.
Penrose, Wm. H., April 9, '65.
Perry, Alex. J., Mar. 13, '65.
Pitcher, Thos. G., Mar. 13, '65.
Poe, Orlando M., Mar. 13, '65.
Porter, Horace, Mar. 13, '65..
Potter, Jos. A., Mar. 13, '65.
Potter, Jos. H., Mar. 13, '65.
Prime, Fred'k E., Mar. 13, '65.
Prince, Henry, Mar. 13, '65.
Raynolds, Wm. F., Mar. 13, '65.
Reese, C. B., Mar. 13, '65.
Reeve, I. V. D., Mar. 13, '65.
Roberts, Jos., Mar. 13, '65.
Robertson, J. M., Mar. 13, '65.
Rodenbough, T. F., Mar. 13, '65.
Rodman, Thos. J., Mar. 13, '65.
Ruff, Chas. F., Mar. 13, '65.
Ruggles, Geo. D., Mar. 13, '65.

Satterlee, R. S., Sept. 2, '64.
Sawtelle, C. G., Mar. 13, '65.
Seawell, Wash., Mar. 13, '65.
Shepherd, O. L., Mar. 13, '65.
Sibley, Caleb C., Mar. 13, '65.
Sidell, Wm. H., Mar. 13, '65.
Simonson, J. S., Mar. 13, '65.
Simpson, J. H., Mar. 13, '65.
Slemmer, A. J., Mar. 13, '65.
Small, M. P., April 9, '65.
Smith, Joseph R., April 9, '65.
Sweitzer, N. B., Mar. 13, '65.
Thayer, Syl., May 31, '63.
Thom, George, Mar. 13, '65.
Thornton, W. A., Mar. 13, '65.
Tompkins, C. H., Mar. 13, '65.
Totten, James, Mar. 13, '65.
Townsend, Fred., Mar. 13, '65.
Tripler, Chas. S., Mar. 13, '65.
Vincent, T. M., Mar. 13, '65.
Vogdes, Israel B., April 9, '65.
Waite, C. A., Mar. 13, '65.
Wallen, Henry D., Mar. 13, '62.
Warner, Jas. M., April 9, '65.
Watkins, L. D., Mar. 13, '65.
Wessells, H. W., Mar. 13, '65.
Whiteley, R. H. K., Mar. 13, '65.
Williams, Rbt., Mar. 13, '65.
Wilson, Thos., Mar. 13, '65.
Wood, Rbt. C., Mar. 13, '65.
Woodruff, I. C., Mar. 13, '65.
Wright, George, Dec. 10, '64.
Wright, Jas. J. B., Mar. 13, '65.

BRIGADIER-GENERALS
U. S. Volunteers
(Full Rank)

Ammen, Jacob, July 16, '62.
Baker, Edw. D., May 17. '61.
Baker, L. C., April 26, '65.
Bayard, Geo. D., April 28, '62.
Beatty, John, Nov. 29, '62.
Biddle, Chas. J., Aug. 31, '61.
Bidwell, D. D., Aug. 11, '64.
Blenker, Louis, Aug. 9, '61.
Bohlen, Henry, April 28, '62.
Boyle, J. T., Nov. 4, '61.
Bragg, Edw. S., June 25, '64.
Bramlette, T. E., April 24, '63.
Briggs, Henry S., July 17, '62.
Brown, Egbert B., Nov. 29, '62.
Buckingham, C. P., July 16, '62.
Burbridge, S. G., June 9, '62.
Burnham, H., April 27, '64.
Bustee, Rich., Aug. 7, '62.
Campbell, C. T., Nov. 29, '62.
Campbell, W. B., June 30, '62.
Catterson, R. F., May 31, '65.
Chambers, Alex., Aug. 11, '63.
Champlin, S. G., Nov. 29, '62.
Chapin, Edw. P., June 27, '63.
Clayton, Powell, Aug. 1, '64.
Cluseret, G. P., Oct. 14, '62.
Cochrane, John, July 17, '62.
Conner, Seldon, June 11, '64.
Cooper, James, May 17, '61.
Cooper, Jos. A., July 21, '64.
Copeland, Jos. T., Nov. 29, '62.
Corcoran, M., July 21, '61.

Cowdin, Robt., Sept. 26, '62.
Craig, James, Mar. 21, '62.
Crittenden, T. T., April 28, '62.
Crocker, M. M., Nov. 29, '62.
Davis, E. J., Nov. 10, '64.
Deitzler, Geo. W., Nov. 29, '62.
Denver, Jas. W., Aug. 14, '61.
Dewey, J. A., Nov. 20, '65.
Dodge, Chas. C., Nov. 29, '62.
Dow, Neal, April 28, '62.
Duffie, Alfred N., June 23, '63.
Dumont, E., Sept. 3, '61.
Dwight, Wm., Nov. 29, '62.
Edwards, John, Sept. 26, '64.
Ellett, Alfred W., Nov. 1, '62.
Este, Geo. P., May 31, '65.
Eustis, H. L., Sept. 12, '63.
Ewing, Charles, Mar. 8, '65.
Fairchild, Lucius, Oct. 19, '65.
Farnsworth, E. J., June 29, '63.
Farnsworth, J. F., Nov. 29, '62.
Fry, Speed S., Mar. 21, '62.
Gamble, Wm., Sept. 25, '65.
Garrard, Th. T., Nov. 29, '62.
Gilbert, Chas. C., Sept. 9, '62.
Gorman, W. A., Sept. 7, '61.
Hackleman, P. A., April 28, '62.
Hamilton, A. J., Nov. 14, '62.
Harding, A. C., Mar. 13, '63.
Harker, Chas. G., Sept. 20, '63.
Harland, Edw., Nov. 29, '62.
Harrow, William, Nov. 29, '62.
Hascall, Milo S., April 25, '62.
Haupt, Herman, Sept. 5, '62.
Haynie, I. N., Nov. 29, '62.
Heckman, C. A., Nov. 29, '62.
Hicks, Thos. H., July 22, '62.
Hobson, Edw. H., Nov. 29, '62.
Hovey, A. P., April 28, '62.
Howell, J. B., Sept. 12, '64.
Jackson, C. F., July 17, '62.
Jackson, Jas. S., July 16, '62.
Jamison, C. D., Sept. 3, '61.
Johnson, Andrew, Mar. 4, '62.
Jones, Patrick H., Dec. 6, '64.
Judah, H. M., Mar. 21, '62.
Kaemerling, Guitar, Jan. 5, '64.
Keim, Wm. H., Dec. 20, '61.
Kiernan, James L., Aug. 1, '63.
King, Rufus, May 17, '61.
Kirby, Edmund, May 23, '63.
Kirk, E. N., Nov. 29, '62.
Knipe, Joseph F., Nov. 29, '62.
Krzyanowski, W., Nov. 29, '62.
Lander, F. W., May 17, '61.
Ledlie, James H., Dec. 24, '62.
Lee, Albert L., Nov. 29, '62.
Lightburn, J. A. J., Mar.14, '63.
Lockwood, H. H., Aug. 8, '61.
Lowell, Chas. R., Oct. 19, '64.
Lyon, Nath'l., May 17, '61.
Lytle, William H., Nov. 29, '62.
McCall, G. A., May 17, '61.
McCandless, W., July 21, '64.
McCook, Daniel, July 16, '64.
McCook, R. L., Mar. 21, '62.
McGinnis, G. P., Nov. 29, '62.
McKinstry, J., Sept. 12, '61.
McLean, N. C., Nov. 29, '62.
Maltby, J. A., Aug. 4, '63.
Manson, M. D., Mar. 24, '62.
Marston, G., Nov. 29, '62.
Matthies, C. L., Nov. 29, '62.

TRUMAN SEYMOUR
Captain at Fort Sumter in 1861;
Later a Brigade Commander
in Army of the Potomac.

EDWIN H. STOUGHTON
Originally Colonel of the 4th
Vermont; Later commanded
the Second Vermont Brigade.

EDWARD H. RIPLEY
Commanded a Brigade in the
24th Corps.

ANDREW J. HAMILTON
Brigadier-General, 1862; Resigned, 1865.

GEORGE J. STANNARD
Led his Brigade against the
Flank of Pickett's Column
at Gettysburg.

JAMES M. WARNER
Colonel of the 1st Regiment
of Artillery.

JOHN W. PHELPS
Commander of a New England
Brigade in Operations on
the Gulf in 1861-2.

EDMUND J. DAVIS
Colonel 1st Texas Cavalry,
1862; Brigadier-General,
1864.

FEDERAL

GENERALS

No. 27—TEXAS

(TWO ABOVE)

VERMONT

(NINE TO LEFT)

B. S. ROBERTS
Colonel 4th Regiment.

GEORGE WRIGHT
Colonel 9th U. S. Infantry.

STEPHEN THOMAS
Colonel of the 8th Regiment.

Meagher, T. F., Feb. 3, '62.
Meredith, S. A., Nov. 29, '62.
Miller, Stephen, Oct. 26, '63.
Mitchell, R. B., April 8, '62.
Montgomery, W. R., May 17, '61.
Morgan, Geo. W., Nov. 12, '61.
Nagle, James, Sept. 10, '62.
Naglee, H. M., Feb. 4, '62.
Nickerson, F. S., Nov. 29, '62.
Orme, Wm. W., Nov. 29, '62.
Owens, Joshua T., Nov. 29, '62.
Paine, Eleazer, Sept. 3, '61.
Patterson, F. E., April 11, '62.
Phelps, John S., July 19, '62.
Phelps, John W., May 17, '61.
Piatt, Abraham, April 28, '62.
Plummer, J. B., Oct. 22, '61.
Porter, Andrew, May 17, '61.
Pratt, Calvin E., Sept. 10, '62.
Quinby, Isaac F., Mar. 17, '62.
Raum, Green B., Feb. 15, '65.
Reid, Hugh T., Mar. 13, '63.
Reilly, James W., July 30, '64.
Revere, J. W., Oct. 25, '62.
Rodman, Isaac P., April 28, '62.
Ross, Leonard F., April 25, '62.
Rowley, T. A., Nov. 29, '62.
Rice, Americus V., May 31, '65.
Rice, James C., Aug. 17, '63.
Rice, Samuel A., Aug. 4, '63.
Richardson, W. A., Sept. 3, '61.
Rutherford, F. S., June 27, '64.
Sanders, Wm. P., Oct. 18, '63.
Scammon, E. P., Oct. 15, '62.
Schimmelpfennig, Alex., Nov. 29, '62.
Schoepf, Albin, Sept. 30, '61.
Seward, W. H., Jr., Sept. 13, '64.
Shackelford, J. M., Jan. 2, '63.
Shepard, Isaac F., Oct. 27, '63.
Shepley, Geo. F., July 18, '62.
Sherman, F. T., July 21, '65.
Shields, James, Aug. 19, '61.
Sill, Joshua W., July 16, '62.
Slough, John B., Aug. 25, '62.
Smith, G. A., Sept. 19, '62.
Smith, Morgan L., July 16, '62.
Smith, T. C. H., Nov. 29, '62.
Smith, Wm. S., April 15, '62.
Spears, James G., Mar. 5, '62.
Spinola, F. B., June 8, '65.
Sprague, John W., July 21, '64.
Sprague, Wm., May 17, '61.
Starkweather, J. C., July 17, '63.
Stevenson, T. G., Mar. 14, '63.
Stokes, James H., July 20, '65.
Stolbrand, C. J., Feb. 18, '65.
Stone, C. P., May 17, '61.
Stoughton, E. H., Nov. 5, '62.
Strong, Wm. K., Sept. 28, '61.
Stuart, D., Nov. 29, '62.
Stumbaugh, F. S., Nov. 29, '62.
Sullivan, J. C., April 28, '62.
Sweeney, T. W., Nov. 29, '62.
Taylor, Geo. W., May 9, '62.
Taylor, Nelson, Sept. 7, '62.
Terrill, Wm. R., Sept. 9, '62.
Terry, Henry D., July 17, '62.
Thomas, Stephen, Feb. 1, '65.
Thurston, C. M., Sept. 7, '61.

Todd, John B. S., Sept. 19, '65.
Turchin, John B., July 17, '62.
Tuttle, James M., June 9, '62.
Tyler, Daniel, Mar. 13, '62.
Van Allen, J. H., April 15, '62.
Van Derveer, F., Oct. 4, '64.
Van Wyck, C. H., Sept. 27, '65.
Viele, Egbert L., Aug. 17, '61.
Vincent, Strong, July 3, '63.
Vinton, F. L., Sept. 19, '62.
Vogdes, Israel, Nov. 29, '62.
Von Steinwehr, Adolph, Oct. 12, '61.
Wade, M. S., Oct. 1, '61.
Wagner, Geo. D., Nov. 29, '62.
Wallace, W. H. L., Mar. 21, '62.
Ward, John H. H., Oct. 4, '62.
Weber, Max, April 28, '62.
Weed, Stephen H., June 6, '63.
Welsh, Thomas, Mar. 13, '63.
Wild, Edw. A., April 24, '63.
Williams, D. H., Nov. 29, '62.
Williams, Thos., Sept. 28, '61.
Wistar, Isaac, Nov. 29, '62.

BRIGADIER–GENERALS
U. S. VOLUNTEERS
(By Brevet)

Abbott, Ira C., Mar. 13, '65.
Abbott, J. C., Jan. 5, '65.
Abert, Wm. S., Mar. 13, '65.
Acker, Geo. S., Mar. 13, '65.
Adams, A. W., Mar. 13, '65.
Adams, Chas. F., Mar. 13, '65.
Adams, Chas. P., Mar. 13, '65.
Adams, Chas. W., Feb. 13, '65.
Adams, Robt. N., Mar. 13, '65.
Adams, Will. A., Mar. 13, '65.
Agnus, Felix, Mar. 13, '65.
Albright, Chas., Mar. 7, '65.
Alden, Alonzo, Jan. 15, '65.
Allaire, A. J., June 28, '65.
Allcock, Thos. R., Mar. 13, '65.
Allen, Harrison, Mar. 13, '65.
Allen, Thos. S., Mar. 13, '65.
Ames, John W., Jan. 15, '65.
Ames, William, Mar. 13, '65.
Amory, Thos. J. C., Oct. 7, '64.
Anderson, A. L., Mar. 13, '65.
Anderson, J. F., April 2, '65.
Anderson, W. B., Mar. 13, '65.
Anthony, DeW. C., Mar. 13, '65.
Appleton, J. F., Mar. 13, '65.
Armstrong, S. C., Mar. 13, '65.
Askew, Franklin, July 14, '65.
Astor, John J., Jr., Mar. 13, '65.
Aukeny, Rollin V., Mar. 13, '65.
Averill, John T., Oct. 18, '65.
Avery, Mat. H., Mar. 13, '65.
Babcock, W., Sept. 19, '65.
Bailey, Silas M., Mar. 13, '65.
Baker, James H., Mar. 13, '65.
Balch, Joseph P., Mar. 13, '65.
Baldey, George, Mar. 13, '65.
Baldwin, Chas. P., April 1, '65.
Baldwin, Wm. H., Aug. 22, '65.
Ball, Wm. H., Oct. 19, '64.
Ballier, John F., July 13, '64.
Ballock, G. W., Mar. 13, '65.
Bangs, Isaac S., Mar. 13, '65.
Bankhead, H. C., April 1, '65.

Barber, G. M., Mar. 13, '65.
Barnes, Charles, Sept. 28, '65.
Barney, A. M., Mar. 11, '65.
Barney, B. G., Mar. 13, '65.
Barnett, James, Mar. 13, '65.
Barrett, Theo. H., Mar. 13, '65.
Barrett, W. W., Mar. 13, '65.
Barstow, Wilson, April 2, '65.
Barstow, S. F., Mar. 13, '65.
Bartholomew, O. A., Mar. 13, '65.
Bartlett, C. G., Mar. 13, '65.
Bartlett, Wm. C., Mar. 13, '65.
Barton, Wm B., Mar. 13, '65.
Bassett, Isaac C., Dec. 12, '64.
Batchelder, R. N., Mar. 13, '65.
Bates, Delavan, July 30, '64.
Bates, Erastus N., Mar. 13, '65.
Baxter, D. W. C., Mar. 13, '65.
Beadis, John E., Mar. 13, '65.
Beadle, W. H. H., Mar. 16, '66.
Beaver, James A., Aug. 1, '64.
Bedel, John, Jan. 5, '65.
Beecher, James C., Mar. 13, '65.
Bell, John H., Nov. 30, '65.
Bell, J. W., Feb. 13, '65.
Bendix, John E., Mar. 13, '65.
Benedict, Lewis, April 9, '64.
Benjamin, W. H., Mar. 13, '65.
Bennett, John E., April 6, '65.
Bennett, T. W., Mar. 5, '65.
Bennett, Wm. T., May 25, '65.
Bentley, R. H., Mar. 13, '65.
Bentley, R. C., Mar. 13, '65.
Benton, Jr., T. H., Dec. 15, '64.
Berdan, Hiram, Mar. 13, '65.
Bertram, Henry, Mar. 13, '65.
Beveridge, J. L., Feb. 7, '65.
Biddle, James, Mar. 13, '65.
Biggs, Herman, Mar. 8, '65.
Biggs, Jonathan, Mar. 13, '65.
Biles, E. R., Mar. 13, '65.
Bingham, H. H., April 9, '65.
Bintliff, James, April 2, '65.
Bishop, J. W., June 7, '65.
Black, J. C., Mar. 13, '65.
Blackman, A. M., Oct. 27, '64.
Blair, C. W., Feb. 13, '65.
Blair, Louis J., Mar. 13, '65.
Blair, W. H., Mar. 13, '65.
Blaisdell, W., Jan. 23, '64.
Blakeslee, E., Mar. 13, '65.
Blanchard, J. W., Mar. 13, '65.
Blanden, L., Mar. 26, '65.
Bloomfield, Ira J., Mar. 13, '65.
Blunt, Asa P., Mar. 13, '65.
Bodine, R. L., Mar. 13, '65.
Bolinger, H. C., Mar. 13, '65.
Bolles, John A., July 17, '65.
Bolton, Wm. J., Mar. 13, '65.
Bond, John R., Mar. 13, '65.
Bonham, Edw., Mar. 13, '65.
Boughton, H., Mar. 11, '65.
Bouton, Edw., Feb. 28, '65.
Bowen, T. M., Feb. 13, '65.
Bowerman, R. N., April 1, '65.
Bowie, Geo. W., Mar. 13, '65.
Bowman, S. M., Mar. 13, '65.
Bowyer, Eli, Mar. 13, '65.
Boyd, Joseph F., Mar. 13, '65.
Boynton, H. V. N., Mar. 13, '65.

Boynton, H., Mar. 13, '65.
Bradshaw, R. C., Mar. 13, '65.
Brady, T. J., Mar. 13, '65.
Brailey, M. R., Mar. 13, '65.
Brayton, C. R., Mar. 13, '65.
Brewster, W. R., Dec. 2, '64.
Brinkerhoff, R., Sept. 20, '65.
Briscoe, Jas. C., Mar. 13, '65.
Broadhead, T. F., Aug. 30, '62.
Bronson, S., Sept. 28, '65.
Browne, T. M., Mar. 13, '65.
Browne, W. H., Mar. 13, '65.
Brown, C. E., Mar. 13, '65.
Brown, H. L., Sept. 3, '64.
Brown, J. M., Mar. 13, '65.
Brown, L. G., Mar. 13, '65.
Brown, O., Jan. 6, '66.
Brown, P. P., Mar. 13, '65.
Brown, S. B., Jr., Mar. 13, '65.
Brown, S. L., Mar. 13, '65.
Brown, T. F., Mar. 13, '65.
Brown, Wm. R., Mar. 13, '65.
Brownlow, J. P., Mar. 13, '65.
Bruce, John, Mar. 13, '65.
Brumback, J., Mar. 13, '65.
Brush, D. H., Mar. 13, '65.
Bukey, Van H., Mar. 13, '65.
Burke, J. W., Mar. 13, '65.
Burling, G. C., Mar. 13, '65.
Burnett, H. L., Mar. 13, '65.
Busey, S. T., April 9, '65.
Butler, T. H., Mar. 13, '65.
Callis, J. B., Mar. 13, '65.
Cameron, D., Mar. 13, '65.
Cameron, Hugh, Mar. 13, '65.
Campbell, C. J., Mar. 13, '65.
Campbell, E. L., June 2, '65.
Campbell, J. M., Mar. 13, '65.
Campbell, J. A., Mar. 13, '65.
Candy, Charles, Mar. 13, '65.
Capron, Horace, Feb. 13, '65.
Carle, James, Mar. 13, '65.
Carleton, C. A., Mar. 13, '65.
Carman, Ezra A., Mar. 13, '65.
Carnahan, R. H., Oct. 28, '65.
Carruth, Sumner, April 2, '65.
Carson, Chris., Mar. 13, '65.
Case, Henry, Mar. 16, '65.
Casement, J. S., Jan. 25, '65.
Cassidy, A. L., Mar. 13, '65.
Cavender, J. S., Mar. 13, '65.
Chamberlain, S. E., Feb. 24, '65.
Champion, T. E., Feb. 20, '65.
Chickering, T. E., Mar. 13, '65.
Chipman, H. L., Mar. 13, '65.
Chipman, N. P., Mar. 13, '65.
Christ, B. C., Aug. 1, '64.
Christensen, C. T., Mar. 13, '65.
Christian, W. H., Mar. 13, '65.
Churchill, M., Mar. 13, '65.
Cilly, J. P., June 2, '65.
Cist, H. M., Mar. 13, '65.
Clapp, D. E., Mar. 13, '65.
Clark, G. W., Mar. 13, '65
Clark, J. S., Mar. 13, '65.
Clarke, Gideon, Mar. 13, '65.
Clarke, Wm. H., Mar. 13, '65.
Clay, Cecil, Mar. 13, '65.
Clendenin, D. R., Feb. 20, '65
Clough, J. M., Mar. 13, '65.
Coates, B. F., Mar. 13, '65.

Edward S. Bragg Commanded the
Iron Brigade.

Lysander Cutler Commanded a Brigade at Gettysburg.

Lucius Fairchild, Colonel of the 2d
Regiment.

FEDERAL

GENERALS

Frederick Salomon, Orig-
inally Colonel of the 9th
Regiment of Infantry.

Jeremiah M. Rusk, Orig-
inally Lieut.-Colonel
of the 25th Regiment.

No. 28

WISCONSIN

Charles S. Hamilton Com-
manded a Division
at Corinth.

John C. Starkweather Com-
manded a Brigade
at Perryville.

Halbert E. Paine Com-
manded a Division
at Port Hudson.

Rufus King Commanded a Division in the Army
of the Potomac.

The Union Generals

Coates, J. H., Mar. 13, '65.
Cobb, Amasa, Mar. 13, '65.
Cobham, G. A., Jr., July 19, '64.
Coburn, J., Mar. 13, '65.
Cockerill, J. R., Mar. 13, '65.
Coggswell, W., Dec. 15, '64.
Coit, J. B., Mar. 13, '65.
Colgrove, Silas, Aug. 4, '64.
Collier, F. H., Mar. 13, '65.
Colville, Jr., W., Mar. 3, '65.
Comly, J. M., Mar. 13, '65.
Commager, H. S., Mar. 13, '65.
Congdon, J. A., Mar. 13, '65.
Conklin, J. T., Mar. 13, '65.
Conrad, J., Mar. 13, '65.
Cook, Edw. F., Mar. 13, '65.
Coon, D. E., Mar. 8, '65.
Corbin, H. C., Mar. 13, '65.
Coughlin, John, April 9, '65.
Cowan, B. R., Mar. 13, '65.
Cox, John C., July 4, '63.
Cox, Rob't C., April 2, '65.
Cram, Geo. H., Mar. 13, '62.
Cramer, F. L., Mar. 13, '65.
Crandal, F. M., Oct. 24, '65.
Crane, M. M., Mar. 13, '65.
Cranor, Jonathan, Mar. 3, '65.
Crawford, S. J., Mar. 13, '65.
Crocker, J. S., Mar. 13, '65.
Crowinshield, C., Mar. 13, '65.
Cummings, Alex., Apr. 19, '65.
Cummings, G. W., Mar. 13, '65.
Cummins, J. E., Mar. 13, '65.
Cunningham, J. A., Apr. 1, '65.
Curly, Thos., Mar. 13, '65.
Curtin, John J., Oct. 12, '64.
Curtis, A. R., Mar. 13, '65.
Curtis, G. S., Mar. 13, '65.
Curtis, J. F., Mar. 13, '65.
Curtis, Wm. B., Mar. 13, '65.
Curtiss, J. E., Mar. 13, '65.
Cutcheon, B. M., Mar. 13, '65.
Cutting, Wm., April 2, '65.
Cutts, R. D., Mar. 13, '65.
Daggett, A. S., Mar. 13, '65.
Daggett, Rufus, Jan. 15, '65.
Dana, E. L., July 26, '65.
Darr, Francis, Mar. 13, '65.
Dawson, A. R. Z., Nov. 21, '65.
Davis, E. P., Oct. 19, '64.
Davis, Hasbrook, Feb. 13, '65.
Davis, H. G., Mar. 13, '65.
Davis, W. W. H., Mar. 13, '65.
Day, Henry M., Mar. 26, '65.
Day, Nich. W., Mar. 13, '65.
Dayton, Oscar V., Mar. 13, '65.
Dawes, R. R., Mar. 18, '65.
Deems, J. M., Mar. 13, '65.
De Groat, C. H., Mar. 13, '65.
De Hart, R. P., Mar. 13, '65.
De Lacey, Wm., Mar. 13, '65.
De Land, C. V., Mar. 13, '65.
Dennis, John B., Mar. 13, '65.
Devereux, A. F., Mar. 13, '65.
De Witt, D. P., Mar. 13, '65.
Dick, Geo. F., Mar. 13, '65.
Dickerson, C. J., Mar. 13, '65.
Dickey, Wm. H., Mar. 13, '65.
Dickinson, Jos., Mar. 13, '65.
Dilworth, C. J., Mar. 13, '65.
Dixon, C. A. R., Mar. 13, '65.
Diven, Alex. S., Aug. 30, '64.
Diven, C. W., Mar. 25, '65.

Dixon, Wm. D., Mar. 13, '65.
Doan, A. W., Mar. 13, '65.
Dodd, Levi A., April 2, '65.
Dodge, Geo. S., Jan. 15, '65.
Donohue, M. T., Mar. 13, '65.
Doster, Wm. E., Mar. 13, '65.
Doubleday, U., Mar. 11, '65.
Dox, Ham. B., Feb. 13, '65.
Drake, Francis M., Feb. 22, '65.
Drake, Geo. B., Mar. 13, '65.
Draper, Alonzo G., Oct. 28, '64.
Draper, W. F., Mar. 13, '65.
Drew, C. W., Mar. 13, '65.
Ducat, A. C., Mar. 13, '65.
Dudley, N. A. M., Jan. 19, '65.
Dudley, Wm. W., Mar. 13, '65.
Duer, John O., July 12, '65.
Duff, Wm. L., Mar. 13, '65.
Dunham, T. H., Jr., Mar. 13, '65.
Dunlap, H. C., Mar. 13, '62.
Dunlap, James, Mar. 13, '65.
Duryea, Hiram, Mar. 13, '65.
Duryee, J. E., Mar. 13, '65.
Dustin, Daniel, Mar. 13, '65.
Dutton, A. H., May 16, '64.
Dutton, E. F., Mar. 16, '65.
Duval, Hiram F., Mar. 13, '65.
Dye, Wm. McE., Mar. 13, '65.
Dyer, Isaac, Mar. 13, '65.
Eaton, Chas. G., Mar. 13, '65.
Eaton, John, Jr., Mar. 13, '65.
Eckert, Thos. T., Mar. 13, '65.
Edgerton, A. J., Mar. 13, '65.
Edmonds, J. C., Mar. 13, '65.
Edwards, C. S., Mar. 13, '65.
Eggleston, B. B., Mar. 13, '62.
Eldridge, H. N., Mar. 13, '65.
Elliott, I. H., Mar. 13, '65.
Elliott, S. M., Mar. 13, '65.
Ellis, A. VanHorn, July 2, '63.
Ellis, Theo. G., Mar. 13, '65.
Elstner, G. R., Aug. 8, '64.
Elwell, J. J., Mar. 13, '65.
Ely, Ralph, April 2, '65.
Ely, Wm. C., April 13, '65.
Engleman, A., Mar. 13, '65.
Enochs, Wm. H., Mar. 13, '65.
Ent, W. H., Mar. 13, '65.
Enyart, D. A., Mar. 13, '62.
Erskine, Albert, Feb. 13, '65.
Estes, L. G., Mar. 13, '65.
Evans, George S., Mar. 13, '65.
Everett, Charles, Mar. 13, '65.
Fairchild, C., Mar. 13, '65.
Fairchild, H. S., Mar. 13, '65.
Fallows, Samuel, Oct. 24, '65.
Fardella, Enrico, Mar. 13, '65.
Farnum, J. E., Jan. 3, '66.
Farnsworth, A., Sept. 27, '65.
Farrar, B. G., Mar. 9, '65.
Fearing, Benj. D., Dec. 2, '64.
Fisher, Benj. F., Mar. 13, '65.
Fisher, Joseph W., Nov. 4, '65.
Fisk, Henry C., April 6, '65.
Fiske, Frank S., Mar. 13, '65.
Fiske, Wm. O., Mar. 13, '65.
Fitzsimmons, C., Mar. 13, '65.
Flanigan, Mark, Mar. 13, '65.
Fleming, R. E., Mar. 13, '64.
Fletcher, T. C., Mar. 13, '65.
Flood, Martin, Mar. 13, '65.
Flynn, John, Mar. 13, '65.

Fonda, John G., June 28, '65.
Ford, James H., Dec. 10, '65.
Forsyth, Geo. A., Feb. 13, '65.
Foster, Geo. P., Aug. 1, '64.
Foster, John A., Sept. 28, '65.
Foust, B. F., Mar. 13, '65.
Fowler, Edw. B., Mar. 13, '65.
Franchot, R., Mar. 13, '65.
Francine, Louis R., July 2, '63.
Frank, Paul, Mar. 13, '65.
Frankle, Jones, Sept. 3, '65.
Frazer, D., Mar. 13, '65.
Frazer, John, Mar. 13, '65.
Frederick, C. H., Mar. 13, '65.
French, W. B., Mar. 13, '65.
Frink, Henry A., Oct. 4, '65.
Frisbie, H. N., Mar. 13, '65.
Fritz, Peter, Jr., Mar. 13, '65.
Frizell, J. W., Mar. 13, '65.
Frohock, Wm. T., Mar. 13, '65.
Fuller, H. W., Mar. 13, '65.
Fullerton, J. S., Mar. 13, '65.
Funke, Otto, Feb. 13, '65.
Fyffe, Edw. P., Mar. 13, '65.
Gage, Joseph S., June 15, '65.
Gallagher, T. F., Mar. 13, '65.
Gallup, Geo. W., Mar. 13, '62.
Gansevoort, H. S., June 24, '64.
Gardiner, Alex., Sept. 19, '64.
Garrard, Israel, June 20, '65.
Garrard, Jephtha, Mar. 13, '65.
Gates, Theo. B., Mar. 13, '65.
Geddes, James L., June 5, '65.
Gerhardt, Joseph, Mar. 13, '65.
Gibson, H. G., Mar. 13, '65.
Gibson, Wm. H., Mar. 13, '65.
Giesy, Henry H., May 28, '64.
Gilbert, S. A., Mar. 13, '65.
Gilchrist, C. A., Mar. 26, '65.
Gile, Geo. W., May 6, '65.
Ginty, Geo. C., Sept. 28, '65.
Given, Josiah, Mar. 13, '65.
Given, William, Mar. 13, '65.
Glasgow, S. L., Dec. 19, '64.
Gleason, Newell, Mar. 13, '65.
Glenny, Wm., Mar. 13, '65.
Gobin, J. P. S., Mar. 13, '65.
Goddard, Wm., Mar. 13, '65.
Godman, J. H., Mar. 13, '65.
Goff, Nathan, Jr., Mar. 13, '65.
Goodell, A. A., Mar. 13, '65.
Goodyear, E. D. S., April 2, '65.
Gowan, Geo. W., April 2, '65.
Graham, Harvey, July 25, '65.
Graham, Samuel, Mar. 13, '65.
Granger, Geo. F., June 12, '65.
Greeley, Edwin S., Mar. 13, '65.
Green, Wm. M., May 14, '64.
Gregg, Wm. M., April 2, '65.
Grier, D., Mar. 26, '65.
Griffin, Dan'l F., Mar. 13, '65.
Grindlay, James, Mar. 13, '65.
Grosvenor, C. H., Mar. 13, '65.
Grosvenor, T. W., Feb. 13, '65.
Grover, Ira G., Mar. 13, '65.
Grubb, E. Burd, Mar. 13, '65.
Guiney, P. R., Mar. 13, '65.
Guppy, Joshua J., Mar. 13, '65.
Gurney, William, May 19, '65.
Hall, Caldwell K., Mar. 13, '65.
Hall, Cyrus, Mar. 13, '65.
Hall, H. Seymour, Mar. 13, '65.
Hall, Jas. A., Mar. 3, '65.

Hall, James F., Feb. 24, '65.
Hall, Jarius W., Mar. 13, '65.
Hall, Rob't M., Mar. 13, '65.
Hallowell, E. N., June 27, '65.
Halpine, C. G., Mar. 13, '65.
Hamilton, W. D., April 9, '65.
Hamlin, Chas., Mar. 13, '65.
Hammell, John S., Mar. 13, '65.
Hammond, J. H., Oct. 31, '64.
Hammond, John, Mar. 13, '65.
Hanbreght, H. A., June 7, '65.
Hanna, Wm., Mar. 13, '65.
Hardenbergh, J. B., Mar. 13, '65.
Harding, C., Jr, May 27, '65.
Harlin, E. B., Mar. 13, '65.
Harnden, Henry, Mar. 13, '65.
Harriman, Sam'l, April 2, '65.
Harriman, W., Mar. 13, '65.
Harris, A. L., Mar. 13, '65.
Harris, Benj. F., Mar. 13, '65.
Harris, Chas. L., Mar. 13, '65.
Harrison, Benj., Jan. 23, '65.
Harrison, M. LaRue, Mar. 13, '65.
Harrison, T. J., Jan. 31, '65.
Hart, James H., Mar. 13, '65.
Hart, O. H., Mar. 13, '65.
Hartshorne, W. R., Mar. 13, '65.
Hartsuff, Wm., Jan. 24, '64.
Hartwell, A. S., Dec. 30, '64.
Hartwell, C. A., Dec. 2, '65.
Haskill, L. F., Mar. 13, '65.
Hastings, R., Mar. 13, '65.
Haughton, Nath'l, Mar. 13, '65.
Hawkes, Geo. P., Mar. 13, '65.
Hawkins, I. R., Mar. 13, '65.
Hawkins, R. C., Mar. 13, '65.
Hawley, William, Mar. 16, '65.
Hayes, P. C., Mar. 13, '65.
Hayman, S. B., Mar. 13, '65.
Hays, E. L., Jan. 12, '65.
Hazard, J. G., Mar. 13, '65.
Healy, R. W., Mar. 13, '65.
Heath, Francis, Mar. 13, '65.
Heath, Thomas T., Dec. 15, '64.
Hedrick, J. M., Mar. 13, '65.
Heine, Wm., Mar. 13, '65.
Heinrichs, Gus., Mar. 13, '65.
Henderson, R. M., Mar. 13, '65.
Henderson, T. J., Nov. 30, '64.
Hendrickson, J., Mar. 13, '65.
Hennessey, J. A., Mar. 13, '65.
Henry, Guy V., Oct. 28, '64.
Henry, Wm. W., Mar. 7, '65.
Herrick, W. F., May 13, '65.
Herring, Chas. P., Mar. 13, '65.
Hickenlooper, A., Mar. 13, '65.
Hill, Jonathan A., April 9, '65.
Hill, Sylvester G., Dec. 15, '64.
Hillis, David B., Mar. 13, '65.
Hillyer, W. S., Mar. 13, '65.
Hitchcock, G. H., Mar. 13, '65.
Hobart, H. C., Jan. 12, '65.
Hobson, Wm., April 6, '65.
Hoffman, H. C., Mar. 13, '65.
Hoffman, Wm. J., Aug. 1, '64.
Hoge, Geo. B., Mar. 13, '65.
Hoge, George W., Mar. 13, '65.
Holbrook, M. T., Mar. 13, '65.
Holloway, E. S., Mar. 13, '65.

David H. Strother, of Virginia, Originally Colonel 3d West Virginia Cavalry.

Thomas M. Harris, of West Virginia, Originally Colonel of the 10th Infantry.

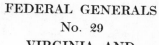

Lawrence P. Graham, of Virginia, Organized and Led a Cavalry Brigade in the Army of the Potomac.

FEDERAL GENERALS
No. 29
VIRGINIA AND
WEST VIRGINIA

Henry Capehart, of West Virginia, Colonel 1st Cavalry.

John W. Davidson, of Virginia, Promoted for the Capture of Little Rock.

Henry B. Carrington, Originally Colonel of the 18th West Virginia Infantry.

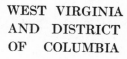

James A. Hardie, of West Virginia, Brevetted for Distinguished Services.

Robert C. Buchanan, of District of Columbia, Brevetted for Gallantry.

WEST VIRGINIA
AND DISTRICT
OF COLUMBIA

Richard H. Jackson, of District of Columbia, Brevetted for Gallantry During the War.

Holman, J. H., Mar. 13, '65.
Holt, Thomas, Mar. 13, '65.
Holter, M. J. W., Mar. 13, '65.
Hooker, A. E., Mar. 13, '65.
Horn, John W., Oct. 19, '64.
Hotchkiss, C. T., Mar. 13, '65.
Hough, John, March 13, '65.
Houghtaling, Chas., Feb. 13, '65.
Houghton, M. B., Mar. 13, '65.
Howard, Chas. H., Aug. 15, '65.
Howe, John H., Mar. 13, '65.
Howland, H. N., Mar. 13, '62.
Howland, Joseph, Mar. 13, '65.
Hoyt, Chas. H., Mar. 13, '65.
Hoyt, Geo. H., Mar. 13, '65.
Hoyt, Henry M., Mar. 13, '65.
Hubbard, James, April 6, '65.
Hubbard, L. F., Dec. 16, '64.
Hubbard, T. H., June 30, '65.
Hudnutt, Jos. O., Mar. 13, '65.
Hudson, John G., Mar. 13, '65.
Huey, Pennock, Mar. 13, '65.
Hugunin, J. R., Mar. 13, '65.
Humphrey, T. W., June 10, '65.
Humphrey, Wm., Aug. 1, '64.
Hunt, Lewis C., Mar. 13, '65.
Hunter, M. C., Mar. 13, '65.
Hurd, John R., Mar. 13, '65.
Hurst, Samuel H., Mar. 13, '65.
Hutchins, Rue P., Mar. 13, '65.
Hutchinson, F. S., May 24, '65.
Hyde, Thomas W., April 2, '65.
Ingraham, T., Oct. 2, '65.
Innes, Wm. P., Mar. 13, '65.
Irvine, Wm., March 13, '65.
Irvin, William H., Mar. 13, '65.
Ives, Brayton, March 13, '65.
Jacobs, Ferris, Jr., Mar. 13, '65.
Jackson, S. M., March 13, '64.
Jackson, Jos. C., Mar. 13, '65.
James, W. L., March 1, '66.
Jardine, Edw., Nov. 2, '65.
Jarvis, Dwight, Jr., Mar. 13, '65.
Jeffries, Noah L., Mar. 30, '65.
Jenkins, H., Jr., March 13, '65.
Jennison, S. P., March 13, '65.
Johnson, Chas. A., Mar. 13, '65.
Johnson, G. M. L., March 13, '65.
Johnson, J. M., March 13, '65.
Johnson, Lewis, March 13, '65.
Johnson, Robert, Mar. 13, '65.
Johns, Thos. D., March 13, '65.
Jones, J. B., March 13, '65.
Jones, Edward F., Mar. 13, '65.
Jones, Fielder A., Mar. 13, '65.
Jones, John S., March 13, '65.
Jones, Samuel B., Mar. 31, '65.
Jones, Theodore, Mar. 13, '65.
Jones, Wells S., Mar. 13, '65.
Jones, Wm. P., March 13, '65.
Jordan, Thos. J., Feb. 25, '65.
Judson, R. W., July 28, '66.
Judson, Wm. R., Mar. 13, '65.
Karge, Jonah, March 13, '65.
Keily, D. J., March 13, '65.
Kellogg, John A., April 9, '65.
Kelly, John H., Feb. 13, '65.
Kennedy, R. P., March 13, '65.
Kent, Loren, March 22, '65.
Kennett, H. G., March 13, '65.
Ketner, James, March 13, '65.

Kidd, James H., Mar. 13, '65.
Kilgour, Wm. M., June 20, '65.
Kimball, John W., Mar. 13, '65.
Kimball, Wm. R., Mar. 13, '65.
Kimberly, R. L., Mar. 13, '65.
King, Adam E., Mar. 13, '65.
King, John F., March 13, '65.
King, Wm. S., March 13, '65.
Kingsbury, H. D., Mar. 10, '65.
Kinney, T. J., March 26, '65.
Kinsey, Wm. B., Mar. 13, '65.
Kirby, Byron, Sept. 6, '65.
Kirby, Dennis T., Mar. 13, '65.
Kirby, Isaac M., Jan. 12, '65.
Kise, Reuben C., Mar. 13, '65.
Kitchell, Edward, Mar. 13, '65.
Kitching, J. H., Aug. 1, '64.
Kneffner, Wm. C., Mar. 13, '65.
Knefler, Fred'k, Mar. 13, '65.
Knowles, Oliv. B., Mar. 13, '65.
Kozlay, E. A., March 13, '65.
Krez, Conrad, March 26, '65.
Lafflin, Byron, March 13, '65.
Lagow, C. B., March 13, '65.
La Grange, O. H., Mar. 13, '65.
La Motte, C. E., Mar. 13, '65.
Landram, Wm. J., Mar. 13, '62.
Lane, John Q., March 13, '65.
Langdon, E. Bassett, Mar. 13, '65.
Lansing, H. S., Mar. 13, '65.
Laselle, Wm. P., Mar. 13, '65.
Laughlin, R. G., Mar. 13, '65.
Latham, Geo. R., Mar. 13, '65.
Lawrence, A. G., Mar. 25, '65.
Lawrence, Wm. Henry, Mar. 13, '65.
Lawrence, Wm. Hudson, Mar. 13, '65.
Leake, Jos. B., March 13, '65.
Le Duc, Wm. G., Mar. 13, '65.
Lee, Horace C., Mar. 13, '65.
Lee, Edward M., Mar. 13, '65.
Lee, John C., March 13, '65.
Lee, Wm. R., March 13, '65.
Le Favour, H., March 13, '65.
Le Gendre, C. W., Mar. 13, '65.
Leech, Wm. A., Mar. 13, '65.
Leib, Herman, March 13, '65.
Leiper, Chas. L., Mar. 13, '65.
Lewis, Chas. W., Mar. 13, '65.
Lewis, John R., March 13, '65.
Lewis, W. D., Jr., Mar. 13, '65.
Lincoln, Wm. S., June 23, '65.
Locke, Fred'k. T., April 1, '65.
Lockman, J. T., March 13, '65.
Loomis, Cyrus O., June 20, '65.
Lord, T. Ellery, Mar. 13, '65.
Love, George M., Mar. 7, '65.
Lovell, Fred'k S., Oct. 11, '65.
Lindley, J. M., March 13, '65.
Lippincott, C. E., Feb. 17, '65.
Lippitt, Francis J., Mar. 3, '65.
Lister, Fred. W., Mar. 13, '65.
Litchfield, A. C., Mar. 13, '65.
Littell, John S., Jan. 15, '65.
Littlejohn, De Witt C., Mar. 13, '65.
Littlefield, M. S., Nov. 26, '65.
Livingston, R. R., June 21, '65.
Ludington, M. J., Mar. 13, '65.
Ludlow, Benj. C., Oct. 28, '64.
Lyle, Peter, Mar. 13, '65.

Lyman, Luke, Mar. 13, '65.
Lynch, Jas. C., Mar. 13, '65.
Lynch, Wm. F., Jan. 31, '65.
Lyon, Wm. P., Oct. 26, '65.
McArthur, W. M., Mar. 13, '65.
McBride, J. D., Mar. 13, '65.
McCall, W. H. H., April 2, '65.
McCalmont, A. B., Mar. 13, '65.
McCleery, Jas., Mar. 13, '65.
McCleunen, M. R., April 2, '65.
McClurg, A. C., Sept. 18, '65.
McConihe, John, June 1, '64.
McConihe, Sam., Mar. 13, '65.
McConnell, H. K., Mar. 13, '65.
McConnell, John, Mar. 13, '65.
McCook, A. G., Mar. 13, '65.
McCormick, Chas. C., Mar. 13, '65.
McCoy, Daniel, Mar. 13, '65.
McCoy, Rob't A., Mar. 13, '65.
McCoy, Thos. F., April 1, '65.
McCreary, D. B., Mar. 13, '65.
McCrillis, L., Sept. 4, '64.
McDougall, C. D., Feb. 25, '65.
McEwen, Matt., Mar. 13, '65.
McGarry, Ed., Mar. 13, '65.
McGowan, J. E., Mar. 13, '65.
McGregor, J. D., Mar. 13, '65.
McGroarty, S. J., May 1, '65.
McKenny, T. J., Mar. 13, '65.
McKibbin, G. H., Dec. 2, '64.
McLaren, R. N., Dec. 14, '65.
McMahon, J., June 30, '65.
McNary, Wm. H., Mar. 13, '65.
McNaught, T. A., Aug. 4, '65.
McNett, A. J., July 28, '66.
McNulta, John, Mar. 13, '65.
McQueen, A. G., Mar. 13, '65.
McQueston, J. C., Mar. 13, '65.
Mackey, A. J., Mar. 13, '65.
Macauley, Dan., Mar. 13, '65.
Magee, David W., Mar. 13, '65.
Malloy, Adam G., Mar. 13, '65.
Manderson, C. F., Mar. 13, '65.
Mank, Wm. G., Mar. 13, '65.
Mann, Orrin L., Mar. 13, '65.
Manning, S. H., Mar. 13, '65.
Mansfield, John, Mar. 13, '65.
Markoe, John, Mar. 13, '65.
Marple, Wm. W., Mar. 13, '65.
Marshall, W. R., Mar. 13, '65.
Martin, Jas., Feb. 28, '65.
Martin, John A., Mar. 13, '65.
Martin, Wm. H., June 8, '65.
Mason, Ed. C., June 3, '65.
Mather, T. S., Sept. 28, '65.
Matthews, J. A., April 2, '65.
Matthews, Sol. S., Mar. 13, '65.
Mattocks, C. P., Mar. 13, '65.
Maxwell, N. J., April 18, '65.
Maxwell, O. C., Mar. 13, '65.
May, Dwight, Mar. 13, '65.
Mehringer, John, Mar. 13, '65.
Merrill, Lewis, Mar. 13, '65.
Mersey, August, Mar. 13, '65.
Messer, John, Mar. 13, '65.
Meyers, Edw. S., Mar. 13, '65.
Michie, Peter S., Jan. 1, '65.
Miller, A. O., Mar. 13, '65.
Miller, Madison, Mar. 13, '65.
Mills, Jas. K., Mar. 13, '65.
Mintzer, Wm. M., Mar. 13, '65.
Mitchell, G. M., Aug. 22, '65.

Mitchell, W. G., Mar. 13, '65.
Mix, Elisha, Mar. 13, '65.
Mizner, H. R., Mar. 13, '65.
Mizner, John K., Mar. 13, '65.
Moffitt, Stephen, Mar. 13, '65.
Monroe, Geo. W., Mar. 13, '62.
Montgomery, M., Mar. 13, '65.
Moody, G., Jan. 12, '65.
Moon, John C., Nov. 21, '65.
Moonlight, Thos., Feb. 13, '65.
Moor, Augustus, Mar. 13, '65.
Moore, David, Feb. 21, '65.
Moore, Fred'k W., Mar. 26, '65.
Moore, Jesse H., May 15, '65.
Moore, Jon. B., Mar. 26, '65.
Moore, Tim. C., Mar. 13, '65.
Morehead, T. G., Mar. 13, '65.
Morgan, G. N., Mar. 13, '65.
Morgan, Thos. J., Mar. 13, '65.
Morgan, Wm. H., April 20, '65.
Morgan, Wm. H., Mar. 13, '65.
Morrill, John, Mar. 13, '65.
Morrison, D., Mar. 13, '65.
Morrison, Jos. J., Mar. 13, '65.
Morse, Henry B., Mar. 13, '65.
Mott, Sam'l R., Mar. 13, '65.
Mudgett, Wm. S., Mar. 13, '65.
Mulcahey, Thos., Mar. 13, '65.
Mulford, J. E., July 4, '64.
Mulligan, J. A., July 23, '65.
Mundee, Chas., April 2, '65.
Murphy, John K., Mar. 13, '65.
Murray, Benj. B., Mar. 13, '65.
Murray, Edw., Mar. 13, '65.
Murray, Ely H., Mar. 25, '65.
Murray, John B., Mar. 13, '65.
Mussey, R. D., Mar. 13, '65.
Myers, Geo. R., Mar. 13, '65.
Nase, Adam, Mar. 13, '65.
Neafie, Alfred, Mar. 13, '65.
Neff, Andrew J., Mar. 13, '65.
Neff, Geo. W., Mar. 13, '65.
Neide, Horace, Mar. 13, '65.
Nettleton, A. B., Mar. 13, '62.
Newbury, W. C., Mar. 31, '65.
Newport, R. M., Mar. 13, '65.
Nichols, Geo. F., Mar. 13, '65.
Nichols, Geo. S., Mar. 13, '65.
Niles, Nat., Mar. 13, '65.
Noble, John W., Mar. 13, '65.
Noble, Wm. H., Mar. 13, '65.
Northcott, R. S., Mar. 13, '65.
Norton, Chas. B., Mar. 13, '65.
Noyes, Edw. F., Mar. 13, '65.
Nugent, Robert, Mar. 13, '65.
O'Beirne, J. R., Sept. 26, '65.
O'Brien, Geo. M., Mar. 13, '65.
O'Dowd, John, Mar. 13, '65.
Oley, John H., Mar. 13, '65.
Oliphant, S. D., June 27, '65.
Oliver, Paul A., Mar. 8, '65.
Olmstead, W. A., April 9, '65.
Ordway, Albert, Mar. 13, '65.
Osband, E. D., Oct. 5, '64.
Osborn, F. A., Mar. 13, '65.
Otis, Calvin N., Mar. 13, '65.
Otis, Elwell S., Mar. 13, '65.
Otis, John L., Mar. 13, '65.
Ozburn, Lyndorf, Mar. 13, '65.
Packard, Jasper, Mar. 13, '65.
Painter, Wm., Mar. 13, '65.
Palfrey, F. W., Mar. 13, '65.
Palmer, Oliver H., Mar. 13, '65.

Walter P. Lane Led a Brigade of Cavalry West of the Mississippi.

William P. Hardeman Led a Brigade in Magruder's Army.

Lawrence S. Ross Commanded a Brigade in Wheeler's Cavalry.

Walter H. Stevens, Chief Engineer, Army of Northern Virginia.

Elkanah Greer Commanded the Reserve Corps, Trans-Mississippi Department.

A. P. Bagby, Originally Colonel of the 7th Cavalry; Later Led a Division.

John A. Wharton Commanded a Division of Wheeler's Cavalry in Tennessee.

James E. Harrison Commanded a Brigade of Polignac's Division in Louisiana.

William H. Young Led a Brigade in the Army of Tennessee.

John W. Whitfield Commanded a Brigade of Texas Cavalry.

Joseph L. Hogg Led a Brigade in the Army of the West.

Samuel Bell Maxcy, Originally Colonel of the 9th Infantry.

William Steele Led a Brigade at Shreveport in 1864.

CONFEDERATE GENERALS—No. 21—TEXAS

Palmer, Wm. J., Nov. 6, '64.
Partridge, F. W., Mar. 13, '65.
Partridge, B. F., Mar. 31, '65.
Parish, Chas. S., Mar. 13, '65.
Parrott, Jas. C., Mar. 13, '65.
Park, Sidney W., Mar. 13, '65.
Parkhurst, J. G., May 22, '65.
Pardee, D. A., Mar. 13, '65.
Pardee, Ario, Jr., Jan. 12, '65.
Parry, Aug. C., Mar. 13, '65.
Pattee, John, Mar. 13, '65.
Pattee, Jos. B., April 9, '65.
Patterson, R. F., Mar. 13, '65.
Patterson, R. E., Mar. 13, '65.
Patterson, J. N., Mar. 13, '65.
Patten, H. L., Sept. 10, '64.
Paul, Frank, Mar. 13, '65.
Payne, Eugene B., Mar. 13, '65.
Payne, Oliver H., Mar. 13, '65.
Pearsall, Uri B., Mar. 13, '65.
Pearson, Rbt. N., Mar. 13, '65.
Pearce, John S., Mar. 13, '65.
Pease, Phineas, Mar. 13, '65.
Pease, Wm. R., Mar. 13, '65.
Peck, Frank H., Sept. 19, '65.
Pennington, A. C. M., July 16, '65.
Perkins, H. W., Mar. 13, '65.
PerLee, Sam'l R., Mar. 13, '65.
Phelps, Chas. E., Mar. 13, '65.
Phelps, John E., Mar. 13, '65.
Phelps, W., Jr., Mar. 13, '65.
Phillips, Jesse L., Mar. 13, '65.
Pickett, Josiah, Mar. 13, '65.
Pierson, Chas. L., Mar. 13, '65.
Pierson, J. Fred., Mar. 13, '65.
Pierson, Wm. S., Mar. 13, '65.
Pierce, F. E., Mar. 13, '65.
Pinckney, Jos. C., Mar. 13, '65.
Pinto, F. E., Mar. 13, '64.
Platner, John S., Mar. 13, '65.
Pleasants, H., Mar. 13, '65.
Pollock, S. M., Mar. 13, '65.
Pomutz, Geo., Mar. 13, '65.
Pope, Ed. M., Mar. 13, '65.
Porter, Sam'l A., Mar. 13, '65.
Post, P. Sidney, Dec. 16, '64.
Potter, Carroll H., Mar. 13, '65.
Powell, Eugene, Mar. 13, '65.
Price, Francis, Mar. 13, '65.
Price, W. R., Mar. 13, '65.
Price, S. W., Mar. 13, '62.
Price, Rich'd B., Mar. 13, '65.
Pritchard, B. D., May 10, '65.
Proudfit, J. L., Mar. 13, '65.
Pratt, Benj. F., Mar. 13, '65.
Preston, S. M., Dec. 30, '65.
Prescott, Geo. L., June 18, '64.
Prevost, C. M., Mar. 13, '65.
Pugh, Isaac C., Mar. 10, '65.
Pulford, John, Mar. 13, '65.
Quincy, S. M., Mar. 13, '65.
Randall, Geo. W., Mar. 13, '65.
Randol, A. M., June 24, '65.
Ratliff, Rbt. W., Mar. 13, '65.
Raynor, Wm. H., Mar. 13, '65.
Read, S. Tyler, Mar. 13, '65.
Read, Theo., Sept. 29, '64.
Remick, D., Mar. 13, '65.
Reno, M. A., Mar. 13, '65.
Revere, W. R., Jr., Mar. 13, '65.
Revere, P. J., July 2, '65.

Reynolds, Jos. S., July 11, '65.
Richardson, H., Mar. 13, '65.
Richardson, W. P., Dec. 7, '64.
Richmond, Lewis, Mar. 13, '65.
Riggin, John, Mar. 13, '65.
Rinaker, J. I., Mar. 13, '65.
Ripley, Edw. H., Aug. 1, '64.
Ripley, Theo. A., Mar. 13, '65.
Risdon, O. C., Mar. 13, '65.
Ritchie, John, Feb. 21, '65.
Robbins, W. R., Mar. 13, '65.
Roberts, Chas. W., Mar. 13, '65.
Roberts, S. H., Oct. 28, '64.
Robeson, W. P., Jr., April 1, '65.
Robinson, G. D., Mar. 13, '65.
Robinson, H. L., Mar. 13, '65.
Robinson, M. S., Mar. 13, '65.
Robinson, W. A., Mar. 13, '65.
Robison, J. K., Mar. 13, '65.
Rockwell, A. P., Mar. 13, '65.
Rodgers, H., Jr., Mar. 13, '65.
Rodgers, H. C., Mar. 13, '65.
Rogers, Jas. C., Mar. 13, '65.
Rogers, George, Mar. 13, '65.
Rogers, Geo. C., Mar. 13, '65.
Rogers, Wm. F., Mar. 13, '65.
Roome, Chas., Mar. 13, '65.
Rose, Thos. E., July 22, '65.
Ross, Samuel, April 13, '65.
Ross, W. E. W., Mar. 11, '65.
Rowett, Rich'd, Mar. 13, '65.
Rowley, Wm. R., Mar. 13, '65.
Ruggles, Jas. M., Mar. 13, '65.
Rusk, Jer. M., Mar. 13, '65.
Rusling, Jas. F., Feb. 16, '66.
Russell, Chas. S., July 30, '64.
Russell, Hy. S., Mar. 13, '65.
Rust, John D., Mar. 13, '65.
Rust, H., Jr., Mar. 13, '65.
Rutherford, Allen, Mar. 13, '65.
Rutherford, G. V., Mar. 13, '65.
Rutherford, R. C., Mar. 13, '65.
Sackett, Wm. H., June 10, '64.
Salm Salm, F. P., April 13, '65.
Salomon, C. E., Mar. 13, '65.
Salomon, E. S., Mar. 13, '65.
Sanborn, Wm., Mar. 13, '65.
Sanders, A. H., Mar. 13, '65.
Sanders, H. T., April 19, '65.
Sanderson, T. W., Mar. 13, '65.
Sanford, E. S., Mar. 13, '65.
Sargent, H. B., Mar. 21, '64.
Sawyer, Frank, Mar. 13, '65.
Scates, W. B., Mar. 13, '65.
Schmitt, Wm. A., Mar. 13, '65.
Schneider, E. F., Mar. 13, '65.
Schofield, H., Mar. 13, '65.
Schofield, Geo. W., Jan. 26, '65.
Schwenk, S. K., July 24, '65.
Scribner, B. F., Aug. 8, '64.
Scott, Geo. W., Mar. 13, '65.
Scott, Rufus, Mar. 13, '65.
Seaver, Joel J., Mar. 13, '65.
Seawall, Thos. D., Mar. 13, '65.
Selfridge, J. L., Mar. 16, '65.
Serrell, Edw. W., Mar. 13, '65.
Sewall, F. D., July 21, '65.
Shaffer, G. T., Mar. 13, '65.
Shaffer, J. W., Mar. 13, '65.
Shafter, Wm. R., Mar. 13, '65.
Sharpe, Jacob, Mar. 13, '65.
Shaurman, N., Mar. 13, '65.

Shaw, Jas., Jr., Mar. 13, '65.
Shedd, Warren, Mar. 13, '65.
Sheets, Benj. F., Mar. 13, '65.
Sheets, Josiah A., Mar. 13, '65.
Sheldon, Chas. S., Mar. 13, '65.
Sheldon, L. A., Mar. 13, '65.
Shepherd, R. B., Mar. 13, '65.
Sherwood, I. R., Feb. 27, '65.
Sherwin, T., Jr., Mar. 13, '65.
Shoup, Sam'l, Mar. 13, '65.
Shunk, David, Feb. 9, '65.
Shurtleff, G. W., Mar. 13, '65.
Sickles, H. F., Mar. 13, '65.
Sigfried, J. K., Aug. 1, '64.
Simpson, S. P., Mar. 13, '65.
Sleven, P. S., Mar. 13, '65.
Slocum, Willard, Mar. 13, '65.
Smith, Arthur A., Mar. 13, '65.
Smith, Al. B., Mar. 13, '65.
Smith, Benj. F., Mar. 26, '65.
Smith, Chas. E., Mar. 13, '65.
Smith, E. W., Mar. 13, '65.
Smith, F. C., Mar. 13, '65.
Smith, Geo. W., Mar. 13, '65.
Smith, Gus. A., Mar. 13, '65.
Smith, Israel C., Mar. 13, '65.
Smith, James, Mar. 13, '65.
Smith, John C., June 20, '65.
Smith, Jos. S., July 11, '65.
Smith, Orlando, Mar. 13, '65.
Smith, Orlow, Mar. 13, '65.
Smith, Robert F., Mar. 13, '65.
Smith, Rbt. W., Feb. 13, '65.
Smith, Wm. J., July 16, '65.
Sniper, Gustavus, Mar. 13, '65.
Sowers, Edgar, Mar. 13, '65.
Sprague, A. B. R., Mar. 13, '65.
Sprague, Ezra T., June 20, '65.
Spalding, George, Mar. 21, '65.
Spaulding, Ira, April 9, '65.
Spaulding, O. L., June 25, '65.
Spencer, Geo. E., Mar. 13, '65.
Spear, Ellis, Mar. 13, '65.
Spear, Sam'l P., Mar. 13, '65.
Spicely, Wm. T., Aug. 26, '65.
Spurling, A. B., Mar. 26, '65.
Spofford, John P., Mar. 13, '65.
Stafford, Jacob A., Mar. 13, '65.
Stager, Anson, Mar. 13, '65.
Stagg, Peter, Mar. 30, '65.
Stanley, Tim. L., Mar. 13, '65.
Stanton, David L., April 1, '65.
Starbird, I. W., Mar. 13, '65.
Starring, F. A., Mar. 13, '65.
Stedman, G. A., Jr., Aug. 5, '64.
Stedman, Wm., Mar. 13, '65.
Steers, Wm. H. P., Mar. 13, '65.
Steiner, John A., Mar. 13, '65.
Stephenson, L., Jr., Mar. 13, '64.
Stevens, Aaron F., Dec. 8, '64.
Stevens, A. A., Mar. 7, '65.
Stevens, Hazard, April 2, '65.
Stevenson, R. H., Mar. 13, '65.
Stewart, Jas., Jr., Mar. 13, '65.
Stewart, W. S., Mar. 13, '65.
Stewart, Wm. W., Mar. 13, '65.
Stibbs, John H., Mar. 13, '65.
Stiles, Israel N., Jan. 31, '64.
Stockton, Jos., Mar. 13, '65.
Stokes, Wm. B., Mar. 13, '65.
Stone, Geo. A., Mar. 13, '65.

Stone, Roy, Sept. 7, '64.
Stone, Wm. M., Mar. 13, '65.
Stough, Wm., Mar. 13, '65.
Stoughton, C. B., Mar. 13, '65.
Stout, Alex. W., Mar. 13, '62.
Stratton, F. A., Mar. 13, '65.
Streight, Abel D., Mar. 13, '65.
Strickland, S. A., Mar. 13, '65.
Strong, Jas. C., Mar. 13, '65.
Strong, Thos. J., Mar. 13, '65.
Strong, Wm. E., Mar. 21, '65.
Strother, D. H., Aug. 23, '65.
Sumner, E. V., Jr., Mar. 13, '65.
Sullivan, P. J., Mar. 13, '65.
Sweet, Benj., Dec. 20, '64.
Sweitzer, J. B., Mar. 13, '65.
Swift, Fred. W., Mar. 13, '65.
Switzler, T. A., Mar. 13, '65.
Sypher, J. Hale, Mar. 13, '65.
Talbot, Thos. H., Mar. 13, '65.
Talley, Wm. C., Mar. 13, '65.
Tarbell, Jon., Mar. 13, '65.
Taylor, Ezra, Feb. 13, '65.
Taylor, J. E., Mar. 13, '65.
Taylor, John P., Aug. 4, '65.
Taylor, Thos. T, Mar. 13, '65.
Tevis, W. Carroll, Mar. 13, '65.
Tew, Geo. W., Mar. 13, '65.
Thomas, De Witt C., Mar. 13, '65.
Thomas, M. T., Feb. 10, '65.
Thomas, Samuel, Mar. 13, '65.
Thompson, C. R., April 13, '65.
Thompson, D., Mar. 13, '65.
Thompson, H. E., Mar. 13, '65.
Thompson, J. L., Mar. 13, '65.
Thompson, J. M., Mar. 13, '65.
Thompson, R., Mar. 13, '65.
Thompson, Wm., Mar. 13, '65.
Thorp, Thos. J., Mar. 13, '65.
Throop, Wm. A., Mar. 13, '65.
Thruston, G. P., Mar. 13, '65.
Thurston, W. H., Mar. 13, '65.
Tilden, Chas. W., Mar. 13, '65.
Tilghman, B. C., April 13, '65.
Tillson, John, Mar. 10, '65.
Tilton, Wm. S., Sept. 9, '64.
Titus, Herbert B., Mar. 13, '65.
Tompkins, C. H., Aug. 1, '64.
Tourtelotte, J. E., Mar. 13, '65.
Tracy, B. F., Mar. 13, '65.
Trauernicht, T., Mar. 13, '65.
Tremaine, H. E., Nov. 30, '65.
Trotter, F. E., Mar. 13, '65.
True, Jas. M., Mar. 6, '65.
Truex, William S., April 2, '65.
Trumbull, M. M., Mar. 13, '65.
Turley, John A., Mar. 13, '65.
Turner, Charles, Mar. 26, '65.
Van Antwerp, V., Feb. 13, '65.
VanBuren, D. T., Mar. 13, '65.
VanBuren, J. L., April 2, '65.
VanBuren, T. B., Mar. 13, '65.
Van Schrader, A., Mar. 13, '65.
Varney, Geo., Mar. 13, '65.
Van Petten, J. V., Mar. 13, '65.
Van Shaak, G. W., Mar. 13, '65.
Vail, Jacob G., Mar. 13, '65.
Vail, Nicholas J., Mar. 13, '65.
Vaughn, Sam'l K., Aug. 9, '65.
Vickers, David, Mar. 13, '65.
Vifquain, V., Mar. 13, '65.
Von Blessingh, L., Mar. 13, '65.

Richard M. Gano Led a Brigade of Morgan's Cavalry.

Matthew D. Ector Led a Brigade in the Army of Tennessee.

Richard Waterhouse Led a Brigade of Infantry and Cavalry.

Thomas Harrison Led a Brigade in the Army of Tennessee.

Felix H. Robertson Led a Brigade of Cavalry in the Army of Tennessee.

John C. Moore Led a Brigade in the Army of the West.

John R. Baylor, Conspicuous in Operations in Texas and New Mexico in 1861–62.

Henry E. McCulloch, Texas Brigade and District Commander.

Louis T. Wigfall, Bearer of a Flag of Truce at Fort Sumter.

Thomas N. Waul, Colonel of Waul's Texas Legion.

Jerome B. Robertson Led a Brigade in Hood's Division.

CONFEDERATE GENERALS

—No. 22—

TEXAS (CONTINUED)

The Union Generals

Von Egloffstein, F. W., Mar. 13, '65.
Von Vegesack, E., Mar. 13, '65.
Vreeland, M. J., Mar. 13, '65.
Wade, Jas. F., Feb. 13, '64.
Wagner, Louis, Mar. 13, '65.
Waite, Charles, April 2, '65.
Waite, John M., Feb. 13, '65.
Wainwright, C. S., Aug. 1, '64.
Wainwright, W. P., Mar. 13, '65.
Walcutt, C. F., April 9, '65.
Walker, D. S., Mar. 13, '65.
Walker, F. A., Mar. 31, '65.
Walker, M. B., Mar. 27, '65.
Walker, Samuel, Mar. 13, '65.
Walker, Thos. M., July 5, '65.
Wallace, M. R. M., Mar. 13, '65.
Wangelin, Hugo, Mar. 13, '65.
Warner, D. B., Feb. 13, '65.
Ward, Durbin, Oct. 18, '65.
Ward, Geo. H., July 2, '63.
Ward, Henry C., Nov. 29, '65.
Ward, Lyman M., Mar. 13, '65.
Warner, A. J., Mar. 13, '65.
Warner, Edw. R., April 9, '65.
Warren, L. H., Mar. 13, '65.
Washburn, F., April 6, '65.
Washburn, G. A., Mar. 13, '65.

Wass, Ansell D., Mar. 13, '65.
Waters, L. H., June 18, '65.
Weaver, Jas. B., Mar. 13, '65.
Webber, Jules C., Mar. 13, '65.
Webber, A. W., Mar. 26, '65.
Weld, S. M., Jr., Mar. 13, '65.
Welles, Geo. E., Mar. 13, '65.
Wells, Geo. D., Oct. 12, '64.
Wells, Henry H., June 3, '65.
Wells, Milton, Mar. 13, '65.
Wentworth, M. F., Mar. 13, '65.
Welsh, William, Mar. 13, '65.
West, Edward W., Mar. 13, '65.
West, Francis H., Mar. 13, '65.
West, Geo. W., Dec. 2, '64.
West, Henry R., July 13, '65.
West, Robert M., April 1, '65.
Wever, Clark R., Feb. 9, '65.
Wheelock, Charles, Aug. 9, '64.
Wherry, Wm. M., April 2, '65.
White, Daniel, Mar. 13, '65.
Whitaker, E. W., Mar. 13, '65.
Whistler, J. N. G., Mar. 13, '65.
Whitbeck, H. N., Mar. 13, '65.
White, Carr B., Mar. 13, '65.
White, David B., Mar. 13, '65.
White, Frank, Mar. 13, '65.
White, Frank J., Mar. 13, '65.
White, Harry, Mar. 2, '65.

Whittier, Chas. A., April 9, '65.
Whittier, F. H., Mar. 13, '65.
Whittlesey, C. H., Mar. 13, '65.
Whittlesey, E., Mar. 13, '65.
Whittlesey, H. M., Mar. 13, '65.
Wilcox, Jas. A., Feb. 13, '65.
Wilcox, John S., Mar. 13, '65.
Wilder, John T., Aug. 7, '64.
Wildes, Thos. F., Mar. 11, '65.
Wildrick, A. C., April 2, '65.
Wiles, G. F., Mar. 13, '65.
Wiley, Aquila, Mar. 13, '65.
Wiley, Dan'l D., Mar. 13, '65.
Williams, A. W., Mar. 13, '65.
Williams, Jas. M., July 13, '65.
Williams, John, Mar. 13, '65.
Williams, R., Mar. 13, '65.
Williams, T. J., Sept. 22, '62.
Willian, John, April 9, '65.
Wilson, J. G., Mar. 13, '65.
Wilson, James, Mar. 13, '65.
Wilson, Lester S., Mar. 13, '65.
Wilson, Thomas, Mar. 13, '65.
Wilson, Wm. T., Mar. 13, '65.
Wilson, Wm., Nov. 13, '65.
Winkler, Fred. C., June 15, '65.
Winslow, Bradley, April 2, '65.
Winslow, E. F., Dec. 12, '64.
Winslow, R. E., Mar. 13, '65.

Wise, Geo. D., Mar. 13, '65.
Wisewell, M. N., Mar. 13, '65.
Wister, L., Mar. 13, '65.
Witcher, John S., Mar. 13, '65.
Withington, W. H., Mar. 13, '65.
Wolfe, Edw. H., Mar. 13, '65.
Wood, Oliver, Mar. 13, '65.
Wood, Wm. D., Mar. 13, '65.
Woodall, Daniel, June 15, '65.
Woodford, S. L., May 12, '65.
Woodhull, M. V. L., Mar. 13, '65.
Woodward, O. S., Mar. 13, '65.
Woolley, John, Mar. 13, '65
Wormer, G. S., Mar. 13, '65.
Wright, Ed., Mar. 13, '65.
Wright, Elias, Jan. 15, '65.
Wright, John G., Mar. 13, '65.
Wright, Thos. F., Mar. 13, '65.
Yates, Henry, Jr., Mar. 13, '65.
Yeoman, S. B., Mar. 13, '65.
Yorke, Louis E., Mar. 13, '65.
Young, S. B. M., April 9, '65.
Young, Thos. L., Mar. 13, '65.
Zahm, Louis, Mar. 13, '62.
Ziegler, Geo. M., Mar. 13, '65.
Zinn, Geo., April 6, '65.
Zulick, Sam'l M., Mar. 13, '65.

D. B. Harris, Colonel in the Engineer Corps; Chief Engineer at Charleston.

Armstead L. Long, Staff Officer to Lee and His Authorized Biographer.

John B. Floyd, in Command in West Virginia in 1861, later at Fort Donelson.

William L. Jackson, Originally Colonel of the 31st Regiment.

CONFEDERATE

GENERALS

No. 23

VIRGINIA

Albert G. Jenkins Led a Command in Southwest Virginia; Wounded at Cloyd's Mountain.

Daniel Ruggles Commanded a Division in General Breckinridge's Army.

Camille J. Polignac, Defender of the Red River Country, Leading in many Battles.

Montgomery D. Corse Battled Heroically at Five Forks and Petersburg.

Richard L. T. Beale Led a Brigade in Lee's Army.

Henry H. Walker Led a Virginia Brigade in Lee's Army.

Joseph R. Anderson Led a Brigade in Lee's Army.

Thomas Jordan, Beauregard's Chief of Staff; Later Fought for "Cuba Libre."

General Officers of the Confederate Army

A FULL ROSTER COMPILED FROM THE OFFICIAL RECORDS

The Confederate titles below derive authority through verification by General Marcus J. Wright, for many years in charge of Confederate records at the United States War Department, Washington. Some ranks appropriate to high commands, and fully justified, were never legally confirmed. In such cases, as those of Joseph Wheeler and John B. Gordon, General Wright has followed the strictest interpretation of the Confederate records below. As for the body of this History it has been thought best to employ the titles most commonly used, and found in the popular reference works. The highest rank attained is given in every case together with the date of the commission conferring such rank.

GENERALS
REGULAR

Beauregard, P. G. T., July 21, '61.
Bragg, Braxton, April 6, '62.
Cooper, Samuel, May 16, '61.
Johnston, A. S., May 30, '61.
Johnston, J. E., July 4, '61.
Lee, Robert E., June 14, '61.

GENERAL
PROVISIONAL ARMY

Smith, E. Kirby, Feb. 19, '64.

GENERALS
PROVISIONAL ARMY
(With Temporary Rank)

Hood, John B., July 18, '64.

LIEUTENANT-GENERALS
PROVISIONAL ARMY

Buckner, S. B., Sept. 20, '64.
Ewell, Richard S., May 23, '63.
Forrest, N. B., Feb. 28, '65.
Hampton, Wade, Feb. 14, '65.
Hardee, Wm. J., Oct. 10, '62.
Hill, Ambrose P., May 24, '63.
Hill, Daniel H., July 11, '63.
Holmes, T. H., Oct. 13, '62.
Jackson, T. J., Oct. 10, '62.
Lee, Stephen D., June 23, '64.
Longstreet, James, Oct. 9, '62.
Pemberton, J. C., Oct. 10, '62.
Polk, Leonidas, Oct. 10, '62.
Taylor, Richard, April 8, '64.

LIEUTENANT-GENERALS
PROVISIONAL ARMY
(With Temporary Rank)

Anderson, R. H., May 31, '64.
Early, Jubal A., May 31, '64.
Stewart, A. P., June 23, '64.

MAJOR-GENERALS
PROVISIONAL ARMY

Anderson, J. P., Feb. 17, '64.
Bate, William B., Feb. 23, '64.
Bowen, John S., May 25, '63.

Breckinridge, J. C., Apr. 14, '62.
Butler, M. C., Sept. 19, '64.
Cheatham, B. F., Mar. 10, '62.
Churchill, T. J., Mar. 17, '65.
Crittenden, G. B., Nov. 9, '61.
Cleburne, P. R., Dec. 13, '62.
Cobb, Howell, Sept. 9, '63.
Donelson, D. S., Jan. 17, '63.
Elzey, Arnold, Dec. 4, '62.
Fagan, James F., April 25, '64.
Field, Chas. W., Feb. 12, '64.
Forney, John H., Oct. 27, '62.
French, S. G., Aug. 31, '62.
Gardner, F., Dec. 13, '62.
Grimes, Bryan, Feb. 15, '65.
Gordon, John B., May 14, '64.
Heth, Henry, Oct. 10, '62.
Hindman, T. C., April 14, '62.
Hoke, Robert F., April 20, '64.
Huger, Benj., Oct. 7, '61.
Johnson, B. R., May 21, '64.
Johnson, Edward, Feb. 28, '63.
Jones, David R., Oct. 11, '62.
Jones, Samuel, Mar. 10, '62.
Kemper, J. L., Sept. 19, '64.
Kershaw, J. B., May 18, '64.
Lee, Fitzhugh, Aug. 3, '63.
Lee, G. W. Custis, Oct. 20, '64.
Lee, W. H. F., Apr. 23, '64.
Loring, W. W., Feb. 17, '62.
Lovell, Mansfield, Oct. 7, '61.
McCown, John P., Mar. 10, '62.
McLaws, L., May 23, '62.
Magruder, J. B., Oct. 7, '61.
Mahone, William, July 30, '64.
Marmaduke, J. S., Mar. 17, '65.
Martin, Will T., Nov. 10, '63.
Maury, D. H., Nov. 4, '62.
Polignac, C. J., April 8, '64.
Pender, W. D., May 27, '63.
Pickett, George E., Oct. 10, '62.
Price, Sterling, Mar. 6, '62.
Ransom, R., Jr., May 26, '63.
Rodes, Robert E., May 2, '63.
Smith, G. W., Sept. 19, '61.
Smith, Martin L., Nov. 4, '62.
Smith, William, Aug. 12, '63.
Stevenson, C. L., Oct. 10, '62.
Stuart, J. E. B., July 25, '62.
Taylor, Richard, July 28, '62.
Trimble, Isaac R., Jan. 17, '63.
Twiggs, D. F., May 22, '61.
Van Dorn, Earl, Sept. 19, '61.
Walker, John G., Nov. 8, '62.
Walker, W. H. T., May 23, '63.
Wharton, John A., Nov. 10, '63.
Wheeler, Joseph, Jan. 20, '64.
Whiting, W. H. C., Apr. 22, '63.
Withers, Jones M., April 6, '62.
Wilcox, C. M., Aug. 3, '63.

MAJOR-GENERALS
PROVISIONAL ARMY
(With Temporary Rank)

Allen, William W., Mar. 4, '65.
Brown, John C., Aug. 4, '64.
Clayton, Henry D., July 7, '64.
Lomax, L. L., Aug. 10, '64.
Ramseur, S. D., June 1, '64.
Rosser, T. L., Nov. 1, '64.
Walthall, E. C., July 6, '64.
Wright, A. R., Nov. 26, '64.
Young, P. M. B., Dec. 20, '64.

MAJOR-GENERAL
FOR SERVICE WITH VOLUN-TEER TROOPS
(With Temporary Rank)

Gilmer, J. F., Aug. 25, '63.

BRIGADIER-GENERALS
PROVISIONAL ARMY

Adams, Daniel W., May 23, '62.
Adams, John, Dec. 29, '62.
Adams, Wirt, Sept. 25, '63.
Allen, Henry W., Aug. 19, '63.
Anderson, G. B., June 9, '62.
Anderson, J. R., Sept. 3, '61.
Anderson, S. R., July 9, '61.
Armistead, L. A., April 1, '62.
Armstrong, F. C., April 20, '63.
Anderson, G. T., Nov. 1, '62.
Archer, James J., June 3, '62.
Ashby, Turner, May 23, '62.
Baker, Alpheus, Mar. 5, '64.
Baker, L. S., July 23, '63.
Baldwin, W. E., Sept. 19, '62.
Barksdale, W., Aug. 12, '62.
Barringer, Rufus, June 1, '64.
Barton, Seth M., Mar. 11, '62.
Battle, Cullen A., Aug. 20, '63.
Beall, W. N. R., April 11, '62.
Beale, R. L. T., Jan. 6, '65.
Bee, Barnard E., June 17, '61.
Bee, Hamilton P., Mar. 4, '62.
Bell, Tyree H., Feb. 28, '65.
Benning, H. L., Jan. 17, '63.
Boggs, William R., Nov. 4, '62.
Bonham, M. L., April 23, '61.
Blanchard, A. G., Sept. 21, '61.
Buford, Abraham, Sept. 2, '62.
Branch, L. O. B., Nov. 16, '61.
Brandon, Wm. L., June 18, '64.
Bratton, John, May 6, '64.
Brevard, T. W., Mar. 22, '65.
Bryan, Goode, Aug. 29, '63.
Cabell, Wm. A., Jan. 20, '63.
Campbell, A. W., Mar. 1, '65.
Cantey, James, Jan. 8, '63.

Capers, Ellison, Mar. 1, '65.
Carroll, Wm. H., Oct. 26, '61.
Chalmers, J. R., Feb. 13, '62.
Chestnut, J., Jr., April 23, '64.
Clark, Charles, May 22, '61.
Clark, John B., Mar. 8, '64.
Clanton, J. H., Nov. 16, '63.
Clingman, T. L., May 17, '62.
Cobb, T. R. R., Nov. 1, '62.
Cockrell, F. M., July 18, '63.
Cocke, P. St. G., Oct. 21, '61.
Colston, R. E., Dec. 24, '61.
Cook, Philip, Aug. 5, '64.
Cooke, John R., Nov. 1, '62.
Cooper, D. H., May 2, '63.
Colquitt, A. H., Sept. 1, '62.
Corse, M. D., Nov. 1, '62.
Cosby, Geo. B., Jan. 20, '63.
Cumming, Alfred, Oct. 29, '62.
Daniel, Junius, Sept. 1, '62.
Davidson, H. B., Aug. 18, '63.
Davis, Wm. G. M., Nov. 4, '62.
Davis, J. R., Sept. 15, '62.
Deas, Z. C., Dec. 13, '62.
De Lagnel, J. A., April 15, '62.
Deshler, James, July 28, '63.
Dibrell, Geo. G., July 26, '64.
Dockery, T. P., Aug. 10, '63.
Doles, George, Nov. 1, '62.
Drayton, T. F., Sept. 25, '61.
Duke, Basil W., Sept. 15, '64.
Duncan, J. K., Jan. 7, '62.
Echols, John, April 16, '62.
Ector, M. D., Aug. 23, '62.
Evans, C. A., May 19, '64.
Evans, Nathan G., Oct. 21, '61.
Farney, Wm. H., Feb. 15, '65.
Featherson, W. S., Mar. 4, '62.
Ferguson, S. W., July 23, '63.
Finegan, Joseph, April 5, '62.
Finley, Jesse J., Nov. 16, '63.
Floyd, John B., May 23, '61.
Forney, John H., Mar. 10, '62.
Frazer, John W., May 19, '63.
Frost, Daniel M., Mar. 3, '62.
Gano, Rich. M., Mar. 17, '65.
Gardner, Wm. M., Nov. 14, '61.
Garland, Sam., Jr., May 23, '62.
Garnett, Rich. B., Nov. 14, '61.
Garnett, Robt. S., June 6, '61.
Garrott, I. W., May 28, '63.
Gartrell, Lucius J., Aug. 22, '64.
Gary, Martin W., May 19, '64.
Gatlin, Richard C., July 8, '61.
Gholson, S. J., May 6, '64.
Gist, States R., Mar. 20, '62.
Gladden, A. H., Sept. 30, '61.
Godwin, Arch. C., Aug. 5, '64.
Gordon, James B., Sept. 28, '63.
Govan, Dan'l C., Dec. 29, '63.

David A. Weisinger, Defender of the Petersburg Crater.

Gabriel C. Wharton, in the Shenandoah Valley in 1864.

Philip St. G. Cocke, First Defender of Virginia, in 1861.

Patrick T. Moore, in Command of Reserves Defending Richmond.

CONFEDERATE

GENERALS

No. 24

VIRGINIA

Edwin G. Lee, On Special Service.

James B. Terrell Led Pegram's Old Brigade at the Wilderness.

Robert H. Chilton, Lee's Adjutant-General.

Seth M. Barton Led a Brigade in Lee's Army.

George W. Randolph, Secretary of War in 1862.

William C. Wickham Fought Sheridan Before Richmond.

Eppa Hunton Led a Brigade in Pickett's Division.

Gracie, Arch., Jr., Nov. 4, '63.
Gray, Henry, Mar. 17, '65.
Grayson, John B., Aug. 15, '61.
Green, Martin E., July 21, '62.
Green, Thomas, May 20, '63.
Greer, Elkanah, Oct. 8, '62.
Gregg, John, Aug. 29, '62.
Gregg, Maxcy, Dec. 14, '61.
Griffith, Rich., Nov. 2, '61.
Hagood, Johnson, July 21, '62.
Hanson, Roger W., Dec. 13, '62.
Hardeman, W. P., Mar. 17, '65.
Harris, Nat. H., Jan. 20, '64.
Harrison, J. E., Dec. 22, '64.
Hays, Harry T., July 25, '62.
Hatton, Robert, May 23, '62.
Hawes, James M., Mar. 5, '62.
Hawthorne, A. T., Feb. 18, '64.
Helm, Ben. H., Mar. 14, '62.
Hebert, Louis, May 26, '62.
Hebert, Paul O., Aug. 17, '61.
Higgins, Edward, Oct. 29, '63.
Hodge, Geo. B., Nov. 20, '63.
Hogg, Joseph L., Feb. 14, '62.
Hoke, Robert F., Jan. 17, '63.
Hood, John B., Mar. 3, '62.
Huger, Benjamin, June 17, '61.
Humes, W. Y. C., Nov. 16, '63.
Humphreys, B. G., Aug. 12, '63.
Hunton, Eppa, Aug. 9, '63.
Iverson, Alfred, Nov. 1, '62.
Jackson, Alfred E., Feb. 9, '63.
Jackson, H. R., June 4, '61.
Jackson, John K., Feb. 13, '62.
Jackson, Wm. A., Dec. 19, '61.
Jackson, Wm. H., Dec. 29, '62.
Jenkins, Albert G., Aug. 5, '62.
Jenkins, Micah, July 22, '62.
Johnston, R. D., Sept. 1, '63.
Jones, John M., May 15, '63.
Jones, John R., June 23, '62.
Jones, William E., Sept. 19, '62.
Jordan, Thomas, April 14, '62.
Kelly, John H., Nov. 16, '63.
Kirkland, W. W., Aug. 29, '63.
Lane, James H., Nov. 1, '62.
Lane, Walter P., Mar. 17, '65.
Law, Evander M., Oct. 3, '62.
Lawton, Alex. R., April 13, '61.
Leadbetter, D., Feb. 27, '62.
Lee, Edwin G., Sept. 20, '64.
Lewis, Joseph H., Sept. 30, '63.
Liddell, St. J. R., July 12, '62.
Little, Henry, April 16, '62.
Logan, T. M., Feb. 15, '65.
Lowrey, Mark. P., Oct. 4, '63.
Lowry, Robert, Feb. 4, '65.
Lyon, Hylan B., June 14, '64.
McCausland, J., May 18, '64.
McComb, Wm., June 30, '65.
McCulloch, H. E., Mar. 14, '62.
McCullough, Ben., May 11, '61.
McGowan, S., Jan. 17, '63.
McIntosh, James, Jan. 24, '62.
McNair, Evander, Nov. 4, '62.
McRae, Dandridge, Nov. 5, '62.
Mackall, Wm. W., Feb. 27, '62.
Major, James P., July 21, '63.
Maney, George, April 16, '62.
Manigault, A. M., April 26, '63.
Marshall, H., Oct. 30, '61.
Martin, James G., May 15, '62.
Maxey, S. B., Mar. 4, '62.

Mercer, Hugh W., Oct. 29, '61.
Moody, Young M., Mar. 4, '65.
Moore, John C., May 26, '62.
Moore, P. T., Sept. 20, '64.
Morgan, John H., Dec. 11, '62.
Morgan, John T., June 6, '63.
Mouton, Alfred, April 16, '62.
Nelson, Allison, Sept. 12, '62.
Nicholls, F. T., Oct. 14, '62.
O'Neal, Ed. A., June 6, '63.
Parsons, M. M., Nov. 5, '62.
Paxton, E. F., Nov. 1, '61.
Peck, Wm. R., Feb. 18, '65.
Pegram, John, Nov. 7, '62.
Pendleton, W. N., Mar. 26, '62.
Perrin, Abner, Sept. 10, '63.
Perry, Ed. A., Aug. 28, '62.
Perry, Wm. F., Feb. 21, '65.
Pettigrew, J. J., Feb. 26, '62.
Pettus, E. W., Sept. 18, '63.
Pike, Albert, Aug. 15, '61.
Pillow, Gideon J., July 9, '61.
Polk, Lucius E., Dec. 13, '62.
Preston, William, April 14, '62.
Pryor, Roger A., April 16, '62.
Quarles, Wm. A., Aug. 25, '63.
Rains, G. J., Sept. 23, '61.
Rains, James E., Nov. 4, '62.
Randolph, G. W., Feb. 12, '62.
Ransom, M. W., June 13, '63.
Reynolds, A. W., Sept. 14, '63.
Richardson, R. V., Dec. 1, '63.
Ripley, Roswell S., Aug. 15, '61.
Roberts, Wm. P., Feb. 21, '65.
Robertson, B. H., June 9, '62.
Robertson, J. B., Nov. 1, '62.
Roddy, Philip D., Aug. 3, '63.
Roane, John S., Nov. 20, '62.
Ross, Lawrence S., Dec. 21, '63.
Ruggles, Daniel, Aug. 9, '61.
Rust, Albert, Mar. 4, '62.
Scales, Alfred M., June 3, '63.
Scott, T. M., May 10, '64.
Scurry, Wm. R., Sept. 12, '62.
Sears, Claudius W., Mar. 1, '64.
Semmes, Paul J., Mar. 11, '62.
Shelby, Joseph O., Dec. 15, '63.
Shoup, Francis A., Sept. 12, '62.
Sibley, H. H., June 17, '61.
Simms, James P., Dec. 4, '64.
Slack, William Y., April 12, '62.
Slaughter, J. E., Mar. 8, '62.
Smith, James A., Sept. 30, '63.
Smith, Preston, Oct. 27, '62.
Smith, Wm. D., Mar. 7, '62.
Stafford, Leroy A., Oct. 8, '63.
Starke, Peter B., Nov. 4, '64.
Starke, Wm. E., Aug. 6, '62.
Steele, William, Sept. 12, '62.
Sterling, A. M. W., Jan. 7, '62.
Steuart, Geo. H., Mar. 6, '62.
Stevens, C. H., Jan. 20, '64.
Stovall, M. A., April 23, '63.
Strahl, Otho F., July 28, '63.
Taliaferro, Wm. B., Mar. 4, '62.
Tappan, James C., Nov. 5, '62.
Taylor, T. H., Nov. 4, '62.
Thomas, Allen, Feb. 4, '64.
Thomas, Ed. L., Nov. 1, '62.
Toombs, Robert, July 19, '61.
Tilghman, Lloyd, Oct. 18, '61.
Tracy, Edward D., Aug. 16, '62.
Trapier, James H., Oct. 21, '61.

Tucker, Wm. F., Mar. 1, '64.
Tyler, Robert C., Feb. 23, '64.
Vance, Robert B., Mar. 4, '63.
Vaughn, A. J., Jr., Nov. 18, '63.
Vaughn, J. C., Sept. 22, '62.
Villepigue, J. B., Mar. 13, '62.
Walker, H. H., July 1, '63.
Walker, James A., May 15, '63.
Walker, Leroy P., Sept. 17, '61.
Walker, L. M., April 11, '62.
Walker, Wm. S., Oct. 30, '62.
Waterhouse, R., Mar. 17, '65.
Watie, Stand, May 6, '64.
Waul, Thomas N., Sept. 18, '63.
Wayne, Henry C., Dec. 16, '61.
Weisiger, D. A., July 30, '64.
Wharton, G. C., July 8, '63.
Whitfield, John W., May 9, '63.
Wickham, W. C., Sept. 1, '63.
Wigfall, Louis T., Oct. 2, '61.
Williams, John S., April 16, '62.
Wilson, C. C., Nov. 16, '63.
Winder, Chas. S., Mar. 1, '62.
Winder, John H., June 21, '61.
Wise, Henry A., June 5, '61.
Woffard, Wm. T., Jan. 17, '63.
Wood, S. A. M., Jan. 7, '62.
Wright, Marcus J., Dec. 13, '62.
Zollicoffer, Felix K., July 9, '61.

BRIGADIER-GENERALS OF ARTILLERY

PROVISIONAL ARMY

Alexander, Ed. P., Feb. 26, '64.
Long, A. L., Sept. 21, '63.
Walker, R. L., Feb. 18, '65.

BRIGADIER-GENERAL (COMMISSARY GENERAL)

PROVISIONAL ARMY

St. John, Isaac M., Feb. 16, '65.

BRIGADIER-GENERALS (Special Appointments)

PROVISIONAL ARMY

Imboden, John D., Jan. 28, '63.
Johnson, Adam R., June 1, '64.

BRIGADIER-GENERALS (Special)

PROVISIONAL ARMY

Benton, Samuel, July 26, '64.
Chambliss, J. R., Jr., Dec. 19, '63.
Chilton, R. H., Oct. 20, '62.
Connor, James, June 1, '64.
Elliott, S., Jr., May 24, '64.
Fry, Birkett D., May 24, '64.
Gibson, R. L., Jan. 11, '64.
Goggin, James M., Dec. 4, '64.
Gorgas, Josiah, Nov. 10, '64.
Granberry, H. B., Feb. 29, '64.
Hodge, Geo. B., Aug. 2, '64.
Leventhorpe, C., Feb. 3, '65.
McRae, William, Nov. 4, '64.
Northrop, L. B., Nov. 26, '64.
Page, Richard L., Mar. 1, '64.
Payne, Wm. H., Nov. 1, '64.

Posey, Carnot, Nov. 1, '62.
Preston, John S., June 10, '64.
Reynolds, D. H., Mar. 5, '64.
Stevens, W. H., Aug. 28, '64.
Terry, William, May 19, '64.

BRIGADIER-GENERALS

PROVISIONAL ARMY

(With Temporary Rank)

Anderson, R. H., July 26, '64.
Barry, John D., Aug. 3, '64.
Brantly, Wm. F., July 26, '64.
Browne, Wm. M., Nov. 11, '64.
Bullock, Robert, Nov. 29, '64.
Carter, John C., July 7, '64.
Cox, William R., May 31, '64.
Dubose, D. M., Nov. 16, '64.
Dunnovant, John, Aug. 22, '64.
Girardey, V. J. B., July 30, '64.
Gordon, Geo. W., Aug. 15, '64.
Harrison, T., Jan. 14, '65.
Hill, Benjamin J., Nov. 30, '64.
Holtzclaw, J. T., July 7, '64.
Johnson, B. T., June 28, '64.
Johnson, G. D., July 26, '64.
Kennedy, J. D., Dec. 22, '64.
Lewis, Wm. G., May 31, '64.
Lilley, Robt. D., May 31, '64.
Miller, William, Aug. 2, '64.
Palmer, Joseph B., Nov. 15, '64.
Robertson, F. H., July 26, '64.
Sanders, J. C. C., May 31, '64.
Sharp, Jacob H., July 26, '64.
Shelley, Chas. M., Sept. 17, '64.
Smith, T. B., July 29, '64.
Sorrell, G. Moxley, Oct. 27, '64.
Terrill, James B., May 31, '64.
Terry, Wm. R., May 31, '64.
Toon, Thomas F., May 31, '64.
Wallace, Wm. H., Sept. 20, '64.
York, Zebulon, May 31, '64.
Young, Wm. H., Aug. 15, '64.

BRIGADIER-GENERALS

FOR SERVICE WITH VOLUNTEER TROOPS

(With Temporary Rank)

Armstrong, F. C., Jan. 20, '63.
Dearing, James, April 29, '64.
Thomas, Bryan M., Aug. 4, '64.

The following were assigned to duty as general officers by Gen. E. Kirby Smith commanding the Trans-Mississippi Department, and served as such.

Green, Cullen.
Gordon, B. Frank.
Harrison, G. P. J.
Jackman, S. D.
Lewis, Leven M.
Maclay, Robt. P.
Munford, Thomas T.
Pearce, N. B.
Randall, Horace.

Assigned to duty as brigadier-general by Major-General Fitzhugh Lee and served as such though not appointed by the President or confirmed.

Terrell, Alex. W., May 16, '65.

Richard L. Page Commanded the Defenses of Mobile Bay.

Carter L. Stevenson, Active Division Leader in the West.

Henry A. Wise, Defender of Petersburg in 1864.

CONFEDERATE GENERALS

No. 25

VIRGINIA (CONTINUED)

William Terry Led a Brigade in Lee's Army.

James E. Slaughter, Inspector-General of the Army of Tennessee.

John McCausland, Cavalry Leader in the Shenandoah Valley.

William H. Payne, Leader of the Black Horse Cavalry.

Alexander W. Reynolds Led a Brigade in the Army of Tennessee.

The Photographic History
of The Civil War

Two Volumes in One.
Poetry and Eloquence

ACKNOWLEDGMENT

All rights on selections in this volume are reserved by the holders of the copyrights. The publishers and others named in the following list are the proprietors, either in their own right or as agents for the authors, of the selections of which the authorship and titles are given, and of which the ownership is thus specifically noted and is hereby acknowledged.

The Bobbs-Merrill Company, Indianapolis.—"One Country," by Frank Lebby Stanton.

The Century Company, New York.—"Farragut," by William Tuckey Meredith, from "The Century Magazine."

Doubleday, Page & Company, New York.—"Lee on 'Traveller,'" from "Recollections and Letters of General Lee."

Henry Holt & Company, New York.—"The Blue and the Gray," by Francis Miles Finch.

Houghton Mifflin Company, Boston.—"Sherman," "On the Life Mask of Abraham Lincoln," from "Poems," by Richard Watson Gilder; "John Burns of Gettysburg," "A Second Review of the Grand Army," "The Aged Stranger," from "Poems," by Bret Harte; "Brother Jonathan's Lament," by Oliver Wendell Holmes; "Battle-Hymn of the Republic," from "From Sunset Ridge," and "Robert E. Lee," from "At Sunset," by Julia Ward Howe; "Ode Recited at the Harvard Commemoration," by James Russell Lowell; "The Bivouac in the Snow," by Margaret Junkin Preston; "Kearny at Seven Pines," by Edmund Clarence Stedman; "To the South," from "Poems," by Maurice Thompson; "A Message," from "Poetic Studies," by Elizabeth Stuart Phelps Ward.

The B. F. Johnson Publishing Company, Richmond, Virginia.—"Charleston," and "Ode at Magnolia Cemetery," by Henry Timrod.

P. J. Kenedy & Sons, New York.—"The Conquered Banner," from "Poems: Patriotic, Religious, Miscellaneous," by Abram Joseph Ryan.

The J. B. Lippincott Company, Philadelphia.—"Sheridan's Ride," from "Poetical Works of Thomas Buchanan Read"; "A Georgia Volunteer," from "Poems," by Mary Ashley Townsend.

Little, Brown & Company, Boston.—"The Volunteer," from "War Poems," by Elbridge Jefferson Cutler.

Moffat, Yard & Company, New York.—"After All," from "Poems," by William Winter.

The John Murphy Company, Baltimore.—"Ashby," by John Reuben Thompson, from "Southern Poems of the War," collected by Emily Mason.

The Neale Publishing Company, New York.—"Little Giffen," from "The Poems of Francis Orray Ticknor."

G. P. Putnam's Sons, New York.—"United," from "From Cliff and Scaur," by Benjamin Sledd; "A Soldier's Grave," from "Poems," by John Albee.

Charles Scribner's Sons, New York.—"Keenan's Charge," "Gettysburg: A Battle Ode," by George Parsons Lathrop; "The Dying Words of Stonewall Jackson," and "The Tournament," by Sidney Lanier.

The John C. Winston Company, Philadelphia.—"The Picket Guard," from "All Quiet Along the Potomac," by Ethel Lynn Beers.

In addition to the above, the Editor begs to acknowledge permission from the following to use the selections named.

Henry Abbey, for "On a Great Warrior."

Charles Francis Adams, for "A New England Tribute to Lee," from "Three Phi Beta Kappa Addresses," published by Houghton Mifflin Co.

Matthew Page Andrews, Editor of "Poems of James Ryder Randall," for "My Maryland," and "Pelham."

Samuel H. M. Byers, for "Sherman's March to the Sea," from his "The Happy Isles, and other Poems."

General Frederick Dent Grant, for "Let Us Have Peace," from "Personal Memoirs of U. S. Grant."

John Howard Jewett, for "Those Rebel Flags."

William Gordon McCabe, for "Christmas Night of '62," and "Dreaming in the Trenches."

Dr. Edward Mayes, for text of Lamar's "Eulogy of Sumner."

Mrs. Eva M. O'Connor, for "The General's Death," by Joseph O'Connor.

Mrs. William C. Palmer, for "Stonewall Jackson's Way," by John Williamson Palmer.

General Horace Porter, for the "Eulogy of Ulysses S. Grant."

Wallace Rice, for "Wheeler's Brigade at Santiago."

John Jerome Rooney, for "Joined the Blues."

Clinton Scollard, for "The Daughter of the Regiment," from "Ballads of Valor and Victory," by Wallace Rice and Clinton Scollard.

Kate Brownlee Sherwood, for "Albert Sidney Johnston," and "Thomas at Chickamauga."

Henry Jerome Stockard, for "Over their Graves."

Will Henry Thompson, for "The High Tide at Gettysburg."

Horace Traubel, for "Bivouac on a Mountainside," "Cavalry Crossing a Ford," and "O Captain! My Captain!" from "Leaves of Grass," by Walt Whitman.

Robert Burns Wilson, for "Such is the Death the Soldier Dies."

IN VIRGINIA—1865

WHAT THE WAR BROUGHT TO THE SOUTH—RUINS OF A MILL AT PETERSBURG JUST AFTER
THE CAPTURE OF THE TOWN BY GRANT'S ARMY

To study this scene at the close of the war reveals the spirit of this volume. Within the stone walls of the woolen mill that now gape empty to Heaven, many a gray blanket and uniform had been woven for Lee's devoted army. Many a wheel had been turned by the stream that now plays but an idle part in the dreamy landscape. Yet the magnificent Army of the Potomac, as it rushed through the city in hot pursuit of the men soon to wear gray no longer, brought in its train an enduring prosperity. Half a century later, Petersburg, with thousands of other cities in Virginia and its sister Southern States once trampled by armies, hummed again with industry under the very flag once borne against them. North and South had learned the lasting meaning of Blue and Gray—symbols of principle and love of home, emblems of the heroism proclaimed by poets and orators of a nation united.

The Photographic History of The Civil War

Complete and Unabridged

TWO VOLUMES IN ONE.

Volume 5
The Armies and Leaders
* Poetry and Eloquence

EDITOR

DUDLEY H. MILES, PH.D.

Sometime University Fellow in Comparative Literature, Columbia University

FOREWORD BY

WILLIAM P. TRENT, LL.D.

Professor of English in Columbia University

WITH AN APPENDIX
"Songs of the War Days"
EDITED BY
JEANNE ROBERT FOSTER

THE BLUE & GREY PRESS

CONTENTS

Contents

FOREWORD

THE spirit in which Dr. Miles has written his introduction and made his selections from the prose and poetry inspired by our Civil War, seems to me so admirable and so characteristically American as to need no praise and to suggest little comment that would not be superfluous. As is the case with the other volumes of this PHOTOGRAPHIC HISTORY OF THE CIVIL WAR, the present anthology brings out clearly two facts in our national history that give us great encouragement as a people—the fact that, even when the flames of war burned most fiercely, the fraternal feeling between Americans of all sections showed no signs of perishing completely, and the fact that, despite the mistakes made during the period of Reconstruction, the reestablishment of sympathy and confidence between the sections went forward with a speed and a thoroughness not previously experienced after civil wars. On these two facts alone one might base a justification of our experiment, if that word be applicable since 1865, in democratic government; and it is pleasant for the literary student to think that these facts are facts partly because of the beneficent influence exerted by our literature in affording our people an opportunity to express their better selves.

These better selves, Northern and Southern, are so well expressed in Dr. Miles' selections that one wonders why the material he has gathered has not been made more of a common literary heritage through the medium of that universally circulated book, the school-reader. Just after the war the sectional origin of most of the pieces, such as " The Blue and the Gray " and " Pelham," stood in the way of their use for national educational purposes, but now that we are truly one people in one great country, such considerations do not count, and the time seems to have come when the literature of our most heroic period should be rendered accessible to the children and grandchildren of the men and women who made that period memorable in the annals of human fortitude and patience. Surely no better year than the semi-centennial of the beginning of the great struggle can be found for the publication of Dr. Miles' essentially reconciliatory volume. May it stimulate our patriotism, our sense of brotherhood, our pride in our great past, and, what is more, that spirit of tolerant sympathy, which not even the passions of civil war could utterly destroy!

In the light of what has just been said we may infer that it is difficult for the American reader, to whom patriotic considerations are naturally paramount, to judge the poetry and prose gathered in this volume as dispassionately as he can judge the literature produced, let us say, during the English Civil War. I well remember, for example, how in my youth I committed the indiscretion of comparing, with some reserve of praise for the native product, certain verses produced by militant cavaliers of the South with other verses produced by English and Scotch cavaliers in the seventeenth century, and how roundly I was assured by some compatriots that I had no taste in poetry. My impression is that I was but voicing, unnecessarily perhaps, a preference for more or less original seventeenth century verse over somewhat derivative mid-nineteenth century verse, but I doubtless seemed to be combining treason with bad taste.

My taste has not sufficiently improved to enable me to prefer the poetical products of the later and much greater struggle, but I trust that I have learned to express my preferences with more suavity than of yore, and that the less perfervid American reader of to-day, who, notwithstanding the control he has acquired over his unsophisticated emotions, still values our native poetry above any foreign productions in verse, at least will stop short of feeling it necessary to assert that any

Foreword

one who does not agree with him is a combination of a fool and
a traitor. Quarreling over matters of politics is bad enough;
quarreling over matters of taste is too absurd. It is all very
well to be patriotic and to cherish our literature, but for the
sake of that literature we ought to strive to pass disinterested
and, as far as possible, strictly critical judgments upon the
works that constitute it, even when, as in the present case, they
deal with the gravest issue in our national life and represent
that finest of all our achievements, national reconciliation. For
we must do justice to ourselves and to posterity as well as to
our ancestors, and we must also do justice to ourselves as
individuals endowed with esthetic ideals, not merely to ourselves as patriotic citizens. A tolerant spirit makes for peace
and for many other good things, but, while it is always to be
preferred to contentiousness, especially in matters of taste, too
often it makes for the triumph of intolerable mediocrity. In
literature as in life it will not do to assume unreservedly that
the fittest will survive, and then to argue that because something has survived, it has proved its fitness.

It will be gathered from the tone of these remarks that I
do not think that much of the poetry Dr. Miles has included,
suitable though it is for the present work, would find a place in
a volume edited with an exigence equal to that manifested by
the late Mr. Palgrave in his " Golden Treasury." But if Dr.
Miles had proved as exigent an editor as Mr. Palgrave, he
would have been left at the end of his labors, through no fault of
his own, without a volume to give us. That would surely have
been a pity, for the writers included are thoroughly representative of their time, and they display as a rule clarity of thought,
rightness of feeling, and creditable powers of expression.

They rarely attain, however, in my judgment, to consummate felicity of cadence and phrase or to notable imaginative
utterance. With a few exceptions such as Lincoln's " Gettysburg Address," Lowell's " Commemoration Ode," Timrod's

[13]

Foreword

" Ode at Magnolia Cemetery," and Randall's " My Maryland," the poetry and prose of the war period, like the rest of our
literature, is adequate or good, rather than remarkable or great.

One ought to add immediately that, like the rest of our
literature, that produced during and shortly after the Civil
War seems to have been excellently adapted to the needs of the
democratic public for which it was primarily written. It has
democratic soundness of substance in thought and feeling, even
if it rarely possesses aristocratic distinction of style. We do
right to collect it and to emphasize the great part it has played
in our history, as well as the great part it can play now, particularly in this semi-centennial year, in stimulating our sense
of civic brotherhood. We do right, also, to acknowledge its
esthetic limitations, but we ought, at the same time, to point to
the fact that the American is perhaps of all men the most determined to put up with nothing less than the best. As he
learns to demand more of his writers, they will learn to answer
more and more satisfactorily his legitimate demands.

NEW YORK, May 23, 1911.   W. P. TRENT.

INTRODUCTION

THE SPIRIT OF NATIONALITY

THE END OF THE WAR—CANNON USELESS SAVE
TO BE MELTED FOR PLOWSHARES

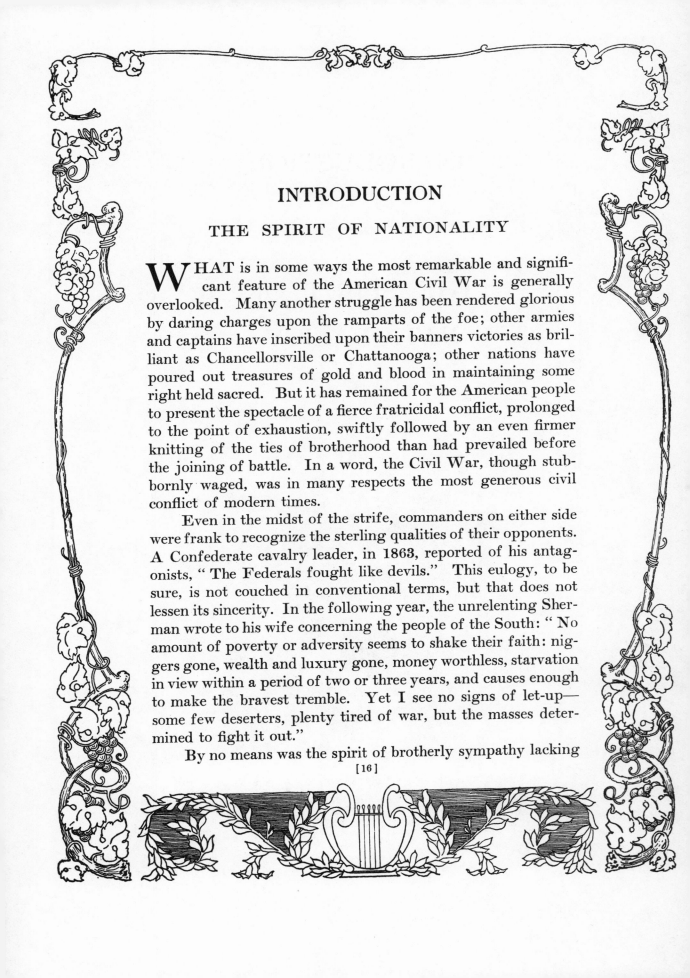

INTRODUCTION

THE SPIRIT OF NATIONALITY

WHAT is in some ways the most remarkable and significant feature of the American Civil War is generally overlooked. Many another struggle has been rendered glorious by daring charges upon the ramparts of the foe; other armies and captains have inscribed upon their banners victories as brilliant as Chancellorsville or Chattanooga; other nations have poured out treasures of gold and blood in maintaining some right held sacred. But it has remained for the American people to present the spectacle of a fierce fratricidal conflict, prolonged to the point of exhaustion, swiftly followed by an even firmer knitting of the ties of brotherhood than had prevailed before the joining of battle. In a word, the Civil War, though stubbornly waged, was in many respects the most generous civil conflict of modern times.

Even in the midst of the strife, commanders on either side were frank to recognize the sterling qualities of their opponents. A Confederate cavalry leader, in 1863, reported of his antagonists, "The Federals fought like devils." This eulogy, to be sure, is not couched in conventional terms, but that does not lessen its sincerity. In the following year, the unrelenting Sherman wrote to his wife concerning the people of the South: "No amount of poverty or adversity seems to shake their faith: niggers gone, wealth and luxury gone, money worthless, starvation in view within a period of two or three years, and causes enough to make the bravest tremble. Yet I see no signs of let-up—some few deserters, plenty tired of war, but the masses determined to fight it out."

By no means was the spirit of brotherly sympathy lacking

JULIA WARD HOWE IN 1861

The author of the magnificent "Battle-Hymn of the Republic" was born in New York in 1819, a daughter of the banker Samuel Ward. In 1843 she married the philanthropist, Dr. S. G. Howe, best known as the head of Perkins Institute for the Blind. She assisted him in editing his anti-slavery journal, the *Boston Commonwealth*. In 1861, at the time of this picture, she made her first trip to Washington, where her husband became interested in the work of the Sanitary Commission. During the visit the party was invited to a military review in the Virginia camps. On the way back she and the others in the carriage sang "John Brown's Body" to the applause of the soldiers by the roadside. Her pastor, who was in the party, suggested that she invent better words for the tune. That night the inspiration came; she wrote the best known of her poems and one of the finest products of the whole Civil War period. Her later life was devoted largely to the cause of woman suffrage. She died at Newport, October 17, 1910.

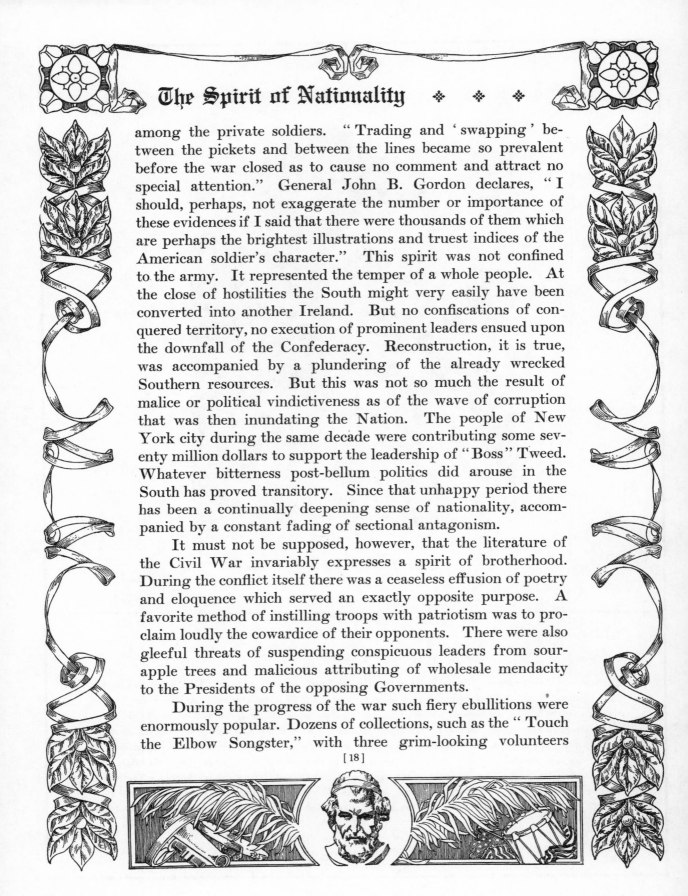

among the private soldiers. "Trading and 'swapping' between the pickets and between the lines became so prevalent before the war closed as to cause no comment and attract no special attention." General John B. Gordon declares, "I should, perhaps, not exaggerate the number or importance of these evidences if I said that there were thousands of them which are perhaps the brightest illustrations and truest indices of the American soldier's character." This spirit was not confined to the army. It represented the temper of a whole people. At the close of hostilities the South might very easily have been converted into another Ireland. But no confiscations of conquered territory, no execution of prominent leaders ensued upon the downfall of the Confederacy. Reconstruction, it is true, was accompanied by a plundering of the already wrecked Southern resources. But this was not so much the result of malice or political vindictiveness as of the wave of corruption that was then inundating the Nation. The people of New York city during the same decade were contributing some seventy million dollars to support the leadership of "Boss" Tweed. Whatever bitterness post-bellum politics did arouse in the South has proved transitory. Since that unhappy period there has been a continually deepening sense of nationality, accompanied by a constant fading of sectional antagonism.

It must not be supposed, however, that the literature of the Civil War invariably expresses a spirit of brotherhood. During the conflict itself there was a ceaseless effusion of poetry and eloquence which served an exactly opposite purpose. A favorite method of instilling troops with patriotism was to proclaim loudly the cowardice of their opponents. There were also gleeful threats of suspending conspicuous leaders from sour-apple trees and malicious attributing of wholesale mendacity to the Presidents of the opposing Governments.

During the progress of the war such fiery ebullitions were enormously popular. Dozens of collections, such as the " Touch the Elbow Songster," with three grim-looking volunteers

JAMES RYDER RANDALL

THE AUTHOR OF "MY MARYLAND," AT TWENTY-TWO

In 1861, just as he looked when he wrote his famous battle-cry, "My Maryland," James Ryder Randall, the youthful poet, faces the reader. Randall was born in Baltimore the first day of 1839. His early schooling was under Joseph H. Clark, a former teacher of Edgar Allan Poe. At Georgetown College he was the smallest boy that had ever been received as a student. After becoming known as the poet of the college, he traveled extensively in the West Indies and South America, landing in 1858 in New Orleans on his return. Then he accepted the chair of English literature at Poydras College, a flourishing Creole institution at Pointe Coupée, Louisiana. He was still teaching there when he learned through the New Orleans *Delta* of the attack on the Sixth Massachusetts in Baltimore on April 19, 1861. That night he wrote the verses that ran like wildfire through the South and were parodied numberless times in the North. The remainder of his days were chiefly spent in newspaper work, largely in Georgia. He became indifferent to his poetical work, and it was owing to the insistence of his friend, Miss Lillian McGregor Shepherd, that his verse was collected. Through her courtesy is here reproduced the intimate and appealing photograph above, a gift to her from the poet himself. He died in 1908 in Augusta, Georgia.

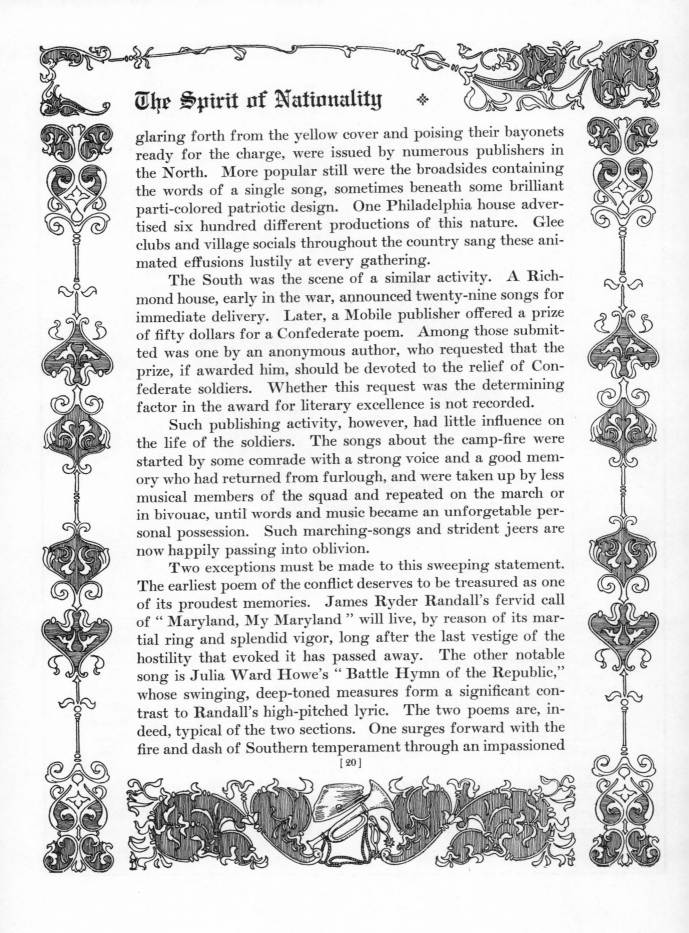

glaring forth from the yellow cover and poising their bayonets ready for the charge, were issued by numerous publishers in the North. More popular still were the broadsides containing the words of a single song, sometimes beneath some brilliant parti-colored patriotic design. One Philadelphia house advertised six hundred different productions of this nature. Glee clubs and village socials throughout the country sang these animated effusions lustily at every gathering.

The South was the scene of a similar activity. A Richmond house, early in the war, announced twenty-nine songs for immediate delivery. Later, a Mobile publisher offered a prize of fifty dollars for a Confederate poem. Among those submitted was one by an anonymous author, who requested that the prize, if awarded him, should be devoted to the relief of Confederate soldiers. Whether this request was the determining factor in the award for literary excellence is not recorded.

Such publishing activity, however, had little influence on the life of the soldiers. The songs about the camp-fire were started by some comrade with a strong voice and a good memory who had returned from furlough, and were taken up by less musical members of the squad and repeated on the march or in bivouac, until words and music became an unforgetable personal possession. Such marching-songs and strident jeers are now happily passing into oblivion.

Two exceptions must be made to this sweeping statement. The earliest poem of the conflict deserves to be treasured as one of its proudest memories. James Ryder Randall's fervid call of " Maryland, My Maryland " will live, by reason of its martial ring and splendid vigor, long after the last vestige of the hostility that evoked it has passed away. The other notable song is Julia Ward Howe's " Battle Hymn of the Republic," whose swinging, deep-toned measures form a significant contrast to Randall's high-pitched lyric. The two poems are, indeed, typical of the two sections. One surges forward with the fire and dash of Southern temperament through an impassioned

WALT WHITMAN DURING THE WAR

The most individual of American poets was born at Westhills, Long Island, in 1809, the son of a carpenter. He early learned the trade of printing; at twenty he was editor and publisher of a paper. For many years he was traveling all over the West of that day, from New Orleans to Canada. In 1855 he brought out the first edition of "Leaves of Grass," at first a thin volume of ninety-four pages, later growing until it had become several times the size of the original. At the end of the second year of the Civil War, Whitman went to Washington to care for his brother, who had been wounded in the battle of Fredericksburg. For the next three years he served as an army nurse, chiefly in the hospitals of Washington. The literary outcome of this experience was "Drum Taps," from which the poems in the present volume are taken, and which he described as "a little book containing life's darkness and blood-dripping wounds and psalms of the dead." For several years after the war he remained in Government employ in Washington, but in 1873 he moved to Camden, New Jersey, where in 1892 he died in cheerful poverty.

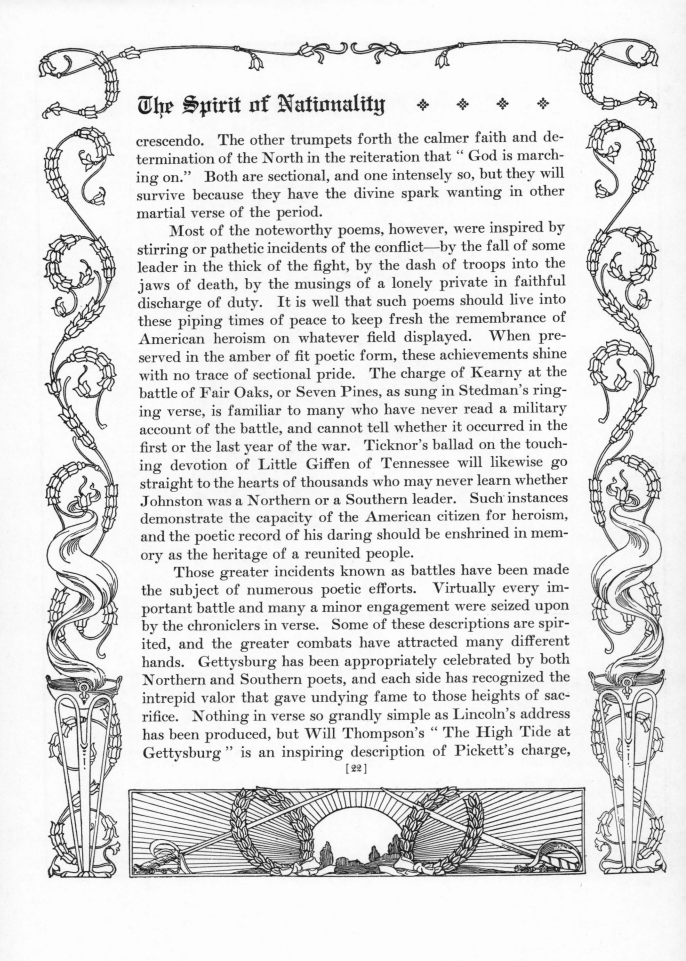

crescendo. The other trumpets forth the calmer faith and determination of the North in the reiteration that "God is marching on." Both are sectional, and one intensely so, but they will survive because they have the divine spark wanting in other martial verse of the period.

Most of the noteworthy poems, however, were inspired by stirring or pathetic incidents of the conflict—by the fall of some leader in the thick of the fight, by the dash of troops into the jaws of death, by the musings of a lonely private in faithful discharge of duty. It is well that such poems should live into these piping times of peace to keep fresh the remembrance of American heroism on whatever field displayed. When preserved in the amber of fit poetic form, these achievements shine with no trace of sectional pride. The charge of Kearny at the battle of Fair Oaks, or Seven Pines, as sung in Stedman's ringing verse, is familiar to many who have never read a military account of the battle, and cannot tell whether it occurred in the first or the last year of the war. Ticknor's ballad on the touching devotion of Little Giffen of Tennessee will likewise go straight to the hearts of thousands who may never learn whether Johnston was a Northern or a Southern leader. Such instances demonstrate the capacity of the American citizen for heroism, and the poetic record of his daring should be enshrined in memory as the heritage of a reunited people.

Those greater incidents known as battles have been made the subject of numerous poetic efforts. Virtually every important battle and many a minor engagement were seized upon by the chroniclers in verse. Some of these descriptions are spirited, and the greater combats have attracted many different hands. Gettysburg has been appropriately celebrated by both Northern and Southern poets, and each side has recognized the intrepid valor that gave undying fame to those heights of sacrifice. Nothing in verse so grandly simple as Lincoln's address has been produced, but Will Thompson's "The High Tide at Gettysburg" is an inspiring description of Pickett's charge,

JAMES RUSSELL LOWELL IN 1863

The poet who recited his ode at the Harvard Commemoration looked thus on that memorable occasion. He was born in 1819 at Cambridge, Massachusetts, of a long line of eminent New Englanders. In Harvard he was poet of his class. During the Mexican War he won immense popularity by his series of satirical poems in Yankee dialect, collected in 1848 as "The Biglow Papers." In 1855 he was appointed to succeed Longfellow in the Smith Professorship of Modern Languages. The additional distinction he had gained as editor of *The Atlantic Monthly* and later of *The North American Review* made him the logical poet at the commemoration service held by Harvard University on July 21, 1865, for its students and graduates who had perished in the war. His ode, not very enthusiastically received that day, has made him the foremost poet of American patriotism. His later life was filled with varied activities. From 1877 to 1885 he represented this country at Madrid and London. He continued to publish poetry and prose that made him at his death in 1891 the most eminent man of letters in America.

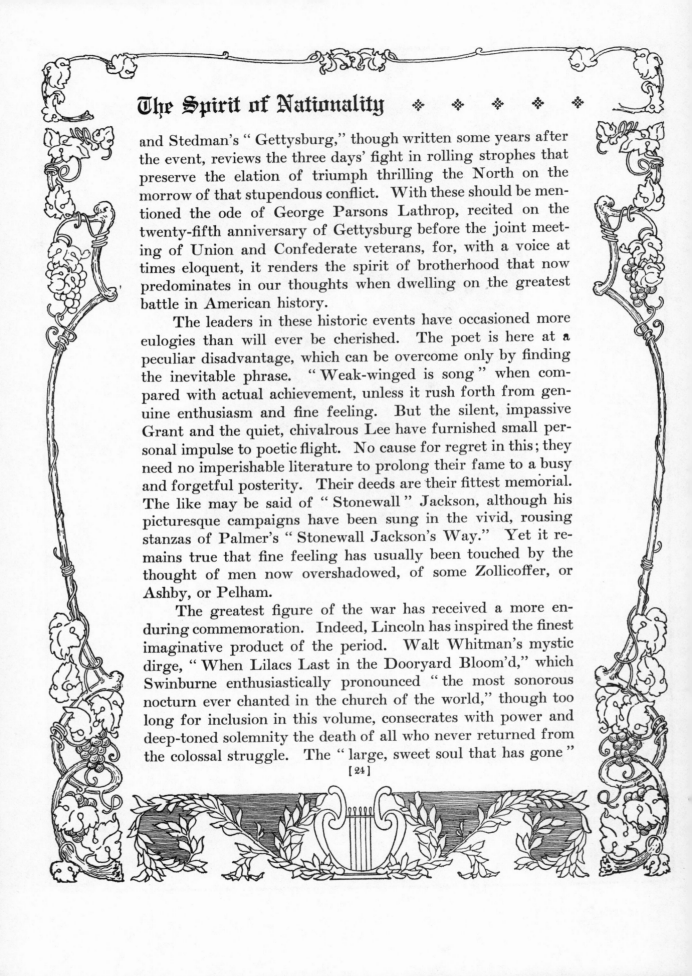

and Stedman's "Gettysburg," though written some years after the event, reviews the three days' fight in rolling strophes that preserve the elation of triumph thrilling the North on the morrow of that stupendous conflict. With these should be mentioned the ode of George Parsons Lathrop, recited on the twenty-fifth anniversary of Gettysburg before the joint meeting of Union and Confederate veterans, for, with a voice at times eloquent, it renders the spirit of brotherhood that now predominates in our thoughts when dwelling on the greatest battle in American history.

The leaders in these historic events have occasioned more eulogies than will ever be cherished. The poet is here at a peculiar disadvantage, which can be overcome only by finding the inevitable phrase. "Weak-winged is song" when compared with actual achievement, unless it rush forth from genuine enthusiasm and fine feeling. But the silent, impassive Grant and the quiet, chivalrous Lee have furnished small personal impulse to poetic flight. No cause for regret in this; they need no imperishable literature to prolong their fame to a busy and forgetful posterity. Their deeds are their fittest memorial. The like may be said of "Stonewall" Jackson, although his picturesque campaigns have been sung in the vivid, rousing stanzas of Palmer's "Stonewall Jackson's Way." Yet it remains true that fine feeling has usually been touched by the thought of men now overshadowed, of some Zollicoffer, or Ashby, or Pelham.

The greatest figure of the war has received a more enduring commemoration. Indeed, Lincoln has inspired the finest imaginative product of the period. Walt Whitman's mystic dirge, "When Lilacs Last in the Dooryard Bloom'd," which Swinburne enthusiastically pronounced "the most sonorous nocturn ever chanted in the church of the world," though too long for inclusion in this volume, consecrates with power and deep-toned solemnity the death of all who never returned from the colossal struggle. The "large, sweet soul that has gone"

SIDNEY LANIER IN 1879

Sidney Lanier's war poems "The Death of Stonewall Jackson" and "The Tournament" appear in this volume. Lanier was born in Macon, Georgia, February 3, 1842. In early childhood he developed a passion for music, learning to play on many instruments without instruction. At eighteen he graduated from Oglethorpe University with the highest honors in his class. Soon after the war broke out he marched to the front with the Second Georgia Battalion of the Macon Volunteers, served through the Seven Days' Battles before Richmond, then spent two exciting years along the James in the Confederate Signal Service, and in August, 1864, was transferred to a blockade runner plying between Wilmington, North Carolina, and the Bermudas, which was captured in November of the same year. Thereafter Lanier was imprisoned for four months in Point Lookout Prison, Maryland. On securing his freedom he was emaciated to a skeleton, with the seeds of tuberculosis already developing. After the war he studied law with his father and practised for a time, but when it became apparent that he might not survive for many years, he courageously determined to devote his powers to music and literature. He settled in Baltimore in 1873 as first flute in the Peabody Symphony Concerts, eagerly studied the two arts of his love, attracted attention by his poems, and received national recognition in 1876 through the invitation to write the Centennial "Cantata." A noble feature of his writings is the absence of all sectionalism and the broadly national spirit that breathes through his verse. In 1879 he was appointed to a lectureship in literature in the recently founded Johns Hopkins University. He was winning recognition when the end came in 1881 in the mountains of North Carolina.

was there mourned in a symbolic way, but Whitman spoke in a poignant, personal way in "O Captain, My Captain," which, partly on that account and partly because of its more conventional poetic form, has become much more popular. Loftier in its flight is the ode recited by Lowell at the Harvard commemoration for her sons slain in battle. The idealism of the poet there attained its most inspired utterance, and in particular the section on Lincoln has been taken up by the whole Nation as the highest and truest characterization of the martyred President.

The features thus commemorated, however, are not peculiar to our Civil War. There have been other occasions for the display of heroism, other fields where pathetic incidents call for tears, other conflicts where leaders have arisen whom whole nations have delighted to honor. What is peculiar to the American Civil War is the generous feeling of reconciliation—the spirit of nationality which has developed since the close of hostilities.

When once the battle was joined, the forces of common tradition and of common blood asserted themselves inevitably. Numerous poems depicted scenes on the battlefield where sons of the same mother clutched each other in the death-grapple. A Southern production, popular throughout the land, was John Reuben Thompson's "Music in Camp," which in simple rimes pictured the soldiers of the recently contending hosts as hushed into silence by their recollections of home. But it is a striking fact that, in the beginning of hostilities, the poems on the Southern side were much more intense and inspired than those produced in the North. Only the fear of dissolution aroused in all its strength the latent devotion to the central Government. Only then throughout the North—

> They closed the ledger and they stilled the loom,
>   The plough left rusting in the prairie farm;
> They saw but "Union" in the gathering gloom;
>   The tearless women helped the men to arm.

[26]

HENRY TIMROD IN 1865

Henry Timrod, born in Charleston, South Carolina, in 1829, devoted himself during all his brief life to the service of his native city and State. During his early education in the Charleston schools his love of poetry was already apparent. After leaving the University of Georgia, on account of ill-health and lack of means, he studied law for a time in Charleston. His poetic convictions led him to withdraw from the profession and accept a position as private tutor. Among the literary men of the city he soon became known as one of the choicest spirits. At the outbreak of the Civil War he entered service as a volunteer, but was ordered back by the physician as soon as he reached the front. He fired Southern hearts with several martial lyrics, proclaiming the resolution of the Confederacy to fight to the death and inspiring thousands to an intenser determination. Up to 1864 he was an army correspondent. In that year he settled in Columbia as an editor of the *South Carolinian*. In 1867 he died of tuberculosis, courageous to the end. His biographer records that "His latest occupation was correcting the proof-sheets of his own poems, and he passed away with them by his side, stained with his life-blood."

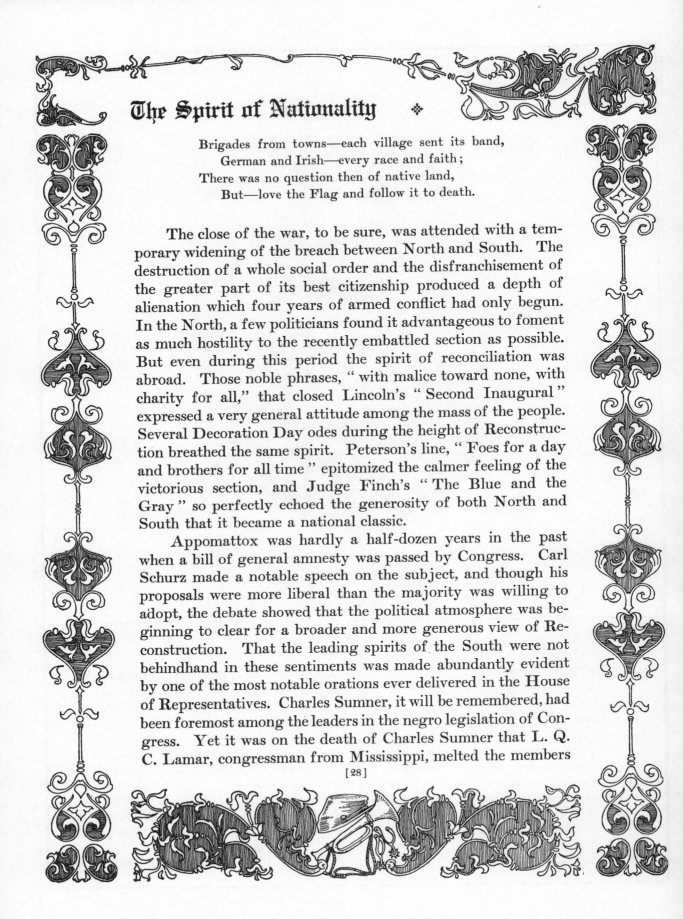

The Spirit of Nationality ❖

Brigades from towns—each village sent its band,
   German and Irish—every race and faith;
There was no question then of native land,
   But—love the Flag and follow it to death.

The close of the war, to be sure, was attended with a temporary widening of the breach between North and South. The destruction of a whole social order and the disfranchisement of the greater part of its best citizenship produced a depth of alienation which four years of armed conflict had only begun. In the North, a few politicians found it advantageous to foment as much hostility to the recently embattled section as possible. But even during this period the spirit of reconciliation was abroad. Those noble phrases, " with malice toward none, with charity for all," that closed Lincoln's " Second Inaugural" expressed a very general attitude among the mass of the people. Several Decoration Day odes during the height of Reconstruction breathed the same spirit. Peterson's line, " Foes for a day and brothers for all time" epitomized the calmer feeling of the victorious section, and Judge Finch's " The Blue and the Gray" so perfectly echoed the generosity of both North and South that it became a national classic.

Appomattox was hardly a half-dozen years in the past when a bill of general amnesty was passed by Congress. Carl Schurz made a notable speech on the subject, and though his proposals were more liberal than the majority was willing to adopt, the debate showed that the political atmosphere was beginning to clear for a broader and more generous view of Reconstruction. That the leading spirits of the South were not behindhand in these sentiments was made abundantly evident by one of the most notable orations ever delivered in the House of Representatives. Charles Sumner, it will be remembered, had been foremost among the leaders in the negro legislation of Congress. Yet it was on the death of Charles Sumner that L. Q. C. Lamar, congressman from Mississippi, melted the members

LUCIUS Q C. LAMAR IN 1879

Taken only five years after his "Eulogy of Sumner," this photograph preserves the noble features of Lamar as he stood before the House of Representatives in 1874. He was born in Georgia in 1825, studied at Emory College in that State, graduating at twenty; and soon began the practice of law. In a few years he moved to Oxford, Mississippi, where he became a professor of mathematics in the State University, and continued his legal practice. His reputation as a speaker dates from 1851, when he met Senator Foote in joint debate and ⌐ borne from the platform in triumph by the students of the University. Six years later he went to Congress from that district. During the war he served in the army until his health gave way, when he was sent as commissioner to Russia. In 1872 he was elected to Congress. Two years later, he was the best known Southerner in Washington because of his "Eulogy of Sumner." From 1877 to 1885 he represented Mississippi in the Senate. In 1885 he became Secretary of the Interior under Cleveland, and in 1887 he was appointed to the Supreme Court, where he served with distinction. His death in 1893 called forth tributes to his noble character and high patriotism from North and South alike.

of the House to tears and woke the applause of the Nation by a eulogy conceived in the most magnanimous temper and closing with a plea for a fuller understanding and a closer union.

How quickly the prayer was being answered appeared in 1876. The hundredth anniversary of the signing of the Declaration of Independence was celebrated by the International Industrial Exhibition at Philadelphia. The honor of writing the official cantata for this national occasion was conferred upon the Southern poet, Sidney Lanier. The cantata, composed for Dudley Buck's music, was sung " in the open air, by a chorus of many hundred voices, and with the accompaniment of a majestic orchestra." Daniel Coit Gilman thus describes the occasion: " The devotional exercises awakened no sentiment of reverence. At length came the cantata. From the overture to the closing cadence it held the attention of the vast throng of listeners, and when it was concluded loud applause rang through the air. A noble conception had been nobly rendered." The same glorification of American freedom was expressed by Lanier in the freer poetic form of the " Psalm of the West," and by including the revised ballad, " The Tournament," he voiced his own joy at the uniting of the recently antagonistic sections.

The celebration itself, followed by the immense wave of enthusiasm that ran over the country, and taken in connection with the withdrawal of Federal troops from the South in the early weeks of the Hayes administration, was significant in many ways. In the South, it marked the return to power of the responsible classes; in the North, the return of political parties to something nearer equality; and in the country as a whole, the confirmation of a conviction, arising from the panic of 1873, that problems unconnected with the war were in most pressing need of solution. The resulting consciousness of national unity, deeper and broader than had existed before, was hastened by the gathering of economic forces for an unparalleled material development. The civilization of the South was in a few

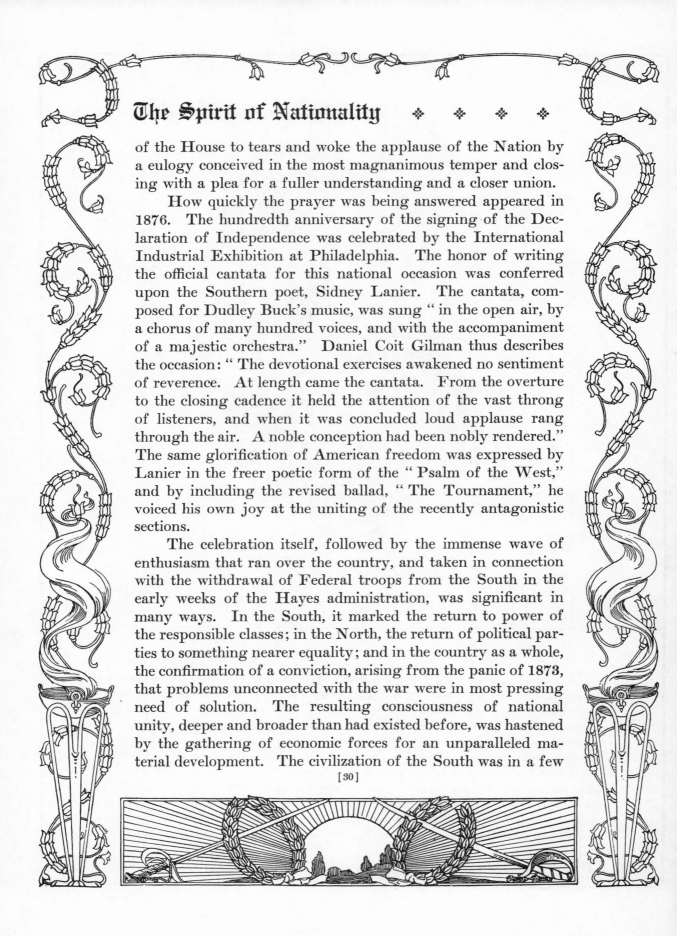

HENRY WOODFIN GRADY
THE HERALD OF THE NEW SOUTH

The Southerner who made himself famous, in 1886, by his New York address on "The New South" was born in Athens, Georgia, in 1851. After graduating at the University of Georgia, in his native town, he studied in the University of Virginia. His qualities of leadership appeared at an early age while he was editing the *Courier* of Rome, Georgia. The proprietor would not allow him to print an article denouncing a political ring, whereupon young Grady bought two other papers of the town, combined them, and carried on his campaign. After some experience on the New York *Herald* he served as reporter on the Atlanta *Constitution*. In 1880 he purchased a fourth interest in the paper and became the managing editor. He was soon recognized as a moving spirit in the progress of his city and the whole South. The reputation he gained as a speaker and editor secured him the invitation from the New England Society of New York to respond to the toast, "The South," at its banquet on December 22, 1886. The response, which was largely impromptu, was copied all over the country and brought him to a position of national importance. Some critics, however, consider his speech before the Merchants' Association of Boston in December, 1889, a superior performance, It was also his last. Hardly had he returned home when the whole Nation was grieved by the news of his death, on December 23, 1889. Every leading newspaper in the country commented upon his labors for the progress of brotherly feeling between the North and the South.

years transformed from the purely agricultural condition of ante-bellum times. Coal and iron were found in untold quantities beneath the fertile soil. Manufactures developed with astonishing rapidity. Railways and telegraph lines spread a network over the entire section. Millions of Northern capital were poured in a quickening stream upon these newly springing industries. Amid such absorbing and multifarious activities, the old alienation receded into a hazy background. The South was no longer a peculiar section founded on a distinct civilization. It shared the interests of the whole mighty and growing Republic, and it became proud of this unification, eager to have its part in the national life everywhere recognized.

The most conspicuous Southern leader in the progress of nationalization was Henry W. Grady, of Georgia. His father, a Confederate soldier on the staff of General Gordon, met his death at Petersburg in the attack on Fort Stedman only two weeks before the surrender at Appomattox. Yet the son looked back on the conflict with no feeling of bitterness. "With the eyes of a statesman and the heart of a patriot," he lent his great energy, his talent for organization, his influence as a journalist to fostering the spirit of activity that had now awakened throughout his section. Better still, in all his public speeches he endeavored to bring about a more thorough understanding between the North and the South. A recognition of his prominence came in the first invitation extended a Southerner to address the New England Society of New York city. His address on the evening of December 22, 1886, not only brought him national renown, but became one of the most important events in the unification of the once-sundered sections.

The illness and death of Grant, in 1885, had already shown to what extent cordiality of feeling was displacing the old antagonism and alienation. From all over the country came messages of sympathy during the last months of his life, especially at the time when it was thought he was at death's door. Among his last words were: "I am thankful for the providential

OLIVER WENDELL HOLMES IN WAR-TIME

Something of Holmes' gracious personality and his fastidious care for personal appearance may be traced in the portrait. The writer of "Brother Jonathan," the first selection in this volume, was born in Cambridge, Massachusetts, in 1809. He graduated from Harvard at the age of twenty. At twenty-one he was famous for the stirring verses, "Old Ironsides," which preserved the old frigate *Constitution* from destruction. In 1836, after several years spent in studying medicine both in Harvard and abroad, he began practice in Boston. It is said that he made the announcement, "The smallest fevers thankfully received." Certainly he is best known as a humorist. After some twenty years he was an honored professor in the Harvard Law School and a much sought after poet for social occasions. But in 1857 his series of essays in *The Atlantic Monthly*, under the title "The Autocrat of the Breakfast Table," brought him national recognition. Their wit and humor have made them the most popular essays written in America, and they have gained wide reception in England. He also wrote three novels, the best known of which is "Elsie Venner." Many of his poems, such as "The Last Leaf" and "Dorothy" will long continue to give him a warm place in the public heart. The poem in this volume, "Brother Jonathan's Lament for Sister Caroline," is characteristic of Holmes' kindly disposition—striking as a piece of prophecy before the war had really begun. The last thirty-four years of his life, ending in 1894, were filled with a large variety of literary work.

extension of my time to enable me to continue my work. I am further thankful, and in a much greater degree thankful, because it has enabled me to see for myself the happy harmony which has so suddenly sprung up between those engaged but a few short years ago in deadly conflict." Grant's gratitude was well founded. With only insignificant exceptions, the Southern press showed that the harmony was real. So representative a newspaper as *The Mobile Register* used this language: " The South unites with the North in paying tribute to his memory. He saved the Union. For this triumph—and time has shown it to be a triumph for the South as well as the North—he is entitled to, and will receive, the grateful tribute of the millions who in the course of time will crowd this continent with a hundred imperial States, and spread to the world the blessings of republican freedom."

Grant's thankfulness for the spirit of brotherhood was shared by the survivors of the hosts he led. From July 2 to 4, 1887, was held the most impressive celebration of the decade, the joint meeting on the field of Gettysburg of the survivors of the Philadelphia brigade of the Union army and of Pickett's division of the Confederate army. As part of the program, it was intended to return the Confederate standards captured by the Pennsylvania troops. The plan failed because of the political turmoil of the time, but the failure did not lessen the heartiness of the good feeling that characterized the occasion. The next year, the Grand Army of the Republic furthered these cordial relations by holding a reunion with the veterans of the Confederate armies on the twenty-fifth anniversary of the great battle. Some three thousand old soldiers were in attendance. The well-known Georgian, General John B. Gordon, delivered an earnest and eloquent address. The New Englander, George William Curtis, followed him. One who was present reports that " his tribute to Confederate valor and the purity of Confederate motives was all that any Southerner could have desired, and brought a genuine glow of pleasure over Longstreet's

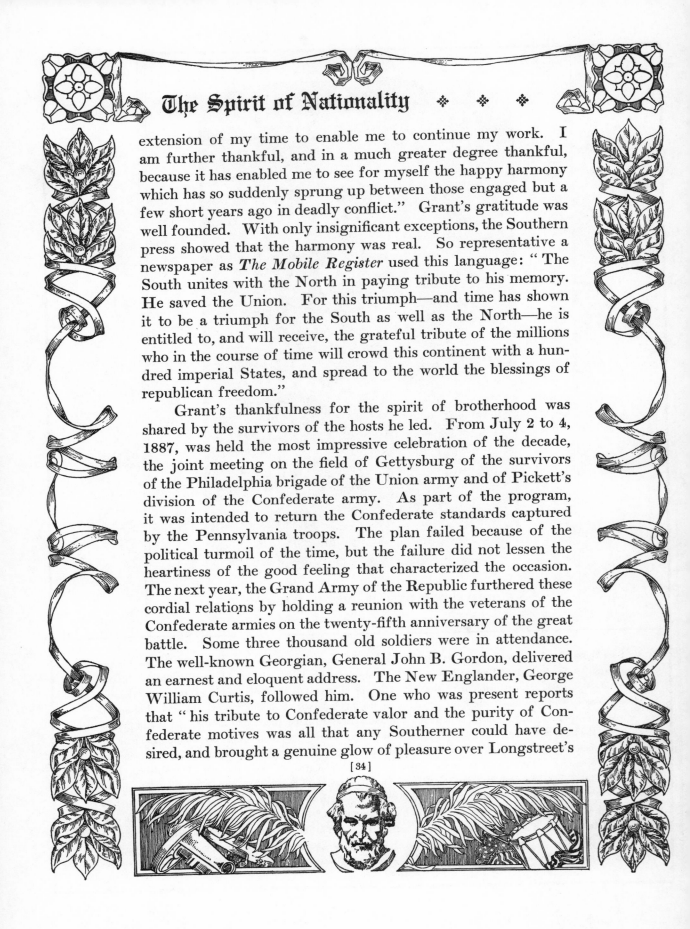

BRET HARTE

One of the most American of American authors, the novelist Francis Bret Harte is represented in this volume by three poems that reveal the lighter vein of his versifying. "The Aged Stranger" is purposely humorous. "John Burns of Gettysburg" is half-humorous. "A Second Review of the Grand Army" has touches of wit in spite of its solemn subject. Harte was born in Albany, New York, in 1839. The gold-fever caught him at fifteen; he wandered to California, where he made more at school-teaching than at gold-digging. At eighteen, he entered newspaper life as a typesetter, and soon worked up to the position of editor-in-chief of the *Weekly Californian*. From 1864 to 1867, while secretary of the United States Mint in San Francisco, he wrote most of his Civil War poems and many humorous verses that made his name familiar in both East and West. During the next two years he was editor of the *Overland Monthly*, publishing in it his best-known stories—"The Luck of Roaring Camp" and "The Outcasts of Poker Flat." In 1871, he left for New York, to devote all his time to writing. Beginning with 1878, he held a succession of consular appointments. In 1885 he settled in England, where he lived till his death in 1902. A born story-teller; Harte put into his vividly realistic scenes from early California life a racy swing combined with universal sentiment that made him popular both at home and abroad.

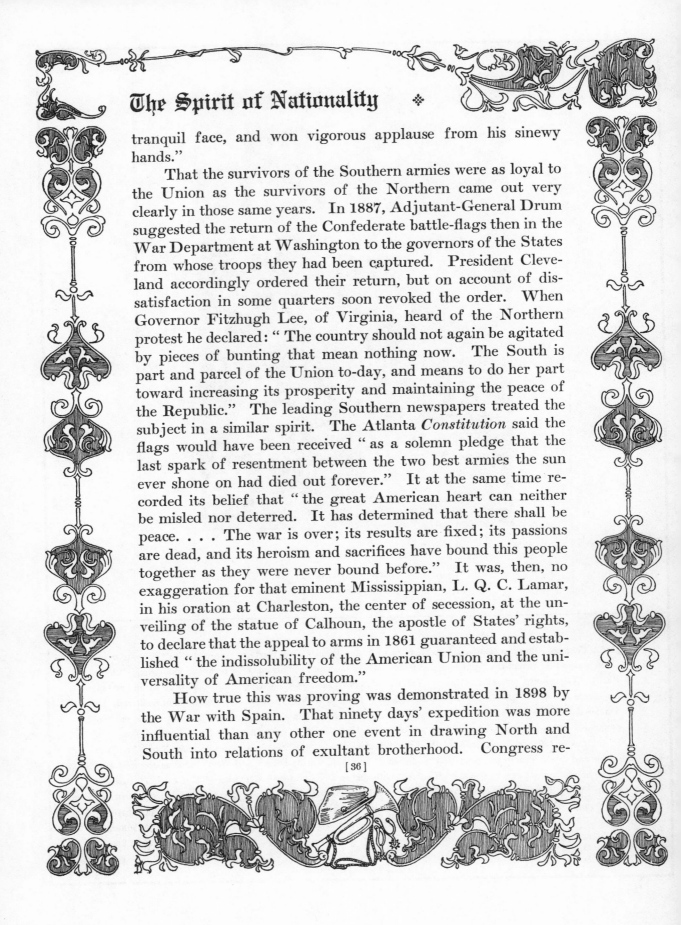

tranquil face, and won vigorous applause from his sinewy hands."

That the survivors of the Southern armies were as loyal to the Union as the survivors of the Northern came out very clearly in those same years. In 1887, Adjutant-General Drum suggested the return of the Confederate battle-flags then in the War Department at Washington to the governors of the States from whose troops they had been captured. President Cleveland accordingly ordered their return, but on account of dissatisfaction in some quarters soon revoked the order. When Governor Fitzhugh Lee, of Virginia, heard of the Northern protest he declared: " The country should not again be agitated by pieces of bunting that mean nothing now. The South is part and parcel of the Union to-day, and means to do her part toward increasing its prosperity and maintaining the peace of the Republic." The leading Southern newspapers treated the subject in a similar spirit. The Atlanta *Constitution* said the flags would have been received " as a solemn pledge that the last spark of resentment between the two best armies the sun ever shone on had died out forever." It at the same time recorded its belief that " the great American heart can neither be misled nor deterred. It has determined that there shall be peace. . . . The war is over; its results are fixed; its passions are dead, and its heroism and sacrifices have bound this people together as they were never bound before." It was, then, no exaggeration for that eminent Mississippian, L. Q. C. Lamar, in his oration at Charleston, the center of secession, at the unveiling of the statue of Calhoun, the apostle of States' rights, to declare that the appeal to arms in 1861 guaranteed and established " the indissolubility of the American Union and the universality of American freedom."

How true this was proving was demonstrated in 1898 by the War with Spain. That ninety days' expedition was more influential than any other one event in drawing North and South into relations of exultant brotherhood. Congress re-

Born in Bordentown, New Jersey, on February 8, 1844, Richard Watson Gilder was educated at Bellvue Seminary, an institution conducted by his father in Flushing, Long Island. At the age of twelve he was publishing a newspaper—a sheet a foot square, entitled *The St. Thomas Register*, for which he wrote all the articles, set all the type, and performed all the press-work. As a member of Landis's Philadelphia battery, he enlisted for the "emergency campaign" of the summer of 1863, and took part in the defense of Carlisle, Pennsylvania, when Lee made the invasion of the North ending at Gettysburg. His long editorial career began the next year, when he joined the staff of the *Newark Advertiser*, of Newark, N. J.

In 1869 he became editor of *Hours at Home*. When it was absorbed by the old *Scribner's Monthly*, Doctor J. G. Holland retained young Gilder as managing editor. Thus at twenty-six he had attained high literary influence. On the death of Doctor Holland, in 1881, Gilder became editor-in-chief of the same magazine, re-named *The Century*. His many poems, chiefly lyrical, gave him distinguished standing among American poets. But his interests exceeded the bounds of literature. All kinds of civic progress engaged his energies. He rendered valuable service in tenement-house reform in New York City and in promoting civil-service reform over the country at large. He died on November 18, 1909.

RICHARD WATSON
GILDER

AS A CADET OF
THE WAR DAYS

moved all discrimination against former Confederate officers, and one of the conspicuous Southern leaders entered the service of the armies against Spain. Newspapers and magazines were filled with expressions of cordiality, such as "Joined the Blues" and "Wheeler at Santiago." This new patriotism was no spasmodic affair of the moment. Political parties were still fervidly debating about imperialism and the colonial policy when the assassination of McKinley, in 1901, startled the whole country. Professor William P. Trent, an acute observer, remarked to me in conversation: "I recall vividly how I had to make a flying trip from North to South at the time, and how impressed I was with the fact that *not a particle of difference* could be noticed between the sections—both were deep in grief. . . . I should say that few events of our time have brought out our essential unity more clearly than his assassination."

The justice of Professor Trent's observation is apparent from a dramatic episode of the next year. When General Charles Francis Adams, a veteran of the Union armies, a New Englander, and the descendant of a long line of distinguished New Englanders, delivered his eulogy on Robert E. Lee, in 1902, it was a sign that extremes had indeed been reconciled. More expressive of popular feeling was an incident almost unnoticed at the time. On February 24, 1905, a bill for returning the Confederate flags was passed in Congress without a single dissenting vote, without even a single moment's debate. This action was the result, not of careful prearrangement, but of spontaneous unanimity among the representatives of an harmonious people. With this impressive proof of the completeness of American union, this record appropriately closes.

DUDLEY H. MILES.

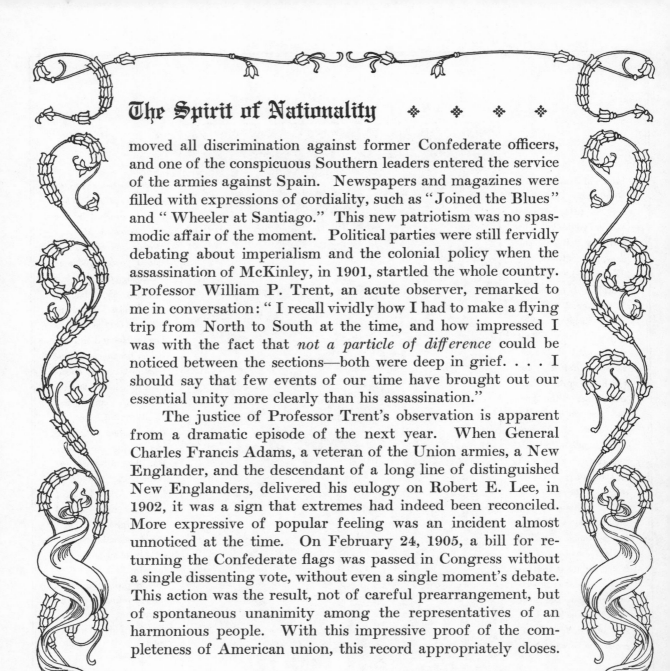

I

SEPARATION
AND
REUNION

"IN VAIN IS
THE STRIFE"
—*Holmes*

RUINS OF CHARLESTON, 1865
FROM THE CIRCULAR CHURCH

SCENES OF '61 THAT QUICKLY FOLLOWED "BROTHER JONA- THAN" (PAGE 44)

The upper photograph shows Confederates on Monday the fifteenth of April, 1861 — one day after the momentous event which Holmes dimly prophesied in "Brother Jonathan" (page 44). The picture below, with the two following, were made on the 16th. As April wore on, North and South alike had been reluctant to strike first. When Major Robert Anderson, on December 26, 1860, removed to Fort Sumter, on an island at the entrance to Charleston

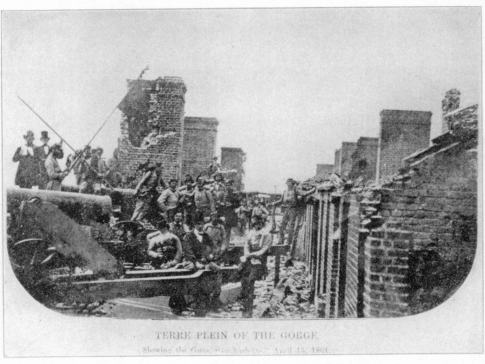

TERRE PLEIN OF THE GORGE.
Showing the Guns, &c. April 15, 1861.

CONFEDERATES IN SUMTER THE DAY AFTER ANDERSON LEFT

NORTHEASTERN ANGLE AND EASTERN FACE OF FORT SUMTER

A GUN TRAINED ON CHARLESTON BY ANDERSON

Harbor, he placed himself in a position to withstand long attack. But he needed supplies. The Confederates would allow none to be landed. When at length rumors of a powerful naval force to relieve the fort reached Charleston, the Confederates demanded the surrender of the garrison. Anderson promised to evacuate by April 15th if he received no additional supplies. His terms were rejected. At half-past four on the morning of April 12th a shell from Fort Johnson "rose high in air, and curving in its course, burst almost directly over the fort." The mighty war had begun.

TWO DAYS AFTER THE BOMBARDMENT OF SUMTER, APRIL 16, 1861

Wade Hampton (the tallest figure) and other leading South Carolinians inspecting the effects of the cannonading that had forced Major Anderson to evacuate, and had precipitated the mightiest conflict of modern times—two days before.

GUNS THAT FIRED ON SUMTER

Below are some of the Confederate guns in the battery near Fort Moultrie that bore upon the fort pictured above. It was the hot shot from Fort Moultrie itself that set fire to the barracks in Fort Sumter about eight o'clock on the morning of April 13th. When the Confederate commanders saw the black smoke rise from the fort, they doubled the fire of the batteries to keep the flames from being extinguished. Sumter did not cease replying, although the intervals between shots became longer as the garrison dashed from spot to spot checking the flames.

NORTH-WEST ANGLE, SHOWING CASEMATES

**THE STARS AND BARS
WAVING OVER THE CAPTURED FORT**

SOUTH-WESTERN ANGLE,
Showing Sand-bag Defences and Columbiads bearing on Fort Sumter, April 16, 1861.

CONFEDERATE GUNS THAT FIRED ON SUMTER

The South Carolinians showed their admiration for their dauntless antagonists by cheering at every shot that replied to them. About half-past twelve of that day the flagstaff on Sumter was shot away. General Beauregard, who was in charge of the operations of Charleston, at once sent three of his aides to inquire if Major Anderson would accept assistance in subduing the flames and to offer terms of surrender. The terms, which allowed the gallant garrison to march out with the honors of war, were at length accepted. The first step in the war had been irrevocably taken.

The damage done by those first guns of the war, "the shots heard around the world," is shown in these faded photographs of April 16, 1861. By five A.M. of April 12th the Confederate batteries were directing a converging fire on Sumter. The garrison did not immediately reply; it had been subsisting on half rations and on this particular morning made a breakfast off pork and damaged rice. At seven it began to return the fire. During the day the duel was unremitting. The whole city poured out to witness the spectacle. The Battery, the fashionable promenade of Charleston, was thronging with

INTERIOR FACE OF GORGE.
Showing Officer's Quarters and Gate-way.

**THE OFFICERS' QUARTERS
WHERE THE FIRE STARTED**

ladies in holiday attire. Early on the next day the officers' quarters in Sumter caught fire from some shells or hot shot. Flames soon spread to the barracks. So fierce was the conflagration that the magazine had to be closed. The men threw themselves on the ground to avoid suffocation. Then Beauregard's terms of evacuation were accepted. On Sunday, April 14th, with colors flying and drums beating, Major Anderson and his little company marched out with a salute to the flag of fifty guns. That day the whole North was steeled to live up to the spirit of Holmes' poem.

WESTERN BARRACKS AND PARADE

THE SHATTERED FLAGSTAFF (TO THE RIGHT)

SEPARATION AND REUNION

BROTHER JONATHAN'S LAMENT FOR SISTER CAROLINE

Both a record and a prophecy are contained in these lines by the New England poet, Oliver Wendell Holmes. A state convention meeting in Charleston had on December 20, 1860, unanimously passed an ordinance of secession, and during January and February six other states had followed. Early in February the Confederate Government had been organized at Montgomery, Alabama, with Jefferson Davis as President. Holmes dated this poem March 25, 1861. Four days later the new President of the United States, Abraham Lincoln, ordered relief to be sent to Fort Sumter in Charleston Harbor. On April 12th the attack on Sumter was made, and the war begun. How fully the sentiment of brotherhood here expressed by Holmes has been realized among the American people it has been the purpose of the Introduction to this volume and of the following selections to show.

She has gone,—she has left us in passion and pride,—
Our stormy-browed sister, so long at our side!
She has torn her own star from our firmament's glow,
And turned on her brother the face of a foe!

O Caroline, Caroline, child of the sun,
We can never forget that our hearts have been one,—
Our foreheads both sprinkled in Liberty's name,
From the fountain of blood with the finger of flame!

You were always too ready to fire at a touch;
But we said: " She is hasty,—she does not mean much."
We have scowled when you uttered some turbulent threat;
But Friendship still whispered: " Forgive and forget! "

Has our love all died out? Have its altars grown cold?
Has the curse come at last which the fathers foretold?
Then Nature must teach us the strength of the chain
That her petulant children would sever in vain.

THE RUINS OF SECESSION HALL, CHARLESTON—1865

Three months before Holmes' poem, South Carolinians had cast the die of separation in Secession Hall. It appears to the right of the Circular Church, across the narrow graveyard, its walls blasted by the fire of December, 1861. Here the vote was taken on December 20, 1860, declaring that "the union now subsisting between South Carolina and the other States under the name of the 'United States of America' is hereby dissolved." The secession convention was composed of the most experienced men in the State—men who had represented it in the national Congress, judges in the highest courts, eminent divines, and wealthy planters. On the fourth day of its session, at twelve o'clock, the ordinance quoted from above was read with flashing eyes by the venerable judge of chancery, Chancellor Inglis. At a quarter past one it was passed unanimously. The doorkeeper passed the word to the policeman without; he called to another, and so on until the sentinel at the massive iron gate proclaimed it to the impatient populace. The bells in every rocking steeple mingled their notes with the shouts of the excited throngs that filled the streets. There was no dissent in the secession sentiments here.

"THOUGH DARKENED WITH SULPHUR"

THE CHARLESTON RAILROAD DEPOT.   DESTROYED BY EXPLOSION IN 1865

These ruins form an impressive fulfilment of the prophecy in Oliver Wendell Holmes' poem.   But it was not till near the end that the scene here preserved could meet the eye.   It resulted from the evacuation of the city by the Confederate forces on February 17, 1865.   This step had been taken with great reluctance.   The movement of secession had begun at Charleston.   The city was dear to every Southern heart.   Yet military policy clearly dictated that the scattered troops in the Carolinas be concentrated against Sherman.   Indeed, it would have been better policy to evacuate earlier.   But sentiment is always powerful.   Even Jefferson Davis said, "Such full preparation had been made that I had hoped for other and better results, and the disappointment to me is extremely bitter."   When the Union troops from Morris Island arrived in Charleston the next morning, they found that the commissary depot had been blown up with the loss of two hundred lives, mostly of women and children.   An officer reported "Public buildings, stores, warehouses, private dwellings, shipping, etc., were burning and being burned by armed Confederates."   All the Negroes in the city were impressed by the Union officers to work the fire apparatus until all the fires were extinguished. But some of the fairest sections of Charleston were already in ruins.

"IN VAIN IS THE STRIFE"

THE ROMAN CATHOLIC CATHEDRAL OF ST. JOHN AND ST. FINBAR, DESTROYED BY THE FIRE OF DECEMBER, 1861—MOST OF THE ABLE BODIED
CITIZENS WERE SERVING AS SOLDIERS, AND THE FLAMES RAGED UNCHECKED.

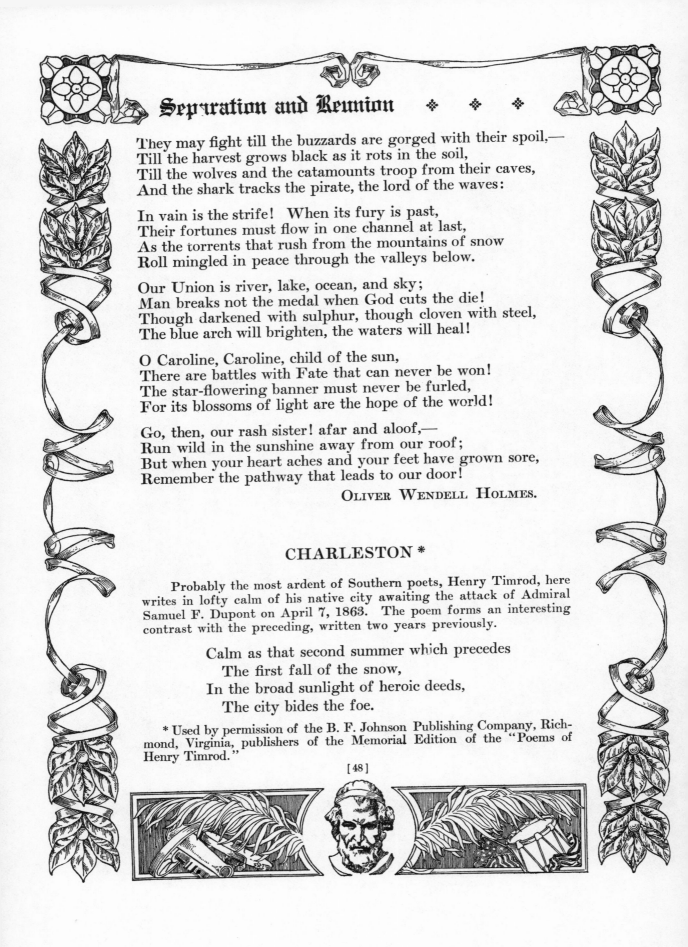

Separation and Reunion ❖ ❖ ❖

They may fight till the buzzards are gorged with their spoil,—
Till the harvest grows black as it rots in the soil,
Till the wolves and the catamounts troop from their caves,
And the shark tracks the pirate, the lord of the waves:

In vain is the strife! When its fury is past,
Their fortunes must flow in one channel at last,
As the torrents that rush from the mountains of snow
Roll mingled in peace through the valleys below.

Our Union is river, lake, ocean, and sky;
Man breaks not the medal when God cuts the die!
Though darkened with sulphur, though cloven with steel,
The blue arch will brighten, the waters will heal!

O Caroline, Caroline, child of the sun,
There are battles with Fate that can never be won!
The star-flowering banner must never be furled,
For its blossoms of light are the hope of the world!

Go, then, our rash sister! afar and aloof,—
Run wild in the sunshine away from our roof;
But when your heart aches and your feet have grown sore,
Remember the pathway that leads to our door!

OLIVER WENDELL HOLMES.

CHARLESTON *

Probably the most ardent of Southern poets, Henry Timrod, here writes in lofty calm of his native city awaiting the attack of Admiral Samuel F. Dupont on April 7, 1863. The poem forms an interesting contrast with the preceding, written two years previously.

Calm as that second summer which precedes
    The first fall of the snow,
In the broad sunlight of heroic deeds,
    The city bides the foe.

* Used by permission of the B. F. Johnson Publishing Company, Richmond, Virginia, publishers of the Memorial Edition of the "Poems of Henry Timrod."

[48]

"THE CITY BIDES THE FOE"

The picture of Confederate artillerymen sighting a field-piece in the outskirts of Charleston shows that there were active preparations for the expected attack. The city had, indeed, been put in a thorough state of defense by General Beauregard, who had assumed command on September 15, 1862. The forts at the entrance to the harbor were strengthened or partly rebuilt, and the waters sown with torpedoes and obstructions. The poet therefore had good reason for awaiting so calmly the naval attack of April 7, 1863. In the lower photograph, St. Michael's and the principal street of Charleston are preserved for us by the Confederate photographer Cook, just as they appeared when Timrod wrote his lines. The city was indeed a very busy one, for constant blockade-running had brought in ample munitions of war and many luxuries. It was no idle boast that Summer was brought to her courts, for silks and spices came in with every cargo. Later on, the blockading fleet, though it did not succeed in reducing Charleston, made blockade-running so dangerous that a constantly decreasing number of laden vessels arrived at the piers.

"THROUGH STREETS STILL ECHOING WITH TRADE"

CHARLESTON IN WAR TIME

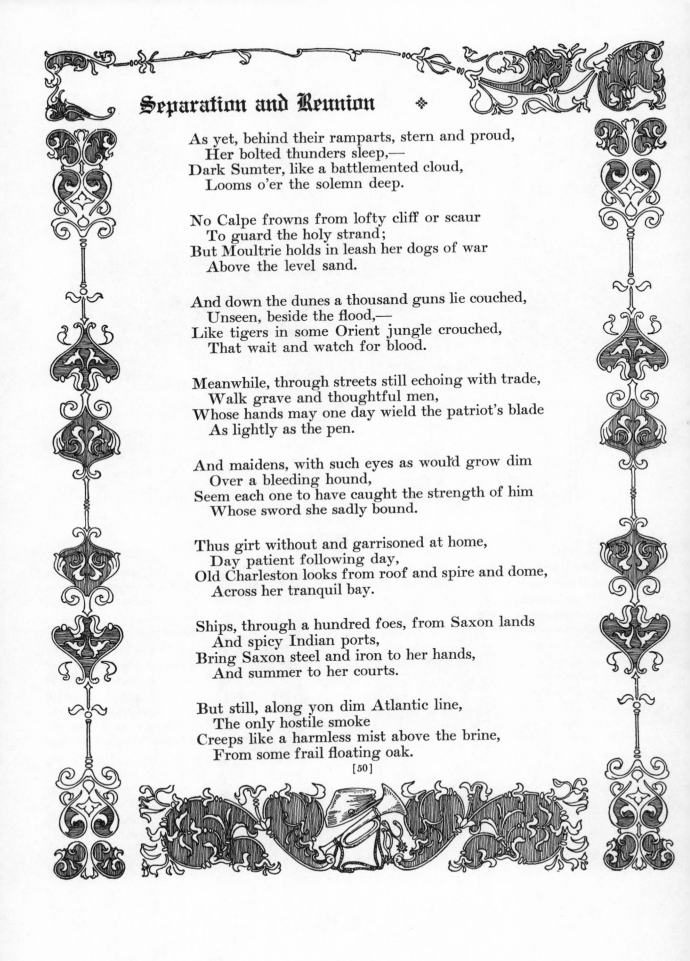

Separation and Reunion ❖

As yet, behind their ramparts, stern and proud,
    Her bolted thunders sleep,—
Dark Sumter, like a battlemented cloud,
    Looms o'er the solemn deep.

No Calpe frowns from lofty cliff or scaur
    To guard the holy strand;
But Moultrie holds in leash her dogs of war
    Above the level sand.

And down the dunes a thousand guns lie couched,
    Unseen, beside the flood,—
Like tigers in some Orient jungle crouched,
    That wait and watch for blood.

Meanwhile, through streets still echoing with trade,
    Walk grave and thoughtful men,
Whose hands may one day wield the patriot's blade
    As lightly as the pen.

And maidens, with such eyes as would grow dim
    Over a bleeding hound,
Seem each one to have caught the strength of him
    Whose sword she sadly bound.

Thus girt without and garrisoned at home,
    Day patient following day,
Old Charleston looks from roof and spire and dome,
    Across her tranquil bay.

Ships, through a hundred foes, from Saxon lands
    And spicy Indian ports,
Bring Saxon steel and iron to her hands,
    And summer to her courts.

But still, along yon dim Atlantic line,
    The only hostile smoke
Creeps like a harmless mist above the brine,
    From some frail floating oak.

"SHE WAITS THE TRIUMPH OR THE TOMB"

THE BOMBARDED GRAVEYARD OF THE CENTRAL CHURCH AT CHARLESTON

The event awaited by Timrod with faith and resignation is here directly illustrated. A sacred spot in the beautiful city of Charleston has been visited by Federal bombs. The tombs of its honored ancestors lie shattered where the ruins of fair mansions look down upon the scene. The cannonading that wrought this havoc was conducted by the Federal army under General Q. A. Gillmore after the failure of Admiral S. F. Du Pont's attack of April 7, 1863. The bombardment of the city was begun on August 21, 1863, by the famous gun, the "Swamp Angel," to enforce the evacuation of Fort Sumter. But Sumter, though reduced to a shapeless mass of ruins, did not surrender. On September 7, 1863, however, Gillmore succeeded in capturing Battery Wagner and Battery Gregg, on the northern part of Morris Island. One 30-pounder Parrott gun sent 4,523 shells toward the city, many of them landing within it destructively.

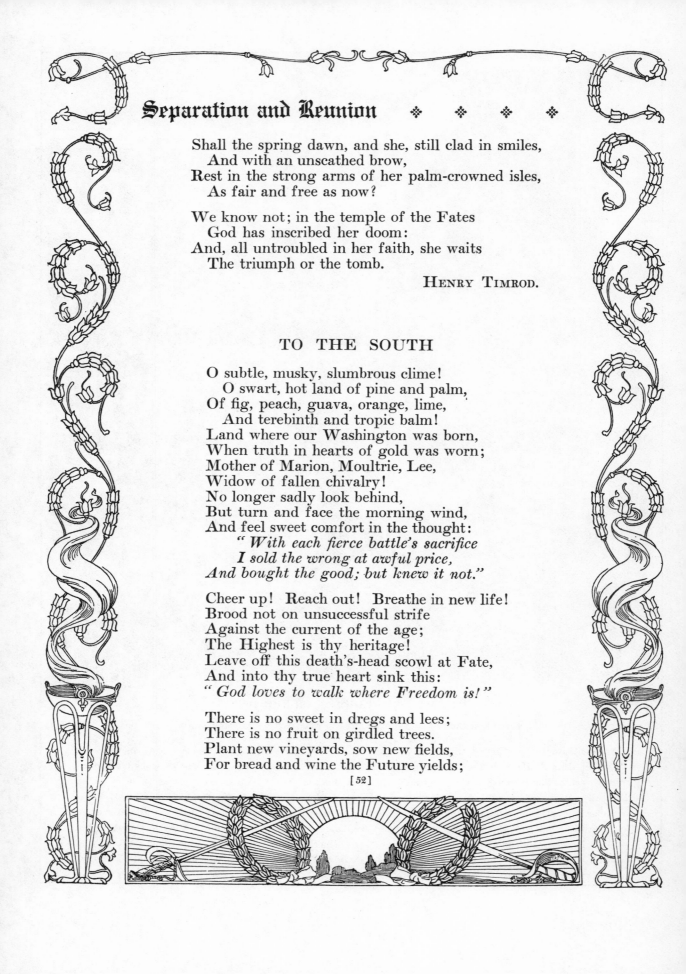

Separation and Reunion ❖ ❖ ❖ ❖

Shall the spring dawn, and she, still clad in smiles,
  And with an unscathed brow,
Rest in the strong arms of her palm-crowned isles,
  As fair and free as now?

We know not; in the temple of the Fates
  God has inscribed her doom:
And, all untroubled in her faith, she waits
  The triumph or the tomb.

                                      HENRY TIMROD.

TO THE SOUTH

O subtle, musky, slumbrous clime!
  O swart, hot land of pine and palm,
Of fig, peach, guava, orange, lime,
  And terebinth and tropic balm!
Land where our Washington was born,
When truth in hearts of gold was worn;
Mother of Marion, Moultrie, Lee,
Widow of fallen chivalry!
No longer sadly look behind,
But turn and face the morning wind,
And feel sweet comfort in the thought:
    *"With each fierce battle's sacrifice
    I sold the wrong at awful price,
And bought the good; but knew it not."*

Cheer up! Reach out! Breathe in new life!
Brood not on unsuccessful strife
Against the current of the age;
The Highest is thy heritage!
Leave off this death's-head scowl at Fate,
And into thy true heart sink this:
"God loves to walk where Freedom is!"

There is no sweet in dregs and lees;
There is no fruit on girdled trees.
Plant new vineyards, sow new fields,
For bread and wine the Future yields;

"O SUBTLE, MUSKY, SLUMBEROUS CLIME"

Down the lofty nave of this forest cathedral, gleams under the open sky the tomb of some long-honored fore-father of Savannah.   The gigantic live-oaks of the stately plantation, festooned with the long Spanish moss, shadow the fragrant shrubbery growing at their feet.   The whole scene breathes the "subtle, musky, slum-berous" atmosphere sung by the poet Thompson.   Savannah, situated inland on the Savannah River, was through four years of the war unvisited by hostile armies.   But in December, 1864, it fell into the hands of Sherman's troops.   Many another lovely spot in the Southland passed through the conflict with its beauties undisturbed, as if to remind its brave people of the unbounded lavishness of nature amid the wreckage of war.   Bravely have they answered the mute appeal of such surroundings.   To-day the South can point, not only to the charms of its almost tropical clime, but to the material achievements which link it inseparably with the rapidly developing North and West.   Its people have even come to feel a thankfulness for the out-come of the war.   Typical are the whole-hearted vigorous lines of Maurice Thompson printed opposite.

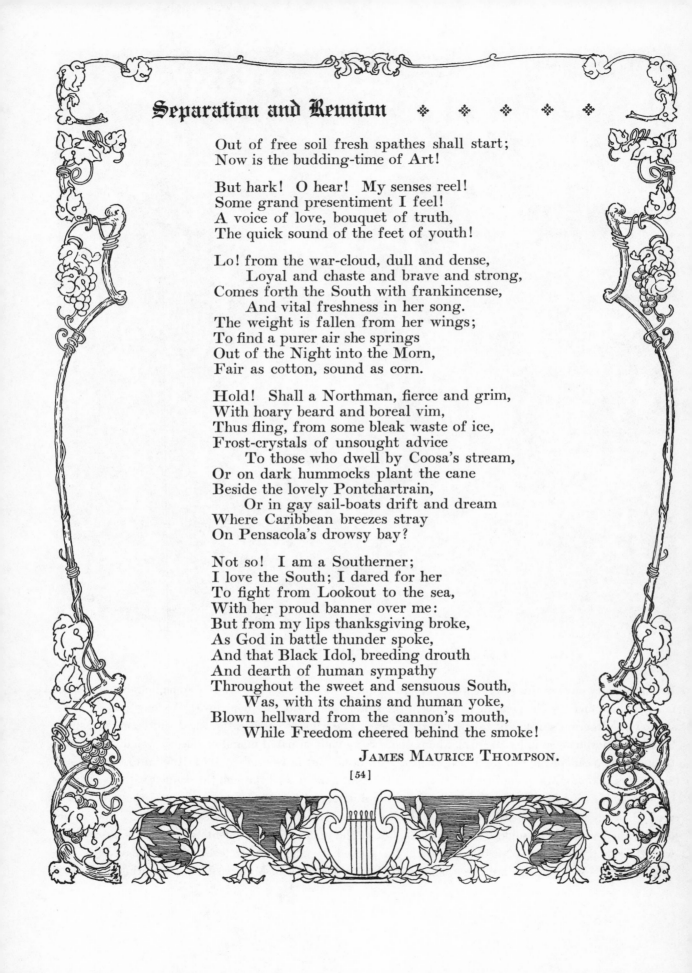

Separation and Reunion ✦ ✦ ✦ ✦ ✦

Out of free soil fresh spathes shall start;
Now is the budding-time of Art!

But hark! O hear! My senses reel!
Some grand presentiment I feel!
A voice of love, bouquet of truth,
The quick sound of the feet of youth!

Lo! from the war-cloud, dull and dense,
    Loyal and chaste and brave and strong,
Comes forth the South with frankincense,
    And vital freshness in her song.
The weight is fallen from her wings;
To find a purer air she springs
Out of the Night into the Morn,
Fair as cotton, sound as corn.

Hold! Shall a Northman, fierce and grim,
With hoary beard and boreal vim,
Thus fling, from some bleak waste of ice,
Frost-crystals of unsought advice
    To those who dwell by Coosa's stream,
Or on dark hummocks plant the cane
Beside the lovely Pontchartrain,
    Or in gay sail-boats drift and dream
Where Caribbean breezes stray
On Pensacola's drowsy bay?

Not so! I am a Southerner;
I love the South; I dared for her
To fight from Lookout to the sea,
With her proud banner over me:
But from my lips thanksgiving broke,
As God in battle thunder spoke,
And that Black Idol, breeding drouth
And dearth of human sympathy
Throughout the sweet and sensuous South,
    Was, with its chains and human yoke,
Blown hellward from the cannon's mouth,
    While Freedom cheered behind the smoke!

JAMES MAURICE THOMPSON.

[54]

II

DEEDS
OF
VALOR

"WHEN GALLANT BURNSIDE MADE DASH UPON
NEW BERNE'

FEDERAL BARRACKS AT NEW BERNE, NORTH CAROLINA, 1862

DEEDS OF VALOR

KEARNY AT SEVEN PINES

Stedman's stirring poem was suggested by a newspaper account of the ringing retort made by General Kearny to a colonel. The military historian, John C. Ropes, writing of the battle at Chantilly, September 1, 1862, says: "The gallant Kearny also was killed, while reconnoitering in front of his troops; a loss which was very deeply felt. He was a man who was made for the profession of arms. In the field he was always ready, always skilful, always brave, always untiring, always hopeful, and always vigilant and alert."

So that soldierly legend is still on its journey,—
    That story of Kearny who knew not to yield!
'Twas the day when with Jameson, fierce Berry, and Birney,
    Against twenty thousand he rallied the field.
Where the red volleys poured, where the clamor rose highest,
    Where the dead lay in clumps through the dwarf oak and
        pine,
Where the aim from the thicket was surest and nighest,—
    No charge like Phil Kearny's along the whole line.

When the battle went ill, and the bravest were solemn,
    Near the dark Seven Pines, where we still held our ground,
He rode down the length of the withering column,
    And his heart at our war-cry leapt up with a bound;
He snuffed, like his charger, the wind of the powder,—
    His sword waved us on and we answered the sign;
Loud our cheer as we rushed, but his laugh rang the louder.
    "There's the devil's own fun, boys, along the whole line!"

How he strode his brown steed! How we saw his blade brighten
    In the one hand still left,—and the reins in his teeth!
He laughed like a boy when the holidays heighten,
    But a soldier's glance shot from his visor beneath.
Up came the reserves to the mellay infernal,
    Asking where to go in,—through the clearing or pine?
"O, anywhere! Forward! 'Tis all the same, Colonel:
    You'll find lovely fighting along the whole line!"

[56]

KEARNY—"HOW WE SAW HIS BLADE BRIGHTEN"

In Brigadier-General Philip Kearny, Stedman selected as the hero of his poem one of the most dashing veteran soldiers in the Civil War. He had entered the army in 1838, at the age of twenty-two, but soon went to France to study cavalry methods. After several months in the school at Saumur he entered the French service and fought with conspicuous gallantry along with veterans of Napoleon in the Arab war against Abd-el-Kader that won Algeria to France. In the American-Mexican War, at the close of the battle of Churubusco, he made a charge into Mexico City, during which he received a wound that necessitated the amputation of an arm. His love of fighting led him across the Atlantic in 1859 to take part in the Italian War against the Austrians. His bravery at Magenta and elsewhere won him the cross of the Legion of Honor. At the outbreak of the Civil War he returned—to his death.

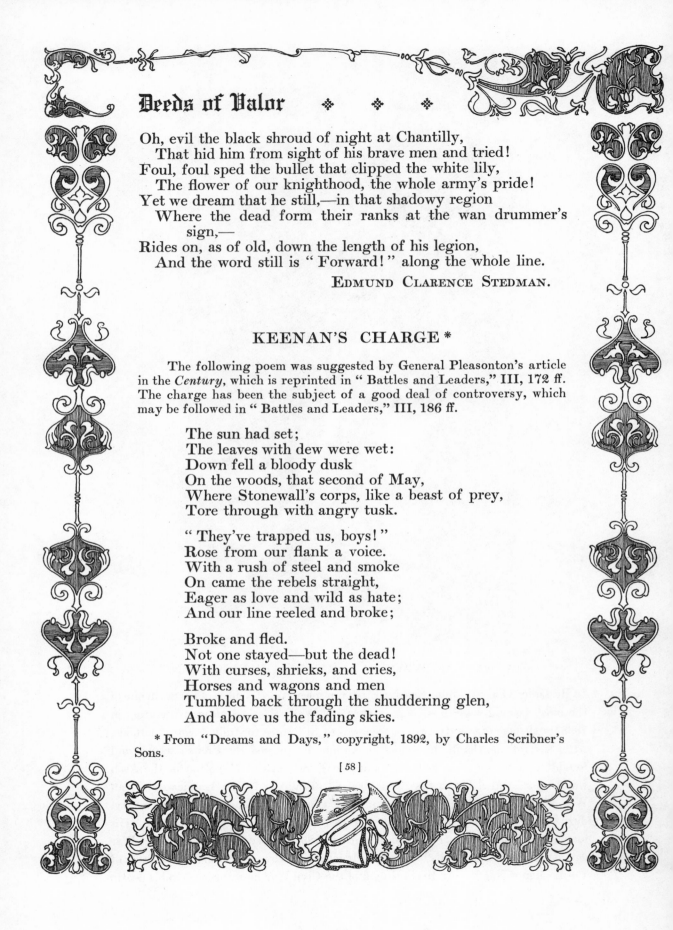

Deeds of Valor ❖ ❖ ❖

Oh, evil the black shroud of night at Chantilly,
    That hid him from sight of his brave men and tried!
Foul, foul sped the bullet that clipped the white lily,
    The flower of our knighthood, the whole army's pride!
Yet we dream that he still,—in that shadowy region
    Where the dead form their ranks at the wan drummer's
        sign,—
Rides on, as of old, down the length of his legion,
    And the word still is "Forward!" along the whole line.

                 EDMUND CLARENCE STEDMAN.

KEENAN'S CHARGE *

    The following poem was suggested by General Pleasonton's article in the *Century*, which is reprinted in "Battles and Leaders," III, 172 ff. The charge has been the subject of a good deal of controversy, which may be followed in "Battles and Leaders," III, 186 ff.

The sun had set;
The leaves with dew were wet:
Down fell a bloody dusk
On the woods, that second of May,
Where Stonewall's corps, like a beast of prey,
Tore through with angry tusk.

"They've trapped us, boys!"
Rose from our flank a voice.
With a rush of steel and smoke
On came the rebels straight,
Eager as love and wild as hate;
And our line reeled and broke;

Broke and fled.
Not one stayed—but the dead!
With curses, shrieks, and cries,
Horses and wagons and men
Tumbled back through the shuddering glen,
And above us the fading skies.

   * From "Dreams and Days," copyright, 1892, by Charles Scribner's Sons.

[58]

KEARNY'S MEN AFTER THE BATTLE OF FAIR OAKS

This photograph directly illustrates Stedman's poem. It is June, 1862. Men of Kearny's brigade, one seated, others standing and sitting by, are gathered before the Widow Allen's house, now used as a hospital after those bloody days, May 31st and June 1st—the battle of Fair Oaks or Seven Pines. McClellan had advanced up the Peninsula to within five miles of Richmond. About noon of May 31st the Confederate attack on the Union troops about Seven Pines threatened to become heavy, but the message for reënforcements did not reach the commanding officer in the rear till three o'clock. General Kearny was sent forward. He thus reports: "On arriving at the field of battle we found certain zigzag rifle-pits sheltering crowds of men, and the enemy firing from abatis and timber in their front. General Casey remarked to me on coming up, 'If you will regain our late camp, the day will still be ours.' I had but the Third Michigan up, but they moved forward with alacrity, dashing into the felled timber, and commenced a desperate but determined contest, heedless of the shell and ball which rained upon them. . . . I directed General Berry [with the Fifth Michigan] to turn the slashings and, fighting, gain the open ground on the enemy's right flank. This was perfectly accomplished. The Thirty-seventh New York was arranged in column to support the attack. Its services in the sequel proved invaluable. In the meanwhile my remaining brigade, the One hundred and fifth and Sixty-third Pennsylvania, came up, under General Jameson. . . . Eight companies of the Sixty-third Pennsylvania, led by Lieutenant-Colonel Morgan and most spiritedly headed by General Jameson, aided by his daring chief of staff, Captain Potter, were pushed through the abatis (the portions never until now occupied by us), and nobly repelled a strong body of the enemy, who, though in a strong line and coming up rapidly and in order, just failed to reach to support this position in time, but who, nothing daunted and with a courage worthy a united cause, halted in battle array and poured in a constant heavy roll of musketry fire."

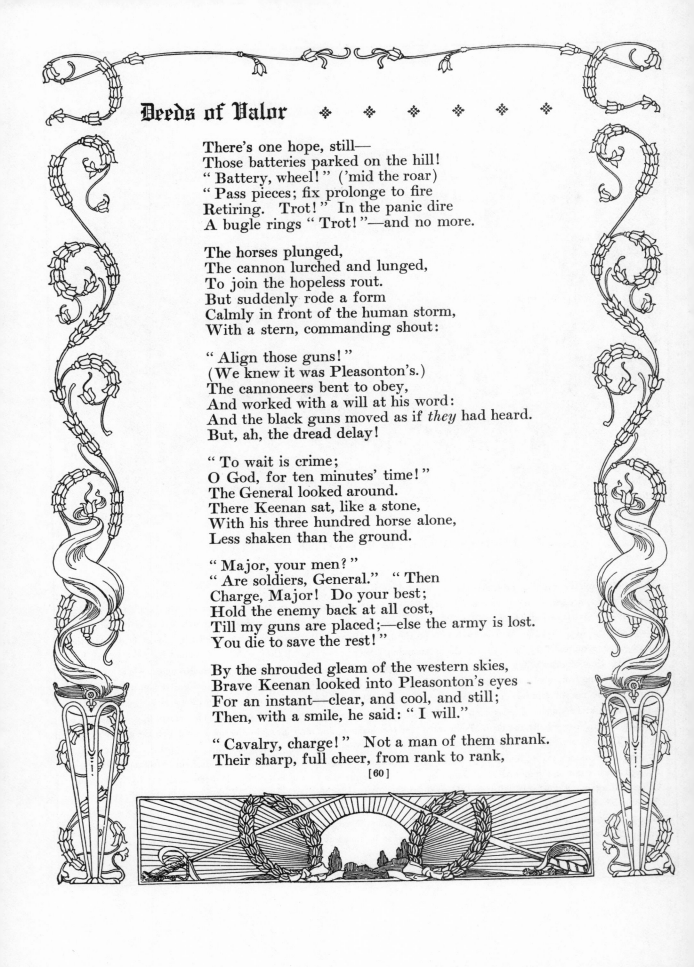

Deeds of Valor ❖ ❖ ❖ ❖ ❖ ❖

There's one hope, still—
Those batteries parked on the hill!
" Battery, wheel! " ('mid the roar)
" Pass pieces; fix prolonge to fire
Retiring. Trot! " In the panic dire
A bugle rings " Trot! "—and no more.

The horses plunged,
The cannon lurched and lunged,
To join the hopeless rout.
But suddenly rode a form
Calmly in front of the human storm,
With a stern, commanding shout:

" Align those guns! "
(We knew it was Pleasonton's.)
The cannoneers bent to obey,
And worked with a will at his word:
And the black guns moved as if *they* had heard.
But, ah, the dread delay!

" To wait is crime;
O God, for ten minutes' time! "
The General looked around.
There Keenan sat, like a stone,
With his three hundred horse alone,
Less shaken than the ground.

" Major, your men? "
" Are soldiers, General."   " Then
Charge, Major! Do your best;
Hold the enemy back at all cost,
Till my guns are placed;—else the army is lost.
You die to save the rest! "

By the shrouded gleam of the western skies,
Brave Keenan looked into Pleasonton's eyes
For an instant—clear, and cool, and still;
Then, with a smile, he said: " I will."

" Cavalry, charge! " Not a man of them shrank.
Their sharp, full cheer, from rank to rank,

[60]

The pictures of the battery at "action front" and of the Germanna Plank Road as seen from the hill near the Lacy house, recall vividly the two notable events of Chancellorsville that form the theme of Lathrop's poem. On May 2, 1863, "Stonewall" Jackson had marched around the right flank of the Union army and late in the afternoon had fallen with terrific force upon Howard's (Eleventh) Corps, driving it along in confusion. Pleasonton had started out at four o'clock to pursue the Confederate wagon-train, since Jackson was supposed to be in retreat for Gordonsville, but about six he discovered that his force was needed to repel an attack. His official report runs: "I immediately ordered the Eighth Pennsylvania Cavalry to proceed at a gallop, attack the rebels, and check the attack at any cost until we could get ready for them. This service was splendidly performed, but with heavy loss, and I gained some fifteen minutes to bring Martin's battery into position facing the woods, to reverse a battery of your corps, to detach some cavalry to stop runaways, and to secure more guns from our retreating forces. . . . Time was what we most wanted. Fortunately, I succeeded, before

THE GERMANNA PLANK ROAD IN 1864

"WHERE 'STONEWALL'S' CORPS, LIKE A BEAST OF PREY TORE THROUGH WITH ANGRY TUSK"

the advancing columns of the enemy came in sight, in placing twenty-two pieces of artillery in position, double-shotted with canister, and bearing on the direction the rebels were pursuing. To support this force, I had two small squadrons of cavalry, ready to charge upon any attempt made to take the guns.

My position was upon the extreme left of the line of the Eleventh Corps, and as it recoiled from the fierce onset of the rebels through and over my guns, it was soon apparent we must meet the shock. In rear of the Eleventh Corps the rebels came on rapidly, but now in silence. . . . I ordered all the guns to fire as they were advancing. This terrible discharge staggered them and threw the heads of their columns back on the woods, from which they opened a tremendous fire of musketry, bringing up fresh forces constantly, and striving to advance as fast as they we were swept back by our guns." In another place he adds: "Suspecting that they might play the trick of having their men lie down, draw the fire of artillery, then jump up and charge before the pieces could be reloaded, I poured in the canister for about twenty minutes, and the affair was over."

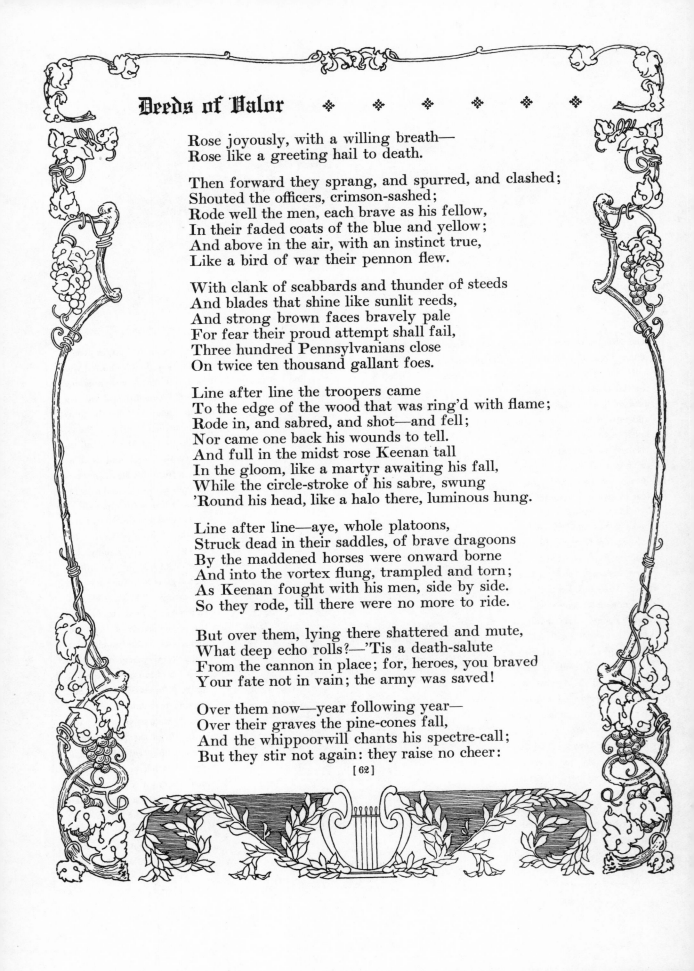

Deeds of Valor ❖ ❖ ❖ ❖ ❖ ❖

Rose joyously, with a willing breath—
Rose like a greeting hail to death.

Then forward they sprang, and spurred, and clashed;
Shouted the officers, crimson-sashed;
Rode well the men, each brave as his fellow,
In their faded coats of the blue and yellow;
And above in the air, with an instinct true,
Like a bird of war their pennon flew.

With clank of scabbards and thunder of steeds
And blades that shine like sunlit reeds,
And strong brown faces bravely pale
For fear their proud attempt shall fail,
Three hundred Pennsylvanians close
On twice ten thousand gallant foes.

Line after line the troopers came
To the edge of the wood that was ring'd with flame;
Rode in, and sabred, and shot—and fell;
Nor came one back his wounds to tell.
And full in the midst rose Keenan tall
In the gloom, like a martyr awaiting his fall,
While the circle-stroke of his sabre, swung
'Round his head, like a halo there, luminous hung.

Line after line—aye, whole platoons,
Struck dead in their saddles, of brave dragoons
By the maddened horses were onward borne
And into the vortex flung, trampled and torn;
As Keenan fought with his men, side by side.
So they rode, till there were no more to ride.

But over them, lying there shattered and mute,
What deep echo rolls?—'Tis a death-salute
From the cannon in place; for, heroes, you braved
Your fate not in vain; the army was saved!

Over them now—year following year—
Over their graves the pine-cones fall,
And the whippoorwill chants his spectre-call;
But they stir not again: they raise no cheer:

[62]

"SO THEY RODE, TILL THERE WERE NO MORE TO RIDE"

THE CHANCELLORSVILLE BATTLEFIELD, WHERE "KEENAN'S CHARGE" HAD SWEPT ON MAY 2, 1863

Across this spot swept the charge of the Eighth Pennsylvania Cavalry, celebrated in Lathrop's lines. Major Pennock Huey thus reported the affair: "We moved off briskly to the right, and found General Howard had fallen back, and the enemy's skirmish-line had crossed the road on which we were moving, throwing us between their skirmishers and battle-line. The whole regiment made a desperate charge on the main column of Jackson's corps, who were crossing the road in our front, completely checking the enemy, losing Major Keenan, Captain Arrowsmith, and Adjutant Haddock, with about 30 men and about 80 horses. I immediately re-formed the regiment to support the reserve artillery. We afterward moved back, and formed across the roads, to stop stragglers of the Eleventh Corps. Here we remained all night." But in the words of the poet, "The rush of their charge is resounding still."

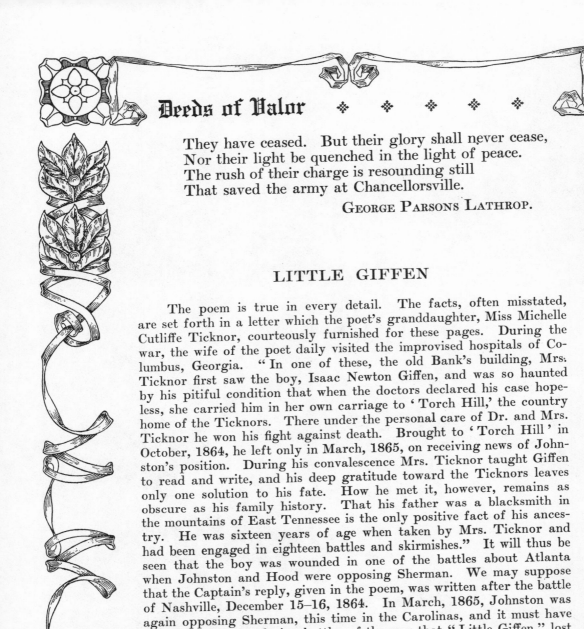

They have ceased. But their glory shall never cease,
Nor their light be quenched in the light of peace.
The rush of their charge is resounding still
That saved the army at Chancellorsville.

GEORGE PARSONS LATHROP.

LITTLE GIFFEN

The poem is true in every detail. The facts, often misstated, are set forth in a letter which the poet's granddaughter, Miss Michelle Cutliffe Ticknor, courteously furnished for these pages. During the war, the wife of the poet daily visited the improvised hospitals of Columbus, Georgia. " In one of these, the old Bank's building, Mrs. Ticknor first saw the boy, Isaac Newton Giffen, and was so haunted by his pitiful condition that when the doctors declared his case hopeless, she carried him in her own carriage to 'Torch Hill,' the country home of the Ticknors. There under the personal care of Dr. and Mrs. Ticknor he won his fight against death. Brought to 'Torch Hill' in October, 1864, he left only in March, 1865, on receiving news of Johnston's position. During his convalescence Mrs. Ticknor taught Giffen to read and write, and his deep gratitude toward the Ticknors leaves only one solution to his fate. How he met it, however, remains as obscure as his family history. That his father was a blacksmith in the mountains of East Tennessee is the only positive fact of his ancestry. He was sixteen years of age when taken by Mrs. Ticknor and had been engaged in eighteen battles and skirmishes." It will thus be seen that the boy was wounded in one of the battles about Atlanta when Johnston and Hood were opposing Sherman. We may suppose that the Captain's reply, given in the poem, was written after the battle of Nashville, December 15–16, 1864. In March, 1865, Johnston was again opposing Sherman, this time in the Carolinas, and it must have been in one of the closing battles of the war that " Little Giffen " lost his life.

Out of the focal and foremost fire,
Out of the hospital walls as dire,
Smitten of grape-shot and gangrene,
(Eighteenth battle, and *he* sixteen!)
Spectre! such as you seldom see,
Little Giffen, of Tennessee.

"TO THE EDGE OF THE WOOD THAT WAS RINGED WITH FLAME"

WILDERNESS TREES AFTER THE ARTILLERY FIRING THAT FOLLOWED THE CAVALRY CHARGE

Blasted by the artillery fire that saved the Federals at Chancellorsville, the Wilderness woods, only a couple of hundred yards south of the plank road, reveal the desperate nature of the conflict in the early evening of May 2, 1863. Of the close of the fight, the Union General Alfred Pleasonton reported: "It was now dark, and their presence could only be ascertained by the flash of their muskets, from which a continuous stream of fire was seen encircling us, and gradually extending to our right, to cut us off from the army. This was at last checked by our guns, and the rebels withdrew. Several guns and caissons were then recovered from the woods where the enemy had been posted. Such was the fight at the head of Scott's Run. Artillery against infantry at 300 yards; the infantry in the woods, the artillery in the clearing. War presents many anomalies, but few so curious and strange in its results."

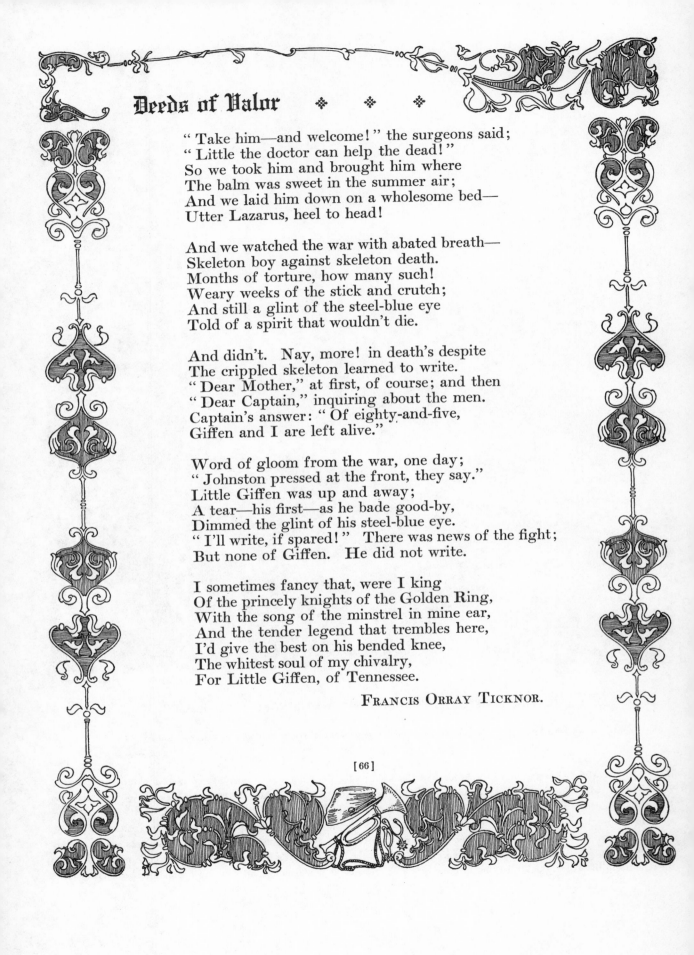

Deeds of Valor ❖ ❖ ❖

"Take him—and welcome!" the surgeons said;
"Little the doctor can help the dead!"
So we took him and brought him where
The balm was sweet in the summer air;
And we laid him down on a wholesome bed—
Utter Lazarus, heel to head!

And we watched the war with abated breath—
Skeleton boy against skeleton death.
Months of torture, how many such!
Weary weeks of the stick and crutch;
And still a glint of the steel-blue eye
Told of a spirit that wouldn't die.

And didn't. Nay, more! in death's despite
The crippled skeleton learned to write.
"Dear Mother," at first, of course; and then
"Dear Captain," inquiring about the men.
Captain's answer: "Of eighty-and-five,
Giffen and I are left alive."

Word of gloom from the war, one day;
"Johnston pressed at the front, they say."
Little Giffen was up and away;
A tear—his first—as he bade good-by,
Dimmed the glint of his steel-blue eye.
"I'll write, if spared!" There was news of the fight;
But none of Giffen. He did not write.

I sometimes fancy that, were I king
Of the princely knights of the Golden Ring,
With the song of the minstrel in mine ear,
And the tender legend that trembles here,
I'd give the best on his bended knee,
The whitest soul of my chivalry,
For Little Giffen, of Tennessee.

FRANCIS ORRAY TICKNOR.

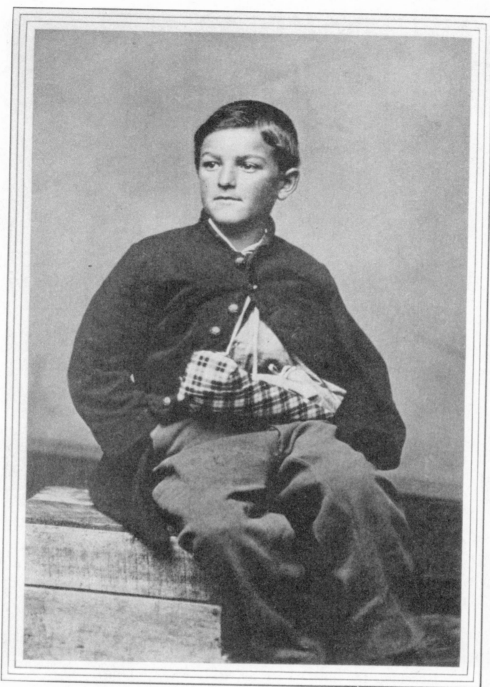

WILLIAM BLACK, THE YOUNGEST WOUNDED SOLDIER REPORTED

Lest the instance of "Little Giffen" seem an uncommon one, there is presented here the winning face of little William Black. He was the youngest boy, it is true, to be reported "wounded." Yet General Charles King's researches on "Boys of the War Days" in Volume VIII brings out the fact that "over 800,000 lads of seventeen or less were found in the ranks of the Union army, that over 200,000 were no more than sixteen, that there were even 100,000 on the Union rolls who were no more than fifteen."

THE DAUGHTER OF THE REGIMENT
(FIFTH RHODE ISLAND)

The young lady here celebrated had attracted attention in New York as the troops passed through the city on the way to the front. The *New York Herald* of April 25, 1861, said:

"The volunteers bring along with them two very prepossessing young women, named Martha Francis and Katey Brownell, both of Providence, who propose to act as 'daughters of the regiment,' after the French plan."

Who with the soldiers was stanch danger-sharer,—
　Marched in the ranks through the shriek of the shell?
Who was their comrade, their brave color-bearer?
　Who but the resolute Kady Brownell!

Over the marshland and over the highland,
　Where'er the columns wound, meadow or dell,
Fared she, this daughter of little Rhode Island,—
　She, the intrepid one, Kady Brownell!

While the mad rout at Manassas was surging,
　When those around her fled wildly, or fell,
And the bold Beauregard onward was urging,
　Who so undaunted as Kady Brownell!

When gallant Burnside made dash upon Newberne,
　Sailing the Neuse 'gainst the sweep of the swell,
Watching the flag on the heaven's broad blue burn,
　Who higher hearted than Kady Brownell?

In the deep slough of the springtide debarking,
　Toiling o'er leagues that are weary to tell,
Time with the sturdiest soldiery marking,
　Forward, straight forward, strode Kady Brownell.

Reaching the lines where the army was forming,
　Forming to charge on those ramparts of hell,
When from the wood came her regiment swarming,
　What did she see there—this Kady Brownell?

[68]

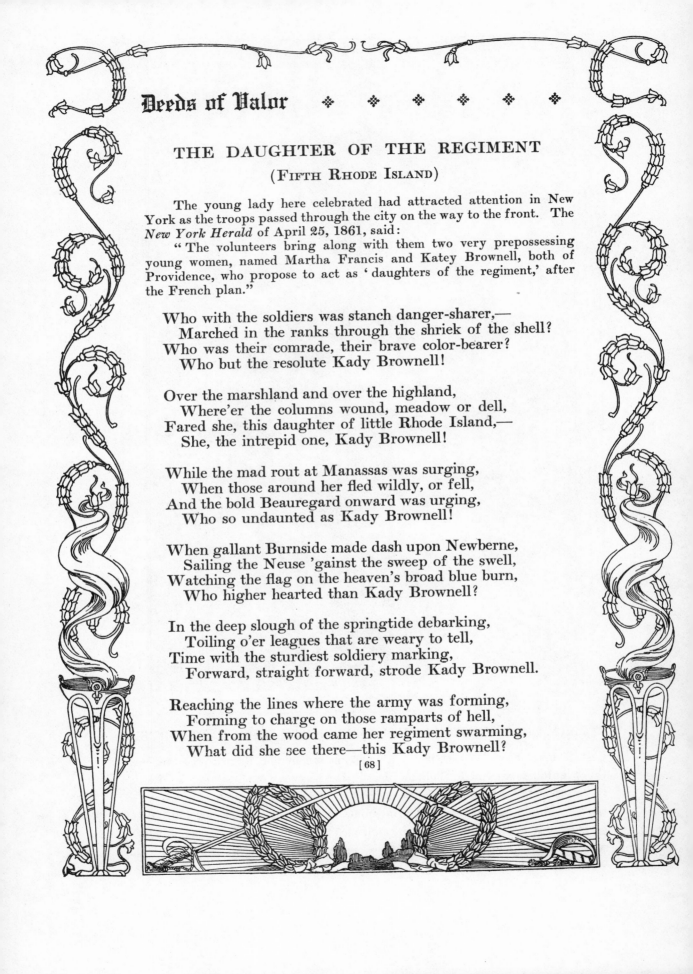

"GALLANT BURNSIDE" AT THE HEIGHT OF HIS CAREER

PHOTOGRAPHED EIGHT MONTHS AFTER THE EVENTS OF SCOLLARD'S POEM; WHILE WITH HIS STAFF-OFFICERS AT WARRENTON, VIRGINIA, NOVEMBER 14, 1862

General Burnside entered the war in May, 1861, as colonel of the First Rhode Island Volunteers. At Bull Run, July 21, 1861, he at first commanded the brigade in which the regiment was serving, but was soon called upon to take charge of the Second (Hunter's) division in the presence of the opposing Confederates. Under his command, Kady Brownell showed herself "so undaunted"; the two Rhode Island regiments in the battle were in his brigade, the colonel of the Second losing his life early in the action. On August 6, 1861, Burnside was commissioned brigadier-general of volunteers, and from January to July,

1862, commanded the Department of North Carolina. He captured Roanoke Island, occupied New Berne in the manner alluded to in Scollard's poem, and forced the evacuation of Fort Macon, at Beaufort. In July, as major-general of volunteers, he was asked to take chief command of the Army of the Potomac, but he refused. In September the offer was renewed, and again refused. Finally, on November 9th, he accepted. His disastrous repulse a month later at Fredericksburg was followed by his resignation as chief, though he served no less faithfully, both as department and corps commander, to the end of the war.

Deeds of Valor ❖ ❖ ❖ ❖ ❖ ❖

See! why she saw that their friends thought them foemen;
    Muskets were levelled, and cannon as well!
Save them from direful destruction would no men?
    Nay, but this woman would,—Kady Brownell!

Waving her banner she raced for the clearing;
    Fronted them all, with her flag as a spell;
Ah, what a volley—a volley of cheering—
    Greeted the heroine, Kady Brownell!

Gone (and thank God!) are those red days of slaughter!
    Brethren again we in amity dwell;
Just one more cheer for the Regiment's Daughter!—
    Just one more cheer for her, Kady Brownell!

CLINTON SCOLLARD.

SHERIDAN'S RIDE

Up from the South, at break of day,
Bringing to Winchester fresh dismay,
The affrighted air with a shudder bore,
Like a herald in haste to the chieftain's door,
The terrible grumble, and rumble, and roar,
Telling the battle was on once more,
    And Sheridan twenty miles away.

And wider still those billows of war
Thundered along the horizon's bar;
And louder yet into Winchester rolled
The roar of that red sea uncontrolled,
Making the blood of the listener cold,
As he thought of the stake in that fiery fray,
    With Sheridan twenty miles away.

But there is a road from Winchester town,
A good, broad highway leading down:
And there, through the flush of the morning light,
A steed as black as the steeds of night
Was seen to pass, as with eagle flight;

[70]

"OVER THE MARSHLAND AND OVER THE HIGHLAND"

FEDERAL FORTIFICATIONS NEAR THE RAILROAD, SOUTH OF NEW BERNE

This view recalls the incident of March 14, 1862, described by Clinton Scollard in "The Daughter of the Regiment." Burnside's attack on New Berne was part of the blockading movement which sought to close every port along the Southern coasts. The Fifth Rhode Island was in General John G. Parke's brigade. The soldiers were so eager to engage the enemy that many of them leaped from the ship into the water and waded waist-deep to the shore, and during the day often waded knee-deep in mud. The next morning little could be seen in the "open piney woods," owing to the dense fog. This condition accounts for the confusion that might have proved serious but for Kady Brownell. The brigade marched on out of the woods, and charged the Confederate works. Burnside himself reported: " Too much praise cannot be awarded to the officers and men for their untiring exertion and unceasing patience in accomplishing this work. The effecting of the landing and the approach to within a mile and a half of the enemy's work on the 13th I consider as great a victory as the engagement of the 14th. Owing to the difficult nature of the landing, our men were forced to wade ashore waist-deep, march through mud to a point twelve miles distant, bivouac in low, marshy ground in a rain-storm for the night, engage the enemy at daylight in the morning, fighting them for four hours amid a dense fog that prevented them from seeing the position of the enemy, and finally advancing rapidly over bad roads upon the city. In the midst of all this, not a complaint was heard; the men were only eager to accomplish their work." Burnside's success was rewarded by the rank of major-general of volunteers.

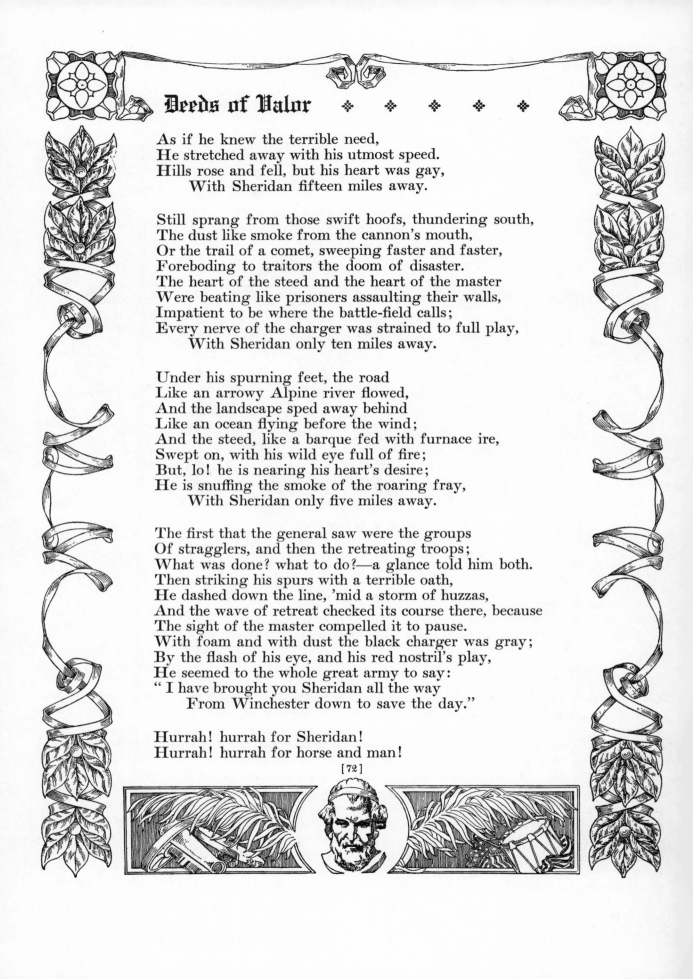

Deeds of Valor ❖ ❖ ❖ ❖ ❖

As if he knew the terrible need,
He stretched away with his utmost speed.
Hills rose and fell, but his heart was gay,
    With Sheridan fifteen miles away.

Still sprang from those swift hoofs, thundering south,
The dust like smoke from the cannon's mouth,
Or the trail of a comet, sweeping faster and faster,
Foreboding to traitors the doom of disaster.
The heart of the steed and the heart of the master
Were beating like prisoners assaulting their walls,
Impatient to be where the battle-field calls;
Every nerve of the charger was strained to full play,
    With Sheridan only ten miles away.

Under his spurning feet, the road
Like an arrowy Alpine river flowed,
And the landscape sped away behind
Like an ocean flying before the wind;
And the steed, like a barque fed with furnace ire,
Swept on, with his wild eye full of fire;
But, lo! he is nearing his heart's desire;
He is snuffing the smoke of the roaring fray,
    With Sheridan only five miles away.

The first that the general saw were the groups
Of stragglers, and then the retreating troops;
What was done? what to do?—a glance told him both.
Then striking his spurs with a terrible oath,
He dashed down the line, 'mid a storm of huzzas,
And the wave of retreat checked its course there, because
The sight of the master compelled it to pause.
With foam and with dust the black charger was gray;
By the flash of his eye, and his red nostril's play,
He seemed to the whole great army to say:
" I have brought you Sheridan all the way
    From Winchester down to save the day."

Hurrah! hurrah for Sheridan!
Hurrah! hurrah for horse and man!

GENERAL

P. H. SHERIDAN

IN 1864

WITH THE HAT

HE WORE ON HIS

FAMOUS "RIDE"

The most dramatic deed of a Federal general in the Valley of Virginia is recorded in Read's poem. In September, 1864, Sheridan had driven the Confederates up the Valley, and in early October had retreated northward. Early followed, but he was soon out of supplies. He was obliged to fight or fall back. At an early hour on the foggy morning of October 19th, he attacked the unsuspecting Union army encamped along Cedar Creek and drove it back in confusion. General Sheridan, who had made a flying visit to Washington, spent the night of the 18th at Winchester on his way back to the army. At Mill Creek, half a mile south of Winchester, he came in sight of the fugitives. An officer who was at the front gives this account: "Far away in the rear was heard cheer after cheer. What was the cause? Were reënforcements coming? Yes, Phil Sheridan was coming, and he was a host. . . . Dashing along the pike, he came upon the line of battle. 'What troops are those?' shouted Sheridan. 'The Sixth Corps,' was the response from a hundred voices. 'We are all right,' said Sheridan, as he swung his old hat and dashed along the line toward the right. 'Never mind, boys, we'll whip them yet; we'll whip them yet! We shall sleep in our old quarters to-night!' were the encouraging words of the chief, as he rode along, while the men threw their hats high in air, leaped and danced and cheered in wildest joy." The victory was so complete that the campaign was virtually at an end. Three weeks of occasional skirmishing and the last action in the Valley was over.

SHERIDAN'S WINCHESTER CHARGER, IN 1869

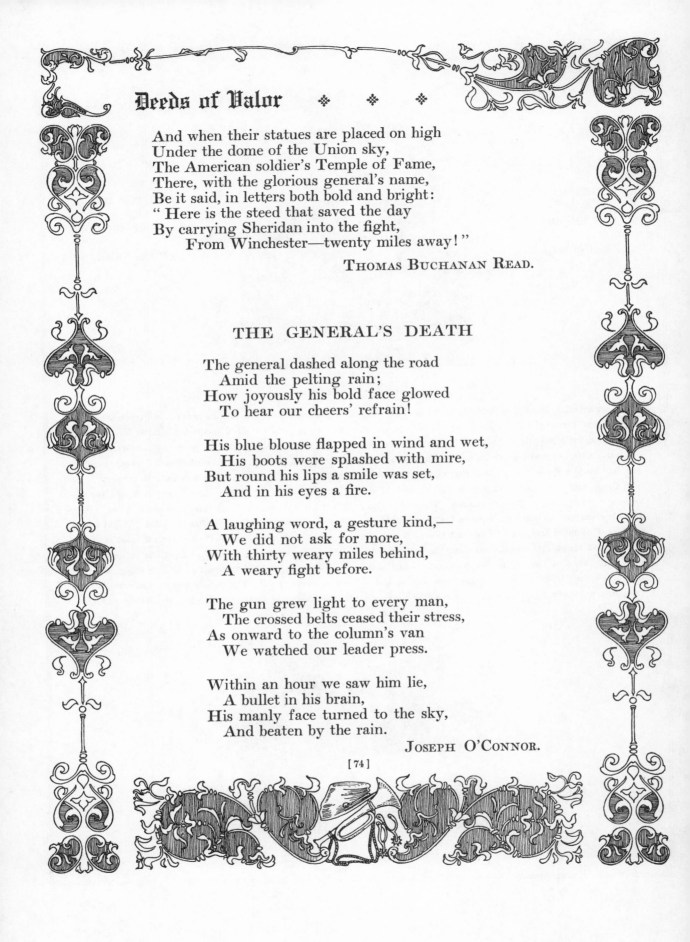

Deeds of Valor ❖ ❖ ❖

And when their statues are placed on high
Under the dome of the Union sky,
The American soldier's Temple of Fame,
There, with the glorious general's name,
Be it said, in letters both bold and bright:
" Here is the steed that saved the day
By carrying Sheridan into the fight,
    From Winchester—twenty miles away!"

THOMAS BUCHANAN READ.

THE GENERAL'S DEATH

The general dashed along the road
    Amid the pelting rain;
How joyously his bold face glowed
    To hear our cheers' refrain!

His blue blouse flapped in wind and wet,
    His boots were splashed with mire,
But round his lips a smile was set,
    And in his eyes a fire.

A laughing word, a gesture kind,—
    We did not ask for more,
With thirty weary miles behind,
    A weary fight before.

The gun grew light to every man,
    The crossed belts ceased their stress,
As onward to the column's van
    We watched our leader press.

Within an hour we saw him lie,
    A bullet in his brain,
His manly face turned to the sky,
    And beaten by the rain.

JOSEPH O'CONNOR.

[74]

"THE GENERAL'S DEATH"

This sylvan scene, as it looked a few months after the death of General George W. Taylor, on August 27, 1862, recalls Pope's Virginia campaign. "Stonewall" Jackson in a series of forced marches had swept round to the rear of Pope's army, seized the railroad, and then captured the immense depot of supplies at Manassas Station. To meet him, after an all-day's march from near Alexandria on August 26th, Union troops under General Taylor crossed Bull Run near the spot pictured above. They advanced about two miles to occupy the important point Taylor made all the dispositions for an attack on the Confederate force, which at once opened upon the advancing brigade with a heavy discharge of round-shot, shell, and grape. The men nevertheless moved forward undaunted and defiant. Within 300 yards of the earthworks Taylor discovered that he was greatly outnumbered. A force of cavalry was making for his rear. He stood in danger of being surrounded. Nothing was left but to regain the bridge. While directing the movement, Taylor received a wound from which he soon died. Assistance arrived, and he was carried across the stream, begging the officers to rally the men of his brigade and prevent another Bull Run.

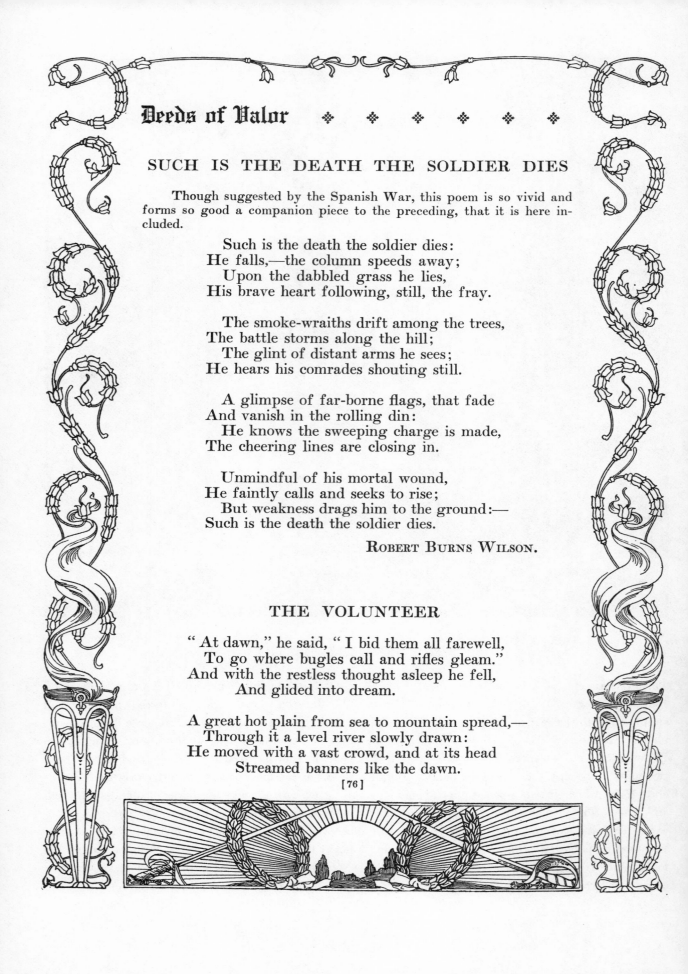

Deeds of Valor ✦ ✦ ✦ ✦ ✦ ✦

SUCH IS THE DEATH THE SOLDIER DIES

Though suggested by the Spanish War, this poem is so vivid and forms so good a companion piece to the preceding, that it is here included.

Such is the death the soldier dies:
He falls,—the column speeds away;
Upon the dabbled grass he lies,
His brave heart following, still, the fray.

The smoke-wraiths drift among the trees,
The battle storms along the hill;
The glint of distant arms he sees;
He hears his comrades shouting still.

A glimpse of far-borne flags, that fade
And vanish in the rolling din:
He knows the sweeping charge is made,
The cheering lines are closing in.

Unmindful of his mortal wound,
He faintly calls and seeks to rise;
But weakness drags him to the ground:—
Such is the death the soldier dies.

ROBERT BURNS WILSON.

THE VOLUNTEER

" At dawn," he said, " I bid them all farewell,
To go where bugles call and rifles gleam."
And with the restless thought asleep he fell,
And glided into dream.

A great hot plain from sea to mountain spread,—
Through it a level river slowly drawn:
He moved with a vast crowd, and at its head
Streamed banners like the dawn.

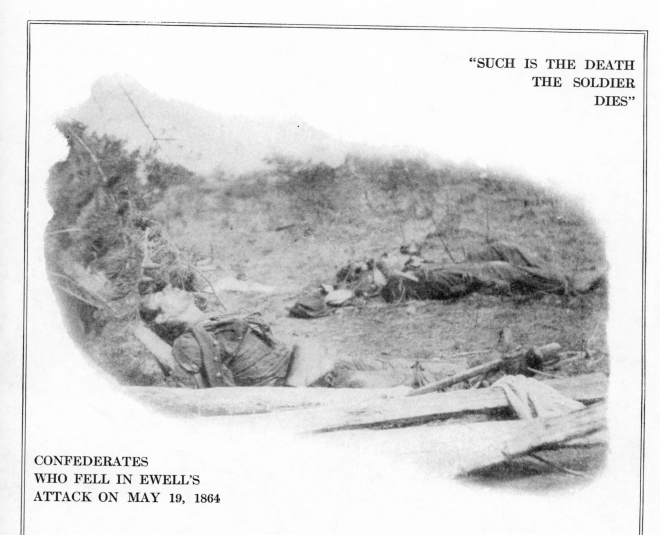

CONFEDERATES
WHO FELL IN EWELL'S
ATTACK ON MAY 19, 1864

His musket dropped across him as he fell, its hammer down as it had clicked in that last unavailing shot—here lies one of the 900 men in gray and behind him another comrade, left on the last Spotsylvania battlefield. In the actions about Spotsylvania Court House, of which this engagement was the close, the Union army lost about fifteen thousand. With sympathy for the last moments of each soldier, such as Robert Burns Wilson has put into his poem opposite, the horror of war becomes all too vivid. Ewell's attack illustrates the sudden facing of death that may come to every soldier. The desperate fighting about Spotsylvania had been prolonged ten days and more, when General Lee thought the Union army was withdrawing to his right. To ascertain whether this was true he directed Ewell to feel out the Federal position. After a long detour through roads nearly impassable, Ewell came upon the enemy ready to receive him. The object of his movement thus accomplished, he prepared to return, but found himself fiercely attacked. It was necessary then to make a stand, for no effective fighting can be done in retreat. The late afternoon and the early evening were filled with the fierce encounter. Only when darkness came was Ewell able in safety to withdraw.

"WHERE BUGLES CALL AND RIFLES GLEAM"

The men of the 74th New York Infantry, as they drill in their camp of 1861, exemplify the martial splendor of Cutler's poem; nor was its hero animated by a more unflinching resolve than they. The regiment's record tells the story. It was organized in New York and till August 20th was stationed at Camp Scott, on Staten Island, as the fifth in Sickles' "Excelsior Brigade." Barely a month after Bull Run, the first overwhelming Federal defeat, this regiment was on its way to Washington. The fall of the year, as the picture shows, was spent in the constant marching and drilling by which McClellan forged that fighting instrument known to fame as the Army of the Potomac. The volunteers were indeed where bugles called and rifles gleamed, but they were impatient for service on the "great hot plain" to hear the "dissonant cries of triumph and dismay." Marching about under the leafless trees over

ILLUSTRATION FOR "THE VOLUNTEER"

ground frequently covered with snow did not satisfy their notions of the glory of military service. The next year brought to both officers and men the long-wished-for opportunity. In April, 1862, they floated down the Potomac to take part in McClellan's Peninsula campaign. At the battle of Williamsburg, May 5th, the regiment performed distinguished service, fighting behind an abatis of felled timber and holding a position against the main force of the Confederate army. Of 36 of its number the regiment might report, "And with the dead he lay," and the total loss mounted to 143. Through the rest of the campaign, at Fair Oaks and during the Seven Days' Battles, it was in the hard fighting. At Chancellorsville it served under General Berry, who was killed on May 3, 1863. At Gettysburg it appeared with ranks thinned by two years of continuous service, yet sustained a loss of eighty-nine.

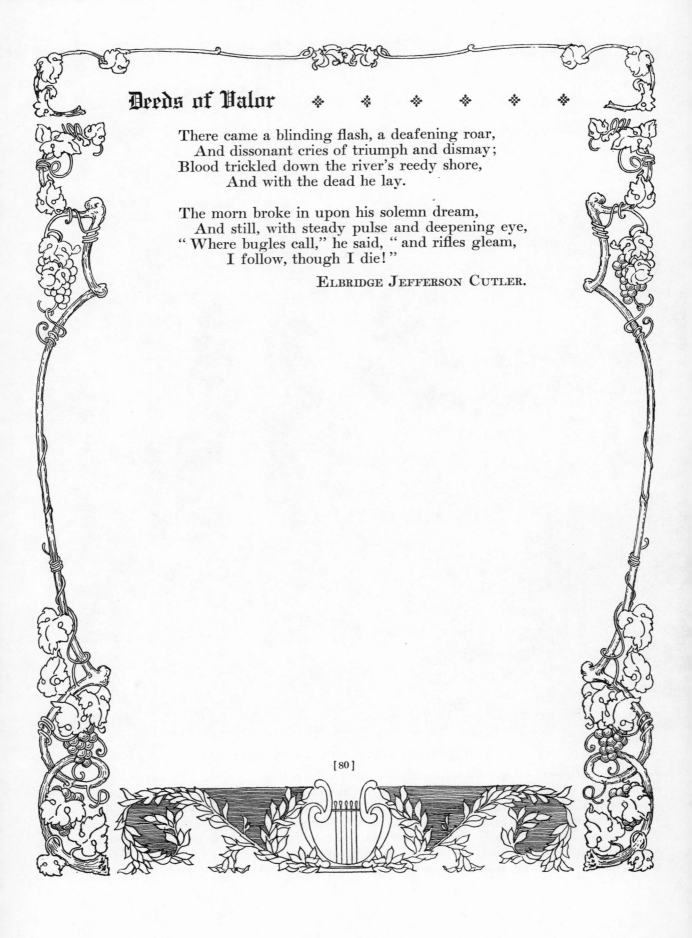

Deeds of Valor ❖ ❖ ❖ ❖ ❖ ❖

There came a blinding flash, a deafening roar,
  And dissonant cries of triumph and dismay;
Blood trickled down the river's reedy shore,
  And with the dead he lay.

The morn broke in upon his solemn dream,
  And still, with steady pulse and deepening eye,
"Where bugles call," he said, "and rifles gleam,
  I follow, though I die!"

ELBRIDGE JEFFERSON CUTLER.

III

IN

MEMORIAM

THE RUINED BRIDGE AT BULL RUN

ON THE HEIGHTS ABOVE, YOUNG PELHAM,
HERO OF RANDALL'S POEM FOLLOWING,
WON HIS FIRST LAURELS

IN MEMORIAM

PELHAM

Just as the spring came laughing through the strife,
    With all its gorgeous cheer,
In the bright April of historic life
    Fell the great cannoneer.

The wondrous lulling of a hero's breath
    His bleeding country weeps;
Hushed, in the alabaster arms of Death,
    Our young Marcellus sleeps.

Nobler and grander than the child of Rome,
    Curbing his chariot steeds,
The knightly scion of a Southern home
    Dazzled the land with deeds.

Gentlest and bravest in the battle's brunt—
    The Champion of the Truth—
He bore his banner in the very front
    Of our immortal youth.

A clang of sabres 'mid Virginian snow,
    The fiery pang of shells—
And there's a wail of immemorial woe
    In Alabama dells.

The pennon droops that led the sacred band
    Along the crimson field;
The meteor blade sinks from the nerveless hand
    Over the spotless shield.

We gazed and gazed upon that beauteous face,
    While, round the lips and eyes,
Couched in their marble slumber, flashed the grace
    Of a divine surprise.

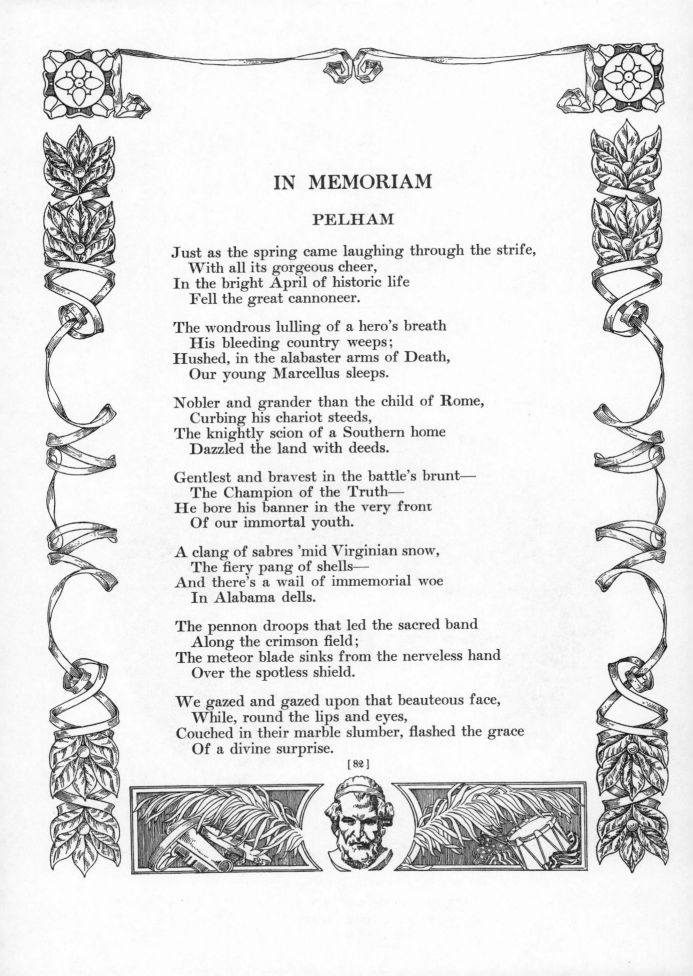

PELHAM, "THE GREAT CANNONEER"

Randall's poem was such a tribute as few young soldiers have ever received, and this is true also of General "Jeb" Stuart's order of March 20, 1863, after Pelham's death: "The major-general commanding approaches with reluctance the painful duty of announcing to the division its irreparable loss in the death of Major John Pelham, commanding the Horse Artillery. He fell mortally wounded in the battle of Kellysville, March 17, with the battle-cry on his lips and the light of victory beaming from his eye. To you, his comrades, it is needless to dwell upon what you have so often witnessed, his prowess in action, already proverbial. . . . His eye had glanced over every battle-field of this army from the First Manassas to the moment of his death, and he was, with a single exception, a brilliant actor in all. The memory of 'the gallant Pelham,' his many manly virtues, his noble nature and purity of character, are enshrined as a sacred legacy in the hearts of all who knew him. His record has been bright and spotless, his career brilliant and successful. He fell the noblest of sacrifices on the altar of his country, to whose glorious service he had dedicated his life from the beginning of the war." To this General Lee added an unusual endorsement: "Respectfully forwarded for the information of the department. I feel deeply the loss of the noble dead, and heartily concur in the commendation of the living. R. E. Lee, General." All Virginia concurred in these sentiments.

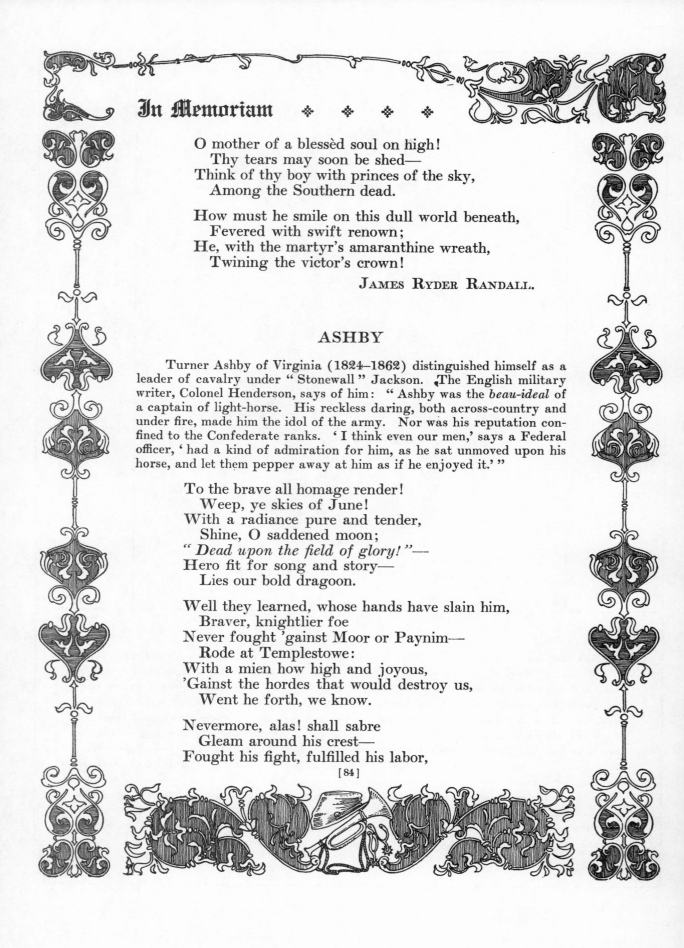

In Memoriam ✦ ✦ ✦ ✦

O mother of a blessèd soul on high!
Thy tears may soon be shed—
Think of thy boy with princes of the sky,
Among the Southern dead.

How must he smile on this dull world beneath,
Fevered with swift renown;
He, with the martyr's amaranthine wreath,
Twining the victor's crown!

JAMES RYDER RANDALL.

ASHBY

Turner Ashby of Virginia (1824–1862) distinguished himself as a leader of cavalry under "Stonewall" Jackson. The English military writer, Colonel Henderson, says of him: "Ashby was the *beau-ideal* of a captain of light-horse. His reckless daring, both across-country and under fire, made him the idol of the army. Nor was his reputation confined to the Confederate ranks. 'I think even our men,' says a Federal officer, 'had a kind of admiration for him, as he sat unmoved upon his horse, and let them pepper away at him as if he enjoyed it.'"

To the brave all homage render!
Weep, ye skies of June!
With a radiance pure and tender,
Shine, O saddened moon;
"*Dead upon the field of glory!*"—
Hero fit for song and story—
Lies our bold dragoon.

Well they learned, whose hands have slain him,
Braver, knightlier foe
Never fought 'gainst Moor or Paynim—
Rode at Templestowe:
With a mien how high and joyous,
'Gainst the hordes that would destroy us,
Went he forth, we know.

Nevermore, alas! shall sabre
Gleam around his crest—
Fought his fight, fulfilled his labor,

[84]

WHERE PELHAM FIRST "DAZZLED THE LAND WITH DEEDS"

The Henry house on the Bull Run battlefield, the site of John Pelham's first effort.   At that time he was only twenty, having been born in Calhoun County, Alabama, about 1841.   At the outbreak of the war he had left West Point to enter the Southern army.   Of his conduct near the ruins above, "Stonewall" Jackson reported: "Nobly did the artillery maintain its position for hours against the enemy's advancing thousands."   Soon he won the command of a battery of horse artillery, to serve with General "Jeb" Stuart's cavalry. Stuart officially reported of the battle of Williamsburg, May 5, 1862: "I ordered the horse artillery at once into action; but before the order could be given, Pelham's battery was speaking to the enemy in thunder-tones of defiance, its maiden effort on the field, thus filling its function of unexpected arrival with instantaneous execution and sustaining in gallant style the fortunes of the day, keeping up a destructive fire upon the enemy until our infantry, having re-formed, rushed onward, masking the pieces.   I directed Captain Pelham then to take a position farther to the left and open a cross-fire on the Telegraph Road, which he did as long as the presence of the enemy warranted the expenditure of ammunition."   At Antietam, Stuart again reports: "The gallant Pelham displayed all those noble qualities which have made him immortal.   He had under his command batteries from every portion of General Jackson's command.   The batteries of Poague, Pegram, and Carrington (the only ones which now recur to me) did splendid service, as also did the Stuart horse artillery, all under Pelham.   The hill held on the extreme left so long and so gallantly by artillery alone, was essential to the maintenance of our position."   It is surprising to remember that these reports are not of a war-grimed veteran but of a youth of twenty.

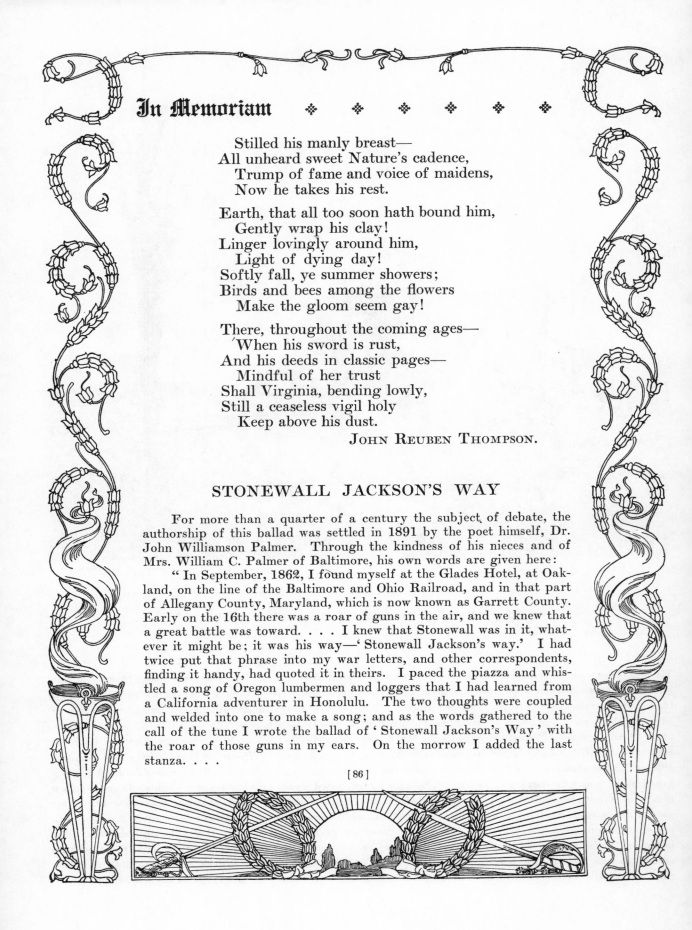

Stilled his manly breast—
All unheard sweet Nature's cadence,
    Trump of fame and voice of maidens,
    Now he takes his rest.

Earth, that all too soon hath bound him,
    Gently wrap his clay!
Linger lovingly around him,
    Light of dying day!
Softly fall, ye summer showers;
Birds and bees among the flowers
    Make the gloom seem gay!

There, throughout the coming ages—
    'When his sword is rust,
And his deeds in classic pages—
    Mindful of her trust
Shall Virginia, bending lowly,
Still a ceaseless vigil holy
    Keep above his dust.

JOHN REUBEN THOMPSON.

STONEWALL JACKSON'S WAY

For more than a quarter of a century the subject of debate, the authorship of this ballad was settled in 1891 by the poet himself, Dr. John Williamson Palmer. Through the kindness of his nieces and of Mrs. William C. Palmer of Baltimore, his own words are given here:

" In September, 1862, I found myself at the Glades Hotel, at Oakland, on the line of the Baltimore and Ohio Railroad, and in that part of Allegany County, Maryland, which is now known as Garrett County. Early on the 16th there was a roar of guns in the air, and we knew that a great battle was toward. . . . I knew that Stonewall was in it, whatever it might be; it was his way—'Stonewall Jackson's way.' I had twice put that phrase into my war letters, and other correspondents, finding it handy, had quoted it in theirs. I paced the piazza and whistled a song of Oregon lumbermen and loggers that I had learned from a California adventurer in Honolulu. The two thoughts were coupled and welded into one to make a song; and as the words gathered to the call of the tune I wrote the ballad of 'Stonewall Jackson's Way' with the roar of those guns in my ears. On the morrow I added the last stanza. . . .

WHERE JACKSON PLAYED WITH FEDERAL ARMIES

THE MASSANNUTTEN MOUNTAINS, IN THE CENTER OF THE SHENANDOAH VALLEY, 1884

"Stonewall Jackson's Way" came to be known amid this fertile valley and noble range. The English military authority, Colonel Henderson, writes that "The Valley campaign saved Richmond. In a few short months the quiet gentleman of Lexington became, in the estimation of friend and foe, a very thunderbolt of war; and his name, which a year previous had hardly been known beyond the Valley, was already famous." Jackson had been in command of the Southern forces in the Valley since the beginning of 1862. For the Confederate Government the Shenandoah region was of the greatest importance; it afforded an easy avenue of advance into Maryland and the rear of Washington, and was the granary for all the Virginia armies. When McClellan with his hundred thousand men was advancing upon Richmond, which seemed certain to fall before superior numbers, Jackson prevented the junction of the Union armies by a series of startling achievements. On May 8th, by a forced march, he took the Federal force at McDowell by surprise, and despite a four hours' resistance drove it back in defeat. He followed up the retreating troops. In the early morning of May 23d, at Fort Royal, the clear notes of the bugle, followed by the crash of musketry, startled the Union camp. The hastily formed line was sturdily repelling the charge when the appearance of cavalry in its rear caused it to fall back. But Jackson was soon following the dust of the retreating column down the road to Winchester. There Banks, who was "fond of shell," was attacked with artillery on the morning of May 25th, after which ten thousand bayonets rushed forward to the ringing "rebel yell" in a charge that drove everything before them. Jackson, rising in his stirrups, shouted to his officers, "Press forward to the Potomac!" The troops that had marched thirty miles in thirty hours pressed forward; but, the cavalry not assisting, Banks made good his escape across the broad river. During the month of June, Jackson kept three armies busy in the Shenandoah; then, vanishing as by magic, he joined Lee in driving McClellan from within five miles of Richmond to his gunboats on the James. Henderson exclaims, "75,000 men absolutely paralyzed by 16,000! Only Napoleon's campaign of 1814 affords a parallel to this extraordinary spectacle." Jackson's death was like the loss of an army.

In Memoriam ❖ ❖ ❖ ❖ ❖ ❖ ❖

" In Baltimore I told the story of the song to my father, and at his request made immediately another copy of it. This was shown cautiously to certain members of the Maryland Club; and a trusty printer was found who struck off a dozen slips of it, principally for private distribution. That first printed copy of the song was headed 'Found on a Rebel Sergeant of the old Stonewall Brigade, Taken at Winchester.' The fabulous legend was for the misleading of the Federal provost marshal, as were also the address and date: ' Martinsburg, Sept. 13, 1862.' "

Come, stack arms, men! pile on the rails,
 Stir up the camp-fire bright;
No growling if the canteen fails,
 We'll make a roaring night.
Here Shenandoah brawls along,
There burly Blue Ridge echoes strong,
To swell the Brigade's rousing song
 Of " Stonewall Jackson's way."

We see him now—the queer slouched hat
 Cocked o'er his eye askew;
The shrewd, dry smile; the speech so pat,
 So calm, so blunt, so true.
The " Blue-light Elder " knows 'em well;
Says he, " That's Banks—he's fond of shell;
Lord save his soul! we'll give him—" well!
 That's " Stonewall Jackson's way."

Silence! ground arms! kneel all! caps off!
 Old Massa's goin' to pray.
Strangle the fool that dares to scoff!
 Attention! it's his way.
Appealing from his native sod
In forma pauperis to God:
" Lay bare Thine arm; stretch forth Thy rod!
 Amen! "—That's " Stonewall's way."

He's in the saddle now. Fall in!
 Steady! the whole brigade!
Hill's at the ford, cut off; we'll win
 His way out, ball and blade!
What matter if our shoes are worn?
What matter if our feet are torn?

WHERE "STONEWALL" JACKSON FELL

In this tangled nook Lee's right-hand man was shot through a terrible mistake of his own soldiers. It was the second of May, 1863. After his brilliant flank march, the evening attack on the rear of Hooker's army had just been driven home. About half-past eight, Jackson had ridden beyond his lines to reconnoiter for the final advance. A single rifle-shot rang out in the darkness. The outposts of the two armies were engaged. Jackson turned toward his own line, where the Eighteenth North Carolina was stationed. The regiment, keenly on the alert and startled by the group of strange horsemen riding through the gloom, fired a volley that brought several men and horses to the earth. Jackson was struck once in the right hand and twice in the left arm, a little below the shoulder. His horse dashed among the trees; but with his bleeding right hand Jackson succeeded in seizing the reins and turning the frantic animal back into the road. Only with difficulty was the general taken to the rear so that his wounds might be dressed. To his attendants he said, "Tell them simply that you have a wounded Confederate officer." To one who asked if he was seriously hurt, he replied: "Don't bother yourself about me. Win the battle first and attend to the wounded afterward." He was taken to Guiney's Station. At first it was hoped that he would recover, but pneumonia set in and his strength gradually ebbed. On Sunday evening, May 10th, he uttered the words which inspired the young poet, Sidney Lanier, to write his elegy, beautiful in its serene resignation.

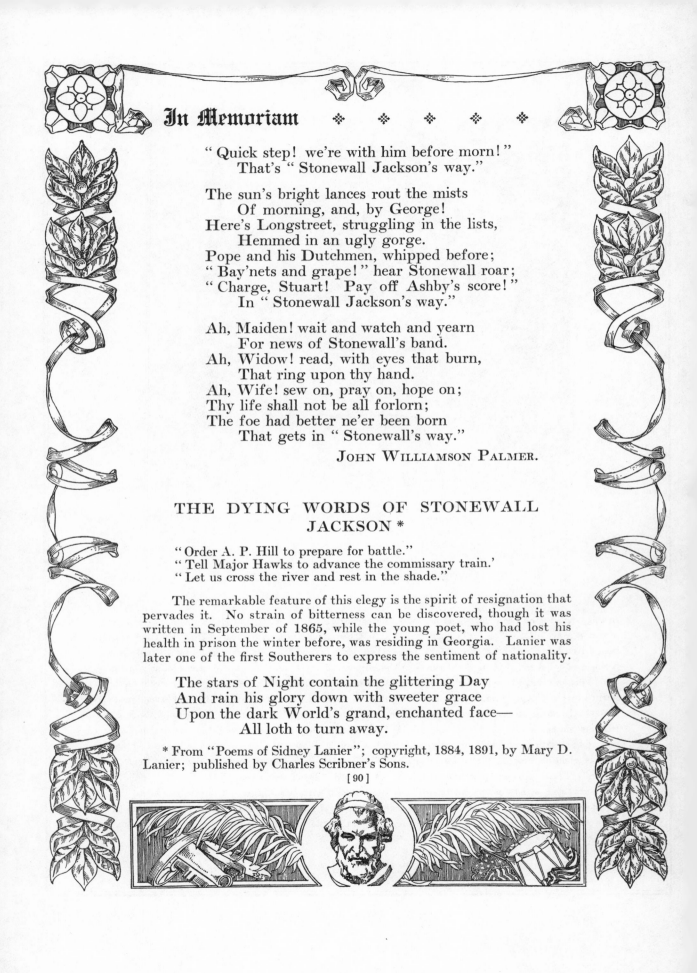

In Memoriam ❖ ❖ ❖ ❖ ❖

"Quick step! we're with him before morn!"
    That's "Stonewall Jackson's way."

The sun's bright lances rout the mists
    Of morning, and, by George!
Here's Longstreet, struggling in the lists,
    Hemmed in an ugly gorge.
Pope and his Dutchmen, whipped before;
"Bay'nets and grape!" hear Stonewall roar;
"Charge, Stuart! Pay off Ashby's score!"
    In "Stonewall Jackson's way."

Ah, Maiden! wait and watch and yearn
    For news of Stonewall's band.
Ah, Widow! read, with eyes that burn,
    That ring upon thy hand.
Ah, Wife! sew on, pray on, hope on;
Thy life shall not be all forlorn;
The foe had better ne'er been born
    That gets in "Stonewall's way."

JOHN WILLIAMSON PALMER.

THE DYING WORDS OF STONEWALL JACKSON *

"Order A. P. Hill to prepare for battle."
"Tell Major Hawks to advance the commissary train.'
"Let us cross the river and rest in the shade.''

The remarkable feature of this elegy is the spirit of resignation that pervades it. No strain of bitterness can be discovered, though it was written in September of 1865, while the young poet, who had lost his health in prison the winter before, was residing in Georgia. Lanier was later one of the first Southerers to express the sentiment of nationality.

The stars of Night contain the glittering Day
And rain his glory down with sweeter grace
Upon the dark World's grand, enchanted face—
    All loth to turn away.

* From "Poems of Sidney Lanier"; copyright, 1884, 1891, by Mary D. Lanier; published by Charles Scribner's Sons.

From this humble grave on the green Virginia hillside, Jackson rises before the American people as one of the mightiest figures of a mighty conflict. When he died on May 10, 1863, in the little town of Guiney's Station, not far from the battlefield of Chancellorsville, his remains were taken to Richmond. In the Hall of Representatives the body lay in state while the sorrowing throngs passed by the open coffin in silence. In the Military Institute at Lexington, which Jackson had left two years before as an obscure professor, the remains of the illustrious leader were under the charge of the cadets, until his burial in the quiet cemetery above the town. The pure

"STONEWALL" JACKSON

"STILL SHINE THE WORDS
THAT MINIATURE
HIS DEEDS"

and noble words of Lanier need no comment. A few lines from an Englishman, Colonel G. F. R. Henderson, declare Jackson's life a message not for America alone. "The hero who lies buried at Lexington, in the Valley of Virginia, belongs to a race that is not confined to a single continent; and to those who speak the same tongue, and in whose veins the same blood flows, his words come home like an echo of all that is noblest in their history: 'What is life without honor? Degradation is worse than death. We must think of the living and of those who are to come after us, and see that by God s blessing we transmit to them the freedom we have ourselves inherited '"

JACKSON'S GRAVE AT LEXINGTON, VIRGINIA

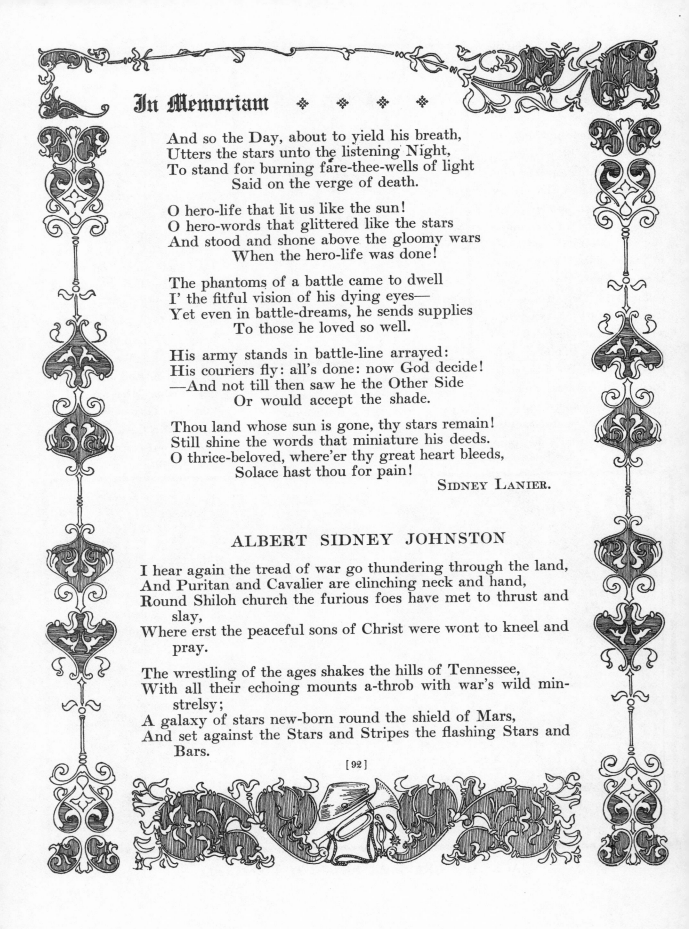

In Memoriam ✦ ✦ ✦ ✦

And so the Day, about to yield his breath,
Utters the stars unto the listening Night,
To stand for burning fare-thee-wells of light
    Said on the verge of death.

O hero-life that lit us like the sun!
O hero-words that glittered like the stars
And stood and shone above the gloomy wars
    When the hero-life was done!

The phantoms of a battle came to dwell
I' the fitful vision of his dying eyes—
Yet even in battle-dreams, he sends supplies
    To those he loved so well.

His army stands in battle-line arrayed:
His couriers fly: all's done: now God decide!
—And not till then saw he the Other Side
    Or would accept the shade.

Thou land whose sun is gone, thy stars remain!
Still shine the words that miniature his deeds.
O thrice-beloved, where'er thy great heart bleeds,
    Solace hast thou for pain!

SIDNEY LANIER.

ALBERT SIDNEY JOHNSTON

I hear again the tread of war go thundering through the land,
And Puritan and Cavalier are clinching neck and hand,
Round Shiloh church the furious foes have met to thrust and
    slay,
Where erst the peaceful sons of Christ were wont to kneel and
    pray.

The wrestling of the ages shakes the hills of Tennessee,
With all their echoing mounts a-throb with war's wild min-
    strelsy;
A galaxy of stars new-born round the shield of Mars,
And set against the Stars and Stripes the flashing Stars and
    Bars.

ALBERT SIDNEY JOHNSTON

The man who, at the opening of hostilities, was regarded as the most formidable general in the Confederacy is commemorated in the poem opposite by a woman long prominent in the relief work of the Grand Army of the Republic. Johnston, whose father was a Connecticut Yankee, won distinction in the Black Hawk War, entered the army of Texas in its struggle for independence, succeeded Sam Houston as commander-in-chief, fought in the War with Mexico, and was recommended for the grade of brigadier-general for his conduct at Monterey. When he heard that his adopted state, Texas, had passed the ordinance of secession, he resigned from the Department of the Pacific. He was assured that he might have the highest position in the Federal service. Sorrowfully he declined, writing at the time: "No one could feel more sensibly the calamitous condition of our country than myself, and whatever part I may take hereafter, it will always be a subject of gratulation with me that no act of mine ever contributed to bring it about. I suppose the difficulties now will only be adjusted by the sword. In my humble judgment, that was not the remedy." Johnston counted for more, said Jefferson Davis, than an army of 10,000.

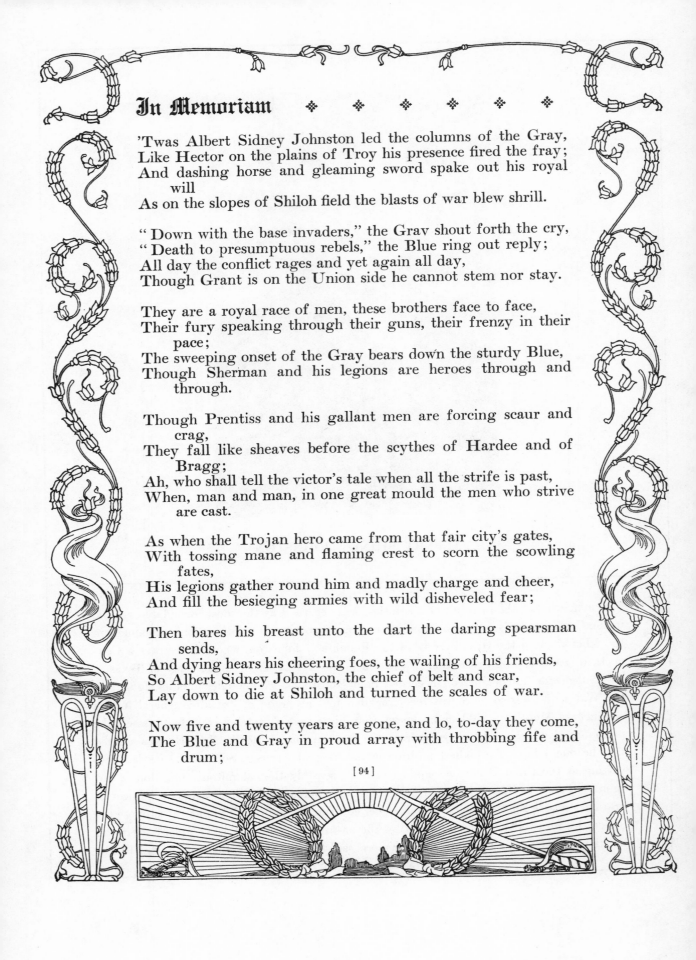

In Memoriam ✦ ✦ ✦ ✦ ✦ ✦

'Twas Albert Sidney Johnston led the columns of the Gray,
Like Hector on the plains of Troy his presence fired the fray;
And dashing horse and gleaming sword spake out his royal
    will
As on the slopes of Shiloh field the blasts of war blew shrill.

" Down with the base invaders," the Gray shout forth the cry,
" Death to presumptuous rebels," the Blue ring out reply;
All day the conflict rages and yet again all day,
Though Grant is on the Union side he cannot stem nor stay.

They are a royal race of men, these brothers face to face,
Their fury speaking through their guns, their frenzy in their
        pace;
The sweeping onset of the Gray bears down the sturdy Blue,
Though Sherman and his legions are heroes through and
        through.

Though Prentiss and his gallant men are forcing scaur and
        crag,
They fall like sheaves before the scythes of Hardee and of
        Bragg;
Ah, who shall tell the victor's tale when all the strife is past,
When, man and man, in one great mould the men who strive
        are cast.

As when the Trojan hero came from that fair city's gates,
With tossing mane and flaming crest to scorn the scowling
        fates,
His legions gather round him and madly charge and cheer,
And fill the besieging armies with wild disheveled fear;

Then bares his breast unto the dart the daring spearsman
        sends,
And dying hears his cheering foes, the wailing of his friends,
So Albert Sidney Johnston, the chief of belt and scar,
Lay down to die at Shiloh and turned the scales of war.

Now five and twenty years are gone, and lo, to-day they come,
The Blue and Gray in proud array with throbbing fife and
        drum;

[94]

"ON THE SLOPES OF SHILOH FIELD"
PITTSBURG LANDING—A FEW DAYS AFTER THE BATTLE

By the name of "Pittsburg Landing," this Tennessee River point, Southerners designate the conflict of April 6 and 7, 1862. The building upon the left and one farther up the bank were the only ones standing at the time of the battle. Of the six steamers, the name of the *Tycoon*, which brought hospital supplies from the Cincinnati branch of the Sanitary Commission, is visible. Johnston's plan in the attack on the Federal forces was to pound away on their left until they were driven away from the Landing and huddled in the angle between the Tennessee River and Snake Creek. The onset of the Confederates was full of dash. Sherman was at length driven from Shiloh Church, and the command of Prentiss was surrounded and forced to surrender. It looked as if Johnston would crush the left. Just at this point he was struck down by a minie-ball from the last line of a Federal force that he had victoriously driven back. The success of the day now begins to tell on the Confederate army. Many of the lines show great gaps. But the men in gray push vigorously toward the point where these boats lie anchored. Some heavy guns are massed near this point. Reënforcements are arriving across the river, but General Beauregard, who succeeds Johnston in command, suspends the battle till the morrow. During the night 24,000 fresh troops are taken across the river by the transports here pictured. They successfully withstand the attempt of Beauregard, and with the arrival of Lew Wallace from up the river victory shifts to the Stars and Stripes.

In Memoriam ✦ ✦ ✦ ✦ ✦ ✦ ✦

But not as rivals, not as foes, as brothers reconciled,
To twine love's fragrant roses where the thorns of hate grew
  wild.

They tell the hero of three wars, the lion-hearted man,
Who wore his valor like a star—uncrowned American;
Above his heart serene and still the folded Stars and Bars,
Above his head, like mother-wings, the sheltering Stripes and
  Stars.

Aye, five and twenty years, and lo, the manhood of the South
Has held its valor stanch and strong as at the cannon's mouth,
With patient heart and silent tongue has kept its true parole,
And in the conquests born of peace has crowned its battle roll.

But ever while we sing of war, of courage tried and true,
Of heroes wed to gallant deeds, or be it Gray or Blue,
Then Albert Sidney Johnston's name shall flash before our
  sight
Like some resplendent meteor across the sombre night.

America, thy sons are knit with sinews wrought of steel,
They will not bend, they will not break, beneath the tyrant's
  heel;
But in the white-hot flame of love, to silken cobwebs spun,
They whirl the engines of the world, all keeping time as one.

To-day they stand abreast and strong, who stood as foes of
  yore,
The world leaps up to bless their feet, heaven scatters blessings
  o'er;
Their robes are wrought of gleaming gold, their wings are
  freedom's own,
The trampling of their conquering hosts shakes pinnacle and
  throne.

Oh, veterans of the Blue and Gray, who fought on Shiloh field,
The purposes of God are true, His judgment stands revealed;
The pangs of war have rent the veil, and lo, His high decree:
One heart, one hope, one destiny, one flag from sea to sea.

KATE BROWNLEE SHERWOOD.

[96]

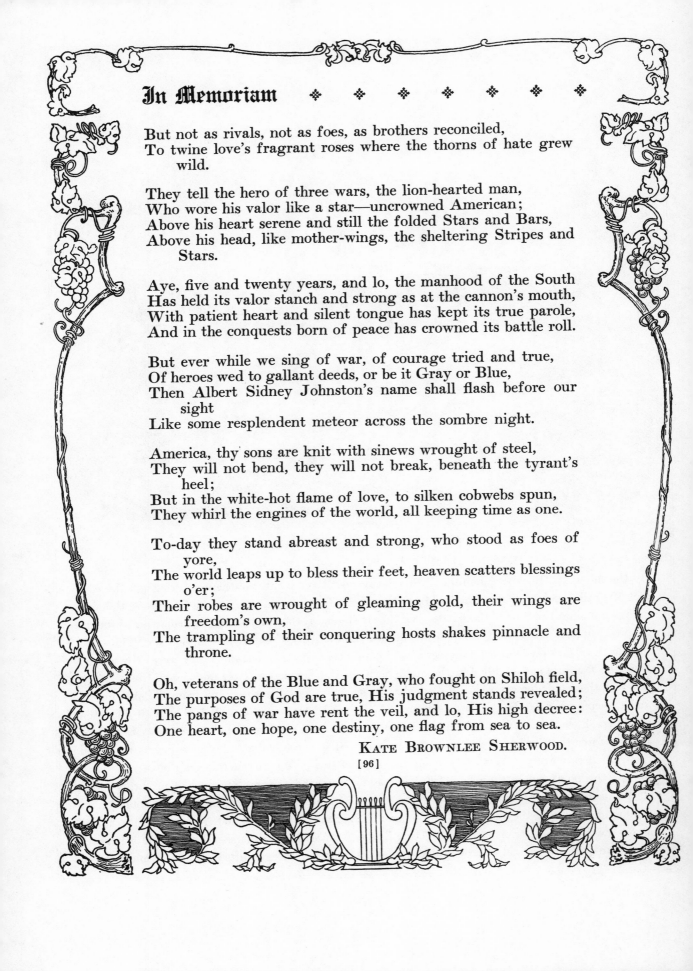

GRANT

HIS APPEARANCE AT SHILOH
—HIS EARLIEST PORTRAIT
AS MAJOR-GENERAL

"THOUGH GRANT IS ON
THE UNION SIDE HE CAN-
NOT STEM NOR STAY"

These rare photographs preserve the grim determination that steeled both of these young leaders during their first great battle, while gallantly facing Albert Sidney Johnston, as celebrated by the poem opposite. Grant was already known to fame. His brilliant capture of Forts Henry and Donelson in February, 1862, had focussed the eyes of the Nation upon him. In executing a movement against Corinth the battle of April 6th–7th was fought. Grant arrived on the field about eight o'clock, and with the quick judgment of a soldier at once organized an ammunition train to supply the men on the firing-line. During the rest of the day he rode along the front, smoking a cigar and encouraging both officers and men at every point. The second day's battle was a complete victory for his army, but he was traduced by the press universally and came near terminating his military career by resigning from the service. The picture of Sherman in August, 1862, at Memphis, was the first to show the three stars on his shoulder straps. Sherman's troops plunged into the very heaviest of the fighting at Shiloh. Three horses were shot under him. He was himself wounded in two places. For his gallant services he was commissioned major-general of volunteers. The carnage produced a profound effect on both Sherman and Grant. It was then Grant first saw that the conflict would be long and bitter. Four days after the battle Sherman wrote his wife: "I still feel the horrid nature of this war, and the piles of dead and wounded and maimed makes me more anxious than ever for some hope of an end, but I know such a thing cannot be for a long, long time. Indeed I never expect it, or to survive it." But both survived in great honor.

SHERMAN

SOON AFTER SHILOH—BEFORE
WAR HAD AGED AND
GRIZZLED HIM

"THOUGH SHERMAN AND
HIS LEGIONS ARE HEROES
THROUGH AND THROUGH"

THOMAS AT CHICKAMAUGA

It was that fierce contested field when Chickamauga lay
Beneath the wild tornado that swept her pride away;
Her dimpling dales and circling hills dyed crimson with the
    flood
That had its sources in the springs that throb with human
    blood.

" Go say to General Hooker to reinforce his right!"
Said Thomas to his aide-de-camp, when wildly went the fight;
In front the battle thundered, it roared both right and left,
But like a rock " Pap " Thomas stood upon the crested cleft.

" Where will I find you, General, when I return?" The aide
Leaned on his bridle-rein to wait the answer Thomas made;
The old chief like a lion turned, his pale lips set and sere,
And shook his mane, and stamped his foot, and fiercely an-
    swered, *" Here!"*

The floodtide of fraternal strife rolled upward to his feet,
And like the breakers on the shore the thunderous clamors beat;
The sad earth rocked and reeled with woe, the woodland
    shrieked in pain,
And hill and vale were groaning with the burden of the slain.

Who does not mind that sturdy form, that steady heart and
    hand,
That calm repose and gallant mien, that courage high and
    grand?—
O God, who givest nations men to meet their lofty needs,
Vouchsafe another Thomas when our country prostrate bleeds!

They fought with all the fortitude of earnest men and true—
The men who wore the rebel gray, the men who wore the blue;
And those, they fought most valiantly for petty state and clan,
And these, for truer Union and the brotherhood of man.

[98]

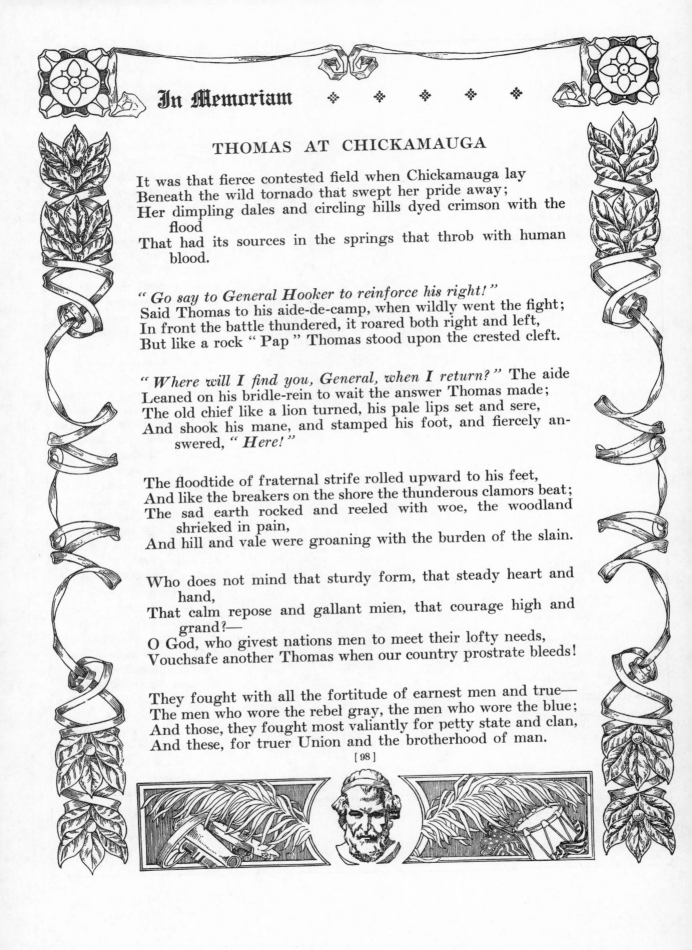

COPYRIGHT, 1911. REVIEW OF REVIEWS CO.

BEFORE CHICKAMAUGA—IN THE RUSH OF EVENTS

Rarely does the camera afford such a perfectly contemporaneous record of the march of events so momentous. This photograph shows the hotel at Stevenson, Alabama, during the Union advance that ended in Chickamauga. Sentinels are parading the street in front of the hotel, several horses are tied to the hotel posts, and the officers evidently have gone into the hotel headquarters. General Alexander McDowell McCook, commanding the old Twentieth Army Corps, took possession of the hotel as temporary headquarters on the movement of the Army of the Cumberland from Tullahoma. On August 29, 1863, between Stevenson and Caperton's Ferry, on the Tennessee River, McCook gathered his boats and pontoons, hidden under the dense foliage of overhanging trees, and when ready for his crossing suddenly launched them into and across the river. Thence the troops marched over Sand Mountain and at length into Lookout Valley. During the movements the army was in extreme peril, for McCook was at one time three days' march from Thomas, so that Bragg might have annihilated the divisions in detail. Finally the scattered corps were concentrated along Chickamauga Creek, where the bloody struggle of September 19th and 20th was so bravely fought.

[J—7]

In Memoriam ❖ ❖ ❖ ❖

They come, those hurling legions, with banners crimson-
　　splashed,
Against our stubborn columns their rushing ranks are dashed,
Till 'neath the blistering iron hail the shy and frightened deer
Go scurrying from their forest haunts to plunge in wilder
　　fear.

Beyond, our lines are broken; and now in frenzied rout
The flower of the Cumberland has swiftly faced about;
And horse and foot and color-guard are reeling, rear and van,
And in the awful panic man forgets that he is man.

Now Bragg, with pride exultant above our broken wings,
The might of all his army against "Pap" Thomas brings;
They're massing to the right of him, they're massing to the
　　left,
Ah, God be with our hero, who holds the crested cleft!

Blow, blow, ye echoing bugles! give answer, screaming shell!
Go, belch your murderous fury, ye batteries of hell!
Ring out, O impious musket! spin on, O shattering shot,—
Our smoke-encircled hero, he hears but heeds ye not!

Now steady, men! now steady! make one more valiant stand,
For gallant Steedman's coming, his forces well in hand!
Close up your shattered columns, take steady aim and true,
The chief who loves you as his life will live or die with you!

By solid columns, on they come; by columns they are hurled,
As down the eddying rapids the storm-swept booms are
　　whirled;
And when the ammunition fails—O moment drear and dread—
The heroes load their blackened guns from rounds of soldiers
　　dead.

God never set His signet on the hearts of braver men,
Or fixed the goal of victory on higher heights than then;
With bayonets and muskets clubbed, they close the rush and
　　roar;
Their stepping-stones to glory are their comrades gone before.

[100]

ON THE WAY TO CHICKAMAUGA

This solitary observer, if he was standing here September 20, 1863, shortly before this was photographed, certainly gazed at the base of the hill to the left. For through the pass called Rossville Gap a column in blue was streaming—Steedman's Division of the Reserve Corps, rushing to aid Thomas, so sore pressed at Chickamauga. Those slopes by Chickamauga Creek witnessed the deadliest battle in the West and the highest in percentage of killed and wounded of the entire war. It was fought as a result of Rosecrans' attempt to maneuver Bragg out of Chattanooga. The Federal army crossed the Tennessee River west of the city, passed through the mountain-ranges, and came upon Bragg's line of communications. Finding his position untenable, the Southern leader moved southward and fell upon the united forces of Rosecrans along Chickamauga Creek. The vital point in the Federal line was the left, held by Thomas. Should that give way, the army would be cut off from Chattanooga, with no base to fall back on. The heavy fighting of September 19th showed that Bragg realized the situation. Brigades and regiments were shattered. For a time, the Union army was driven back. But at nightfall Thomas had regained the lost ground. He re-formed during the night in order to protect the road leading into Chattanooga. Since the second day was foggy till the middle of the forenoon, the fighting was not renewed till late. About noon a break was made in the right of the Federal battle-line, into which the eager Longstreet promptly hurled his men. Colonel Dodge writes: "Everything seems lost. The entire right of the army, with Rosecrans and his staff, is driven from the field in utter rout. But, unknown even to the commanding general, Thomas, the Rock of Chickamauga, stands there at bay, surrounded, facing two to one. Heedless of the wreck of one-half the army, he knows not how to yield."

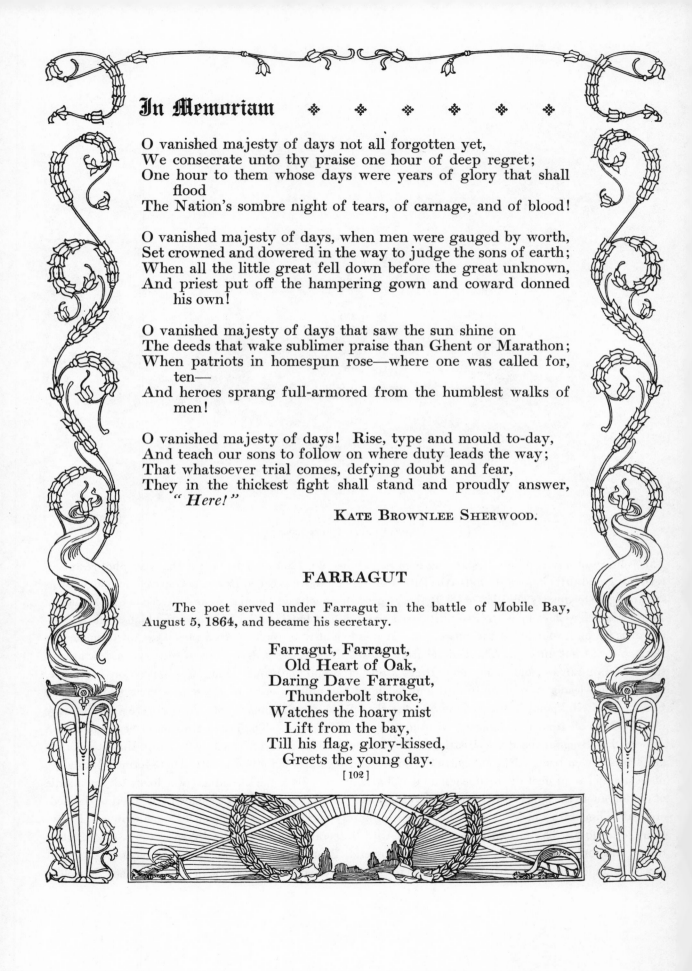

In Memoriam ❖ ❖ ❖ ❖ ❖ ❖

O vanished majesty of days not all forgotten yet,
We consecrate unto thy praise one hour of deep regret;
One hour to them whose days were years of glory that shall
    flood
The Nation's sombre night of tears, of carnage, and of blood!

O vanished majesty of days, when men were gauged by worth,
Set crowned and dowered in the way to judge the sons of earth;
When all the little great fell down before the great unknown,
And priest put off the hampering gown and coward donned
    his own!

O vanished majesty of days that saw the sun shine on
The deeds that wake sublimer praise than Ghent or Marathon;
When patriots in homespun rose—where one was called for,
    ten—
And heroes sprang full-armored from the humblest walks of
    men!

O vanished majesty of days! Rise, type and mould to-day,
And teach our sons to follow on where duty leads the way;
That whatsoever trial comes, defying doubt and fear,
They in the thickest fight shall stand and proudly answer,
  " Here!"

              KATE BROWNLEE SHERWOOD.

FARRAGUT

The poet served under Farragut in the battle of Mobile Bay,
August 5, 1864, and became his secretary.

Farragut, Farragut,
  Old Heart of Oak,
Daring Dave Farragut,
  Thunderbolt stroke,
Watches the hoary mist
  Lift from the bay,
Till his flag, glory-kissed,
  Greets the young day.

[102]

GENERAL GEORGE H. THOMAS

"Pap" Thomas is the name Sherwood's poem gives this massive, stern warrior; for thus he was affectionately known among his devoted soldiers. Colonel T. F. Dodge has written of him: "He was essentially cast in a large mold, in mind and body; so modest that he shrunk from command, to which he was peculiarly fitted; with courage of the stamp that ignores self; possessing steadfastness in greater measure than audacity, he yet lacked none of that ability which can deal heavy blows; while no antagonist was ever able to shake his foothold. Honesty in thought, word, and deed was constitutional with him. A thorough military training, added to a passionate love of his profession and great natural powers, made him peer of any soldier. Sedate in mind and physically slow in movement, he yet aroused great enthusiasm."

In Memoriam ✦ ✦ ✦ ✦ ✦ ✦ ✦

Far, by gray Morgan's walls,
    Looms the black fleet.
Hark, deck to rampart calls
    With the drums' beat!
Buoy your chains overboard,
    While the steam hums;
Men! to the battlement,
    Farragut comes.

See, as the hurricane
    Hurtles in wrath
Squadrons of clouds amain
    Back from its path!
Back to the parapet,
    To the guns' lips,
Thunderbolt Farragut
    Hurls the black ships.

Now through the battle's roar
    Clear the boy sings,
" By the mark fathoms four,"
    While his lead swings.
Steady the wheelmen five
    " Nor' by East keep her."
" Steady," but two alive:
    How the shells sweep her!

Lashed to the mast that sways
    Over red decks,
Over the flame that plays
    Round the torn wrecks,
Over the dying lips
    Framed for a cheer,
Farragut leads his ships,
    Guides the line clear.

On by heights cannon-browed,
    While the spars quiver;
Onward still flames the cloud
    Where the hulks shiver.

THE MOST FAMOUS OF AMERICAN NAVAL OFFICERS AND ONE OF HIS MOST DARING FEATS

In his admiral's uniform, "Dave" Farragut might contrast with pride his start in life, in an obscure Tennessee town at the opening of the century. The son of a veteran of the Revolutionary War, he early entered the navy, and while yet a lad of thirteen took distinguished part in the battle between the *Essex* and the British vessels, *Phœbe* and *Cherub*. After cruising all over the world, he was stationed, at the opening of the Civil War, in the navy-yard in Norfolk, Virginia. Though bound to the South by birth and strong family ties, he remained in the national service without wavering. His capture of New Orleans in April, 1862, when he ran by two forts

"DARING DAVE FARRAGUT"
TO ILLUSTRATE MEREDITH'S POEM OPPOSITE

under terrific fire and worked havoc in a Confederate fleet of thirteen vessels, is one of the most thrilling actions in naval warfare. Its importance to the Federal cause lay in the opening of the port of New Orleans and securing control of the lower Mississippi. Farragut was of service to the army in opening the whole river and thus cutting the Confederacy in two. The closing of Mobile Bay in August, 1864, was another daring exploit. He had long planned to attack the forts at the entrance of the bay, but not till August was the necessary fleet ready. The battery pictured below was one of the features to be reckoned with. Here at the water's edge the Confederates mounted seven guns. During the engagement the gunners were driven from their posts again and again by the broadsides of the fleet, only to return with fresh men—but in vain.

THE CAPTURED WATER BATTERY AT FORT MORGAN, 1864

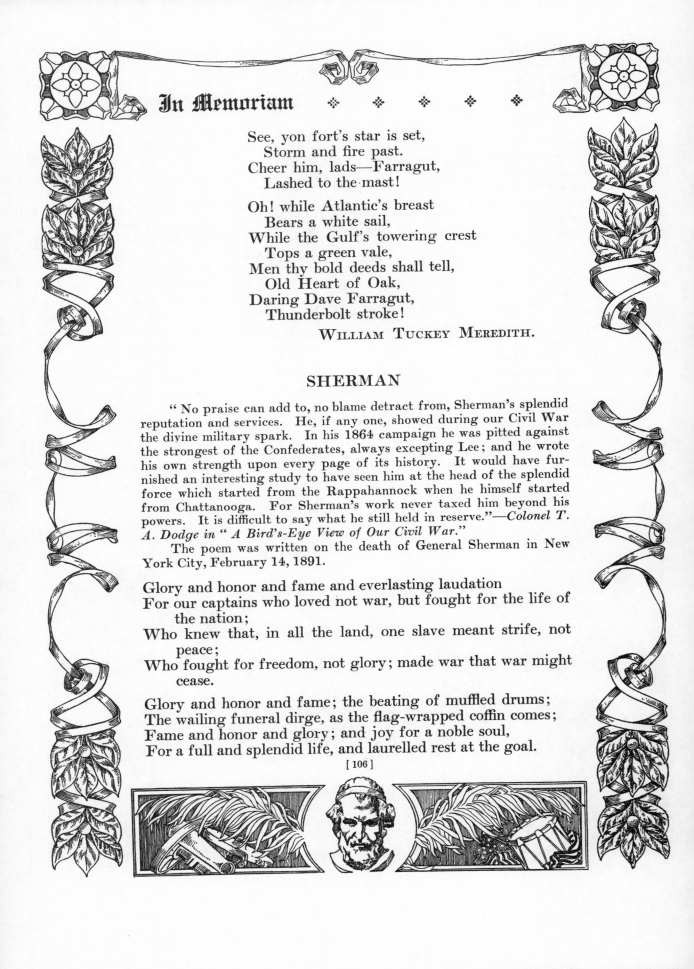

See, yon fort's star is set,
   Storm and fire past.
Cheer him, lads—Farragut,
   Lashed to the mast!

Oh! while Atlantic's breast
   Bears a white sail,
While the Gulf's towering crest
   Tops a green vale,
Men thy bold deeds shall tell,
   Old Heart of Oak,
Daring Dave Farragut,
   Thunderbolt stroke!

           WILLIAM TUCKEY MEREDITH.

SHERMAN

"No praise can add to, no blame detract from, Sherman's splendid reputation and services. He, if any one, showed during our Civil War the divine military spark. In his 1864 campaign he was pitted against the strongest of the Confederates, always excepting Lee; and he wrote his own strength upon every page of its history. It would have furnished an interesting study to have seen him at the head of the splendid force which started from the Rappahannock when he himself started from Chattanooga. For Sherman's work never taxed him beyond his powers. It is difficult to say what he still held in reserve."—*Colonel T. A. Dodge in "A Bird's-Eye View of Our Civil War."*

The poem was written on the death of General Sherman in New York City, February 14, 1891.

Glory and honor and fame and everlasting laudation
For our captains who loved not war, but fought for the life of
    the nation;
Who knew that, in all the land, one slave meant strife, not
    peace;
Who fought for freedom, not glory; made war that war might
    cease.

Glory and honor and fame; the beating of muffled drums;
The wailing funeral dirge, as the flag-wrapped coffin comes;
Fame and honor and glory; and joy for a noble soul,
For a full and splendid life, and laurelled rest at the goal.

[106]

"FAR BY GRAY MORGAN'S WALLS"—THE MOBILE BAY FORT, BATTERED BY FARRAGUT'S GUNS

How formidable was Farragut's undertaking in forcing his way into Mobile Bay is apparent from these photographs. For wooden vessels to pass Morgan and Gaines, two of the strongest forts on the coast, was pronounced by experts most foolhardy. Besides, the channel was planted with torpedoes that might blow the ships to atoms, and within the bay was the Confederate ram *Tennessee*, thought to be the most powerful ironclad ever put afloat. In the arrangements for the attack, Farragut's flagship, the *Hartford*, was placed second, the *Brooklyn* leading the line of battleships, which were preceded by four monitors. At a quarter before six, on the morning of August 5th, the fleet moved. Half an hour later it came within range of Fort Morgan. The whole undertaking was then threatened with disaster. The monitor *Tecumseh*, eager to engage the Confederate ram *Tennessee* behind the line of torpedoes, ran straight ahead, struck a torpedo, and in a few minutes went down with most of the crew. As the monitor sank, the *Brooklyn* recoiled. Farragut signaled: "What's the trouble?" "Torpedoes," was the answer.

WHERE BROADSIDES STRUCK

"Damn the torpedoes!" shouted Farragut. "Go ahead, Captain Drayton. Four bells." Finding that the smoke from the guns obstructed the view from the deck, Farragut ascended to the rigging of the main mast, where he was in great danger of being struck and of falling to the deck. The captain accordingly ordered a quartermaster to tie him in the shrouds. The *Hartford*, under a full head of steam, rushed over the torpedo ground far in advance of the fleet. The battle was not yet over. The Confederate ram, invulnerable to the broadsides of the Union guns, steamed alone for the ships, while the ramparts of the two forts were crowded with spectators of the coming conflict. The ironclad monster made straight for the flagship, attempting to ram it and paying no attention to the fire or the ramming of the other vessels. Its first effort was unsuccessful, but a second came near proving fatal. It then became a target for the whole Union fleet; finally its rudder-chain was shot away and it became unmanageable; in a few minutes it raised the white flag. No wonder Americans call Farragut the greatest of naval commanders.

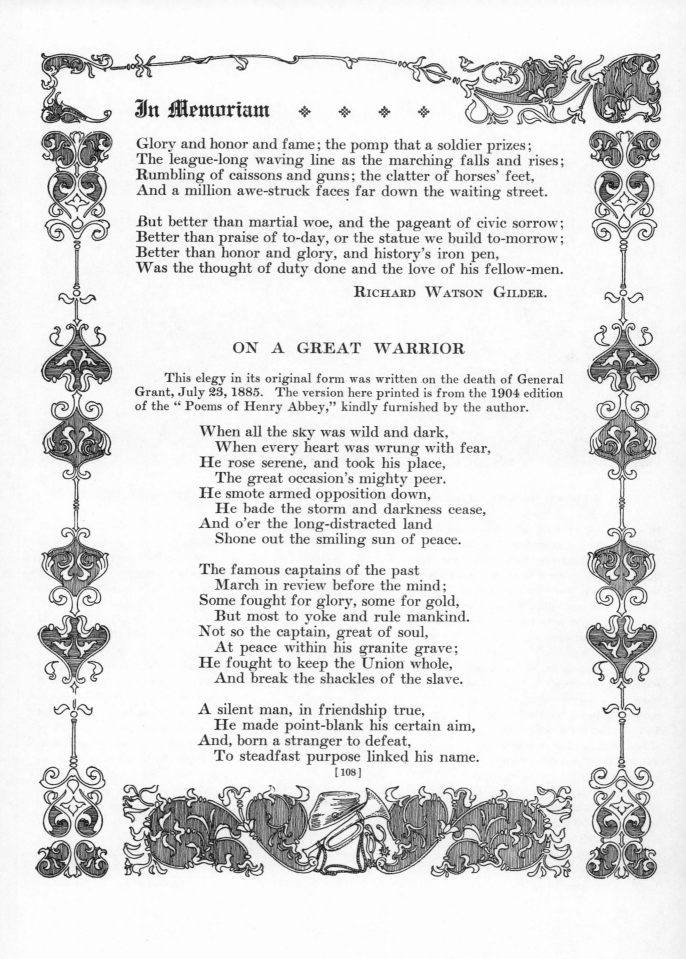

In Memoriam ✦ ✦ ✦ ✦

Glory and honor and fame; the pomp that a soldier prizes;
The league-long waving line as the marching falls and rises;
Rumbling of caissons and guns; the clatter of horses' feet,
And a million awe-struck faces far down the waiting street.

But better than martial woe, and the pageant of civic sorrow;
Better than praise of to-day, or the statue we build to-morrow;
Better than honor and glory, and history's iron pen,
Was the thought of duty done and the love of his fellow-men.

RICHARD WATSON GILDER.

ON A GREAT WARRIOR

This elegy in its original form was written on the death of General
Grant, July 23, 1885. The version here printed is from the 1904 edition
of the " Poems of Henry Abbey," kindly furnished by the author.

When all the sky was wild and dark,
    When every heart was wrung with fear,
He rose serene, and took his place,
    The great occasion's mighty peer.
He smote armed opposition down,
    He bade the storm and darkness cease,
And o'er the long-distracted land
    Shone out the smiling sun of peace.

The famous captains of the past
    March in review before the mind;
Some fought for glory, some for gold,
    But most to yoke and rule mankind.
Not so the captain, great of soul,
    At peace within his granite grave;
He fought to keep the Union whole,
    And break the shackles of the slave.

A silent man, in friendship true,
    He made point-blank his certain aim,
And, born a stranger to defeat,
    To steadfast purpose linked his name.

[108]

"THE LEAGUE–LONG WAVING LINE AS THE MARCHING FALLS AND RISES"

AN ILLUSTRATION FOR GILDER'S ELEGY ON THE DEATH OF

GENERAL WILLIAM TECUMSEH SHERMAN

Veterans of the Sixth Corps, Army of the Potomac, are here seen marching down Pennsylvania Avenue in the National Capital on June 8, 1865. In the immediate foreground, at the left, the very sway and swing of the leading files is recorded on the glass plate as the column executes "platoons, right wheel." The masses in the advancing column almost seem to fall and rise. Up the long street the eye sweeps to catch the dim outlines of the Capitol. Here are no "awe-struck faces," for this is the moment of the nation's rejoicing. But twenty-six years later, when General Sherman died, some of the same men who passed when this picture was taken marched in the solemn procession that attended the last rites of the distinguished chieftain, Sherman.

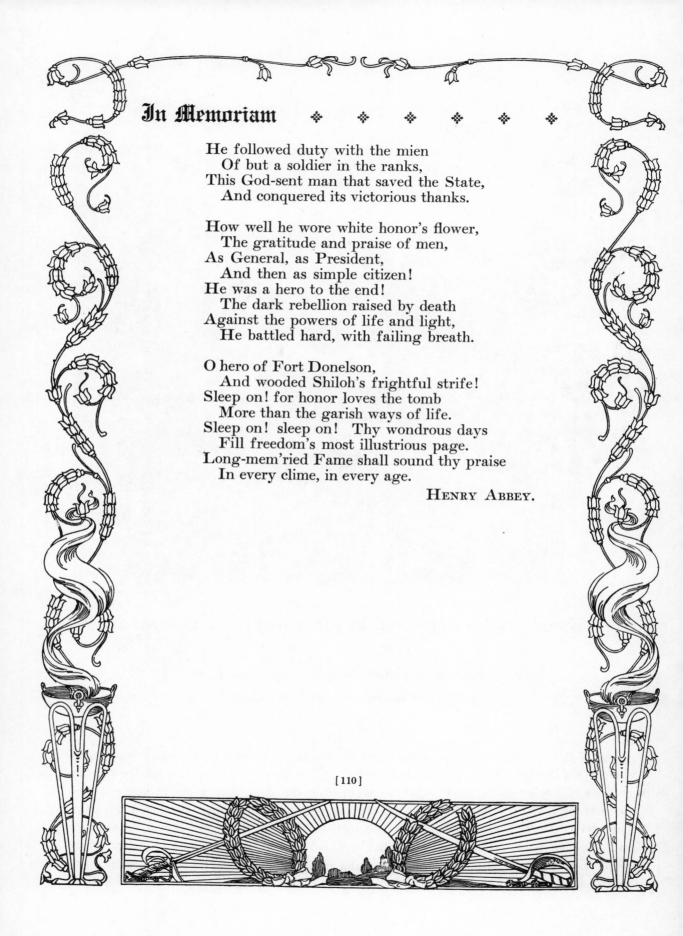

In Memoriam ❖ ❖ ❖ ❖ ❖ ❖

He followed duty with the mien
    Of but a soldier in the ranks,
This God-sent man that saved the State,
    And conquered its victorious thanks.

How well he wore white honor's flower,
    The gratitude and praise of men,
As General, as President,
    And then as simple citizen!
He was a hero to the end!
    The dark rebellion raised by death
Against the powers of life and light,
    He battled hard, with failing breath.

O hero of Fort Donelson,
    And wooded Shiloh's frightful strife!
Sleep on! for honor loves the tomb
    More than the garish ways of life.
Sleep on! sleep on! Thy wondrous days
    Fill freedom's most illustrious page.
Long-mem'ried Fame shall sound thy praise
    In every clime, in every age.

HENRY ABBEY.

[110]

"WITH THE MIEN OF BUT A SOLDIER IN THE RANKS"

THE COMMANDER OF THE ARMIES GRANT IN JULY, 1864

Here Grant's dress is nearer uniform than usual. A veteran recalls that it consisted ordinarily of a plain old army hat—"slouch," as it was called—and fatigue coat, pretty well worn, with very little insignia of rank for outward show. Thus he was frequently taken by the soldiers along the line for some old cavalryman who was investigating affairs he knew nothing about. In his tours General Grant was often stopped by the guards around the camps and compelled to identify himself before the men would permit him to pass. It sometimes happened that the sentries knew the General well enough by sight, but since he was not in full uniform and bore no insignia of rank, they would solemnly compel him to halt until they could call for the officer of the guard, who would formally examine the general as to his identity.

EULOGY OF ULYSSES S. GRANT

The speech was delivered at the banquet of the Army of the Tennessee, upon the occasion of the inauguration of the Grant Equestrian Statue, at Chicago, October 8, 1891. The address is the tribute of one who was for years Grant's trusted military aide and close personal associate. That he has not been unduly influenced by personal feeling may be seen from the judgment of the Confederate general, James Longstreet: " As the world continues to look at and study the grand combinations and strategy of General Grant, the higher will be his award as a great soldier."

The text here followed was kindly furnished by General Porter, by whose permission it is reproduced.

ALMOST all the conspicuous characters in history have risen to prominence by gradual steps, but Ulysses S. Grant seemed to come before the people with a sudden bound. The first sight they caught of him was in the flashes of his guns, and the blaze of his camp fires, those wintry days and nights in front of Donelson. From that hour until the closing triumph at Appomattox he was the leader whose name was the harbinger of victory. From the final sheathing of his sword until the tragedy on Mount McGregor he was the chief citizen of the Republic and the great central figure of the world. The story of his life savors more of romance than reality. It is more like a fabled tale of ancient days than the history of an American citizen of the nineteenth century. As light and shade produce the most attractive effects in a picture, so the singular contrasts, the strange vicissitudes in his marvelous career, surround him with an interest which attaches to few characters in history. His rise from an obscure lieutenancy to the command of the veteran armies of the Republic; his transition from a one-company post of the untrodden West to the executive mansion of the nation; at one time sitting in his little store in Galena, not even known to the Congressman of his district; at another time striding through the palaces of the Old World, with the descendants of a line of kings rising and standing uncovered in his presence—these are some of the features of his extraordinary career which appeal to the imagination, excite men's wonder, and fascinate all who read the story of his life.

"FRIENDS WHO LOVED HIM FOR HIS OWN SAKE"

GRANT AND HIS STAFF IN 1864—BY THE TENT POLE SITS HORACE PORTER,
AUTHOR OF THE ADDRESS REPRODUCED OPPOSITE

The roll-call of those present at City Point in June, 1864, is impressive. Sitting on the bench at the left is Lieutenant-General Grant, with his familiar slouch hat on his knee. By him is Brigadier-General J. A. Rawlins, his chief-of-staff. To the left of the latter sits Lieutenant-Colonel W. L. Duff, assistant inspector-general. By the tent-pole is Lieutenant-Colonel Horace Porter, the author of the address here reprinted. At the right is Captain Ely S. Parker, a full-blooded Indian. Standing behind Grant is one of his secretaries, Lieutenant-Colonel Adam Badeau, who later wrote a military biography of the general. Behind Rawlins is Lieutenant-Colonel C. B. Comstock, noted as an engineer. By Duff stands Lieutenant-Colonel F. T. Dent. Between Porter and Parker is Lieutenant-Colonel O. E. Babcock. All were faithful, in the war and later.

General Grant possessed in a striking degree all the characteristics of the successful soldier. His methods were all stamped with tenacity of purpose, with originality and ingenuity. He depended for his success more upon the powers of invention than of adaptation, and the fact that he has been compared at different times to nearly every great commander in history is perhaps the best proof that he was like none of them. He was possessed of a moral and physical courage which was equal to every emergency in which he was placed; calm amidst excitement, patient under trials, never unduly elated by victory or depressed by defeat. While he possessed a sensitive nature and a singularly tender heart, yet he never allowed his sentiments to interfere with the stern duties of the soldier. He knew better than to attempt to hew rocks with a razor. He realized that paper bullets cannot be fired in warfare. He felt that the hardest blows bring the quickest results; that more men die from disease in sickly camps than from shot and shell in battle.

His magnanimity to foes, his generosity to friends, will be talked of as long as manly qualities are honored. You know after Vicksburg had succumbed to him he said in his order: " The garrison will march out to-morrow. Instruct your commands to be quiet and orderly as the prisoners pass by, and make no offensive remarks." After Lee's surrender at Appomattox, when our batteries began to fire triumphal salutes, he at once suppressed them, saying in his order: " The war is over; the rebels are again our countrymen; the best way to celebrate the victory will be to abstain from all demonstrations in the field." After the war General Lee and his officers were indicted in the civil courts of Virginia by direction of a President who was endeavoring to make treason odious, but succeeded in making nothing so odious as himself. General Lee appealed to his old antagonist for protection. He did not appeal to that heart in vain. General Grant at once took up the cudgels in his defense, threatened to resign his office if such officers were indicted while they continued to obey their paroles, and such was the logic of his argument and the force of his character that those indictments were soon after quashed. So that he penned no idle platitude, he fashioned no stilted epigram, he spoke the earnest convictions of an honest heart when he said, " Let us have peace." He never tired of giving

"ON THE HEIGHTS OF CHATTANOOGA"—A LANDMARK IN GRANT'S RISE TO FAME

The view from Lookout Mountain, showing the very ground over which the Federal soldiers scrambled in their charge, illustrates Porter's reference to the battle of November 23–25, 1863. Grant's own account thus describes the concluding charge: "Discovering that the enemy in his desperation to defeat or resist the progress of Sherman was weakening his center on Missionary Ridge, determined me to order the advance at once. Thomas was accordingly directed to move forward his troops, constituting our center, Baird's division (Fourteenth Corps), Wood's and Sheridan's divisions (Fourth Corps), and Johnston's division (Fourteenth Corps), with a double line of skirmishers thrown out, followed in easy supporting distance by the whole force, and carry the rifle-pits at the foot of Missionary Ridge, and, when carried, to re-form his lines on the rifle-pits with a view to carrying the top of the ridge. These troops moved forward, drove the enemy from the rifle-pits at the base of the ridge like bees from a hive—stopped but a moment until the whole were in line—and commenced the ascent of the mountain from right to left almost simultaneously, following closely the retreating enemy, without further orders. They encountered a fearful volley of grape and canister from near thirty pieces of artillery and musketry from still well-filled rifle-pits, on the summit of the ridge. Not a waver, however, was seen in all that long line of brave men. Their progress was steadily onward until the summit was in their possession." Three months later Grant became the first lieutenant-general since Washington.

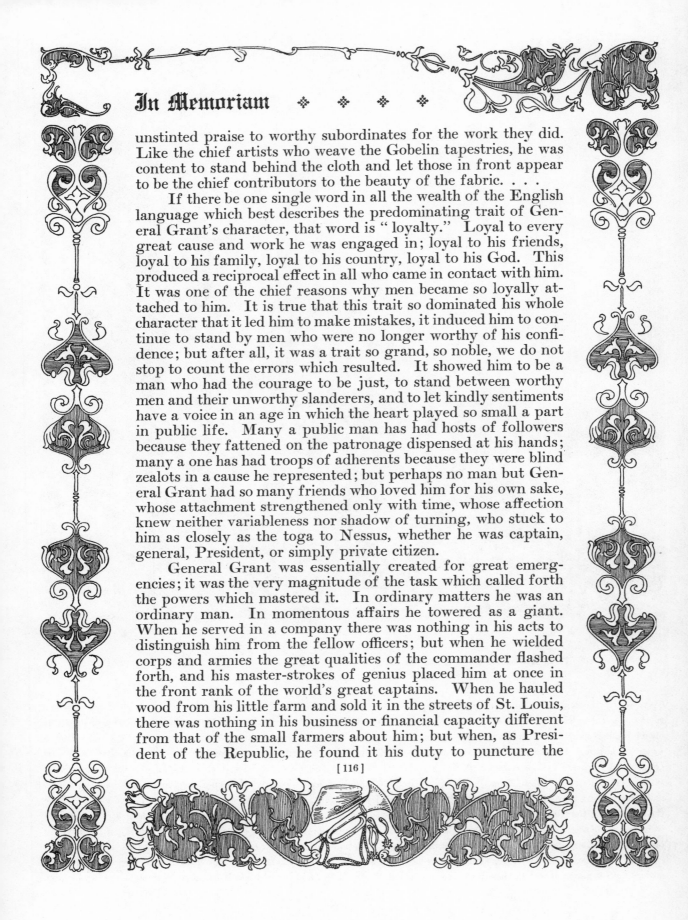

unstinted praise to worthy subordinates for the work they did. Like the chief artists who weave the Gobelin tapestries, he was content to stand behind the cloth and let those in front appear to be the chief contributors to the beauty of the fabric. . . .

If there be one single word in all the wealth of the English language which best describes the predominating trait of General Grant's character, that word is " loyalty." Loyal to every great cause and work he was engaged in; loyal to his friends, loyal to his family, loyal to his country, loyal to his God. This produced a reciprocal effect in all who came in contact with him. It was one of the chief reasons why men became so loyally attached to him. It is true that this trait so dominated his whole character that it led him to make mistakes, it induced him to continue to stand by men who were no longer worthy of his confidence; but after all, it was a trait so grand, so noble, we do not stop to count the errors which resulted. It showed him to be a man who had the courage to be just, to stand between worthy men and their unworthy slanderers, and to let kindly sentiments have a voice in an age in which the heart played so small a part in public life. Many a public man has had hosts of followers because they fattened on the patronage dispensed at his hands; many a one has had troops of adherents because they were blind zealots in a cause he represented; but perhaps no man but General Grant had so many friends who loved him for his own sake, whose attachment strengthened only with time, whose affection knew neither variableness nor shadow of turning, who stuck to him as closely as the toga to Nessus, whether he was captain, general, President, or simply private citizen.

General Grant was essentially created for great emergencies; it was the very magnitude of the task which called forth the powers which mastered it. In ordinary matters he was an ordinary man. In momentous affairs he towered as a giant. When he served in a company there was nothing in his acts to distinguish him from the fellow officers; but when he wielded corps and armies the great qualities of the commander flashed forth, and his master-strokes of genius placed him at once in the front rank of the world's great captains. When he hauled wood from his little farm and sold it in the streets of St. Louis, there was nothing in his business or financial capacity different from that of the small farmers about him; but when, as President of the Republic, he found it his duty to puncture the

"TO THE EXECUTIVE MANSION OF THE NATION"

GRANT'S INAUGURATION AS PRESIDENT—MARCH 4, 1869

The inauguration of Ulysses S. Grant was a particularly impressive ceremony. When he was nominated in May, 1868, his letter of acceptance had closed with the phrase, "Let us have peace," which became the slogan of the campaign. The ceremonies on March 4th were marked by intense enthusiasm. The recent contest between the President and Congress had made the people more than responsive to the prayer, "Let us have peace"; they looked forward with eagerness for this hero of war, the youngest of their Presidents, to allay the bitterness of partisan strife and sectional animosity. This was so much the purpose of Grant's own heart that, out of all his public utterances, this was chosen for inscription on his tomb on Riverside Drive in New York. Grant is one of the few captains in the history of the world who "made war that war might cease." The story of his career forms more than military history; it is an example for all ages.

fallacy of the inflationists, to throttle by a veto the attempt of unwise legislators to tamper with the American credit, he penned a State paper so logical, so masterly, that it has ever since been the pride, wonder, and admiration of every lover of an honest currency. He was made for great things, not for little. He could collect for the nation $15,000,000 from Great Britain in settlement of the *Alabama* claims; he could not protect his own personal savings from the miscreants who robbed him in Wall Street. . . .

During his last illness an indescribably touching incident happened which will ever be memorable, and which never can be effaced from the memory of those who witnessed it. Even after this lapse of years I can scarcely trust my own feelings to recall it. It was on Decoration Day in the city of New York, the last one he ever saw on earth. That morning the members of the Grand Army of the Republic, the veterans in that vicinity, arose earlier than was their wont. They seemed to spend more time that morning in unfurling the old battle flags, in burnishing the medals of honor which decorated their breasts, for on that day they had determined to march by the house of their dying commander to give him a last marching salute. In the streets the columns were forming; inside the house, on that bed from which he was never to rise again, lay the stricken chief. The hand which had received the surrendered swords of countless thousands could scarcely return the pressure of a friendly grasp. The voice which had cheered on to triumphant victory the legions of America's manhood could no longer call for the cooling draught that slaked the thirst of a fevered tongue; and prostrate on that bed of anguish lay the form which in the New World had ridden at the head of conquering columns, which in the Old World had been deemed worthy to stand with head covered and feet sandled in the presence of princes, kings, and emperors. Now his ear caught the sound of martial music. Bands were playing the same strains which had mingled with the echoes of his guns at Vicksburg, the same quicksteps to which his men had sped in hot haste in pursuit of Lee through Virginia. And then came the heavy, measured steps of moving columns, a step which can be acquired only by years of service in the field. He recognized it all now. It was the tread of his old veterans. With his little remaining strength he arose and dragged himself to the window. As he gazed upon those battle flags

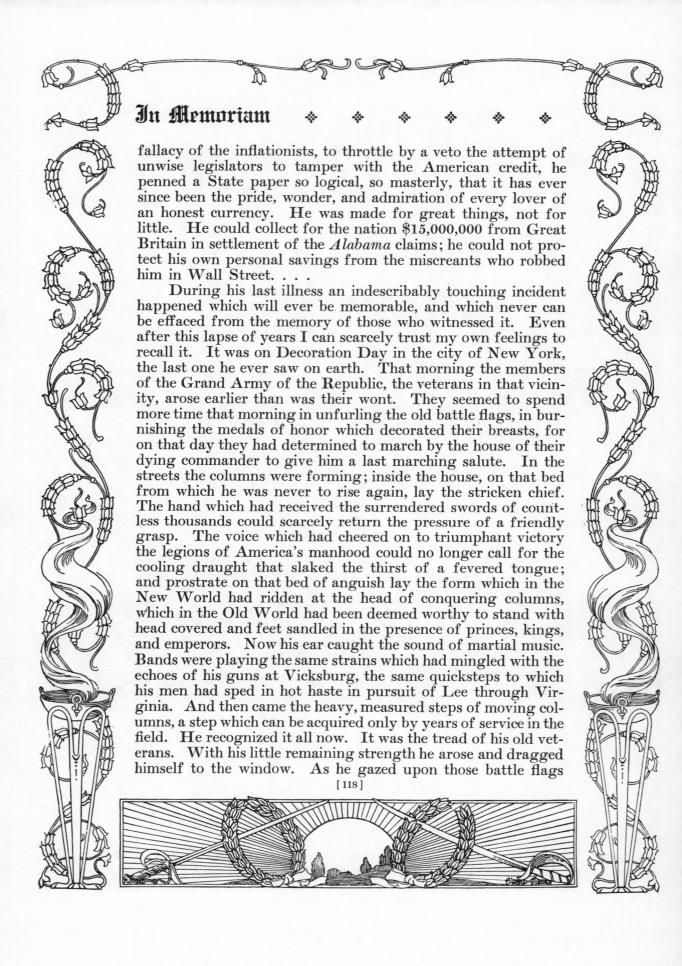

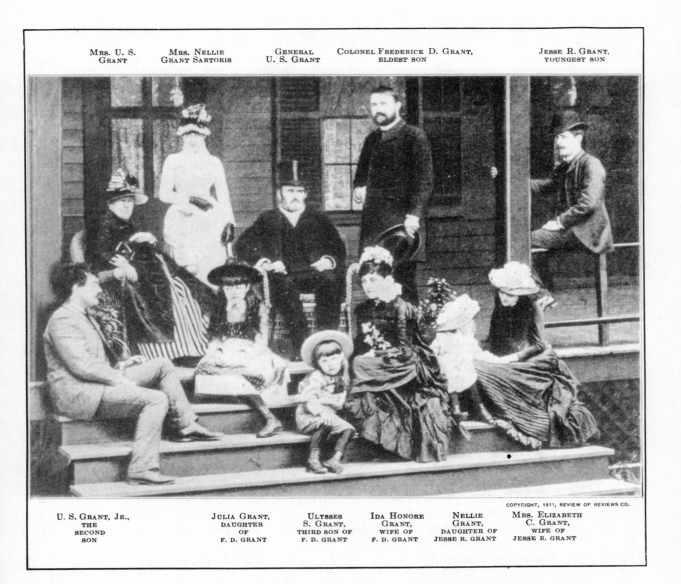

MRS. U. S.   MRS. NELLIE   GENERAL   COLONEL FREDERICK D. GRANT,   JESSE R. GRANT,
GRANT   GRANT SARTORIS   U. S. GRANT   ELDEST SON   YOUNGEST SON

COPYRIGHT, 1911, REVIEW OF REVIEWS CO.

U. S. GRANT, JR.,   JULIA GRANT,   ULYSSES   IDA HONORE   NELLIE   MRS. ELIZABETH
THE   DAUGHTER   S. GRANT,   GRANT,   GRANT,   C. GRANT,
SECOND   OF   THIRD SON OF   WIFE OF   DAUGHTER OF   WIFE OF
SON   F. D. GRANT   F. D. GRANT   F. D. GRANT   JESSE R. GRANT   JESSE R. GRANT

"THE TRAGEDY AT MOUNT McGREGOR"—GRANT AND HIS FAMILY, JULY 19, 1885

On July 16th, three days before this photograph was taken, the general was removed to a summer cottage on Mount McGregor, near Saratoga Springs. Exactly a week later, July 23, 1885, he breathed his last amid the family here assembled. No period of Ulysses S. Grant's life was more heroic than its closing months. He had remained in excellent health up to Christmas of 1883. In the summer of 1884 he was annoyed by unpleasant sensations in his throat. He paid little attention to the symptoms until autumn. A physician, calling one day in October, made an examination that alarmed him. He advised that a specialist be called at once. Cancer of the throat had set in. The annoying sensations at length became painful, and in December the disease had so far advanced that to drink even liquid food was torture. General Badeau says: "He was in no way dismayed, but the sight was to me the most appalling I had ever witnessed—the conqueror looking at his own inevitable conqueror; the stern soldier to whom so many armies had surrendered, watching the approach of that enemy before whom even he must yield." Yet the stricken chief continued work upon his "Memoirs." He could not now dictate to an amanuensis, so he wrote with a hand quivering with pain upon pads placed in his lap. There is something peculiarly noble in this determination to provide by his own efforts a competence for his family. What effect his departure had on the country is told in the Introduction to this volume, but the demonstrations were not confined to America. On August 4th a memorial service was held in the English temple of fame, Westminster Abbey. No less a dignitary than Canon Farrar delivered the funeral address. The civilized world joined in the mourning. Tributes to his memory extended over many years. In 1896, the Chinese statesman, Li Hung Chang, left a memorial at his tomb on Riverside Drive, New York City. Grant's fame is a secure American possession.

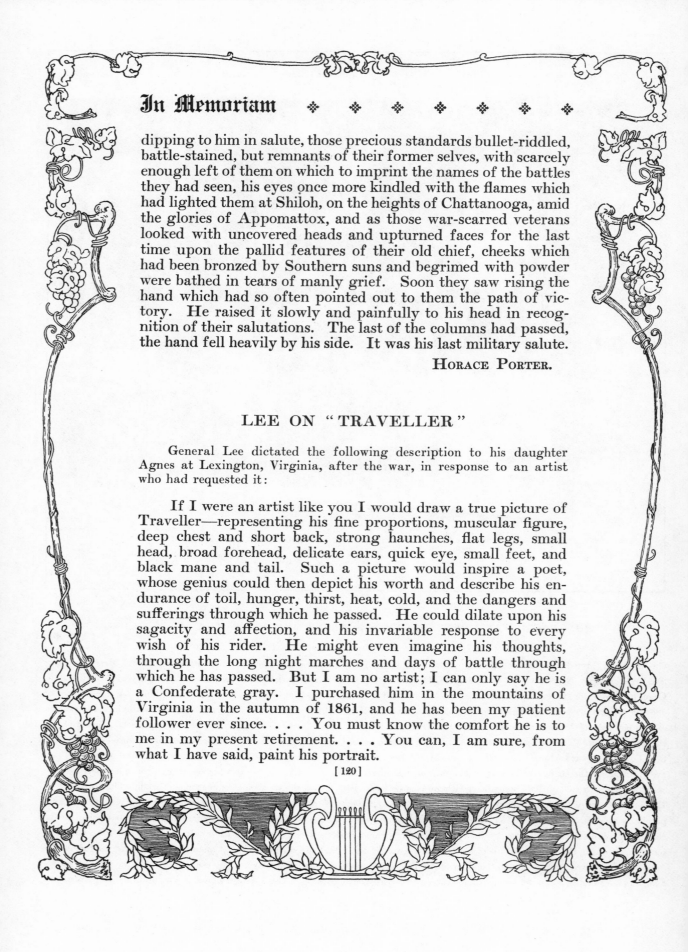

dipping to him in salute, those precious standards bullet-riddled, battle-stained, but remnants of their former selves, with scarcely enough left of them on which to imprint the names of the battles they had seen, his eyes once more kindled with the flames which had lighted them at Shiloh, on the heights of Chattanooga, amid the glories of Appomattox, and as those war-scarred veterans looked with uncovered heads and upturned faces for the last time upon the pallid features of their old chief, cheeks which had been bronzed by Southern suns and begrimed with powder were bathed in tears of manly grief. Soon they saw rising the hand which had so often pointed out to them the path of victory. He raised it slowly and painfully to his head in recognition of their salutations. The last of the columns had passed, the hand fell heavily by his side. It was his last military salute.

HORACE PORTER.

LEE ON "TRAVELLER"

General Lee dictated the following description to his daughter Agnes at Lexington, Virginia, after the war, in response to an artist who had requested it:

If I were an artist like you I would draw a true picture of Traveller—representing his fine proportions, muscular figure, deep chest and short back, strong haunches, flat legs, small head, broad forehead, delicate ears, quick eye, small feet, and black mane and tail. Such a picture would inspire a poet, whose genius could then depict his worth and describe his endurance of toil, hunger, thirst, heat, cold, and the dangers and sufferings through which he passed. He could dilate upon his sagacity and affection, and his invariable response to every wish of his rider. He might even imagine his thoughts, through the long night marches and days of battle through which he has passed. But I am no artist; I can only say he is a Confederate gray. I purchased him in the mountains of Virginia in the autumn of 1861, and he has been my patient follower ever since. . . . You must know the comfort he is to me in my present retirement. . . . You can, I am sure, from what I have said, paint his portrait.

[120]

"I CAN ONLY SAY HE IS A CONFEDERATE GRAY"—LEE ON "TRAVELLER"

This famous photograph of Lee on "Traveller" was taken by Miley, of Lexington, in September, 1866. In July of that year Brady, Gardner, and Miley had tried to get a photograph of the general on his horse, but the weather was so hot and the flies accordingly so annoying that the pictures were very poor. But the September picture has become probably the most popular photograph in the South. In the Army of Northern Virginia the horse was almost as well known as his master. It was foaled near the White Sulphur Springs in West Virginia, and attracted the notice of General Lee in 1861. Lee's affection for it was very deep and strong. On it he rode from Richmond to Lexington to assume his duties as president of Washington College. During the remainder of his life "Traveller" was his constant companion. His son records that the general enjoyed nothing more than a long ride, which gave him renewed energy for his work. In one of his letters while away from home he said: "How is Traveller? Tell him I miss him dreadfully, and have repented of our separation but once—and that is the whole time since we parted."

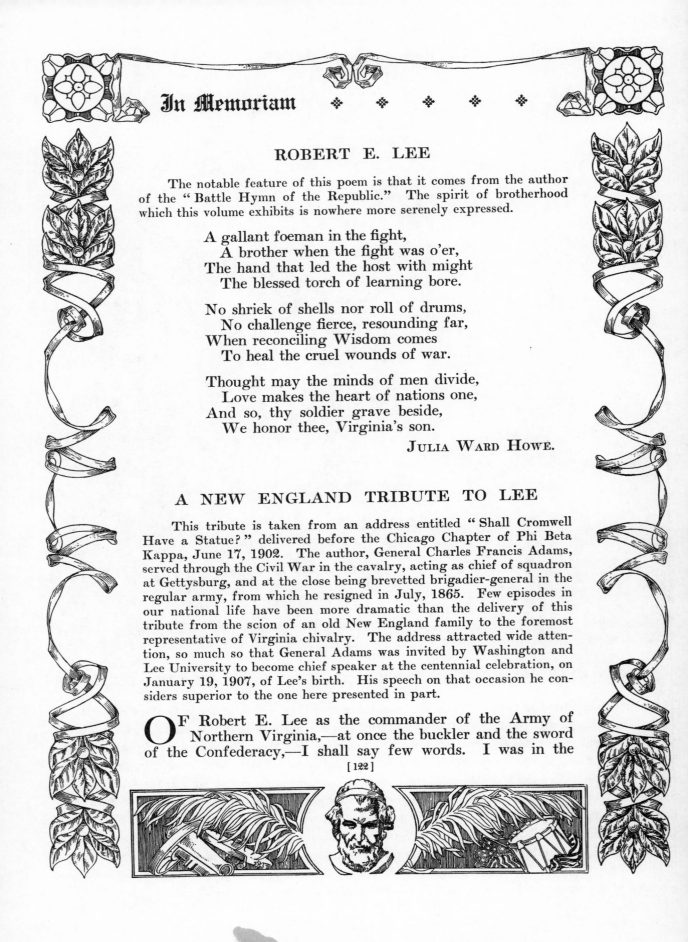

In Memoriam ❖ ❖ ❖ ❖ ❖

ROBERT E. LEE

The notable feature of this poem is that it comes from the author of the "Battle Hymn of the Republic." The spirit of brotherhood which this volume exhibits is nowhere more serenely expressed.

A gallant foeman in the fight,
    A brother when the fight was o'er,
The hand that led the host with might
    The blessed torch of learning bore.

No shriek of shells nor roll of drums,
    No challenge fierce, resounding far,
When reconciling Wisdom comes
    To heal the cruel wounds of war.

Thought may the minds of men divide,
    Love makes the heart of nations one,
And so, thy soldier grave beside,
    We honor thee, Virginia's son.

JULIA WARD HOWE.

A NEW ENGLAND TRIBUTE TO LEE

This tribute is taken from an address entitled "Shall Cromwell Have a Statue?" delivered before the Chicago Chapter of Phi Beta Kappa, June 17, 1902. The author, General Charles Francis Adams, served through the Civil War in the cavalry, acting as chief of squadron at Gettysburg, and at the close being brevetted brigadier-general in the regular army, from which he resigned in July, 1865. Few episodes in our national life have been more dramatic than the delivery of this tribute from the scion of an old New England family to the foremost representative of Virginia chivalry. The address attracted wide attention, so much so that General Adams was invited by Washington and Lee University to become chief speaker at the centennial celebration, on January 19, 1907, of Lee's birth. His speech on that occasion he considers superior to the one here presented in part.

OF Robert E. Lee as the commander of the Army of Northern Virginia,—at once the buckler and the sword of the Confederacy,—I shall say few words. I was in the

LEE IN '63—"EVERY INCH A SOLDIER"

The words of General Charles Francis Adams are fittingly borne out by this magnificent likeness, taken by Vannerson of Richmond in 1863, when Lee was at the height of his military power. He wears a handsome sword and sash presented to him by ladies of Baltimore just previously. Some of the ladies of Richmond had made a set of shirts for their hero, and asked him for his portrait on one of his visits to Richmond. Out of compliment to the ladies, General Lee wore one here; the turnover collar, high in the neck, clearly identifies this portrait.

ranks of those opposed to him. For years I was face to face with some fragment of the Army of Northern Virginia, and intent to do it harm; and during those years there was not a day when I would not have drawn a deep breath of relief and satisfaction at hearing of the death of Lee, even as I did draw it at hearing of the death of Jackson. But now, looking back through a perspective of nearly forty years, I glory in it, and in them as foes,—they were worthy of the best of steel. I am proud now to say that I was their countryman. Whatever differences of opinion may exist as to the course of Lee when his choice was made, of Lee as a foe and the commander of an army, but one opinion can be entertained. Every inch a soldier, he was an opponent not less generous and humane than formidable, a type of highest martial character; cautious, magnanimous and bold, a very thunderbolt in war, he was self-contained in victory, but greatest in defeat. To that escutcheon attaches no stain.

I now come to what I have always regarded—shall ever regard—as the most creditable episode in all American history, —an episode without a blemish,—imposing, dignified, simple, heroic. I refer to Appomattox. Two men met that day, representative of American civilization, the whole world looking on. The two were Grant and Lee,—types each. Both rose, and rose unconsciously, to the full height of the occasion,— and than that occasion there has been none greater. About it, and them, there was no theatrical display, no self-consciousness, no effort at effect. A great crisis was to be met; and they met that crisis as great countrymen should. Consider the possibilities; think for a moment of what that day might have been; you will then see cause to thank God for much.

That month of April saw the close of exactly four years of persistent strife,—a strife which the whole civilized world had been watching intently. Democracy—the capacity of man in his present stage of development for self-government—was believed to be on trial. The wish the father to the thought, the prophets of evil had been liberal in prediction. It so chances that my attention has been especially drawn to the European utterances of that time; and, read in the clear light of subsequent history, I use words of moderation when I say that they are now both inconceivable and ludicrous. Staid journals, grave public men seemed to take what was little less than

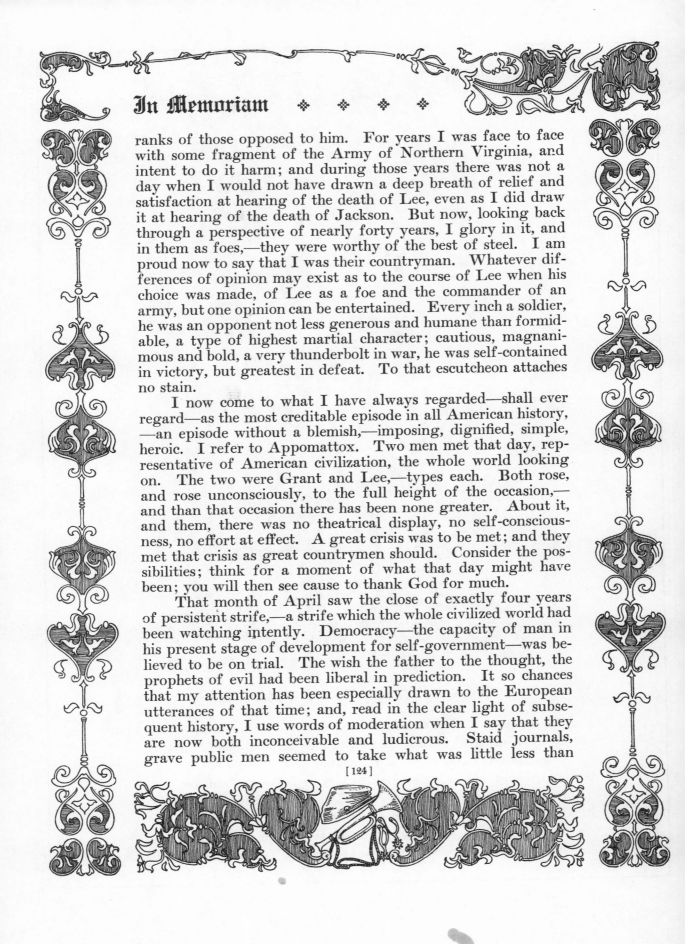

"WITH A HOME NO LONGER HIS"

The massive Doric pillars of the home of Robert E. Lee are, in June, 1864, the background for a group of Federal soldiers. Around this splendid colonial mansion cluster memories of the whole course of American history. It was built by the adopted son of Washington, George Washington Parke Custis, grandson of his wife Martha Custis. On the death of Martha Washington in 1802, he erected this lordly mansion with the front in imitation of the Temple of Theseus at Athens. Within were stored memorials brought from Mount Vernon—pictures, silver-service, and furniture. Here Custis entertained with a lavish hospitality. Lafayette was a guest of honor on his visit to this country. In 1831, in the room to the left of the main hall, the only daughter of the house was married to Lieutenant Robert E. Lee. In 1861 the estate was confiscated and occupied by Federal troops. The family heirlooms were removed, many of them eventually finding their way to the National Museum in Washington and others to their original abiding-place, Mount Vernon. The grounds became a national cemetery; the first person buried there being a Confederate soldier. In 1864 the estate was sold at auction for delinquent taxes for $26,100 to the National Government. After the war General Lee made small effort to recover the property, but in 1877 George Washington Custis Lee, the heir under the law, established his title to the place and received therefor $150,000. Thus the resting-place of some 20,000 American soldiers passed permanently into the possession of the American nation.

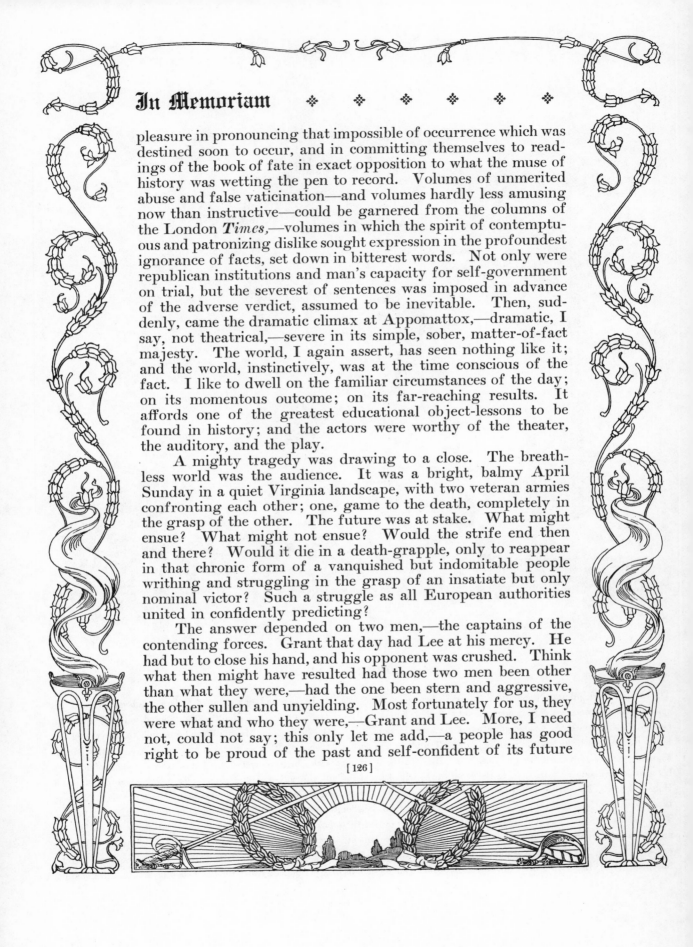

pleasure in pronouncing that impossible of occurrence which was destined soon to occur, and in committing themselves to readings of the book of fate in exact opposition to what the muse of history was wetting the pen to record. Volumes of unmerited abuse and false vaticination—and volumes hardly less amusing now than instructive—could be garnered from the columns of the London *Times,*—volumes in which the spirit of contemptuous and patronizing dislike sought expression in the profoundest ignorance of facts, set down in bitterest words. Not only were republican institutions and man's capacity for self-government on trial, but the severest of sentences was imposed in advance of the adverse verdict, assumed to be inevitable. Then, suddenly, came the dramatic climax at Appomattox,—dramatic, I say, not theatrical,—severe in its simple, sober, matter-of-fact majesty. The world, I again assert, has seen nothing like it; and the world, instinctively, was at the time conscious of the fact. I like to dwell on the familiar circumstances of the day; on its momentous outcome; on its far-reaching results. It affords one of the greatest educational object-lessons to be found in history; and the actors were worthy of the theater, the auditory, and the play.

A mighty tragedy was drawing to a close. The breathless world was the audience. It was a bright, balmy April Sunday in a quiet Virginia landscape, with two veteran armies confronting each other; one, game to the death, completely in the grasp of the other. The future was at stake. What might ensue? What might not ensue? Would the strife end then and there? Would it die in a death-grapple, only to reappear in that chronic form of a vanquished but indomitable people writhing and struggling in the grasp of an insatiate but only nominal victor? Such a struggle as all European authorities united in confidently predicting?

The answer depended on two men,—the captains of the contending forces. Grant that day had Lee at his mercy. He had but to close his hand, and his opponent was crushed. Think what then might have resulted had those two men been other than what they were,—had the one been stern and aggressive, the other sullen and unyielding. Most fortunately for us, they were what and who they were,—Grant and Lee. More, I need not, could not say; this only let me add,—a people has good right to be proud of the past and self-confident of its future

SOLDIER AND CITIZEN BEFORE THE APPOMATTOX COURT HOUSE

This picture and the next one reveal contrasting scenes at the close of the greatest civil conflict of modern times—the soldiers of the Union army after Lee's surrender grouped before Appomattox Court House, and citizens of the hitherto quiet village gathered in front of the village inn. Grant himself did not remain long after the negotiations were concluded. As he left the McLean house a little after four in the afternoon he heard the firing of salutes in the Union camp in celebration of the news of surrender. He at once issued orders to discontinue it. "The war is over," he said, "the rebels are our countrymen again, and the best sign of rejoicing after the victory will be to abstain from all demonstrations." The next morning he rode to the Confederate lines and held a last interview with Lee, after which he returned to the McLean house before setting out for Washington. Many of his staff were disappointed, but Grant had no curiosity to look upon the conquered army. He was much more eager to restore harmony and prosperity to the reunited nation.

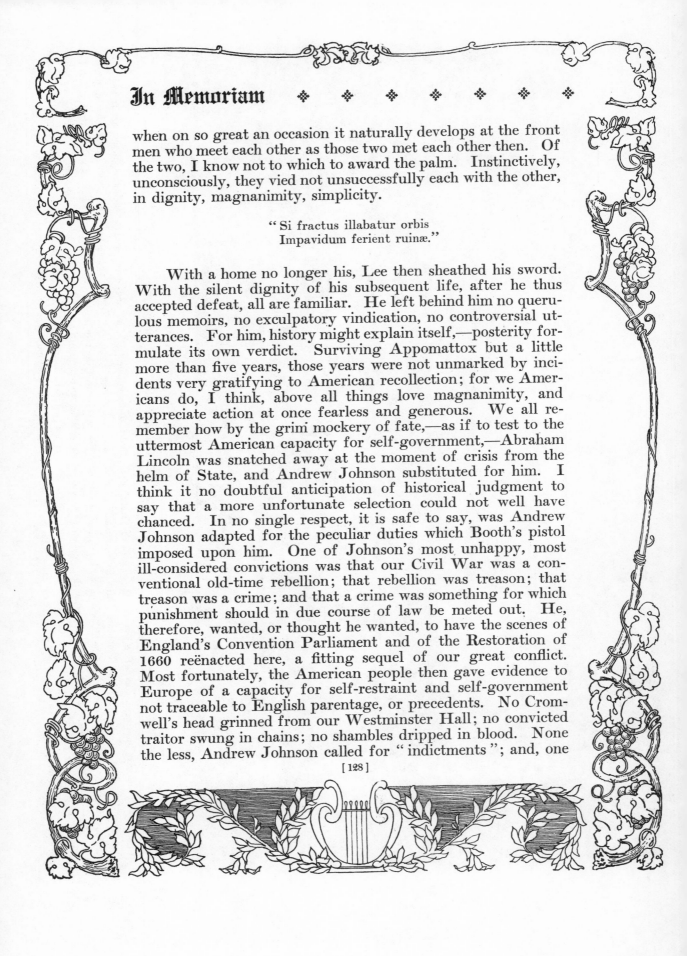

when on so great an occasion it naturally develops at the front men who meet each other as those two met each other then. Of the two, I know not to which to award the palm. Instinctively, unconsciously, they vied not unsuccessfully each with the other, in dignity, magnanimity, simplicity.

> "Si fractus illabatur orbis
> Impavidum ferient ruinæ."

With a home no longer his, Lee then sheathed his sword. With the silent dignity of his subsequent life, after he thus accepted defeat, all are familiar. He left behind him no querulous memoirs, no exculpatory vindication, no controversial utterances. For him, history might explain itself,—posterity formulate its own verdict. Surviving Appomattox but a little more than five years, those years were not unmarked by incidents very gratifying to American recollection; for we Americans do, I think, above all things love magnanimity, and appreciate action at once fearless and generous. We all remember how by the grim mockery of fate,—as if to test to the uttermost American capacity for self-government,—Abraham Lincoln was snatched away at the moment of crisis from the helm of State, and Andrew Johnson substituted for him. I think it no doubtful anticipation of historical judgment to say that a more unfortunate selection could not well have chanced. In no single respect, it is safe to say, was Andrew Johnson adapted for the peculiar duties which Booth's pistol imposed upon him. One of Johnson's most unhappy, most ill-considered convictions was that our Civil War was a conventional old-time rebellion; that rebellion was treason; that treason was a crime; and that a crime was something for which punishment should in due course of law be meted out. He, therefore, wanted, or thought he wanted, to have the scenes of England's Convention Parliament and of the Restoration of 1660 reënacted here, a fitting sequel of our great conflict. Most fortunately, the American people then gave evidence to Europe of a capacity for self-restraint and self-government not traceable to English parentage, or precedents. No Cromwell's head grinned from our Westminster Hall; no convicted traitor swung in chains; no shambles dripped in blood. None the less, Andrew Johnson called for "indictments"; and, one

APPOMATTOX—IN THE SUNSHINE OF PEACE

The quaint costumes of the groups before the village inn—the flaring skirt of the woman by the gate and the queer pinafores and roundabouts of the children standing by their father near the tree—all mark the year of 1865. These spectators cannot realize the immensity of the event they have witnessed. But the wisest heads are thankful that peace has returned to their land. They are ready to become once more citizens of the United States of America, and to contribute by their industry and loyalty to the future of a common country. The record of the South since Appomattox shows how faithfully its sons have kept the terms accepted there by Robert E. Lee, and turned defeat into victory.

day, demanded that of Lee. Then outspoke Grant,—General of the Army. Lee, he declared, was his prisoner. He had surrendered to him, and in reliance on his word. He had received assurance that so long as he quietly remained at his home, and did not offend against the law, he should not be molested. He had done so; and, so long as Grant held his commission, molested he should not be. Needless, as pleasant, to say, what Grant then grimly intimated did not take place. Lee was not molested; nor did the General of the Army indignantly fling his commission at an accidental President's feet. That, if necessary, he would have so done, I take to be quite indubitable.

Of Lee's subsequent life, as head of Washington College, I have but one incident to offer. I believe it to be typical. A few months ago I received a letter from a retired army officer. It is needless to give his name; but, from his letter, I extract the following:

"Lee was essentially a Virginian. His sword was Virginia's, and I fancy the State had higher claims upon him than had the Confederacy, just as he supposed it had than the United States. But, after the surrender, he stood firmly and unreservedly in favor of loyalty to the Nation. A gentleman told me this anecdote: As a boy he ran away from his Kentucky home, and served the last two years in the rebel ranks. After the war he resumed his studies under Lee's presidency; and, on one occasion, delivered as a college exercise an oration with eulogistic reference to the 'Lost Cause,' and what it meant. Later, General, then President, Lee sent for the student; and, after praising his composition and delivery, seriously warned him against holding or advancing such views, impressing strongly upon him the unity of the Nation, and urging him to devote himself loyally to maintain the integrity and the honor of the United States. The kindly paternal advice thus given was, I imagine, typical of his whole *post-bellum* life." Let this one anecdote suffice. Here was magnanimity, philosophy, true patriotism: the pure American spirit. Accepting the situation loyally and in a manly, silent way,—without self-consciousness or mental reservation,—he sought by precept, and yet more by a great example, to build up the shattered community of which he was the most observed representative in accordance with the new conditions imposed by fate.

CHARLES FRANCIS ADAMS.

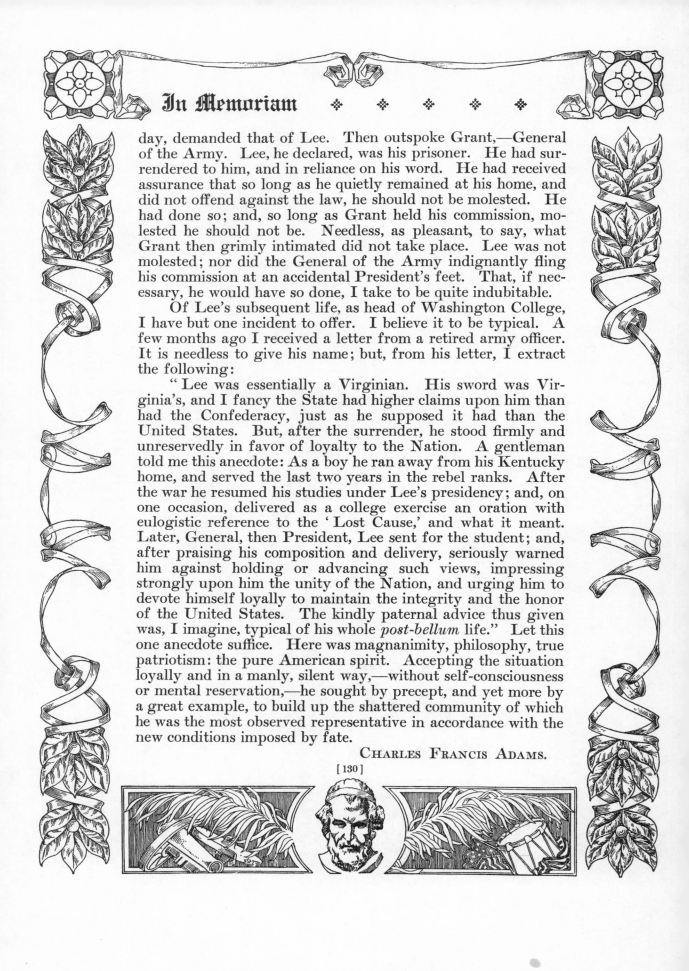

IV

SCENES FROM
SOLDIER
LIFE

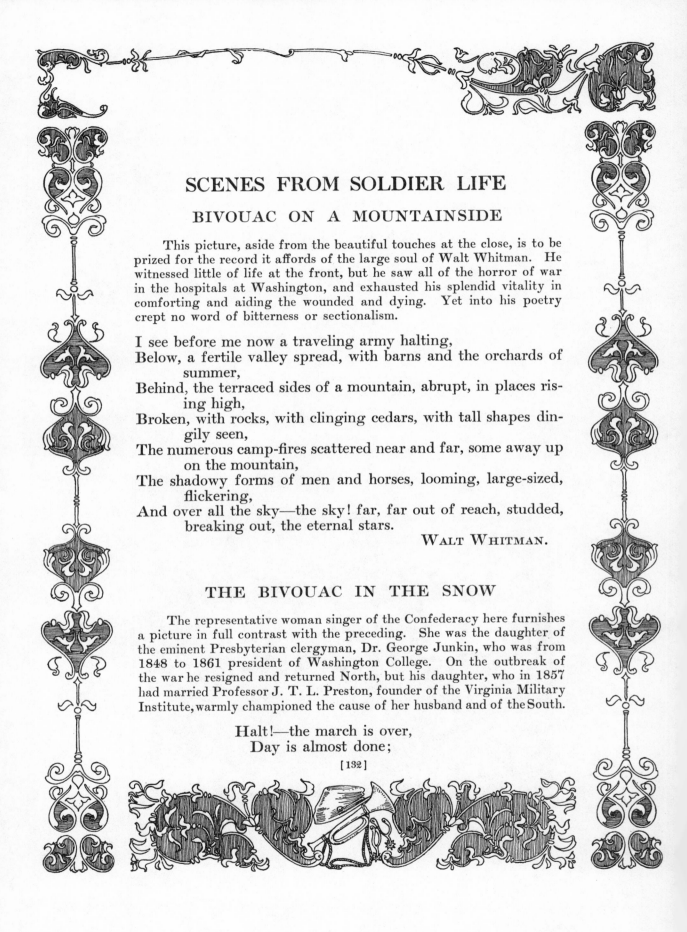

SCENES FROM SOLDIER LIFE

BIVOUAC ON A MOUNTAINSIDE

This picture, aside from the beautiful touches at the close, is to be prized for the record it affords of the large soul of Walt Whitman. He witnessed little of life at the front, but he saw all of the horror of war in the hospitals at Washington, and exhausted his splendid vitality in comforting and aiding the wounded and dying. Yet into his poetry crept no word of bitterness or sectionalism.

I see before me now a traveling army halting,
Below, a fertile valley spread, with barns and the orchards of
      summer,
Behind, the terraced sides of a mountain, abrupt, in places ris-
      ing high,
Broken, with rocks, with clinging cedars, with tall shapes din-
      gily seen,
The numerous camp-fires scattered near and far, some away up
      on the mountain,
The shadowy forms of men and horses, looming, large-sized,
      flickering,
And over all the sky—the sky! far, far out of reach, studded,
      breaking out, the eternal stars.

WALT WHITMAN.

THE BIVOUAC IN THE SNOW

The representative woman singer of the Confederacy here furnishes a picture in full contrast with the preceding. She was the daughter of the eminent Presbyterian clergyman, Dr. George Junkin, who was from 1848 to 1861 president of Washington College. On the outbreak of the war he resigned and returned North, but his daughter, who in 1857 had married Professor J. T. L. Preston, founder of the Virginia Military Institute, warmly championed the cause of her husband and of the South.

Halt!—the march is over,
  Day is almost done;

"BIVOUAC"

TO ILLUSTRATE
THE POEM BY
WHITMAN

The encampment of the Army of the Potomac at Cumberland Landing is a scene strikingly similar to that described by Whitman. With the shadowy soldiers in the foreground one can gaze upon the camp that fills the plain. The ascending smoke from the camp-fires drifts about in the still air, while the horses stand at their fodder and the men await the evening meal. Away to the left the low ground is covered with a pool of water formed by the rain that has fallen most of that day. To-morrow the wagon-trains in the distance will again move slowly along the heavy roads, and the soldiers will trudge forward toward Richmond. This picture shows a scene in the famous Peninsula campaign, when the boys in blue were jubilantly responding to the demand of the North, "On to Richmond." When this view was taken the army had covered more than half the distance. The soldiers' hopes rise with the smoke of the camp-fires all over the peaceful plain.

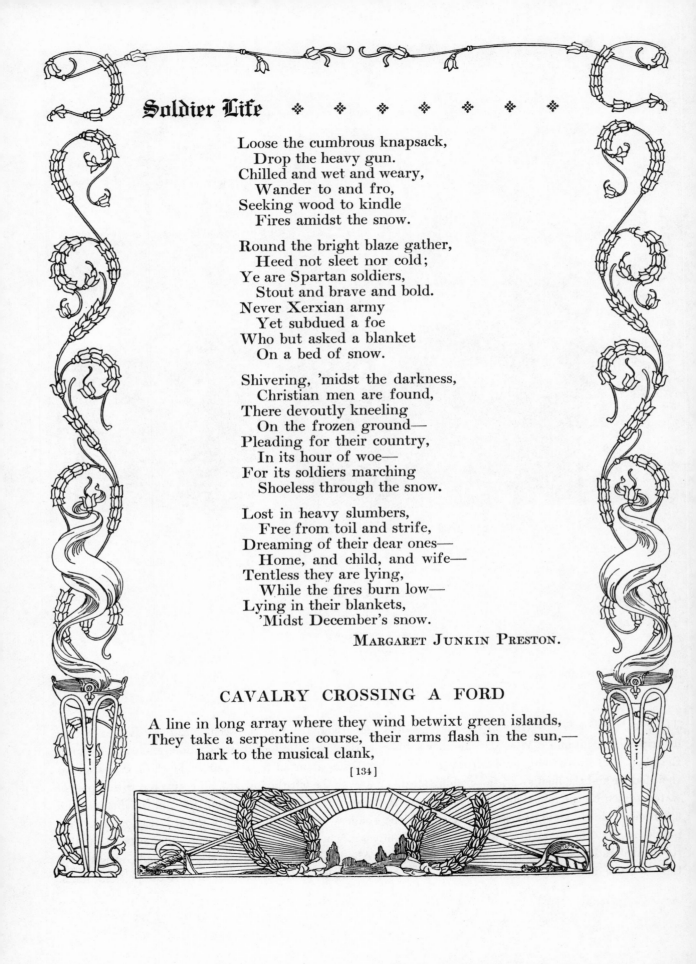

Soldier Life ✦ ✦ ✦ ✦ ✦ ✦ ✦

Loose the cumbrous knapsack,
  Drop the heavy gun.
Chilled and wet and weary,
  Wander to and fro,
Seeking wood to kindle
  Fires amidst the snow.

Round the bright blaze gather,
  Heed not sleet nor cold;
Ye are Spartan soldiers,
  Stout and brave and bold.
Never Xerxian army
  Yet subdued a foe
Who but asked a blanket
  On a bed of snow.

Shivering, 'midst the darkness,
  Christian men are found,
There devoutly kneeling
  On the frozen ground—
Pleading for their country,
  In its hour of woe—
For its soldiers marching
  Shoeless through the snow.

Lost in heavy slumbers,
  Free from toil and strife,
Dreaming of their dear ones—
  Home, and child, and wife—
Tentless they are lying,
  While the fires burn low—
Lying in their blankets,
  'Midst December's snow.

MARGARET JUNKIN PRESTON.

CAVALRY CROSSING A FORD

A line in long array where they wind betwixt green islands,
They take a serpentine course, their arms flash in the sun,—
  hark to the musical clank,

"THE SHADOWY FORMS OF HORSES"

These scenes from a bivouac of McClellan's army, in 1862, reveal, in much the same spirit as Whitman's poem, the actual life of the soldier. At the end of a hard day's march, officers and men were tired, and horses and mules were willing to be unhitched and to nibble on the fodder by the wagon-tongue, or in the rear of the vehicle. The teamsters, meanwhile, were gathered about the twinkling camp-fires that Whitman brings before our eyes. Night will soon fall, and the army will pass into the land of dreams. Little it realizes the dangers of the road to Richmond.

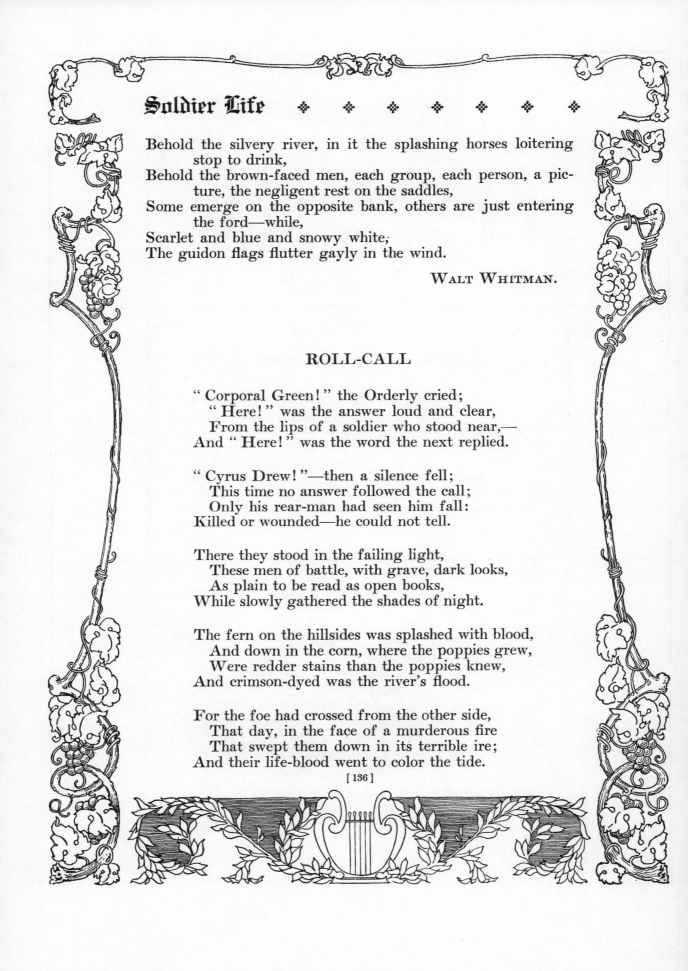

Soldier Life ✦ ✦ ✦ ✦ ✦ ✦ ✦

Behold the silvery river, in it the splashing horses loitering
    stop to drink,
Behold the brown-faced men, each group, each person, a pic-
    ture, the negligent rest on the saddles,
Some emerge on the opposite bank, others are just entering
    the ford—while,
Scarlet and blue and snowy white,
The guidon flags flutter gayly in the wind.

WALT WHITMAN.

ROLL-CALL

" Corporal Green!" the Orderly cried;
    " Here!" was the answer loud and clear,
    From the lips of a soldier who stood near,—
And " Here!" was the word the next replied.

" Cyrus Drew!"—then a silence fell;
    This time no answer followed the call;
    Only his rear-man had seen him fall:
Killed or wounded—he could not tell.

There they stood in the failing light,
    These men of battle, with grave, dark looks,
    As plain to be read as open books,
While slowly gathered the shades of night.

The fern on the hillsides was splashed with blood,
    And down in the corn, where the poppies grew,
    Were redder stains than the poppies knew,
And crimson-dyed was the river's flood.

For the foe had crossed from the other side,
    That day, in the face of a murderous fire
    That swept them down in its terrible ire;
And their life-blood went to color the tide.

[136]

"KILLED OR WOUNDED—HE COULD NOT TELL"

As a companion to the sad lines of the poem "Roll Call," this Confederate soldier, fallen on the field of Spotsylvania, speaks more clearly than words. He is but one of 200,000 "killed and died of wounds" during the war; yet there is a whole world of pitifulness in his useless trappings, his crumpled hat, his loosened straps and haversack. Here the young soldier lies in the gathering twilight, while his companions far away answer to their names. The empty canteen will never more wet the lips of the upturned face, nor shall the long musket dropped in the moment of falling speak again to the foe.

"THERE THEY STOOD
IN THE FAILING LIGHT
THESE MEN OF BATTLE, WITH GRAVE DARK LOOKS"

The spirit of Shepherd's somber poem, "Roll Call," lives in this group—from the spadesmen whose last services to their comrades have been performed, to the solemn bearers of the muffled drums. Many more such occasions were to arise; for these soldiers belonged to the brigade that suffered the greatest loss of life of any one brigade during the war; 1,172 of its men were either killed in battle or died of wounds. The same five regiments that lay in Camp Griffin when this picture was taken in 1861 marched together in the Grand Review on Pennsylvania Avenue in Washington, in 1865. When their term of enlistment expired in 1864, they had all re-enlisted and preserved the existence of the brigade. It was famous also for being composed entirely of troops from one State. It contained the Second, Third, Fourth, Fifth and Sixth Vermont Infantry, and later the First Vermont Heavy Artillery. It was in this respect conspicuous in the Union army, which did not adopt the Confederate policy of grouping regiments from the same

BURIAL PARTY,
OLD VERMONT BRIGADE,
CAMP GRIFFIN, NEAR WASHINGTON, 1861

State in brigades. The gallant record of the Vermont brigade was nowhere more conspicuous than in the Wilderness campaign. The first five regiments lost in the battle of the Wilderness, May 5-6, 1864, 195 killed, 1,017 wounded, and 57 missing, making a total of 1,269. Within a week its loss had amounted to 58 per cent. of the number engaged. The words of the poet are therefore no merely fanciful picture of frightful loss in battle. There were a dozen battles in which the Federal armies alone lost more than 10,000 men, enough in each case to populate a city, and it has been estimated that the totals on both sides amounted to more than 700,000 killed and wounded. When it is recalled that most of these were young men, who in the natural course of events had many years of usefulness yet to live for their country, the cost to the American nation is simply appalling. This is entirely aside from the many sorrowing mourners for the heroes of the Old Vermont Brigade and for many others who failed on any battlefield to answer "Here" at roll-call.

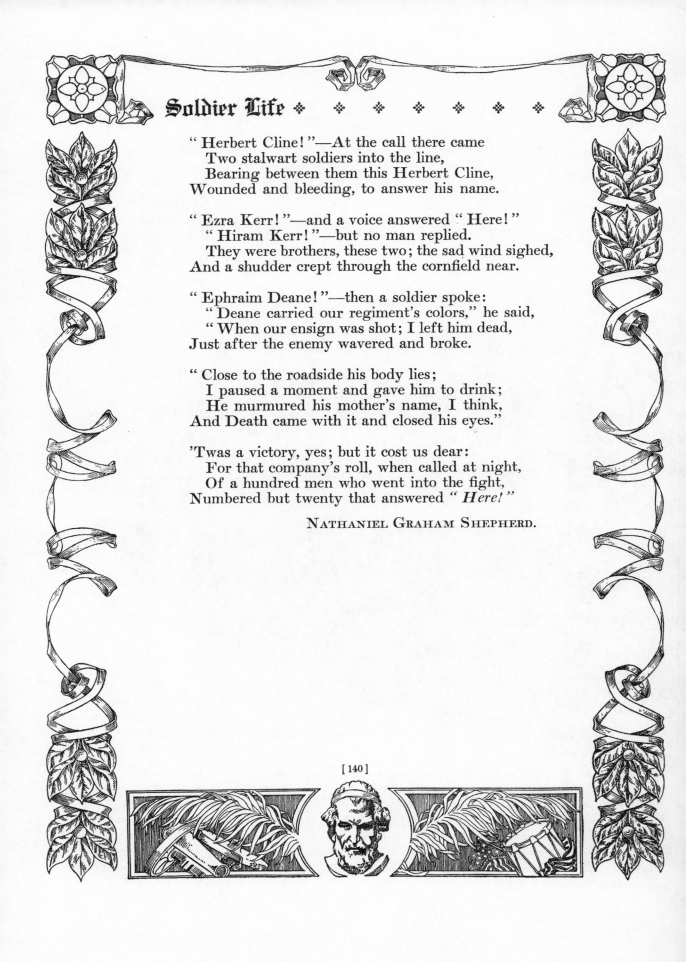

Soldier Life ❖ ❖ ❖ ❖ ❖ ❖

"Herbert Cline!"—At the call there came
  Two stalwart soldiers into the line,
  Bearing between them this Herbert Cline,
Wounded and bleeding, to answer his name.

"Ezra Kerr!"—and a voice answered "Here!"
  "Hiram Kerr!"—but no man replied.
  They were brothers, these two; the sad wind sighed,
And a shudder crept through the cornfield near.

"Ephraim Deane!"—then a soldier spoke:
  "Deane carried our regiment's colors," he said,
  "When our ensign was shot; I left him dead,
Just after the enemy wavered and broke.

"Close to the roadside his body lies;
  I paused a moment and gave him to drink;
  He murmured his mother's name, I think,
And Death came with it and closed his eyes."

'Twas a victory, yes; but it cost us dear:
  For that company's roll, when called at night,
  Of a hundred men who went into the fight,
Numbered but twenty that answered "*Here!*"

NATHANIEL GRAHAM SHEPHERD.

V

WIVES
AND
SWEETHEARTS

AT ANTIETAM BRIDGE

A UNION SOLDIER AFTER THE BATTLE, IN SEPTEM-
BER, 1862, OCCUPIED WITH DIFFERENT "DUTIES"

WIVES AND SWEETHEARTS

THE PICKET-GUARD

The authorship of this production has occasioned more dispute than any other poem of the conflict. Very plausible details of its composition on August 2, 1861, were given by Lamar Fontaine. Joel Chandler Harris, who declared he would be glad to claim the poem as a specimen of Southern literature, concluded for five separate reasons that it was the production of Mrs. Ethelinda Beers. Mrs. Beers in a private letter to Mrs. Helen Kendrick Johnson said: "The poor 'Picket' has had so many authentic claimants, and willing sponsors, that I sometimes question myself whether I did really write it that cool September morning, after reading the stereotyped 'All quiet, etc.', to which was added in small type 'A picket shot.'" The lines first appeared in *Harper's Weekly* for November 30, 1861.

"All quiet along the Potomac," they say,
   "Except now and then a stray picket
Is shot, as he walks on his beat to and fro,
   By a rifleman hid in the thicket.
'Tis nothing: a private or two now and then
   Will not count in the news of the battle;
Not an officer lost—only one of the men,
   Moaning out, all alone, the death-rattle."

All quiet along the Potomac to-night,
   Where the soldiers lie peacefully dreaming;
Their tents in the rays of the clear autumn moon,
   Or the light of the watch-fire, are gleaming.
A tremulous sigh of the gentle night-wind
   Through the forest leaves softly is creeping;
While the stars up above, with their glittering eyes,
   Keep guard, for the army is sleeping.

There's only the sound of the lone sentry's tread,
   As he tramps from the rock to the fountain,
And thinks of the two in the low trundle-bed
   Far away in the cot on the mountain.

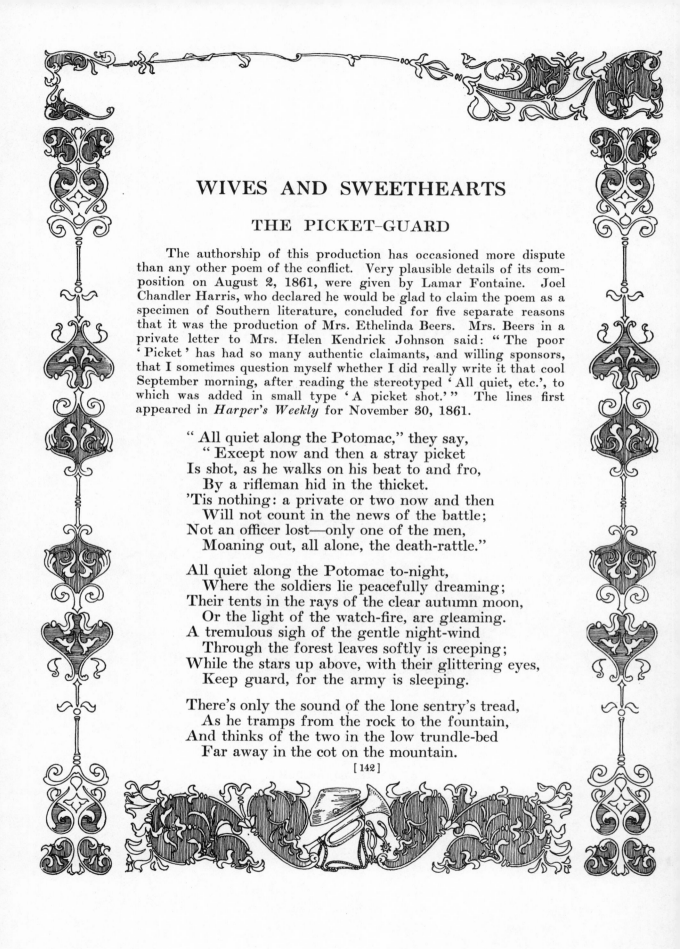

"ALL QUIET   A CIVIL–WAR

ALONG   SENTRY

THE POTOMAC"   ON HIS BEAT

This Union picket by the Potomac River bank, clasping his musket in the chilling blast as he tramps his beat, conjures up the original of Ethel Beers' historic poem. The sympathy of the poet was not misplaced. Picket duty was an experience in every soldier's life. Regiments were detailed at stated intervals to march from their camps to the outer lines and there disposition would be made of the men in the following order: about one half of the regiment would be placed in what was known as the "reserve," while the balance of the men would be taken, by the officer of the guard designated for that purpose, to the extreme outpost, either relieving another regiment or forming new outposts, according to the necessities or changes of position. The period of the poem is the fall of 1861. The battle of Bull Run had been fought in the summer, and thereafter there was very little military activity along the Potomac. McClellan was doing what was absolutely necessary to effective operations—he was drilling the raw recruits into professional soldiers. The public at large, whose impatience had brought on the disaster of Bull Run before either side was prepared for battle, was naturally exasperated. But the author—a woman—was more impressed by the fate of the lonely sentinel.

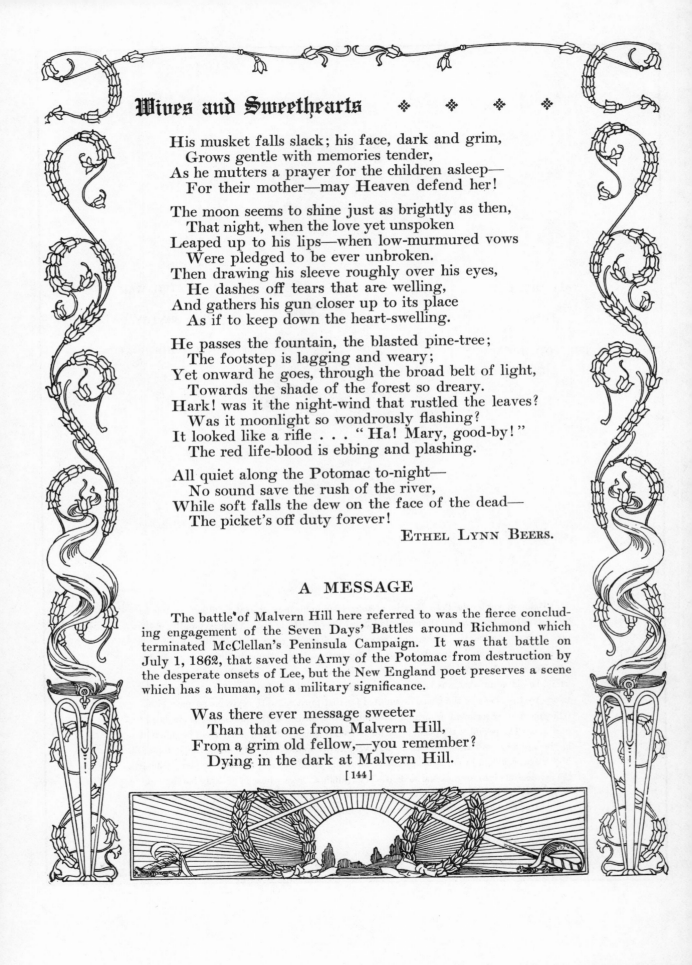

Wives and Sweethearts ❖ ❖ ❖ ❖

His musket falls slack; his face, dark and grim,
   Grows gentle with memories tender,
As he mutters a prayer for the children asleep—
   For their mother—may Heaven defend her!

The moon seems to shine just as brightly as then,
   That night, when the love yet unspoken
Leaped up to his lips—when low-murmured vows
   Were pledged to be ever unbroken.
Then drawing his sleeve roughly over his eyes,
   He dashes off tears that are welling,
And gathers his gun closer up to its place
   As if to keep down the heart-swelling.

He passes the fountain, the blasted pine-tree;
   The footstep is lagging and weary;
Yet onward he goes, through the broad belt of light,
   Towards the shade of the forest so dreary.
Hark! was it the night-wind that rustled the leaves?
   Was it moonlight so wondrously flashing?
It looked like a rifle . . . "Ha! Mary, good-by!"
   The red life-blood is ebbing and plashing.

All quiet along the Potomac to-night—
   No sound save the rush of the river,
While soft falls the dew on the face of the dead—
   The picket's off duty forever!

                ETHEL LYNN BEERS.

A MESSAGE

The battle of Malvern Hill here referred to was the fierce concluding engagement of the Seven Days' Battles around Richmond which
terminated McClellan's Peninsula Campaign. It was that battle on
July 1, 1862, that saved the Army of the Potomac from destruction by
the desperate onsets of Lee, but the New England poet preserves a scene
which has a human, not a military significance.

Was there ever message sweeter
   Than that one from Malvern Hill,
From a grim old fellow,—you remember?
   Dying in the dark at Malvern Hill.

"THEIR SEARCHING MESSAGE FROM THOSE DISTANT HOURS"

OFF TO THE WAR—EMBARKATION OF NINTH ARMY CORPS AT AQUIA CREEK LANDING, IN FEBRUARY, 1863

Elizabeth Stuart Phelps' poem "A Message" breathes a faith that inspired the mothers of many men who stand expectantly in this picture, and of many thousands more who, like them, were "off to the war" in '61–'65. Proud, indeed, were the sweethearts and wives of their "heroes" marching away to the big camps or floating down the stream on the transports. Honor and glory awaited these sons and brothers who were helping to serve their cause. To each fond heart came the hope: "Soon the nation will be ringing with my boy's praise, and his name will be repeated with blessings by unnumbered tongues." But there was also the sickening dread that he might never again be heard of, that stalking disease might single him out in the camp, that he might fall unnoticed when on lonely picket service, that in the wild tumult of the cannonading or the panting rush of the bayonet charge he might be forgotten by his comrades. Mrs. Ward voiced the desire of all true women, both North and South. Though the hero in Blue or in Gray was not to fill the pages of history with deathless deeds, these women believed that at least he would find an honored grave and rise to a higher bliss than this world gives.

Wives and Sweethearts ❖ ❖ ❖ ❖ ❖

With his rough face turned a little,
    On a heap of scarlet sand,
They found him, just within the thicket,
    With a picture in his hand,—

With a stained and crumpled picture
    Of a woman's aged face;
Yet there seemed to leap a wild entreaty,
    Young and living—tender—from the face
When they flashed the lantern on it,
    Gilding all the purple shade,
And stooped to raise him softly,—
    " That's my mother, sir," he said.

" Tell her "—but he wandered, slipping
    Into tangled words and cries,—
Something about Mac and Hooker,
    Something dropping through the cries
About the kitten by the fire,
    And mother's cranberry-pies; and there
The words fell, and an utter
    Silence brooded in the air.

Just as he was drifting from them,
    Out into the dark, alone
(Poor old mother, waiting for your message,
    Waiting with the kitten, all alone!),
Through the hush his voice broke,—" Tell her—
    Thank you, Doctor—when you can,—
Tell her that I kissed her picture,
    And wished I'd been a better man."

Ah, I wonder if the red feet
    Of departed battle-hours
May not leave for us their searching
    Message from those distant hours.
Sisters, daughters, mothers, think you,
    Would your heroes now or then,
Dying, kiss your pictured faces,
    Wishing they'd been better men?

ELIZABETH STUART PHELPS WARD.

[146]

"THE WINTRY BLAST GOES WAILING BY"

Like a vision evoked by Gordon McCabe's verse rises this encampment of the Forty-fourth New York on the Virginia plains.   The snow that covers the foreground suggests of itself the faint smoke that rises from the camp and hovers like a veil over the hillside beyond.   One may suppose that "the owl, for all his feathers is a-cold," and that hares go limping through the frozen grass.   Yet it is not so much the effort to keep warm amid the bleak surroundings that brings gloom to the soldier's heart.   It is rather the emotions which the Southern poet has expressed in Tennysonian stanzas.   Distant from home, or with no home to return to, the soldier feels the loss of those domestic relations which fill life with warmth and hope.   The patriotism that leads to enlistment, or the ardor that springs from war's wild alarms, must sooner or later give way for a time to the simple human emotions that even a child can share and understand.   "East, west, home's best."

CHRISTMAS NIGHT OF '62

William Gordon McCabe entered the Confederate Army in the artillery and rose from private to captain. At the time of writing this poem he was with the Army of Northern Virginia encamped about Fredericksburg. The sanguinary repulse of Burnside was only twelve days in the past, but the thoughts of the soldiers were turned toward family and home.

The wintry blast goes wailing by,
 The snow is falling overhead;
 I hear the lonely sentry's tread,
And distant watch-fires light the sky.

Dim forms go flitting through the gloom;
 The soldiers cluster round the blaze
 To talk of other Christmas days,
And softly speak of home and home.

My sabre swinging overhead
 Gleams in the watch-fire's fitful glow,
 While fiercely drives the blinding snow,
And memory leads me to the dead.

My thoughts go wandering to and fro,
 Vibrating 'twixt the Now and Then;
 I see the low-browed home again,
The old hall wreathed with mistletoe.

And sweetly from the far-off years
 Comes borne the laughter faint and low,
 The voices of the Long Ago!
My eyes are wet with tender tears.

I feel again the mother-kiss,
 I see again the glad surprise
 That lightened up the tranquil eyes
And brimmed them o'er with tears of bliss,

As, rushing from the old hall-door,
 She fondly clasped her wayward boy—
 Her face all radiant with the joy
She felt to see him home once more.

[148]

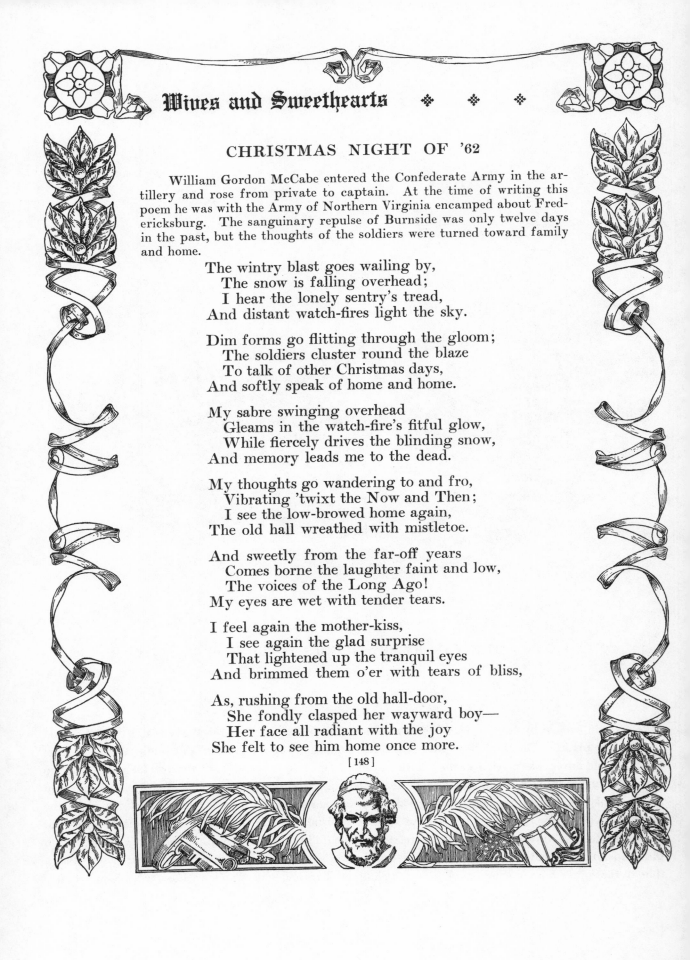

"THE SOLDIERS CLUSTER ROUND THE BLAZE"

As if made for Gorden McCabe's poem, this photograph shows vividly a group of pickets in winter. Pickets were the "eyes" of the army, to observe all movements made by the enemy and to give warning of the approach of any force from the direction of his lines. The particular picket here is a soldier who, after lonely outpost duty on the hilltop just beyond his companions, has returned to warm his hands over their fire. "It was fortunate for these boys," remarked a veteran, "that they had a little hill between themselves and the enemy so that a fire might be made without observation." In general, when facing the foe, pickets upon the outer lines were allowed no fires of any kind. The utmost vigilance was required, no matter what the state of the weather. In many instances during the war soldiers were found frozen to death at their posts of duty, leaning against trees, or as they had fallen while marching on their beats.

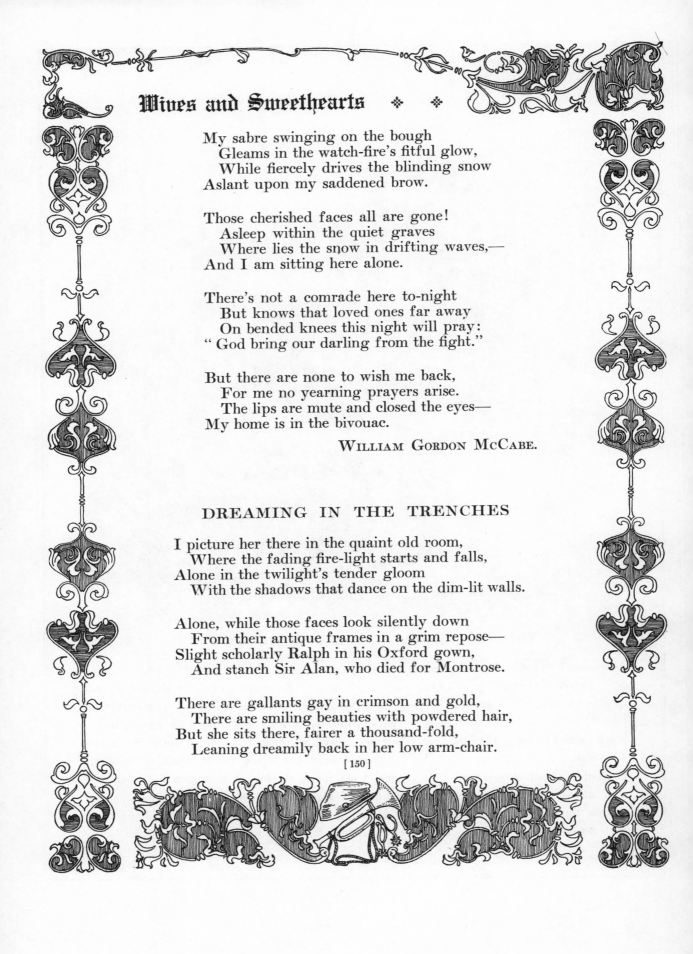

Wives and Sweethearts ❖ ❖

My sabre swinging on the bough
   Gleams in the watch-fire's fitful glow,
   While fiercely drives the blinding snow
Aslant upon my saddened brow.

Those cherished faces all are gone!
   Asleep within the quiet graves
   Where lies the snow in drifting waves,—
And I am sitting here alone.

There's not a comrade here to-night
   But knows that loved ones far away
   On bended knees this night will pray:
" God bring our darling from the fight."

But there are none to wish me back,
   For me no yearning prayers arise.
   The lips are mute and closed the eyes—
My home is in the bivouac.

          WILLIAM GORDON McCABE.

DREAMING IN THE TRENCHES

I picture her there in the quaint old room,
   Where the fading fire-light starts and falls,
Alone in the twilight's tender gloom
   With the shadows that dance on the dim-lit walls.

Alone, while those faces look silently down
   From their antique frames in a grim repose—
Slight scholarly Ralph in his Oxford gown,
   And stanch Sir Alan, who died for Montrose.

There are gallants gay in crimson and gold,
   There are smiling beauties with powdered hair,
But she sits there, fairer a thousand-fold,
   Leaning dreamily back in her low arm-chair.

"THE VOICES OF THE LONG AGO"

The war-time home scene from Virginia gives McCabe's line a more touching pathos. The old-fashioned croquet on the lawn, where the little girl has sat down and delayed the game, is in keeping with the quaint hats and crinoline skirts. The house and its vine-clad arbor have the "home" feeling that emphasizes one of the sorest deprivations of a soldier's life. All the poems in this section record some phase of the loneliness of the tented field, where thousands are gathered from many sections. Differ as much as they may in age, previous occupation, and whole manner of life, they are all moved by the recollection of loved ones afar, who will give a joyous welcome on their return. McCabe's verses on this theme are classic.

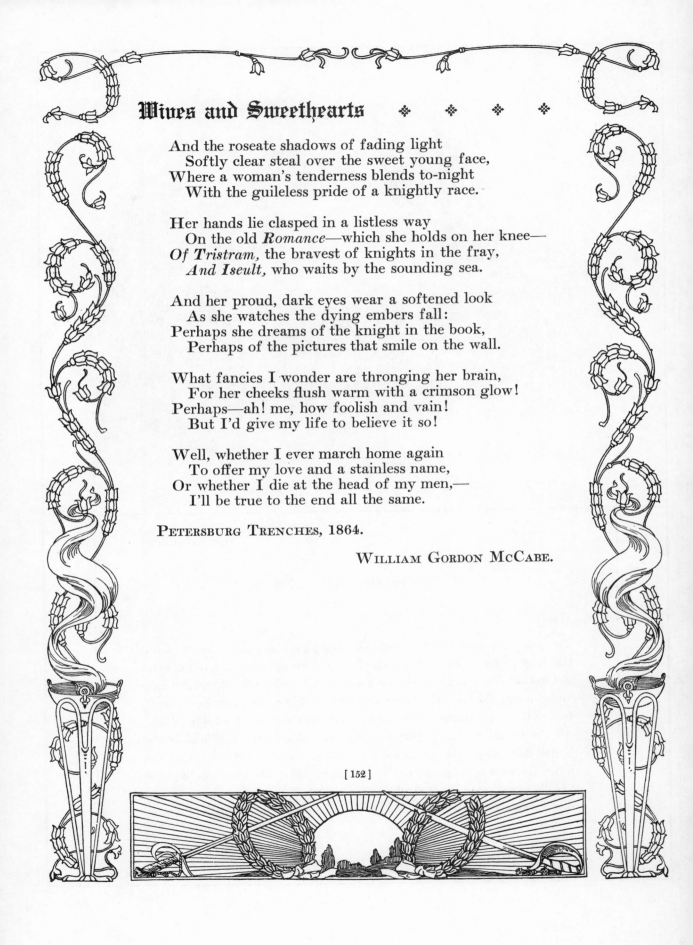

Wives and Sweethearts ❖ ❖ ❖ ❖

And the roseate shadows of fading light
   Softly clear steal over the sweet young face,
Where a woman's tenderness blends to-night
   With the guileless pride of a knightly race.

Her hands lie clasped in a listless way
   On the old *Romance*—which she holds on her knee—
Of Tristram, the bravest of knights in the fray,
   And Iseult, who waits by the sounding sea.

And her proud, dark eyes wear a softened look
   As she watches the dying embers fall:
Perhaps she dreams of the knight in the book,
   Perhaps of the pictures that smile on the wall.

What fancies I wonder are thronging her brain,
   For her cheeks flush warm with a crimson glow!
Perhaps—ah! me, how foolish and vain!
   But I'd give my life to believe it so!

Well, whether I ever march home again
   To offer my love and a stainless name,
Or whether I die at the head of my men,—
   I'll be true to the end all the same.

PETERSBURG TRENCHES, 1864.

WILLIAM GORDON McCABE.

[152]

VI

LYRICS

A SOLDIER GROUP IN A MOMENT FIT FOR SONG—THE 170TH NEW YORK
ON RESERVE PICKET DUTY

THE BATTLE HYMN OF THE REPUBLIC—"A HUNDRED CIRCLING CAMPS"

The time of this photograph and its actors connect directly with Julia Ward Howe's inspiration for her "Battle Hymn." The author, in the late fall of 1861, had made her first visit to Washington in company with her pastor, James Freeman Clarke, Governor Andrew of Massachusetts, and her husband, Dr. Howe, who, already past the age of military service, rendered valuable aid as an officer of the Sanitary Commission. Of her visit she writes in her "Reminiscences": "On the return from the review of troops near the city, to beguile the rather tedious drive, we sang from time to time snatches of the army songs so popular at that time, concluding, I think, with 'John Brown's body.' The soldiers . . . answered back, 'Good for you!' Mr. Clarke said, 'Mrs. Howe, why do you not write some good words for that stirring tune?' I replied that I had often wished to do this, but had not as yet found in my mind any leading toward it. I went to bed that night as usual, and slept, according to my wont, quite soundly. I awoke in the gray of the morning twilight; and as I lay waiting for the dawn, the long lines of the desired poem began to twine themselves in my mind. Having thought out all the stanzas, I said to myself, 'I must get up and write those verses down, lest I fall asleep and forget them.' So, with a sudden effort, I sprang out of bed, and found in the dimness an old stump of a pen which I remembered to have used the day before. I scrawled the verses almost without looking at the paper. I had learned to do this when, on previous occasions, attacks of versification had visited me in the night, and I feared to have recourse to a light lest I should wake the baby, who slept near me. I was always obliged to decipher my scrawl before another night should intervene, as it was only legible while the matter was fresh in my mind. At this

THE FIFTH VERMONT IN 1861, WITH THEIR COLONEL, L. A. GRANT

time, having completed my writing, I returned to bed and fell asleep, saying to myself, 'I like this better than most things that I have written.'" In 1861 the Fifth Vermont lay near Camp Griffin. It was on the outskirts of the encampments in Virginia, near Washington, and consequently subject to attacks by the Confederates. Its career throughout the war is proof that the spirit of the "Battle-Hymn" animated these boys in blue. Its Lieutenant-Colonel, L. A. Grant, who sits on his charger to the right, became famous later as the general commanding the "Vermont Brigade." To the left is Major Redfield Proctor. Leaving Camp Griffin on March 10, 1862, the regiment moved to the Peninsula. Its name became known at Yorktown and Savage's Station, at Antietam, Fredericksburg, and Gettysburg. In the Wilderness campaign, in the battle of May 5th, it assisted in checking the advance of the Confederates along the plank road in time for the Second Corps to take a strong position. It was in the heavy fighting of the succeeding day, and at the "Bloody Angle" at Spotsylvania was engaged for eight hours in the desperate and determined contest. The brigade commander reported: "It was emphatically a hand-to-hand fight. Scores were shot down within a few feet of the death-dealing muskets." After battling all the way down to Petersburg, the Fifth Vermont was suddenly rushed to Washington to repel Early's attack. It then engaged in the thrilling victories of Sheridan in the Valley. In December, it returned to Petersburg and ended its active service only with the surrender at Appomattox. During these four years of service, the regiment lost eleven officers and 202 enlisted men killed and mortally wounded, and one officer and 124 enlisted men by disease. Its total loss was therefore 338, worthy of the famous "Vermont Brigade."

LYRICS

BATTLE–HYMN OF THE REPUBLIC

The unusual circumstances under which this national classic was written are recounted under the picture of the Fifth Vermont in '61, with their Colonel, L. A. Grant, on the immediately preceding page.

Mine eyes have seen the glory of the coming of the Lord:
He is trampling out the vintage where the grapes of wrath are
    stored;
He hath loosed the fateful lightning of his terrible swift sword:
    His truth is marching on.

I have seen Him in the watch-fires of a hundred circling camps;
They have builded Him an altar in the evening dews and
    damps;
I can read His righteous sentence by the dim and flaring
    lamps.
    His day is marching on.

I have read a fiery gospel, writ in burnished rows of steel:
" As ye deal with my contemners, so with you my grace shall
    deal;
Let the Hero, born of woman, crush the serpent with his heel,
    Since God is marching on."

He has sounded forth the trumpet that shall never call retreat;
He is sifting out the hearts of men before his judgment-seat:
Oh! be swift, my soul, to answer Him! be jubilant, my feet!
    Our God is marching on.

In the beauty of the lilies Christ was born across the sea,
With a glory in his bosom that transfigures you and me:
As He died to make men holy, let us die to make men free,
    While God is marching on.

JULIA WARD HOWE.

"IN BURNISHED ROWS OF STEEL"

As pictured above, the Seventeenth New York Infantry at Minor's Hill marches along the rolling Virginia fields to the inspiring music of the military band. This regiment, with its bright array, lives up to its spirited name, "Westchester Chasseurs." Well might such a pageant have inspired Mrs. Howe to write the resonant war-song to which her name is forever linked. But these New Yorkers saw much severe service. They went with McClellan on the Peninsula campaign in 1862, and back toward Washington in time to fight in the second battle of Bull Run and to see service in the bloody conflict at Antietam, September 16–17, 1862. They were in the sanguinary repulse at Fredericksburg, December 13, 1862. They remained at Falmouth, across the river from Fredericksburg, till Chancellorsville. Its three-years men then went to the 146th New York.

"HIS TRUTH IS MARCHING ON"

In the earnest spirit of Mrs. Howe's poem, the Ninth Vermont Infantry, as pictured vividly below, marches out of camp in North Carolina, 1863. Its career of only a year has been unusual. It had barely entered active service in 1862 when it was transferred to Harper's Ferry. There it was captured by "Stonewall" Jackson on September 15, 1862, and was paroled the next day. Its military career was apparently cut short. It was used, however, to guard Confederate prisoners at Camp Douglas, Chicago, until March 28, 1863. In January of that year, it had been declared exchanged and in the fall was at length sent to New Berne, North Carolina, where it was on duty in the Newport Barracks till July, 1864. There it engaged in various expeditions into the vicinity, destroying salt-works and capturing turpentine. There the photograph here reproduced was taken.

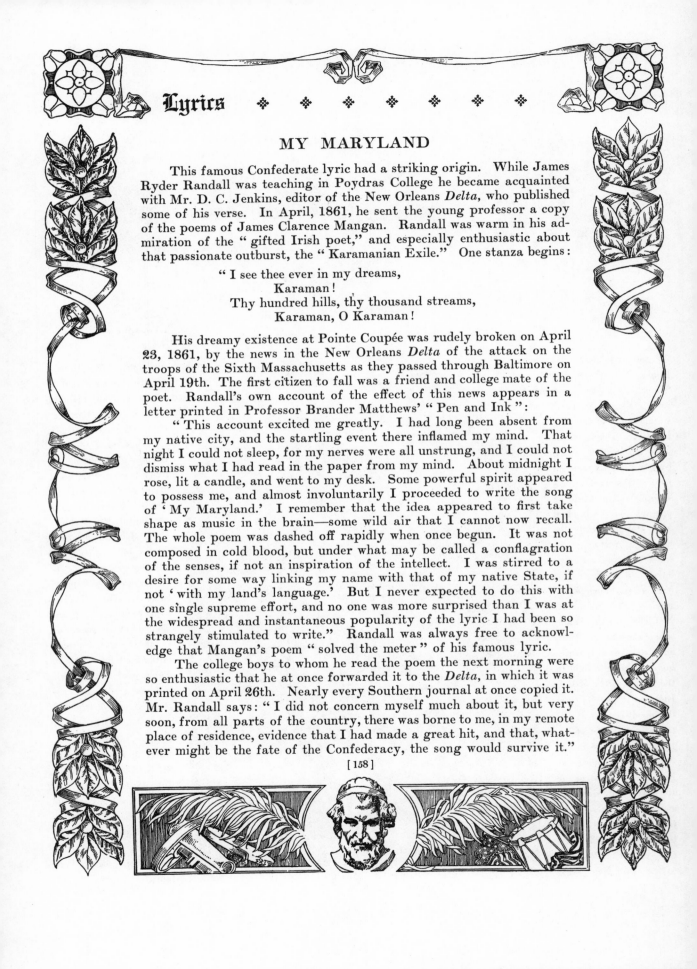

MY MARYLAND

This famous Confederate lyric had a striking origin. While James Ryder Randall was teaching in Poydras College he became acquainted with Mr. D. C. Jenkins, editor of the New Orleans *Delta*, who published some of his verse. In April, 1861, he sent the young professor a copy of the poems of James Clarence Mangan. Randall was warm in his admiration of the " gifted Irish poet," and especially enthusiastic about that passionate outburst, the " Karamanian Exile." One stanza begins:

> " I see thee ever in my dreams,
>   Karaman!
> Thy hundred hills, thy thousand streams,
>   Karaman, O Karaman!

His dreamy existence at Pointe Coupée was rudely broken on April 23, 1861, by the news in the New Orleans *Delta* of the attack on the troops of the Sixth Massachusetts as they passed through Baltimore on April 19th. The first citizen to fall was a friend and college mate of the poet. Randall's own account of the effect of this news appears in a letter printed in Professor Brander Matthews' " Pen and Ink ":

" This account excited me greatly. I had long been absent from my native city, and the startling event there inflamed my mind. That night I could not sleep, for my nerves were all unstrung, and I could not dismiss what I had read in the paper from my mind. About midnight I rose, lit a candle, and went to my desk. Some powerful spirit appeared to possess me, and almost involuntarily I proceeded to write the song of ' My Maryland.' I remember that the idea appeared to first take shape as music in the brain—some wild air that I cannot now recall. The whole poem was dashed off rapidly when once begun. It was not composed in cold blood, but under what may be called a conflagration of the senses, if not an inspiration of the intellect. I was stirred to a desire for some way linking my name with that of my native State, if not ' with my land's language.' But I never expected to do this with one single supreme effort, and no one was more surprised than I was at the widespread and instantaneous popularity of the lyric I had been so strangely stimulated to write." Randall was always free to acknowledge that Mangan's poem " solved the meter " of his famous lyric.

The college boys to whom he read the poem the next morning were so enthusiastic that he at once forwarded it to the *Delta*, in which it was printed on April 26th. Nearly every Southern journal at once copied it. Mr. Randall says: " I did not concern myself much about it, but very soon, from all parts of the country, there was borne to me, in my remote place of residence, evidence that I had made a great hit, and that, whatever might be the fate of the Confederacy, the song would survive it."

"THE DESPOT'S HEEL IS ON THY SHORE"

THE NEW YORK "SEVENTH" IN MARYLAND

These Union soldiers at Federal Hill, Maryland, in 1862, are the Gun Squad of the Fifth Company in New York's representative "Seventh" regiment. Sergeant-Major Rathbone is handing an order to Captain Spaight. Personally, the invaders were far from "despots," as Southerners soon ascertained. In the picture below are veterans of this same "Seventh" regiment, as they appeared seventeen years later in a different rôle—hosts and escorts of the Gate City Guard. In 1861, this had been the first body of troops to enter Confederate service from Atlanta. In 1879, its neighborly call upon New York City was met by one courtesy after another, under the auspices of the "Seventh." The *New York Sun* said: "The visit among us of the Gate City Guard will do more to bring about an understanding between North and South than the legislation of a century." Other newspapers commented on the event in a similar cordial spirit of friendship.

Lyrics ❖ ❖ ❖ ❖ ❖

The despot's heel is on thy shore,
    Maryland!
His torch is at thy temple door,
    Maryland!
Avenge the patriotic gore
That flecked the streets of Baltimore,
And be the battle-queen of yore,
    Maryland, my Maryland!

Hark to an exiled son's appeal,
    Maryland!
My Mother State, to thee I kneel,
    Maryland!
For life and death, for woe and weal,
Thy peerless chivalry reveal,
And gird thy beauteous limbs with steel,
    Maryland, my Maryland!

Thou wilt not cower in the dust,
    Maryland!
Thy beaming sword shall never rust,
    Maryland!
Remember Carroll's sacred trust,
Remember Howard's warlike thrust,
And all thy slumberers with the just,
    Maryland, my Maryland!

Come! 'tis the red dawn of the day,
    Maryland!
Come with thy panoplied array,
    Maryland!
With Ringgold's spirit for the fray,
With Watson's blood at Monterey,
With fearless Lowe and dashing May,
    Maryland, my Maryland!

Come! for thy shield is bright and strong,
    Maryland!
Come! for thy dalliance does thee wrong,
    Maryland!

"BURST THE TYRANT'S CHAIN"

NORTHERN OFFICERS AT A MARYLAND HOME IN PLEASANT VALLEY, AFTER THE BATTLE OF ANTIETAM

The young Maryland girl with the charming ruffles has evidently discovered at least one Northerner not a "tyrant" or otherwise disagreeable. The scene is at the Lee homestead near the battlefield of Antietam; the time, October, 1862. Two members of General Burnside's staff and one of General McClellan's are here seen talking with the family, who were furnishing a temporary home for Mrs. McClellan after Antietam. One would never surmise that, a short time before, the fiercest single day's action of the war had been fought. Many another hospitable home among the beautiful rolling hills of Maryland entertained the same kindly feelings for the "despots" of whom Randall sang. Many another young lady, like the one sitting in her crinoline and ruffles opposite the handsome young officer, held a similar admiration for some leader in blue. Maryland, even in war-time, was always conscious of the bond of brotherhood that linked its people with the American Union. The group on the vine-shadowed veranda was but a prophecy of a day when all can admire the martial ring of "My Maryland" without losing pride in the greatness of the American Republic.

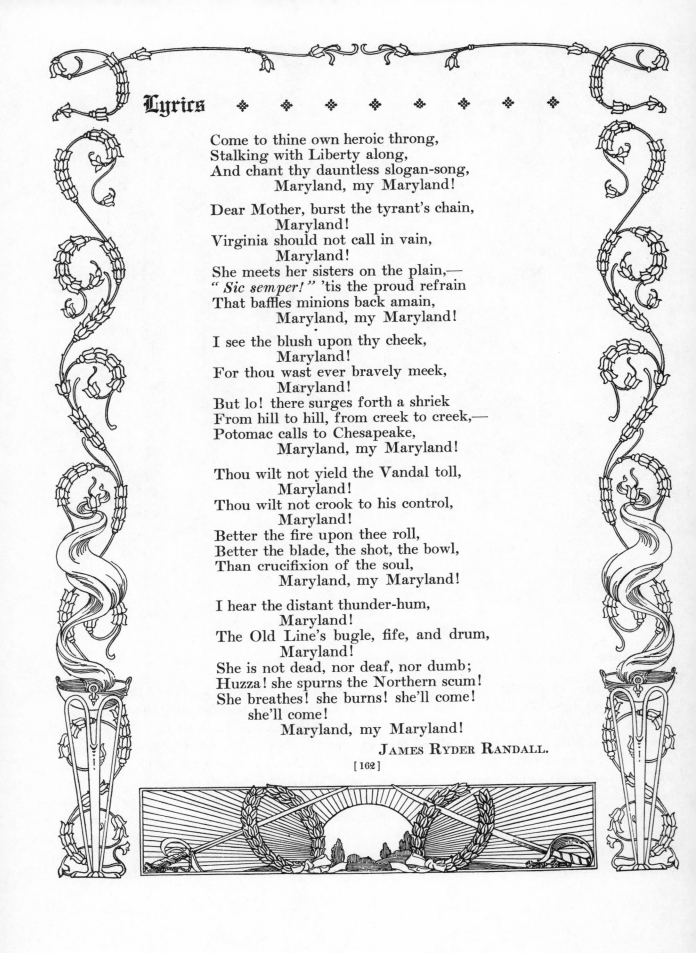

Lyrics ❖ ❖ ❖ ❖ ❖ ❖ ❖

Come to thine own heroic throng,
Stalking with Liberty along,
And chant thy dauntless slogan-song,
    Maryland, my Maryland!

Dear Mother, burst the tyrant's chain,
    Maryland!
Virginia should not call in vain,
    Maryland!
She meets her sisters on the plain,—
" *Sic semper!* " 'tis the proud refrain
That baffles minions back amain,
    Maryland, my Maryland!

I see the blush upon thy cheek,
    Maryland!
For thou wast ever bravely meek,
    Maryland!
But lo! there surges forth a shriek
From hill to hill, from creek to creek,—
Potomac calls to Chesapeake,
    Maryland, my Maryland!

Thou wilt not yield the Vandal toll,
    Maryland!
Thou wilt not crook to his control,
    Maryland!
Better the fire upon thee roll,
Better the blade, the shot, the bowl,
Than crucifixion of the soul,
    Maryland, my Maryland!

I hear the distant thunder-hum,
    Maryland!
The Old Line's bugle, fife, and drum,
    Maryland!
She is not dead, nor deaf, nor dumb;
Huzza! she spurns the Northern scum!
She breathes! she burns! she'll come!
    she'll come!
    Maryland, my Maryland!

                JAMES RYDER RANDALL.

[162]

"ADVANCE

THE FLAG

OF

DIXIE"

A HOPEFUL

CONFEDERATE

GROUP

OF '61

Actual photographs of the Confederate flags raised within the Confederate fortifications are rare indeed. This photograph was taken by Edwards, the New Orleans artist, inside the Confederate lines at Pensacola, Florida. The cannon, at whose "ringing voices" Pike sang "The South's great heart rejoices," are shining in the warm Southern sunlight that brightens the flag in the color-bearer's hands. All is youth and hope.

DIXIE

Southrons, hear your country call you!
Up, lest worse than death befall you!
    To arms! To arms! To arms, in Dixie!
Lo! all the beacon-fires are lighted,—
Let all hearts be now united!
    To arms! To arms! To arms, in Dixie!
      Advance the flag of Dixie!
          Hurrah! hurrah!
For Dixie's land we take our stand,
    And live or die for Dixie!
        To arms! To arms!
And conquer peace for Dixie!
        To arms! To arms!
And conquer peace for Dixie!

Hear the Northern thunders mutter!
Northern flags in South winds flutter!
Send them back your fierce defiance!
Stamp upon the accursed alliance!

Fear no danger! Shun no labor!
Lift up rifle, pike, and sabre!
Shoulder pressing close to shoulder,
Let the odds make each heart bolder!

How the South's great heart rejoices
At your cannons' ringing voices!
For faith betrayed, and pledges broken,
Wrongs inflicted, insults spoken.

Strong as lions, swift as eagles,
Back to their kennels hunt these beagles!
Cut the unequal bonds asunder!
Let them hence each other plunder!

Swear upon your country's altar
Never to submit or falter,
Till the spoilers are defeated,
Till the Lord's work is completed!

"NORTHERN FLAGS

IN

SOUTH WINDS

FLUTTER"

UNION GUNBOATS

ON THE

MISSISSIPPI

AND THE JAMES

These views of Federal gunboats flying the Stars and Stripes preserve such scenes as inspired Albert Pike's stanzas to the tune of "Dixie." The ram *Vindicator* above is particularly apt, since "Dixie" first appeared in a "River" town, being printed in the *Natchez Courier* on April 30, 1862. It is a curious fact that the author was born in Boston and attended Harvard. The tune itself had a Northern origin. Daniel Decatur Emmet, who had traveled a great deal with circus bands and a minstrel company of his own, and was already known as the composer of "Old Dan Tucker," joined the famous Bryant's Minstrels in 1857. He not only appeared in the performances, but composed airs for the entertainments. The closing number on each occasion was known as a "walk-around," in which all members of the company would appear. One Saturday night, September 17, 1859, Emmet was told to prepare a new walk-around for the following Monday rehearsal. Sunday was gloomy, with a cold rain falling. As Emmet looked out the window an expression with which he had become familiar in his circus experience flashed across his memory,—"I wish I was in Dixie." Dixie referred to the South, where many companies

spent the winter on the road. Emmet at once took up his fiddle and began to work out the melody along with the words. The melody which he used is supposed to have been an old Northern Negro air, associated with the name of one Dix or Dixy, who had a large plantation, some say on Manhattan Island, others on Staten Island. When the progress of abolition sentiment obliged him to migrate southward, his slaves looked back to their old home as a paradise. But with years the term Dixie's Land was transferred to their new home and was taken up by both white and black as a name for the South. Emmet's production was sung for the first time on Monday night, September 19, 1859, at 472 Broadway, New York City, where Bryant's Minstrels were then showing. It enjoyed instant popularity. Its vogue in the South was begun in New Orleans in the Spring of 1861. Mrs. John Woods was then playing at the New Orleans Varieties Theater in John Brougham's burlesque of "Pocahontas." In the last scene was a zouave march. At the first performance the zouaves were led by Miss Susan Denin, singing "Dixie," and reappearing seven times in answer to the persistent applause. The whole South took it up.

Halt not till our Federation
Secures among earth's powers its station!
Then at peace, and crowned with glory,
Hear your children tell the story!

If the loved ones weep in sadness,
Victory soon shall bring them gladness,—
　　　To arms!
Exultant pride soon vanish sorrow;
Smiles chase tears away to-morrow.
　　To arms! To arms! To arms, in Dixie!
　　　Advance the flag of Dixie!
　　　　Hurrah! hurrah!
For Dixie's land we take our stand,
　　And live or die for Dixie!
　　　To arms! To arms!
　　And conquer peace for Dixie!
　　　To arms! To arms!
　　And conquer peace for Dixie!

ALBERT PIKE.

SHERMAN'S MARCH TO THE SEA

The song that made Sherman's march famous, according to the General, who remarked to George Cary Eggleston: "It was this poem, with its phrase ' march to the sea,' that threw a glamor of romance over the movement which it celebrates. The movement was nothing more than a change of base, an operation perfectly familiar to every military man. But a poet got hold of it, gave it the captivating title, ' The March to the Sea,' and the unmilitary public made a romance out of it." The author was regimental adjutant of the Fifth Iowa Infantry when he was captured in a charge at the battle of Missionary Ridge, November 24, 1863. He was confined successively in six Southern prisons, escaping three times and being each time recaptured. While imprisoned at Columbia, South Carolina, one chilly morning in a little wedge tent he wrote the song here reprinted. Meagre reports of Sherman's leaving Atlanta had come through a daily paper, which a kindly disposed negro stuffed into a loaf of bread furnished to a mess of the Union prisoners who were fortunate enough to have a little money to pay for it. Through

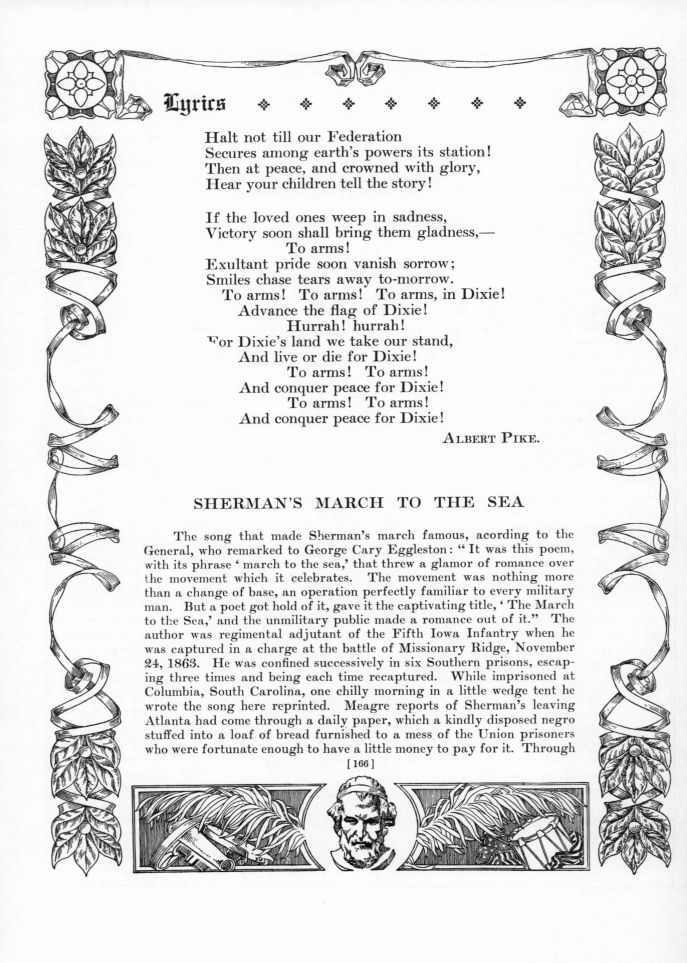

"AND WE STORMED THE WILD HILLS OF RESACA"

A SCENE AFTER SHERMAN'S MARCH

This freshly turned earth on the entrenchments at Resaca, over which the weeds have shot up in the spring weather of 1864, witnessed the even-handed struggle of May 14–15th, to which Byers refers. The heavy timber made the movement of troops very difficult, but it was of advantage to the Confederates behind their fortifications. In one case the attackers under General Henry M. Judah were moving up a valley to storm a salient, when they were met by a murderous fire from the edge of the woods in front as well as from the right. The bluffs proved too steep for even their dash and courage. At another point General J. D. Cox's men charged directly upon the entrenchments and drove the opposing force out after a fierce struggle. Artillery from higher up the slope then opened upon the Federals, so that they had to use the reverse of the work just captured, strengthening it with small timber, like that in the picture, till reënforcements came. All the fighting was of this nature. As soon as Sherman got into position to march across the river to Johnston's rear, that wary general retreated, leaving all the "wild hills" in the possession of the Federals.

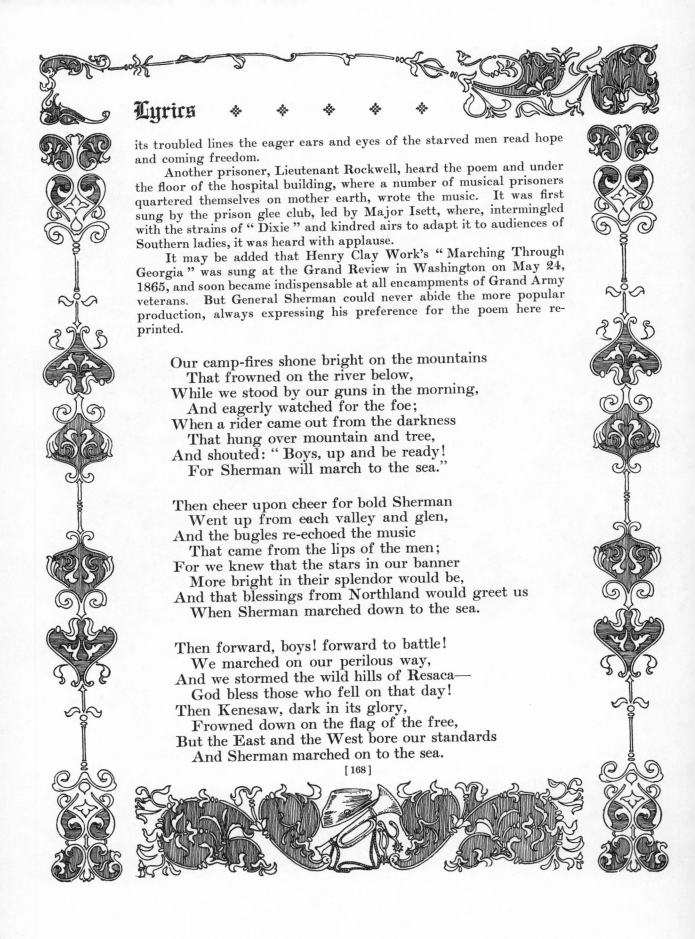

its troubled lines the eager ears and eyes of the starved men read hope and coming freedom.

Another prisoner, Lieutenant Rockwell, heard the poem and under the floor of the hospital building, where a number of musical prisoners quartered themselves on mother earth, wrote the music. It was first sung by the prison glee club, led by Major Isett, where, intermingled with the strains of "Dixie" and kindred airs to adapt it to audiences of Southern ladies, it was heard with applause.

It may be added that Henry Clay Work's "Marching Through Georgia" was sung at the Grand Review in Washington on May 24, 1865, and soon became indispensable at all encampments of Grand Army veterans. But General Sherman could never abide the more popular production, always expressing his preference for the poem here reprinted.

Our camp-fires shone bright on the mountains
    That frowned on the river below,
While we stood by our guns in the morning,
    And eagerly watched for the foe;
When a rider came out from the darkness
    That hung over mountain and tree,
And shouted: "Boys, up and be ready!
    For Sherman will march to the sea."

Then cheer upon cheer for bold Sherman
    Went up from each valley and glen,
And the bugles re-echoed the music
    That came from the lips of the men;
For we knew that the stars in our banner
    More bright in their splendor would be,
And that blessings from Northland would greet us
    When Sherman marched down to the sea.

Then forward, boys! forward to battle!
    We marched on our perilous way,
And we stormed the wild hills of Resaca—
    God bless those who fell on that day!
Then Kenesaw, dark in its glory,
    Frowned down on the flag of the free,
But the East and the West bore our standards
    And Sherman marched on to the sea.

"WHEN SHERMAN MARCHED DOWN TO THE SEA"

This somber view of Fort McAllister, on the Great Ogeechee River, was taken soon after the termination of Sherman's famous march. As Byers sings of the achievement, the movement began in May, 1864, with the advance against Johnston, but the usual understanding is of the march from Atlanta, which began on November 15th. On December 10th, Sherman's army had closed in on the works around Savannah. The general's first move was to make connections with the fleet and its supplies. The country about Savannah afforded nothing but rice, which did not satisfy an army that for a month had been living on pigs, chickens, and turkeys. But the only convenient channel of communication was the Great Ogeechee, guarded by the fort that had defied the navy for two years. Its storming by Hazen, on December 17th, was welcome to Sherman's men above most victories. A foraging party had rowed down the river into Ossabaw Sound and met a steamer coming in, the crew of which said that it was the *Nemeha* and had Major-General Foster on board. The party answered: "Oh, we've got twenty-seven major-generals up at camp. What we want is hardtack!" On December 21st, the army entered Savannah. Sherman's achievement was world-famous.

"OUR CAMP-FIRES SHONE BRIGHT ON THE MOUNTAIN"

The war-time view of the Chattanooga River, from Lookout Mountain, gives a good notion of the country through which Sherman advanced on the first half of his "march to the sea." Byers reckons this famous military operation as beginning with the campaign against Joseph E. Johnston. Sherman's forces were centered at Ringgold, a little south of the point here pictured. The fighting in this campaign was of the most picturesque variety. Johnston was a master of defensive warfare. The mountainous nature of the country enabled him to entrench his forces at every step. He could always wait to be attacked, could always be sure of having the advantage in position, and could retreat through the passes to a new stand before the Federal forces could arrive. The Union troops, on the other hand, must advance along the railway to keep in touch with their base of supplies in the rear, must fight their way through forests, over boulders, across torrents and broad rivers, ever in the face of a vigilant foe. Thus from May 6th to September 2d, 1864, Sherman fought every foot of his way into the city of Atlanta. "Each valley and glen" had seen some of his sturdy followers fall, but his victorious banners fluttered in the breeze on every mountain side.

"BUT TO–DAY FAIR SAVANNAH IS OURS"

Byers' line celebrates a triumph fresh when this charming view of the Savannah River was taken. Drooping live-oaks and tangled vines give the scene an air of almost tropical luxuriance. The far gleam of the river from across the level marshes adds just the picture to accompany the song "that echoed o'er river and lea." The march from Atlanta to Savannah is the operation usually thought of when the famous phrase, "March to the Sea" is uttered. It was November 15, 1864, when Sherman's army "swept out from Atlanta's grim walls" after the total destruction of the military resources of the city. The undertaking was considered one of unparalleled daring. For more than a month the North heard not a word of Sherman and his men. Conjectures as to his whereabouts and activities were of the wildest. But, as a matter of fact, the undertaking was proving one long holiday. There were no Confederate troops sufficient to check the Northern forces. Their foraging parties provided all the soldiers could desire. Indeed, Sherman wrote his wife, "We have lived sumptuously,—turkeys, chickens, and sweet potatoes all the way." Yet the greatness of the expedition grew on him. Before the end of the year he wrote, "Like one who has walked a narrow plank, I look back and wonder if I really did it." He did well to wonder. The journals of the civilized world were loud in his praise. Scores of poems heralded him. Byers' song gave additional fame by its captivatingly romantic title.

Lyrics ❖ ❖ ❖ ❖ ❖ ❖

Still onward we pressed till our banners
　　Swept out from Atlanta's grim walls,
And the blood of the patriot dampened
　　The soil where the traitor flag falls.
We paused not to weep for the fallen,
　　Who sleep by each river and tree,
But we twined them a wreath of the laurel,
　　And Sherman marched on to the sea.

Oh, proud was our army that morning,
　　That stood where the pine darkly towers,
When Sherman said, "Boys, you are weary,
　　But to-day fair Savannah is ours."
Then sang we a song for our chieftain,
　　That echoed o'er river and lea,
And the stars in our banner shone brighter
　　When Sherman marched down to the sea.

SAMUEL HAWKINS MARSHALL BYERS.

[172]

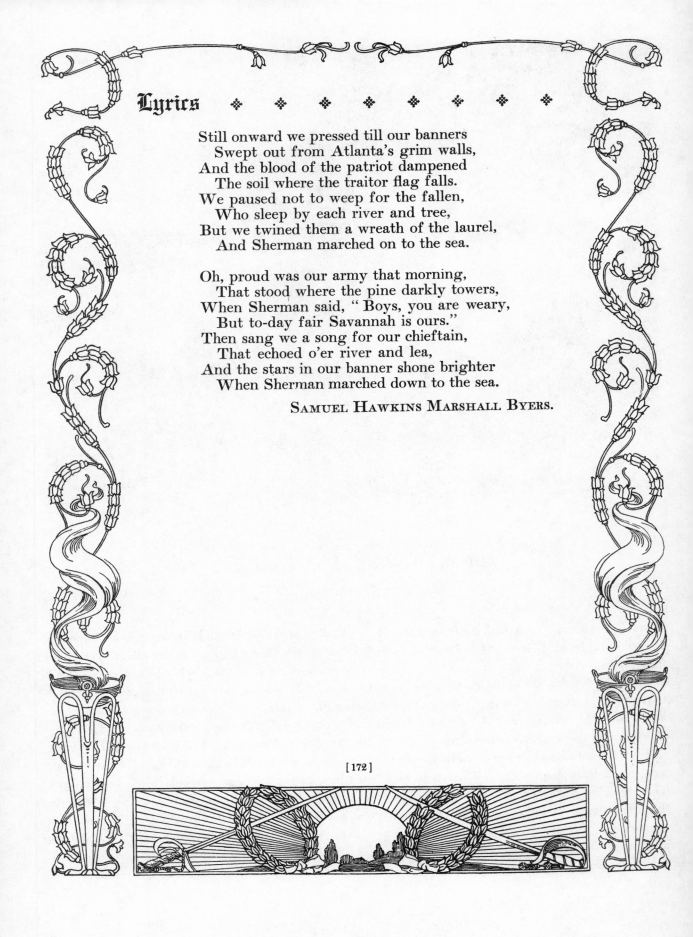

VII

THE
LIGHTER
SIDE

"SAMBO'S RIGHT TO BE KILT"

COLORED TROOPS AT DRILL—VICKSBURG, 1864

TO ILLUSTRATE "SAMBO'S RIGHT TO BE KILT"

A beautiful Southern mansion stands in flickering shadows of walnut and elm and white oak, and in front are some of the negro troops that have been formed from "contrabands." The passions of the period waxed particularly bitter over the question of employing Negroes in warfare. Charles Graham Halpine comes to the rescue, in his poem that follows on page 176, with a saving sense of Irish humor. He suggests that "men who object to Sambo should take his place and fight." As for himself, he will object not at all "if Sambo's body

GUARD OF COLORED TROOPS AT THE PROVOST–MARSHAL'S—BEAUFORT, NORTH CAROLINA, 1864

should stop a ball that was coming for me direct." This recalls Artemas Ward's announcement of his own patriotism, which he said he had carried so far that he was willing for all his wife's relatives to go to the front! The human side of this problem helps to solve it, as with others. Certainly, the line above presents a firm and soldierly front. Many of the colored regiments came to be well-disciplined and serviceable. Their bravery is attested by the loss of life at Battery Wagner and in the charges at the Petersburg crater.

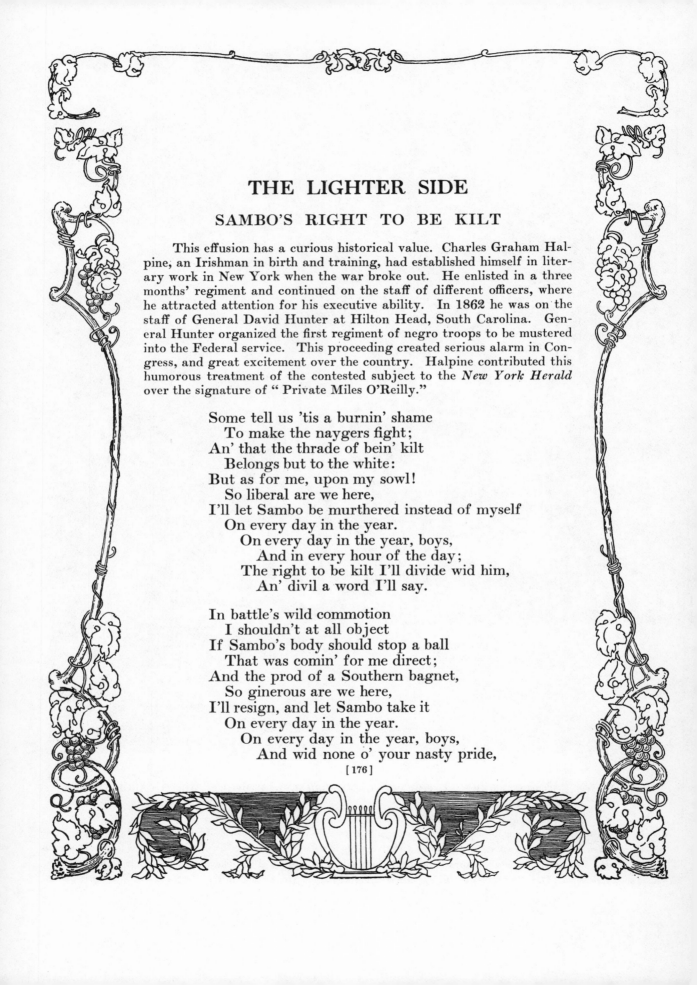

THE LIGHTER SIDE

SAMBO'S RIGHT TO BE KILT

This effusion has a curious historical value. Charles Graham Halpine, an Irishman in birth and training, had established himself in literary work in New York when the war broke out. He enlisted in a three months' regiment and continued on the staff of different officers, where he attracted attention for his executive ability. In 1862 he was on the staff of General David Hunter at Hilton Head, South Carolina. General Hunter organized the first regiment of negro troops to be mustered into the Federal service. This proceeding created serious alarm in Congress, and great excitement over the country. Halpine contributed this humorous treatment of the contested subject to the *New York Herald* over the signature of " Private Miles O'Reilly."

Some tell us 'tis a burnin' shame
  To make the naygers fight;
An' that the thrade of bein' kilt
  Belongs but to the white:
But as for me, upon my sowl!
  So liberal are we here,
I'll let Sambo be murthered instead of myself
  On every day in the year.
    On every day in the year, boys,
      And in every hour of the day;
    The right to be kilt I'll divide wid him,
      An' divil a word I'll say.

In battle's wild commotion
  I shouldn't at all object
If Sambo's body should stop a ball
  That was comin' for me direct;
And the prod of a Southern bagnet,
  So ginerous are we here,
I'll resign, and let Sambo take it
  On every day in the year.
    On every day in the year, boys,
      And wid none o' your nasty pride,

"I'LL LET SAMBO BE MURTHERED INSTEAD OF MYSELF"
COLORED INFANTRY AT FORT LINCOLN, 1862

This picture possesses especial interest as the subject of the following comment by Major George Haven Putnam (a contributor to Volume I of this HISTORY) from his experience as a Federal officer in charge of colored troops: Late in the war, when the Confederacy was sadly in need of fresh supplies of men, the proposition was more than once brought up in the Confederate Congress and elsewhere for the arming of the slaves or of a selection of the slaves.   But such a step was never ventured upon.   On the Northern side, as early as 1862, regiments were formed of the colored residents of the North, the first two being the famous Fifty-fourth and Fifty-fifth Massachusetts.   These men represented, of course, a fairly high average of intelligence and of education, and they did brilliant fighting.   In the course of the succeeding two years many regiments were organized out of the plantation negroes as they made their way across into Federal lines, or as Federal control extended over plantation country.   These men also rendered earnest, faithful, and usually effective service. They lacked, as was quite natural, individual initiative.   They did not do good fighting in a skirmish-line. They wanted to be in touch, shoulder to shoulder, and within immediate reach of the commander's word; but there is hardly an instance in which, when once under fire, they did not fulfil their duty pluckily and persistently.   The army rosters show that more than 150,000 colored men fought under the Stars and Stripes.

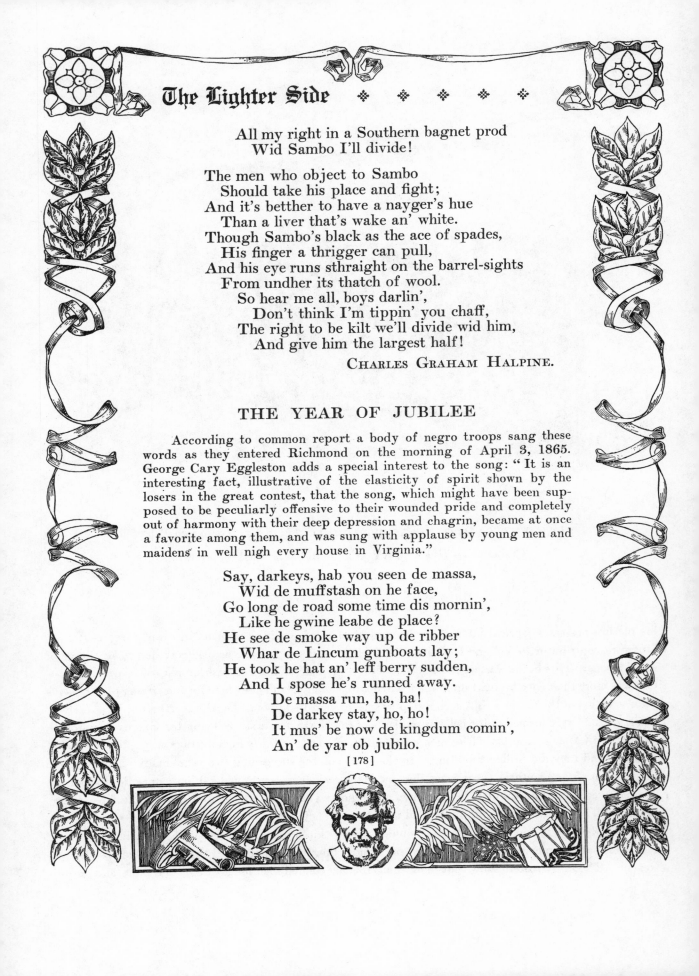

All my right in a Southern bagnet prod
  Wid Sambo I'll divide!

The men who object to Sambo
  Should take his place and fight;
And it's betther to have a nayger's hue
  Than a liver that's wake an' white.
Though Sambo's black as the ace of spades,
  His finger a thrigger can pull,
And his eye runs sthraight on the barrel-sights
  From undher its thatch of wool.
    So hear me all, boys darlin',
      Don't think I'm tippin' you chaff,
    The right to be kilt we'll divide wid him,
      And give him the largest half!

CHARLES GRAHAM HALPINE.

THE YEAR OF JUBILEE

According to common report a body of negro troops sang these
words as they entered Richmond on the morning of April 3, 1865.
George Cary Eggleston adds a special interest to the song: "It is an
interesting fact, illustrative of the elasticity of spirit shown by the
losers in the great contest, that the song, which might have been supposed to be peculiarly offensive to their wounded pride and completely
out of harmony with their deep depression and chagrin, became at once
a favorite among them, and was sung with applause by young men and
maidens in well nigh every house in Virginia."

Say, darkeys, hab you seen de massa,
  Wid de muffstash on he face,
Go long de road some time dis mornin',
  Like he gwine leabe de place?
He see de smoke way up de ribber
  Whar de Lincum gunboats lay;
He took he hat an' leff berry sudden,
  And I spose he's runned away.
    De massa run, ha, ha!
    De darkey stay, ho, ho!
    It mus' be now de kingdum comin',
    An' de yar ob jubilo.

"AND HIS EYE RUNS STHRAIGHT ON THE BARREL SIGHTS"

These Negro pickets near Dutch Gap Canal in 1864 were posing proudly for their photograph, unconscious that they were illustrating Halpine's line so closely. The natural love of the Negro for imitating the white folks was not the only trait that distinguished the colored troops at Dutch Gap. Work on the canal proved to be very dangerous. The Confederate sharpshooters in the vicinity were continually firing at the men from tree-tops, and several mortars were continually dropping bombs among the squads, who had to seek refuge in dug-outs. In the fall of 1864 most of the labor was performed by colored troops. General P. S. Michie reports that they "displayed the greatest courage and fortitude, and maintained under the most trying circumstances their usual good humor and cheerful disposition." Such a record may encourage their well-wishers.

The Lighter Side ❖ ❖ ❖

He six foot one way an' two foot todder,
    An' he weigh six hundred poun';
His coat so big he couldn't pay de tailor,
    An' it won't reach half way roun';
He drill so much dey calls him cap'n,
    An' he git so mighty tanned,
I spec he'll try to fool dem Yankees,
    For to tink he contraband.
            De massa run, ha, ha!
            De darkey stay, ho, ho!
            It mus' be now de kingdum comin',
            An' de yar ob jubilo.

De darkeys got so lonesome libb'n
    In de log hut on de lawn,
Dey moved dere tings into massa's parlor
    For to keep it while he gone.
Dar's wine and cider in de kitchin,
    An' de darkeys dey hab some,
I spec it will be all fiscated
    When de Lincum sojers come.
            De massa run, ha, ha!
            De darkey stay, ho, ho!
            It mus' be now de kingdum comin',
            An' de yar ob jubilo.

De oberseer he makes us trubble,
    An' he dribe us roun' a spell,
We lock him up in de smoke-house cellar,
    Wid de key flung in de well.
De whip am lost, de han'-cuff broke,
    But de massy hab his pay;
He big an' ole enough for to know better
    Dan to went an' run away.
            De massa run, ha, ha!
            De darkey stay, ho, ho!
            It mus' be now de kingdum comin',
            An' de yar ob jubilo.

HENRY CLAY WORK.

"CONTRABAN"

NEGRO TEAMSTERS NEAR BUTLER'S SIGNAL TOWER, BERMUDA HUNDRED, 1864

The history and nature of "contraband of war," so expressively illustrated by this photograph, are thus explained by George Haven Putnam: Early in the war, General Benjamin F. Butler invented the term "contraband," which came to be accepted as the most convenient classification for the colored refugee who had made his way within the Federal lines and who, while no longer a slave or a piece of property, was not yet accepted as a person. It was the legal theory of Butler that the property rights in the refugee who had been a slave had, under war conditions, been annulled. Throughout the war, the information of happenings within the enemy's lines was frequently enough brought to our headquarters by the (more or less) "intelligent contraband." As far as my experience goes, the colored reporter was always willing and eager to help. I know of no single instance on record in which false or misleading information was knowingly given by the colored man; but this information was, nevertheless, in a large number of cases by no means trustworthy. The darkey had no capacity for accuracy of observation or for precision of statement. An enormous allowance had to be made for his imagination when he was describing to us the number of the enemy's troops that were in position or that possibly were advancing to the attack. His imagination worked most frequently on the apprehensive side. His experience had made hopefulness somewhat difficult for him.

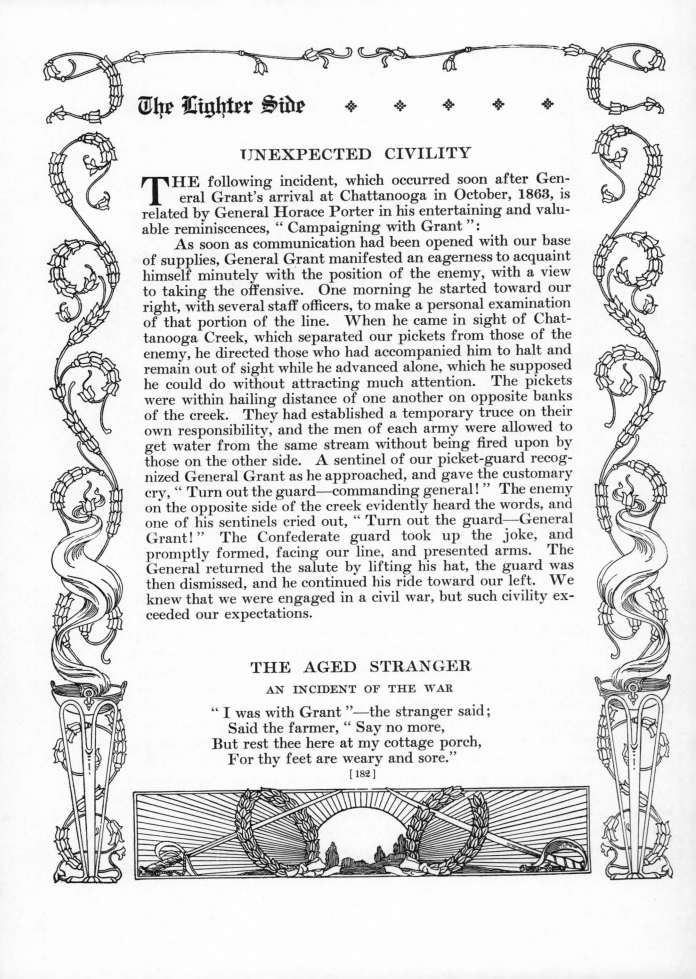

The Lighter Side ❖ ❖ ❖ ❖ ❖

UNEXPECTED CIVILITY

THE following incident, which occurred soon after General Grant's arrival at Chattanooga in October, 1863, is related by General Horace Porter in his entertaining and valuable reminiscences, "Campaigning with Grant":

As soon as communication had been opened with our base of supplies, General Grant manifested an eagerness to acquaint himself minutely with the position of the enemy, with a view to taking the offensive. One morning he started toward our right, with several staff officers, to make a personal examination of that portion of the line. When he came in sight of Chattanooga Creek, which separated our pickets from those of the enemy, he directed those who had accompanied him to halt and remain out of sight while he advanced alone, which he supposed he could do without attracting much attention. The pickets were within hailing distance of one another on opposite banks of the creek. They had established a temporary truce on their own responsibility, and the men of each army were allowed to get water from the same stream without being fired upon by those on the other side. A sentinel of our picket-guard recognized General Grant as he approached, and gave the customary cry, " Turn out the guard—commanding general! " The enemy on the opposite side of the creek evidently heard the words, and one of his sentinels cried out, " Turn out the guard—General Grant! " The Confederate guard took up the joke, and promptly formed, facing our line, and presented arms. The General returned the salute by lifting his hat, the guard was then dismissed, and he continued his ride toward our left. We knew that we were engaged in a civil war, but such civility exceeded our expectations.

THE AGED STRANGER

AN INCIDENT OF THE WAR

" I was with Grant "—the stranger said;
Said the farmer, " Say no more,
But rest thee here at my cottage porch,
For thy feet are weary and sore."

[182]

"DE DARKEYS GOT SO LONESOME"

ILLUSTRATION FOR "THE YEAR OF JUBILEE"

The crinoline of the old "auntie" in the center and the quaint sunbonnets of her companions are distinguishing marks of the war-time scene—a Mississippi plantation, where the darkies have gathered to relieve some of the lonesomeness of which Work writes.   It was one of the noteworthy features of the war that the people who, before the conflict, had been supposed to be on the point of rising and inaugurating a race-war, remained quietly at work on the large plantations.   Frequently only women were left to direct the labor of the slaves.   Several diaries from various parts of the South tell of the continued affection and even devotion of these colored people.   It is only of the close of the war that the scenes in "The Year of Jubilee" can be imagined.   But the picture above is typical of all the four years of the conflict and of later negro life.

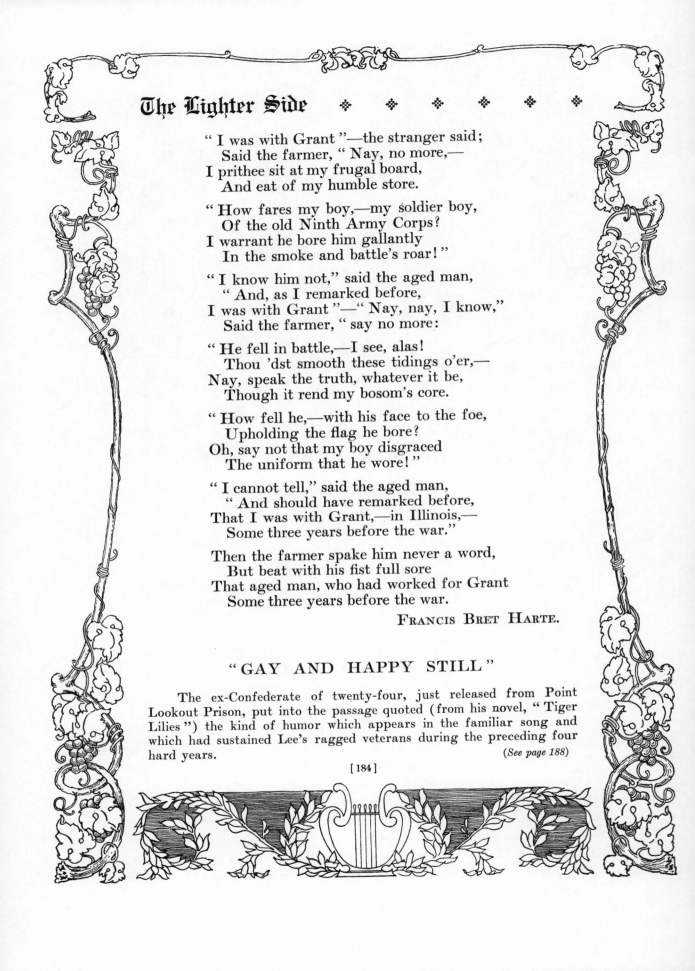

" I was with Grant "—the stranger said;
　Said the farmer, " Nay, no more,—
I prithee sit at my frugal board,
　And eat of my humble store.

" How fares my boy,—my soldier boy,
　Of the old Ninth Army Corps?
I warrant he bore him gallantly
　In the smoke and battle's roar! "

" I know him not," said the aged man,
　" And, as I remarked before,
I was with Grant "—" Nay, nay, I know,"
　Said the farmer, " say no more:

" He fell in battle,—I see, alas!
　Thou 'dst smooth these tidings o'er,—
Nay, speak the truth, whatever it be,
　Though it rend my bosom's core.

" How fell he,—with his face to the foe,
　Upholding the flag he bore?
Oh, say not that my boy disgraced
　The uniform that he wore! "

" I cannot tell," said the aged man,
　" And should have remarked before,
That I was with Grant,—in Illinois,—
　Some three years before the war."

Then the farmer spake him never a word,
　But beat with his fist full sore
That aged man, who had worked for Grant
　Some three years before the war.

FRANCIS BRET HARTE.

" GAY AND HAPPY STILL "

　The ex-Confederate of twenty-four, just released from Point
Lookout Prison, put into the passage quoted (from his novel, " Tiger
Lilies ") the kind of humor which appears in the familiar song and
which had sustained Lee's ragged veterans during the preceding four
hard years. *(See page 188)*

IMPOSING OFFICERS AND FOREIGN ATTACHÉS—

WHO UNBEND BETWEEN BATTLES—FALMOUTH, VIRGINIA, APRIL, 1863

Lest the reader suppose the life of the Civil War soldier was unrelieved by any sallies of playfulness, these photographs of 1863 are reproduced. No schoolboys in their wildest larks could engage in a struggle of more mock-desperate nature than that waged by these officers of the Army of the Potomac, with the English, French, and Austrian attachés come to report to their Governments how Americans made war. Boxes and chairs have been scattered hither and yon; swords are slashing in deadly combat; bottles are wielded by some in the hand-to-hand mêlée. The burly attaché at the right is even preparing to dig a grave for the unfortunate slain in the combat.

AT THE SUTLER'S STORE

A LIFELIKE GROUP

A high degree of artistic feeling and skill was shown by the war photographer who preserved this band of joking soldiers beside a sutler's store. Few photographic feats are as difficult, even to-day, as the successful portraying of such a number of different subjects, in poses so remarkably diversified, and under such abrupt color contrasts of light and shadow. Evidently, the army was in a permanent camp when this picture was taken; for it was then that the sutlers would open up their stocks of canned goods, soft drinks, playing cards, handkerchiefs, paper collars, and such luxuries, enjoyed by the boys of '61 only at infrequent intervals. Sometimes the soldiers rebelled against the storekeeper's extortionate prices, and once in a while, on the eve of a forward movement, they would sack the little shanty of its contents by way of reprisal.

CAMP HUMOR

FACETIOUSNESS OF A SUTLER WITH THE WESTERN ARMIES

The signs about this sutler's store in Tennessee display the rude wit of the soldier in camp. The name over the little shanty contains an affectation of French elegance that is amusing even to-day. The misspelling in the announcement, "Meels at all Ours," may not have appealed to all the frequenters as strongly as to us, but the imposing declaration that it was kept on the European plan came to be understood by everyone. There was no humor at all in some of the signs, such as the warning over the door "No Tick," as many a lad with empty pockets must have found when he felt very thirsty for "XXXX Ale." No one can be so sure of the other sign "No Licker Sold to Soljers." Probably the arrangements could be made in the dark of the moon for suspension of this grim regulation. The sutler's store was a center of the social life of the squad in off hours. Here they would gather to chat over the events of the last campaign, to compare notes on the various leaders, to discuss the probabilities of the next advance, and to swap yarns from all possible sources.

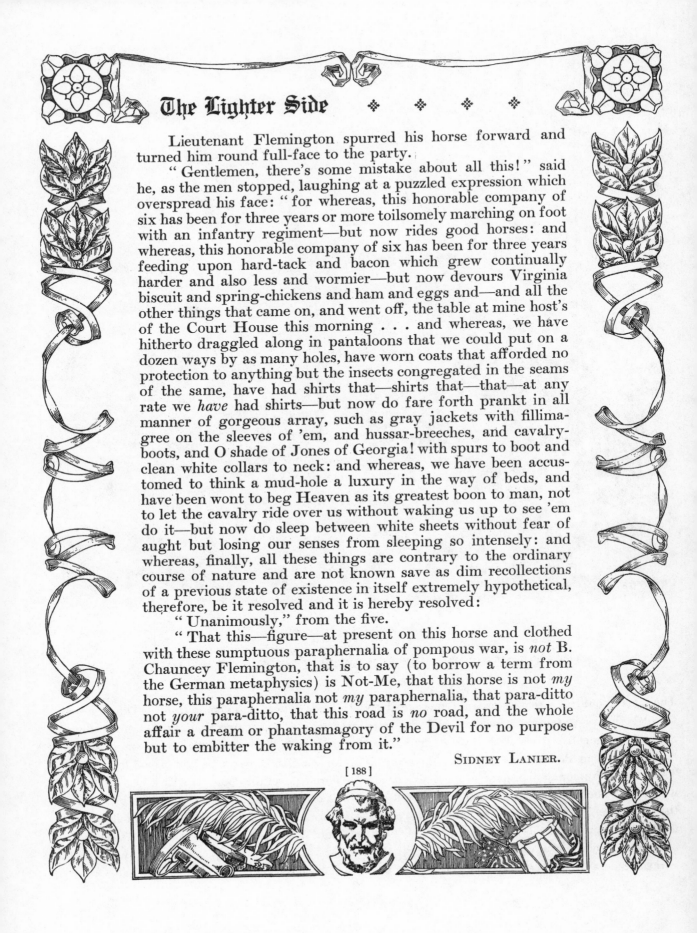

The Lighter Side ❖ ❖ ❖ ❖

Lieutenant Flemington spurred his horse forward and turned him round full-face to the party.

"Gentlemen, there's some mistake about all this!" said he, as the men stopped, laughing at a puzzled expression which overspread his face: "for whereas, this honorable company of six has been for three years or more toilsomely marching on foot with an infantry regiment—but now rides good horses: and whereas, this honorable company of six has been for three years feeding upon hard-tack and bacon which grew continually harder and also less and wormier—but now devours Virginia biscuit and spring-chickens and ham and eggs and—and all the other things that came on, and went off, the table at mine host's of the Court House this morning . . . and whereas, we have hitherto draggled along in pantaloons that we could put on a dozen ways by as many holes, have worn coats that afforded no protection to anything but the insects congregated in the seams of the same, have had shirts that—shirts that—that—at any rate we *have* had shirts—but now do fare forth prankt in all manner of gorgeous array, such as gray jackets with fillima-gree on the sleeves of 'em, and hussar-breeches, and cavalry-boots, and O shade of Jones of Georgia! with spurs to boot and clean white collars to neck: and whereas, we have been accustomed to think a mud-hole a luxury in the way of beds, and have been wont to beg Heaven as its greatest boon to man, not to let the cavalry ride over us without waking us up to see 'em do it—but now do sleep between white sheets without fear of aught but losing our senses from sleeping so intensely: and whereas, finally, all these things are contrary to the ordinary course of nature and are not known save as dim recollections of a previous state of existence in itself extremely hypothetical, therefore, be it resolved and it is hereby resolved:

"Unanimously," from the five.

"That this—figure—at present on this horse and clothed with these sumptuous paraphernalia of pompous war, is *not* B. Chauncey Flemington, that is to say (to borrow a term from the German metaphysics) is Not-Me, that this horse is not *my* horse, this paraphernalia not *my* paraphernalia, that para-ditto not *your* para-ditto, that this road is *no* road, and the whole affair a dream or phantasmagory of the Devil for no purpose but to embitter the waking from it."

SIDNEY LANIER.

[188]

VIII

BETWEEN
BATTLES

"THE SCREAMING MISSILES FELL"

THIS LINE FROM "THE PRIDE OF BATTERY B," AN EPISODE OF ANTIETAM
(PAGE 196), IS ILLUSTRATED BY THE HUMBLE DUNKER CHURCH AROUND
WHICH RAGED THE CENTER OF THE CONFLICT—THE PHOTOGRAPH
FOLLOWED SOON, BEFORE THE SHOT HOLES HAD BEEN REPAIRED

BETWEEN BATTLES

UNITED

All day it shook the land—grim battle's thunder tread;
And fields at morning green, at eve are trampled red.
But now, on the stricken scene, twilight and quiet fall;
Only, from hill to hill, night's tremulous voices call;
And comes from far along, where campfires warning burn,
The dread, hushed sound which tells of morning's sad return.

Timidly nature awakens; the stars come out overhead,
And a flood of moonlight breaks like a voiceless prayer for the
    dead.
And steals the blessed wind, like Odin's fairest daughter,
In viewless ministry, over the fields of slaughter;
Soothing the smitten life, easing the pang of death,
And bearing away on high the passing warrior's breath.

Two youthful forms are lying apart from the thickest fray,
The one in Northern blue, the other in Southern gray.
Around his lifeless foeman the arms of each are pressed,
And the head of one is pillowed upon the other's breast.
As if two loving brothers, wearied with work and play,
Had fallen asleep together, at close of the summer day.
Foeman were they, and brothers?—Again the battle's din,
With its sullen, cruel answer, from far away breaks in.

BENJAMIN SLEDD.

MUSIC IN CAMP

The setting of this poem is immediately after the battle of Chancellorsville, May 1–4, 1863. For some three weeks the armies were encamped on opposite banks of the Rappahannock, before Lee's invasion of the North ending in the battle of Gettysburg. Historically, the intercourse between the soldiers had been much freer during the preceding winter and spring, between the battle of Fredericksburg and the opening of the Chancellorsville campaign.

[190]

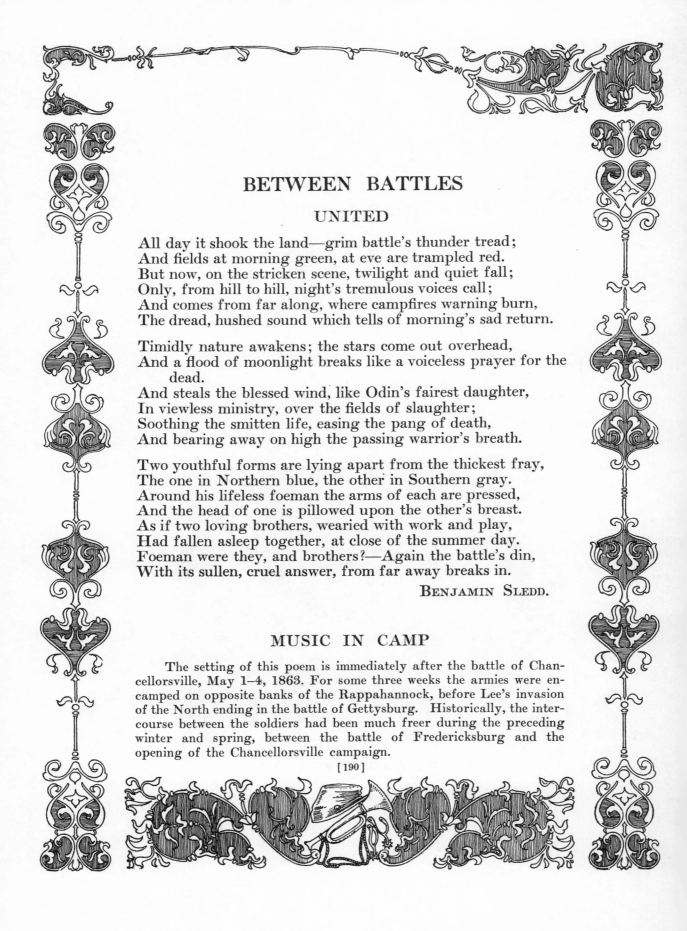

"APART FROM THE THICKEST FRAY"—A SCENE OF '65

CONFEDERATE AND UNION DEAD, SIDE BY SIDE, IN THE TRENCHES AT FORT MAHONE

This spectacle of April 3d, the day after Grant's army stormed the Petersburg defenses, is a strikingly real illustration for the poem "United." With "U. S." on his haversack lies a Union soldier; beyond, a booted Confederate. Every field of the war was a reminder of the brotherhood of the opponents. The same cast of features indicated their common descent. The commands heard above the roar of cannonading or in the midst of desperate charges revealed the identity of their language and heritage from a heroic past. The unyielding fortitude and unhesitating fidelity displayed by the private in the ranks as he followed his appointed leaders was merely additional proof of the Anglo-Saxon blood that flowed in the veins of the embattled countrymen. During the conflict there was, naturally, a great deal of hostility. The ranks opposed were the ranks of the enemy, no matter how close the bonds of relationship, and against the enemy the utmost destruction must be hurled. Yet in the Eastern and Western armies, friendly relations were established whenever the camps of opposing forces were stationed near each other for any length of time. Since the war this feeling has grown until the saddest feature of the irrepressible conflict is that it was waged between brothers, that every battlefield furnished many a spot like the one above.

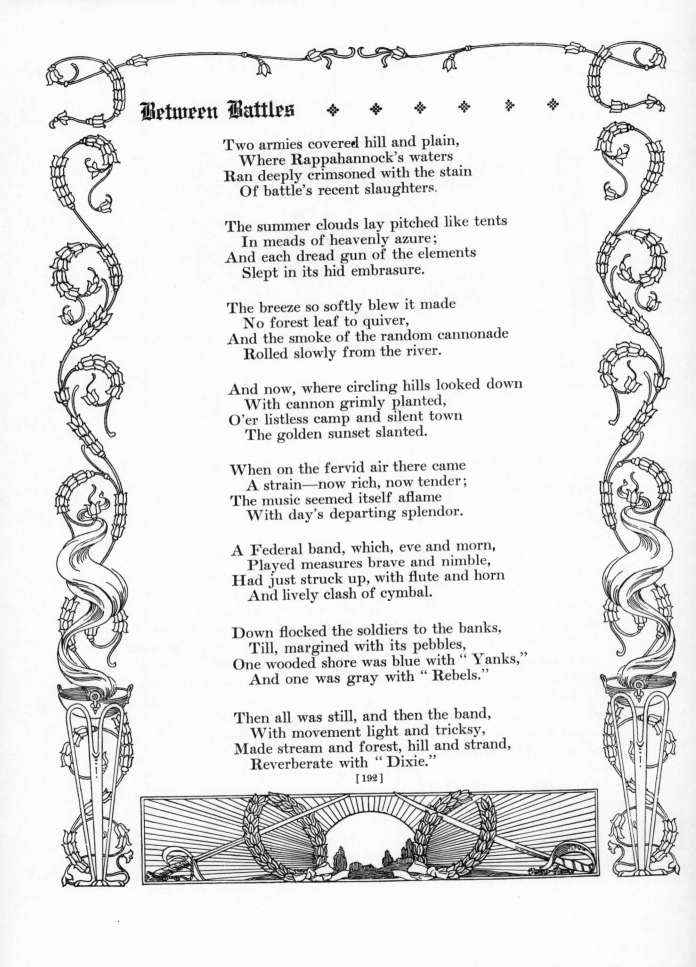

Between Battles ✦ ✦ ✦ ✦ ✦ ✦

Two armies covered hill and plain,
 Where Rappahannock's waters
Ran deeply crimsoned with the stain
 Of battle's recent slaughters.

The summer clouds lay pitched like tents
 In meads of heavenly azure;
And each dread gun of the elements
 Slept in its hid embrasure.

The breeze so softly blew it made
 No forest leaf to quiver,
And the smoke of the random cannonade
 Rolled slowly from the river.

And now, where circling hills looked down
 With cannon grimly planted,
O'er listless camp and silent town
 The golden sunset slanted.

When on the fervid air there came
 A strain—now rich, now tender;
The music seemed itself aflame
 With day's departing splendor.

A Federal band, which, eve and morn,
 Played measures brave and nimble,
Had just struck up, with flute and horn
 And lively clash of cymbal.

Down flocked the soldiers to the banks,
 Till, margined with its pebbles,
One wooded shore was blue with " Yanks,"
 And one was gray with " Rebels."

Then all was still, and then the band,
 With movement light and tricksy,
Made stream and forest, hill and strand,
 Reverberate with " Dixie."

[192]

"WHERE RAPPAHANNOCK'S WATERS RAN DEEPLY CRIMSONED"

These two views, the lower being the right half of the panorama, are a truly remarkable illustration of Thompson's lines. "Taken during the battle of May 3, 1863" is the legend written on the print by the Government photographer, Captain A. J. Russell. In the early morning of that day, Gibbon had encrimsoned the stream at this point in crossing the river to cooperate with Sedgwick to attack the Confederate positions on the heights of Fredericksburg. When this picture was taken, Sedgwick was some nine miles away, fighting desperately along a crest near Salem Chapel, from which he was at length driven slowly back through the woods. Sedgwick held his ground through the next day; but on the night of May 4th he recrossed the Rappahannock, this time above Fredericksburg, while the Confederate batteries shelled the bridges over which his troops were marching. The waters were indeed "crimsoned by battle's recent slaughters." To the right in the lower half of the panorama are the stone piers of the bridge in the telephoto picture on the next page.

PANORAMA (WITH PICTURE ABOVE) OF FREDERICKSBURG FROM LACY HOUSE

Between Battles

The conscious stream with burnished glow
    Went proudly o'er its pebbles,
But thrilled throughout its deepest flow
    With yelling of the Rebels.

Again a pause, and then again
    The trumpets pealed sonorous,
And " Yankee Doodle " was the strain
    To which the shore gave chorus.

The laughing ripple shoreward flew,
    To kiss the shining pebbles;
Loud shrieked the swarming Boys in Blue
    Defiance to the Rebels.

And yet once more the bugles sang
    Above the stormy riot;
No shout upon the evening rang—
    There reigned a holy quiet.

The sad, slow stream its noiseless flood
    Poured o'er the glistening pebbles;
All silent now the Yankees stood,
    And silent stood the Rebels.

No unresponsive soul had heard
    That plaintive note's appealing,
So deeply " Home, Sweet Home " had stirred
    The hidden founts of feeling.

Or Blue or Gray, the soldier sees,
    As by the wand of fairy,
The cottage 'neath the live-oak trees,
    The cabin by the prairie.

Or cold or warm, his native skies
    Bend in their beauty o'er him;
Seen through the tear-mist in his eyes,
    His loved ones stand before him.

"AND ONE WAS GRAY WITH REBELS"

The photograph of Confederates on the Fredericksburg end of the ruined railroad bridge is one of the first telephoto photographs anywhere taken. On page 26, Volume I, of this HISTORY is reproduced a photograph made by climbing out along the portion of the bridge standing on the eastern bank of the river. At the left of this picture, the end of a bridge-beam is seen roughly projected against the brick wall. The photograph is proof of the friendly relations existing between the two armies encamped on opposite banks of the Rappahannock. Men in gray, both officer and private, are actually posing before the Federal camera. General Gordon says: "This rollicking sort of intercourse would have been alarming in its intimacy, but for the perfect confidence which the officers of both sides had in their men. Even officers on the opposite banks of this narrow stream would now and then declare a truce among themselves, in order that they might bathe in the little river. Where the water was shallow they would wade in and meet each other in the center and shake hands and 'swap' newspapers and barter Southern tobacco for Yankee coffee. Where the water was deep so that they could not wade in and 'swap,' they sent the articles of traffic across in miniature boats, laden on the southern shore with tobacco and sailed across to the Union side. These little boats were unloaded by the Union soldiers, reloaded, and sent back with Yankee coffee for the Confederates." He then tells of finding a Union soldier lying in the weeds, who said that he came across the river see the Johnnies for a little while, since there was no battle in progress. When General Gordon threatened to send the scantily clad visitor to prison, his own soldiers protested so stoutly that he allowed the "Yank" to swim back to his camp.

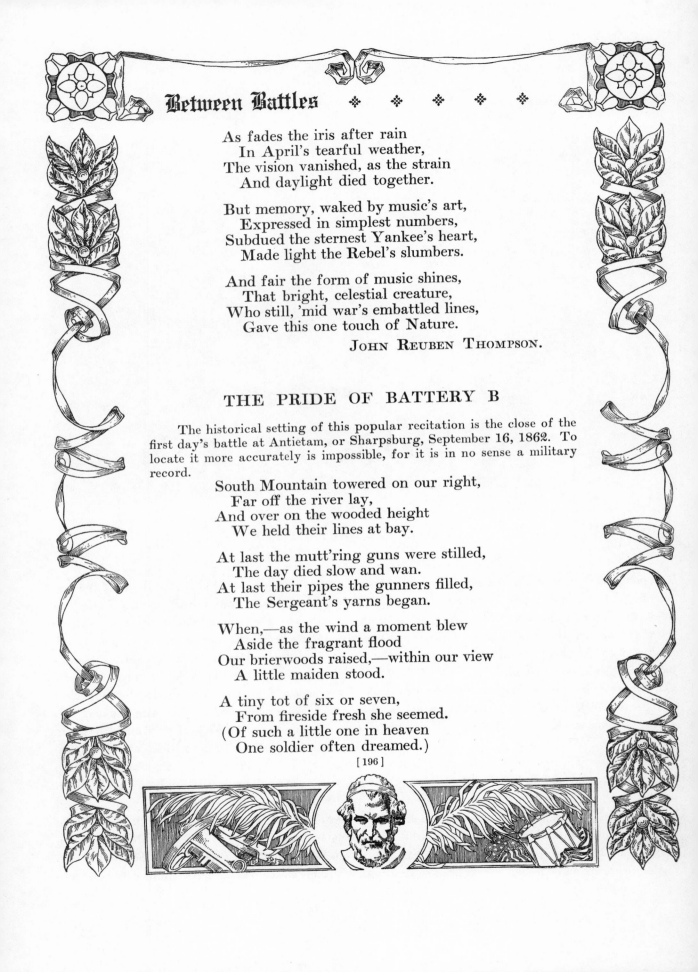

Between Battles ❖ ❖ ❖ ❖ ❖

As fades the iris after rain
　　In April's tearful weather,
The vision vanished, as the strain
　　And daylight died together.

But memory, waked by music's art,
　　Expressed in simplest numbers,
Subdued the sternest Yankee's heart,
　　Made light the Rebel's slumbers.

And fair the form of music shines,
　　That bright, celestial creature,
Who still, 'mid war's embattled lines,
　　Gave this one touch of Nature.

　　　　　　　JOHN REUBEN THOMPSON.

THE PRIDE OF BATTERY B

　　The historical setting of this popular recitation is the close of the
first day's battle at Antietam, or Sharpsburg, September 16, 1862. To
locate it more accurately is impossible, for it is in no sense a military
record.

South Mountain towered on our right,
　　Far off the river lay,
And over on the wooded height
　　We held their lines at bay.

At last the mutt'ring guns were stilled,
　　The day died slow and wan.
At last their pipes the gunners filled,
　　The Sergeant's yarns began.

When,—as the wind a moment blew
　　Aside the fragrant flood
Our brierwoods raised,—within our view
　　A little maiden stood.

A tiny tot of six or seven,
　　From fireside fresh she seemed.
(Of such a little one in heaven
　　One soldier often dreamed.)

[196]

UNION SOLDIERS IN THE JUST DESERTED CONFEDERATE
CAMP AT FREDERICKSBURG

The camera has caught a dramatic moment in the period of Thompson's "Music in Camp." It is May 3, 1863, and Sedgwick has carried the heights of Fredericksburg, impregnable to six assaults in December. One who was present reported: "Upon reaching the summit of the sharp hill, after passing through the extensive and well-wooded grounds of the Marye house, an exciting scene met the eye. A single glance exhibited to view the broad plateau alive with fleeing soldiers, riderless horses, and artillery and wagon-trains on a gallop." As no cavalry was at hand, the troops that carried the heights, "exhausted by the night march, the weight of several days' rations and sixty rounds of ammunition, and by the heat, fatigue, and excitement of battle, were allowed to halt for a short time. Many were soon asleep, while others made coffee and partook of their first meal that day." Captain A. J. Russell, the Government photographer who followed the army in its movements, dated this picture, May 3d, the very same day. The soldiers so confident in the picture were obliged to retreat across the Rappahannock, where, in a week or so, Thompson imagines the events of "Music in Camp" to take place. In a month these men were to fight the decisive battle of the war—Gettysburg.

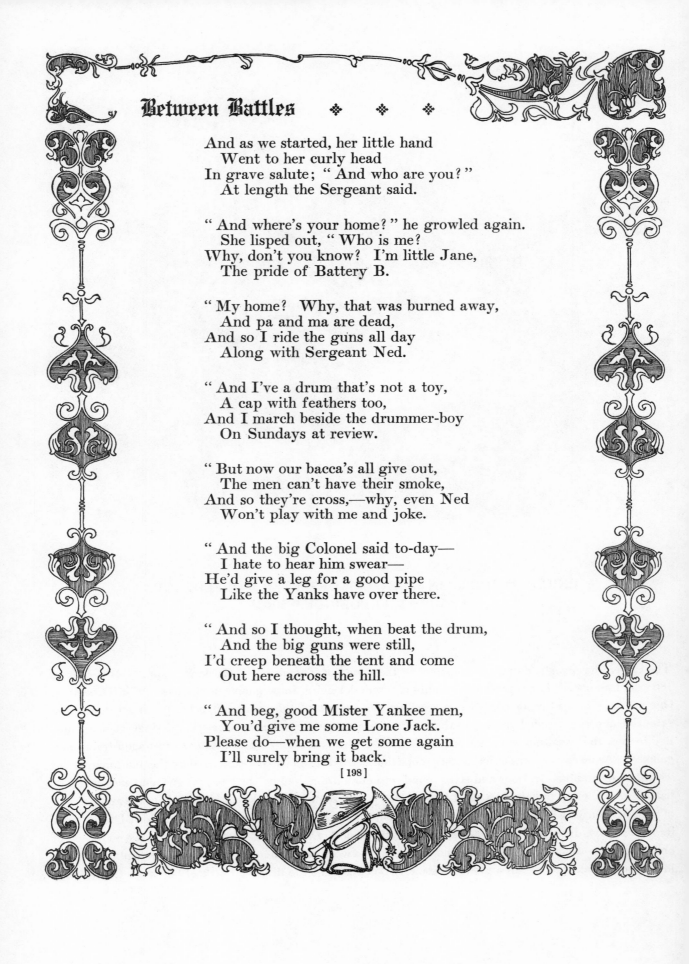

Between Battles   ❖   ❖   ❖

And as we started, her little hand
   Went to her curly head
In grave salute; "And who are you?"
   At length the Sergeant said.

"And where's your home?" he growled again.
   She lisped out, "Who is me?
Why, don't you know? I'm little Jane,
   The pride of Battery B.

"My home? Why, that was burned away,
   And pa and ma are dead,
And so I ride the guns all day
   Along with Sergeant Ned.

"And I've a drum that's not a toy,
   A cap with feathers too,
And I march beside the drummer-boy
   On Sundays at review.

"But now our bacca's all give out,
   The men can't have their smoke,
And so they're cross,—why, even Ned
   Won't play with me and joke.

"And the big Colonel said to-day—
   I hate to hear him swear—
He'd give a leg for a good pipe
   Like the Yanks have over there.

"And so I thought, when beat the drum,
   And the big guns were still,
I'd creep beneath the tent and come
   Out here across the hill.

"And beg, good Mister Yankee men,
   You'd give me some Lone Jack.
Please do—when we get some again
   I'll surely bring it back.

[198]

"FAR OFF
THE RIVER LAY"
ANTIETAM CREEK IN 1862

BURNSIDE'S
BRIDGE—WHERE
THE FIGHTING RAGED

Thus the placid stream flowed on to join the far Potomac after the sanguinary battle sung by Gassaway in "The Pride of Battery B." In neither the white sunlight falling upon the pillars nor the cool reflection of the foliage is there a suggestion of the death and wounds suffered by nearly 25,000 men in Blue and Gray. Around this very spot some of the hottest fighting raged. Along the hills on either side of the stream were ranged hundreds of guns. All through the first day of the battle, September 16, 1862, they volleyed and thundered at each other across the narrow valley. Both Union and Confederate armies were well supplied with artillery, which was so well served that every one tried to keep behind the crests of the ridges. At the termination of this long-continued duel, the incident of little Jane's visit to the Union battery is described by Gassaway as occurring in the vicinity of the peaceful scene here reproduced, from a photograph taken a few days after the battle.

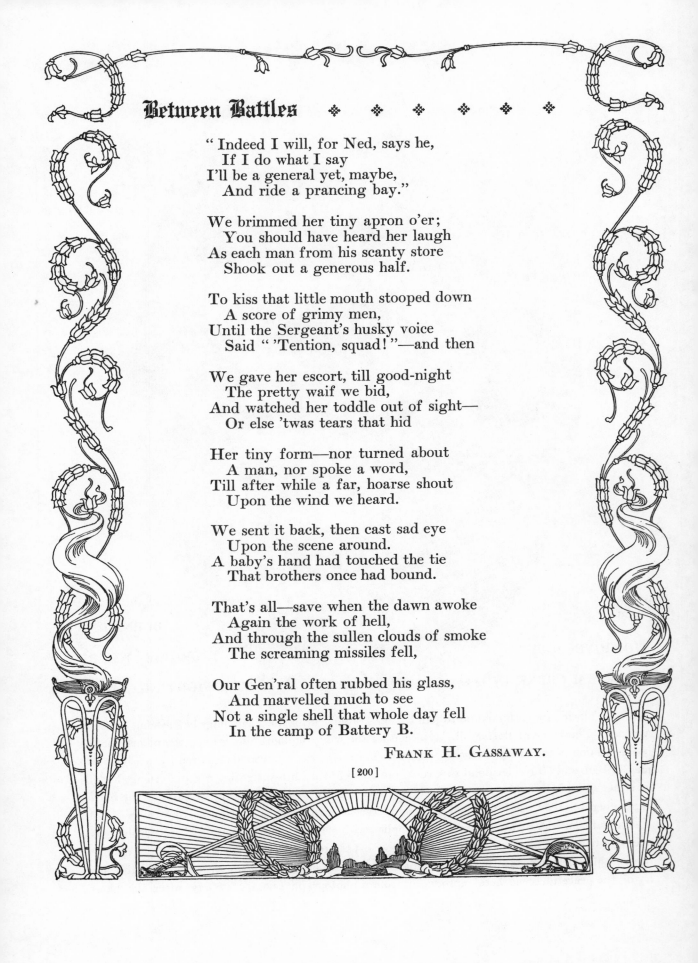

Between Battles ❖ ❖ ❖ ❖ ❖ ❖

"Indeed I will, for Ned, says he,
　　If I do what I say
I'll be a general yet, maybe,
　　And ride a prancing bay."

We brimmed her tiny apron o'er;
　　You should have heard her laugh
As each man from his scanty store
　　Shook out a generous half.

To kiss that little mouth stooped down
　　A score of grimy men,
Until the Sergeant's husky voice
　　Said " 'Tention, squad!"—and then

We gave her escort, till good-night
　　The pretty waif we bid,
And watched her toddle out of sight—
　　Or else 'twas tears that hid

Her tiny form—nor turned about
　　A man, nor spoke a word,
Till after while a far, hoarse shout
　　Upon the wind we heard.

We sent it back, then cast sad eye
　　Upon the scene around.
A baby's hand had touched the tie
　　That brothers once had bound.

That's all—save when the dawn awoke
　　Again the work of hell,
And through the sullen clouds of smoke
　　The screaming missiles fell,

Our Gen'ral often rubbed his glass,
　　And marvelled much to see
Not a single shell that whole day fell
　　In the camp of Battery B.

　　　　　　　FRANK H. GASSAWAY.

[200]

"AGAIN THE WORK OF HELL"

With painful realism the camera has furnished an illustration for Gassaway's line in "The Pride of Battery B." But even the horror of this view fails to give a true idea of the fearful slaughter at this point of the battlefield. About nine o'clock the Confederates fighting in the vicinity of the little Dunker Church heard the shout, "They are flanking us!" "This cry spread like an electric shock along the ranks. In a moment they broke and fell to the rear," says General D. H. Hill. In the rear of the fleeing companies General Rodes immediately formed a line along an old sunken road. The soldiers rendered the position more secure by piling rails upon the ridge. Some of these rails are seen scattered along the edge of the ditch. General Hill continues: "It was now apparent that the grand attack would be made upon my position, which was the center of the line. Before reenforcements arrived a heavy force advanced in three parallel lines, with all the precision of a parade day, upon my two brigades. They met with a galling fire, however, recoiled, and fell back; again advanced and again fell back, and finally lay down behind the crest of the hill and kept up an irregular fire." Owing to an unfortunate blunder, Rodes's men retreated, whereupon the Federal troops charged and after a fierce struggle drove the Confederate force from its position. General Hill concludes: "The unparalleled loss of the division shows that, spite of hunger and fatigue, the officers and men fought most heroically." The "Bloody Lane" was full of the men who had defended their position to the bitter end.

CIVIL WAR

This famous piece, frequently called "The Fancy Shot," appeared originally in the London "Once a Week" with the title "Civile Bellum," and dated "From the Once United States." The implied prophecy failed of fulfilment, and the concealed authorship has usually been cleared up by attributing the poem to Charles Dawson Shanly.

"Rifleman, shoot me a fancy shot
   Straight at the heart of yon prowling vidette;
Ring me a ball in the glittering spot
   That shines on his breast like an amulet!"

"Ah, captain! here goes for a fine-drawn bead,
   There's music around when my barrel's in tune!"
Crack! went the rifle, the messenger sped,
   And dead from his horse fell the ringing dragoon.

"Now, rifleman, steal through the bushes, and snatch
   From your victim some trinket to handsel first blood;
A button, a loop, or that luminous patch
   That gleams in the moon like a diamond stud!"

"O captain! I staggered, and sunk on my track,
   When I gazed on the face of that fallen vidette,
For he looked so like you, as he lay on his back,
   That my heart rose upon me, and masters me yet.

"But I snatched off the trinket,—this locket of gold;
   An inch from the centre my lead broke its way,
Scarce grazing the picture, so fair to behold,
   Of a beautiful lady in bridal array."

"Ha! rifleman, fling me the locket!—'tis she,
   My brother's young bride, and the fallen dragoon
Was her husband—Hush! soldier, 'twas Heaven's decree,
   We must bury him there, by the light of the moon!

"But hark! the far bugles their warnings unite;
   War is a virtue,—weakness a sin;
There's a lurking and loping around us to-night;
   Load again, rifleman, keep your hand in!"

CHARLES DAWSON SHANLY.

[202]

X

GETTYSBURG

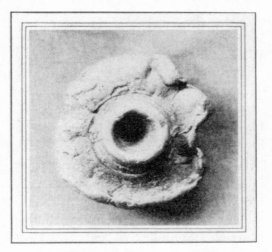

GETTYSBURG
THE HIGH–WATER MARK OF THE WAR

TWO HOSTILE BULLETS IN MID-AIR
TOGETHER SHOCKED
AND SWIFT WERE LOCKED
FOREVER IN A FIRM EMBRACE
—*Lathrop*

This is a picture of which Captain Gordon McCabe of Richmond, Virginia, writes: "I send photographs of two bullets, one Federal, the other Confederate, that met in mid-air and flattened out against each other. The bullets were picked up in 1865 between the 'lines' immediately after the evacuation of Petersburg."

GETTYSBURG

GETTYSBURG

Military critics have generally settled upon the battle of Gettysburg, July 1–3, 1863, as the decisive battle of the war, and the greatest battle in American history. It ended Lee's second invasion of the North, and, together with the fall of Vicksburg, threw the Confederacy upon the defensive and shut out hope of foreign intervention. The poem was written for the dedication of the High Water Mark Monument, July 2, 1892.

There was no union in the land,
  Though wise men labored long
With links of clay and ropes of sand
  To bind the right and wrong.

There was no temper in the blade
  That once could cleave a chain;
Its edge was dull with touch of trade
  And clogged with rust of gain.

The sand and clay must shrink away
  Before the lava tide:
By blows and blood and fire assay
  The metal must be tried.

Here sledge and anvil met, and when
  The furnace fiercest roared,
God's undiscerning workingmen
  Reforged His people's sword.

Enough for them to ask and know
  The moment's duty clear—
The bayonets flashed it there below,
  The guns proclaimed it here:

To do and dare, and die at need,
  But while life lasts, to fight—
For right or wrong a simple creed,
  But simplest for the right.

"BUT WHILE LIFE LASTS, TO FIGHT"

Such was the fate of many of the 5,000 and more Confederates of whom no returns were made after the fighting at Gettysburg. This young soldier was one of the sharpshooters posted in the "Devil's Den," the only position captured and held by the Confederates in the fighting at the Round Tops. In their lonely fastness these boys in gray sent many a swift messenger of death into the Federal lines that were fighting on the near-by crest. Then at last a Federal shell, bursting over this lad, wounded him in the head, but was not merciful enough to kill him outright. He was evidently able to spread his blanket and must have lain there alone for hours in his death agony. The photographer who took this picture, just after the battle in July, attended the dedication of the National Cemetery at Gettysburg, in November, and again penetrated to this rocky spot. The musket, rusted by many storms, still leaned against the rock; the remains of the boy soldier lay undisturbed within the mouldering uniform. No burial party had found him. The only news that his loved ones got was the single word, "Missing." A tale like this is true for 5,000 more.

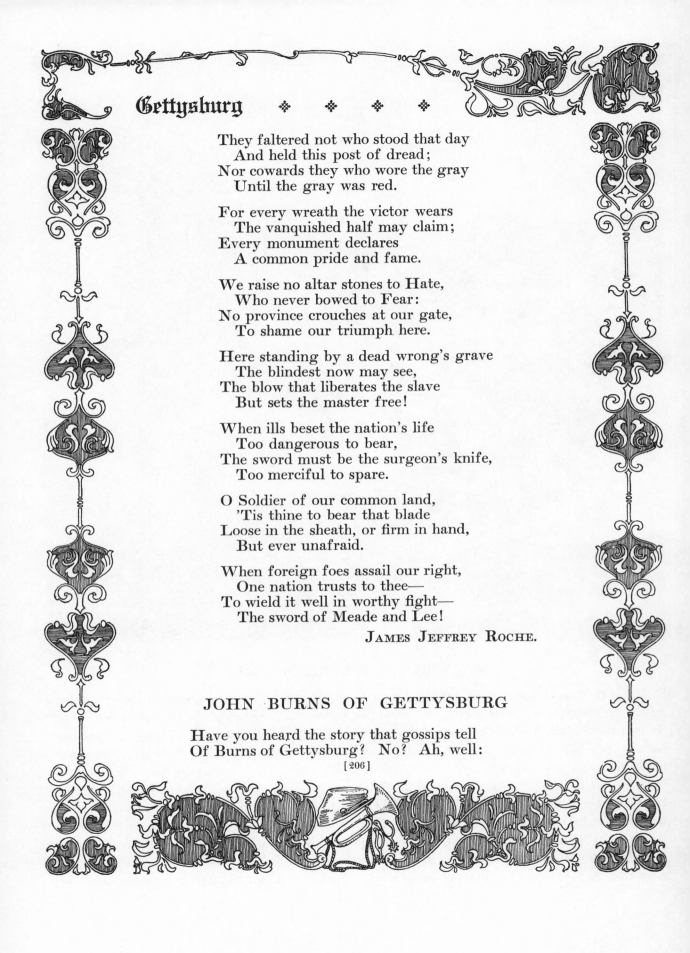

Gettysburg ❖ ❖ ❖

They faltered not who stood that day
   And held this post of dread;
Nor cowards they who wore the gray
   Until the gray was red.

For every wreath the victor wears
   The vanquished half may claim;
Every monument declares
   A common pride and fame.

We raise no altar stones to Hate,
   Who never bowed to Fear:
No province crouches at our gate,
   To shame our triumph here.

Here standing by a dead wrong's grave
   The blindest now may see,
The blow that liberates the slave
   But sets the master free!

When ills beset the nation's life
   Too dangerous to bear,
The sword must be the surgeon's knife,
   Too merciful to spare.

O Soldier of our common land,
   'Tis thine to bear that blade
Loose in the sheath, or firm in hand,
   But ever unafraid.

When foreign foes assail our right,
   One nation trusts to thee—
To wield it well in worthy fight—
   The sword of Meade and Lee!

                 JAMES JEFFREY ROCHE.

JOHN BURNS OF GETTYSBURG

Have you heard the story that gossips tell
Of Burns of Gettysburg? No? Ah, well:

"TO DO AND DARE, AND DIE AT NEED"

These sharpshooters, prone beside the mossy boulders and scrub trees of "Devil's Den" are among the most daring of those who fought at Gettysburg. They have paid the penalty so often attending such duty. At the beginning of the war it was argued that individual and unattached riflemen should be regarded as murderers and shot if captured; but this was never done, since sharpshooters came to play an important part on both sides. In the Confederate ranks they were men from Alabama, Mississippi, and Texas—men whose outdoor life made them experts with the rifle. Seeing the value of such a force, the Federals early organized a regiment of sharpshooters, enlisting men from each of the Federal States. These brought their own rifles, and most of them could snuff out a candle at a hundred yards. Often far in advance of the line, the sharpshooters chose their own positions, sometimes climbing into trees and lashing themselves to the branches to avoid a fall in case they should be wounded. Thousands paid the price of their daring.

Gettysburg ✦ ✦ ✦ ✦ ✦ ✦ ✦

Brief is the glory that hero earns,
Briefer the story of poor John Burns:
He was the fellow who won renown,—
The only man who didn't back down
When the rebels rode through his native town;
But held his own in the fight next day,
When all his townsfolk ran away.
That was in July, sixty-three,—
The very day that General Lee,
Flower of Southern chivalry,
Baffled and beaten, backward reeled
From a stubborn Meade and a barren field.

I might tell how, but the day before,
John Burns stood at his cottage-door,
Looking down the village street,
Where, in the shade of his peaceful vine,
He heard the low of his gathered kine,
And felt their breath with incense sweet;
Or I might say, when the sunset burned
The old farm gable, he thought it turned
The milk that fell like a babbling flood
Into the milk-pail, red as blood!
Or how he fancied the hum of bees
Were bullets buzzing among the trees.
But all such fanciful thoughts as these
Were strange to a practical man like Burns,
Who minded only his own concerns,
Troubled no more by fancies fine
Than one of his calm-eyed, long-tailed kine,
Quite old-fashioned and matter-of-fact,
Slow to argue, but quick to act.
That was the reason, as some folks say,
He fought so well on that terrible day.

And it was terrible. On the right
Raged for hours the heady fight,
Thundered the battery's double bass,—
Difficult music for men to face;

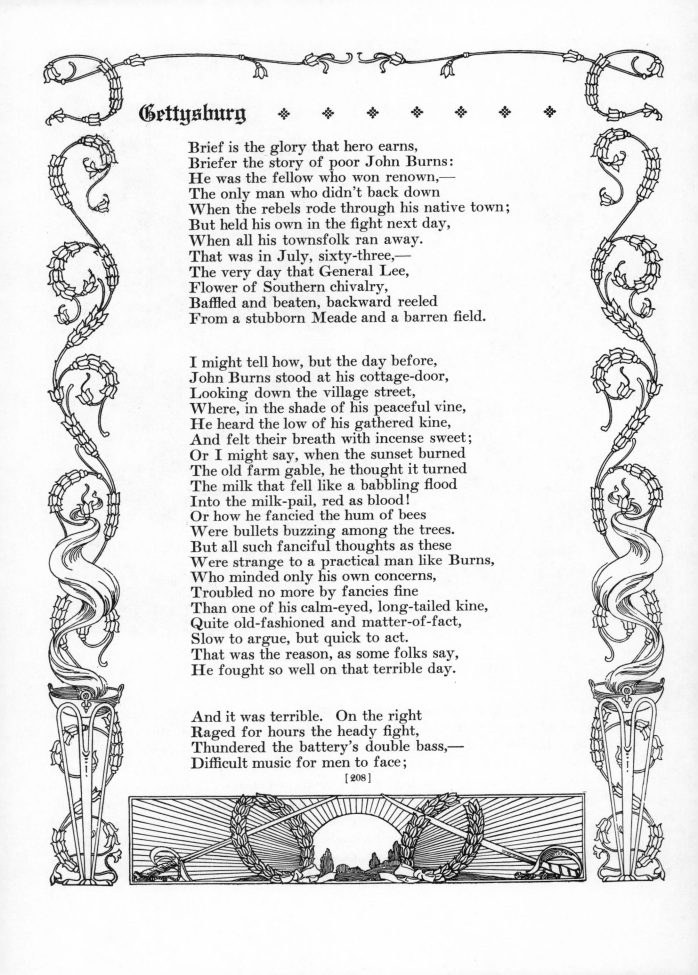

"WITH HIS LONG BROWN RIFLE"—JOHN BURNS OF GETTYSBURG

The old hero of Gettysburg sits here by his cottage. On one side is the old-fashioned gun Harte speaks of, on the other, the crutches he needed after the battle. Sergeant George Eustice, of Company F, Seventh Wisconsin Volunteers, in "Battles and Leaders" describes John Burns' action in the ranks of that regiment: "It must have been about noon when I saw a little old man coming up in the rear of Company F. In regard to the peculiarities of his dress, I remember he wore a swallow-tailed coat with smooth brass buttons. He had a rifle on his shoulder. We boys began to poke fun at him as soon as he came amongst us, as we thought no civilian in his senses would show himself in such a place. . . . Bullets were flying thicker and faster, and we hugged the ground about us as close as we could. Burns got behind a tree and surprised us all by not taking a double-quick to the rear. He was as calm and collected as any veteran."

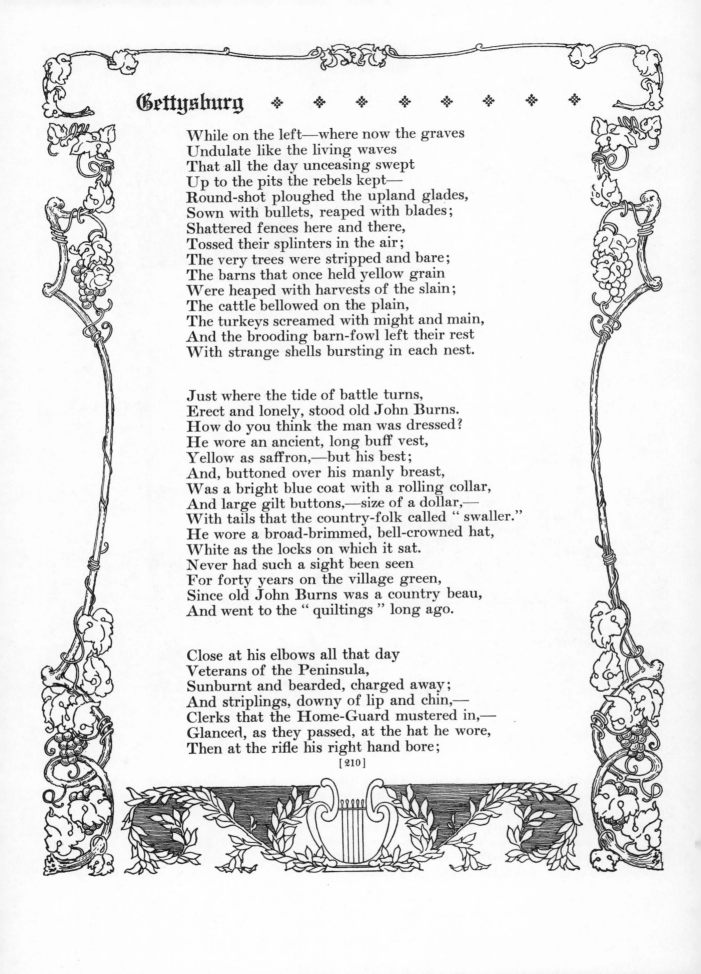

Gettysburg ❖ ❖ ❖ ❖ ❖ ❖ ❖ ❖

While on the left—where now the graves
Undulate like the living waves
That all the day unceasing swept
Up to the pits the rebels kept—
Round-shot ploughed the upland glades,
Sown with bullets, reaped with blades;
Shattered fences here and there,
Tossed their splinters in the air;
The very trees were stripped and bare;
The barns that once held yellow grain
Were heaped with harvests of the slain;
The cattle bellowed on the plain,
The turkeys screamed with might and main,
And the brooding barn-fowl left their rest
With strange shells bursting in each nest.

Just where the tide of battle turns,
Erect and lonely, stood old John Burns.
How do you think the man was dressed?
He wore an ancient, long buff vest,
Yellow as saffron,—but his best;
And, buttoned over his manly breast,
Was a bright blue coat with a rolling collar,
And large gilt buttons,—size of a dollar,—
With tails that the country-folk called " swaller."
He wore a broad-brimmed, bell-crowned hat,
White as the locks on which it sat.
Never had such a sight been seen
For forty years on the village green,
Since old John Burns was a country beau,
And went to the " quiltings " long ago.

Close at his elbows all that day
Veterans of the Peninsula,
Sunburnt and bearded, charged away;
And striplings, downy of lip and chin,—
Clerks that the Home-Guard mustered in,—
Glanced, as they passed, at the hat he wore,
Then at the rifle his right hand bore;

"JOHN BURNS STOOD AT HIS COTTAGE DOOR"

These photographs present at his home the man of whom Harte wrote the half-humorous poem. According to common report, Burns was seventy years old when the battle was fought. In the war of 1812, though still a youth, he had been among the first to volunteer; and he took part in the battles of Plattsburg, Queenstown, and Lundy's Lane. In 1846 he again volunteered for service in the American armies, and served through the Mexican War. At the beginning of the Civil War he tried to enlist once more, but the officer told him that a man of sixty-seven was not acceptable for active service. He did, however, secure employment for a time as a teamster but was finally sent home to Gettysburg. To keep him contented his townsmen elected him constable of the then obscure village. He took his duties very seriously. When General Lee's troops entered the place in June, 1863, Burns asserted his authority in opposition to that of the Confederate provost-guard and was accordingly locked up. But no sooner had the troops left the town than he began to arrest the stragglers of the army. On July 1st, the first day of the battle of Gettysburg, the old man borrowed a rifle and ammunition from a Federal soldier who had been wounded, went west of the town to the point of heaviest fighting, and asked to be given a place in the line. The colonel of the Seventh Wisconsin handed him a long-range rifle and allowed him to join the other troops. There he fought like a veteran. When the Union forces were driven back by superior numbers, Burns fell into the hands of the Confederates and came very near being executed as an ununiformed combatant. Though wounded in three places, he recovered and lived here until his death in 1872.

WITH HIS WIFE AFTER THE BATTLE

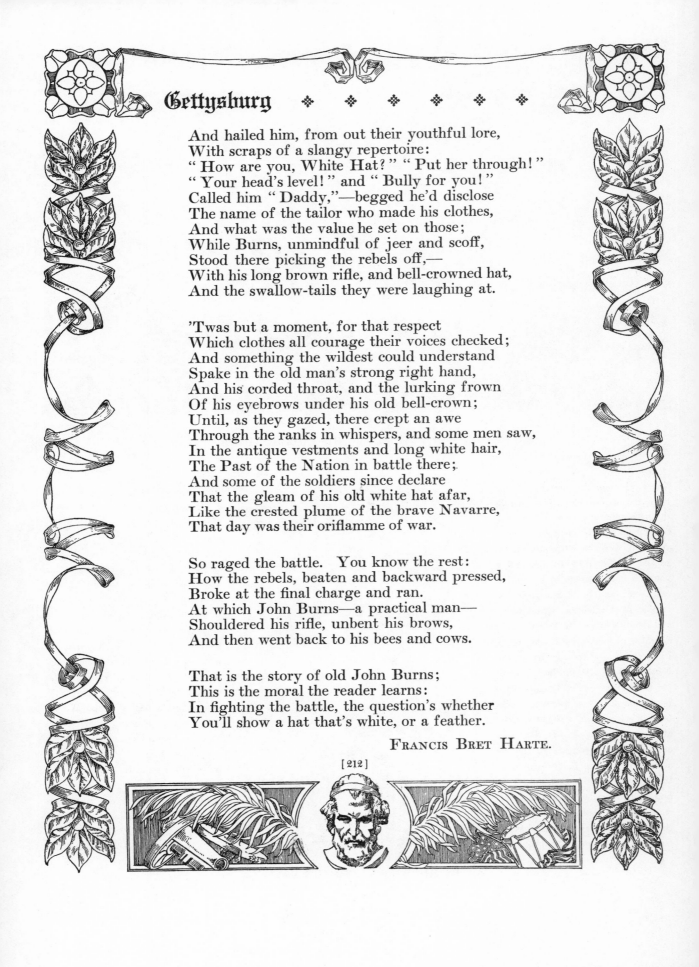

Gettysburg ✦ ✦ ✦ ✦ ✦ ✦

And hailed him, from out their youthful lore,
With scraps of a slangy repertoire:
" How are you, White Hat? " " Put her through! "
" Your head's level! " and " Bully for you! "
Called him " Daddy,"—begged he'd disclose
The name of the tailor who made his clothes,
And what was the value he set on those;
While Burns, unmindful of jeer and scoff,
Stood there picking the rebels off,—
With his long brown rifle, and bell-crowned hat,
And the swallow-tails they were laughing at.

'Twas but a moment, for that respect
Which clothes all courage their voices checked;
And something the wildest could understand
Spake in the old man's strong right hand,
And his corded throat, and the lurking frown
Of his eyebrows under his old bell-crown;
Until, as they gazed, there crept an awe
Through the ranks in whispers, and some men saw,
In the antique vestments and long white hair,
The Past of the Nation in battle there;
And some of the soldiers since declare
That the gleam of his old white hat afar,
Like the crested plume of the brave Navarre,
That day was their oriflamme of war.

So raged the battle. You know the rest:
How the rebels, beaten and backward pressed,
Broke at the final charge and ran.
At which John Burns—a practical man—
Shouldered his rifle, unbent his brows,
And then went back to his bees and cows.

That is the story of old John Burns;
This is the moral the reader learns:
In fighting the battle, the question's whether
You'll show a hat that's white, or a feather.

FRANCIS BRET HARTE.

"THE VERY TREES WERE STRIPPED AND BARE"

This picture of cannonaded trees on Culp's Hill, and the views herewith of Round Top and Cemetery Ridge, carry the reader across the whole battlefield. Culp's Hill was the scene of a contest on the second day. Lee's plan on that day was to attack the right and left flanks of the Union army at the same time. Longstreet's attack on the left, at Little Round Top, approached a victory. Ewell's attack on the right at Culp's Hill, although made later than intended, came near complete success. His cannonading, the effects of which appear in the picture, was soon silenced, but the infantry forces that assaulted the positions on the extreme right found them nearly defenseless because the troops had been sent to reënforce the left. About sunset General Edward Johnson led this attack, which was repulsed by the thin but well fortified line under command of General George S. Greene. About nine o'clock Johnson walked into the undefended works of the extreme right. The next morning he was soon driven out, but the Union peril had been great.

THE HIGH TIDE AT GETTYSBURG

Pickett's charge, the subject of these lines, was made on the afternoon of the third day's battle, July 3, 1863, and ended the stubborn conflict. The author became a Confederate soldier at fifteen, in the
Fourth Georgia, and fought until disabled in 1865.

A cloud possessed the hollow field,
The gathering battle's smoky shield:
 Athwart the gloom the lightning flashed,
 And through the cloud some horsemen dashed,
And from the heights the thunder pealed.

Then, at the brief command of Lee,
Moved out that matchless infantry,
 With Pickett leading grandly down,
 To rush against the roaring crown
Of those dread heights of destiny.

Far heard above the angry guns
A cry across the tumult runs,—
 The voice that rang through Shiloh's woods
 And Chickamauga's solitudes,
The fierce South cheering on her sons!

Ah, how the withering tempest blew
Against the front of Pettigrew!
 A Khamsin wind that scorched and singed
 Like that infernal flame that fringed
The British squares at Waterloo!

A thousand fell where Kemper led;
A thousand died where Garnett bled:
 In blinding flame and strangling smoke
 The remnant through the batteries broke
And crossed the works with Armistead.

"Once more in Glory's van with me!"
Virginia cried to Tennessee;
 "We two together, come what may,
 Shall stand upon these works to-day!"
(The reddest day in history.)

[214]

"WITH PICKETT LEADING GRANDLY DOWN"

Thompson's description of Pickett's charge, with this martial portrait, calls for little explanation. A few words from an English army officer who was present, Arthur J. Fremantle, will describe Lee's share in the record of nobility. General Lee's conduct after the charge, writes the English colonel, "was perfectly sublime. He was engaged in rallying and in encouraging the broken troops, and was riding about a little in front cf the wood, quite alone, the whole of his staff being engaged in a similar manner further to the rear. His face, which is always placid and cheerful, did not show signs of the slightest disappointment, care, or annoyance; and he was addressing to every soldier he met a few words of encouragement, such as, 'All this will come right in the end—we'll talk it over afterward; but, in the mean time, all good men must rally—we want all good and true men just now,' etc. He spoke to all the wounded men that passed him, and the slightly wounded he exhorted 'to bind up their hurts and take up a musket' in this emergency. Very few failed to answer his appeal, and I saw many badly wounded men take off their hats and cheer him. He said to me, 'This has been a very sad day for us, Colonel, a sad day; but we can't expect always to gain victories.' . . . I saw General Wilcox come up to him, and explain, almost crying, the state of his brigade. General Lee immediately shook hands with him and said, cheerfully, 'Never mind, General, all this has been *my* fault; it is *I* that have lost this fight, and you must help me out of it in the best way you can.'"

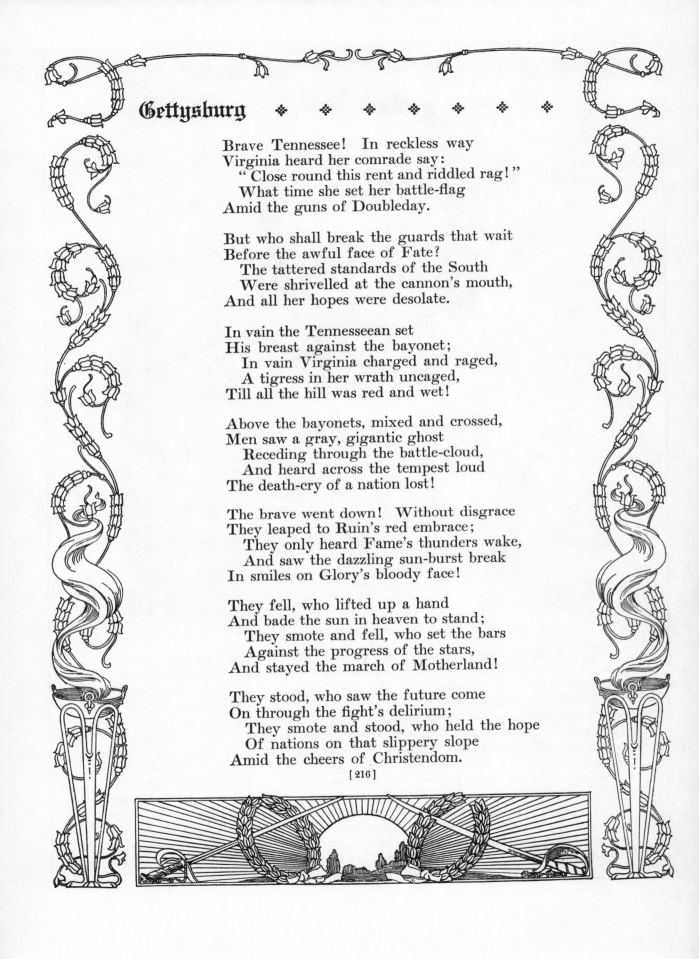

Gettysburg ❖ ❖ ❖ ❖ ❖ ❖ ❖

Brave Tennessee! In reckless way
Virginia heard her comrade say:
   "Close round this rent and riddled rag!"
   What time she set her battle-flag
Amid the guns of Doubleday.

But who shall break the guards that wait
Before the awful face of Fate?
   The tattered standards of the South
   Were shrivelled at the cannon's mouth,
And all her hopes were desolate.

In vain the Tennesseean set
His breast against the bayonet;
   In vain Virginia charged and raged,
   A tigress in her wrath uncaged,
Till all the hill was red and wet!

Above the bayonets, mixed and crossed,
Men saw a gray, gigantic ghost
   Receding through the battle-cloud,
   And heard across the tempest loud
The death-cry of a nation lost!

The brave went down! Without disgrace
They leaped to Ruin's red embrace;
   They only heard Fame's thunders wake,
   And saw the dazzling sun-burst break
In smiles on Glory's bloody face!

They fell, who lifted up a hand
And bade the sun in heaven to stand;
   They smote and fell, who set the bars
   Against the progress of the stars,
And stayed the march of Motherland!

They stood, who saw the future come
On through the fight's delirium;
   They smote and stood, who held the hope
   Of nations on that slippery slope
Amid the cheers of Christendom.

[216]

A GUN AND GUNNERS THAT REPULSED PICKETT'S CHARGE

FROM A PHOTOGRAPH TREASURED NEARLY HALF A CENTURY BY THE CAPTAIN OF THIS BATTERY

This photograph of a gun and cannoneers that helped to check Pickett's charge at Gettysburg was preserved for nearly fifty years by Andrew Cowan, captain of the battery containing this gun. From that bloody angle on Cemetery Ridge his life was spared, although the commanders of the batteries to right and left of him, Lieutenant Alonzo H. Cushing and Captain James Rorty, both were killed. At the very height of the action, General Henry J. Hunt, chief of artillery of the army, rode into the battery and fired his revolver at the oncoming gray line, exclaiming: "See 'em! See 'em! See 'em!" A moment later, Cowan ordered his guns to cease firing, for fear of injuring the men of the Sixty-ninth Pennsylvania at the wall in their front. The Sixty-ninth suddenly swung to the right, leaving the guns uncovered. The Confederates came rushing on from behind a slight elevation, covered with bushes and rocks, where they had crouched. A Confederate officer shouted, "Take the guns!" They were double-loaded, with canister. Some of the brave assailants were within 10 yards of the muzzles when Captain Cowan shouted, "Fire!" Two hundred and twenty chunks of lead burst from the muzzles of each of the five guns. Before the deadly storm, the line in gray withered and was no more. "We buried that officer with honor," wrote Captain Cowan, to whom readers are indebted for both the photograph and this account. "I returned his sword to survivors of Pickett's division on the same ground, twenty-five years afterward." At Cedar Creek, six months after this photograph, Sergeant William E. Uhlster (A) was crippled and Corporal Henry J. Tucker (B) was killed.

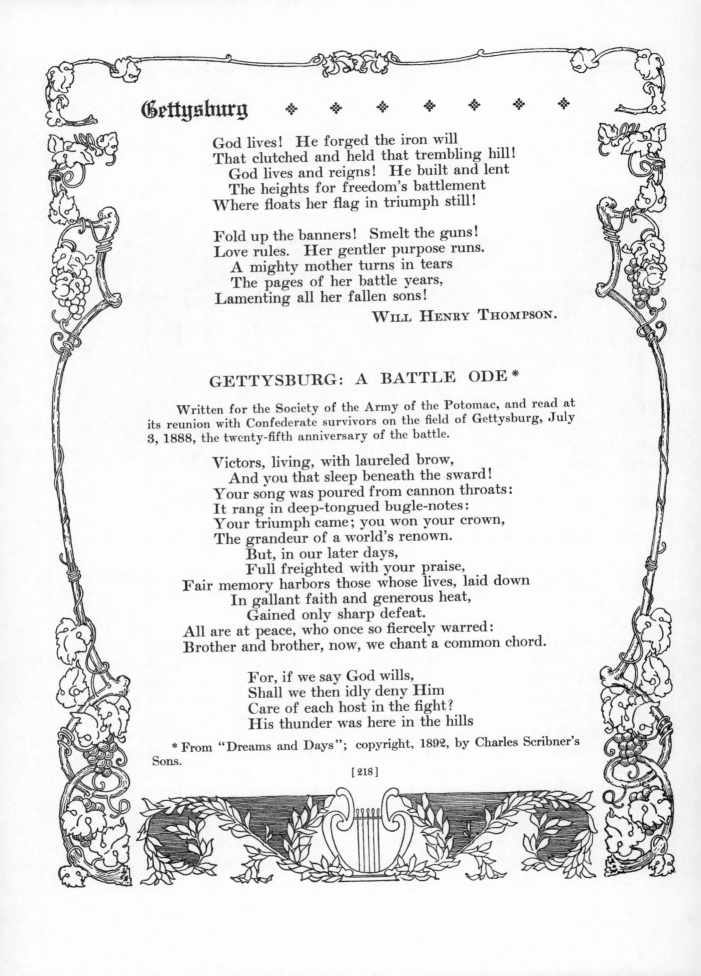

Gettysburg ✦ ✦ ✦ ✦ ✦ ✦ ✦

God lives! He forged the iron will
That clutched and held that trembling hill!
  God lives and reigns! He built and lent
  The heights for freedom's battlement
Where floats her flag in triumph still!

Fold up the banners! Smelt the guns!
Love rules. Her gentler purpose runs.
  A mighty mother turns in tears
  The pages of her battle years,
Lamenting all her fallen sons!

WILL HENRY THOMPSON.

GETTYSBURG: A BATTLE ODE *

Written for the Society of the Army of the Potomac, and read at
its reunion with Confederate survivors on the field of Gettysburg, July
3, 1888, the twenty-fifth anniversary of the battle.

Victors, living, with laureled brow,
  And you that sleep beneath the sward!
Your song was poured from cannon throats:
It rang in deep-tongued bugle-notes:
Your triumph came; you won your crown,
The grandeur of a world's renown.
    But, in our later days,
    Full freighted with your praise,
Fair memory harbors those whose lives, laid down
  In gallant faith and generous heat,
    Gained only sharp defeat.
All are at peace, who once so fiercely warred:
Brother and brother, now, we chant a common chord.

    For, if we say God wills,
    Shall we then idly deny Him
    Care of each host in the fight?
    His thunder was here in the hills

* From "Dreams and Days"; copyright, 1892, by Charles Scribner's
Sons.

[218]

"FOLD UP THE BANNERS, SMELT THE GUNS"

The tangled heap is all that remains of hundreds of captured Confederate artillery carriages, gathered at the Watervliet Arsenal in Troy, New York, and burned for the iron. A more impressive illustration of the line quoted from the stirring battle-ballad could hardly exist. But Thompson's words were used in a higher sense. Never more shall Americans level artillery or musketry upon their fellow-countrymen. Gettysburg virtually decided that. Not only so, but the people shall be bound together by active pride in their common blood and common traditions which finds expression in common hopes and aspirations for the future. America has become a single country, with a central Government wielding sovereign power and holding among the nations of the earth a position of world-wide honor and influence. One of the foremost New England historians, Professor Albert Bushnell Hart of Harvard, declares: "The keynote to which intelligent spirits respond most quickly in the United States is Americanism; no nation is more conscious of its own existence and its importance in the universe, more interested in the greatness, the strength, the pride, the influence, and the future of the common country."

Gettysburg ✤ ✤ ✤ ✤ ✤ ✤

When the guns were loud in July;
And the flash of the musketry's light
Was sped by a ray from God's eye.
In its good and its evil the scheme
Was framed with omnipotent hand,
Though the battle of men was a dream
That they could but half understand.
Can the purpose of God pass by him?
Nay; it was sure, and was wrought
Under inscrutable powers:
Bravely the two armies fought
And left the land, that was greater than they, still theirs
and ours!

Lucid, pure, and calm and blameless
   Dawned on Gettysburg the day
That should make the spot, once fameless,
   Known to nations far away.
Birds were caroling, and farmers
   Gladdened o'er their garnered hay,
When the clank of gathering armors
   Broke the morning's peaceful sway;
And the living lines of foemen
   Drawn o'er pasture, brook, and hill,
Formed in figures weird of omen
   That should work with mystic will
Measures of a direful magic—
   Shattering, maiming—and should fill
Glades and gorges with a tragic
   Madness of desire to kill.
Skirmishers flung lightly forward
   Moved like scythemen skilled to sweep
Westward o'er the field and nor'ward,
   Death's first harvest there to reap.
You would say the soft, white smoke-puffs
   Were but languid clouds asleep,
Here on meadows, there on oak-bluffs,
   Fallen foam of Heaven's blue deep.
Yet that blossom-white outbreaking
   Smoke wove soon a martyr's shroud.

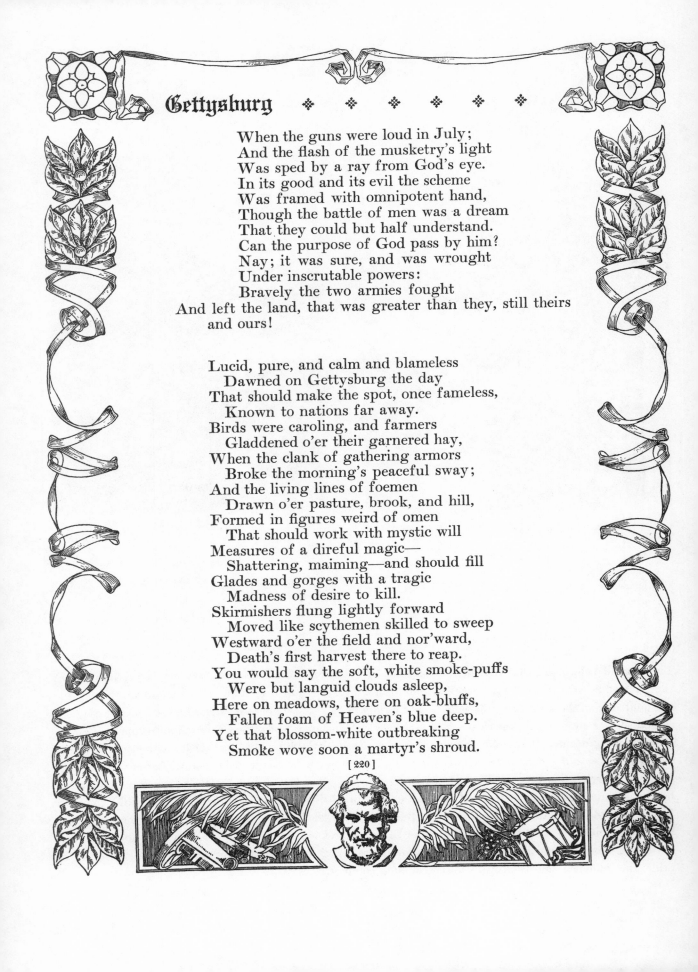

AFTER THE BATTLE—ROUND TOP, SOUTHERN END OF THE FEDERAL LINE

From these rocks of Round Top, as seen from Little Round Top, echoed the cannonading at Gettysburg—the heaviest ever heard on this continent, and seldom equaled anywhere. For two miles the Confederate line was planted thick with cannon. General Hancock's official account gives a clear notion of this part of the battle: "From 11 A.M. until 1 P.M. there was an ominous stillness. About 1 o'clock, apparently by a given signal, the enemy opened upon our front with the heaviest artillery fire I have ever known. Their guns were in position at an average distance of about 1,400 yards from my line, and ran in a semi-circle from the town of Gettysburg to a point opposite Round Top Mountain. Their number is variously estimated at from one hundred and fif-

ABNER DOUBLEDAY

DEFENDER OF CEMETERY RIDGE, THE NORTHERN END
OF MEADE'S LINE

teen to one hundred and fifty. The air was filled with projectiles, there being scarcely an instant but that several were seen bursting at once. No irregularity of ground afforded much protection, and the plain in rear of the line of battle was soon swept of everything movable. The infantry troops maintained their position with great steadiness, covering themselves as best they might by the temporary but trifling defenses they had erected and the accidents of the ground. Scarcely a straggler was seen, but all waited the cessation of the fierce cannonade, knowing well what it foreshadowed. The artillery of the corps, imperfectly supplied with ammunition, replied to the enemy most gallantly, maintaining the unequal contest in a manner that reflected the highest honor on this arm."

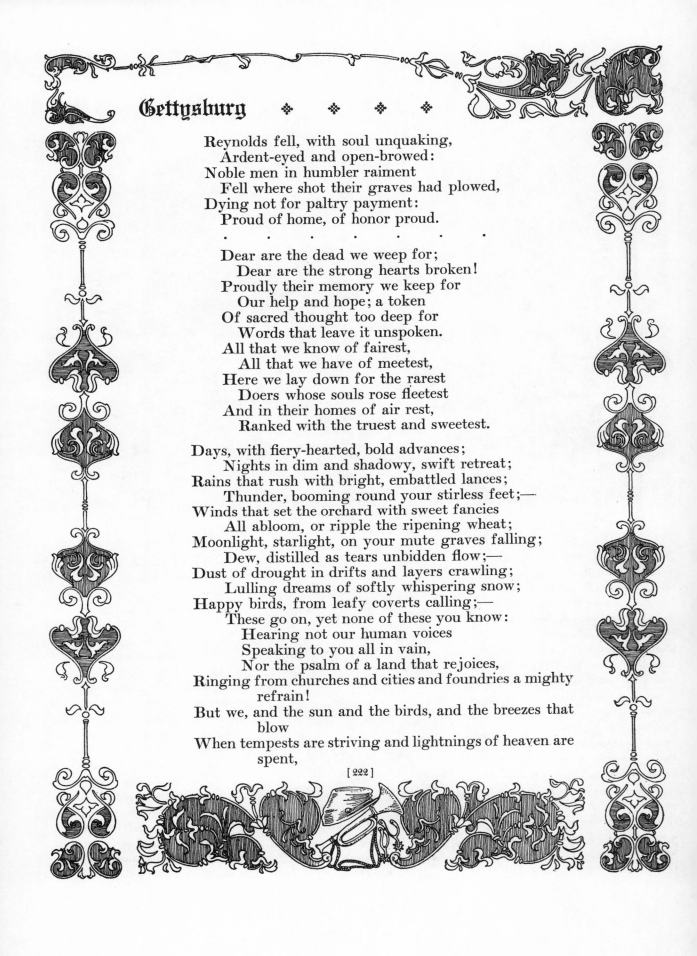

Gettysburg ❖ ❖ ❖ ❖

Reynolds fell, with soul unquaking,
  Ardent-eyed and open-browed:
Noble men in humbler raiment
  Fell where shot their graves had plowed,
Dying not for paltry payment:
  Proud of home, of honor proud.

. . . .

Dear are the dead we weep for;
  Dear are the strong hearts broken!
Proudly their memory we keep for
  Our help and hope; a token
Of sacred thought too deep for
  Words that leave it unspoken.
All that we know of fairest,
  All that we have of meetest,
Here we lay down for the rarest
  Doers whose souls rose fleetest
And in their homes of air rest,
  Ranked with the truest and sweetest.

Days, with fiery-hearted, bold advances;
  Nights in dim and shadowy, swift retreat;
Rains that rush with bright, embattled lances;
  Thunder, booming round your stirless feet;—
Winds that set the orchard with sweet fancies
  All abloom, or ripple the ripening wheat;
Moonlight, starlight, on your mute graves falling;
  Dew, distilled as tears unbidden flow;—
Dust of drought in drifts and layers crawling;
  Lulling dreams of softly whispering snow;
Happy birds, from leafy coverts calling;—
  These go on, yet none of these you know:
    Hearing not our human voices
    Speaking to you all in vain,
    Nor the psalm of a land that rejoices,
Ringing from churches and cities and foundries a mighty
    refrain!
But we, and the sun and the birds, and the breezes that
    blow
When tempests are striving and lightnings of heaven are
    spent,

"REYNOLDS FELL, WITH SOUL UNQUAKING"

MCPHERSON'S WOODS AT GETTYSBURG—ILLUSTRATION FOR LATHROP'S "ODE"

Matthew Brady, the wizard who preserved so many war scenes, is here gazing across the field toward the woods where Reynolds fell. About ten o'clock in the morning, July 1st, the brigade of the Confederate General Archer and the Federal "Iron Brigade," directed by General Reynolds, were both trying to secure control of this strip. Reynolds was on horseback in the edge of the woods, impatient for the troops to come up so that he could make the advance. As he turned once to see how close they were, a Confederate sharpshooter from the depths of the thicket hit him in the back of the head. He fell dead without a word. General Hunt says of him: "He had opened brilliantly a battle which required three days of hard fighting to close with a victory. To him may be applied in a wider sense than in its original one, Napier's happy eulogium on Ridge: 'No man died on that field with more glory than he, yet many died, and there was much glory.'" Thus his name is inseparably linked with the history of his country at a turning-point in its course.

Gettysburg ✦ ✦ ✦ ✦ ✦ ✦ ✦

With one consent
Make unto them
Who died for us eternal requiem.

Lovely to look on, O South,
No longer stately-scornful
But beautiful still in pride,
Our hearts go out to you as toward a bride!
Garmented soft in white,
Haughty, and yet how love-imbuing and tender!
You stand before us with your gently mournful
Memory-haunted eyes and flower-like mouth,
Where clinging thoughts—as bees a-cluster
Murmur through the leafy gloom,
Musical in monotone—
Whisper sadly. Yet a lustre
As of glowing gold-gray light
Shines upon the orient bloom,
Sweet with orange-blossoms, thrown
Round the jasmine-starred, deep night
Crowning with dark hair your brow.
Ruthless, once, we came to slay,
And you met us then with hate.
Rough was the wooing of war: we won you,
Won you at last, though late!
Dear South, to-day,
As our country's altar made us
One forever, so we vow
Unto yours our love to render:
Strength with strength we here endow,
And we make your honor ours.
Happiness and hope shall sun you:
All the wiles that half betrayed us
Vanish from us like spent showers.

Two hostile bullets in mid-air
Together shocked,
And swift were locked
Forever in a firm embrace.
Then let us men have so much grace

[224]

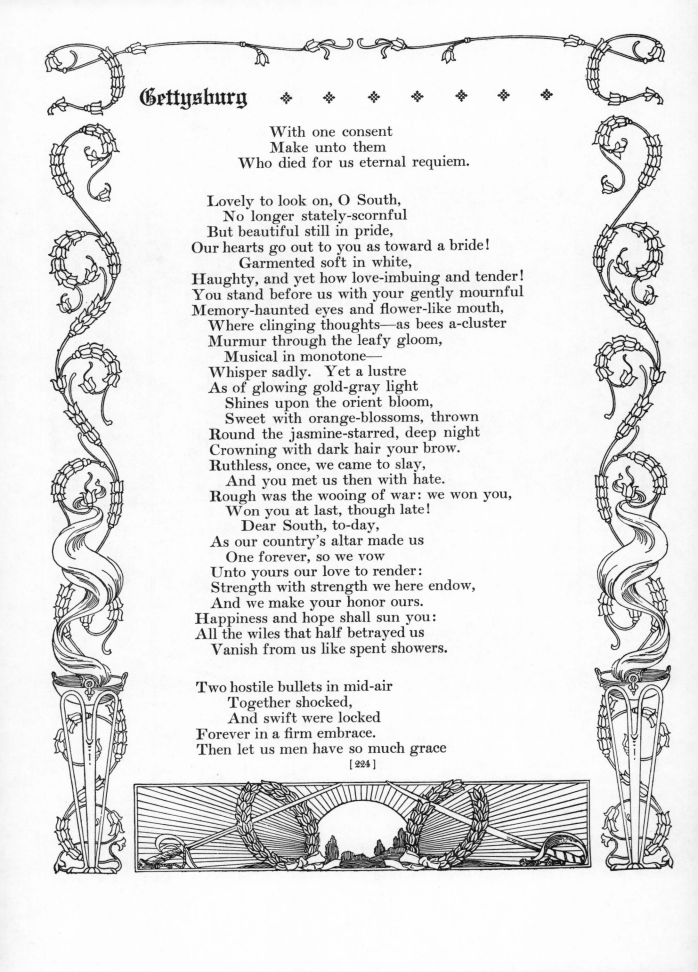

"NOBLE MEN IN HUMBLER RAIMENT FELL"

A CONFEDERATE SHARPSHOOTER KILLED AT THE BATTLE OF GETTYSBURG

The words from Lathrop's poem on "Gettysburg" apply to the 7,058 soldiers who fell in this deadliest of American battles. The point photographed is "Devil's Den," a rocky height rising sharply on the east and sloping gradually to the plain on the west. Its northern point was composed of huge rocks and boulders with numberless crevices and holes such as the one that yawns at the left of the picture. The whole region is covered with similar boulders, which afforded retreats for sharpshooters on both sides. Five hundred yards east, and a hundred feet higher than "Devil's Den," was Little Round Top, the key to the entire Federal position along Cemetery Ridge. Lee's tactics on the second day were to drive back a Federal force on the plain near "Devil's Den" and secure Little Round Top and the whole Union position. His troops formed in the woods, far outflanking the opposing troops on the plain. They were almost at Little Round Top before General G. K. Warren discovered that a single signal-man was there to defend the height. Only by marvelous exertions were defenders secured in time to meet the attack. Longstreet's men, however, gained possession of "Devil's Den." A multitude of sharpshooters clambered into the lurking-places among the boulders, whence they could not be dislodged by artillery fire or by sharpshooting. These men were especially successful in picking off the cannoneers on Little Round Top. At one time three were shot down in quick succession, and only the fourth succeeded in firing the piece. When night closed on the scene the Confederates still held the "Den" and the ground at the foot of Little Round Top, but many of the defenders were dead or dying. And yet another day of carnage was to come.

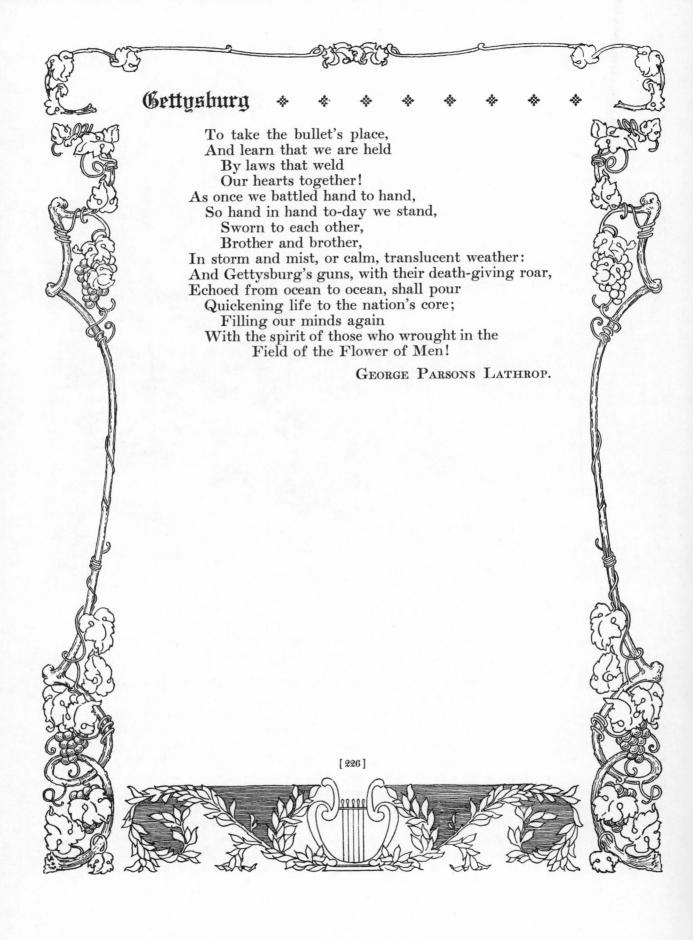

Gettysburg ❖ ❖ ❖ ❖ ❖ ❖ ❖ ❖

To take the bullet's place,
And learn that we are held
　　By laws that weld
　　Our hearts together!
As once we battled hand to hand,
　So hand in hand to-day we stand,
　　Sworn to each other,
　　Brother and brother,
In storm and mist, or calm, translucent weather:
And Gettysburg's guns, with their death-giving roar,
Echoed from ocean to ocean, shall pour
　Quickening life to the nation's core;
　　Filling our minds again
With the spirit of those who wrought in the
　　Field of the Flower of Men!

GEORGE PARSONS LATHROP.

X

THE END
OF THE STRUGGLE

HISTORIC FORT MOULTRIE AT CHARLESTON IN RUINS—1865

ILLUSTRATIONS FOR MARGARET PRESTON'S LINES "A PAST WHOSE MEMORY MAKES US THRILL"—THIS STRONGHOLD, NAMED FOR WILLIAM MOULTRIE, THE YOUNG SOUTH CAROLINIAN WHO DEFENDED IT IN 1776 AGAINST THE BRITISH, WAS 85 YEARS LATER HELD BY SOUTH CAROLINIANS AGAINST FELLOW-AMERICANS —IN THE PICTURE IT IS ONCE MORE UNDER THE FLAG OF A UNITED LAND.

[J—15]

"A PAST WHOSE MEM-ORY MAKES US THRILL"

WAR-TIME SCENES IN VIR-GINIA ASSOCIATED WITH THE FATHER OF HIS COUNTRY

The picture below of Washington's headquarters recalls his advance to fame. He had proceeded with Braddock as aide-de-camp on the ill-fated expedition ending in the battle of the Monongahela, July 9, 1755. Owing to Washington's conspicuous gallantry in that engagement, he was assigned the duty of reorganizing the provincial troops. During this period his headquarters were in the little stone house by the tree. In the church below, a second period of his life was inaugurated. Here he was married on January 6, 1759, to

THE RICHMOND STATUE

Mrs. Martha Custis, a young widow with two children. Already a member of the House of Burgesses of Virginia, he soon came to be recognized as one of the leading men in the colony. Important trusts were frequently laid upon him, and he was often chosen as an arbitrator. The statue at the top of the page, standing in Capitol Square in Richmond, commemorates Washington as leader of the colonial forces in the Revolution. With a few ill-trained and ill-equipped troops he maintained a long struggle against one of the great military powers of the day and won American Independence. Every Virginian has a right to thrill at the honored name of Washington, be he Southerner or Northerner.

SAINT PETER'S CHURCH—UNION SOLDIERS

WASHINGTON'S HEADQUARTERS IN RICHMOND

"A PAST WHOSE MEMORY MAKES US THRILL"—THE JAMESTOWN CHURCH

The pictures on this page bring back vividly the history of Virginia. First is the ruins of the church at Jamestown, the first permanent English settlement within the limits of the United States. The church was built about a century before the Declaration of Independence, while the little village on the James was still the capital of Virginia. Below it appears St. John's Church, Richmond, the scene of Patrick Henry's immortal oration. The First Continental Congress had met in Philadelphia in September, 1774, and the colonies were drifting toward war. But many were very timid about taking such a step. Some were directly opposed to any break with Great Britain. Patrick Henry was far in advance of his fellow-colonists, when the Second Revolutionary Convention of Virginia met in this church on March 20, 1775. The event of the week was a set of resolutions offered on March 23d "for embodying, arming, and disciplining such a number of men as may be sufficient" to put the colony in a posture of defense. This was Henry's opportunity.

WHERE PATRICK HENRY SPOKE

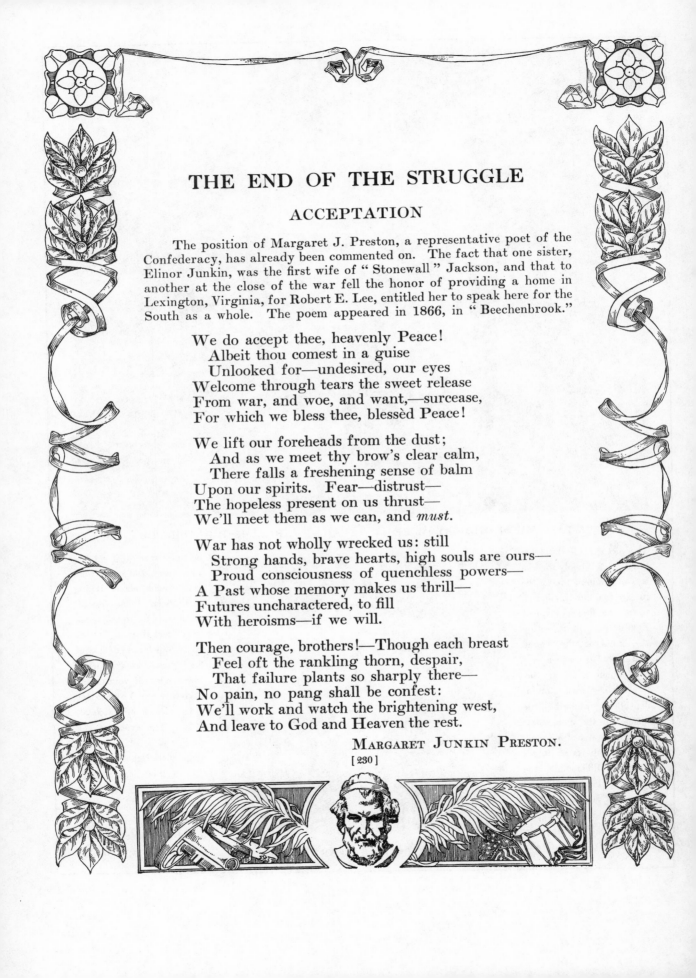

THE END OF THE STRUGGLE

ACCEPTATION

The position of Margaret J. Preston, a representative poet of the Confederacy, has already been commented on. The fact that one sister, Elinor Junkin, was the first wife of " Stonewall " Jackson, and that to another at the close of the war fell the honor of providing a home in Lexington, Virginia, for Robert E. Lee, entitled her to speak here for the South as a whole. The poem appeared in 1866, in " Beechenbrook."

We do accept thee, heavenly Peace!
    Albeit thou comest in a guise
    Unlooked for—undesired, our eyes
Welcome through tears the sweet release
From war, and woe, and want,—surcease,
For which we bless thee, blessèd Peace!

We lift our foreheads from the dust;
    And as we meet thy brow's clear calm,
    There falls a freshening sense of balm
Upon our spirits. Fear—distrust—
The hopeless present on us thrust—
We'll meet them as we can, and *must*.

War has not wholly wrecked us: still
    Strong hands, brave hearts, high souls are ours—
    Proud consciousness of quenchless powers—
A Past whose memory makes us thrill—
Futures uncharactered, to fill
With heroisms—if we will.

Then courage, brothers!—Though each breast
    Feel oft the rankling thorn, despair,
    That failure plants so sharply there—
No pain, no pang shall be confest:
We'll work and watch the brightening west,
And leave to God and Heaven the rest.

MARGARET JUNKIN PRESTON.

[230]

MOURNING WOMEN AMONG THE RICHMOND RUINS—APRIL, 1865

A SOMBER PICTURE THAT VISUALIZES MARGARET PRESTON'S POEM "ACCEPTATION"

" .   .   .   Our Eyes
Welcome Through Tears the Sweet Release
From War."

The End of the Struggle ✦ ✦

A SECOND REVIEW OF THE GRAND ARMY

I read last night of the Grand Review
   In Washington's chiefest avenue,—
Two hundred thousand men in blue,
   I think they said was the number,—
Till I seemed to hear their trampling feet,
The bugle blast and the drum's quick beat,
The clatter of hoofs in the stony street,
The cheers of the people who came to greet,
And the thousand details that to repeat
   Would only my verse encumber,—
Till I fell in a revery, sad and sweet,
   And then to a fitful slumber.

When, lo! in a vision I seemed to stand
In the lonely Capitol. On each hand
Far stretched the portico, dim and grand
Its columns ranged, like a martial band
Of sheeted spectres whom some command
   Had called to a last reviewing.
And the streets of the city were white and bare;
No footfall echoed across the square;
But out of the misty midnight air
I heard in the distance a trumpet blare,
And the wandering night-winds seemed to bear
   The sound of a far tattooing.

Then I held my breath with fear and dread;
For into the square, with a brazen tread,
There rode a figure whose stately head
   O'erlooked the review that morning,
That never bowed from its firm-set seat
When the living column passed its feet,
Yet now rode steadily up the street
   To the phantom bugle's warning:

Till it reached the Capitol square, and wheeled,
And there in the moonlight stood revealed
A well known form that in State and field

"TWO HUNDRED THOUSAND MEN IN BLUE"

MARCHING UP PENNSYLVANIA AVENUE, IN MAY, 1865

Bret Harte's poem sounds the note of sorrow amid the national rejoicing at the splendor of the Grand Review. Those who never returned from the field of battle, or returned only to die of their wounds, formed a greater host than that which marched from the recently completed Capitol to the reviewing stand in front of the Executive Mansion. In the Federal army 110,070 were killed in battle or died of their wounds; 199,720 died of disease; 24,866 died in Confederate prisons; other causes of mortality bring the total up to 359,528. The estimates for the Confederate losses are less definite; but probably 94,000 were killed in action, 59,297 died of disease, 4,000 died in prison, and other causes would probably bring the total up to 250,000. Over 600,000 lives were therefore lost to the country by the necessities of warfare. When it is remembered that not only thousands of homes were cast in gloom but that most of these men were young, the cost of the war is apparent.

The End of the Struggle

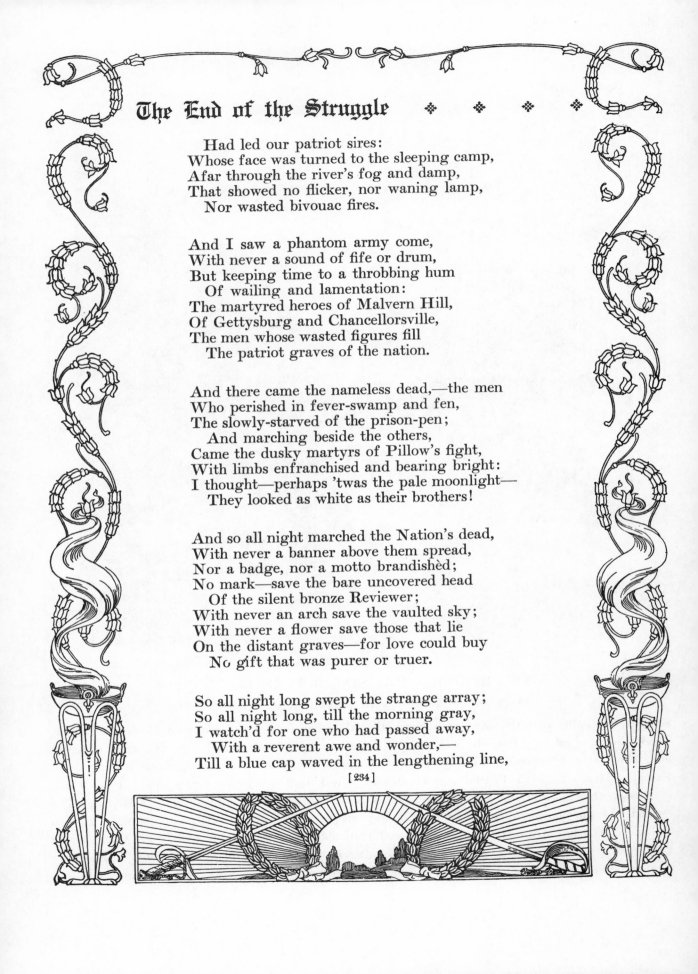

Had led our patriot sires:
Whose face was turned to the sleeping camp,
Afar through the river's fog and damp,
That showed no flicker, nor waning lamp,
    Nor wasted bivouac fires.

And I saw a phantom army come,
With never a sound of fife or drum,
But keeping time to a throbbing hum
    Of wailing and lamentation:
The martyred heroes of Malvern Hill,
Of Gettysburg and Chancellorsville,
The men whose wasted figures fill
    The patriot graves of the nation.

And there came the nameless dead,—the men
Who perished in fever-swamp and fen,
The slowly-starved of the prison-pen;
    And marching beside the others,
Came the dusky martyrs of Pillow's fight,
With limbs enfranchised and bearing bright:
I thought—perhaps 'twas the pale moonlight—
    They looked as white as their brothers!

And so all night marched the Nation's dead,
With never a banner above them spread,
Nor a badge, nor a motto brandishèd;
No mark—save the bare uncovered head
    Of the silent bronze Reviewer;
With never an arch save the vaulted sky;
With never a flower save those that lie
On the distant graves—for love could buy
    No gift that was purer or truer.

So all night long swept the strange array;
So all night long, till the morning gray,
I watch'd for one who had passed away,
    With a reverent awe and wonder,—
Till a blue cap waved in the lengthening line,

[234]

These shifting crowds on Pennsylvania Avenue, watching the Grand Review on May 23–24, 1865, seem like visions evoked by Bret Harte's lines. Part of the multitude of visitors to this most imposing fête day in American history are gathered near the reviewing-stand, before which the lines of men in blue are marching with military precision. Below the majestic elms and horse-chestnuts cavalrymen are trotting to the martial music of the band on the double-quick in the rear. The weather was perfect. Scores of bands filled the air with familiar tunes, and the choruses of "When this cruel war is over," "When Johnny comes marching home," and "Tramp, tramp, tramp, the boys are marching," were sung

"THE CHEERS OF THE PEOPLE WHO CAME TO GREET"

"I SEEMED TO HEAR THEIR TRAMPLING FEET"

lustily by the enthusiastic onlookers. Popular leaders were received with the most boisterous demonstrations. When Meade appeared at the head of the column, his pathway was strewn with flowers, and garlands were placed upon him and his horse. On the second day, Sherman was eagerly waited for, and he had advanced but a little way when flowers and wreaths almost covered him and his horse. When the bands at the reviewing stand struck up "Marching through Georgia," the people cheered wildly with delight. This was no Roman triumph. It was the rejoicing over the return of peace and the saving of the nation's life.

The End of the Struggle ❖ ❖ ❖ ❖

And I knew that one who was kin of mine
Had come; and I spake—and lo! that sign
Awakened me from my slumber.

FRANCIS BRET HARTE.

DRIVING HOME THE COWS

Out of the clover and blue-eyed grass
    He turned them into the river-lane;
One after another he let them pass,
    Then fastened the meadow-bars again.

Under the willows, and over the hill,
    He patiently followed their sober pace;
The merry whistle for once was still,
    And something shadowed the sunny face.

Only a boy! and his father had said
    He never could let his youngest go:
Two already were lying dead
    Under the feet of the trampling foe.

But after the evening work was done,
    And the frogs were loud in the meadow-swamp,
Over his shoulder he slung his gun,
    And stealthily followed the foot-path damp,

Across the clover, and through the wheat,
    With resolute heart and purpose grim,
Though cold was the dew on his hurrying feet,
    And the blind bat's flitting startled him.

Thrice since then had the lanes been white,
    And the orchards sweet with apple-bloom;
And now, when the cows came back at night,
    The feeble father drove them home.

For news had come to the lonely farm
    That three were lying where two had lain;
And the old man's tremulous, palsied arm
    Could never lean on a son's again.

[236]

"IN WASHINGTON'S CHIEFEST AVENUE"

Thus appeared the crowds that greeted the army whose home-coming inspired Bret Harte's poem. From the steps of the Treasury building the impatient people gaze down Pennsylvania Avenue on the morning of June 8, 1865, awaiting the march of the Sixth Corps of the Army of the Potomac, which had been prevented by duty in Virginia from participating in the Grand Review of May 23rd. The scene is similar. The women and children in the foreground, the senators and important citizens in silk hats, the throng surging far out into the street beneath the fluttering banners, the general restlessness and impatience are the same as on the earlier and more famous gala occasion. The pomp and panoply of war are here in the parades and the blare of trumpets and the admiring hosts that line the street—not in the actual service in the field. Harte writes of actual warfare as a sad business, which only the preservation of a nation's existence or honor can justify.

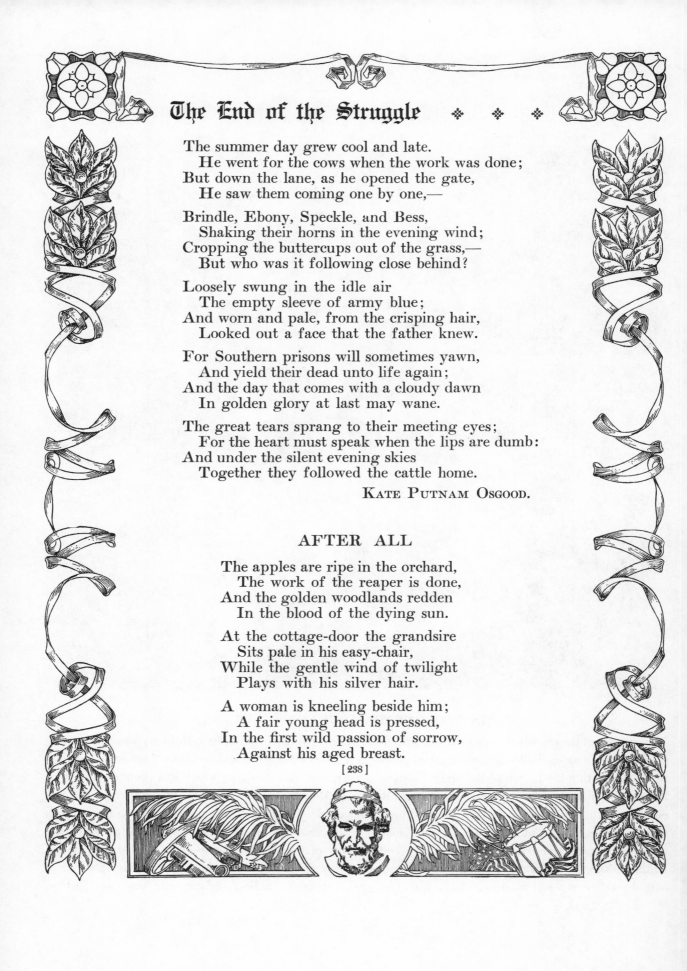

The End of the Struggle ❖ ❖ ❖

The summer day grew cool and late.
  He went for the cows when the work was done;
But down the lane, as he opened the gate,
  He saw them coming one by one,—

Brindle, Ebony, Speckle, and Bess,
  Shaking their horns in the evening wind;
Cropping the buttercups out of the grass,—
  But who was it following close behind?

Loosely swung in the idle air
  The empty sleeve of army blue;
And worn and pale, from the crisping hair,
  Looked out a face that the father knew.

For Southern prisons will sometimes yawn,
  And yield their dead unto life again;
And the day that comes with a cloudy dawn
  In golden glory at last may wane.

The great tears sprang to their meeting eyes;
  For the heart must speak when the lips are dumb:
And under the silent evening skies
  Together they followed the cattle home.

KATE PUTNAM OSGOOD.

AFTER ALL

The apples are ripe in the orchard,
  The work of the reaper is done,
And the golden woodlands redden
  In the blood of the dying sun.

At the cottage-door the grandsire
  Sits pale in his easy-chair,
While the gentle wind of twilight
  Plays with his silver hair.

A woman is kneeling beside him;
  A fair young head is pressed,
In the first wild passion of sorrow,
  Against his aged breast.

[238]

WAITING FOR NEWS OF THE BATTLE

WAR-TIME GROUPS NEAR RICHMOND

AT HANOVER JUNCTION A BATTLE GROUND FOUGHT OVER MANY TIMES

These views of the station at Hanover Junction, in Virginia, bring back in pictorial form the emotions of war-time, much as do the accompanying poems of Kate Putnam Osgood and William Winter. The shabby building with the crowd about it, the queer little engine drawing old-fashioned coaches, on the last of which a man leans out from the steps, and behind, in the chilly gray atmosphere of autumn, the wooded Virginia hills—these details make more real the men and women who suffered in the days of 1861. On the platform, at the left, stands an old soldier whose white beard and venerable face contrast with the hearty content of the man whose hands are in the pockets of his conspicuously checked trousers. At the other end, on the steps, is a wounded officer painfully making his way with the aid of two canes. Grouped by the doorway stand some mothers, wives, and sweethearts, dressed in the ancient poke-bonnets and rustling crinoline of fifty years ago. Some poems in this chapter express phases of the anguish that came to many a fond heart in those four endless years. But the women in the picture are more fortunate than most. They can go to the front to be with the wounded son or brother. Thousands had to wait on the hillside farm, or in the cabin on the prairie, or near the cottage by the live-oaks, while weeks and months of dread uncertainty brought no solace to eyes that watched through the darkness and hearts that suffered on in silence until the news arrived.

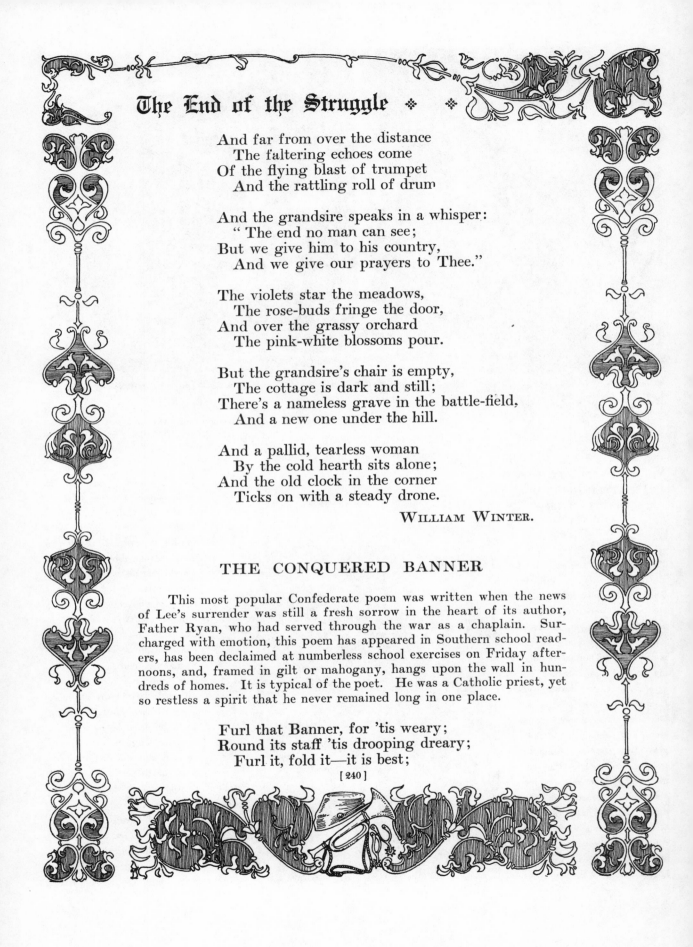

The End of the Struggle ❖ ❖

And far from over the distance
    The faltering echoes come
Of the flying blast of trumpet
    And the rattling roll of drum

And the grandsire speaks in a whisper:
    " The end no man can see;
But we give him to his country,
    And we give our prayers to Thee."

The violets star the meadows,
    The rose-buds fringe the door,
And over the grassy orchard
    The pink-white blossoms pour.

But the grandsire's chair is empty,
    The cottage is dark and still;
There's a nameless grave in the battle-field,
    And a new one under the hill.

And a pallid, tearless woman
    By the cold hearth sits alone;
And the old clock in the corner
    Ticks on with a steady drone.

WILLIAM WINTER.

THE CONQUERED BANNER

This most popular Confederate poem was written when the news of Lee's surrender was still a fresh sorrow in the heart of its author, Father Ryan, who had served through the war as a chaplain. Surcharged with emotion, this poem has appeared in Southern school readers, has been declaimed at numberless school exercises on Friday afternoons, and, framed in gilt or mahogany, hangs upon the wall in hundreds of homes. It is typical of the poet. He was a Catholic priest, yet so restless a spirit that he never remained long in one place.

Furl that Banner, for 'tis weary;
Round its staff 'tis drooping dreary;
    Furl it, fold it—it is best;

"THERE'S A NAMELESS GRAVE IN THE BATTLEFIELD"

This mute reminder of Antietam s awful cost suggests how many thousand homes were sunk in grief such as the poem "After All" describes. The soldiers themselves shared this grief. One of their saddest duties was the burial of comrades. When the graves had been dug, if there was found on their person any means of identifying them or if any one knew who they were, little pieces of board were secured and placed at the head of each. On these little boards, pieces of cracker-box, generally, would be placed the name and regiment of the deceased comrade written in pencil. Under the rain and the snows the writing would be obliterated or the boards themselves tumble down, and those lying in their graves on the battlefield would pass into the number of the great "unknown." There were no opportunities afforded in these burial details to go through any religious forms. The numbers forbade. Yet the lads who formed burial parties always gave their meed of reverence.

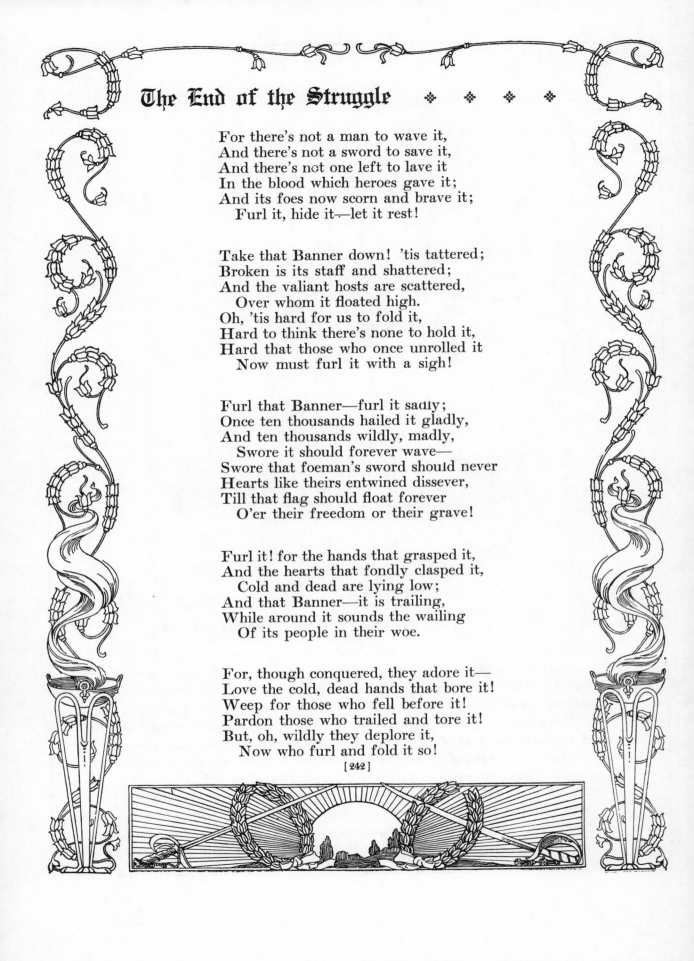

The End of the Struggle ✦ ✦ ✦ ✦

For there's not a man to wave it,
And there's not a sword to save it,
And there's not one left to lave it
In the blood which heroes gave it;
And its foes now scorn and brave it;
    Furl it, hide it—let it rest!

Take that Banner down! 'tis tattered;
Broken is its staff and shattered;
And the valiant hosts are scattered,
    Over whom it floated high.
Oh, 'tis hard for us to fold it,
Hard to think there's none to hold it,
Hard that those who once unrolled it
    Now must furl it with a sigh!

Furl that Banner—furl it sadly;
Once ten thousands hailed it gladly,
And ten thousands wildly, madly,
    Swore it should forever wave—
Swore that foeman's sword should never
Hearts like theirs entwined dissever,
Till that flag should float forever
    O'er their freedom or their grave!

Furl it! for the hands that grasped it,
And the hearts that fondly clasped it,
    Cold and dead are lying low;
And that Banner—it is trailing,
While around it sounds the wailing
    Of its people in their woe.

For, though conquered, they adore it—
Love the cold, dead hands that bore it!
Weep for those who fell before it!
Pardon those who trailed and tore it!
But, oh, wildly they deplore it,
    Now who furl and fold it so!

[242]

"THE VALIANT HOSTS ARE SCATTERED"

HERE PASSED THE MOST FAMOUS ARMY OF ALL THAT HAD FOUGHT FOR "THE CONQUERED BANNER"

This tragic still-life near Stony Creek, Virginia, is a witness to the turmoil of Lee's retreat. The caisson of a gun that tumbled into Chamberlain's Run on March 31, 1865, and was there abandoned, remains to tell of the last great battle. Through March Lee recognized that his only hope was to join Johnston in the Carolinas. Grant had spent many a sleepless night, fearing always that the next morning would bring him a report of Lee's retreat. To prevent this, he ordered Sheridan to destroy the railroads west of Petersburg. But on March 30th Sheridan was met at Five Forks by the Confederates under command of Fitzhugh Lee, and the next day was driven back southward to within half a mile of Dinwiddie Court House. In this engagement, W. H. F. Lee was sent along a wooded road leading south from Five Forks west of Chamberlain Bed, a creek running into Stony Creek near Dinwiddie Court House. After failing at one crossing, he succeeded in reaching the east bank at Danse's Crossing. All of Sheridan's cavalry corps then fell back on Dinwiddie Court House. Of this attack the single wheel of a caisson is the silent reminder. That night Sheridan was reënforced by the Fifth Corps; the next day, April 1st, he carried the Confederate position at Five Forks, and took nearly five thousand prisoners. The next morning, April 2d, the Petersburg entrenchments were carried by storm. The day after, the whole Confederate army was hastening westward. Seven days after this engagement came Appomattox. Lee's valiant hosts were indeed scattered, returning to their homes in a land that was once more united.

THE CONQUERED BANNER—WAVING FREE IN '61

The first Confederate flag made in Augusta, Georgia, swells in the May breeze of 1861. It has two red bars, with a white in the middle, and a union of blue with seven stars. The men who so proudly stand before it near the armory at Macon are the Clinch Rifles, forming Company A of the Fifth Georgia Infantry. The organization was completed on the next day—May 11th. It first went to Pensacola. From after the battle of Shiloh to July, 1864, it served in the Army of Tennessee, when it was sent to the Georgia coast, later serving under General Joseph E. Johnston in the final campaign in the Carolinas. It was conspicuous at Chickamauga, where its colonel commanded a brigade. His account of the action on September 20, 1863, is well worth quoting: "The brigade, with the battery in the center, moved forward in splendid style about 100 yards, when the enemy opened a galling fire from the front and left flank, enfilading the entire

"ONCE TEN THOUSANDS HAILED IT GLADLY"

line with canister and small-arms. The engagement now became terrific and the position of my brigade extremely critical. The troops, however, stood nobly to the work before them, and, steadily advancing, surmounted the hill on which the enemy's breastworks were, the battery moving with the line, and rendering effective service. The enemy were driven from their breastworks, and Brigadier-General Maney's brigade coming up at this opportune moment, charged them, and the contest was over. At daylight on Monday morning the enemy was found to have sought safety in flight under the cover of darkness." During the battle the regiment lost 194 men, a percentage of 54.95. The next highest recorded loss was 42.78. Ryan's words, "Those who once unrolled it," can appropriately be quoted under this spirited scene. And another phrase, "Cold and dead are lying now," fits too sadly well the careers of these volunteers from Georgia.

THE CONQUERED BANNER—"THERE'S 'NOT A SWORD TO SAVE IT"

As these rows and rows of cannon stretch across the arsenal grounds at Baton Rouge, soon after their surrender on May 4, 1865, by the Confederate general, Richard Taylor, a dramatic illustration appears of "The Conquered Banner" in war and in peace. The large building at the right, the arsenal of war times, was transformed, 45 years later, into dormitories for the Louisiana State University. It had been a military center under no less than five flags. The smaller buildings at the left, formerly used as powder-houses, later became model dairies in the agricultural department of the university work. Thus destruction gave place to training for citizenship and service. As soon as General Taylor heard of the capitulation of General Joseph E. Johnston in North Carolina, he surrendered, on May 4, 1865, at Citronelle, Alabama, not far from Mobile, all the remaining forces of the Confederacy east of the Mississippi River to the Federal General E. R. S. Canby. Canby had advanced from Dauphine Island, at the entrance to Mobile Bay, to the

THE GUNS OF THE LARGEST CONFEDERATE ARMY THAT SURRENDERED

Spanish Fort across from Mobile and had reduced it on April 8th, marching into the deserted works on the day that General Lee surrendered at Appomattox. At the same time, General Frederick Steele had advanced from Pensacola against Blakely, a little farther north than the Spanish Fort, and had captured it on the afternoon of Lee's surrender. On the morning of May 12th the Union forces under General Gordon Granger crossed the bay and found that the Confederate General Dabney H. Maury had marched out with his whole force. Maury succeeded in reaching Meridian in safety. During these operations the celebrated Confederate cavalry General Nathan B. Forrest had been defeated by the Federal cavalry under General James H. Wilson, and Selma, Alabama, with its fortifications, foundries, and workshops, had fallen into his hands. He entered Montgomery the same day that Granger entered Mobile. Taylor surrendered 42,293 men, the largest aggregation anywhere laying down their arms at the close of the war.

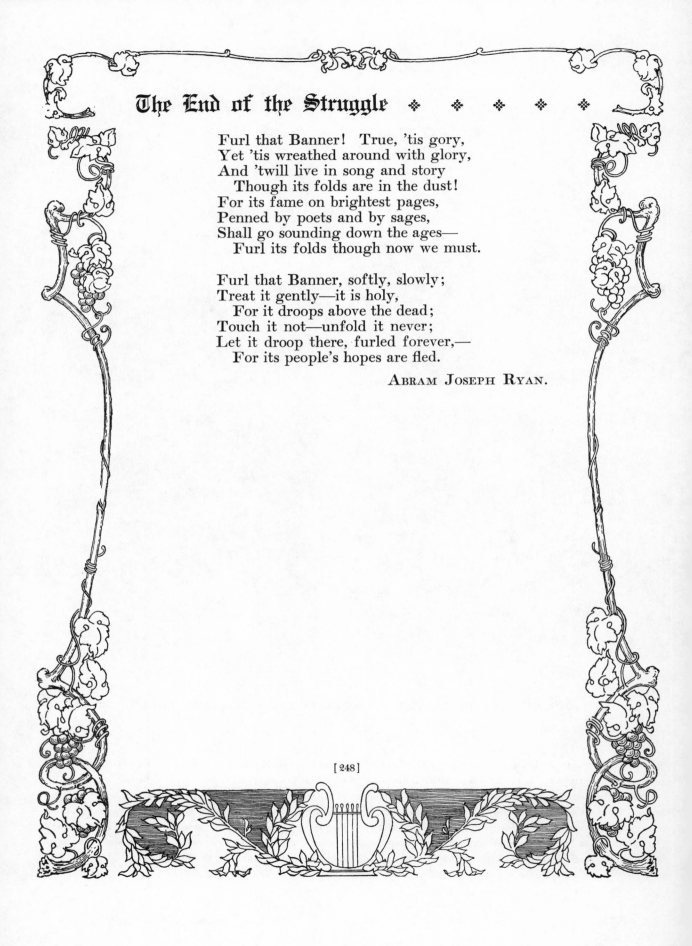

The End of the Struggle ❖ ❖ ❖ ❖ ❖

Furl that Banner! True, 'tis gory,
Yet 'tis wreathed around with glory,
And 'twill live in song and story
   Though its folds are in the dust!
For its fame on brightest pages,
Penned by poets and by sages,
Shall go sounding down the ages—
   Furl its folds though now we must.

Furl that Banner, softly, slowly;
Treat it gently—it is holy,
   For it droops above the dead;
Touch it not—unfold it never;
Let it droop there, furled forever,—
   For its people's hopes are fled.

ABRAM JOSEPH RYAN.

[248]

LINCOLN

THE FUNERAL PROCESSION OF THE MARTYRED PRESIDENT
IN NEW YORK CITY, APRIL 25TH, 1865

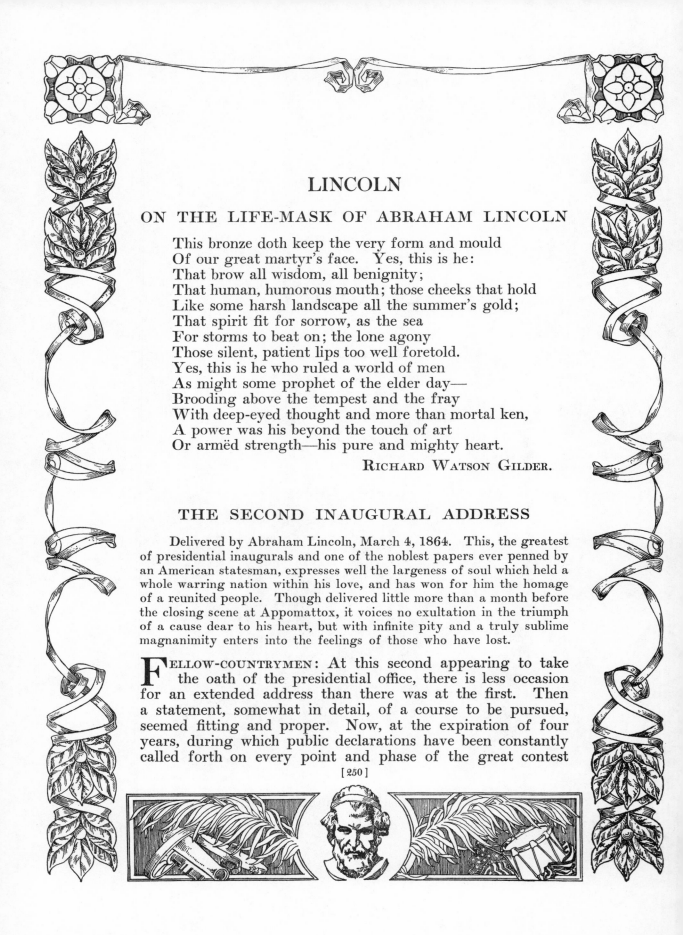

LINCOLN

ON THE LIFE-MASK OF ABRAHAM LINCOLN

This bronze doth keep the very form and mould
Of our great martyr's face. Yes, this is he:
That brow all wisdom, all benignity;
That human, humorous mouth; those cheeks that hold
Like some harsh landscape all the summer's gold;
That spirit fit for sorrow, as the sea
For storms to beat on; the lone agony
Those silent, patient lips too well foretold.
Yes, this is he who ruled a world of men
As might some prophet of the elder day—
Brooding above the tempest and the fray
With deep-eyed thought and more than mortal ken,
A power was his beyond the touch of art
Or armëd strength—his pure and mighty heart.

RICHARD WATSON GILDER.

THE SECOND INAUGURAL ADDRESS

Delivered by Abraham Lincoln, March 4, 1864. This, the greatest
of presidential inaugurals and one of the noblest papers ever penned by
an American statesman, expresses well the largeness of soul which held a
whole warring nation within his love, and has won for him the homage
of a reunited people. Though delivered little more than a month before
the closing scene at Appomattox, it voices no exultation in the triumph
of a cause dear to his heart, but with infinite pity and a truly sublime
magnanimity enters into the feelings of those who have lost.

FELLOW-COUNTRYMEN: At this second appearing to take
the oath of the presidential office, there is less occasion
for an extended address than there was at the first. Then
a statement, somewhat in detail, of a course to be pursued,
seemed fitting and proper. Now, at the expiration of four
years, during which public declarations have been constantly
called forth on every point and phase of the great contest

LINCOLN IN JUNE, 1860—TWO MONTHS AFTER VOLK MADE THE LIFE MASK

GILDER, WHOSE POEM OPPOSITE WAS INSPIRED BY THE MASK, WAS ALWAYS PARTICULARY ATTRACTED TO IT, AND
KEPT A COPY OF IT IN HIS EDITORIAL SANCTUM AT THE *Century Magazine* OFFICES

In 1860, Lincoln had been a national figure only two years, since his campaign against Stephen A. Douglas for the Senate in Illinois. Indeed, his name meant little in the East till the early months of this very year. In February, he had appeared before a New York audience at Cooper Union to explain the purposes of the recently organized Republican party. The larger part of those present expected something "wild and woolly"—certainly nothing of much moment for the cultivated citizens of the East. When they saw the gaunt figure, six feet four inches tall, the large feet and clumsy hands, the jutting eyebrows and small blue eyes, the narrow forehead surmounted by the shock of unkempt hair—in a word, the man of the photograph on this page—the audience put him down for anything but a statesman. But he had not spoken long before it was plain that here stood a leader of the people indeed. The speech shaped the presidential campaign of that year. It resulted in giving Lincoln the Republican nomination at Chicago on May 16th, about a month before this photograph was made. When the ballot-boxes were opened on the first Tuesday of the following November, it was found that Abraham Lincoln was elected President of the United States. That meant war—and eventual Union of the warring elements.

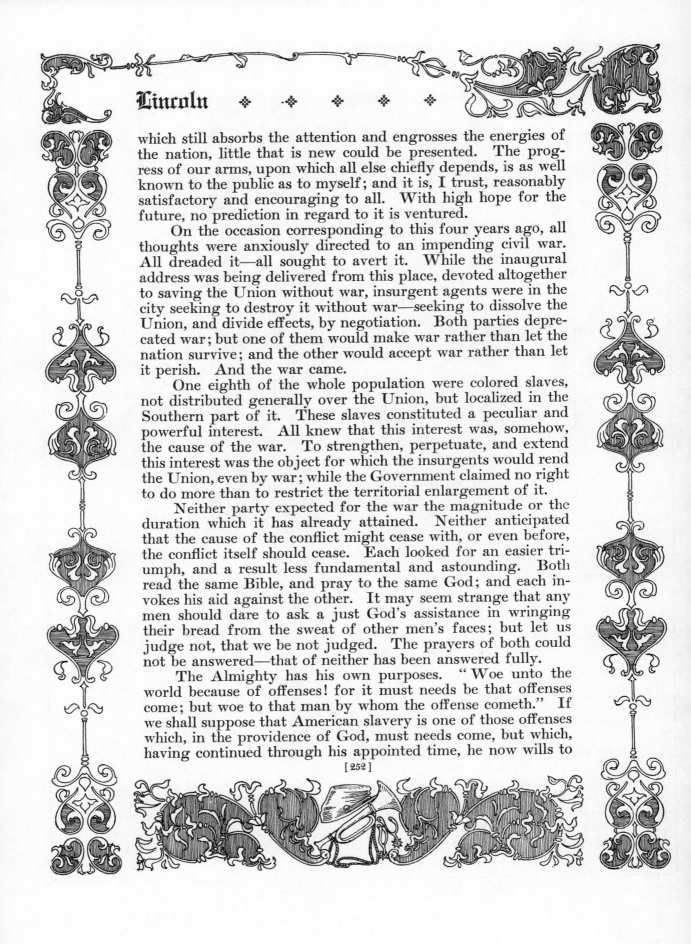

which still absorbs the attention and engrosses the energies of the nation, little that is new could be presented. The progress of our arms, upon which all else chiefly depends, is as well known to the public as to myself; and it is, I trust, reasonably satisfactory and encouraging to all. With high hope for the future, no prediction in regard to it is ventured.

On the occasion corresponding to this four years ago, all thoughts were anxiously directed to an impending civil war. All dreaded it—all sought to avert it. While the inaugural address was being delivered from this place, devoted altogether to saving the Union without war, insurgent agents were in the city seeking to destroy it without war—seeking to dissolve the Union, and divide effects, by negotiation. Both parties deprecated war; but one of them would make war rather than let the nation survive; and the other would accept war rather than let it perish. And the war came.

One eighth of the whole population were colored slaves, not distributed generally over the Union, but localized in the Southern part of it. These slaves constituted a peculiar and powerful interest. All knew that this interest was, somehow, the cause of the war. To strengthen, perpetuate, and extend this interest was the object for which the insurgents would rend the Union, even by war; while the Government claimed no right to do more than to restrict the territorial enlargement of it.

Neither party expected for the war the magnitude or the duration which it has already attained. Neither anticipated that the cause of the conflict might cease with, or even before, the conflict itself should cease. Each looked for an easier triumph, and a result less fundamental and astounding. Both read the same Bible, and pray to the same God; and each invokes his aid against the other. It may seem strange that any men should dare to ask a just God's assistance in wringing their bread from the sweat of other men's faces; but let us judge not, that we be not judged. The prayers of both could not be answered—that of neither has been answered fully.

The Almighty has his own purposes. "Woe unto the world because of offenses! for it must needs be that offenses come; but woe to that man by whom the offense cometh." If we shall suppose that American slavery is one of those offenses which, in the providence of God, must needs come, but which, having continued through his appointed time, he now wills to

LINCOLN AND HIS SON "TAD"

This photograph of Lincoln and little "Tad" was taken in 1861, when the four years of war were yet to burden the heart of the great President. In 1865, only a few days before his assassination, Lincoln for the last time entered the Brady gallery in Washington, and again sat for his picture with "Tad." The scene is touching beyond words.

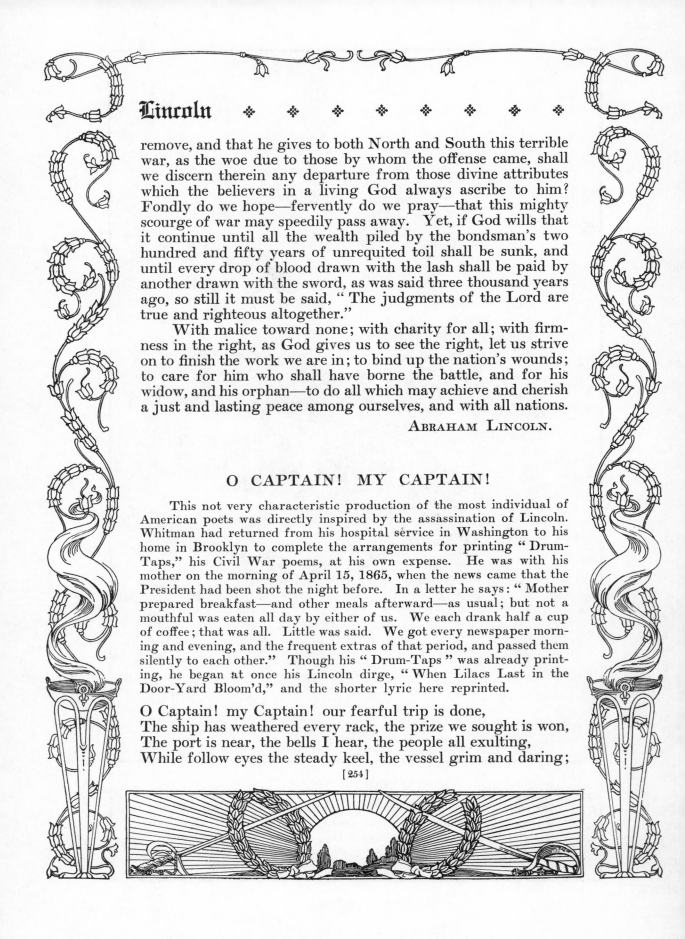

remove, and that he gives to both North and South this terrible war, as the woe due to those by whom the offense came, shall we discern therein any departure from those divine attributes which the believers in a living God always ascribe to him? Fondly do we hope—fervently do we pray—that this mighty scourge of war may speedily pass away. Yet, if God wills that it continue until all the wealth piled by the bondsman's two hundred and fifty years of unrequited toil shall be sunk, and until every drop of blood drawn with the lash shall be paid by another drawn with the sword, as was said three thousand years ago, so still it must be said, " The judgments of the Lord are true and righteous altogether."

With malice toward none; with charity for all; with firmness in the right, as God gives us to see the right, let us strive on to finish the work we are in; to bind up the nation's wounds; to care for him who shall have borne the battle, and for his widow, and his orphan—to do all which may achieve and cherish a just and lasting peace among ourselves, and with all nations.

ABRAHAM LINCOLN.

O CAPTAIN! MY CAPTAIN!

This not very characteristic production of the most individual of American poets was directly inspired by the assassination of Lincoln. Whitman had returned from his hospital service in Washington to his home in Brooklyn to complete the arrangements for printing " Drum-Taps," his Civil War poems, at his own expense. He was with his mother on the morning of April 15, 1865, when the news came that the President had been shot the night before. In a letter he says: " Mother prepared breakfast—and other meals afterward—as usual; but not a mouthful was eaten all day by either of us. We each drank half a cup of coffee; that was all. Little was said. We got every newspaper morning and evening, and the frequent extras of that period, and passed them silently to each other." Though his " Drum-Taps " was already printing, he began at once his Lincoln dirge, " When Lilacs Last in the Door-Yard Bloom'd," and the shorter lyric here reprinted.

O Captain! my Captain! our fearful trip is done,
The ship has weathered every rack, the prize we sought is won,
The port is near, the bells I hear, the people all exulting,
While follow eyes the steady keel, the vessel grim and daring;

WHILE LINCOLN

SPOKE AT

GETTYSBURG,

NOVEMBER

19, 1863

DURING THE

FAMOUS ADDRESS

IN DEDICATION

OF THE

CEMETERY

The most important American address is brief: "Fourscore and seven years ago our fathers brought forth on this continent a new nation, conceived in liberty, and dedicated to the proposition that all men are created equal. Now we are engaged in a great civil war, testing whether that nation, or any nation so conceived and so dedicated, can long endure. We are met on a great battlefield of that war. We have come to dedicate a portion of that field as a final resting-place for those who here gave their lives that that nation might live. It is altogether fitting and proper that we should do this. But in a larger sense, we cannot dedicate, we cannot consecrate, we cannot hallow this ground. The brave men, living and dead, who struggled here, have consecrated it far above our poor power to add or detract. The world will little note, nor long remember, what we say here, but it can never forget what they did here. It is for us, the living, rather, to be dedicated here to the unfinished work which they who fought here have thus far so nobly advanced. It is rather for us to be here dedicated to the great task remaining before us;—that from these honored dead, we take increased devotion to that cause for which they gave the last full measure of devotion;—that we here highly resolve that these dead shall not have died in vain, that this nation, under God, shall have a new birth of freedom, and that government of the people, by the people, for the people, shall not perish from the earth."

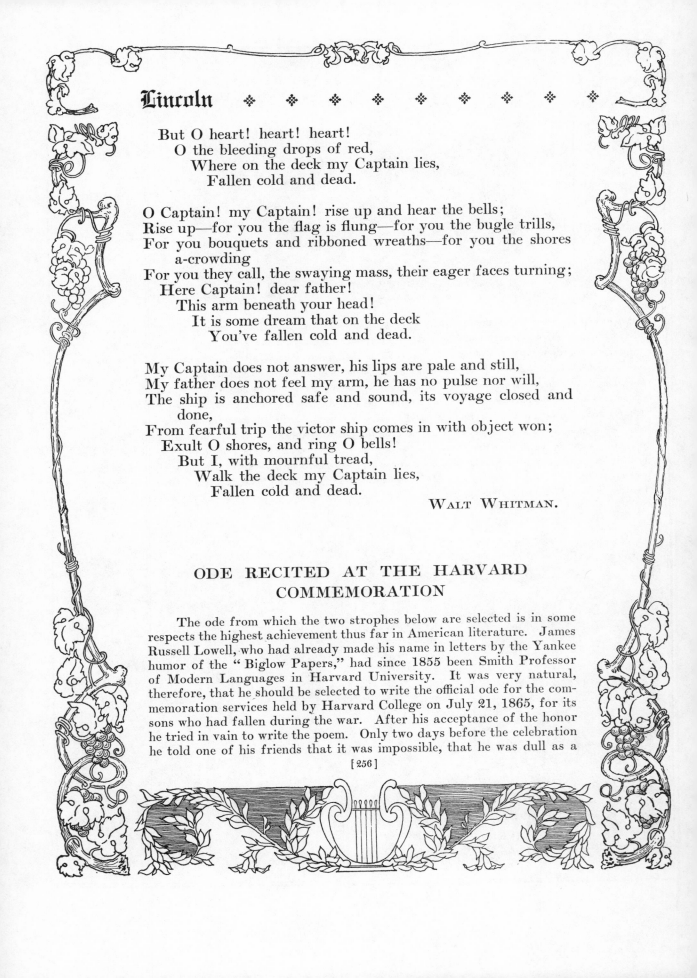

Lincoln ✦ ✦ ✦ ✦ ✦ ✦ ✦

But O heart! heart! heart!
  O the bleeding drops of red,
    Where on the deck my Captain lies,
    Fallen cold and dead.

O Captain! my Captain! rise up and hear the bells;
Rise up—for you the flag is flung—for you the bugle trills,
For you bouquets and ribboned wreaths—for you the shores
    a-crowding
For you they call, the swaying mass, their eager faces turning;
  Here Captain! dear father!
    This arm beneath your head!
      It is some dream that on the deck
      You've fallen cold and dead.

My Captain does not answer, his lips are pale and still,
My father does not feel my arm, he has no pulse nor will,
The ship is anchored safe and sound, its voyage closed and
    done,
From fearful trip the victor ship comes in with object won;
  Exult O shores, and ring O bells!
    But I, with mournful tread,
      Walk the deck my Captain lies,
      Fallen cold and dead.

                         WALT WHITMAN.

ODE RECITED AT THE HARVARD COMMEMORATION

The ode from which the two strophes below are selected is in some respects the highest achievement thus far in American literature. James Russell Lowell, who had already made his name in letters by the Yankee humor of the "Biglow Papers," had since 1855 been Smith Professor of Modern Languages in Harvard University. It was very natural, therefore, that he should be selected to write the official ode for the commemoration services held by Harvard College on July 21, 1865, for its sons who had fallen during the war. After his acceptance of the honor he tried in vain to write the poem. Only two days before the celebration he told one of his friends that it was impossible, that he was dull as a

LINCOLN

THE LAST SITTING—ON THE DAY OF LEE'S SURRENDER

On April 9, 1865, the very day of the surrender of Lee at Appomattox, Lincoln, for the last time, went to the photographer's gallery. As he sits in simple fashion sharpening his pencil, the man of sorrows cannot forget the sense of weariness and pain that for four years has been unbroken. No elation of triumph lights the features. One task is ended—the Nation is saved. But another, scarcely less exacting, confronts him. The States which lay "out of their proper practical relation to the Union," in his own phrase, must be brought back into a proper practical relation. But this task was not for him. Only five days later the sad eyes reflected upon this page closed forever upon scenes of earthly turmoil. Bereft of Lincoln's heart and head, leaders attacked problems of reconstruction in ways that proved unwise. As the mists of passion and prejudice cleared away, both North and South came to feel that this patient, wise, and sympathetic ruler was one of the few really great men in history, and that he would live forever in the hearts of men made better by his presence during those four years of storm.

A NATION IN MOURNING—THE WASHINGTON PROCESSION AT LINCOLN'S FUNERAL

After his faithful service, Abraham Lincoln, the leader from whose wisdom and sympathy both North and South had most to hope, was not to survive the completion of his task. An assassin stole into his box at Ford's Theater on the evening of April 14th, shot him in the back of the head, and leaping upon the stage escaped by a rear door. The next morning at seven o'clock the President was dead. The remains were taken to his home in Springfield, Illinois, along the route by which he had traveled in 1861, on his way to take the oath as President. This picture shows the solemn procession that moved toward the railway station in Washington.

ALL PRESENT BUT THE COMMANDER–IN–CHIEF

The Grand Review of the Army, May 23–24, 1865. As two hundred thousand troops marched in the bright May sunshine of 1865 down the main thoroughfare of the National capital, to the strains of martial music, waving their battle-rent flags amid the flashing of sabers and bayonets, one face was missing at the reviewing-stand. Lincoln, the commander-in-chief, who through four years of struggle had kept faith with his army, was absent—dead by an assassin's bullet. Thus one of the mightiest armies ever gathered passed in final review ere it melted into the walks of civil life. No great victorious force ever turned so quickly and completely to the arts of peace.

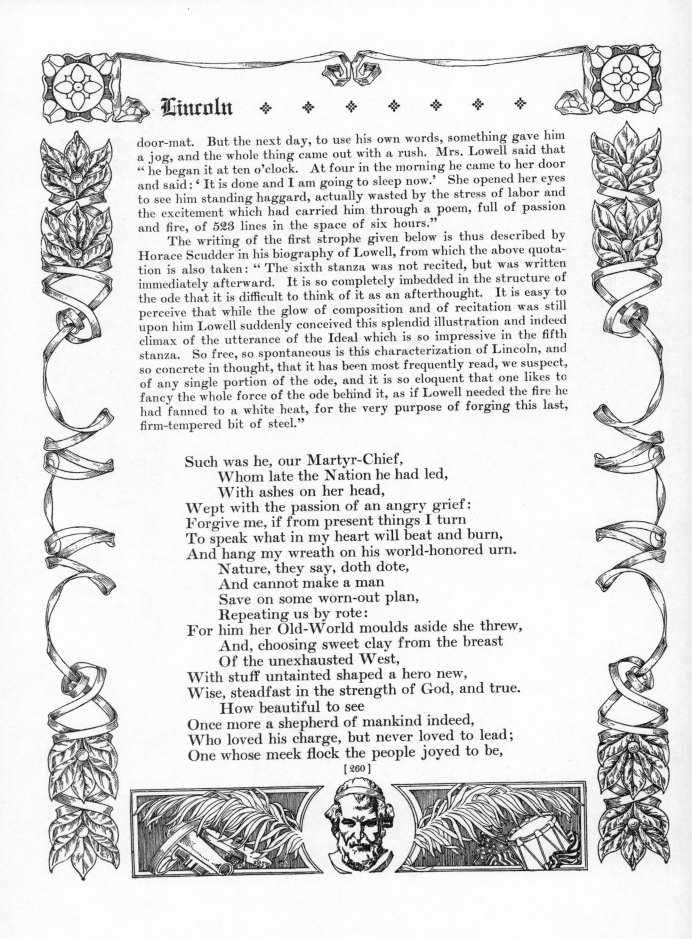

door-mat. But the next day, to use his own words, something gave him a jog, and the whole thing came out with a rush. Mrs. Lowell said that "he began it at ten o'clock. At four in the morning he came to her door and said: 'It is done and I am going to sleep now.' She opened her eyes to see him standing haggard, actually wasted by the stress of labor and the excitement which had carried him through a poem, full of passion and fire, of 523 lines in the space of six hours."

The writing of the first strophe given below is thus described by Horace Scudder in his biography of Lowell, from which the above quotation is also taken: "The sixth stanza was not recited, but was written immediately afterward. It is so completely imbedded in the structure of the ode that it is difficult to think of it as an afterthought. It is easy to perceive that while the glow of composition and of recitation was still upon him Lowell suddenly conceived this splendid illustration and indeed climax of the utterance of the Ideal which is so impressive in the fifth stanza. So free, so spontaneous is this characterization of Lincoln, and so concrete in thought, that it has been most frequently read, we suspect, of any single portion of the ode, and it is so eloquent that one likes to fancy the whole force of the ode behind it, as if Lowell needed the fire he had fanned to a white heat, for the very purpose of forging this last, firm-tempered bit of steel."

Such was he, our Martyr-Chief,
    Whom late the Nation he had led,
    With ashes on her head,
Wept with the passion of an angry grief:
Forgive me, if from present things I turn
To speak what in my heart will beat and burn,
And hang my wreath on his world-honored urn.
    Nature, they say, doth dote,
    And cannot make a man
    Save on some worn-out plan,
    Repeating us by rote:
For him her Old-World moulds aside she threw,
    And, choosing sweet clay from the breast
    Of the unexhausted West,
With stuff untainted shaped a hero new,
Wise, steadfast in the strength of God, and true.
    How beautiful to see
Once more a shepherd of mankind indeed,
Who loved his charge, but never loved to lead;
One whose meek flock the people joyed to be,

"SENDS ALL HER HANDMAID ARMIES BACK TO SPIN"

THE RETURN HOME OF THE SIXTEENTH MASSACHUSETTS INFANTRY, JULY 27, 1864

This scene of 1864, at the corner of Cambridge and Fourth Streets, East Cambridge, is in mournful contrast to the rejoicing which filled the nation the next year while Lowell was reading his ode in Harvard University. As these riders passed through Cambridge the Wilderness campaign had been fought, with little, apparently, accomplished to compensate for the fearful loss of life. Sherman was still struggling in the vicinity of Atlanta, far from his base of supplies, with no certainty of escaping an overwhelming defeat. Early had recently dashed into the outskirts of Washington. In fact an influential political party was about to declare the war a failure. So these Massachusetts troops returned with heavy hearts to be mustered out. Many of them reenlisted, to fight with the armies that captured Petersburg, and to be present at the surrender at Appomattox. Then they could return with those of whom Lowell sang: America "sends all her handmaid armies back to spin."

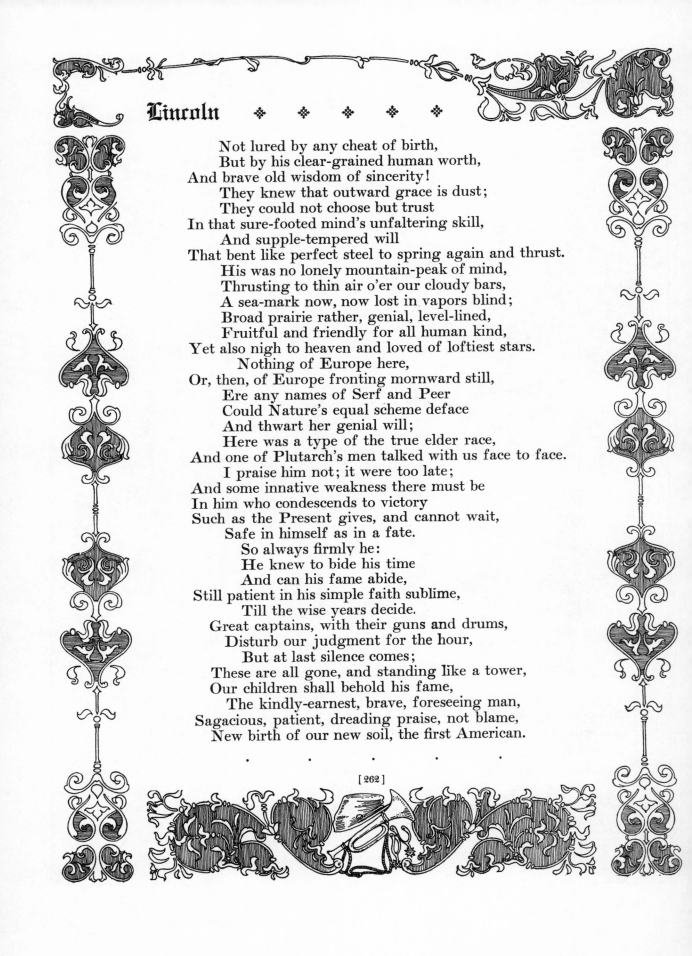

Lincoln ❖ ❖ ❖ ❖ ❖

Not lured by any cheat of birth,
But by his clear-grained human worth,
And brave old wisdom of sincerity!
They knew that outward grace is dust;
They could not choose but trust
In that sure-footed mind's unfaltering skill,
And supple-tempered will
That bent like perfect steel to spring again and thrust.
His was no lonely mountain-peak of mind,
Thrusting to thin air o'er our cloudy bars,
A sea-mark now, now lost in vapors blind;
Broad prairie rather, genial, level-lined,
Fruitful and friendly for all human kind,
Yet also nigh to heaven and loved of loftiest stars.
Nothing of Europe here,
Or, then, of Europe fronting mornward still,
Ere any names of Serf and Peer
Could Nature's equal scheme deface
And thwart her genial will;
Here was a type of the true elder race,
And one of Plutarch's men talked with us face to face.
I praise him not; it were too late;
And some innative weakness there must be
In him who condescends to victory
Such as the Present gives, and cannot wait,
Safe in himself as in a fate.
So always firmly he:
He knew to bide his time
And can his fame abide,
Still patient in his simple faith sublime,
Till the wise years decide.
Great captains, with their guns and drums,
Disturb our judgment for the hour,
But at last silence comes;
These are all gone, and standing like a tower,
Our children shall behold his fame,
The kindly-earnest, brave, foreseeing man,
Sagacious, patient, dreading praise, not blame,
New birth of our new soil, the first American.

.   .   .

"NOT WITHOUT A PROUDER TREAD"—"LIFT THE HEART AND LIFT THE HEAD"

SOLDIERS AT THE DEDICATION OF THE BULL RUN MONUMENT, JUNE 10, 1865

As if to give pictorial expression to Lowell's sonorous lines, these scenes of 1865 have been preserved.   At the top is the Fifth Pennsylvania Heavy Artillery.   A thousand men stepping forward as a single man to the strains of music to which they had marched over the Virginia hills, reveal the practised movements of the veteran.   Below, some of the gaunt and hardened survivors of those four years look out at us.   Tanned by long exposure, toughened by numberless days and nights in sunshine and storm, these are the men who returned home in '65, adding their strength of character to the progress of their country,   Each had earned the right to feel the lofty mood Lowell expressed in his "Ode."   Each could feel the "tumult of elation" and the pride in motherland awaiting the morn of nobler day.

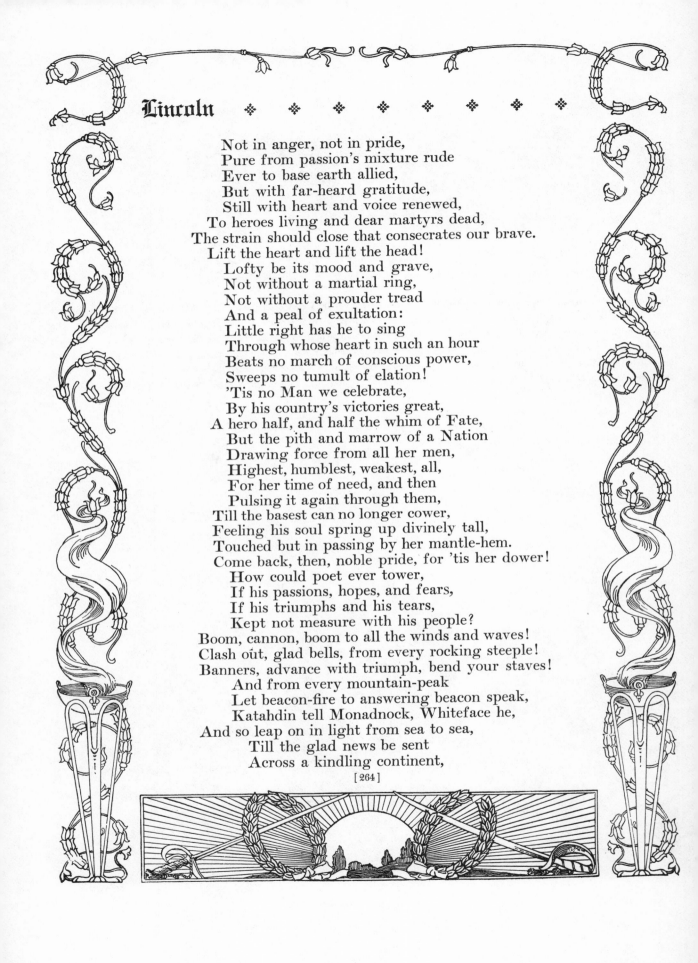

Lincoln ✧ ✧ ✧ ✧ ✧ ✧ ✧

Not in anger, not in pride,
Pure from passion's mixture rude
Ever to base earth allied,
But with far-heard gratitude,
Still with heart and voice renewed,
To heroes living and dear martyrs dead,
The strain should close that consecrates our brave.
Lift the heart and lift the head!
Lofty be its mood and grave,
Not without a martial ring,
Not without a prouder tread
And a peal of exultation:
Little right has he to sing
Through whose heart in such an hour
Beats no march of conscious power,
Sweeps no tumult of elation!
'Tis no Man we celebrate,
By his country's victories great,
A hero half, and half the whim of Fate,
But the pith and marrow of a Nation
Drawing force from all her men,
Highest, humblest, weakest, all,
For her time of need, and then
Pulsing it again through them,
Till the basest can no longer cower,
Feeling his soul spring up divinely tall,
Touched but in passing by her mantle-hem.
Come back, then, noble pride, for 'tis her dower!
How could poet ever tower,
If his passions, hopes, and fears,
If his triumphs and his tears,
Kept not measure with his people?
Boom, cannon, boom to all the winds and waves!
Clash out, glad bells, from every rocking steeple!
Banners, advance with triumph, bend your staves!
And from every mountain-peak
Let beacon-fire to answering beacon speak,
Katahdin tell Monadnock, Whiteface he,
And so leap on in light from sea to sea,
Till the glad news be sent
Across a kindling continent,

"WHERE FELL THE BRAVE"
DEDICATING THE MONUMENT AT BULL RUN, ON JUNE 10, 1865

This shaft was erected by the officers and men of General William Gamble's Separate Cavalry Brigade, stationed at Fairfax Court House during the preceding winter and spring. It is twenty-seven feet high, made of chocolate-colored sandstone, and bears on its top a 100-pound shell. The shells on the pedestals at each corner are of similar size. The inscription reads—"To the memory of the patriots who fell at Bull Run, July 21, 1861." The dedicatory exercises were conducted by the Rev. Dr. McCurdy, who read an appropriate service. After the singing of a special hymn for the occasion, the Fifth Pennsylvania Heavy Artillery executed a military parade and the Sixteenth Massachusetts Battery fired a salute. Judge Olin, who appears in white trousers and high hat, next delivered an eloquent address, and was followed by several generals. A little later in the day a second monument was dedicated on the field of Second Bull Run.

"NOT IN ANGER, NOT IN PRIDE"

Dedication of First Bull Run Monument, June 10, 1865.—A little more than a month before Lowell read his lofty ode for the sons of Harvard who had fallen in the Civil War, the group here preserved by the camera assembled to do honor to the "dear martyrs" who fell in the first great battle of the conflict. The site was on the hillside in front of the stone house, at the spot where on the afternoon of July 21, 1861, Ricketts and Griffin lost their batteries. In that battle the Federal forces had been entirely successful until early in the afternoon. Then the Confederates rallied on the brow of this hill, and the ground on which these men and women are gathered was the scene of a fierce struggle. The batteries were alternately captured by the Confederates and retaken by the Union forces, until the arrival of fresh troops in gray threw the Federal army into confusion and precipitated the panic of retreat. At the time

"TO HEROES LIVING AND DEAR MARTYRS DEAD"

of this picture, four years later, both soldier and citizen are standing calmly in the sunshine of the peaceful June day. "Not in anger, not in pride" do they look into our faces. At the left Judge Olin, with the cane, is standing behind a boy in a white shirt and quaint trousers who almost wistfully is gazing into the distance, as if the call of these mighty events had awakened in him a yearning for fame. To his left are Generals Thomas, Wilcox, Heintzelman, Dyer, and other veterans of many a hard-fought field who can feel the "march of conscious power" of which Lowell speaks. And the women with the flaring crinoline skirts and old-fashioned sleeves certainly may join in the "far-heard gratitude" this celebration was to express. After fifty years their emotions are brought home to the reader with the vividness of personal experience by the art of the photographer.

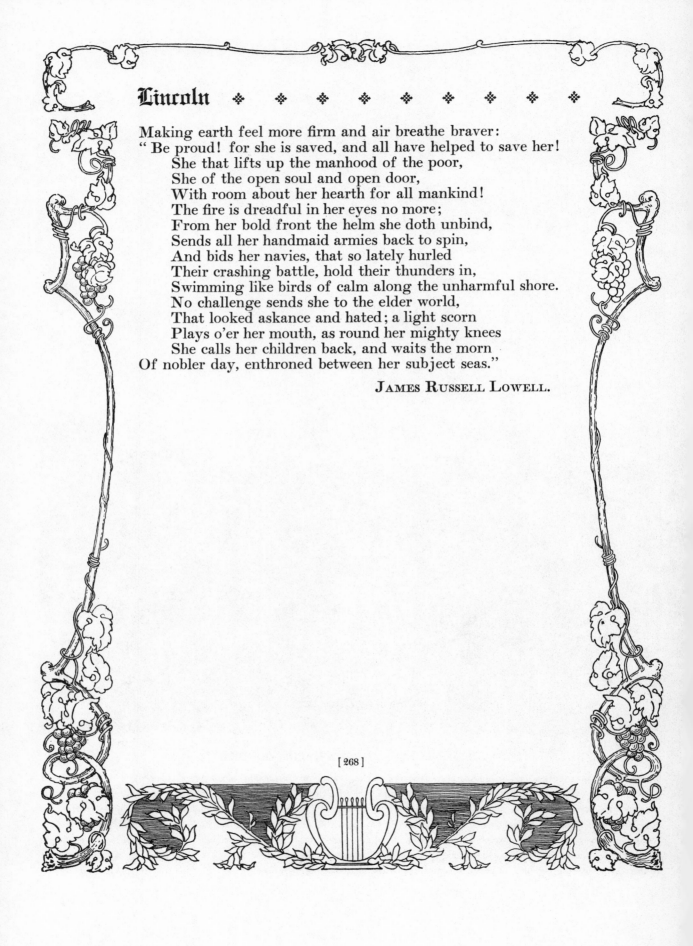

Lincoln ❖ ❖ ❖ ❖ ❖ ❖ ❖ ❖

Making earth feel more firm and air breathe braver:
" Be proud! for she is saved, and all have helped to save her!
　　She that lifts up the manhood of the poor,
　　She of the open soul and open door,
　　With room about her hearth for all mankind!
　　The fire is dreadful in her eyes no more;
　　From her bold front the helm she doth unbind,
　　Sends all her handmaid armies back to spin,
　　And bids her navies, that so lately hurled
　　Their crashing battle, hold their thunders in,
　　Swimming like birds of calm along the unharmful shore.
　　No challenge sends she to the elder world,
　　That looked askance and hated; a light scorn
　　Plays o'er her mouth, as round her mighty knees
　　She calls her children back, and waits the morn
Of nobler day, enthroned between her subject seas."

JAMES RUSSELL LOWELL.

XII

THE
HERITAGE

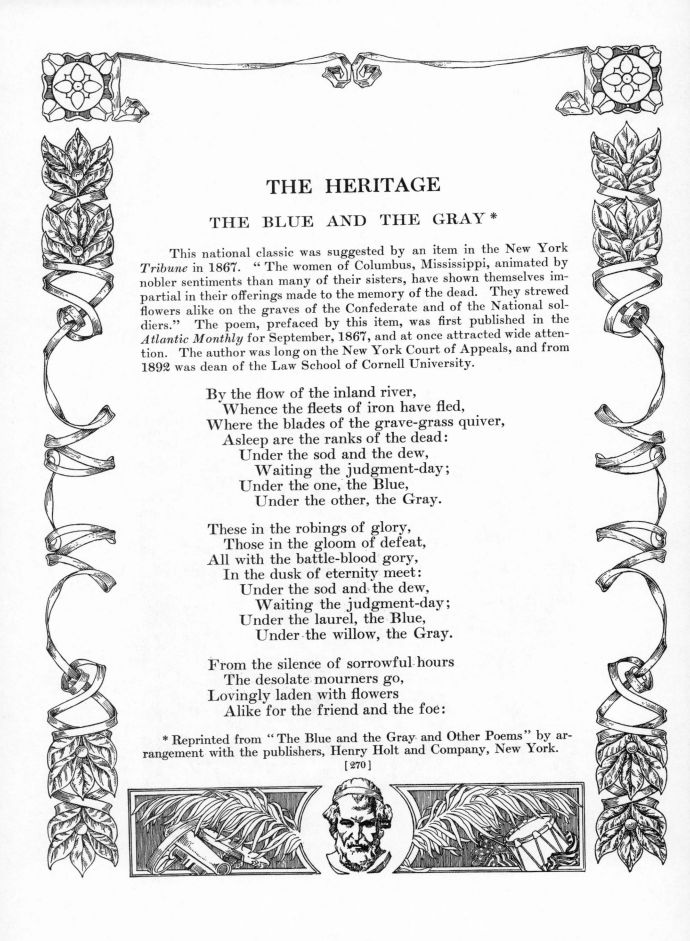

THE HERITAGE

THE BLUE AND THE GRAY *

This national classic was suggested by an item in the *New York Tribune* in 1867. "The women of Columbus, Mississippi, animated by nobler sentiments than many of their sisters, have shown themselves impartial in their offerings made to the memory of the dead. They strewed flowers alike on the graves of the Confederate and of the National soldiers." The poem, prefaced by this item, was first published in the *Atlantic Monthly* for September, 1867, and at once attracted wide attention. The author was long on the New York Court of Appeals, and from 1892 was dean of the Law School of Cornell University.

By the flow of the inland river,
   Whence the fleets of iron have fled,
Where the blades of the grave-grass quiver,
   Asleep are the ranks of the dead:
     Under the sod and the dew,
       Waiting the judgment-day;
     Under the one, the Blue,
       Under the other, the Gray.

These in the robings of glory,
   Those in the gloom of defeat,
All with the battle-blood gory,
   In the dusk of eternity meet:
     Under the sod and the dew,
       Waiting the judgment-day;
     Under the laurel, the Blue,
       Under the willow, the Gray.

From the silence of sorrowful hours
   The desolate mourners go,
Lovingly laden with flowers
   Alike for the friend and the foe:

* Reprinted from "The Blue and the Gray and Other Poems" by arrangement with the publishers, Henry Holt and Company, New York.

THE BLUE AND THE GRAY

"BY THE FLOW OF THE INLAND RIVER—WHENCE THE FLEETS OF IRON HAVE FLED"

Finch's noble lines were evoked by a happening in a Mississippi town, as the opposite page sets forth. The war-time photographs show Union gunboats before they had left the river to peace. The four vessels on this page, *Baron DeKalb*, *Cincinnati*, and *Mound City* at the top, and the *Louisville* at the bottom, were among the most powerful of the Mississippi flotilla. They were all of the same class, 175 feet long and 51½ feet beam. Each carried three bow guns, four broadside guns on each side, and two stern guns. They were in addition plated with 2½-inch iron, yet they drew only six feet of water, and made nine miles an hour. They were constructed in the first year of the war by Captain James B. Eads, and some of them took part in every important action on the western rivers from the evacuation of Fort Henry to the capture of Mobile, 1864.

The Heritage ❖ ❖ ❖ ❖

Under the sod and the dew,
  Waiting the judgment-day;
Under the roses, the Blue,
  Under the lilies, the Gray.

So with an equal splendor,
  The morning sun-rays fall,
With a touch impartially tender,
  On the blossoms blooming for all:
  Under the sod and the dew,
    Waiting the judgment-day;
  Broidered with gold, the Blue,
    Mellowed with gold, the Gray.

So, when the summer calleth,
  On forest and field of grain,
With an equal murmur falleth
  The cooling drip of the rain:
  Under the sod and the dew,
    Waiting the judgment-day;
  Wet with the rain, the Blue,
    Wet with the rain, the Gray.

Sadly, but not with upbraiding,
  The generous deed was done,
In the storm of the years that are fading
  No braver battle was won:
  Under the sod and the dew,
    Waiting the judgment-day;
  Under the blossoms, the Blue,
    Under the garlands, the Gray.

No more shall the war cry sever,
  Or the winding rivers be red;
They banish our anger forever
  When they laurel the graves of our dead!
  Under the sod and the dew,
    Waiting the judgment-day;
  Love and tears for the Blue,
    Tears and love for the Gray.

FRANCIS MILES FINCH.

[272]

"THE BLOSSOMS BLOOMING FOR ALL"

These words of "The Blue and the Gray" might have been written for the tranquil scene here preserved by the war-time camera. All the foreground is bright with daisies, and the three graves under the trees by the cottage shine in the peaceful sunlight of a spring day. Nature asks not to which side belonged those now lying in their lowly beds—nor do we of any who fell in battle or perished in prison. The sentiment of "The Blue and the Gray" is at length the sentiment of the whole American people. The view is typical of the desolation that followed in the wake of the armies. On the right are the ruins of a line of houses; nothing remains but the crumbling foundations and the massive chimneys where hospitable fires once blazed in the wide fireplaces before throngs of merry young people. To the left are the remains of the humbler cottage. In the background are the woods where many a picnic made the days pass happily. The life of ease and quiet among these Arcadian surroundings was rudely ended by grim war. The hamlet lay in the path of a conquering army and was soon a waste place. But the gentle hand of Nature soon covered the unsightly wreckage.

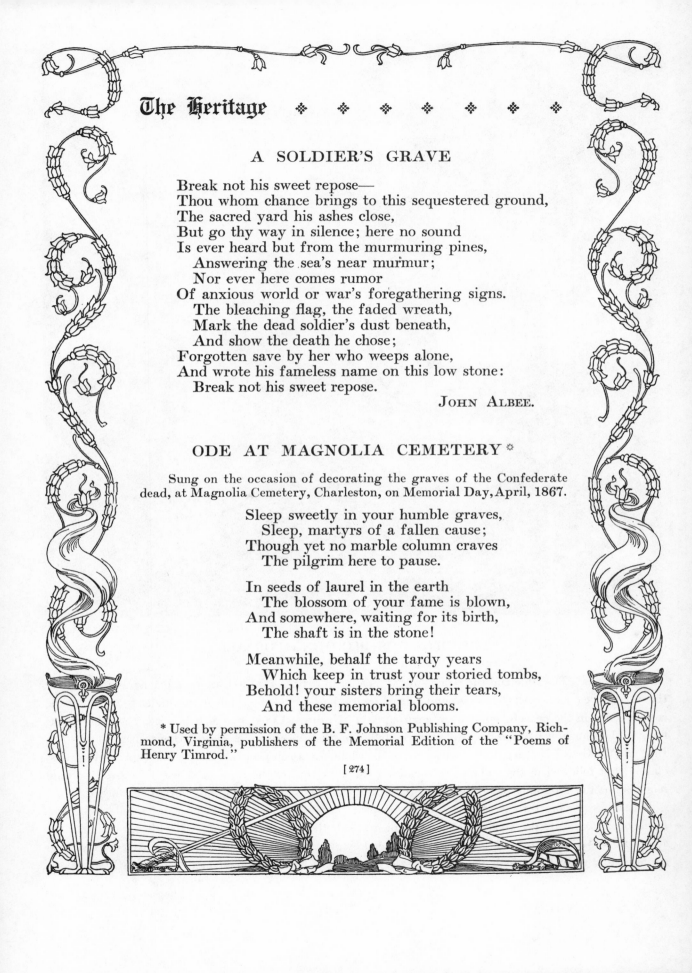

A SOLDIER'S GRAVE

Break not his sweet repose—
Thou whom chance brings to this sequestered ground,
The sacred yard his ashes close,
But go thy way in silence; here no sound
Is ever heard but from the murmuring pines,
 Answering the sea's near murmur;
 Nor ever here comes rumor
Of anxious world or war's foregathering signs.
 The bleaching flag, the faded wreath,
 Mark the dead soldier's dust beneath,
 And show the death he chose;
Forgotten save by her who weeps alone,
And wrote his fameless name on this low stone:
 Break not his sweet repose.

JOHN ALBEE.

ODE AT MAGNOLIA CEMETERY *

Sung on the occasion of decorating the graves of the Confederate
dead, at Magnolia Cemetery, Charleston, on Memorial Day, April, 1867.

Sleep sweetly in your humble graves,
 Sleep, martyrs of a fallen cause;
Though yet no marble column craves
 The pilgrim here to pause.

In seeds of laurel in the earth
 The blossom of your fame is blown,
And somewhere, waiting for its birth,
 The shaft is in the stone!

Meanwhile, behalf the tardy years
 Which keep in trust your storied tombs,
Behold! your sisters bring their tears,
 And these memorial blooms.

 * Used by permission of the B. F. Johnson Publishing Company, Richmond, Virginia, publishers of the Memorial Edition of the "Poems of
Henry Timrod."

"BREAK NOT HIS SWEET REPOSE"

THE BURIAL-GROUND OF SAILORS WHO FELL AT HILTON HEAD IN 1861

This sequestered spot, the burial-place of the sailors who lost their lives in the capture of Hilton Head by the Federal fleet on November 7, 1861, might have been designed to fit the poem by John Albee. The live-oaks droop tenderly above it and cast a gloom around. Through it comes faintly "the sea's near murmur." But though the names of men like these may be unknown to fame, they are not forgotten in their quiet resting-places. Each Memorial Day brings the gratitude of a nation that was saved because they dared to die.

Small tributes! but your shades will smile
　　More proudly on these wreaths to-day,
Than when some cannon-moulded pile
　　Shall overlook this bay.

Stoop, angels, hither from the skies!
　　There is no holier spot of ground
Than where defeated valor lies,
　　By mourning beauty crowned.

HENRY TIMROD.

OVER THEIR GRAVES

Over their graves rang once the bugle's call,
The searching shrapnel and the crashing ball;
　　The shriek, the shock of battle, and the neigh
　　Of horse; the cries of anguish and dismay;
And the loud cannon's thunders that appall.

Now through the years the brown pine-needles fall,
The vines run riot by the old stone wall,
　　By hedge, by meadow streamlet, far away,
　　　　Over their graves.

We love our dead where'er so held in thrall.
Than they no Greek more bravely died, nor Gaul—
　　A love that's deathless!—but they look to-day
　　With no reproaches on us when we say,
" Come, let us grasp your hands, we're brothers all,
　　　　Over their graves!"

HENRY JEROME STOCKARD.

A GEORGIA VOLUNTEER

The author of these verses was born in Lyons, New York, but on her marriage to Gideon Townsend she made her home in New Orleans. How thoroughly she identified herself with her adopted section is evident.

Far up the lonely mountain-side
　　My wandering footsteps led;
The moss lay thick beneath my feet,
　　The pine sighed overhead.

[276]

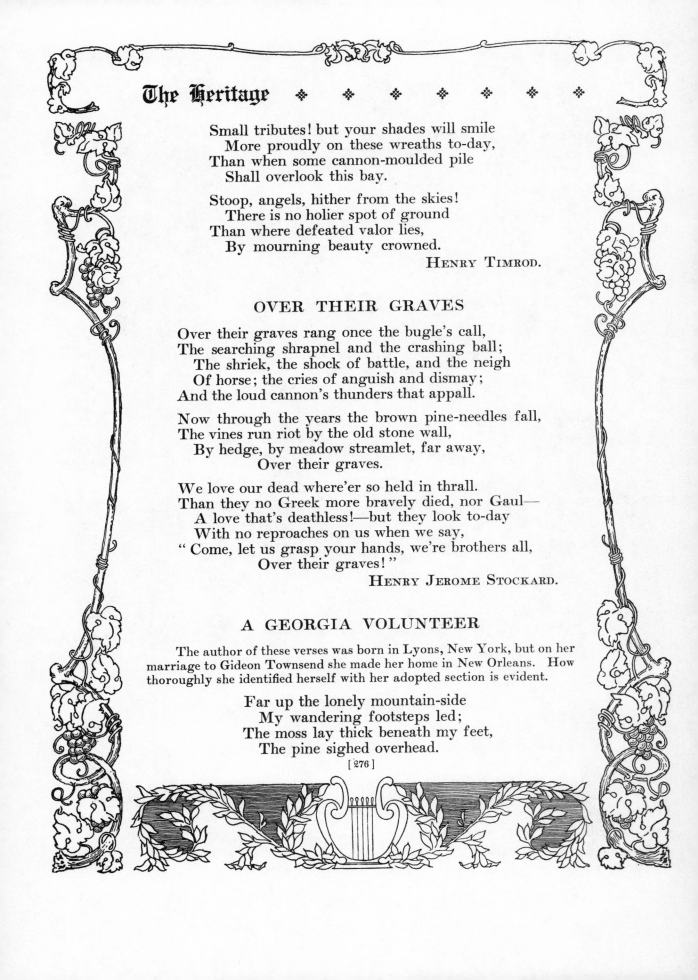

"WHERE DEFEATED VALOR LIES"

MAGNOLIA CEMETERY AT CHARLESTON—HERE TIMROD READ HIS "ODE"

This photograph preserves the resting-place of the Confederate soldiers over whom in 1867 Timrod read his last and finest production—the "Ode" presented opposite. This spreading tree is a fitting place for the utterance of one of the supreme poems in American literature. Timrod had spent his life in singing of his State and the South. He was fired by no ordinary devotion. But in no other effort did he light upon so lofty a subject, and express his emotions with so much of artistic restraint. The view above shows how appropriate to the scene were his lines. The gloom of these towering trees, the glint of marble slabs and columns, evokes at once the tender mood to which the genius of the Southern poet has given classic expression.

The Heritage ✦ ✦ ✦ ✦ ✦ ✦

The trace of a dismantled fort
    Lay in the forest nave,
And in the shadow near my path
    I saw a soldier's grave.

The bramble wrestled with the weed
    Upon the lowly mound;—
The simple head-board, rudely writ,
    Had rotted to the ground;
I raised it with a reverent hand,
    From dust its words to clear,
But time had blotted all but these—
    "A Georgia Volunteer!"

I saw the toad and scaly snake
    From tangled covert start,
And hide themselves among the weeds
    Above the dead man's heart;
But undisturbed, in sleep profound,
    Unheeding, there he lay;
His coffin but the mountain soil,
    His shroud Confederate gray.

I heard the Shenandoah roll
    Along the vale below,
I saw the Alleghanies rise
    Towards the realms of snow.
The "Valley Campaign" rose to mind—
    Its leader's name—and then
I knew the sleeper had been one
    Of Stonewall Jackson's men.

Yet whence he came, what lip shall say—
    Whose tongue will ever tell
What desolated hearths and hearts
    Have been because he fell?
What sad-eyed maiden braids her hair,
    Her hair which he held dear?
One lock of which perchance lies with
    The Georgia Volunteer!

[278]

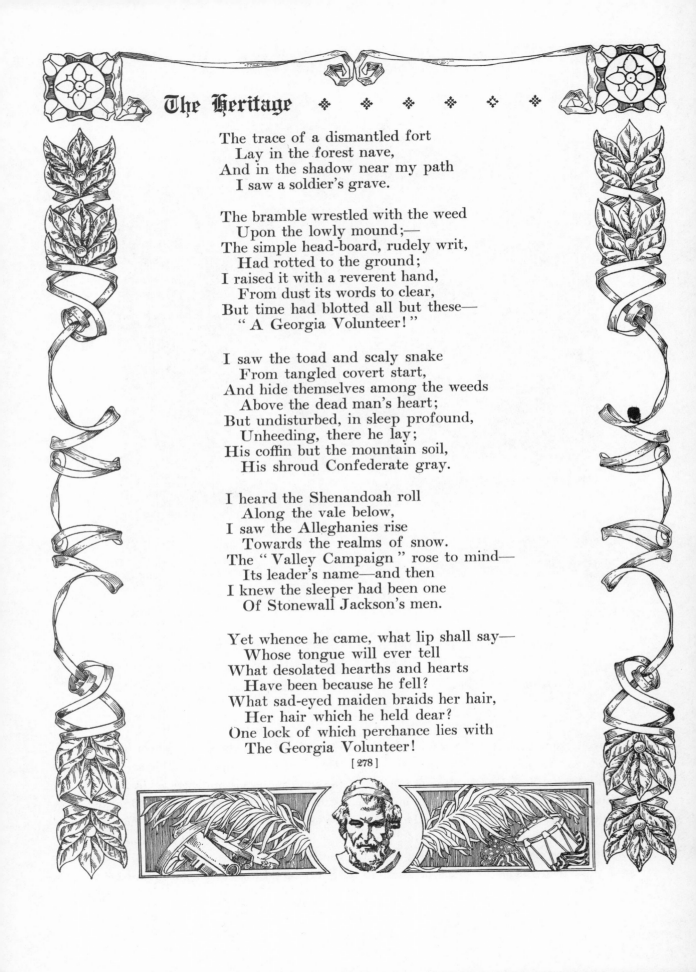

"OVER THEIR GRAVES RANG ONCE THE BUGLE'S CALL"

These resting places of soldiers upon the field of Bull Run, the first severe battle, remind Americans how widely the horror of war visited their land in 1861. Not only by old stone walls such as Stockard speaks of, but also where rude head-boards were erected on the battle-fields, the crash of battle had roared. Since 1862, when these pictures were taken, a grateful nation has converted these wild places into beautiful parks, better fit for preserving the names of those who met death where fell "The searching shrapnel and the crashing ball."

The Heritage ✦ ✦ ✦ ✦

What mother, with long watching eyes,
    And white lips cold and dumb,
Waits with appalling patience for
    Her darling boy to come?
Her boy! whose mountain grave swells up
    But one of many a scar,
Cut on the face of our fair land,
    By gory-handed war.

What fights he fought, what wounds he wore,
    Are all unknown to fame;
Remember, on his lonely grave
    There is not e'en a name!
That he fought well and bravely too,
    And held his country dear,
We know, else he had never been
    A Georgia Volunteer.

He sleeps—what need to question now
    If he were wrong or right?
He knows, ere this, whose cause was just
    In God the Father's sight.
He wields no warlike weapons now,
    Returns no foeman's thrust—
Who but a coward would revile
    An honest soldier's dust?

Roll, Shenandoah, proudly roll,
    Adown thy rocky glen,
Above thee lies the grave of one
    Of Stonewall Jackson's men.
Beneath the cedar and the pine,
    In solitude austere,
Unknown, unnamed, forgotten, lies
    A Georgia Volunteer.

MARY ASHLEY TOWNSEND.

WHERE SOME OF THE HEROIC DEAD LIE IN NATIONAL CEMETERIES

These wildernesses of headstones bring vividly to mind the resting-places of our heroic dead. There were in 1910 eighty-four national cemeteries situated in twenty-eight different States. In them are buried 207,075 known dead and 153,678 unknown, a total of 360,753. Of these the cem-

etery at Soldiers' Home in Washington contains 5,398 known dead, 288 unknown—a total of 5,686; the cemetery at City Point 3,719 known dead, 1,439 unknown—a total of 5,158; the one at Alexandria 3,401 known dead, 123 unknown—a total of 3,524. But these lack much of being the largest. At Vicksburg, 16,615 lie buried; at Nashville, 16,533; at Arlington, Virginia, 16,254; and Fredericksburg, Virginia, 15,273, of whom 12,785 are unknown.

CEMETERY AT SOLDIERS' HOME, WASHINGTON

SOLDIERS' GRAVES AT CITY POINT, VIRGINIA

GRAVES OF FEDERAL SOLDIERS, CHARLESTON, S. C.

IN THE SOLDIERS' CEMETERY AT ALEXANDRIA

A SWEEPING VIEW OF THE ALEXANDRIA "HEROIC DEAD"

ODE FOR DECORATION DAY

One of the earliest poems of its class, this selection from Peterson's Ode manifests a spirit as admirable as it is now general.

O gallant brothers of the generous South,
   Foes for a day and brothers for all time!
I charge you by the memories of our youth,
   By Yorktown's field and Montezuma's clime,
   Hold our dead sacred—let them quietly rest
In your unnumbered vales, where God thought best.
Your vines and flowers learned long since to forgive,
And o'er their graves a broidered mantle weave:
Be you as kind as they are, and the word
Shall reach the Northland with each summer bird,
And thoughts as sweet as summer shall awake
Responsive to your kindness, and shall make
Our peace the peace of brothers once again,
And banish utterly the days of pain.

And ye, O Northmen! be ye not outdone
   In generous thought and deed.
We all do need forgiveness, every one;
   And they that give shall find it in their need.
Spare of your flowers to deck the stranger's grave,
   Who died for a lost cause:—
A soul more daring, resolute, and brave,
   Ne'er won a world's applause.
A brave man's hatred pauses at the tomb.
For him some Southern home was robed in gloom,
Some wife or mother looked with longing eyes
Through the sad days and nights with tears and sighs,
Hope slowly hardening into gaunt Despair.
Then let your foeman's grave remembrance share:
Pity a higher charm to Valor lends,
And in the realms of Sorrow all are friends.

HENRY PETERSON.

[282]

HOLLYWOOD CEMETERY IN RICHMOND, VIRGINIA
1,800 CONFEDERATE SOLDIERS LIE BURIED HERE

CONFEDERATE GRAVES IN THE WILDERNESS
REMINDERS OF THE BATTLE OF MAY 5–6, 1864

GRAVES OF FEDERAL SOLDIERS
NEAR BURNSIDE'S BRIDGE ON THE BATTLEFIELD OF ANTIETAM

A CORNER OF HOLLYWOOD CEMETERY
RICHMOND, VIRGINIA, IN 1865

The cemetery at Antietam, not far from the scene of the photograph above, taken soon after the battle on September 16–17, 1862, contains the graves of 4,684 soldiers, of which 1,829 are marked "unknown." Even a frail memorial like the one at the grave of the "Georgia Volunteer" usually fails to record the native heath of him who lies below, or to give any clue to the campaigns in which he fought. These soldiers, like their companions under the hemlocks in the Wilderness, must await the call of the judgment day. The Hollywood cemetery at Richmond contains a larger host. Eighteen thousand Confederate veterans there sleep in everlasting peace amid beautiful surroundings. Around them lie many of Virginia's famous sons, generation after generation of loved and honored names.

THE TOURNAMENT *

The ballad is a revised form of an early poem by Sidney Lanier. "The Psalm of the West," in which it was inserted, was written in 1876, and was one of the earliest Southern poems to express the feeling of national unity. The bright colors and the medieval simplicity of the treatment lend to this clear and beautiful fragment of allegory a directness of appeal that expresses well the thankfulness in the poet's heart. Though Lanier's thought in 1876 ran in advance of that of contemporaries, Southerners have come to share the joy of these lines and to hold the poet in even higher estimation for the breadth and justice of his views as well as for the artistic quality of his verse.

Lists all white and blue in the skies;
    And the people hurried amain
To the Tournament under the ladies' eyes
    Where jousted Heart and Brain.

Blow, Herald, blow! There entered Heart,
    A youth in crimson and gold.
Blow, Herald, blow! Brain stood apart,
    Steel-armored, glittering cold.

Heart's palfrey caracoled gayly round,
    Heart tra-li-raed merrily;
But Brain sat still, with never a sound—
    Full cynical-calm was he.

Heart's helmet-crest bore favors three
    From his lady's white hand caught;
Brain's casque was bare as Fact—not he
    Or favor gave or sought.

YORKTOWN—THE HOUSE WHERE CORNWALLIS SURRENDERED, 1781

MONUMENT TO HENRY CLAY AT RICHMOND

TOMB OF PRESIDENT POLK AT NASHVILLE

Peterson's poem preceding celebrates the heritage of glorious history common to North and South alike. The war-time views on this page are all Southern; yet every American can share the pride of beholding these spots — the house where Washington received Cornwallis's surrender; the tomb of Polk, leader of the nation when Scott and his soldiers fought in "Montezuma's clime"; the monument to the statesman Henry Clay; and the barracks at Baton Rouge, a stormy point under five flags—French in 1719, British in 1763, Spanish in 1779, American in 1810, and Confederate in 1861. Here nearly every prominent officer in the United States army since the Revolution did duty —Wilkinson and the first Wade Hampton, afterward Gaines and Jesup and Taylor, heroes of 1812. Here Winfield Scott saw his first service. Here Lafayette was received, and Andrew Jackson later. Here was the home of Zachary Taylor, and of his brilliant son "Dick," the Confederate general, who surrendered the largest Southern army.

HISTORIC GROUND AT BATON ROUGE, LOUISIANA

The Heritage ✦ ✦ ✦ ✦ ✦ ✦

Blow, Herald, blow!   Heart shot a glance
    To catch his lady's eye;
But Brain looked straight a-front, his lance
    To aim more faithfully.

They charged, they struck; both fell, both bled;
    Brain rose again, ungloved;
Heart fainting smiled, and softly said,
    "My love to my Beloved!"

Heart and brain! No more be twain;
Throb and think, one flesh again!
Lo! they weep, they turn, they run;
Lo! they kiss: Love, thou art one!

SIDNEY LANIER.

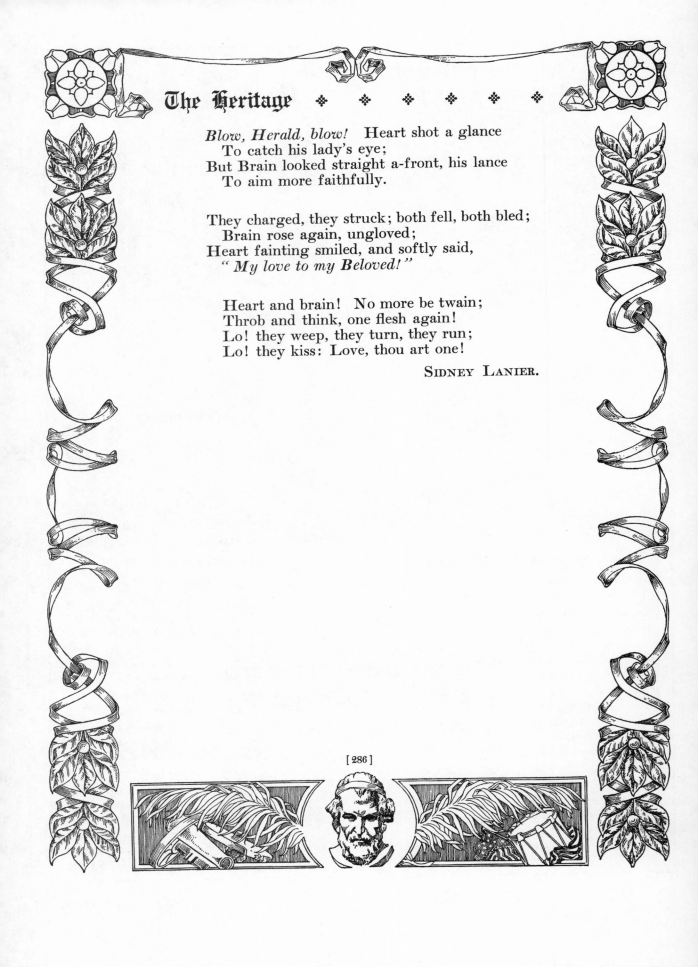

XIII

BROTHERHOOD

"HE REACHES THE HOME
HE LEFT SO PROSPEROUS
AND BEAUTIFUL"—*Grady*

RUINS OF THE
BERNARD HOUSE,
BATTLEFIELD OF
FREDERICKSBURG

THE FUTURE PRESIDENT OF THE CONFEDERACY, WITH HIS WIFE

THE FIRST OF SEVEN SCENES FROM THE LIFE OF JEFFERSON DAVIS

This picture, made from an old daguerreotype, forms as true a document of Jefferson Davis' human side as his letter concerning Grant on page 290. Davis was born in Kentucky the year before Lincoln. His college education began in that State. In 1842 he entered West Point. Army service proved his ability to command. In the Mexican War he won distinction as colonel of the First Mississippi Volunteers by the famous "reëntering angle" at Buena Vista. As Senator from Mississippi and Secretary of War under President Pierce, he became the accepted leader of the Southern party in their insistence on the doctrine of States' rights. His unanimous election as President of the Confederacy on February 8, 1861, by the Congress at Montgomery, Alabama, was unsought. When the permanent government was established in 1862, he entered without opposition upon the six years' term. When the stress of war turned his administration into a virtual dictatorship, he wielded enormous powers with the utmost fidelity. His military training and experience had instilled him with such confidence in his military capacity that he maintained to the end a close control over all his generals. His wife, who possessed all the charm of Southern womanhood, has left an account of her husband that forms one of the most intimate and winning biographies written by an American author.

"THE ROYAL FAMILY"—JEFFERSON DAVIS'S CHILDREN

The second scene in the series from Davis's career brings to mind the private sorrows that fell to his lot. On June 13, 1862, while a hundred thousand Union soldiers pressed at the very gates of Richmond, his infant son, William Howell, lay at the point of death. The harassed statesman and devoted father wrote Mrs. Davis: ". . . My heart sunk within me at the news of the suffering of my angel baby. Your telegram of the 12th gives assurance of the subsidence of disease. But the look of pain and exhaustion, the gentle complaint, 'I am tired,' which has for so many years oppressed me, seems to have been revived; and unless God spares me another such trial, what is to become of me, I don't know. Dr. Garnett will, I hope, reach you this morning. He carried with him what he regarded as a specific remedy. . . . My ease, my health, my property, my life, I can give to the cause of my country. The heroism which could lay my wife and children on any sacrificial altar is not mine. Spare us, good Lord." Yet he was subjected to peculiar trials. During the war a four-year-old son fell from a balcony and was instantly killed. Only two of his children survived him—Margaret, who married J. A. Hayes of Denver, Colorado, in 1877, and Varina Anne Davis, favorably known as a writer, honored at many a veterans' reunion, and beloved throughout the South as "Winnie, the Daughter of the Confederacy."

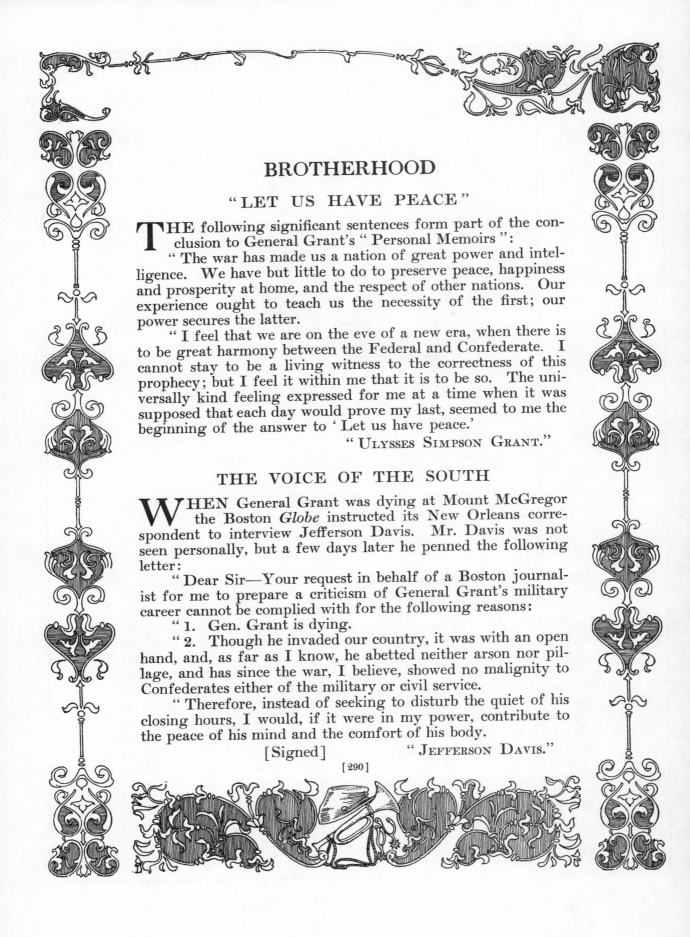

BROTHERHOOD

"LET US HAVE PEACE"

THE following significant sentences form part of the conclusion to General Grant's "Personal Memoirs":

"The war has made us a nation of great power and intelligence. We have but little to do to preserve peace, happiness and prosperity at home, and the respect of other nations. Our experience ought to teach us the necessity of the first; our power secures the latter.

"I feel that we are on the eve of a new era, when there is to be great harmony between the Federal and Confederate. I cannot stay to be a living witness to the correctness of this prophecy; but I feel it within me that it is to be so. The universally kind feeling expressed for me at a time when it was supposed that each day would prove my last, seemed to me the beginning of the answer to 'Let us have peace.'

"ULYSSES SIMPSON GRANT."

THE VOICE OF THE SOUTH

WHEN General Grant was dying at Mount McGregor the Boston *Globe* instructed its New Orleans correspondent to interview Jefferson Davis. Mr. Davis was not seen personally, but a few days later he penned the following letter:

"Dear Sir—Your request in behalf of a Boston journalist for me to prepare a criticism of General Grant's military career cannot be complied with for the following reasons:

"1. Gen. Grant is dying.

"2. Though he invaded our country, it was with an open hand, and, as far as I know, he abetted neither arson nor pillage, and has since the war, I believe, showed no malignity to Confederates either of the military or civil service.

"Therefore, instead of seeking to disturb the quiet of his closing hours, I would, if it were in my power, contribute to the peace of his mind and the comfort of his body.

[Signed] "JEFFERSON DAVIS."

THE INAUGURATION

THIRD OF SEVEN SCENES FROM THE LIFE OF JEFFERSON DAVIS

It is the eighteenth of February, 1861. The clock on the State House of Alabama points to the hour of one. Jefferson Davis is being inaugurated as President of the Confederate States of America. The only photograph of the memorable scene was made by A. C. McIntyre, the principal artist of Montgomery. Davis had been elected on February 9, 1861, by the provisional congress that had met there to form a Confederate Government. Although preferring high rank in the army to political position, Davis accepted. On February 18th he delivered a carefully prepared address to the throng here assembled. At the foot of the slope is the carriage of Judge Benajah Bibb, containing his daughter, who later became president of the Ladies' Memorial Association. On July 20, 1860, the seat of the new Confederate Government was transferred to Richmond, Virginia.

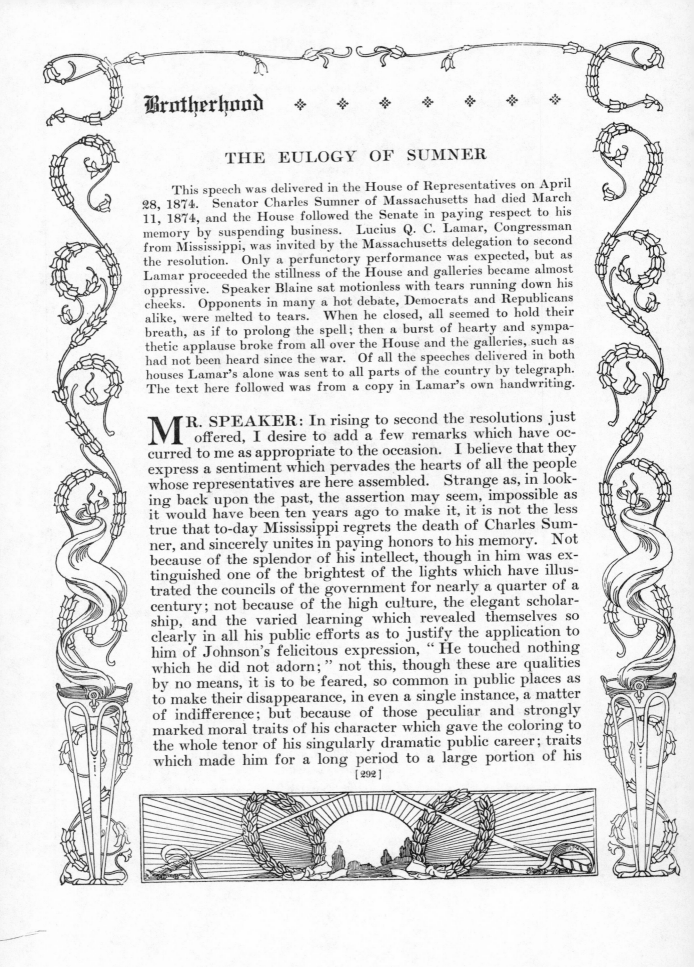

THE EULOGY OF SUMNER

This speech was delivered in the House of Representatives on April 28, 1874. Senator Charles Sumner of Massachusetts had died March 11, 1874, and the House followed the Senate in paying respect to his memory by suspending business. Lucius Q. C. Lamar, Congressman from Mississippi, was invited by the Massachusetts delegation to second the resolution. Only a perfunctory performance was expected, but as Lamar proceeded the stillness of the House and galleries became almost oppressive. Speaker Blaine sat motionless with tears running down his cheeks. Opponents in many a hot debate, Democrats and Republicans alike, were melted to tears. When he closed, all seemed to hold their breath, as if to prolong the spell; then a burst of hearty and sympathetic applause broke from all over the House and the galleries, such as had not been heard since the war. Of all the speeches delivered in both houses Lamar's alone was sent to all parts of the country by telegraph. The text here followed was from a copy in Lamar's own handwriting.

MR. SPEAKER: In rising to second the resolutions just offered, I desire to add a few remarks which have occurred to me as appropriate to the occasion. I believe that they express a sentiment which pervades the hearts of all the people whose representatives are here assembled. Strange as, in looking back upon the past, the assertion may seem, impossible as it would have been ten years ago to make it, it is not the less true that to-day Mississippi regrets the death of Charles Sumner, and sincerely unites in paying honors to his memory. Not because of the splendor of his intellect, though in him was extinguished one of the brightest of the lights which have illustrated the councils of the government for nearly a quarter of a century; not because of the high culture, the elegant scholarship, and the varied learning which revealed themselves so clearly in all his public efforts as to justify the application to him of Johnson's felicitous expression, " He touched nothing which he did not adorn; " not this, though these are qualities by no means, it is to be feared, so common in public places as to make their disappearance, in even a single instance, a matter of indifference; but because of those peculiar and strongly marked moral traits of his character which gave the coloring to the whole tenor of his singularly dramatic public career; traits which made him for a long period to a large portion of his

THE PRESIDENT OF THE CONFEDERACY

THE FOURTH OF SEVEN SCENES FROM THE LIFE OF JEFFERSON DAVIS—HIS WIDOW PRONOUNCED THIS THE ONLY WAR-TIME
PHOTOGRAPH

The trials of the Presidency were particularly severe to one of Davis's delicately balanced temperament. According to Mrs. Davis, "he was abnormally sensitive to disapprobation; even a child's disapproval discomposed him." She relates that one day, during the second year of the war, "he came home, about seven o'clock, from his office, staggered up to a sofa in his little private office and lay down. He declined dinner, and I remained by his side, anxious and afraid to ask what was the trouble which so oppressed him. In an hour or two he told me that the weight of responsibility oppressed him so that he felt he would give all his limbs to have some one with whom he could share it." But she adds in a later chapter, "As hope died out in the breasts of the rank and file of the Confederate army, the President's courage rose, and he was fertile in expedients to supply deficiencies, and calm in the contemplation of the destruction of his dearest hopes, and the violent death he expected to be his." In all his trials his wife was an unfailingly sympathetic companion.

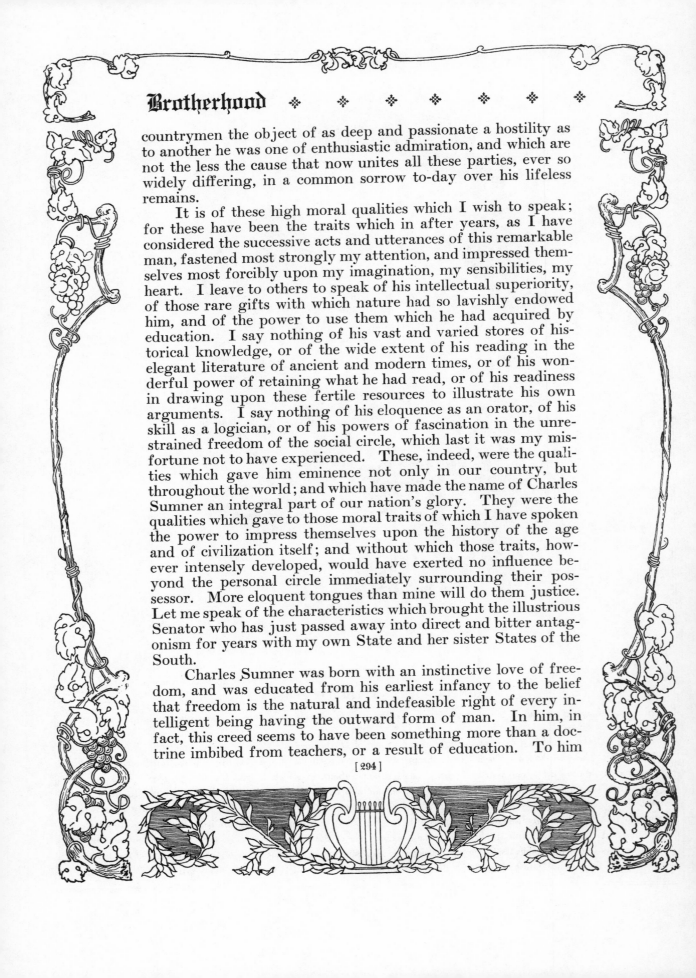

countrymen the object of as deep and passionate a hostility as to another he was one of enthusiastic admiration, and which are not the less the cause that now unites all these parties, ever so widely differing, in a common sorrow to-day over his lifeless remains.

It is of these high moral qualities which I wish to speak; for these have been the traits which in after years, as I have considered the successive acts and utterances of this remarkable man, fastened most strongly my attention, and impressed themselves most forcibly upon my imagination, my sensibilities, my heart. I leave to others to speak of his intellectual superiority, of those rare gifts with which nature had so lavishly endowed him, and of the power to use them which he had acquired by education. I say nothing of his vast and varied stores of historical knowledge, or of the wide extent of his reading in the elegant literature of ancient and modern times, or of his wonderful power of retaining what he had read, or of his readiness in drawing upon these fertile resources to illustrate his own arguments. I say nothing of his eloquence as an orator, of his skill as a logician, or of his powers of fascination in the unrestrained freedom of the social circle, which last it was my misfortune not to have experienced. These, indeed, were the qualities which gave him eminence not only in our country, but throughout the world; and which have made the name of Charles Sumner an integral part of our nation's glory. They were the qualities which gave to those moral traits of which I have spoken the power to impress themselves upon the history of the age and of civilization itself; and without which those traits, however intensely developed, would have exerted no influence beyond the personal circle immediately surrounding their possessor. More eloquent tongues than mine will do them justice. Let me speak of the characteristics which brought the illustrious Senator who has just passed away into direct and bitter antagonism for years with my own State and her sister States of the South.

Charles Sumner was born with an instinctive love of freedom, and was educated from his earliest infancy to the belief that freedom is the natural and indefeasible right of every intelligent being having the outward form of man. In him, in fact, this creed seems to have been something more than a doctrine imbibed from teachers, or a result of education. To him

JEFFERSON DAVIS A PRISONER

PASSING THROUGH MACON, GEORGIA, IN AN AMBULANCE

Thus the motley crowd from street, doorway, and window gazed after the unfortunate President of the Confederate States on May 10, 1865. Davis had left Richmond on the night of April 2d, upon Lee's warning. In Danville, Virginia, he remained for a few days until word was brought of Lee's surrender. At Greensboro, North Carolina, he held a council of war with Generals Johnston and Beauregard, in which he reluctantly made provision for negotiations between Johnston and Sherman. He continued the trip south on April 14th, the day of Lincoln's assassination. At Charlotte, North Carolina, he was called forth by a group of Confederate cavalrymen, when he "expressed his own determination not to despair of the Confederacy but to remain with the last organized band upholding the flag." When he learned of the rejection at Washington of the terms agreed upon by Johnston and Sherman, he ordered Johnston to retreat with his cavalry. On April 26th, Davis continued his own journey. Only ten members of his cavalry escort were retained. In the early light of May 10th Lieut.-Col. B. D. Pritchard and troopers of the Fourth Michigan Cavalry came upon the encampment by the roadside in dense pine woods near Irwinville, Georgia, and captured the whole party.

JEFFERSON DAVIS

IN THE RIDING DRESS
HE WORE WHEN CAPTURED

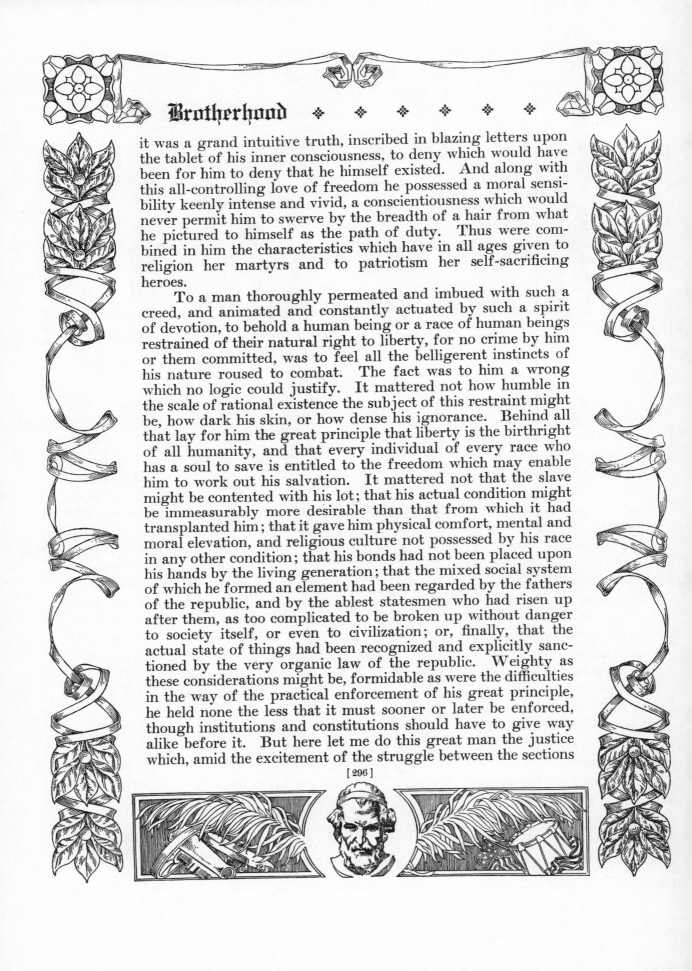

it was a grand intuitive truth, inscribed in blazing letters upon the tablet of his inner consciousness, to deny which would have been for him to deny that he himself existed. And along with this all-controlling love of freedom he possessed a moral sensibility keenly intense and vivid, a conscientiousness which would never permit him to swerve by the breadth of a hair from what he pictured to himself as the path of duty. Thus were combined in him the characteristics which have in all ages given to religion her martyrs and to patriotism her self-sacrificing heroes.

To a man thoroughly permeated and imbued with such a creed, and animated and constantly actuated by such a spirit of devotion, to behold a human being or a race of human beings restrained of their natural right to liberty, for no crime by him or them committed, was to feel all the belligerent instincts of his nature roused to combat. The fact was to him a wrong which no logic could justify. It mattered not how humble in the scale of rational existence the subject of this restraint might be, how dark his skin, or how dense his ignorance. Behind all that lay for him the great principle that liberty is the birthright of all humanity, and that every individual of every race who has a soul to save is entitled to the freedom which may enable him to work out his salvation. It mattered not that the slave might be contented with his lot; that his actual condition might be immeasurably more desirable than that from which it had transplanted him; that it gave him physical comfort, mental and moral elevation, and religious culture not possessed by his race in any other condition; that his bonds had not been placed upon his hands by the living generation; that the mixed social system of which he formed an element had been regarded by the fathers of the republic, and by the ablest statesmen who had risen up after them, as too complicated to be broken up without danger to society itself, or even to civilization; or, finally, that the actual state of things had been recognized and explicitly sanctioned by the very organic law of the republic. Weighty as these considerations might be, formidable as were the difficulties in the way of the practical enforcement of his great principle, he held none the less that it must sooner or later be enforced, though institutions and constitutions should have to give way alike before it. But here let me do this great man the justice which, amid the excitement of the struggle between the sections

SIGNATURES TO THE JEFFERSON DAVIS BAIL—BOND—HORACE GREELEY'S COMES THIRD

Jefferson Davis was captured near Irwinville, Georgia, on May 10, 1865, by a detachment of the Fourth Michigan Cavalry. On the way to Macon the party learned that a reward of $100,000 had been offered for the apprehension of Davis as one of the alleged accomplices of the assassination of Abraham Lincoln. It was later found that the testimony on which the charge was made was untrustworthy, some of the witnesses later retracting their state-

ments. After a two-years' imprisonment in Fort Monroe he was indicted in Richmond for treason and liberated on bail. Of the many names attached to the document, the most conspicuous is that of Horace Greeley, editor of the *New York Tribune*, who had been prominent throughout the war as a molder of Northern sentiment. The passions born of the conflict were still raging, some of them in an intensified form. Greeley displayed unusual courage in subscribing his name to the bond. It appears just above that of Cornelius Vanderbilt, below Gerrit Smith's.

GREELEY READING THE "TRIBUNE"

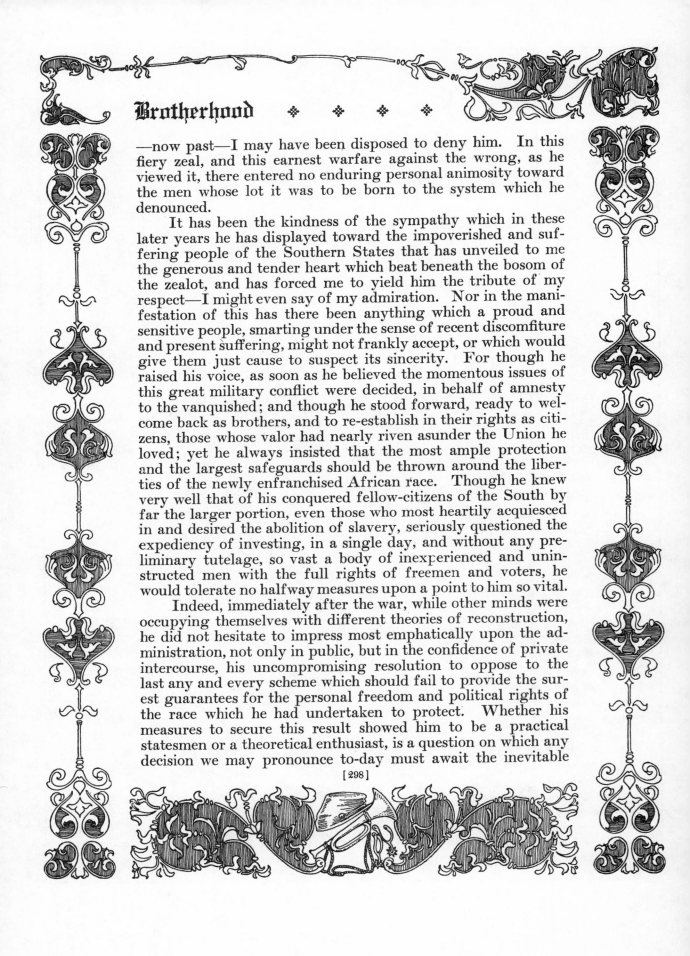

Brotherhood ❖ ❖ ❖ ❖

—now past—I may have been disposed to deny him. In this fiery zeal, and this earnest warfare against the wrong, as he viewed it, there entered no enduring personal animosity toward the men whose lot it was to be born to the system which he denounced.

It has been the kindness of the sympathy which in these later years he has displayed toward the impoverished and suffering people of the Southern States that has unveiled to me the generous and tender heart which beat beneath the bosom of the zealot, and has forced me to yield him the tribute of my respect—I might even say of my admiration. Nor in the manifestation of this has there been anything which a proud and sensitive people, smarting under the sense of recent discomfiture and present suffering, might not frankly accept, or which would give them just cause to suspect its sincerity. For though he raised his voice, as soon as he believed the momentous issues of this great military conflict were decided, in behalf of amnesty to the vanquished; and though he stood forward, ready to welcome back as brothers, and to re-establish in their rights as citizens, those whose valor had nearly riven asunder the Union he loved; yet he always insisted that the most ample protection and the largest safeguards should be thrown around the liberties of the newly enfranchised African race. Though he knew very well that of his conquered fellow-citizens of the South by far the larger portion, even those who most heartily acquiesced in and desired the abolition of slavery, seriously questioned the expediency of investing, in a single day, and without any preliminary tutelage, so vast a body of inexperienced and uninstructed men with the full rights of freemen and voters, he would tolerate no halfway measures upon a point to him so vital.

Indeed, immediately after the war, while other minds were occupying themselves with different theories of reconstruction, he did not hesitate to impress most emphatically upon the administration, not only in public, but in the confidence of private intercourse, his uncompromising resolution to oppose to the last any and every scheme which should fail to provide the surest guarantees for the personal freedom and political rights of the race which he had undertaken to protect. Whether his measures to secure this result showed him to be a practical statesmen or a theoretical enthusiast, is a question on which any decision we may pronounce to-day must await the inevitable

DAVIS AFTER HIS RELEASE FROM PRISON

THE LAST OF SEVEN SCENES FROM THE LIFE OF JEFFERSON DAVIS

On his return from Canada in 1868 Jefferson Davis paid a visit to Baltimore, and stood for this picture. It reveals the lines of pain drawn by the sufferings of three years. Twelve days after his capture he had been imprisoned in Fortress Monroe in a low cell. There he was kept more than four months. Then more comfortable quarters were assigned. His attending physician, though a strong Republican, was completely won by the charm of the Southern gentleman and published an account of his prison life that aroused public sympathy for the most distinguished prisoner ever held in the United States. On May 13, 1867, Davis was indicted for treason in the United States Circuit Court for the district of Virginia, whereupon he was admitted to bail for $100,000, signed by Horace Greeley and fourteen others. When Davis was released he was greeted with deafening cheers, huzzas, and waving of hats. He was included in the general amnesty of Christmas Day, 1868, and was released in February, 1869. The twenty remaining years of his life were spent chiefly in Mississippi.

revision of posterity. The spirit of magnanimity, therefore, which breathes in his utterances and manifests itself in all his acts affecting the South during the last two years of his life, was as evidently honest as it was grateful to the feelings of those toward whom it was displayed.

It was certainly a gracious act toward the South—though unhappily it jarred upon the sensibilities of the people at the other extreme of the Union, and estranged from him the great body of his political friends—to propose to erase from the banners of the national army the mementos of the bloody internecine struggle, which might be regarded as assailing the pride or wounding the sensibilities of the Southern people. That proposal will never be forgotten by that people so long as the name of Charles Sumner lives in the memory of man. But, while it touched the heart of the South, and elicited her profound gratitude, her people would not have asked of the North such an act of self-renunciation.

Conscious that they themselves were animated by devotion to constitutional liberty, and that the brightest pages of history are replete with evidences of the depth and sincerity of that devotion, they cannot but cherish the recollections of sacrifices endured, the battles fought, and the victories won in defense of their hapless cause. And respecting, as all true and brave men must respect, the martial spirit with which the men of the North vindicated the integrity of the Union, and their devotion to the principles of human freedom, they do not ask, they do not wish the North to strike the mementos of her heroism and victory from either records or monuments or battle flags. They would rather that both sections should gather up the glories won by each section: not envious, but proud of each other, and regard them a common heritage of American valor.

Let us hope that future generations, when they remember the deeds of heroism and devotion done on both sides, will speak not of Northern prowess and Southern courage, but of the heroism, fortitude, and courage of Americans in a war of ideas; a war in which each section signalized its consecration to the principles, as each understood them, of American liberty and of the constitution received from their fathers.

It was my misfortune, perhaps my fault, personally never to have known this eminent philanthropist and statesman. The impulse was often strong upon me to go to him and offer him my

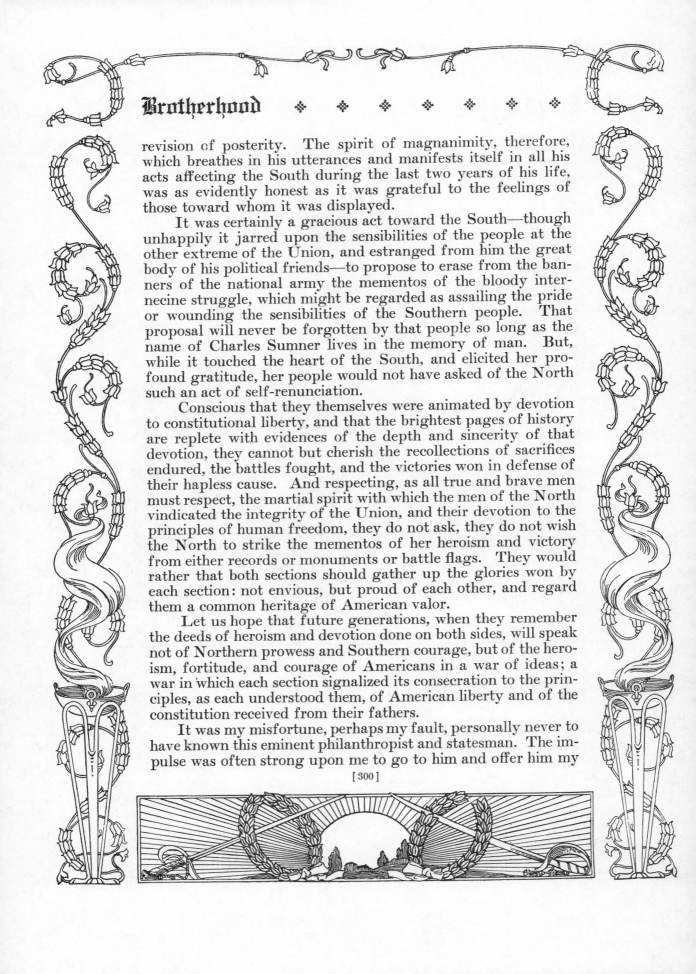

A PICTURE FULL OF MEANING TO READERS OF LAMAR'S "EULOGY"
NEGROES AT THE RUINS OF THE RICHMOND AND PETERSBURG BRIDGE AT RICHMOND IN APRIL, 1865

Everyone knows that the care-free black people sitting before the unruffled pool are in some way connected with the wreck of war that looms behind. A viewpoint of this relation, as warmly human as it is broad and national, is taken by Lamar in his "Eulogy of Sumner." Charles Sumner at the time of his death had for a generation been prominent in anti-slavery agitation. His oration in 1845 on "The True Grandeur of Nations" attracted attention even in England. With his election to the United States Senate, in 1851, at the age of forty, he stepped forward to a position of national leadership. Before and after the war few national figures aroused more opposition in the South than Charles Sumner. He created a storm in 1856 by his speech in the Senate on "The Crime Against Kansas," in which he reflected on South Carolina and on Senator Butler from that State. Preston Brooks, a South Carolina Representative and a relative of Butler, found Sumner alone at his desk in the Senate Chamber, and beat him over the head with a cane until Sumner fell senseless to the floor, receiving spinal injuries from which he never entirely recovered. Sumner, when able some years later to return to his seat, continued his opposition to slavery, and was prominent in securing to the freedmen citizenship and the ballot. No later than 1874, true patriotism had succeeded passion so notably that Lamar's "Eulogy" was greeted with warm applause by representatives of all sections.

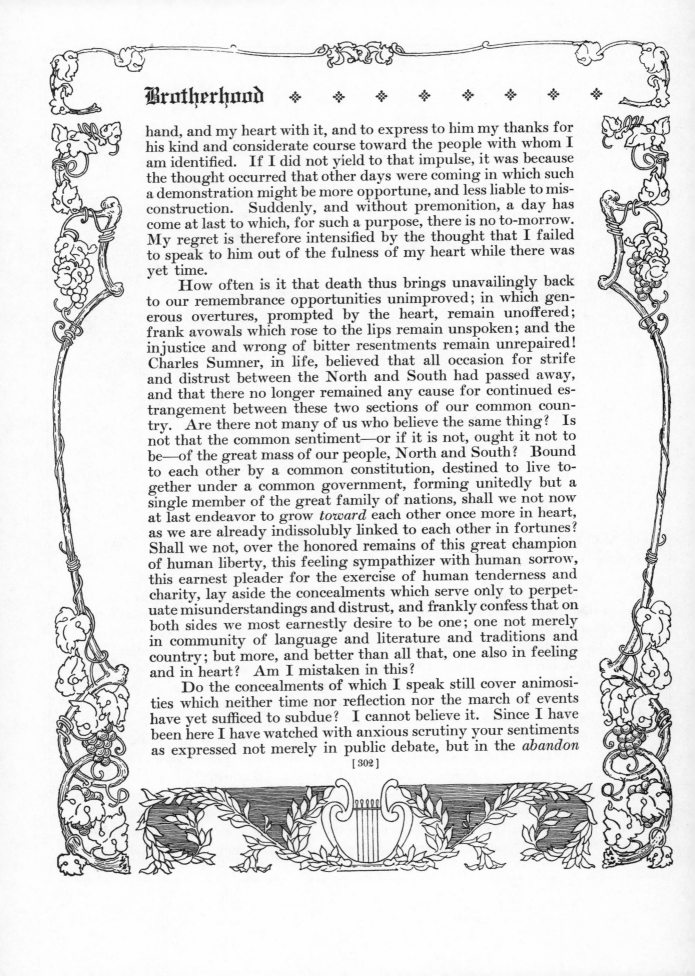

hand, and my heart with it, and to express to him my thanks for his kind and considerate course toward the people with whom I am identified. If I did not yield to that impulse, it was because the thought occurred that other days were coming in which such a demonstration might be more opportune, and less liable to misconstruction. Suddenly, and without premonition, a day has come at last to which, for such a purpose, there is no to-morrow. My regret is therefore intensified by the thought that I failed to speak to him out of the fulness of my heart while there was yet time.

How often is it that death thus brings unavailingly back to our remembrance opportunities unimproved; in which generous overtures, prompted by the heart, remain unoffered; frank avowals which rose to the lips remain unspoken; and the injustice and wrong of bitter resentments remain unrepaired! Charles Sumner, in life, believed that all occasion for strife and distrust between the North and South had passed away, and that there no longer remained any cause for continued estrangement between these two sections of our common country. Are there not many of us who believe the same thing? Is not that the common sentiment—or if it is not, ought it not to be—of the great mass of our people, North and South? Bound to each other by a common constitution, destined to live together under a common government, forming unitedly but a single member of the great family of nations, shall we not now at last endeavor to grow *toward* each other once more in heart, as we are already indissolubly linked to each other in fortunes? Shall we not, over the honored remains of this great champion of human liberty, this feeling sympathizer with human sorrow, this earnest pleader for the exercise of human tenderness and charity, lay aside the concealments which serve only to perpetuate misunderstandings and distrust, and frankly confess that on both sides we most earnestly desire to be one; one not merely in community of language and literature and traditions and country; but more, and better than all that, one also in feeling and in heart? Am I mistaken in this?

Do the concealments of which I speak still cover animosities which neither time nor reflection nor the march of events have yet sufficed to subdue? I cannot believe it. Since I have been here I have watched with anxious scrutiny your sentiments as expressed not merely in public debate, but in the *abandon*

CHARLES SUMNER—THE PORTRAIT BY BRADY

The single-mindedness, the moral grandeur stamped upon Sumner's features are revealed in this lifelike portrait. Even those whose political convictions were different, though equally intense, could agree with the estimate of his biographer, Moorfield Storey: "Charles Sumner was a great man in his absolute fidelity to principle—his un-flinching devotion to duty, his indifference to selfish considerations, his high scorn of anything petty or mean." He had convinced himself that suffrage was a right and not a privilege, and all the force of his intellect and char-acter was devoted to accomplishing what he thought was right. The eulogy by Lamar pays him fitting tribute.

of personal confidence. I know well the sentiments of these, my Southern brothers, whose hearts are so infolded that the feeling of each is the feeling of all; and I see on both sides only the seeming of a constraint, which each apparently hesitates to dismiss. The South—prostrate, exhausted, drained of her lifeblood, as well as of her material resources, yet still honorable and true—accepts the bitter award of the bloody arbitrament without reservation, resolutely determined to abide the result with chivalrous fidelity; yet, as if struck dumb by the magnitude of her reverses, she suffers on in silence. The North, exultant in her triumph, and elated by success, still cherishes, as we are assured, a heart full of magnanimous emotions toward her disarmed and discomfited antagonist; and yet, as if mastered by some mysterious spell, silencing her better impulses, her words and acts are the words and acts of suspicion and distrust.

Would that the spirit of the illustrious dead whom we lament to-day could speak from the grave to both parties to this deplorable discord in tones which should reach each and every heart throughout this broad territory: "My countrymen! *know* one another, and you will *love* one another."

LUCIUS QUINTUS CINCINNATUS LAMAR.

THE NEW SOUTH

Delivered before the New England Society of New York City at the dinner of December 22, 1886. In response to an urgent invitation Henry W. Grady, then managing editor of the Atlanta *Constitution*, attended the banquet, expecting to make a mere formal response to the toast of "The South." But the occasion proved inspiring. The Reverend T. DeWitt Talmage spoke on "Old and New Fashions." Near Grady sat General William Tecumseh Sherman, who had marched through his native State of Georgia with fire and sword. "When I found myself on my feet," he said, describing the scene on his return to Atlanta, " every nerve in my body was strung as tight as a fiddle-string, and all tingling. I knew then that I had a message for that assemblage, and as soon as I opened my mouth it came rushing out." Thus the speech which stirred the whole country was an impromptu effort from beginning to end.

"WHILE OTHER MINDS WERE OCCUPYING THEMSELVES WITH DIFFERENT THEORIES OF RECONSTRUCTION."

A SCENE CONTEMPORARY WITH SUMNER'S "UNCOMPROMISING RESOLUTION" REFERRED TO BY LAMAR

The lively scene in Baton Rouge, Louisiana, just after the war, is typical of early reconstruction in the South. The wagon is filled with a military band, the flags are regimental colors, and the vehicle itself is a military wagon. The music has attracted not only a crowd of boys and men, but a woman with a child in her arms is standing in the door of the bakery where cakes and pies are advertised for sale, and in the second-story window above her another woman is gazing timidly from behind the shutter. Evidently the candidate for the State Senate is making some progress. Reconstruction in the South was not so long a period as some may suppose. The first attempts to reorganize the state governments, like the one here pictured, were under the protection of Federal military forces. The measures taken were sometimes harsh, but the execution of martial law was honest. Most of the governments were left in the hands of civil authorities in 1868. "Carpet-baggers" and "scalawags" then held sway until the better class of citizens could come into control. But in 1874 their power was overthrown, except in Louisiana and South Carolina.

SOUTHERN EXPRESS OFFICE, RICHMOND

MILL ON JAMES RIVER AND KANAWHA CANAL

GALLEGO FLOUR MILLS, JAMES RIVER

GALLEGO FLOUR MILLS FROM THE CANAL

THE RICHMOND AND PETERSBURG RAILROAD STATION

REMAINS OF CARS NEAR THE STATION

"HIS TRADE DESTROYED"—ILLUSTRATIONS FOR GRADY'S WORDS

These few glimpses of ruined industries in the single Southern city of Richmond prove how discouraging a reality confronted the Confederate soldier on his return home. Even the words of the orator Grady are faint in comparison with the almost hopeless future that lay before his people in 1865. All their movable capital was exhausted. The banks had failed. The State and Confederate bonds were worthless. The railroads were ruined; the cities disconsolate; the labor system revolutionized. But, as Henry Watterson says, the South "was poor and in bondage; she was set free, and she had to go to work; she went to work, and she is richer than ever before.

FIRE-SWEPT HOMES

NOTHING BUT BARE WALLS

THE PATH OF DESTRUCTION

WORK OF THE FLAMES

A VISTA OF HAVOC

A ONCE BEAUTIFUL MANSION

"HE FINDS HIS HOUSE IN RUINS"—ILLUSTRATIONS FOR GRADY'S WORDS

On this page appear homes and public buildings wrecked by the conflagration during the evacuation of Richmond on the night of April 2, 1865. The flames swept up from the river, threatening to devour the whole town. The Union troops, arriving about eight o'clock on the morning of April 3d, found the city a scene of wild confusion. They were ordered to press into service every able-bodied man. Only with great difficulty were the flames extinguished by two o'clock. A beautiful residence-district lay utterly devastated.

[J—20]

A DESOLATE GARDEN

In the spring of 1865, this charming Southern garden in Petersburg did not bloom as had been its wont. The thundering cannon of Grant's besieging army had laid in ruins many a noble old mansion. Even where the non-combatants could dwell in comparative safety, they suffered for want of the necessaries of life. In the whole of Virginia there was not enough of either meat or bread to sustain the Confederate troops that had suffered far more severely than the citizens during the unusually hard winter just past. But after the war, the leaders, whose homes were in ruins, did not sit down in despair. The cities of the Southland arose in new beauty, and the manifold problems of a new era were studied with a courage Grady does well to praise. From the exhaustion of merciless war, from wreckage such as this, the South rose renewed like the fabled phenix.

A few steps across the garden, toward the same roofless home of the page facing, opens sadder destruction of the exquisite Georgian architecture. Toward the close of the siege, many scenes like this awaited the army photographer. Homes that had once reposed peacefully in the light of luxury and sparkled with gaiety now stood in ruins, grim tokens that Sherman's terse definition of war is true. And yet the South fought on. Never has the world seen greater devotion to a cause. Grander than this devotion was the resolute meeting of the problems left by the war. An entirely new social order, in which Southern leaders profoundly disbelieved, might well have appalled the stoutest heart. But the present prosperity of the whole section proves that hearts were not appalled. The dauntless energy of the Anglo-Saxon has gained again a victory more precious than any won in war.

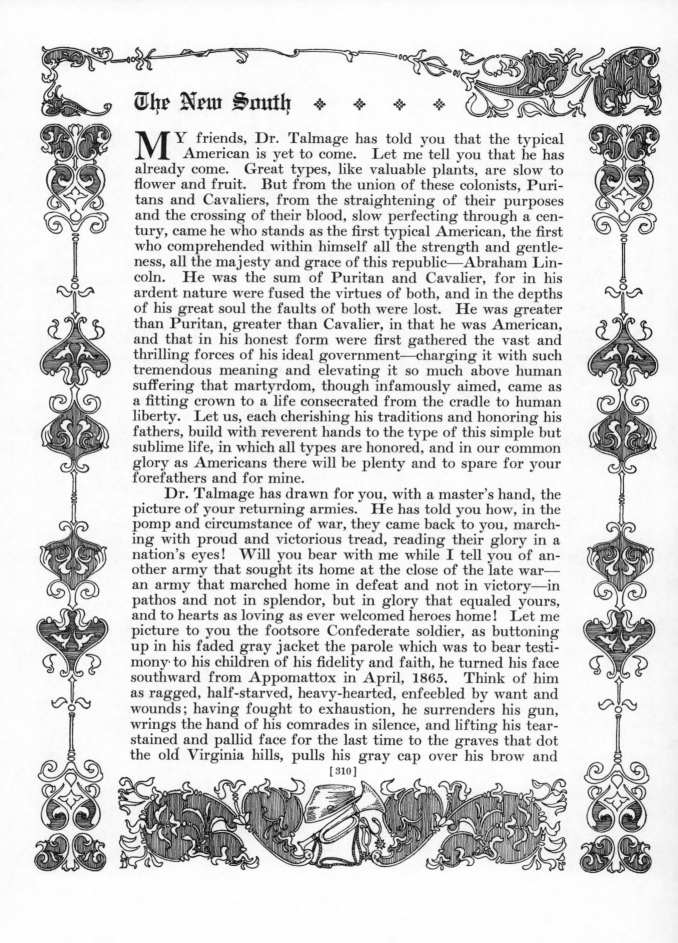

The New South ✦ ✦ ✦ ✦

MY friends, Dr. Talmage has told you that the typical American is yet to come. Let me tell you that he has already come. Great types, like valuable plants, are slow to flower and fruit. But from the union of these colonists, Puritans and Cavaliers, from the straightening of their purposes and the crossing of their blood, slow perfecting through a century, came he who stands as the first typical American, the first who comprehended within himself all the strength and gentleness, all the majesty and grace of this republic—Abraham Lincoln. He was the sum of Puritan and Cavalier, for in his ardent nature were fused the virtues of both, and in the depths of his great soul the faults of both were lost. He was greater than Puritan, greater than Cavalier, in that he was American, and that in his honest form were first gathered the vast and thrilling forces of his ideal government—charging it with such tremendous meaning and elevating it so much above human suffering that martyrdom, though infamously aimed, came as a fitting crown to a life consecrated from the cradle to human liberty. Let us, each cherishing his traditions and honoring his fathers, build with reverent hands to the type of this simple but sublime life, in which all types are honored, and in our common glory as Americans there will be plenty and to spare for your forefathers and for mine.

Dr. Talmage has drawn for you, with a master's hand, the picture of your returning armies. He has told you how, in the pomp and circumstance of war, they came back to you, marching with proud and victorious tread, reading their glory in a nation's eyes! Will you bear with me while I tell you of another army that sought its home at the close of the late war— an army that marched home in defeat and not in victory—in pathos and not in splendor, but in glory that equaled yours, and to hearts as loving as ever welcomed heroes home! Let me picture to you the footsore Confederate soldier, as buttoning up in his faded gray jacket the parole which was to bear testimony to his children of his fidelity and faith, he turned his face southward from Appomattox in April, 1865. Think of him as ragged, half-starved, heavy-hearted, enfeebled by want and wounds; having fought to exhaustion, he surrenders his gun, wrings the hand of his comrades in silence, and lifting his tear-stained and pallid face for the last time to the graves that dot the old Virginia hills, pulls his gray cap over his brow and

"THIS HERO IN GRAY WITH THE HEART OF GOLD"

This portrait of a young Confederate volunteer caught the eye of the New York sculptor Ruckstuhl, while he was designing the magnificent monument to be erected in Baltimore by the Maryland Society of the Daughters of the Confederacy. The photograph was taken in April, 1861, when the boy soldier, Henry Howe Cook, had been promoted at the age of seventeen from the ranks of Company D, First Tennessee Regiment, to a lieutenancy in Company F of the Forty-fourth Tennessee, in B. R. Johnson's brigade. At the outbreak of the war proper arms were scarcer in the Confederacy than uniforms. Private Cook's trig costume contrasts sharply with the big hunting-knife and the old-fashioned pistol with its ramrod and percussion trigger. His glance is direct and fearless; yet he is almost too young to look blood-thirsty, even with the lethal weapon thrust in his belt. Working in the spirit which Grady so eloquently describes, he continued to rise after the war was over. As a lawyer he was eminently successful and in after years was honored by the people of Tennessee with the chancellorship in its court system.

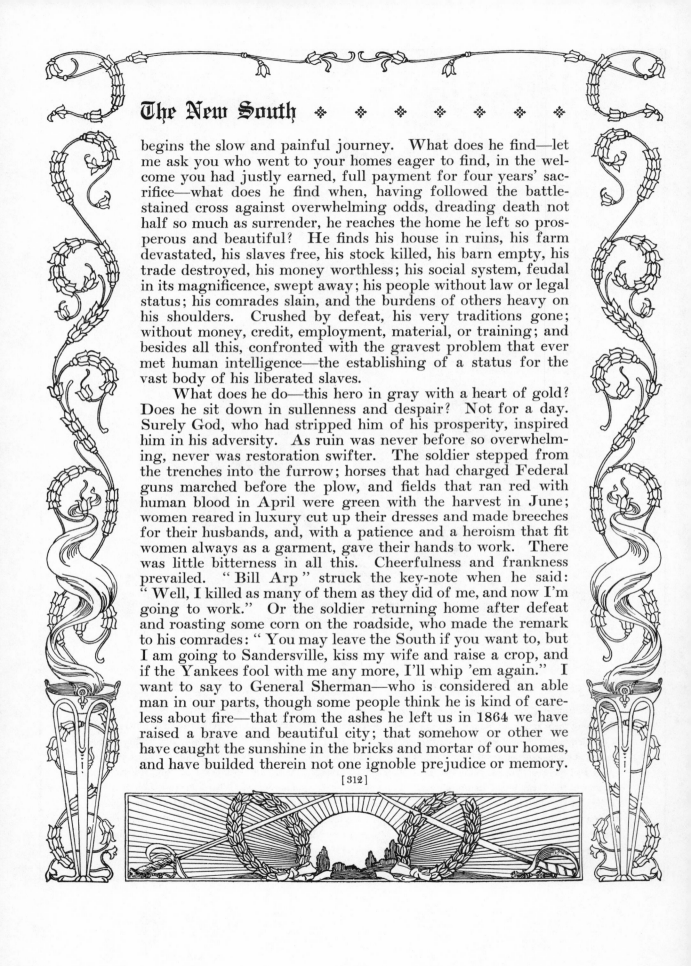

The New South ✦ ✦ ✦ ✦ ✦ ✦ ✦

begins the slow and painful journey. What does he find—let me ask you who went to your homes eager to find, in the welcome you had justly earned, full payment for four years' sacrifice—what does he find when, having followed the battle-stained cross against overwhelming odds, dreading death not half so much as surrender, he reaches the home he left so prosperous and beautiful? He finds his house in ruins, his farm devastated, his slaves free, his stock killed, his barn empty, his trade destroyed, his money worthless; his social system, feudal in its magnificence, swept away; his people without law or legal status; his comrades slain, and the burdens of others heavy on his shoulders. Crushed by defeat, his very traditions gone; without money, credit, employment, material, or training; and besides all this, confronted with the gravest problem that ever met human intelligence—the establishing of a status for the vast body of his liberated slaves.

What does he do—this hero in gray with a heart of gold? Does he sit down in sullenness and despair? Not for a day. Surely God, who had stripped him of his prosperity, inspired him in his adversity. As ruin was never before so overwhelming, never was restoration swifter. The soldier stepped from the trenches into the furrow; horses that had charged Federal guns marched before the plow, and fields that ran red with human blood in April were green with the harvest in June; women reared in luxury cut up their dresses and made breeches for their husbands, and, with a patience and a heroism that fit women always as a garment, gave their hands to work. There was little bitterness in all this. Cheerfulness and frankness prevailed. "Bill Arp" struck the key-note when he said: "Well, I killed as many of them as they did of me, and now I'm going to work." Or the soldier returning home after defeat and roasting some corn on the roadside, who made the remark to his comrades: "You may leave the South if you want to, but I am going to Sandersville, kiss my wife and raise a crop, and if the Yankees fool with me any more, I'll whip 'em again." I want to say to General Sherman—who is considered an able man in our parts, though some people think he is kind of careless about fire—that from the ashes he left us in 1864 we have raised a brave and beautiful city; that somehow or other we have caught the sunshine in the bricks and mortar of our homes, and have builded therein not one ignoble prejudice or memory.

"HIS SOCIAL SYSTEM, FEUDAL IN ITS MAGNIFICENCE, SWEPT AWAY"

WADE HAMPTON'S GARDEN IN COLUMBIA, SOUTH CAROLINA

The plantation of the Hamptons, one of the finest in the whole South, fittingly illustrates Grady's allusion. The Wade Hampton here spoken of was not a states-right's man, but when secession was decided on he entered energetically into the preparations for war. "Hampton's Legion," raised and equipped from his private wealth, was prominent throughout the conflict. Hampton himself fought with them at Bull Run and up to the time he was wounded at Fair Oaks, in the Peninsula campaign. He was in the Gettysburg campaign as a leader of cavalry, being wounded three times in the battle. In 1864 he became especially distinguished for his fights against Sheridan in the Shenandoah. The ability displayed there was rewarded by Lee, who made him commander of all the cavalry in the Army of Northern Virginia. Hampton fought to the end, commanding the cavalry in Johnston's army at the time of his surrender. Even more creditable was his record after the war. Returning to the beautiful home where he had been reared in the "feudal magnificence" of the ante-bellum system, he devoted his energies to rebuilding the South and securing full acceptance of the issues of the war. In 1876 he became Governor of South Carolina, and from 1878 to 1891 served as United States Senator. His career bears out Grady's speech.

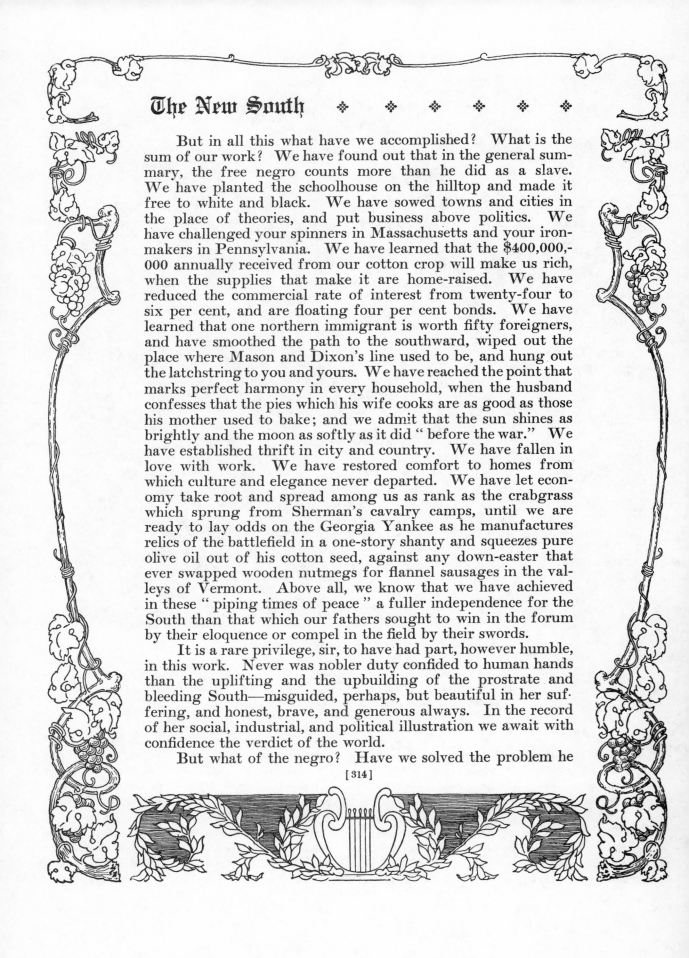

But in all this what have we accomplished? What is the sum of our work? We have found out that in the general summary, the free negro counts more than he did as a slave. We have planted the schoolhouse on the hilltop and made it free to white and black. We have sowed towns and cities in the place of theories, and put business above politics. We have challenged your spinners in Massachusetts and your iron-makers in Pennsylvania. We have learned that the $400,000,-000 annually received from our cotton crop will make us rich, when the supplies that make it are home-raised. We have reduced the commercial rate of interest from twenty-four to six per cent, and are floating four per cent bonds. We have learned that one northern immigrant is worth fifty foreigners, and have smoothed the path to the southward, wiped out the place where Mason and Dixon's line used to be, and hung out the latchstring to you and yours. We have reached the point that marks perfect harmony in every household, when the husband confesses that the pies which his wife cooks are as good as those his mother used to bake; and we admit that the sun shines as brightly and the moon as softly as it did "before the war." We have established thrift in city and country. We have fallen in love with work. We have restored comfort to homes from which culture and elegance never departed. We have let economy take root and spread among us as rank as the crabgrass which sprung from Sherman's cavalry camps, until we are ready to lay odds on the Georgia Yankee as he manufactures relics of the battlefield in a one-story shanty and squeezes pure olive oil out of his cotton seed, against any down-easter that ever swapped wooden nutmegs for flannel sausages in the valleys of Vermont. Above all, we know that we have achieved in these "piping times of peace" a fuller independence for the South than that which our fathers sought to win in the forum by their eloquence or compel in the field by their swords.

It is a rare privilege, sir, to have had part, however humble, in this work. Never was nobler duty confided to human hands than the uplifting and the upbuilding of the prostrate and bleeding South—misguided, perhaps, but beautiful in her suffering, and honest, brave, and generous always. In the record of her social, industrial, and political illustration we await with confidence the verdict of the world.

But what of the negro? Have we solved the problem he

SHOT–RIDDLED HOMES IN FREDERICKSBURG, VIRGINIA

How widespread was the condition of affairs described by Grady as confronting the Confederate soldier on his return home, appears in such pictures. The havoc was the result of Burnside's bombardment of December 11, 1862. When the Confederate sharpshooters from the roofs and windows of the houses in Fredericksburg opened fire on the pontoniers, the Federal artillery at once returned the fire, at 7 A.M., and continued it incessantly until one o'clock in the afternoon. Despite a bombardment which laid the town in ruins, volunteers from the Seventh Michigan and Nineteenth Massachusetts finally had to be sent over to drive off the stubborn sharpshooters.

presents, or progressed in honor and equity toward solution?
Let the record speak to the point. No section shows a more
prosperous laboring population than the negroes of the South,
none in fuller sympathy with the employing and land-owning
class. He shares our school fund, has the fullest protection of
our laws and the friendship of our people. Self-interest, as well
as honor, demand that he should have this. Our future, our
very existence depends upon our working out this problem in
full and exact justice. We understand that when Lincoln
signed the emancipation proclamation, your victory was assured, for he then committed you to the cause of human liberty,
against which the arms of man cannot prevail—while those of
our statesmen who trusted to make slavery the corner-stone of
the Confederacy doomed us to defeat as far as they could, committing us to a cause that reason could not defend or the sword
maintain in the sight of advancing civilization.

Had Mr. Toombs said, which he did not say, " that he
would call the roll of his slaves at the foot of Bunker Hill," he
would have been foolish, for he might have known that whenever slavery became entangled in war it must perish, and that
the chattel in human flesh ended forever in New England when
your fathers—not to be blamed for parting with what didn't
pay—sold their slaves to our fathers—not to be praised for
knowing a paying thing when they saw it. The relations of
the Southern people with the negro are close and cordial. We
remember with what fidelity for four years he guarded our defenseless women and children, whose husbands and fathers were
fighting against his freedom. To his eternal credit be it said
that whenever he struck a blow for his own liberty he fought
in open battle, and when at last he raised his black and humble
hands that the shackles might be struck off, those hands were
innocent of wrong against his helpless charges, and worthy to
be taken in loving grasp by every man who honors loyalty and
devotion. Ruffians have maltreated him, rascals have misled
him, philanthropists established a bank for him, but the South,
with the North, protests against injustice to this simple and
sincere people. To liberty and enfranchisement is as far as the
law can carry the negro. The rest must be left to conscience and
common sense. It must be left to those among whom his lot is
cast, with whom he is indissolubly connected, and whose prosperity depends upon their possessing his intelligent sympathy

[316]

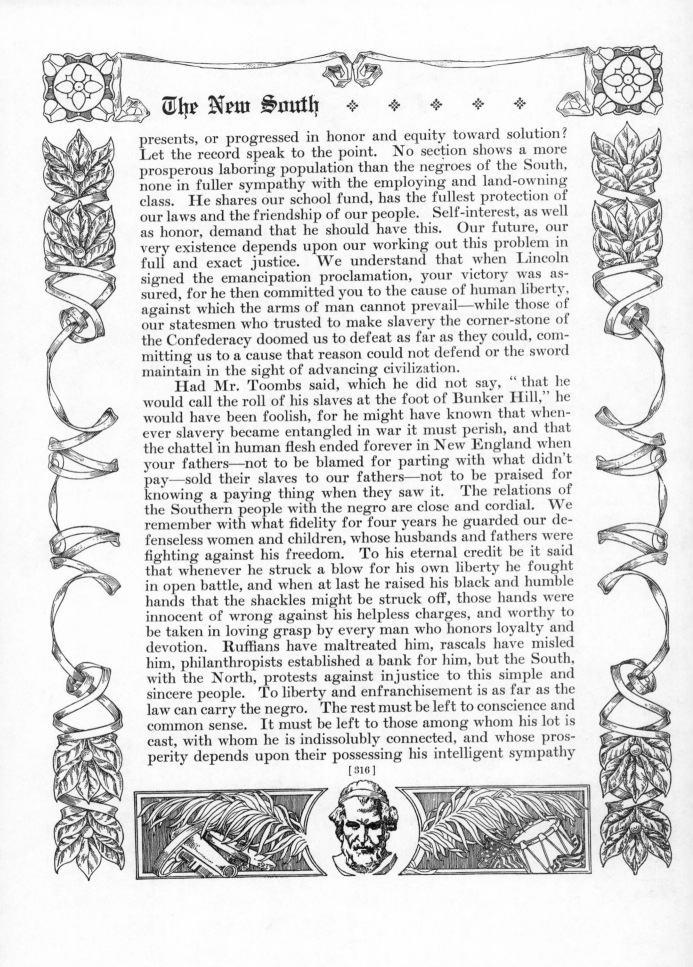

WHAT THE CONFEDERATE SOLDIER FOUND—A MISSISSIPPI VALLEY MILL

This gloomy scene is a reminder of the fate that befell the Mississippi valley and many another fertile region of the South.   Western raids throughout the war destroyed hundreds of miles of railroad, burned the cars, and blew up the locomotives, fell upon tanneries and shoe-factories, wrecked arsenals, captured commissary stores, put the torch to cotton-factories, and in every possible way crippled the resources of the South for continuing the struggle.   General Grant tells of an incident at his capture of Jackson, Mississippi, on May 14, 1863.   Sherman was instructed to destroy "the railroads, bridges, factories, workshops, arsenals, and everything valuable for the support of the enemy."   The two generals went into a very valuable cotton-factory, where the machinery was running at full speed and all the hands were at work, as if the city had not fallen into the hands of the enemy.   While the military leaders stood there, hundreds of yards of canvas rolled out from the looms with the stamp of the Confederate Quartermaster's Department upon it.   It was to be used in tents.   After looking on the busy scene for a few minutes, the order was given for the place to be vacated, and within an hour the building and its warehouses were in flames.   The next day the work of destruction was so thoroughly accomplished that "Jackson as a railroad center or Government depot of stores and military factories," it was reported, could be of little use for at least six months.

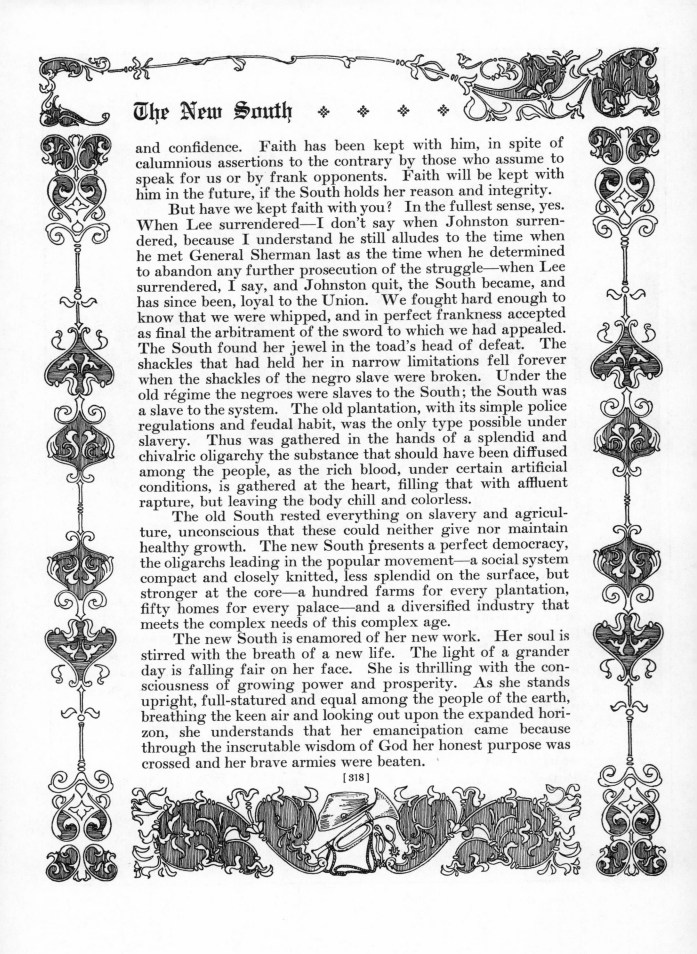

The New South ✦ ✦ ✦ ✦

and confidence. Faith has been kept with him, in spite of calumnious assertions to the contrary by those who assume to speak for us or by frank opponents. Faith will be kept with him in the future, if the South holds her reason and integrity.

But have we kept faith with you? In the fullest sense, yes. When Lee surrendered—I don't say when Johnston surrendered, because I understand he still alludes to the time when he met General Sherman last as the time when he determined to abandon any further prosecution of the struggle—when Lee surrendered, I say, and Johnston quit, the South became, and has since been, loyal to the Union. We fought hard enough to know that we were whipped, and in perfect frankness accepted as final the arbitrament of the sword to which we had appealed. The South found her jewel in the toad's head of defeat. The shackles that had held her in narrow limitations fell forever when the shackles of the negro slave were broken. Under the old régime the negroes were slaves to the South; the South was a slave to the system. The old plantation, with its simple police regulations and feudal habit, was the only type possible under slavery. Thus was gathered in the hands of a splendid and chivalric oligarchy the substance that should have been diffused among the people, as the rich blood, under certain artificial conditions, is gathered at the heart, filling that with affluent rapture, but leaving the body chill and colorless.

The old South rested everything on slavery and agriculture, unconscious that these could neither give nor maintain healthy growth. The new South presents a perfect democracy, the oligarchs leading in the popular movement—a social system compact and closely knitted, less splendid on the surface, but stronger at the core—a hundred farms for every plantation, fifty homes for every palace—and a diversified industry that meets the complex needs of this complex age.

The new South is enamored of her new work. Her soul is stirred with the breath of a new life. The light of a grander day is falling fair on her face. She is thrilling with the consciousness of growing power and prosperity. As she stands upright, full-statured and equal among the people of the earth, breathing the keen air and looking out upon the expanded horizon, she understands that her emancipation came because through the inscrutable wisdom of God her honest purpose was crossed and her brave armies were beaten.

A COLONIAL MANSION IN RUINS—1865

Grady's returning Confederate soldier was a private in the ranks. But Southern officers, as well, rich and poor alike, found desolation at home in 1865. Compare with the preceding scenes the ruins of this handsome residence of the Pinckneys, one of the most distinguished Charleston families. It stood in the middle of a whole square, commanding a fine view of Charleston Harbor. When James Glenn arrived in 1743 as royal governor, he selected this mansion as his official residence. It was occupied in succession by Governors Glenn, Lyttleton, Boone, and Lord Charles Montague, while Charles Pinckney was in Europe and his son was attaining majority. During those years there were many stately dinners here. These ruins were the scene of Charleston's gayest colonial life.

The New South ✦ ✦ ✦ ✦ ✦ ✦

This is said in no spirit of time-serving or apology. The South has nothing for which to apologize. She believes that the late struggle between the States was war and not rebellion, revolution and not conspiracy, and that her convictions were as honest as yours. I should be unjust to the dauntless spirit of the South and to my own convictions if I did not make this plain in this presence. The South has nothing to take back. In my native town of Athens is a monument that crowns its central hill—a plain, white shaft. Deep cut into its shining side is a name dear to me above the names of men, that of a brave and simple man who died in a brave and simple faith. Not for all the glories of New England, from Plymouth Rock all the way, would I exchange the heritage he left me in his soldier's death. To the foot of that shaft I shall send my children's children to reverence him who ennobled their name with his heroic blood. But, sir, speaking from the shadow of that memory which I honor as I do nothing else on earth, I say that the cause in which he suffered and for which he gave his life was adjudged by higher and fuller wisdom than his or mine, and I am glad that the omniscient God held the balance of battle in His Almighty hand and that human slavery was swept forever from American soil—the American·Union was saved from the wreck of war.

This message, Mr. President, comes to you from consecrated ground. Every foot of soil about the city in which I live is sacred as a battle-ground of the republic. Every hill that invests it is hallowed to you by the blood of your brothers who died for your victory, and doubly hallowed to us by the blood of those who died hopeless, but undaunted, in defeat— sacred soil to all of us, rich with memories that make us purer and stronger and better, silent but stanch witnesses in its red desolation of the matchless valor of American hearts and the deathless glory of American arms,—speaking an eloquent witness, in its white peace and prosperity, to the indissoluble union of American States and the imperishable brotherhood of the American people.

Now, what answer has New England to this message? Will she permit the prejudice of war to remain in the hearts of the conquerors, when it has died in the hearts of the conquered? Will she transmit this prejudice to the next generation, that in their hearts, which never felt the generous ardor of conflict, it

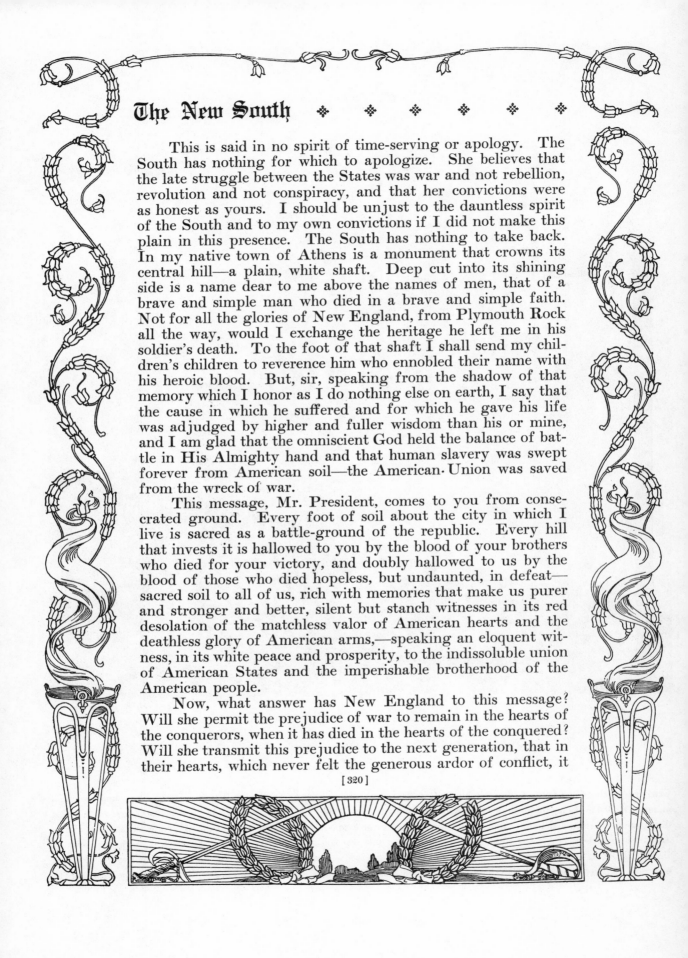

THE PINCKNEY HOUSE IN CHARLESTON, SOUTH CAROLINA

Here lived from 1769 the noted Charles Cotesworth Pinckney, after his return from school at Westminster and Oxford. When the Revolution began he discontinued his practice of law and led a provincial regiment. For two years he was one of Washingon's aides-de-camp. In 1780 his wife was evicted from the mansion by British troops when Sir Henry Clinton and Lord Cornwallis occupied the town. The history of his dwelling-place terminated in December, 1861. A fire began on a wharf by the Cooper River, where some Negroes were cooking their supper. It was blown into a hay store near by; it then spread swiftly before the gale to the banks of the Ashley, leaving behind nothing but a smoking wilderness of ruins. The Pinckney mansion stood in its path. The able-bodied men of the town were in service or drilling in the camps at the race-course, and little could be done to check its course till it reached the Ashley River.

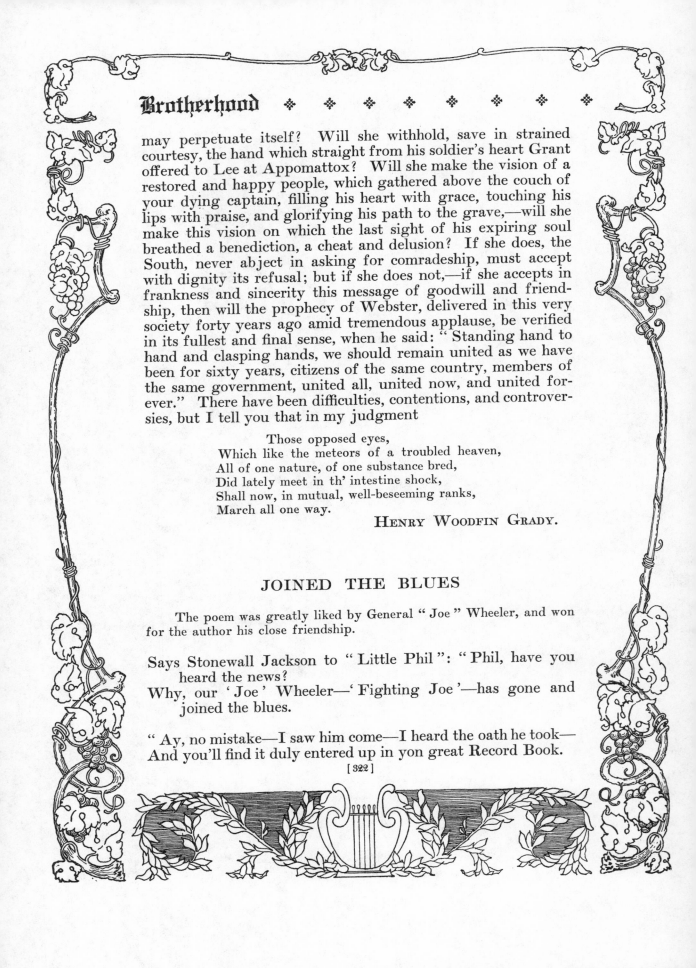

may perpetuate itself? Will she withhold, save in strained courtesy, the hand which straight from his soldier's heart Grant offered to Lee at Appomattox? Will she make the vision of a restored and happy people, which gathered above the couch of your dying captain, filling his heart with grace, touching his lips with praise, and glorifying his path to the grave,—will she make this vision on which the last sight of his expiring soul breathed a benediction, a cheat and delusion? If she does, the South, never abject in asking for comradeship, must accept with dignity its refusal; but if she does not,—if she accepts in frankness and sincerity this message of goodwill and friendship, then will the prophecy of Webster, delivered in this very society forty years ago amid tremendous applause, be verified in its fullest and final sense, when he said: "Standing hand to hand and clasping hands, we should remain united as we have been for sixty years, citizens of the same country, members of the same government, united all, united now, and united forever." There have been difficulties, contentions, and controversies, but I tell you that in my judgment

> Those opposed eyes,
> Which like the meteors of a troubled heaven,
> All of one nature, of one substance bred,
> Did lately meet in th' intestine shock,
> Shall now, in mutual, well-beseeming ranks,
> March all one way.

HENRY WOODFIN GRADY.

JOINED THE BLUES

The poem was greatly liked by General "Joe" Wheeler, and won for the author his close friendship.

Says Stonewall Jackson to "Little Phil": "Phil, have you heard the news?
Why, our 'Joe' Wheeler—'Fighting Joe'—has gone and joined the blues.

"Ay, no mistake—I saw him come—I heard the oath he took—
And you'll find it duly entered up in yon great Record Book.

"FROM THE ASHES LEFT US IN 1864"

The ruins of Atlanta here are the very scenes to which Grady was referring. The destruction of its industries Sherman declared to be a military necessity. Atlanta contained the largest foundries and machine-shops south of Richmond. It formed a railroad center for the central South, where provisions might be gathered and forwarded to the armies at the front. To destroy the Atlanta shops and railroads would therefore cripple the resources of the Confederacy. Railroads had been torn up to the south of the city

even before its capture on September 2, 1864. But it was not until November 15th, when Sherman had completed all his arrangements for the march to the sea, that on every road leading into Atlanta the ties were burned, the rails torn up and then twisted so as to render them permanently useless. The buildings were first burned and the walls afterward razed to the ground. In the fire thus started the exploding of ammunition could be heard all night in the midst of the ruins. The flames soon spread to a block of stores and soon the heart of the city was burned out completely.

RUINS IN RICHMOND

AS THE WAR WAS

DRAWING

TO A CLOSE

ON THE PAGE FACING,

THE SAME SPOT

FORTY-SIX YEARS

LATER

THE USELESS SIGNALS

A RICHMOND PAPER MILL IN 1865

These faithful reproductions show the desolation war leaves in its
track. The paper mill is a mass of ruins, with no power to turn the
burnt and broken rollers. The railroad track is a heap of twisted
wreckage, with the blasted engine hopelessly beyond repair. Of
the bridge nothing remains but a row of granite pillars and the misplaced and useless signals. These views exhibit the stupendous task
that all over the South awaited the returning Confederate soldier who
had received his parole at the final surrenders and begun life again.

THE END OF ITS SERVICE

Below, Grady's declaration finds a vivid example. On the exact spot shown in the central picture of the opposite page has risen a modern mill to replace the blackened ruins. In place of the twisted rails are three well graded tracks. A reënforced concrete bridge replaces the broken causeway. In the distance the tall stacks of a busy city rise against the sky. The South is once more prosperous. Its sons have attacked the problems of the new era and have placed their section upon a basis for permanent advancement. The currents of national life are flowing through every part of its spacious territory, and it feels itself an integral and inseparable

"IT IS A RARE PRIVILEGE, SIR,

TO HAVE HAD ANY PART,

HOWEVER HUMBLE,

IN THIS WORK"

part of the mighty American republic. The hundreds of scenes in this and the preceding volumes have been from photographs taken in war time. Now that the volume is ended and the records of the campaigns are closed, an exception is made to show what the South has accomplished in less than half a century. Proud as all are of the devotion and courage of the South during the four years of war, prouder still should every American be of the splendid record of her peaceful victories in the forty years succeeding. For she has wrung victory from defeat and has provided for the whole world the spectacle of an enduring triumph—a progress without parallel.

FORTY-SIX YEARS AFTER—THE RICHMOND PAPER MILL AND RAILROAD REBUILT

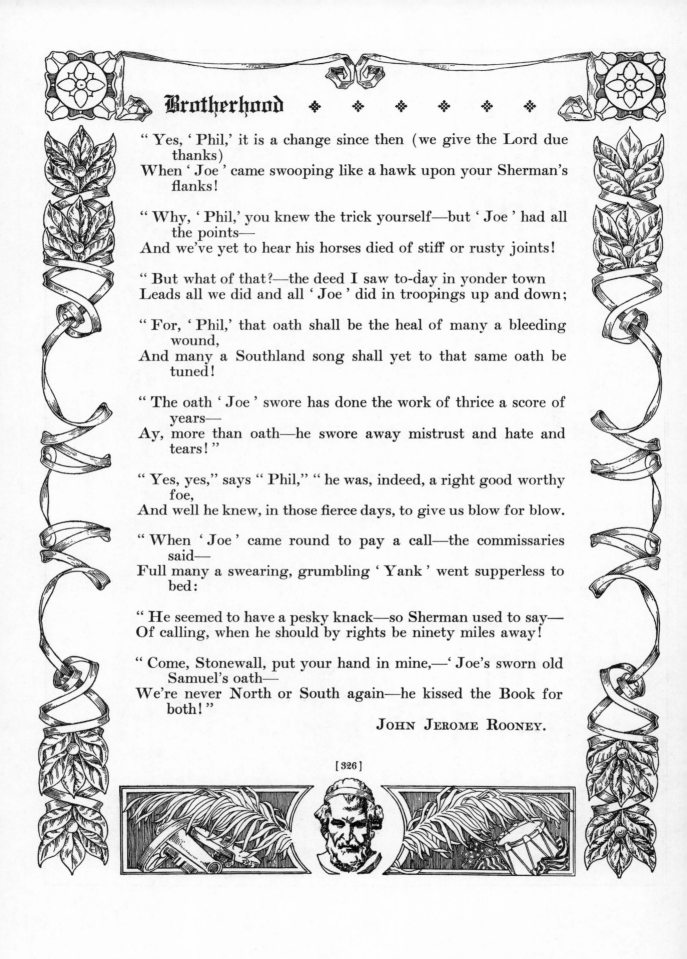

Brotherhood ✦ ✦ ✦ ✦ ✦ ✦

"Yes, 'Phil,' it is a change since then (we give the Lord due
thanks)
When 'Joe' came swooping like a hawk upon your Sherman's
flanks!

"Why, 'Phil,' you knew the trick yourself—but 'Joe' had all
the points—
And we've yet to hear his horses died of stiff or rusty joints!

"But what of that?—the deed I saw to-day in yonder town
Leads all we did and all 'Joe' did in troopings up and down;

"For, 'Phil,' that oath shall be the heal of many a bleeding
wound,
And many a Southland song shall yet to that same oath be
tuned!

"The oath 'Joe' swore has done the work of thrice a score of
years—
Ay, more than oath—he swore away mistrust and hate and
tears!"

"Yes, yes," says "Phil," "he was, indeed, a right good worthy
foe,
And well he knew, in those fierce days, to give us blow for blow.

"When 'Joe' came round to pay a call—the commissaries
said—
Full many a swearing, grumbling 'Yank' went supperless to
bed:

"He seemed to have a pesky knack—so Sherman used to say—
Of calling, when he should by rights be ninety miles away!

"Come, Stonewall, put your hand in mine,—'Joe's sworn old
Samuel's oath—
We're never North or South again—he kissed the Book for
both!"

JOHN JEROME ROONEY.

[326]

"JOE'S SWORN OLD SAMUEL'S OATH"

A post-bellum portrait of General Joseph Wheeler has been chosen to appear here as well as of "that loyal old Reb, Fitzhugh Lee"—in order to illustrate closely the poem. General Joseph Wheeler, a native of Georgia, was a brilliant Confederate cavalry leader in the Civil War. He graduated from West Point in 1859, entered the Confederate service in April, 1861, and fought at the head of a brigade at Shiloh. In the same year he was transferred to the cavalry. In 1863, as major-general, he commanded the cavalry at the battles of Chickamauga and Chattanooga, and protected Bragg's retreat southward. In 1864 he obstructed Sherman in his advance on Atlanta, as alluded to in the poem, and in the march to the sea. In 1865, as lieutenant-general, he commanded the cavalry in Johnston's army up to the surrender.

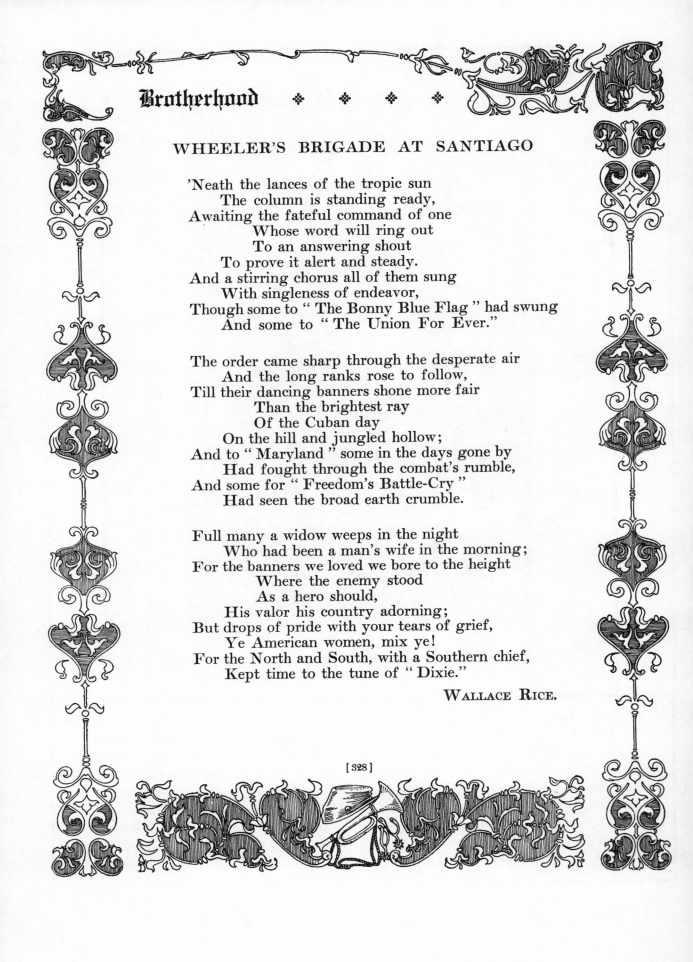

WHEELER'S BRIGADE AT SANTIAGO

'Neath the lances of the tropic sun
 The column is standing ready,
Awaiting the fateful command of one
  Whose word will ring out
  To an answering shout
 To prove it alert and steady.
And a stirring chorus all of them sung
 With singleness of endeavor,
Though some to " The Bonny Blue Flag " had swung
 And some to " The Union For Ever."

The order came sharp through the desperate air
 And the long ranks rose to follow,
Till their dancing banners shone more fair
  Than the brightest ray
  Of the Cuban day
 On the hill and jungled hollow;
And to " Maryland " some in the days gone by
 Had fought through the combat's rumble,
And some for " Freedom's Battle-Cry "
 Had seen the broad earth crumble.

Full many a widow weeps in the night
 Who had been a man's wife in the morning;
For the banners we loved we bore to the height
  Where the enemy stood
  As a hero should,
 His valor his country adorning;
But drops of pride with your tears of grief,
 Ye American women, mix ye!
For the North and South, with a Southern chief,
 Kept time to the tune of " Dixie."

WALLACE RICE.

"FOR THE NORTH AND THE SOUTH, WITH A SOUTHRON CHIEF,

KEPT TIME TO THE TUNE OF 'DIXIE'"

These two figures of '61 and '65 have a peculiar appropriateness for Wallace Rice's "Wheeler's Brigade at Santiago." They recall in detail the fullness of the warlike preparations in those distant days. The Union soldier is equipped with new uniform and shining musket, ready to repel any invader of the Nation's capital. More than once before the close of hostilities such services had been needed in the circle of forts that surrounded the city. The officer stands erect with the intensity and eagerness that characterized Southern troops in battle. A generation later, the Spanish war of 1898 became a magnificent occasion for proof that the hostile relations and feelings of the '60's had melted away. Those who had once stood in opposing ranks, and their sons with them, in '98 marched and fought shoulder to shoulder, inspired by love of the same country and devoted to the same high principles of human freedom.

UNION SOLDIER

ON GUARD OVER A PRISONER

IN WASHINGTON

1865

CONFEDERATE OFFICER

OF THE WASHINGTON ARTILLERY

OF NEW ORLEANS

1861

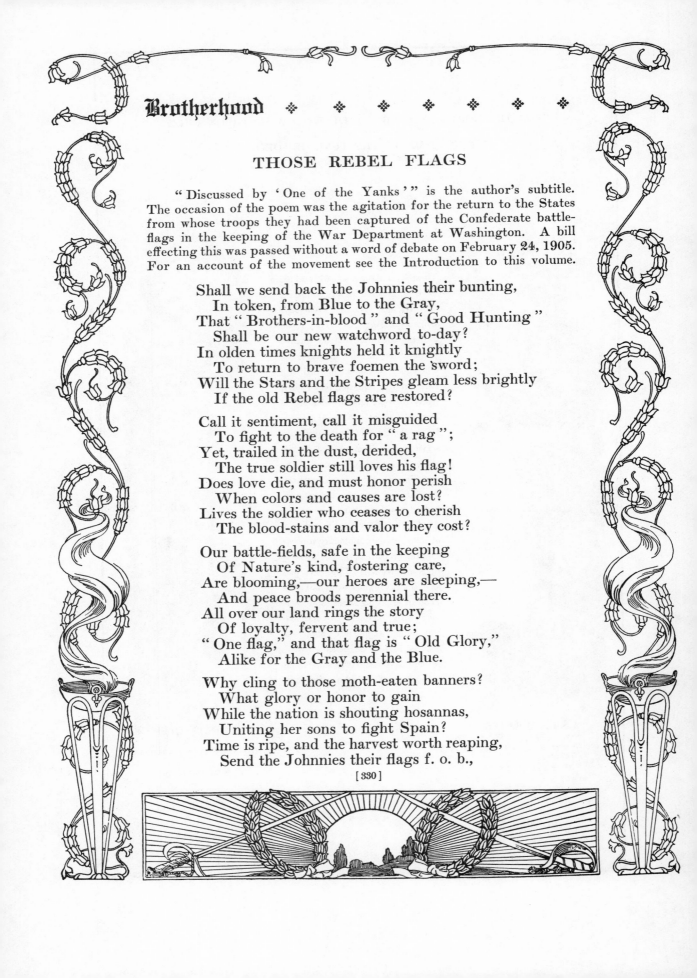

Brotherhood ✦ ✦ ✦ ✦ ✦ ✦ ✦

THOSE REBEL FLAGS

" Discussed by ' One of the Yanks ' " is the author's subtitle.
The occasion of the poem was the agitation for the return to the States
from whose troops they had been captured of the Confederate battle-
flags in the keeping of the War Department at Washington. A bill
effecting this was passed without a word of debate on February 24, 1905.
For an account of the movement see the Introduction to this volume.

Shall we send back the Johnnies their bunting,
    In token, from Blue to the Gray,
That " Brothers-in-blood " and " Good Hunting "
    Shall be our new watchword to-day?
In olden times knights held it knightly
    To return to brave foemen the 'sword;
Will the Stars and the Stripes gleam less brightly
    If the old Rebel flags are restored?

Call it sentiment, call it misguided
    To fight to the death for " a rag ";
Yet, trailed in the dust, derided,
    The true soldier still loves his flag!
Does love die, and must honor perish
    When colors and causes are lost?
Lives the soldier who ceases to cherish
    The blood-stains and valor they cost?

Our battle-fields, safe in the keeping
    Of Nature's kind, fostering care,
Are blooming,—our heroes are sleeping,—
    And peace broods perennial there.
All over our land rings the story
    Of loyalty, fervent and true;
" One flag," and that flag is " Old Glory,"
    Alike for the Gray and the Blue.

Why cling to those moth-eaten banners?
    What glory or honor to gain
While the nation is shouting hosannas,
    Uniting her sons to fight Spain?
Time is ripe, and the harvest worth reaping,
    Send the Johnnies their flags f. o. b.,

[330]

"THAT LOYAL 'OLD REB' FITZHUGH LEE"

Since Jewett's lines apply to the Spanish War period, a portrait of "Fitz" Lee has been selected, taken many years after his days in the saddle as a Confederate cavalry leader.   The nephew of Robert E. Lee was likewise a graduate of West Point, and was instructor in cavalry there from May, 1860, to the outbreak of the war.   In nearly all the movements of the Army of Northern Virginia, he was a dashing cavalry leader.   From March, 1865, to his surrender to General Meade at Farmville, April 7th, he was commander of all the cavalry of the army. That he was "loyal" appeared as early as 1874, when he delivered a patriotic address at Bunker Hill.   His attitude on the return of Confederate battle-flags during his term as Governor of Virginia (1886–1890) is touched on in the Introduction to this volume.   He served his country as consul-general at Havana from 1896, whence he was recalled in April, 1898, to be appointed major-general of volunteers and given command of the Seventh Army Corps.   He too had "joined the Blues."   Moreover, after the war he was made military governor of Havana and subsequently placed in command of the Department of Missouri.   His death in 1905 was mourned nationally.

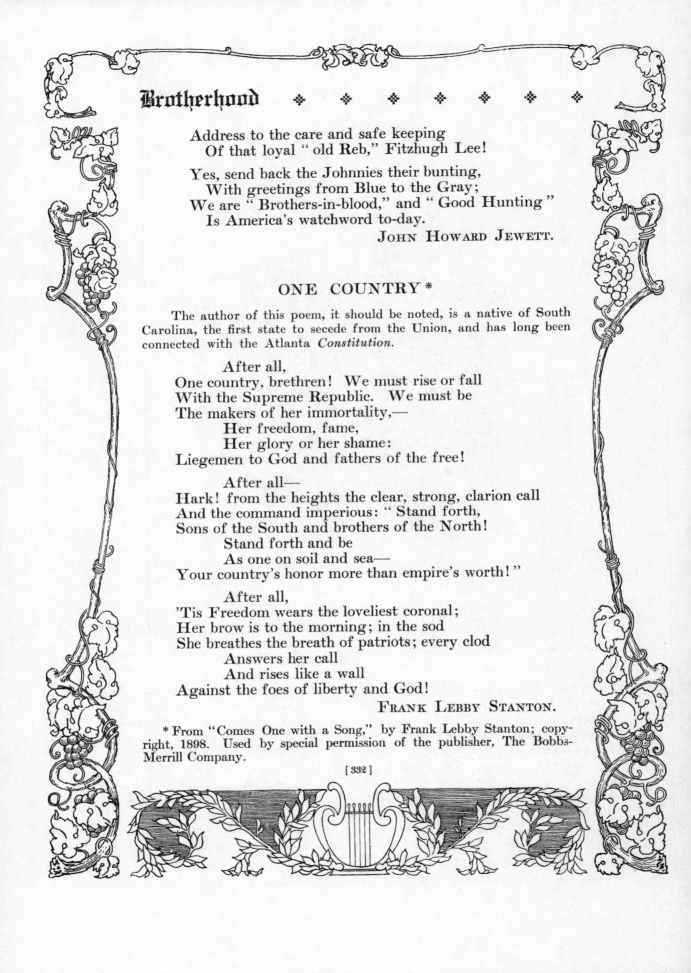

Brotherhood ❖ ❖ ❖ ❖ ❖ ❖ ❖

Address to the care and safe keeping
   Of that loyal " old Reb," Fitzhugh Lee!

Yes, send back the Johnnies their bunting,
   With greetings from Blue to the Gray;
We are " Brothers-in-blood," and " Good Hunting "
   Is America's watchword to-day.

JOHN HOWARD JEWETT.

ONE COUNTRY *

The author of this poem, it should be noted, is a native of South Carolina, the first state to secede from the Union, and has long been connected with the Atlanta *Constitution*.

After all,
One country, brethren! We must rise or fall
With the Supreme Republic. We must be
The makers of her immortality,—
   Her freedom, fame,
   Her glory or her shame:
Liegemen to God and fathers of the free!

After all—
Hark! from the heights the clear, strong, clarion call
And the command imperious: " Stand forth,
Sons of the South and brothers of the North!
   Stand forth and be
   As one on soil and sea—
Your country's honor more than empire's worth! "

After all,
'Tis Freedom wears the loveliest coronal;
Her brow is to the morning; in the sod
She breathes the breath of patriots; every clod
   Answers her call
   And rises like a wall
Against the foes of liberty and God!

FRANK LEBBY STANTON.

* From "Comes One with a Song," by Frank Lebby Stanton; copyright, 1898. Used by special permission of the publisher, The Bobbs-Merrill Company.

"AFTER ALL—ONE COUNTRY"

Here in Charleston, under the sunlight of a cloudless April day, rest the Parrott guns that from Morris Island pulverized the walls of Sumter, that hurled shot and shell across the bay—now silent, "after all." Flecks of shade from the live-oak leaves fall upon the polished barrels that for eighteen months had roared upon the distant foe. Now the silence is broken only by the rustle of the foliage above. Below, the daisies are beginning to hide the newly springing grass. The Stars and Stripes draped above the nearest gun-carriage is once more the flag of the whole American people. Peace has indeed come, and all over the land thanksgiving is ascending like an incense from hearts that have known the anguish of endless separation and the bitterness of unavailing sorrow—thanksgiving, too, for the issue of the conflict, which determined that America should forever wear the coronal of freedom and lead in the vanguard of human liberty.

Although taken long before the days of moving-picture films, this series of photographs preserves the progression of the celebration on April 14, 1865—the fourth anniversary of the evacuation of Sumter. The evening before, the news of Lee's surrender had reached Charleston and made the occasion one of national thanksgiving. The city was gay with flags; patriotic bands filled the air with music, and Dahlgren's fleet opened the day with the full national salute of twenty-one guns from every ship in the harbor. In Fort Sumter the Reverend Matthias Harris, who had helped to raise the flag over the fort, four years before, opened the services with prayer. Dr. Richard S. Storrs read that ever-beautiful passage beginning: "When the Lord turned again the captivity of Zion, we were like them that dream."

RAISING THE NATIONAL FLAG IN SUMTER, JUST FOUR YEARS AFTER ITS EVACUATION

Precisely at noon, General Anderson raised with his own hands the flag which had been lowered in 1861. Long-continued shouting and the boom of guns from every fort about the harbor was the salute to the banner that was held to be a symbol of the restored Union. In the address of Henry Ward Beecher the feeling of brotherhood to the South was prominent. These were his closing words, "We offer to the President of these United States our solemn congratulations that God has sustained his life and health under the unparalleled burdens and sufferings of four bloody years, and permitted him to behold this auspicious consummation of that national unity for which he has waited with so much patience and fortitude, and for which he has labored with such disinterested wisdom."

HENRY WARD BEECHER'S SPEECH OF BROTHERHOOD ON APRIL 14, 1865

WHEN PEACE DWELT AGAIN UPON FORT SUMTER

A spectator before that irregular pile of débris might never imagine that in 1861 Fort Sumter was a formidable work. Its walls then rose to a height of forty feet above high-water. Constructed of the best Carolina gray brick, laid in a mortar of pounded oyster-shells and cement, their thickness of five to ten feet made the stronghold seem impregnable. Despite the appearance in the picture, it proved so. The attack that began the war did very little damage, beyond the burning of the barracks. Two years later, Rear-Admiral Samuel F. Du Pont led a naval attack that was expected to capture the fort with little delay; yet the heavy bombardment made almost no impression. The ironclad that was nearest Sumter, the *Keokuk*, struck ninety times, was so badly injured that it sank the next morning. The *Weehawken* was hit fifty-three times; the *Passaic* thirty-five times, the *Montauk* fourteen times, the *Patapsco*, the fourth vessel in line, forty-seven times; and so on through the entire fleet. The fort, on the other hand, was hardly injured. At one point, where an 11-inch and a 15-inch shell struck at the same point at the same time, the wall was completely breached; on the outside

°THE CRUMBLED WALLS FROM THE SAND BAR—1865

appeared a crater six feet high and eight feet wide. But the destruction shown in the picture was wrought by the bombardment from the land-batteries four months later. General Gillmore's guns opened on August 17th. Major John Johnson in "Battles and Leaders" makes this report of the effect of Gillmore's operations and of the work of the defenders: "When demolished by land-batteries of unprecedented range, the fort endured for more than eighteen months their almost constant fire, and for a hundred days and nights their utmost power until it could with truth be said that it at last tired out, and in this way silenced, the great guns that once had silenced it. From having been a desolate ruin, a shapeless pile of shattered walls and casemates, showing here and there the guns disabled and half-buried in splintered wrecks of carriages, its mounds of rubbish fairly reeking with the smoke and smell of powder, Fort Sumter under fire was transformed within a year into a powerful earthwork, impregnable to assault, and even supporting the other works at the entrance of Charleston harbor with six guns of the heaviest caliber." Above, it is a monument to the wastefulness of warfare.

WITHIN THE DESERTED FORT—1865

Here is the desolation inside the shattered walls of Sumter. The celebration of raising the flag on April 14, 1865, is now in the past. The
benches that had been crowded with listeners eager to catch every word
of the address by Henry Ward Beecher are now empty. The pavilion
in which he spoke is no longer gay with flags. The staff from which
"Old Glory" had floated to the applause of thousands stands bare.
Beyond are the shapeless ruins made by Gillmore's guns. Out in the
bay no ships dressed in flags are to be seen. For the whole nation is in
mourning. On the very evening of the flag-raising the bullet of Booth
had laid low the man through whose patience and statesmanship the
Sumter celebration had become possible. Trials more searching than
those of war awaited his sorrowing people.

APPENDIX

SONGS
OF THE
WAR DAYS

EDITED BY

JEANNE ROBERT FOSTER

"WHEN JOHNNY COMES MARCHING HOME"

THE MOST POPULAR WAR-TIME SONG OF THE MUSTERED-OUT MEN—THUS THEY
LOOKED AS THEY MARCHED HOME FROM TRENCHES AND FORTS, FROM BLOODY BAT-
TLEFIELDS, FROM HOSPITAL AND PRISON—BACK TO CITY, TOWN, AND COUNTRYSIDE

"SUCCESS TO THE ALABAMA"

THE ENGLISH MANOR HOUSE TO WHICH ADMIRAL SEMMES RE-PAIRED AFTER THE FAMOUS BATTLE—HIS CHIEF OFFICER, CAPTAIN KELL, IS STANDING AT THE EXTREME RIGHT.

In this charming photo-graph of Milbrook Manor House near Southampton, Eng-land, appears a scene of 1864 at the quiet country-place to which Admiral Semmes of the Confederate warship, *Ala-bama*, and his chief executive officer, Captain Kell, retired for rest and recuperation after the loss of their vessel in the battle with the U. S. S. *Kear-sarge* off the coast of France. On the right of the picture is Captain Kell, convalescing from his wound in this green, shaded retreat. Exquisitely rendered by the camera are the hoopskirts, the flowing scarfs, and the old-fashioned blouses of the women in the picture. Under a glass the detail comes out with startling reality, and for a moment the atmosphere of the place and the time is re-stored. The beautiful, vine-clad manor house, with the quaint group of women, bring back to remembrance the his-tory of the cruiser and of the *Kearsarge*, and the bravery of the men who fought during the most dramatic naval battle.

Songs of the War Days

Edited by Jeanne Robert Foster

"If a man were permitted to make all the ballads he need not care who should make the laws of a nation."

ANDREW FLETCHER

There is a strange, magical power in songs that spring from the hearts of men passing through great and passionate experience—the power to gather together again in after years a mirage of the emotions that begot them—a remembrance of the enthusiasm that incited men to perilous and heroic deeds. The question of actual literary merit has no place in the consideration of these war-songs; they were chronicles of events; they achieved universality, and on the field of battle they became the sublime pæans of a national crisis. Their words and melodies deserve a place in our records. The songs of the soldier boys, the spirited marching tunes, the sentimental ballads, the outbursts of fiery patriotism, must remain with us a legacy of unfailing inspiration and delight.

WHEN JOHNNY COMES MARCHING HOME

Patrick Sarsfield Gilmore

This rousing war-song was the one most sung by the soldiers returning from service.

When Johnny comes marching home again,
    Hurrah! Hurrah!
We'll give him a hearty welcome then,
    Hurrah! Hurrah!
The men will cheer, the boys will shout,
The ladies they will all turn out.

Chorus—
    And we'll all feel gay,
When Johnny comes marching home.

The old church-bell will peal with joy,
    Hurrah! Hurrah!
To welcome home our darling boy,
    Hurrah! Hurrah!
The village lads and lasses say
With roses they will strew the way.

THE BATTLECRY OF FREEDOM

George Frederick Root

One of the best of the many flag songs written during the war.

Yes, we'll rally round the flag, boys, we'll rally
    once again,
    Shouting the battlecry of freedom,
We will rally from the hillside, we'll gather
    from the plain,
    Shouting the battlecry of freedom.

Chorus—
    The Union forever, hurrah! boys, hurrah!
Down with the traitor, up with the star,

While we rally round the flag, boys,
    Rally once again,
    Shouting the battle cry of Freedom.

We are springing to the call of our
    brothers gone before,
    Shouting the battlecry of freedom.
And we'll fill the vacant ranks with a
    million freemen more,
    Shouting the battlecry of freedom.

MARCHING THROUGH GEORGIA

Henry Clay Work

Written in honor of Sherman's famous march from Atlanta to the sea.

Bring the good old bugle, boys, we'll sing another
    song—
Sing it with a spirit that will start the world
    along—
Sing it as we used to sing it, fifty thousand strong,
While we were marching through Georgia.

Chorus—
    "Hurrah! Hurrah! we bring the jubilee,
    Hurrah! Hurrah! the flag that makes you
      free!"
So we sang the chorus from Atlanta to the sea,
While we were marching through Georgia.

How the darkeys shouted when they heard the
    joyful sound!
How the turkeys gobbled which our commissary
    found!
How the sweet potatoes even started from the
    ground,
While we were marching through Georgia.

THE SOUTHERN MARSEILLAISE

A. E. Blackmar, 1861

This was the rallying song of the Confederacy. It was sung throughout the South as early as 1861 while the soldiers were hurried to Virginia.

Sons of the South, awake to glory,
  A thousand voices bid you rise,
Your children, wives and grandsires hoary,
  Gaze on you now with trusting eyes,
  Gaze on you now with trusting eyes;
Your country every strong arm calling,
  To meet the hireling Northern band
  That comes to desolate the land
With fire and blood and scenes appalling,
  To arms, to arms, ye brave;
  Th' avenging sword unsheath!
March on! March on! All hearts resolved on
  victory or death.
March on! March on! All hearts resolved on
  victory or death.

Now, now, the dangerous storm is rolling,
  Which treacherous brothers madly raise,
The dogs of war let loose, are howling,
  And soon our peaceful towns may blaze,
  And soon our peaceful towns may blaze.
Shall fiends who basely plot our ruin,
  Unchecked, advance with guilty stride
  To spread destruction far and wide,
With Southron's blood their hands embruing?
  To arms, to arms, ye brave!
  Th' avenging sword unsheath!
March on! March on! All hearts resolved on
  victory or death,
March on! March on! All hearts resolved on
  victory or death.

BLUE COATS ARE OVER THE BORDER

Inscribed to Captain Mitchell.

Air—Blue Bonnets are over the Border.

The old song suggested this; a few lines are borrowed from it.

Kentucky's banner spreads
Its folds above our heads;
We are already famous in story.
Mount and make ready then,
Brave Duke and all his men;
Fight for our homes and Kentucky's old glory.

Chorus—

March! March! Brave Duke and all his men!
Haste, brave boys, now quickly march forward in
  order!

March! March! ye men of old Kentuck!
The horrid blue coats are over the border.

Morgan's men have great fame,
There is much in a name;
Ours must shine today as it ever has shone!

"THE SOUTHERN MARSEILLAISE"

These jolly fellows belong to the Fifth Company of the celebrated Washington Artillery. This was a crack regiment of New Orleans, where the Southern Marseillaise was popular, especially at the opening of the war, when this picture was taken. The young Confederates here are relaxing from discipline over their noonday meal. The frying-pan in the hand of the soldier to the right, also the negligent attitudes, reflect a care-free frame of mind. Their uniforms and accouterments still are spick-span and new. But a few weeks later they distinguished themselves at Shiloh.

As it shines o'er our dead,
Who for freedom have bled:
The foe for their deaths have now got to atone.

THE BONNIE BLUE FLAG

Harry Macarthy

South Carolina, the first state to secede from the Union, adopted a blue flag bearing a single white star in the center. Almost simultaneously with this change of flag there appeared the spirited song—"The Bonnie Blue Flag."

We are a band of brothers, and native to the soil,
Fighting for the property we gained by honest
    toil;
And when our rights were threatened, the cry rose
    near and far,
Hurrah for the Bonnie Blue Flag that bears a
    single star!

Chorus—

Hurrah! Hurrah! for Southern Rights, hurrah!
Hurrah! for the Bonnie Blue Flag that bears a
    single star!

As long as the Union was faithful to her trust,
Like friends and like brothers we were kind, we
    were just;
But now when Northern treachery attempts our
    rights to mar,
We hoist on high the Bonnie Blue Flag that bears
    a single star.

VOLUNTEER SONG

Written for the Ladies' Military Fair held at New Orleans, 1861.
Published in *New Orleans Picayune*, April 28th, 1861, and sung
by the regiments departing for Virginia.

1

" Go soldiers, arm you for the fight,
    God shield the cause of Justice, Right;
    May all return with victory crowned,
    May every heart with joy abound,
    May each deserve the laurel crown,
    Nor one to meet his lady's frown.

2

" Your cause is good, 'tis honor bright,
    'Tis virtue, country, home and right;
    Then should you die for love of these,
    We'll waft your names upon the breeze:
    The waves will sing your lullaby,
    Your country mourn your latest sigh."

WE'LL BE FREE IN MARYLAND

ROBERT E. HOLTZ, January 30, 1862

During the years of the war nearly every musician was intent
on composing a new national song. Of the many compositions
offered the public, curiously enough, practically none of the more
ambitious attempts survive, while catchy doggerel such as "We'll
Be Free In Maryland" is still sung far and wide.

The boys down south in Dixie's land,
The boys down south in Dixie's land,
The boys down south in Dixie's land,
Will come and rescue Maryland.

Chorus—

If you will join the Dixie band,
Here's my heart and here's my hand,
If you will join the Dixie band;
We're fighting for a home.

We'll rally to Jeff Davis true,
Beauregard and Johnston, too,
Magruder, Price, and General Bragg,
And give three cheers for the Southern flag.

SLEEPING FOR THE FLAG

HENRY CLAY WORK

Henry C. Work's songs shared popularity during the war with
the melodies of Stephen Foster. "Sleeping For The Flag," "King-
dom Coming," "Brave Boys Are They," and "Marching Through
Georgia" were sung to glory in the '60's.

When the boys come home in triumph, brother,
With the laurels they shall gain;
When we go to give them welcome, brother,
We shall look for you in vain.
We shall wait for your returning, brother,
You were set forever free;
For your comrades left you sleeping, brother,
Underneath a Southern tree.

Chorus—

Sleeping to waken in this weary world no more;
Sleeping for your true lov'd country, brother,
Sleeping for the flag you bore.

You who were the first on duty, brother,
When " to arms " your leader cried,—
You have left the ranks forever,
You have laid your arms aside,
From the awful scenes of battle, brother,
You were set forever free;
When your comrades left you sleeping, brother,
Underneath the Southern tree.

WE ARE COMING, FATHER ABRAHAM

JAMES SLOAN GIBBONS

This song was written in 1862 just after Lincoln had issued his
call for 300,000 volunteers to fill the ranks of the army. It
was first printed in the *Evening Post*, July 16, 1862 and was
afterwards sung by the famous Hutchinson family. Lincoln
listened with bowed head to the song at the White House one
summer morning in 1864.

We are coming, Father Abraham, three hundred
    thousand more,
From Mississippi's winding stream and from New
    England's shore;

We leave our ploughs and workshops, our wives
and children dear,
With hearts too full for utterance, with but a
single tear;
We dare not look behind us, but steadfastly
before:
We are coming, Father Abraham, three hundred
thousand more!

Chorus—
We are coming, we are coming, our Union to
restore:

division on the battlefield of Chickamauga. It is said to have
been sung by Captain Terry's regiment on the battlefield just
previous to the actual engagement.

The morning star is paling; the camp fires flicker
low;
Our steeds are madly neighing; for the bugle bids
us go:
So put the foot in stirrup and shake the bridle
free,
For today the Texas Rangers must cross the
Tennessee.

"FATHER ABRAHAM"

This photograph shows some of the members of the Twenty-second New York Infantry, who fought at the Second Battle of
Bull Run, Antietam, and Chancellorsville. It lost during service eleven officers and sixty-two men killed and mortally wounded
and one officer and twenty-eight enlisted men by disease. Notwithstanding, many of these men were among the first to enlist
again when Lincoln issued his call for 300,000 volunteers to fill the ranks of the army, a call that gave rise to the famous song of
that year, "We're Coming Father Abraham, Three Hundred Thousand Strong." Here they are at Harper's Ferry in '62 enjoying the luxury of a visit from a lady whose light gown is attractively spread out over her ample hoop-skirt at the right of the picture.
It is interesting to study the formal manner in which the men are holding their rifles, and also the grouping around the drum.

We are coming, Father Abraham, three hundred
thousand more,
We are coming, Father Abraham, three hundred
thousand more.

You have called us, and we're coming, by Richmond's bloody tide
To lay us down, for Freedom's sake, our brothers'
bones beside;
Or from foul treason's savage grasp to wrench the
murderous blade,
And in the face of foreign foes its fragments to
parade.
Six hundred thousand loyal men and true have
gone before:
We are coming, Father Abraham, three hundred
thousand more!

SONG OF THE TEXAS RANGERS
Mrs. J. D. Young
Air: *The Yellow Rose of Texas.*
This song was dedicated to Captain Dave Terry, a Texas
Ranger, who was conspicuous for bravery in General Wharton's

With Wharton for our leader, we'll chase the das-
tard foe,
Till our horses bathe their fetlocks in the deep,
blue Ohio.

'Tis joy to be a Ranger! to fight for dear Southland!
'Tis joy to follow Wharton, with his gallant,
trusty band!
'Tis joy to see our Harrison plunge, like a meteor
bright,
Into the thickest of the fray, and deal his deadly
might.
O! who'd not be a Ranger and follow Wharton's
cry!
And battle for his country, and, if needs be, die?

THE ALABAMA
Words by E. King   Music by F. W. Rasier
While the greater number of naval war songs belongs to the
North, crystallizing around the names of Farragut and Winslow,
the heroism displayed by the small, scantily equipped Confederate
Navy, brought forth several lyrical tributes. This roystering

sea-song was dedicated to "Gallant Admiral Semmes of the *Alabama* and to the officers and seamen of the C. S. Navy."

> The wind blows off yon rocky shore,
> Boys, set your sails all free:
> And soon the booming cannon's roar
> Shall ring out merrily.
> Run up your bunting, caught a-peak,
> And swear, lads, to defend her:
> 'Gainst every foe, where'er we go,
> Our motto—" No surrender."

Chorus—

> Then sling the bowl, drink every soul
> A toast to the *Alabama*,
> Whate'er our lot, through storm or shot,
> Here's success to the *Alabama*.

THE SOUTHERN SOLDIER BOY

AIR: *The Boy with the Auburn Hair.*

As sung by Miss Sallie Partington, in the "Virginia Cavalier," Richmond, Va., 1863. Composed by Captain G. W. Alexander. The sentiments of this song pleased the Confederate Soldiers, and for more than a year, the New Richmond Theater was nightly filled by "Blockade Rebels," who greeted with wild hurrahs, "Miss Sallie" the prima donna of the Confederacy.

> Bob Roebuck is my sweetheart's name,
> He's off to the wars and gone,
> He's fighting for his Nannie dear,
> His sword is buckled on;
> He's fighting for his own true love,
> His foes he does defy;
> He is the darling of my heart,
> My Southern soldier boy.

Chorus—

> Yo! ho! yo! ho! yo! ho! ho! ho! ho! ho! ho!
> He is my only joy,
> He is the darling of my heart,
> My Southern soldier boy.

"THE ZOUAVES"

J. HOWARD WAINWRIGHT

Published in New York *Evening Post*, 1861.

"The Zouaves" was one of the many spirited songs sung in memory of Col. Ephraim E. Ellsworth, of the New York Fire Zouaves. The Brooklyn Zouaves attained a place in history at the first day's battle at Gettysburg, by their efficiency under fire and the bravery of their Colonel.

> Onward, Zouaves,—Ellsworth's spirit leads us;
> Onward, Zouaves, for our country needs us;
> Onward, Zouaves, for our banner floats o'er us;
> Onward Zouaves, for the foe is before us.

Chorus—

> Onward Zouaves!
> Do nothing by halves:
> Home to the hilt, with the bay'net, Zouaves.

THE SONGS OF STEPHEN C. FOSTER

Stephen C. Foster, an American song-writer of Irish descent, was the most famous American folk-song writer of his day. While many of the songs antedate the actual years of the war, they were sung far and wide throughout the struggle and have continued to be popular down to the present day. Half a million copies were sold of " Swanee Rubber," and as many more of " My Old Kentucky Home " and " Massa's in the Cold, Cold Ground."

MY OLD KENTUCKY HOME, GOOD NIGHT

> The sun shines bright in the old Kentucky home;
> 'Tis summer, the darkeys are gay,
> The corn-top 's ripe and the meadow 's in the
>   bloom,
> While the birds make music all the day.
> The young folks roll on the little cabin floor,
> All merry, all happy and bright;
> By-'n-by hard times comes a-knocking at the
>   door:—
> Then my old Kentucky home, good-night!

Chorus—
> Weep no more, my lady,
> Oh! weep no more today!
> We will sing one song for the old Kentucky home,
> For the old Kentucky home, far away.

OLD FOLKS AT HOME

> Way down upon de Swanee Ribber,
>   Far, far away,
> Dere's wha my heart is turning ebber,
>   Dere's wha de old folks stay.
> All up and down de whole creation
>   Sadly I roam,
> Still longing for de old plantation,
>   And for de old folks at home!

Chorus—
> All de world am sad and dreary,
>   Ebery where I roam;
> Oh, darkeys, how my heart grows weary,
>   Far from de old folks at home!

CHEER, BOYS, CHEER

"Cheer, Boys, Cheer" was sung by every man who fought in a Southern Kentucky or Tennessee Regiment. General Basil Duke in his account of the battle of Shiloh, says—"Just as Breckinridge's Division was going into action, we came upon the left of it where the Kentucky troops were formed. The bullets commenced to fly thick and fast around us and simultaneously the regiment nearest us struck up the favorite song of the Kentuckians—'Cheer, Boys, Cheer.' The effect was inspiring beyond words."

Several versions of adapted words were sung to the melody of this song. One of the versions was dedicated to Horace Greeley and circulated throughout the north. The original "Cheer, Boys, Cheer," has, however, always remained closely identified with Southern sentiment.

Cheer, boys, cheer! no more of idle sorrow;
Courage! true hearts shall bear us on our way;
Hope points before and shows a bright tomorrow,
Let us forget the darkness of today:
Then farewell, England, much as we may love
      thee,
We'll dry the tears that we have shed before;
We'll not weep to sail in search of fortune;
Then farewell, England, farewell forevermore.

Chorus—
Then cheer, boys, cheer! for England, Mother
      England.
Cheer boys, cheer for the willing strong right
      hand;
Cheer, boys, cheer! there's wealth in honest labor;
Cheer, boys, cheer for the new and happy land.

TO CANAAN

This is an example of the many spontaneous lyrics sung to old tunes,—lyrics that were composed on the spur of occasions and soon afterwards consigned to oblivion.

Where are you going, soldiers,
With banner, gun and sword?
We're marching south to Canaan
To battle for the Lord.
What Captain leads your armies
Along the rebel coasts?
The mighty One of Israel,
His name is Lord of Hosts.

Chorus—
      To Canaan, to Canaan,
      The Lord has led us forth,
      To blow before the heathen walls
      The trumpets of the North.

DIXIE

The Original Version

Dixie was first written as a "walk-a-round" by an Ohioan, Dan Emmet, and was first sung in Dan Bryant's minstrel show on Broadway, New York, shortly before the war. It came into martial usage by accident and its stirring strains inspired the regiments on many a battlefield. Curiously enough it was adapted to patriotic words on both sides and remained popular with North and South alike after the struggle was over. Abraham Lincoln

loved the tune and considered the fact that it was truly representative of the "land of cotton" far more important than its lack of adherence to the strict laws of technical harmony. Twenty-two versions of the Confederate stanzas set to this famous melody have been collected by the Daughters of the Confederacy.

TO CANAAN

"WHERE ARE YOU GOING, SOLDIERS, WITH BANNER, GUN,
AND SWORD?"

These soldiers so brilliant in brass buttons and gold braid, with gun and sword, were "Green Mountain Boys," members of the Sixth Vermont, stationed at Camp Griffin in 1861. The boy in the picture who stands so sturdily between the men has been enthused by the call of patriotism and hurried away from the mountains to join the army, inspired by the leaping rhythm of war songs like "Canaan." Many youngsters like him never returned to their homes after "the trumpets" had blown their final call.

I wish I was in de land ob cotton,
Old times dar am not forgotten;
Look away, look away, look away,
      Dixie Land.
In Dixie Land whar I was born in,
Early on one frosty mornin,'
Look away, look away, look away, Dixie Land.

Chorus—
Den I wish I was in Dixie,
      Hooray! Hooray!

In Dixie Land, I'll took my stand,
To lib and die in Dixie:
Away, away, away, down South in Dixie
Away, away, away, down South in Dixie.

DIXIE

Union adaptation by John Savage—one of the many versions of Dixie sung in the Northern states during the war.

Oh, the Starry Flag is the flag for me;
'Tis the flag of life, 'tis the flag of the free,
Then hurrah, hurrah, for the flag of the Union.
Oh, the Starry Flag is the flag for me.
'Tis the flag of life, 'tis the flag of the free.
We'll raise that starry banner, boys,
Where no power or wrath can face it;

O'er town and field—
The people's shield;
No treason can erase it;
O'er all the land,
That flag must stand,
Where the people's might shall place it.

I GOES TO FIGHT MIT SIGEL

"I goes to fight mit Sigel," is the great war-song of our German Civil War patriots, who fought with exceptional bravery for their beloved General and their adopted "Fatherland."

I've come shust now to tells you how,
I goes mit regimentals,
To schlauch dem voes of Liberty,
Like dem old Continentals,
Vot fights mit England long ago,
To save der Yankee Eagle;
Und now I gets my soldier clothes;
I'm going to fight mit Sigel.

When I comes from der Deutsche Countree,
I vorks sometimes at baking;
Den I keeps a lager beer saloon,
Und den I goes shoe making;
But now I was a sojer been
To save der Yankee Eagle;
To schlauch dem tam secession volks,
I'm going to fight mit Sigel.

TENTING ON THE OLD CAMP GROUND

Walter Kittridge

No song has been so widely sung since the war as "Tenting on the Old Camp Ground." For Memorial Day music, it shares honors with "Soldiers' Farewell."

We're tenting tonight on the old camp ground,
Give us a song to cheer

Our weary hearts, a song of home,
And friends we love so dear.

Chorus—
Many are the hearts that are weary tonight,
Wishing for the war to cease;
Many are the hearts that are looking for the right,
To see the dawn of peace.
Tenting tonight, tenting tonight,
Tenting on the old camp ground.

We've been tenting tonight on the old camp ground,
Thinking of days gone by,
Of the loved ones at home that gave us the hand,
And the tear that said "Good-bye!"

We are tired of war on the old camp ground,
Many are dead and gone,
Of the brave and true who've left their homes;
Others been wounded long.

We've been fighting today on the old camp ground,
Many are lying near;
Some are dead and some are dying,
Many are in tears.

WE HAVE DRUNK FROM THE SAME CANTEEN

Charles Graham Halpine

There are bonds of all sorts in this world of ours,
Fetters of friendship and ties of flowers,
And true lovers' knots, I ween;
The boy and the girl are bound by a kiss,
But there's never a bond, old friend, like this:
We have drunk from the same canteen.

Chorus—
The same canteen, my soldier friend,
The same canteen,
There's never a bond, old friend, like this!
We have drunk from the same canteen.

It was sometimes water, and sometimes milk,
Sometimes applejack, fine as silk,
But whatever the tipple has been,
We shared it together, in bane or bliss,
And I warm to you, friend, when I think of this:
We have drunk from the same canteen.

GAY AND HAPPY

Private Henry Putnam, a descendant of Israel Putnam of historic fame, and a member of a New York regiment, wrote home from Cold Harbor the day before the battle, "We are quite gay in camp despite the prospect for battle to-morrow. To-night we have been singing and telling stories around the camp fire. I send you a paragraph of "Gay and Happy Still," which we sang tonight." The soldier was killed in the trenches the following day by the bullet of a Tennessee rifleman.

1

We're the boys that's gay and happy,
　Wheresoever we may be;
And we'll do our best to please you,
　If you will attentive be.

Chorus—

　So let the wide world wag as it will,
　We'll be gay and happy still,
　Gay and happy, gay and happy,
　We'll be gay and happy still.

2

We envy neither great nor wealthy,
　Poverty we ne'er despise;
Let us be contented, healthy,
　And the boon we dearly prize.

3

The rich have cares we little know of,
　All that glitters is not gold,
Merit's seldom made a show of,
　And true worth is rarely told.

THE GIRL I LEFT BEHIND ME
SAMUEL LOVER

The hour was sad I left the maid, a lingering
　farewell taking,
Her sighs and tears my steps delay'd, I thought
　her heart was breaking;
In hurried words her name I bless'd, I breathed
　the vows that bind me,
And to my heart in anguish press'd the girl I
　left behind me.

Then to the East we bore away, to win a name
　in story,
And there where dawns the sun of day, there
　dawns our sun of glory;
Both blazed in noon on Alma's height, where in
　the post assign'd me,
I shar'd the glory of that fight, Sweet Girl I Left
　Behind Me.

ONE I LEFT THERE

A Southern song of sentiment that equaled "Lorena" in popularity during the war.

1

　Soft blows the breath of morning
　　In my own valley fair,
　For it's there the opening roses
　　With fragrance scent the air,

With fragrance scent the air.
　And with perfume fill the air,
But the breath of one I left there
　Is sweeter far to me.

2

Soft fall the dews of evening
　Around our valley bowers;
And they glisten on the grass plots
　And tremble on the flowers,
　And tremble on the flowers
Like jewels rich to see,
But the tears of one I left there
　Are richer gems to me.

"THE GIRL I LEFT"

It is a strange chance of photography that preserved the wistful face of this wartime Yankee Girl at Fort Monroe, gazing from her window, to appear here. For "The Girl I Left Behind Me" was originally inscribed "To a Yankee Girl at Fort Monroe"! The demure lassie here, with the simple parting of the hair, the little bows and knots of ribbon on her dress, the plaid shawl drawn about her arm, the brocaded curtain above her head—all bring back the days that are gone. The jaunty words of the "Girl I Left Behind Me" bore an undercurrent of sadness, a fear that the waiting sweetheart might by the fortunes of war be condemned to spend a lifetime in unavailing sorrow. The tenderness and pathos of this song have made it live unto a later age. It strikes a note of universal tenderness.

THE FADED COAT OF BLUE
J. H. McNAUGHTON

"The Faded Coat of Blue" was sung extensively throughout the North during the war, in memory of the lads who were gathered with the bivouac of the dead.

My brave lad he sleeps in his faded coat of blue;
In a lonely grave unknown lies the heart that
　　beat so true;
He sank faint and hungry among the famished
　　brave,
And they laid him sad and lonely within his name-
　　less grave.

Chorus—
No more the bugle calls the weary one,
Rest noble spirit, in thy grave unknown!
I'll find you and know you, among the good and
true,
When a robe of white is giv'n for the faded coat
of blue.

He cried, " Give me water and just a little crumb,
And my mother she will bless you through all the
years to come;
Oh! tell my sweet sister, so gentle, good and true,
That I'll meet her up in heaven, in my faded coat
of blue."

LORENA

This was the great sentimental song of the South during the
war period.

The years creep slowly by, Lorena;
    The snow is on the grass again;
The sun's low down the sky, Lorena;
    The frost gleams where the flowers have been.
But the heart throbs on as warmly now
    As when the summer days were nigh;
Oh! the sun can never dip so low
    Adown affection's cloudless sky.

A hundred months have passed, Lorena,
    Since last I held that hand in mine,
And felt the pulse beat fast, Lorena,
    Though mine beat faster far than thine.
A hundred months—'twas flowery May,
    When up the hilly slope we climbed,
To watch the dying of the day
    And hear the distant church bells chime.

MOTHER KISSED ME IN MY DREAM

Set to a plaintive melody—the words of this exquisite lyric
gave comfort to many a lonely soldier. It is recorded that a
wounded private of Colonel Benj. L. Higgins' 86th New York
Infantry sang this song to cheer his comrades while they were
halted in a piece of woods beyond the memorable wheat-field at
Gettysburg, on the morning of July 3d, 1863.

Lying on my dying bed
    Thro' the dark and silent night,
Praying for the coming day,
    Came a vision to my sight.
Near me stood the forms I loved,
    In the sunlight's mellow gleam:
Folding me unto her breast,
    Mother kissed me in my dream.

Comrades, tell her, when you write,
    That I did my duty well;
Say that when the battle raged,
    Fighting, in the van I fell;

Tell her, too, when on my bed
    Slowly ebbed my being's stream,
How I knew no peace until
    Mother kissed me in my dream.

O WRAP THE FLAG AROUND ME, BOYS

R. STEWART TAYLOR

O, wrap the flag around me, boys,
To die were far more sweet,
With Freedom's starry banner, boys,
To be my winding sheet.
In life I lov'd to see it wave,
And follow where it led,
And now my eyes grow dim, my hands
Would clasp its last bright shred.

Chorus—
    Then ⎫
    Yet ⎬ wrap the flag around me, boys,
    So ⎭
To die were far more sweet,
With Freedom's starry emblem, boys,
To be my winding sheet.

COVER THEM OVER WITH BEAUTIFUL FLOWERS
Decoration Hymn.

E. F. STEWART

Cover them over with beautiful flow'rs,
Deck them with garlands, those brothers of ours,
Lying so silently night and day,
Sleeping the years of their manhood away,
Give them the meed they have won in the past,
Give them the honors their future forecast,
Give them the chaplets they won in the strife,
Give them the laurels they lost with their life.

Chorus—
Cover them over, yes, cover them over,
Parent, and husband, brother and lover;
Crown in your hearts those dead heroes of ours,
Cover them over with beautiful flow'rs.

JUST BEFORE THE BATTLE, MOTHER

GEORGE FREDERICK ROOT

Next in popularity to "When This Cruel War Is Over," was
the sentimental song "Just Before The Battle, Mother." Its
pathos and simplicity touched every heart.

Just before the battle, mother,
    I am thinking most of you,
While, upon the field, we're watching,
    With the enemy in view.

Comrades brave are round me lying,
　Filled with thoughts of home and God;
For well they know that, on the morrow,
　Some will sleep beneath the sod.

Chorus—

　Farewell, mother, you may never,
　You may never, mother,
　Press me to your breast again;
　But O, you'll not forget me,
　Mother, you will not forget me
　If I'm number'd with the slain.

LOW IN THE GROUND THEY'RE RESTING

COLLIN COE

Northern sentiment found vent in many beautiful Memorial
Day Odes. Several of these possessed genuine poetic excellence.

　Low in the ground they're resting,
　Proudly the flag waves o'er them;
　Never more 'mid wars contesting
　To save the land that bore them!

Chorus—

Sleep, brave ones, rest, in hallow'd graves!
Our flag now proudly o'er you waves!
Vict'ry and fame, vict'ry and fame,
Loudly forever shall your brave deeds proclaim,
Loudly forever shall your brave deeds proclaim.

WEEPING, SAD AND LONELY

WHEN THIS CRUEL WAR IS OVER

CHARLES CARROLL SAWYER

Most popular of all in North and South alike was the song
known as "When This Cruel War Is Over." It was heard in
every camp, the Southern soldiers inserting "gray" for "blue"
in the sixth line of the first stanza. It is doubtful if any other
American song was ever upon so many tongues. One million
copies were sold during the war.

　Dearest love, do you remember,
　When we last did meet,
　How you told me that you loved me,
　Kneeling at my feet?
　Oh, how proud you stood before me,
　In your suit of blue,
　When you vowed to me and country
　Ever to be true.

Chorus—

　Weeping, sad and lonely,
　Hopes and fears how vain!
　Yet praying, when this cruel war is over,
　Praying that we meet again!

POOR OLD SLAVE

This song, while not directly connected with the events of the
war, was widely popular during the struggle.

　'Tis just one year ago today,
　　That I remember well,
　I sat down by poor Nelly's side
　　And a story she did tell.
　'Twas 'bout a poor unhappy slave,
　　That lived for many a year;
　But now he's dead, and in his grave,
　　No master does he fear.

"WHEN THIS CRUEL WAR IS OVER"

With the quaint style of hair-dressing that ruled in 1864, in
flowered skirt and "Garibaldi blouse," this beautiful woman, the
wife of a Federal army officer, was photographed in front of the
winter quarters of Captain John R. Coxe, in February, at the headquarters of the Army of the Potomac, Brandy Station. She was
even then looking at her soldier husband, who sat near her in his
"suit of blue," or perhaps thinking of the three years of terrific
fighting that had passed. Shiloh, Chickamauga, Chattanooga,
Fredericksburg, Chancellorsville, Gettysburg—all of these had
been fought and the toll of the "cruel war" was not yet complete.

Chorus—

　The poor old slave has gone to rest,
　　We know that he is free;
　Disturb him not but let him rest,
　　Way down in Tennessee.

NEGRO "SPIRITUALS"

Some of the negro chants or "spirituals" are particularly interesting because of their direct connection with the incidents of the Civil War. Their sources were generally obscure; their origin seeming to be either by gradual accretion or by an almost unconscious process of composition.

Colonel T. W. Higginson told the story of the beginning of one of these slave songs as related to him by a sturdy young oarsman of Ladies Island.

"Once we boys" he said "went to tote some rice and de nigger driver he keep a-callin' on us; and I say, 'O, de ole nigger-driver.' Den anudder said, 'Fust ting my mammy tole me was —notin' so bad as nigger drivers.' Den I make a 'sing,' just puttin' a word an' den anudder word." Thus, said Colonel Higginson, almost unconsciously a new song was created, which was repeated the second time with perfect recollection of the original melody and intonations.

The wild, sad strains of these primitive melodies, born of their desire for musical expression amid the dull, daily routine of cotton field and rice swamp, express above and beyond their plaintive lament, a simple trust in the future—in the happy land—the Canaan, toward which their yearning eyes were forever turned.

THE ENLISTED SOLDIERS

Sung by the Ninth Regiment U. S. Colored Troops at Benedict, Maryland, winter of 1863–4. General Armstrong calls this the Negro Battle Hymn. At Petersburg, July 29, 1864, a trooper of General Henry G. Thomas's brigade sat before the camp fire singing this "Negro Battle Hymn," "They look like Men of War." General Thomas describes the scene—the dark men with their white eyes and teeth, crouching over a smouldering camp fire, in dusky shadow, lit only by the feeble rays of the lanterns of the first sergeants dimly showing through the tents. After the terrible "Battle of the Crater" they sang these words no more.

> Hark! listen to the trumpeters,
> They call for volunteers,
> On Zion's bright and flowery mount—
> Behold the officers!

Chorus—
> They look like men,
> They look like men,
> They look like men of war.

MY FATHER, HOW LONG?

This primitive chant is thought by Mr. G. H. Allan, who wrote down the stanzas, to have originated from the Florida plantations. At the outbreak of the Civil War several negroes were thrown into jail at Georgetown, South Carolina, for singing the verses. Although the "spiritual" was an old one, the words were considered as being symbolical of new events. A little colored boy explained the matter tersely to Mr. Allan. "Dey tink de Lord mean fo' to say de Yankees call us."

> We'll fight for liberty,
> We'll fight for liberty,
> We'll fight for liberty,
> When de Lord will call us home.
> And it won't be long,
> And it won't be long,
> And it won't be long,
> When de Lord will call us home.

MANY THOUSAND GO

This "spiritual," to which the Civil War actually gave rise, was composed by nobody knows whom, although it is perhaps the most recent of the slave "spirituals" of which we have record. Lieut. Col. Trowbridge learned that it was first sung on the occasion when General Beauregard gathered the slaves from the Port Royal Islands to build fortifications at Hilton Head and Bay Point.

> No more peck o' corn for me,
> No more, no more;
> No more peck o' corn for me,
> Many tousand go.
>
> No more driver's lash for me,
> No more, no more;
> No more driver's lash for me,
> Many tousand go.

PRAY ON

This curious "spiritual" is one of those arising directly from the events of the war. When the news of 'approaching freedom reached the sea island rice plantations of the Port Royal Islands this chant was sung with great fervor by the negroes. The verses were annotated by Charles Pickard Ware.

> Pray on—pray on;
> Pray on, den light us over;
> Pray on—pray on,
> De Union break of day.
> My sister, you come to see baptize
> In de Union break of day,
> In de Union break of day.

MEET, O LORD

> Meet, O Lord, on de milk-white horse
> An' de nineteen vial in his han'.
> Drop on—drop on de crown on my head,
> And rolly in my Jesus arm;
> In dat mornin' all day,
> In dat mornin' all day,
> In dat mornin' all day,
> When Jesus de Christ been born.

COPYRIGHT, 1911, REVIEW OF REVIEWS CO.

"MEET, O LORD"

HILTON HEAD IN 1861—THE TIME AND PLACE OF THIS NEGRO SONG'S CREATION

This photograph appears here by a curious coincidence. With the presentation of the "spiritual" that commemorates an event of the war connected with the Confederate General Drayton, there has come to light a photograph of his home on Hilton Head in 1861. Through these gates, watched by loving eyes, he rode on the "milk-white horse," the morning of the engagement at Bay Point. Mr. W. F. Allen, who collected many slave-songs, was told that, "When de gun shoot at Bay Pint," General Drayton left a Negro boy holding his white war horse. He never returned to claim his steed and in some way the incident was commemorated in this "spiritual," which is still sung on the plantations of Hilton Head Island. Observe the Negro "mammies" on the porch and at the gate, also the luxuriance of foliage framing the Southern house in a bower of greenery. Members of the Third New Hampshire regiment face the reader; for the house is now a rendezvous of Federal troops.

INDEX

READERS WILL BENEFIT BY A GLANCE AT THE FOLLOWING NOTE, WHICH IMPARTS
SPECIAL MEANING TO THE REFERENCES THAT FOLLOW

Much time is usually lost in referring to an Index of a work as extended and replete with statements of fact as the
PHOTOGRAPHIC HISTORY. The novel plan of these volumes, however, renders it possible for the reader to identify
the nature of each reference, simply by remembering the distinctive character of the volume in question. For convenience,
the titles of the ten volumes will now be repeated:

I. THE OPENING BATTLES
April, 1861—July, 1862

IV. THE CAVALRY

V. FORTS AND ARTILLERY

**VIII. SOLDIER LIFE—SECRET
SERVICE**

II. TWO YEARS OF GRIM WAR
August, 1862—April, 1864

VI. THE NAVIES

IX. POETRY AND ELOQUENCE

III. THE DECISIVE BATTLES
April, 1864—May, 1865

VII. PRISONS AND HOSPITALS

X. ARMIES AND LEADERS

Each volume number constitutes a characterization in itself. Thus, under the heading "Gettysburg" the reference
to " II., 234," clearly indicates the campaign narrative, since Volume II. is that one of the three volumes on BATTLES which covers
the period between August, 1862, and April, 1864, thus including the days of July, 1863, that witnessed the great battle.

But the further reference to Gettysburg, "IV., 238" as clearly indicates a treatment of operations of the Cavalry, since
IV. is the volume on CAVALRY. Again, the reference under this same heading, " V., 40," must indicate the treatment of the
events at Gettysburg in which a part was played by the Artillery, since V. is the ARTILLERY volume.

Thus this History's classification of Civil War matters, volume by volume, has made it possible to present in the Index
that follows a much greater number of items and references for the reader's convenience than has ever been the case previously in a work of this magnitude.

GENERAL OFFICERS. Any general officer, Union or Confederate, who served in the Civil War, not to be found
in the Index that follows, can be placed as regards his full rank, name, and date of appointment by referring to the ROSTER
immediately preceding.

BOLD FACE ARABIC FIGURES INDICATE ILLUSTRATIONS. The Roman numerals indicate the number of the
volume. The Arabic figures in bold face type indicate pages on which photographs appear (text references are in ordinary Roman
type). Thus, under Pleasonton, A., "IV., **237**," means that there is an illustration.